The Palgrave Handbook of Toleration

Mitja Sardoč
Editor

The Palgrave Handbook of Toleration

Volume 1

Editor
Mitja Sardoč
Educational Research Institute
Ljubljana, Slovenia

ISBN 978-3-030-42120-5   ISBN 978-3-030-42121-2   (eBook)
ISBN 978-3-030-42122-9 (print and electronic bundle)
https://doi.org/10.1007/978-3-030-42121-2

© Springer Nature Switzerland AG 2022
This work is subject to copyright. All rights are reserved by the Publisher, whether the whole or part of the material is concerned, specifically the rights of translation, reprinting, reuse of illustrations, recitation, broadcasting, reproduction on microfilms or in any other physical way, and transmission or information storage and retrieval, electronic adaptation, computer software, or by similar or dissimilar methodology now known or hereafter developed.

The use of general descriptive names, registered names, trademarks, service marks, etc. in this publication does not imply, even in the absence of a specific statement, that such names are exempt from the relevant protective laws and regulations and therefore free for general use.

The publisher, the authors, and the editors are safe to assume that the advice and information in this book are believed to be true and accurate at the date of publication. Neither the publisher nor the authors or the editors give a warranty, expressed or implied, with respect to the material contained herein or for any errors or omissions that may have been made. The publisher remains neutral with regard to jurisdictional claims in published maps and institutional affiliations.

This Palgrave Macmillan imprint is published by the registered company Springer Nature Switzerland AG.
The registered company address is: Gewerbestrasse 11, 6330 Cham, Switzerland

Preface

"The safest general characterization of the European philosophical tradition," as Alfred North Whitehead accentuated in *Process and Reality* (based on his *Gifford Lectures Delivered in the University of Edinburgh During the Session 1927–28*) "is that it consists of a series of footnotes to Plato" (1978, p. 39). If one would follow Whitehead's footsteps, contemporary discussions of toleration might best be depicted as didaskalia to the writings of John Locke. Seminal intellectual figures such as Plato and Locke alongside other luminaries from the philosophical tradition provide us with a (giant's) shoulder on which to stand on, while grappling with whatever the task of scholarly research one is focusing on.

As a repository of knowledge on a particular topic, reference works including encyclopedias, handbooks, and companions provide another such shoulder on which to stand upon. Yet, the main goal of this publishing project is not only one of customary purpose reference work has been usually associated with. Ultimately, any author or editor has its own overall plan on how the volume one is either writing or editing should turn out at the end. For example, Ian Fleming supposedly wrote *Casino Royale*, the first of a series of novels on what turned out to be the global franchise of James Bond, to end all spy stories. This reference work obviously does not point in this direction.

The overall aim of this handbook has been to bring together a set of contributions presenting some of the most distinctive, complex, and controversial aspects associated with the idea of toleration. Interestingly enough, there are plenty of these issues around, making the navigation in this area of scholarly research particularly distressing. Its ambivalent character and its enigmatic nature together with its allegedly exotic origins and complex legacy are just some of the character traits toleration has been associated with. The immediate impulse one encounters when faced with the scholarly literature on toleration would most probably resemble Winston Churchill's puzzling observation summed up in the parable of "a riddle wrapped in a mystery inside an enigma." This handbook therefore aims to provide a conceptual cartography that would enable anyone making use of it a safe journey through the many tumultuous issues this area of scholarly research is replete with.

In contrast to some of the other concepts from the pantheon of political ideas, toleration has been graced with a number of monographs, articles, journal special issues, and edited collections that have popped up around the globe. Nevertheless, despite a steady supply of scholarly output, no reference work on toleration has been available to this date. This publishing project aims to fill this gap in the academic market by bringing together more than 50 chapters by leading academics in this area of scholarly research on some of the most pressing and timely issues toleration has been associated with.

Like any scholarly publication, this reference work has its fair share of lost opportunities. They would have been much more numerous if it wouldn't be for the editorial team at Palgrave. In particular, I would like to thank Ambra Finotello, senior commissioning editor in politics at Palgrave, and Michael Hermann, chief editor of the MRW series at Springer, for supporting the idea of this handbook and for helping out in the transition from "book proposal" to "book contract" for this publishing project (usually a distressing period for any author or volume editor). My most profound thanks go to Eleanor Gaffney, editor at Palgrave, for her superb editorial skills, patience, care, and dedication to this handbook. Any author or volume editor could not find better editorial cooperation than Eleanor has provided both to me as volume editor and, I believe, to each of the contributors to this handbook.

Last but not least, I would like to dedicate this handbook to my wife Mojca and our two sons, Žiga and Jakob. It is in their company that the idea for this handbook arose during a summer holiday back in 2018 on the island of Mljet in Croatia. Perhaps more than anyone else, they exemplify a form of "liberal expectancy" the idea of toleration has been associated with. Describing the many nuances of their toleration (alongside their unfailing support and encouragement) would take another volume to straight out.

September 2021   Mitja Sardoč

References

Whitehead N (1978 [1929]) Process and reality (Gifford lectures delivered in the University of Edinburgh during the session 1927–28). Free Press, New York

Contents

Volume 1

1 **The Trouble with Toleration** 1
Mitja Sardoč

2 **Toleration: Concept and Conceptions** 11
Rainer Forst

3 **Defining Toleration** 23
Andrew Jason Cohen

4 **What Toleration Is Not** 53
David Heyd

5 **Toleration** 71
Anna Elisabetta Galeotti

6 **Paradoxes of Toleration** 93
Peter Königs

7 **The Epistemic Justification for Tolerance** 109
Joshua C. Thurow

8 **Political Toleration Explained** 129
Peter Balint

9 **Toleration, Respect for Persons, and the Free Speech
Right to Do Moral Wrong** 149
Kristian Skagen Ekeli

10 **Toleration and Political Change** 173
Lucia M. Rafanelli

11 **Toleration and the Law** 189
Stijn Smet

12 **Toleration and Domination** 209
Monica Mookherjee

vii

13 State Responses to Incongruence: Toleration and Transformation 229
Paul Billingham

14 Toleration and State Neutrality: The Case of Symbolic FGM 249
Federico Zuolo

15 Toleration of Moral Offense 263
Thomas E. Hill Jr

16 Moralism and Anti-Moralism in Theories of Toleration 277
John Christian Laursen and Zachary Dorson

17 Toleration and Neutrality 299
Peter Jones

18 Political Toleration as Substantive Neutrality 325
Bryan T. McGraw

19 Conscientious Exemptions: Between Toleration, Neutrality, and Respect 341
Yossi Nehushtan

20 Toleration and Its Possibilities: Relativism, Skepticism, and Pluralism 363
John William Tate

21 Toleration, Reasonableness, and Power 397
Thomas M. Besch and Jung-Sook Lee

22 Toleration and Reasonableness 419
Roberta Sala

23 International Toleration 439
Pietro Maffettone

24 Toleration and Tolerance in a Global Context 455
Vicki A. Spencer

25 Two Models of Toleration 477
Will Kymlicka

26 Modus Vivendi Toleration 499
Manon Westphal

27 Multiculturalism and Toleration 519
Sune Lægaard

28 Recognition and Toleration 541
Cillian McBride

29 Toleration and Dignity 563
Colin Bird

Contents ix

30 Toleration and Respect 583
John William Tate

Volume 2

31 Toleration and Justice 615
Fabio Macioce

32 The Logic of Intolerance 635
Richard Dees

33 Intolerance and Populism 653
Nenad Miščević

34 Fear and Toleration 673
Robert Paul Churchill

35 Toleration, "Mindsight" and the Epistemic Virtues 699
Colin Farrelly

36 Tough on Tolerance: The Vice of Virtue 719
Thomas Nys and Bart Engelen

37 Toleration and Close Personal Relationships 737
Michael Kühler

38 Hospitality and Toleration 757
Andrew Fiala

39 Toleration and Compassion: A Conceptual Comparison 777
Yossi Nehushtan and Emily Prince

40 Toleration and Religion 797
John William Tate

41 Toleration and Religious Discrimination 827
Andrew Shorten

42 Religious Toleration and Social Contract Theories of Justice 853
Phillip J. Donnelly

43 Toleration and the Protestant Tradition 873
Manfred Svensson

44 Atheist Toleration 887
Charles Devellennes

45 Toleration and the Right to Freedom of Religion in Education ... 905
Zdenko Kodelja

46 Education and Toleration 925
Johannes Drerup

47	**Toleration, Liberal Education, and the Accommodation of Diversity**	951
	Ole Henrik Borchgrevink Hansen	
48	**Toleration Before Toleration**	969
	Cary J. Nederman	
49	**Early Modern Arguments for Toleration**	993
	Andrew R. Murphy	
50	**Thomas Hobbes and the Conditionality of Toleration**	1009
	J. Judd Owen	
51	**John Locke and Religious Toleration**	1023
	John William Tate	
52	**"Stop Being So Judgmental!": A Spinozist Model of Personal Tolerance**	1077
	Justin Steinberg	
53	**Toleration and Liberty of Conscience**	1095
	Jon Mahoney	
54	**Tolerating Racism and Hate Speech: A Critique of C.E. Baker's "Almost" Absolutism**	1115
	Raphael Cohen-Almagor	
55	**Toleration of Free Speech: Imposing Limits on Elected Officials**	1139
	Amos N. Guiora	
Index		1161

About the Editor

Mitja Sardoč (PhD) is senior research associate at the Educational Research Institute in Ljubljana (Slovenia). His research interests and expertise include philosophy of education, political philosophy, and education policy. Over the last two decades he has been member of several (national and international) research projects on multiculturalism, diversity, equality of opportunity, patriotism, citizenship education, etc. During the last few years, his research interest has moved to some of the conceptual and policy-oriented issues associated with radicalization, violent extremism, and conflicting diversity. Between 2018 and 2021, he carried out a research project "Radicalisation and Violent Extremism: Philosophical, Sociological and Educational Perspective(s)" funded by the Slovenian Research Agency as part of its "basic research projects" program (the most selective research funding scheme for basic research in Slovenia). He is author of more than 40 scholarly articles and editor of a number of journal special issues on radicalization and violent extremism, citizenship education, multiculturalism, toleration, the American Dream, equality of opportunity, and patriotism. He acted as an expert for various research initiatives including the Organization for Security and Co-operation in Europe (OSCE), the Council of Europe, and the Slovene Ministry of Foreign Affairs. He also carried out consultancy work for other international institutions (e.g., Cardiff University, ODIHR). He is Managing Editor of *Theory and Research in Education* (http://tre.sagepub.com/), Editor-in-Chief of *The Handbook of Patriotism*, and editor of *The Impacts of Neoliberal Discourse and Language in Education* published by Routledge. Between September and December 2019, he was a visiting fellow at the Robert Schuman Centre for Advanced Studies at the

European University Institute in Florence (Italy). Additional information (including the list of publications) is available at the website: https://www.researchgate.net/profile/Mitja_Sardoc

Contributors

Peter Balint School of Humanities and Social Sciences, UNSW Canberra, Canberra, ACT, Australia

Thomas M. Besch School of Philosophy, Wuhan University, Wuhan, Hubei, China

Department of Philosophy, The University of Sydney, Sydney, NSW, Australia

Paul Billingham Department of Politics and International Relations and Magdalen College, University of Oxford, Oxford, UK

Colin Bird Department of Politics, Program in Political Philosophy, Policy, and Law, University of Virginia, Charlottesville, VA, USA

Robert Paul Churchill Department of Philosophy, George Washington University, Westminster, MD, USA

Andrew Jason Cohen Georgia State University, Atlanta, GA, USA

Raphael Cohen-Almagor University of Hull, Hull, UK

Richard Dees University of Rochester, Rochester, NY, USA

Charles Devellennes University of Kent, Canterbury, UK

Phillip J. Donnelly Baylor University, Waco, TX, USA

Zachary Dorson University of California, Riverside, Riverside, CA, USA

Johannes Drerup Technische Universität Dortmund, Dortmund, Germany

Kristian Skagen Ekeli University of Stavanger, Stavanger, Norway

Bart Engelen Tilburg University, Tilburg, The Netherlands

Colin Farrelly Queen's University, Kingston, Canada

Andrew Fiala Department of Philosophy, California State University, Fresno, CA, USA

Rainer Forst Goethe University, Normative Orders Research Centre, Frankfurt/Main, Germany

Anna Elisabetta Galeotti Università del Piemonte Orientale, Vercelli, Italy

Amos N. Guiora S.J. Quinney College of Law, University of Utah, Salt Lake City, UT, USA

Ole Henrik Borchgrevink Hansen Ostfold University College, School of Education, Ostfold, Norway

David Heyd The Hebrew University of Jerusalem, Jerusalem, Israel

Thomas E. Hill Jr Department of Philosophy, University of North Carolina, Chapel Hill, NC, USA

Peter Jones Newcastle University, Newcastle upon Tyne, UK

Zdenko Kodelja Educational Research Institute, Ljubljana, Slovenia

Peter Königs Human Technology Center, Applied Ethics, RWTH Aachen University, Aachen, Germany

Michael Kühler Department of Philosophy, University of Münster, Münster, Germany

Will Kymlicka Department of Philosophy, Queen's University, Kingston, ON, Canada

Sune Lægaard Department of Communication and Arts, Roskilde University, Roskilde, Denmark

John Christian Laursen University of California, Riverside, Riverside, CA, USA

Jung-Sook Lee School of Social Sciences, UNSW Sydney, Sydney, NSW, Australia

Fabio Macioce Law School, Lumsa University, Rome, Italy

Pietro Maffettone Political Science Department, University of Napoli, Federico II, Naples, Italy

Jon Mahoney Department of Philosophy, Kansas State University, Manhattan, KS, USA

Cillian McBride Queen's University Belfast, Belfast, UK

Bryan T. McGraw Wheaton College, Wheaton, IL, USA

Nenad Miščević University of Maribor, Maribor, Slovenia

Monica Mookherjee School of Social, Political and Global Studies, Keele University, Stoke-on-Trent, Staffordshire, UK

Andrew R. Murphy Department of Political Science, Virginia Commonwealth University, Richmond, VA, USA

Cary J. Nederman Department of Political Science, Texas A&M University, College Station, TX, USA

Yossi Nehushtan Keele University, Newcastle-Under-Lyme, UK

Thomas Nys University of Amsterdam, Amsterdam, The Netherlands

J. Judd Owen Department of Political Science, Emory University, Atlanta, GA, USA

Emily Prince University of Sheffield, Sheffield, UK

Lucia M. Rafanelli The George Washington University, Washington, DC, USA

Roberta Sala Faculty of Philosophy, Vita-Salute San Raffaele University, Milan, Italy

Mitja Sardoč Educational Research Institute, Ljubljana, Slovenia

Andrew Shorten Department of Politics and Public Administration, University of Limerick, Limerick, Ireland

Stijn Smet Faculty of Law, Hasselt University, Hasselt, Belgium

Vicki A. Spencer Politics, School of Social Sciences, University of Otago, Dunedin, New Zealand

Justin Steinberg Brooklyn College and CUNY Graduate Center, New York, NY, USA

Manfred Svensson Department of Philosophy, Universidad de los Andes, Santiago, Chile

John William Tate Discipline of Politics and International Relations, Newcastle Business School, College of Human and Social Futures, University of Newcastle, Newcastle, NSW, Australia

Joshua C. Thurow University of Texas at San Antonio, San Antonio, TX, USA

Manon Westphal Institute of Political Science, University of Münster, Münster, Germany

Federico Zuolo Department of Classics, Philosophy and History, University of Genova, Genova, Italy

The Trouble with Toleration

Mitja Sardoč

Contents

Introduction: The Language of Toleration 2
Summary and Future Directions 7
References 8

Abstract

Both historically and conceptually, toleration has been one of the foundational characteristics that define the very essence of a plurally diverse polity and the basic virtue associated with a liberal conception of citizenship. Despite its central role in contemporary political thought, toleration remains subject to various controversies and disagreements stemming from the many paradoxes, dilemmas, and puzzles associated with it. This chapter identifies some of the distinguishing features of contemporary discussions about toleration as well as elucidates the most pressing and challenging controversies these discussions have been focusing on.

Keywords

Toleration · Diversity · Liberalism · Pluralism · Limits of toleration · Justification of toleration · Critique of toleration

---

M. Sardoč (✉)
Educational Research Institute, Ljubljana, Slovenia
e-mail: mitja.sardoc@guest.arnes.si

© The Author(s), under exclusive licence to Springer Nature Switzerland AG 2022
M. Sardoč (ed.), *The Palgrave Handbook of Toleration*,
https://doi.org/10.1007/978-3-030-42121-2_17

Introduction: The Language of Toleration

As a community of ideas, the pantheon of political concepts has been replete with a variety of problems, challenges, and other conceptual "mishaps" that make the analysis of almost any of its members far more devious than originally envisaged. Alongside ambiguity and confusion, perhaps the most "stable" companions of any conceptual analysis (and the associated disputes), some of the most well-known political concepts are plagued by very peculiar problems and challenges. If being an essentially contested concept is now a household challenge most of the concepts are faced with (Gallie 1955), others are far less straightforward. For example, the "traveling" of a particular concept has been identified as an interesting phenomenon in political science (Sartori 1970). Equality of opportunity and responsibility are just two of the most representative examples of this phenomenon.

Another frequent conceptual "mishap" associated with the "travelling problem" (Sartori 1970) has taken up the form of conceptual stretching. Interestingly enough, writing more than a century apart, the French political scientist Alexis de Tocqueville and the British historian of ideas Isaiah Berlin pointed to this interesting phenomenon that seems to dominate our contemporary discussions. In Book II of *Democracy in America*, Alexis de Tocqueville emphasized eloquently that "[a]n abstract word is like a box with a false bottom: you can put in any ideas you please and take them out again without anyone being the wiser" (de Tocqueville 2000, p. 553). In a similar vein, Isaiah Berlin's essay "Two Concepts of Liberty" points to a vexing problem plaguing the idea of liberty, "[l]ike happiness and goodness, like nature and reality, the meaning of this term is so porous that there is little interpretation that it seems able to resist" (Berlin 2002, p. 181).

At the same time, several concepts face the challenge stemming from the absence of a fixed definition. Interestingly enough, this has had important repercussions outside the "ideal" world of conceptual analysis. A leading example of this challenge has been the lack of a fixed definition of terrorism that has become a sort of trademark of the "War on Terror." As Stephen Nathanson emphasizes, "[c]larity is not everyone's goal, however, because confusion can be politically useful" (Nathanson 2010, p. 20).

Several concepts face another challenging problem. Although the slogan "we recognize violence when we see it" (Bufacchi 2009, p. 293) unequivocally illustrates all the brutality of its consequences, the concept of violence is neither simple nor unproblematic. Due to the sensitive nature of phenomena it may be associated with there is a sort of urgency in having it addressed in a comprehensive manner. Given the fact that it may refer to phenomena as diverse as physical violence, cyber violence, mobbing, domestic violence, bullying, sexual violence, violent [political] extremism, as well as structural violence, symbolic violence, cultural violence, etc., the concept of violence needs to be flexible enough to incorporate all its aberrations. Nevertheless, having it open to as wide a definition as possible, we may ultimately end up with a sort of conceptual inflation. Violence as well as racism are just two of the examples where this problem is of particular salience (Bufacchi 2007; Miles and Brown 1989).

1 The Trouble with Toleration

Among the most unlikely of the conceptual "mishaps" one may encounter has been the one "identified" by Alasdair MacIntyre in his book *After Virtue*. As he accentuates, "rights do not exist as such and to believe in them is similar to believing in witches and unicorns" (MacIntyre 2007, p. 69). Surprisingly enough, this is not the only such example of skeptical "denial" in scholarly research. Radicalization leading to violent extremism has been another such case where "radicalization deniers" (Neumann 2003) have expressed skepticism over the very existence of this phenomenon.

At the same time, the complexity and controversiality of a particular concept could intuitively also be evaluated by either its convergence with or distance from an ordinary language definition of it. In fact, concepts and the ideas they are associated with inhabit not only the pantheon of ideas but have their existence also outside the scholarly discussions and its codified language. There are different ways of depicting the relationship between a scholarly definition of a particular concept and its usage in ordinary language. For some of these concepts, at least on the surface, moving from one language register to another does not represent any major problem. For example, in the case of patriotism [where in both cases patriotism means *love of patria*], there is almost no difference between its use in ordinary language and its definition in the scholarly community [what each of these elements may mean is a completely different endeavor with a set of separate problems].

In contrast, there is a concept where the amplitude between its meaning in the register of ordinary language and its scholarly definition is far from being negligible. It is that of toleration. As Andrew Jason Cohen emphasizes, "[o]utside the academic world of philosophy, the term 'toleration' is often used in different ways" (Cohen 2004, p. 70). Nevertheless, on the side of ordinary language, toleration is straightforwardly unequivocal. Being tolerant, as Wendy Brown somehow subsumes its ordinary language usage, "conjures seemliness, propriety, forbearance, magnanimity, cosmopolitanism, universality, and the large view, while those for whom tolerance is required take their shape as improper, indecorous, urgent, narrow, particular, and often ungenerous or at least lacking in perspective" (Brown 2006, p. 178). On this interpretation, toleration is primarily associated with open-mindedness. As Peter Jones emphasizes, "'[t]olerant', 'tolerance', and 'toleration' are generally used as terms of commendation, while 'intolerant' and 'intolerance' are typically pejorative terms, but that should not mislead us" (Jones 2013, p. 629).

In contrast, a scholarly definition of toleration is crammed with paradoxes, puzzles, and dilemmas, with different conditions and circumstances torn apart by the different conceptions of toleration itself. At the same time, toleration also needs to be discussed alongside concepts and ideas that are part of its gravitational orbit, e.g., civility, dignity, coercion, harm, conflict, disagreement, secularism, orthodoxy, dissent, knowledge, authority, power, domination, trust, restraint, non-interference, neutrality, fairness, reasonableness, pluralism, autonomy, (mutual) respect, recognition, and ultimately diversity itself. In fact, one of the most important issues in discussing a particular concept has been to contextualize it with its immediate surrounding echoing Firth's principle of co-occurrence ["You shall know a word by the company it keeps"] (Firth 1957). This is an important signal for what lies ahead for anyone undertaking either the analysis of a particular aspect of toleration or a comprehensive coverage of this concept.

In fact, the understanding of toleration has never been either simple or straightforward. This comes as no surprise since the history of toleration, one might claim with considerable confidence, has been a history of conflicts. Its long and venerable history spans across some of the most tumultuous periods of human existence going all the way back to the ages of discovery, empire, revolution, the extremes, etc. [to partly paraphrase Eric Hobsbawm's chronological timeline]. As Rainer Forst accentuates, "the history and the present of toleration are always at the same time a history and a present of social struggles" (Forst 2003, p. 2). Furthermore, its "exotic" origins, its enigmatic nature, and complex character, as well as a contentious legacy [at least for its critics] have been a major factor in a somehow puzzling response by almost anyone trying to make sense of out of it.

At the same time, the turn of last decade of the twentieth century has witnessed a theoretical seismic shift of considerable magnitude that had implications for discussions about toleration. If John Locke's *Epistola de Tolerantia [A Letter on Toleration]* first published in 1689 represents some sort of a "Year One" on the calendar of "standard" discussions about toleration, several of the events in 1989 have had a galvanizing effect on discussions about toleration in plurally diverse democracies. In November of that year, following large-scale demonstrations in East Germany, the Berlin Wall fell, leading to the collapse of communism throughout Eastern Europe. This was accompanied by the rise of both xenophobic nationalism and religious fundamentalism that have fueled several subsequent conflicts. Interestingly enough, preceding the fall of the Berlin Wall by just a few weeks, three Muslim girls were suspended in a French public school for wearing the *hijab*. This was a prelude to the headscarf controversy [*l'affaire du foulard*] that remains to this day a landmark event associated with contemporary discussions about toleration (Laborde 2008).

From then on, toleration remained at the forefront of public interest. Cases such as the banning of minarets in some European countries, the display of religious symbols in classrooms, the ban of face covering in public (targeting primarily Muslim women wearing the burka or the niqab), the "gay cake" controversy, cases of cultural appropriation, the disrespectful portrayal of religious figures, etc., are some of the most recent examples where controversies over toleration are at the center of social and political attention. However, these are just some of the most visible cases making it either all the way up to the highest levels of judiciary authority including the US Supreme Court and the European Court of Human Rights or to frontline news (in some cases both).

Furthermore, phenomena as diverse as populism on both the "left" and "right" of the political spectrum (Galston 2018; Müller 2016), the shrinking civic space (Deželan et al. 2020), hate speech (Waldron 2012), fake news [including its various "alternatives," e.g., misinformation, distorted facts, etc.], extremist political movements, "moral panic" and conflicting diversity including radicalization (Sardoč et al. 2021) and violent extremism (Cassam 2021) have also had an important influence on theorizing about toleration. These illiberal forms of authoritarianism are part of the "global authoritarian pushback against democracy and human rights" that has been associated with a global phenomenon of "reverse transitions" (Buyse 2018).

1 The Trouble with Toleration

At the same time, the dominance of the standard liberal conception of civic equality and its uniform treatment approach towards cultural diversity was challenged initially by a handful of scholars arguing that this conception of civic equality failed to recognize the legitimate interest of ethno-cultural groups in a stable cultural context and lacked the means to compensate adequately for individuals' unequal circumstances (e.g., Kymlicka 1989; Spinner-Halev 1994; Taylor 1997 [1992]; Young 1990). Moreover, they also argued that the standard liberal conception of toleration as non-interference did not sufficiently protect the interests of culturally disadvantaged groups, including national minorities, immigrants, and indigenous peoples. On this interpretation, toleration is inconsistent with a commitment to civic equality and a requirement of fairness.

From then on, discussions about toleration (and related issues) have been all but anemic. It therefore comes as no surprise that there has been a steady supply of research monographs (e.g., Balint 2017; Bejan 2017), edited collections (e.g., Drerup and Schweiger 2021; Först 2020), and scholarly articles (e.g., Galeotti 2021; Konigs) addressing these and other phenomena previously thought to be either at the fringes of scholarly interest on toleration or settled for good. In fact, time and again, toleration comes to the forefront as a framework most adequate to makes sense out of the various conflicts, disputes, and other pressing issues.

The events and theoretical developments explicated above have had a decisive influence on subsequent discussions about toleration and have actually contributed to some sort of a renaissance of theorizing over toleration. As "one of the defining topics in political philosophy" (Williams and Waldron 2008, p. 1), toleration remains to this day one of the concepts whose complexity and controversiality can hardly be matched. In fact, both historically and conceptually toleration has been replete with problems, challenges, and paradoxes, few, if any of the other concepts from the pantheon of political ideas are entrusted with.

In particular, the complexity of the foundations, nature and value of toleration and the controversiality of the status, the justification and the limits of what is to be tolerated, raise a number of questions over the basis of toleration in a plurally diverse polity. As the existing literature on this topic clearly exemplifies (e.g., Brown 2014; McKinnon and Castiglione 2003a; Dees 2004; Deveaux 2000; Galeotti 2002; Heyd 1996; Kukathas 2003; McKinnon 2006; Mendus 1989; Newey 1999; Parekh 2000; Rawls 1993; Sardoč 2010; Sardoč 2013; Scanlon 2003; Spencer 2017; Taylor 1997 [1992]; Walzer 1997; Williams and Waldron 2008), the persistence of moral and conceptual objections against toleration confirm that a number of issues associated with the toleration-based approach to diversity remain contested.

For example, toleration is not a universal strategy for each and every conflict we may encounter. Toleration has been a strategy for managing only peculiar conflicts, as conceptual discussions about the conditions of toleration make clear. As Rainer Forst emphasizes eloquently, "toleration is an attitude or practice which is only called for within social conflicts of a certain kind" (2003, p. 1). It therefore remains a contested issue what represents a genuine object of toleration. In particular, the "inflatory use of toleration" (Ceva 2015, p. 633) may ultimately endanger its overall coherence.

This, in turn, opens a set of challenges associated with the limits of toleration. There is an important distinction that needs to be made between the logical and the moral dimension of the limits of toleration. The logical dimension delineates the conditions a particular act needs to fulfill in order to qualify as an act of toleration. For example, liberal and multicultural conceptions of the logical dimension of the limits of toleration differ primarily over what counts as a relevant object of toleration. As has already been emphasized, toleration traditionally dealt with religious and moral conflicts. In contrast, a multicultural conception of toleration can also be directed at identities and not only religious beliefs or other conscience-based commitments of individuals. The logical dimension of the limits of toleration is therefore linked to the status as well as the nature of the object of toleration.

In contrast, the moral dimension of the limits of toleration addresses the problem of which differences should be tolerated and what are the principled bases delineating the limits of toleration. The moral dimension defines the situation where the reasons for the rejection of certain beliefs, practices, or conceptions of the good are stronger than the reasons for their adoption. The moral dimension determines how far the limits of toleration are to be extended. As Rainer Först emphasizes,

> The distinctive feature is that tolerance does not resolve, but merely contains and defuses, the dispute in which it is invoked; the clash of convictions, interests or practices remains, though certain considerations mean that it loses its destructiveness. (Först 2003, p. 1)

While both classical and contemporary proponents of toleration argued succinctly for its necessity for the maintenance of a stable and a peaceful political community, its status, its justification, and the limits of what is to be tolerated remain largely contested.

At the heart of these controversies lie a number of conceptual and moral problems stemming from the many concepts and ideas that are part of its gravitational orbit, e.g., civility, dignity, coercion, harm, power, conflict, disagreement, secularism, orthodoxy, dissent, knowledge, authority, domination, trust, restraint, non-interference, neutrality, fairness, pluralism, autonomy, (mutual) respect, recognition, etc. Moreover, the use and application of toleration has also been questioned as it might represent a form of "liberal expectancy" (Rosenblum 1998, pp. 53–57). This strategy is based on the assumption that toleration will gradually exert a gravitational influence by attracting towards the toleration that what is being tolerated. As Sanford Levinson emphasized, toleration of diversity includes the expectancy that "exposure to diverse beliefs and ways of life over time will shift the tolerated's view towards those of the tolerator" (Levinson 2003, pp. 91–92). Liberals hope and expect, writes Will Kymlicka, "that ethnic, religious, and cultural associations will, over time, voluntarily adjust their practices and beliefs to bring them more in line with the public principles of liberalism, which will reduce the 'incongruence' between associational norms and liberal principles" (Kymlicka 2002, p. 103). Similarly, as Jürgen Habermas emphasizes eloquently,

> [t]he liberal state expects that the religious consciousness of the faithful will become modernized by way of a cognitive adaptation to the individualistic and egalitarian nature of the laws of the secular community. (Habermas 2003, p. 6)

1 The Trouble with Toleration

On this interpretation, toleration would most likely appear as an extension of the classical "formula" advanced by von Clausewitz where war functions as "the continuation of politics by other means." To extend the interpretation further, as an instrument of liberal governance (Brown 2006), toleration would appear as the continuation of war by other means or as some sort of a liberal "Trojan horse" aimed to "colonize" either illiberal or non-liberal communities as some of its critics might argue (Žižek 2008).

It therefore comes as no surprise that despite its political relevance and theoretical import, toleration has found itself in crossfire between the different positions from the political spectrum as its use and application found its way also on the "minefield" of the "War on Terror." For example, toleration has been defined one of the central values aimed to tackle radicalization and violent extremism in a flagship anti-radicalization program that is part of the Prevent strategy by the UK government. As Awan et al. emphasize, "[t]he UK government has defined extremism as the 'vocal or active opposition to fundamental British values, including democracy, the rule of law, individual liberty and mutual respect and tolerance of different faiths and beliefs'" (Awan et al. 2019, p. 10). Here toleration functions primarily as a civilizational discourse (Brown 2006). On this interpretation, toleration appears also as an ideological category as issues as diverse as inequality, exploitation, domination, and discrimination have been recast as problems of toleration. "The language of toleration in liberal democracies," writes Glen Newey, "is vulnerable to political manipulation and that theories that ignore this fact risk becoming, in the pejorative sense, ideological" (Newey 2013, p. 3).

Interestingly enough, the language of toleration has also found its way into the moralizing rhetoric of zero tolerance by becoming a slogan used by public authorities to tackle problems as diverse as violence, drugs, sexual harassment, corruption, etc. As Catriona McKinnon and Dario Castiglione accentuate, "zero tolerance" stands as a slogan "for a less forgiving society" (2003, p. 1). For example, the shift of emphasis here is that the foundational question of toleration, i.e., "what are the limits of toleration" becomes redundant as zero toleration means that any phenomenon identified as the one that is to be tackled, for example, violence or corruption, is equally unacceptable as any other. This opens a range of separate problems with important conceptual and empirical challenges. As Glen Newey emphasizes, "[t]he political rhetoric of 'zero tolerance' provides an expression of this way of thinking, which subverts toleration by appropriating its vocabulary of commendation" (2013, p. 46).

Summary and Future Directions

The main challenge discussions about toleration face is therefore not one of direct criticism addressed in the form of objections but primarily in a range of multitude of shortcomings that might hamper our understanding of toleration in all its complexity. On the one hand, discussions about toleration somehow fail to acknowledge that there is a continuing import of paradoxes, dilemmas, and other conceptual "mishaps." On the other hand, most often when toleration is being discussed, its civilizational import is oftentimes neglected. As Michael Walzer rightly emphasizes,

[t]oleration itself is often underestimated, as if it is the least we can do for our fellows, the most minimal of their entitlements. In fact, [...] even the most grudging forms and precarious arrangements [of toleration] are very good things, sufficiently rare in human history that they require not only practical but also theoretical appreciation. (Walzer 1997, p. xi)

Looking for alternatives for those interested in going beyond toleration would remain at its most productive when its acknowledgment – whatever its faults may be – will be rightly acknowledged. Its continuing relevance is ultimately an important reminder not only of the basic civilizational commitment to "live and let live" but one perhaps much more challenging. The trouble with toleration, as Glen Newey accentuated in his Epilogue to *Toleration in Political Conflict*, "is not just about living with a threatening other, but about living with ourselves" (2013, p. 209).

References

Awan I, Spiller K, Whiting A (2019) Terrorism in the classroom: security, surveillance and a public duty to act. Palgrave Pivot, Cham
Balint P (2017). Respecting Toleration: Traditional Liberalism & Contemporary Diversity. Oxford: Oxford University Press
Bejan T (2017) Mere civility: disagreement and the limits of toleration. Harvard University Press, Cambridge, MA
Berlin I (2002) Two concepts of liberty. In: Hardy H (ed) Isaiah Berlin: liberty. Oxford University Press, Oxford, pp 166–217
Brown W (2006) Regulating aversion: tolerance in the age of identity and empire. Princeton University Press, Princeton
Brown W (2014) The power of tolerance: a debate. Columbia University Press, New York
Bufacchi V (2007) Violence and social justice. Palgrave/Macmillan, New York
Bufacchi V (2009) Introduction: rethinking violence. Global Crime 10(4):293–297
Buyse A (2018) Squeezing civic space: restrictions on civil society organizations and the linkages with human rights. Int J Human Rights 14(5):1–23
Cassam Q (2021) Extremism: a philosophical analysis. Routledge, London
Ceva E (2015) Why toleration is not the appropriate response to dissenting Minorities' claims. Eur J Philos 23(3):633–651
Cohen AJ (2004) What toleration is. Ethics 115(1):68–95
de Tocqueville A (2000) Democracy in America. University of Chicago Press, Chicago
Dees R (2004) Trust and toleration. Routledge, London
Deveaux M (2000) Cultural pluralism and dilemmas of justice. Cornell University Press, Itacha/London
Deželan T, Laker J, Sardoč M (2020) Safeguarding civic space for young people in Europe. European Youth Forum, Brussels
Drerup J, Schweiger G (eds) (2021) Toleration and the challenges to liberalism. Routledge, London
Fiala A (2005) Tolerance and the ethical life. Continuum, London
Firth JR (1957) A synopsis of linguistic theory, 1930–1955. In: Studies in linguistic analysis. Basil Blackwell, Oxford, pp 1–32
Först R (2003) Toleration in conflict: past and present. Cambridge University Press, Cambridge
Först R, (2020). Toleration, Power and the Right to Justification: Rainer Forst in Dialogue. Manchester: Manchester University Press

1 The Trouble with Toleration

Galeotti AE (2002) Toleration as recognition. Cambridge University Press, Cambridge

Galeotti AE (2015) The range of toleration: from toleration as recognition back to disrespectful tolerance. Philos Social Crit 41(2):93–110

Galeotti AE (2021) Rescuing toleration. Crit Rev Int Soc Pol Phil 24(1):87–107

Galeotti AE, Liveriero F (2021) Toleration as the balance between liberty and security. J Ethics 1–19 25:161–179

Gallie WB (1955) Essentially contested concepts. Proc Aristot Soc 56:167–198

Galston WA (2018) Anti-pluralism: the populist threat to liberal democracy. Yale University Press, New Haven

Gaus G, D'Agostino F (eds) (2013) The Routledge companion to social and political philosophy. Routledge, London

Gray J (1996) Berlin. Fontana, London

Gutmann A (ed) (1997) Multiculturalism and the politics of recognition. Princeton University Press, Princeton

Habermas J (2003) Intolerance and discrimination. Int J Constit Law 1(1):2–12

Hardy H (ed) (2002) Isaiah Berlin: liberty. Oxford University Press, Oxford

Haydon G (2006) Respect for persons and for cultures as a basis for national and global citizenship. J Moral Educ 35(4):457–471

Heyd D (ed) (1996) Toleration: an elusive virtue. Princeton University Press, Princeton

Jones P (2006) Toleration, recognition and identity. J Polit Philos 14(2):123–143

Jones P (2013) Toleration. In: Gaus G, D'Agostino F (eds) The Routledge companion to social and political philosophy. Routledge, London, pp 629–639

Kaplan BJ (2010) Divided by faith: religious conflict and the practice of toleration in early modern Europe. Belknap Harvard, Cambridge, MA

Kelly E, McPherson L (2001) On tolerating the unreasonable. J Polit Philos 9(1):38–55

Kühle L, Lindekilde L (2012) Radicalization and the limits of tolerance: a Danish case-study. J Ethn Migr Stud 38(10):1607–1623

Kukathas C (2003) The Liberal archipelago: a theory of diversity and freedom. Oxford University Press, Oxford

Kymlicka W (1989) Liberalism, community and culture. Clarendon Press, Oxford

Kymlicka W (1996) Two models of pluralism and tolerance. In: Heyd D (ed) Toleration: an elusive virtue. Princeton, Princeton University Press, pp 81–105

Kymlicka W (2002) Contemporary political philosophy: an introduction, 2nd edn. Oxford University Press, Oxford

Laborde C (2008) Critical republicanism: the hijab controversy and political philosophy. Oxford University Press, Oxford

Laden AS, Owen D (eds) (2007) Multiculturalism and political theory. Cambridge University Press, Cambridge

Levinson S (2003) Wrestling with diversity. Duke University Press, Durham

MacIntyre A (2007) After virtue: a study in moral theory. University of Notre Dame Press, Notre Dame

McKinnon C (2006) Toleration: a critical introduction. Routledge, London

McKinnon C, Castiglione D (2003a) Introduction: reasonable tolerance. In: McKinnon C, Castiglione D (eds) The culture of toleration in diverse societies. Manchester University Press, Manchester, pp 1–9

McKinnon C, Castiglione D (eds) (2003b) The culture of toleration in diverse societies. Manchester University Press, Manchester

Mendus S (1989) Toleration and the limits of liberalism. Humanities Press International, Atlantic Highlands

Miles R, Brown M (1989) Racism. Routledge, London

Müller J-W (2016) What is populism? University of Pennsylvania Press, Philadelphia

Nathanson S (2010). Terrorism and the Ethics of War. Cambridge: Cambridge University Press

Neumann PR (2003) The trouble with radicalization. Int Aff 89(7):873–893

Newey G (1999) Virtue, reason and toleration: the place of toleration in ethical and political philosophy. Edinburgh University Press, Edinburgh

Newey G (2013) Toleration in political conflict. Cambridge University Press, Cambridge

Parekh B (2000) Rethinking multiculturalism: cultural diversity and political theory. Palgrave, New York

Rawls J (1993) Political liberalism. Columbia University Press, New York

Rosenblum N (1998). Membership and Morals: The Personal Uses of Pluralism in America. Princeton: Princeton University Press

Sardoč M (ed) (2010) Toleration, respect and recognition in education. Wiley-Blackwell, London

Sardoč M (2013) The anatomy of toleration. Annales 23(2):203–214

Sardoč M, Coady CAJ, Bufacchi V, Moghaddam FM, Cassam Q, Silva D, Miščević N, Andrejč G, Kodelja ZV, Boris P, Michael A, Tesar M (2021) Philosophy of education in a new key: on radicalization and violent extremism. Educ Philos Theory. https://doi.org/10.1080/00131857. 2020.1861937

Sartori G (1970) Concept misformation in comparative politics. Am Polit Sci Rev 64(4):1033–1053

Scanlon TM (2003) The difficulty of tolerance: essays in political philosophy. Cambridge University Press, Cambridge

Shorten A (2005) Toleration and cultural controversies. Res Publica 11:275–299

Spencer V (ed) (2017) Toleration in a comparative perspective. Lexington Books, Lanham

Spinner-Halev J (1994) The boundaries of citizenship: race, ethnicity, and nationality in the liberal state. The Johns Hopkins University Press, Baltimore

Taylor C (1997 [1992]) The politics of recognition. In: Gutmann A (ed) Multiculturalism: examining the politics of recognition. Princeton University Press, Princeton, pp 25–74

Waldron J (2012) The harm in hate speech. Harvard University Press, Cambridge, MA

Walzer M (1997) On toleration. Yale University Press, New Haven

Williams M, Waldron J (eds) (2008) Toleration and its Limits. (Vol. 48). New York: NYU Press

Young IM (1990) Justice and the politics of difference. Princeton University Press, Princeton

Zagorin P (2003) How the idea of religious toleration came to the west. Princeton University Press, Princeton

Žižek S (2008) Tolerance as an ideological category. Crit Inq 34(4):660–682

Toleration: Concept and Conceptions

2

Rainer Forst

Contents

Introduction 11
The Concept of Toleration and Its Paradoxes 12
Four Conceptions of Toleration 16
Summary and Future Directions 19
Cross-References 19
References 20

Abstract

In order to do justice to the multiple interpretations of the term toleration, it is useful to distinguish a core concept of toleration from different conceptions of it. Four such conceptions can be defined, each involving different ways to relate to others with whom one disagrees. In addition, toleration should be understood as a normatively dependent concept, i.e., one which must be combined with justifications that stem from other normative sources.

Keywords

Coexistence · Concept of toleration · Justification · Paradoxes of toleration · Permission · Respect

Introduction

The term "toleration" is used in many ways and with very different evaluations, ranging from very positive to extremely negative ones (Forst 2013; Newey 2013). For some, it marks an ideal of pluralist cooperation and mutual esteem, and for

---

R. Forst (✉)
Goethe University, Normative Orders Research Centre, Frankfurt/Main, Germany
e-mail: forst@em.uni-frankfurt.de

© The Author(s), under exclusive licence to Springer Nature Switzerland AG 2022
M. Sardoč (ed.), *The Palgrave Handbook of Toleration*,
https://doi.org/10.1007/978-3-030-42121-2_11

others, a hierarchical form of domination and stigmatization. Therefore, one might be led to assume that there is not just one but many conflicting concepts of toleration, in the sense that Isaiah Berlin (1969) spoke of "two concepts of liberty." However, this assumption is problematic. For, if these usages are to count as understandings of toleration, they must share a core meaning, and this core is the *concept* of toleration. Important differences reside in how this core gets elaborated, thus constituting different *conceptions* of toleration, which, furthermore, are associated with different *justifications* for toleration. Following John Rawls's (1999, p. 5) proposal (apropos the concept of justice), a "concept" includes the central semantic contents of the term, whereas "conceptions" are specific interpretations of the elements contained within the general concept.

The Concept of Toleration and Its Paradoxes

The core concept of toleration is defined by three components, each of which is connected with a particular paradox.

1. Of primary importance for the concept of toleration is the fact that the tolerated convictions or practices are regarded as false or condemned as bad; following Preston King (1976, pp. 44–51), this can be described as the *objection component*. Without this component, one would not speak of toleration but instead either of indifference (the absence of a negative or positive valuation) or of affirmation (the presence of a positive valuation). Although these two attitudes are often confused with toleration, they are in fact incompatible with it.

   Although to demand that the reasons for objection should be "objective" or "capable of being generally shared" seems excessive, nevertheless certain criteria for an acceptable objection are indispensable – at least if we understand tolerance as a virtue (in the following, the term "tolerance" is used primarily to denote a particular attitude and the term "toleration" mainly to refer to a practice, but the conceptual argument holds for both). If the objection rested on mere prejudices, such as belief in the inferiority of certain "races," or even on blind hatred, then the call for tolerance would accept such objections and prejudices as valid judgements to a certain extent. This could lead to the *paradox of the "tolerant racist"* according to which someone with extreme racist antipathies would be described as tolerant provided only that he or she showed restraint in his or her actions (without changing his or her way of thinking). And the more such prejudices the racist had, the greater would be his or her scope for tolerance (Horton 1994, p. 17f.; Newey 1999, p. 107f.). To call on a racist to be tolerant, therefore, seems mistaken; what we should do instead is call upon him or her to repudiate this prejudice and attempt to convince him or her of its groundlessness (Crick 1971). Otherwise, the demand for toleration would be in danger of exerting repressive effects by perpetuating social discrimination and morally demeaning condemnations.

2 Toleration: Concept and Conceptions

Resolving this paradox regarding the virtue of tolerance requires the formulation of minimal conditions for objection judgements, which, to put it negatively, exclude grossly irrational and immoral prejudices. Reasons for objection will, of course, be drawn from particular ethical belief systems; but the key point is that they must not fall below a certain moral threshold beneath which one cannot speak of tolerance as a virtue.

2. In addition to the objection component, toleration also has an *acceptance component* (King 1976, pp. 51–54), which specifies that the tolerated convictions and practices are condemned as false or bad, yet not so false or bad that other, positive reasons do not speak in favor of tolerating them. The important point here is that the positive reasons do not cancel out the negative ones but are set against them in such a way that, although they trump the negative reasons, the objection nevertheless retains its force. The practical reflection of those who exercise tolerance consists in this balancing of reasons.

The nature of the reasons for objection or acceptance remains open at the level of the general definition of the concept. Thus, a negative aesthetic valuation can be offset by a positive ethical or moral evaluation or a religiously grounded objection by other religiously grounded considerations. If the reasons for objection as well as those for acceptance are identified as "moral," the paradox arises how it can be morally right or even obligatory to tolerate what is morally wrong or bad. This paradox, which we can call the *paradox of moral toleration*, has been exhaustively discussed in the literature on toleration and has inspired very different proposals. According to John Horton (1994, p. 13), the paradox can be resolved if either pragmatic reasons speak for toleration or it becomes clear that lack of toleration would jeopardize a higher-level value such as freedom or autonomy. According to Susan Mendus (1989, p. 161f.), we must go beyond liberal justifications and appeal to the idea that tolerating something to which one objects, but which nevertheless is part of people's identities, is imperative if we are to create an inclusive society. Glen Newey (1999, p. 73f.) argues that tolerance must be regarded as a supererogatory attitude on the grounds that the reasons for objections are morally sufficient to repudiate a conviction or practice *pro tanto*, and hence that there cannot be an obligation to tolerate (see also Bejan [2017] on toleration out of a stance of "civility").

This is not the place to examine these (and other) proposals since that would mean examining the full spectrum of justifications for toleration. It becomes apparent, however, that resolving the paradox of moral toleration depends on clarifying how the reasons for objection must be constituted in order to admit a morally (and not just strategically) grounded, higher-level acceptance component without contradiction; and this calls, for example, for a distinction between *ethical* and *moral* reasons and the corresponding judgements concerning "wrong" or "bad" convictions and practices. Thus, a case for toleration arises where one has ethical objections against certain practices as being detrimental to the good life but finds no basic moral fault with them such that they violate essential standards of moral respect. For example, one may find a certain religious way of life wrongheaded but accept it because it does not deny other people's basic rights.

The paradox in question is reflected at the epistemological level. For, if the objection to "wrong" convictions is understood as a function of being convinced of the truth of one's own system of values, then the *paradox of the relativization of truth* follows. According to this, the person who exercises tolerance seems to be compelled to regard her convictions as true in order to arrive at a negative judgement and at the same time to assume that the convictions objected to could also be true if she is to arrive at a judgement of acceptance. This paradox poses a serious problem for the concept of toleration, for it amounts to the demand for a kind of relativization and restriction of one's own convictions which does not fundamentally place one's belief in their truth in question – a *relativization without relativism*, as it were. One of the central issues in discussions of religious toleration, for example, is how toleration is possible without relativism or skepticism (Forst 2013; Rawls 2005).

3. The concept of toleration implies the need to specify the *limits of toleration*. This is a conceptual matter, for toleration involves striking a precarious balance between negative and positive reasons and presupposes the willingness to suspend toleration when the tolerated convictions and practices are judged in such negative terms that the positive reasons are no longer sufficient to counterbalance them. The space of toleration is limited. To want to tolerate "everything" is an incoherent stance, for in that case, one would have to tolerate a practice and at the same time also tolerate it not being tolerated (see Forst 2020 vs. Kukathas 2020). But unlimited toleration is also impossible for practical reasons, for, according to Popper (1994), it would entail the paradox that toleration could disappear altogether: if toleration extends to the enemies of toleration, it leads to its own destruction (this could be called the *paradox of self-destruction*). This paradox is overcome when we acknowledge that toleration is justifiably restricted and we understand it as involving a certain form of reciprocity, so that extreme intolerance does not have to be tolerated (and under certain conditions should not be tolerated either).

How should the limits of toleration be drawn? Here it is important to recognize that, in addition to the reasons for objection and reasons for acceptance, we need a third category of reasons, namely, those for rejecting convictions and practices, where the rejection can no longer be offset by reasons for acceptance. Hence here we can speak of a *rejection component*. The nature of the reasons for rejection is not predetermined: they can be of the same kind as the reasons for objection or the reasons for acceptance, but they can also be of a different kind.

Against this background, we should make a distinction between two boundaries: the first boundary is that between (a) the normative domain of what one agrees with completely, in which there is affirmation and no objection – the domain of what is truly "one's own," as it were – and (b) the domain of what can be tolerated in which there is normative objection and yet also an acceptance which leads to toleration; the second boundary, the true limit of toleration, runs between the latter domain and (c) the domain of what cannot be tolerated, of what

2 Toleration: Concept and Conceptions

is strictly rejected and repudiated. When it comes to toleration, therefore, we must distinguish three normative domains, not just two.

In light of the foregoing, however, the resolution of the paradox of self-destruction seems to give rise to a new paradox. If the concept of toleration implies the necessity of drawing a boundary, then every concretization of the concept leads to the drawing of a boundary which places the tolerant on the "good" side in contrast to those who are labelled as "intolerable" or "intolerant" as a consequence. But then there is no genuine toleration because this one-sided act seems to be itself an act of intolerance and of arbitrary exclusion. What lays claim to the name of toleration merely serves to protect and strengthen one's own evaluative convictions and practices and to claim a higher form of legitimacy for them. Neither side can fall back on such a claim to legitimacy, however. Therefore, the *paradox of drawing the limits* states that toleration must always flip over into its opposite, intolerance, once it traces the inevitable boundary between what can and cannot be tolerated (Fish 1997; Minow 1990).

This paradox points to central difficulties with the concept of toleration. For it can indeed be shown historically that where the maxim "No toleration towards the intolerant!" was filled with content, intolerance all too often crept in and made its presence felt, for example, when the adherents of a particular religion (or atheists) were – and are – distrusted and condemned as a group. There are good reasons for mistrusting the way in which the boundaries separating the "tolerant" from the "intolerant" were drawn historically and continue to be drawn today. Here we should not forget that toleration is always a matter of social power (Brown and Forst 2014).

However, the deconstructivist-skeptical argument that purports to demonstrate the incoherence of toleration must be treated with some skepticism because it conflates two meanings of "intolerance" which should be kept apart. For to describe both the attitude and behavior of those who roundly reject the norm of toleration and the attitude and conduct of those who do not tolerate this alike as "intolerant" presupposes a relativism concerning values which fundamentally doubts the possibility of drawing the limits of toleration in a nonarbitrary and justifiable way. This answer does not resolve the paradox in question, however. Rather, it presupposes the possibility of a nonarbitrary justification of the limits of toleration, so that the identification and critique of intolerance cannot itself be described as similarly "intolerant." Not every rejection could then be criticized as a bad form of intolerance, but only a rejection which lacks good reasons. The normative meaning of the concept of toleration can be rescued only if one succeeds in placing it on a higher-level, generally justifiable foundation which cannot be deconstructed as one-sided and arbitrary.

4. The concept of toleration is further characterized by the fact that tolerance must be exercised *of one's own free will* and may not be coerced. For in that case, one would speak instead of "putting up with" or "bearing" practices against which one is powerless (Garcón Valdéz 1995, p. 471). However, to conclude from this that the tolerating party must actually be in a position of power from which they could effectively prevent the practices in question seems unfounded (Williams 1996).

For a minority who are not equipped with such power can also adopt an attitude of tolerance and be of the (uncoerced) conviction that, if they had sufficient means of power at their disposal, they would not use them to the disadvantage of others.

5. Finally, it is important to keep in mind that the concept itself leaves open the question of which *justification* of toleration is the correct or most appropriate one. Hence, in order to acquire a normative content and to lead to a justified conception, the concept must be filled out with other principles or values – and only in this way does it become a virtue or a particular practice. The concept of toleration itself remains a *normatively dependent concept* which is indeterminate without other normative values or principles. The history of toleration (Forst 2013) can then also be understood as the history of the justifications that have been used to fill the three components of objection, acceptance, and rejection with content.

Four Conceptions of Toleration

In light of this characterization of the central elements of the concept of toleration, we can distinguish four conceptions which provide specific interpretations of these elements. All of them refer to the political context of a state in which the subjects (who are also members of particular communities) exhibit important, profound differences. These conceptions of toleration are not construed as different regimes of toleration, whether in the sense of a historical series or in Michael Walzer's (1997) sense of distinct social arrangements. For, as current discussions of the problem of toleration show, these conceptions exist *simultaneously* in present-day societies. Moreover, many of the heated discussions about what toleration means in concrete terms can be understood as conflicts between advocates of these conceptions.

1. On the first conception, which we can call the *permission conception*, toleration designates the relation between an authority or majority and a minority which does not subscribe to the dominant system of values. Toleration here means that the authority (or majority) grants the minority the permission to live in accordance with its convictions as long as it does not question the predominance of the authority (or majority). The Edict of Nantes of 1598, which was supposed to put an end to the conflicts between Catholics and Huguenots in France, can serve as a historical example. In it Henry IV declared: "[N]ot to leave any occasion of trouble and difference among our Subjects, we have permitted and do permit to those of the Reformed Religion, to live and dwell in all the Cities and places of this our Kingdom and Countreys under our obedience, without being inquired after, vexed, molested, or compelled to do any thing in Religion, contrary to their Conscience, nor by reason of the same be searched after in houses or places where they live" (see Mousnier 1973, pp. 316–347). The more than four centuries that separate us from this edict (which was revoked in 1685) should not mislead us into thinking that this form of toleration has lost its relevance; on the contrary, it is often raised as a minimal demand by oppressed minorities and plays an important role in the interest calculations of states and majority populations within states.

As long as the difference between the minority and the majority remains within limits and a "private matter," so that no demand is made for a public political status based on equal rights, on this conception the minority can be tolerated primarily on pragmatic grounds, although also for reasons of principle. According to the permission conception, therefore, toleration means that the authority or majority which has the power and opportunity to intervene and to coerce the minority into (at least external) conformity, "puts up with" their difference and refrains from intervening, while the minority is forced to accept the authority's position of power. Therefore, the toleration situation is not reciprocal: one side permits the other certain deviations from the dominant practices or beliefs provided that the political dominance of the permission-granting side is not infringed upon. Toleration is accordingly understood as *permissio mali*, as putting up with a conviction or practice which is regarded as neither worthy nor deserving of equal treatment, even though it does not exceed the "limits of the bearable." It is this conception which Goethe had in mind in his dictum concerning toleration as an insult: "Tolerance should be a temporary attitude only; it must lead to recognition. To tolerate means to insult" (Goethe 1998, p. 116; translation amended).

2. The second conception of toleration, the *coexistence conception*, resembles the first in asserting that tolerance counts as an appropriate means of avoiding conflict and pursuing one's own ends and does not itself represent a value or rest on strong values. Toleration is justified primarily in pragmatic and instrumental terms. What is different, however, is the constellation formed by the subjects and objects of toleration. For now, it is not an authority or majority and a minority or minorities which confront one another but groups of approximately equal strengths who recognize that they must exercise tolerance for the sake of social peace. They prefer peaceful coexistence to conflict and consent to the rules of a modus vivendi in the guise of a mutual compromise. The toleration relation is thus no longer a vertical one, as in the permission conception, but a horizontal one: those who exercise tolerance are at the same time also tolerated. The insight into the preferability of a condition of toleration does not have a strong normative character but is rather an insight into practical necessities.

3. By contrast, the *respect conception* of toleration proceeds from a morally grounded form of mutual respect on the part of the individuals or groups who exercise toleration. The tolerating parties respect one another as autonomous persons or as equally entitled members of a political community constituted under the rule of law (Scanlon 1996; Yovel 1998). Although their ethical convictions about the good and worthwhile life and their cultural practices differ profoundly and are in important respects incompatible, they recognize one another – and here an alternative with far-reaching consequences presents itself – as ethically autonomous authors of their own lives (Raz 1988; Weale 1985) *or* as moral and legal equals in the sense that, as they see it, the basic structure of political and social life common to all, which concerns the basic questions of the ascription of rights and the allocation of social resources (Rawls 2005, lec. 7), should be governed by norms which can be accepted by all citizens alike without

privileging any single "ethical community" (e.g., a religious community) (Forst 2013; Habermas 2004). This may be based on respect for the moral autonomy of the individual and her "right to justification" of norms which claim to be reciprocally and generally valid (Forst 2012). Notwithstanding the alternative between justifications based upon a theory that – following classical liberalism – treats the right to be the autonomous author of one's life as central and justifications based upon an approach which emphasizes the principle of the impartial justification of universal norms of justice, the respect conception does not require that the tolerating parties must regard and value each others' conceptions of the good as equally (or in part) true and ethically good; rather, they should be able to view them (and here the alternative again comes into play) as the results of autonomous choices or as not immoral. The person of the other is *respected*; her convictions and actions are *tolerated*.

Two models of the respect conception can be distinguished, that of *formal equality* and that of *qualitative equality*. The former assumes a strict separation between the private and public domains according to which ethical differences between citizens should be confined to the private domain and must not lead to conflicts within the public political sphere. All citizens are equal and, as equals, they stand "outside" or "above" their private convictions. This model can be found in liberal and republican versions depending on whether individual, private liberty or the political equality of the *citoyens* is accorded central importance; an example of the latter is the view of the French authorities that headscarves as a religious symbol have no place in a public school (Galeotti 1993). The model of formal equality, therefore, turns essentially on defending classical liberty rights of citizens and avoiding discrimination on ethical grounds.

The model of qualitative equality, by contrast, is a reaction to the fact that certain strict regulations of formal equality are in danger of giving preference to ethical-cultural forms of life whose convictions and practices can be more easily reconciled with such a separation between "private" and "public" or correspond to the received understanding of this separation. Viewed in this light, the model of formal equality is itself potentially intolerant and discriminatory towards forms of life which lay claim to a kind of public presence that contradicts customary practice and conventional institutions. According to the alternative model, persons respect one another as legal and political equals who nevertheless have different, politically relevant ethical and cultural identities with a special claim to consideration and toleration, because the values and convictions constitutive of these identities have a special existential meaning for persons. This demand for respect in the sense of fairness calls, finally, for particular exceptions to or changes in traditional rules and structures (Laden and Owen 2007; Waldron and Williams 2008).

4. In discussions of the relation between multiculturalism and toleration, a fourth conception is occasionally encountered which can be called the *esteem conception*. It involves a more demanding form of recognition than the respect conception for, according to it, toleration means not only respecting the members of other cultural or religious communities as legal and political equals but also esteeming their

2 Toleration: Concept and Conceptions

convictions and practices as ethically valuable (Apel 1997; Bauman 1991; Kristeva 1991). However, if this is to remain a conception of toleration and the objection component is not to be lost, the esteem in question must be limited or "with reservations," so that the other form of life does not count as equally as good as, or even better than, one's own. One values certain aspects of this form of life while objecting to others; however, the domain of what can be tolerated is defined by the values which one affirms in an ethical sense. Thus, this conception of toleration corresponds, from a liberal perspective, to a version of value pluralism which holds that a rivalry exists within a society between intrinsically worthwhile yet incompatible forms of life (Raz 1988) and, from the communitarian perspective, to the view that there are particular, socially shared notions of the good life whose partial variations can be tolerated (Sandel 1989).

Summary and Future Directions

The conceptual analysis of toleration provides a framework for fleshing out different conceptions of toleration, but given the normative dependency of the concept, the sources of the principles and values used to determine the grounds of objection, acceptance, or rejection are not predetermined by this analysis. Within Western history, one major source for all of the three sets of reasons was religious faith, whether Jewish, Christian, or Muslim. In the course of history, many other foundations were added, and apart from strategic or instrumental considerations, values such as peace, truth, reason, autonomy, community, identity, democracy, human dignity, and the like were used to justify a stance or policies of toleration. Some of these foundations lend themselves more to one rather than another conception, but the range of possible combinations is broad. At this point, normative reflection that is connected but not based on the foregoing analysis becomes necessary. It may be helpful to consider the question of toleration to be a question of *justice* and of the mutual justifiability of a common legal and political normative order, but that question cannot be further explored here (Forst 2013). It remains a matter for further research to discuss the advantages and problems of various justifications for toleration.

Another important direction for further research is to transcend the boundaries of Western traditions and discourses and inquire into the way in which other traditions and reflections dealt with the question of toleration, especially whether there is a particular, similar concept for it or not and how toleration was justified (Chan 2014; Dhouib 2020; Flanagan 2013).

Translated by Ciaran Cronin

Cross-References

▶ Paradoxes of Toleration
▶ Toleration and Justice
▶ Toleration and Liberty of Conscience

- ► Toleration and Neutrality
- ► Toleration and Reasonableness

References

Apel K-O (1997) Plurality of the good? The problem of affirmative tolerance in a multicultural society from an ethical point of view. Ratio Juris 10(2):199–212

Bauman Z (1991) Modernity and ambivalence. Polity, Cambridge, UK

Bejan TM (2017) Mere civility. Harvard University Press, Cambridge, MA

Berlin I (1969) Two concepts of liberty. In: Four essays on liberty. Oxford University Press, Oxford

Brown W, Forst R (2014) The power of tolerance. Columbia University Press, New York

Chan J (2014) Confucian perfectionism. Princeton University Press, Princeton

Crick B (1971) Toleration and tolerance in theory and practice. Gov Oppos 6(2):144–171

Dhouib S (2020) Toleranz in transkultureller Perspektive. Velbrück, Weilerswist

Fish A (1997) Mission impossible: settling the just bounds between Church and State. Columbia Law Rev 97(8):2255–2333

Flanagan O (2013) The view from the East pole: buddhist and confucian tolerance. In: Clarke S et al (eds) Religion, intolerance, and conflict. Oxford University Press, Oxford

Forst R (2012) The right to justification. Columbia University Press, New York

Forst R (2013) Toleration in conflict. Past and present. Cambridge University Press, Cambridge, UK

Forst R (2020) The dialectics of toleration and the power of reason(s). Reply to my critics. In: Forst R (ed) Toleration, power and the right to justification Rainer Forst in dialogue. Manchester University Press, Manchester

Galeotti AE (1993) Citizenship and equality. The place for toleration. Political Theory 21(4):585–605

Garcón Valdéz E (1995) Nimm deine dreckigen Pfoten von meinem Mozart!' Überlegungen zum Begriff der Toleranz. In: Garcón Valdéz E, Zimmerling R (eds) Facetten der Wahrheit. Alber, Freiburg

Goethe JW (1998) Maxims and reflections. Penguin, London

Habermas J (2004) Religious tolerance – the pacemaker for cultural rights. Philosophy 79(307):5–18

Horton J (1994) Three (apparent) paradoxes of toleration. Synth Philos 17(1):7–20

King P (1976) Toleration. St. Martin's Press, New York

Kristeva J (1991) Strangers to ourselves. Discovering the adaptive unconscious. Columbia University Press, New York

Kukathas C (2020) Let's get radical. Extending the reach of Baylean (and Forstian) toleration. In: Forst R (ed) Toleration, power and the right to justification. Rainer Forst in dialogue. Manchester University Press, Manchester

Laden AS, Owen D (eds) (2007) Multiculturalism and political theory. Cambridge University Press, Cambridge, UK

Mendus S (1989) Toleration and the limits of liberalism. Humanities Press, Atlantic Highlands

Minow M (1990) Putting up and putting down. Tolerance reconsidered. In: Tushnet M (ed) Comparative constitutional federalism. Europe and America. Greenwood Press, New York

Mousnier R (1973) The assassination of Henry IV. The tyrannicide problem and the consolidation of the French absolute monarchy in the early seventeenth century. Scribner, New York

Newey G (1999) Virtue, reason and toleration. The place of toleration in ethical and political philosophy. Edinburgh University Press, Edinburgh

Newey G (2013) Toleration in political conflict. Cambridge University Press, Cambridge, UK

Popper K (1994) Toleration and intellectual responsibility (Stolen from Xenophanes and from Voltaire). In: Popper K (ed) In search of a better world lectures and essays from thirty years. Routledge, London

Rawls J (1999) A theory of justice, rev ed. Harvard University Press, Cambridge, MA

Rawls J (2005) Political liberalism, exp ed. Columbia University Press, New York

2 Toleration: Concept and Conceptions

Raz J (1988) Autonomy, toleration and the harm principle. In: Mendus S (ed) Justifying toleration. Conceptual and historical perspectives. Cambridge University Press, Cambridge, UK

Sandel MJ (1989) Moral argument and liberal toleration: abortion and homosexuality. Calif Law Rev 77(3):521–538

Scanlon TM (1996) The difficulty of tolerance. In: Heyd D (ed) Toleration. An elusive virtue. Princeton University Press, Princeton

Waldron J, Williams M (eds) (2008) Toleration and its limits. New York University Press, New York

Walzer M (1997) On toleration. Yale University Press, New Haven

Weale A (1985) Toleration, individual differences, and respect for persons. In: Horton J, Mendus S (eds) Aspects of toleration. Methuen, London

Williams B (1996) Toleration: an impossible virtue? In: Heyd D (ed) Toleration. An elusive virtue. Princeton University Press, Princeton

Yovel Y (1998) Tolerance as grace and as rightful recognition. Soc Res 65(4):897–919

Defining Toleration

3

Andrew Jason Cohen

Contents

Introduction	24
Related Concepts	24
A. Indifference, Simple Noninterference, Resignation	25
B. A *Principle* of Toleration	28
C. Pluralism, Multiculturalism, Diversity	28
D. Permissiveness, Relativism, Pessimism	30
E. Neutrality	31
F. Tolerance	32
The Conditions of Toleration	35
1. *Agent ("an* agent *tolerates when she ...").*	35
2. *Intentional ("an agent tolerates when she* intentionally ...")	36
3. *Value ("an agent tolerates when she intentionally* and on principle ...").	36
4. *Noninterference ("an agent tolerates when she intentionally and on principle* refrains from interfering ...")	41
5. *Opposition ("an agent tolerates when she intentionally and on principle refrains from interfering with an* opposed ...").	43
6. *Object ("an agent tolerates when she intentionally and on principle refrains from interfering with an opposed* other (or their behavior, etc.) ....").	46
7. *Believed Power ("an agent tolerates when she intentionally, and on principle refrains from interfering with an opposed other (or their behavior, etc.), though* she believes she has the power to interfere ").	47
Summary and Future Directions	49
References	51

> **Abstract**
>
> The task of this chapter is to provide what is necessary for a conceptual analysis of toleration such that one would have a clear definition of this central liberal tenet. First, notions related to but different from toleration are discussed; this

---

A. J. Cohen
Georgia State University, Atlanta, GA, USA
e-mail: cohenaj@gsu.edu

© The Author(s), under exclusive licence to Springer Nature Switzerland AG 2022
M. Sardoĉ (ed.), *The Palgrave Handbook of Toleration*,
https://doi.org/10.1007/978-3-030-42121-2_20

provides guidance by introducing the likely definitional conditions of toleration. Next, those conditions are explicated and defended. Putting the conditions together, we can say *an agent tolerates when she intentionally and on principle refrains from interfering with an opposed other (or their behavior,* etc.*), though she believes she has the power to interfere.* This definition is neither normatively loaded nor sufficient for moral or political theory. Readers may also prefer a definition made with some subset of the conditions rather than all.

Keywords

Toleration · Tolerance · Interference · Neutrality · Diversity · Pluralism · Power

---

Introduction

Toleration has been called "the substantive heart of liberalism" (Hampton 1989: 802). This should be understood as precisely as possible. The task of this chapter is thus to provide what is necessary for a conceptual analysis of toleration such that one would have a clear definition of this central liberal tenet. First, notions related to, but different from, toleration are discussed; this provides guidance by introducing the likely definitional conditions of toleration. Next, those conditions are explicated and defended. Putting the conditions together, we can say *an agent tolerates when she intentionally and on principle refrains from interfering with an opposed other (or their behavior,* etc.*), though she believes she has the power to interfere*[1]. This definition is neither normatively loaded nor sufficient for moral or political theory. Readers may also prefer a definition made with some subset of the conditions rather than all.

Related Concepts

While we all likely have some inchoate ideas about toleration, it is also likely that these ideas are somewhat confused. Outside the world of academic philosophy, the term "toleration" is often used in different ways. Since much of that variation finds its way into scholarly thought, it is worth distinguishing toleration from other concepts with which it is often confused before engaging directly in conceptual

---

[1]This is a revision of work in Chaps. 1 and 2 of Cohen (2018), which was itself revised from Cohen (2004a). The definition defended here is thus a modification of that in Cohen (2004a): that an act of toleration is an agent's intentional and principled refraining from interfering with an opposed other (or their behavior, etc.) in situations of diversity, where the agent believes she has the power to interfere. The current version is meant to be substantively equivalent to the 2004a though with the removal of the requirement of "situations of diversity," which now seems to me to add nothing to the definition for reasons I make clear. I am grateful to Taylor and Francis (Routledge) for permission to use the material from Cohen (2018) and *Ethics* for the earlier permission to use the material from Cohen (2004a).

3 Defining Toleration

analysis. This will also provide guidance for determining what the core idea of toleration is as we begin to see conditions necessary for toleration. These, indeed, will appear quite quickly in this discussion; it will nonetheless be worth looking at a number of other concepts that are often confused with toleration. The following list owes much to Robert Paul Churchill 1997 (esp. 193–198). In particular, indifference, resignation, permissiveness, and neutrality are all suggested in his discussion, though they are discussed differently here. Of course, all of these concepts – and the others discussed here – are *related* to toleration. If they were not, there would be no confusion. Some may be on a continuum with toleration, but we need not be concerned with that here.

A. Indifference, Simple Noninterference, Resignation

Toleration is not indifference or simple noninterference. If you see someone playing baseball and have no interest in that American game, you would likely walk past without interfering; when you do, it does not seem right to say you tolerate the behavior. The reason for this seems straightforward: we think of ourselves as tolerating only when we recognize something and disapprove or, at least, dislike it. If someone is throwing a ball against your wall, you may tolerate it (or not) – in part because the behavior annoys. Some negative response is necessary for our lack of interference to count as toleration. Put another way, we must *care* (see Churchill 1997: 193; David Heyd 1996: 4; and Edward Langerak 1997: 111). Absent caring about that with which we refrain from interfering, we are not tolerating it. It may be that we are indifferent to it or that we simply do not notice it.

From this brief discussion, we already see that we are the sorts of beings that can tolerate, that toleration requires noninterference, and that behavior is something that can be tolerated. These three facts seem uncontroversial; they will be conditions one (agent), four (noninterference), and six (object). Also interesting is that toleration requires that the tolerator have some negative response; as Bernard Williams explains, "If you do not care all that much what anyone believes, you do not need . . . toleration . . . Indeed, if I and others in the neighborhood said we were *tolerating* the homosexual relations of the couple next door, our attitude would be thought less than liberal" (Williams 1996: 20). Interestingly, then, a world populated by individuals indifferent to those they do not know and like might be better than a world populated by individuals who know and tolerate those others. One way people can tolerate more often, after all, is to have more negative reactions. Horton notes something similar (1996: 34) which he points out may be thought paradoxical (see Horton 1994). Newey's discussion of the "censorious tolerator" (1999: 107ff and elsewhere) is helpful in dispelling the paradox, but it can also be dispelled by noting that though the agent who has more negative reactions is less *tolerant*, he may *tolerate* more (see the discussion about *tolerance* below). Indeed, Williams's point (above) is simply that "being liberal" (in the colloquial sense) requires being tolerant, not tolerating. The need for a negative reaction – for toleration, not tolerance – will be condition five (opposition).

Having a negative reaction to something is not enough to make noninterference with it toleration. One may refrain from interfering with it, after all, because one recognizes that one has no power to stop the disliked behavior, because the opposed other is physically stronger or, differently, because others have rights "even if they exercise those rights in unattractive ways" (Walzer 1997: 11; see also 59). Noninterference we resign ourselves to because we cannot do otherwise is not toleration but a matter enduring what one does not like – a sort of resignation, "mere restraint" (Heyd 1996: 14), or "a kind of moral stoicism" (Walzer 1997: 11). The person engaging in this form of noninterference resigns herself to living with others for the sake of peace, as if in a sort of modus vivendi (see John Rawls 1999a, esp. 430–433) or "pragmatic compromise" (Heyd 1996: 4; see also Walzer 1997: 10).

If these descriptions are accurate, why don't we consider these activities toleration? Why, that is, does one's resignation to one's inability to prevent some behavior not count as toleration? Simply put, it is because we think toleration is something we do *for the right reasons*. The presence of those reasons matters. We might say that one *endures* what one (believes one) *has to*; one *tolerates* what one (believes one) *should*.

To be clear, etymologically, the Latin root of toleration, "tolerantia," is "broadly intended to label … the general notion of enduring," as Preston King points out (King 1976: 12; see also Creppell 2002: 5). King also notes this, though, as a distinct use. What is here called "resignation," King calls "'acquiescence' or 'sufferance' or 'endurance'"; "toleration" is different and likely requires what is below called the *believed power* condition (King 1976: 21). George Fletcher similarly points out that in German, Hebrew, and Russian, the "same root generates both tolerance and patience" (Fletcher 1996: 237 note 12) but adds that "people [have to] *care* enough to be tolerant rather than indifferent" (237; emphasis added). There are often times when the concepts seem to overlap, at least in ordinary language. We say, for example, that one endures a pain and that one tolerates it (or builds one's tolerance toward it). If something could be done about that pain – taking an analgesic, for example – but one intentionally and on principle refrains from doing so, it may be toleration as well.

Importantly at this point, noninterference must be *valued* or properly *principled* for it to count as toleration. This will be condition three (value). It is obvious, but worth pointing out, that for a case of noninterference to be principled, it must also be intentional – one does not act on one's principles by accident. This will be condition two. (While an action could be intentional and unprincipled, it cannot be principled and unintentional. Hence, we could consider the intentionality requirement a subcondition of the value condition.)

One must refrain from interfering for good reason for one's noninterference to be toleration. That one must act for good reason means that one's belief states matter when determining if one is tolerating or merely not interfering. Belief states matter in a second way. Consider a new example. Say Albert tries to persuade his sister not to have an abortion but then stands aside when she leaves to go to the family planning clinic. Surely, Alex may be tolerating her action. His attempt at rational persuasion –

3 Defining Toleration

which, as will be made clearer in below, should not be considered interference – failed and he does not interfere with her actions, which he nonetheless opposes. Now it may be that Albert is merely enduring his sister's actions – that because he has no (legal) right to interfere, he could do nothing and so must have resigned himself to her action. This *may* be the case, but it need not be. Perhaps Alex mistakenly thinks he does have a (legal) right to interfere. If so, he may not be merely resigning himself to her action. He may be standing aside because, though he believes he *can* interfere, he also believes he *should* not – that is, he may well value his non-interfering or her right to proceed so that his noninterference is based on a principled reason, as indicated is needed in condition three. What we also should notice now is that this case clearly suggests that *believing one has the power to interfere* is relevant to toleration. It will be condition seven (believed power).

The previous paragraph assumed that what was at issue was the lack of a legal right (of Albert's) to interfere with his sister. Some may think it is a moral right that is at issue; that is, they may claim that Albert has no moral right to interfere with his sister's action. For that to make it such that the case is not one of toleration but one of mere resignation to what he cannot change, the moral prohibition indicated by the absence of a right must be accompanied by an internal compulsion to abide by morality. If there were none, he would be able to interfere by disregarding morality. Delving further into this requires looking to the internalism-externalism debate. If someone (a third party to the above debate) were to think that Albert had, in the example, a moral right (perhaps accompanied by a legal right) to interfere, then it is indeed possible that the case is one of toleration.

Two caveats should be recognized at this point. First, as motivations and belief states generally are often mixed and/or confused, there may be cases where determining whether an act is one of mere resignation or one of toleration is near impossible; indeed, it may be that there is no sharp line between the two. Second, complicating the first, there is a common use of the word "tolerance" (itself discussed below) which is equivalent to endurance – one "builds one's level of tolerance/endurance." Given that and the oft conflation of tolerance and toleration, confusions are not infrequent.

We have now (briefly) elucidated the seven likely conditions of toleration. They are:

1. the presence of an *agent*
2. who *intentionally*
3. and *on principle*
4. *refrains from interfering* with
5. an *opposed*
6. *other* (or their behavior, etc.) though
7. she *believes she has the power to interfere*.

Each of these will be examined below. First, though, we continue our examination of concepts that are distinct though related to – and sometimes conflated with – toleration.

B. A *Principle* of Toleration

It will be noted that the seven conditions of toleration do nothing to tell us when we should interfere or refrain from interfering. Their joint presence indicates that toleration is present, not that it *should* be. When we say that toleration is at the heart of liberalism, we mean something like toleration's presence in society is morally important. Indeed, its presence is of paramount moral importance. Its absence suggests a society is not liberal – or rather suggests either that the society is not liberal or that the society is so harmonious that liberalism is irrelevant because none of its members oppose how any of their compatriots live (whether because they are indifferent to many of those compatriots or have universal love toward them). Assuming we will not attain utopia any time soon, liberalism thus must include a view about *when* toleration should be present – no one thinks it should always be present. We should not, for simple examples, tolerate murder and rape. Liberalism thus requires a normative principle (or principles) of toleration to adjudicate interference.

In order to have a *principle of toleration*, one must be clear about what toleration is. With a clear understanding of toleration, we can move on to discuss possible principles and defend one (or more) against others. Toleration itself, then, is not a principle. It is a form of behavior (refraining from interfering). That behavior must be principled, as we saw above and will discuss further below, but that is a different matter. Again, being able to identify toleration is not the same as knowing when we should or must tolerate or knowing when we should or must not. This is why understanding what toleration is cannot be sufficient for moral or political philosophy – in itself, it provides no normative guidance. We need a normative principle (or principles) of toleration for that purpose. (That is not the topic of this chapter, but see Cohen 2014, 55–85.)

C. Pluralism, Multiculturalism, Diversity

Toleration is not pluralism, the view that insists there are multiple genuine values. Nor is it "enthusiastic endorsement of difference" (Walzer 1997: 11; see also Langerak 1997: 111) that might be better associated with multiculturalism.

There may be multiple genuine values and if there are, we ought usually to tolerate (or at least not interfere with) people acting in ways meant to promote those values. This means, though, that pluralism and toleration are distinct. Believing that X is a value (or that X and Y are values), tolerating X (or X and Y), promoting X (or X and Y), and tolerating the promotion of X (or X and Y) are all different. One does not tolerate what one promotes. It may, of course, be that we recognize values without promoting them in any significant way, but to recognize X as a value is to recognize it as something not to oppose. (Should one, perversely, oppose a value, one might be able to tolerate it. Still recognizing it as a value and tolerating it are different. Recognizing that there are multiple values is distinct from toleration.)

Importantly, the claim that there is cultural diversity is distinct from pluralism understood as the view that there are plural values. The first is an empirical claim only. Saying *there is* cultural diversity is not saying there *should be* cultural diversity nor *why* there should be. Multiculturalists presumably believe not only that there is cultural diversity, but also that there *should* be. Some may believe the latter claim because they believe different cultures instantiate different values; some may believe it because they believe different cultures instantiate the same values but in different ways. We need not pursue those questions here.

Cultural diversity itself may or may not be a value. (Arguments in favor are familiar; for an argument against it, see Susan Moller Okin 1999; for a broader discussion, see Chap. 9 of Cohen 2018.) While toleration would make diversity possible, the latter is not required for the former (see Newey 1999: 4 and 28–30). If no one brings different cultural (or other) views to the table, as it were, there likely is simply less to tolerate and the advocate of toleration need not be concerned. Of course, the advocate of multiculturalism may seek to bring different cultures to the table, perhaps wanting to promote them all. The advocate of multiculturalism, that is, promotes multiple cultures. Of course, she is thereby precluded from tolerating them – again, one does not tolerate what one promotes. She may, on the other hand, seek to encourage the toleration of one or more of the cultures she promotes *by others* who oppose those cultures. If she does, she will seek to provide good principled reasons for those with opposition to particular cultures to refrain from interfering with them. Toleration and enthusiastic endorsement of difference may form a spectrum of related responses to diversity.

Those advocating for the value of multiple cultures may wish to make toleration more intertwined with their view. Ingrid Creppell, for example, adds a condition to toleration that she takes to be of fundamental import: "one stays in a relationship with the person or group with whom one is in conflict [i.e., opposes]. … the parties remain in the presence of one another in a nontrivial way" (Creppell 2002: 4). Depending on what is meant by "nontrivial" or "the commonality of the ensuing relationship" (ibid), this may be what might be called a *diversity* condition for toleration (see Cohen 2004a), as discussed below. Creppell's "nontrivial ensuing relationship" seems, though, to mean something more and may be problematic. An act of toleration is, as Creppell notes, "a unilateral act of one person toward another" (ibid) – when one person tolerates another, the other may be tolerating the first or not (indeed, may be doing nothing regarding the first). There thus does remain a relationship, but it remains trivially. It is unclear, then, why the conception of toleration must thereby be "one that acknowledges the fundamental feature of the maintenance of [nontrivial] relationship[s]" as Creppell would prefer. That is, it does not seem that "toleration is about what connects persons to one another in a significant way despite differences and conflict" (Creppell 2002: 6). Toleration is simply one way to react when there are differences – regardless of the presence or absence of a connection. If this is mistaken, it would appear that there is no role for toleration in situations where the two involved groups have no significant connection. To take one simple example, if the USA decided to, it could interfere with, rather than tolerate, Iceland. It could also tolerate Iceland. This is true whether there are any significant connections between the two countries and their peoples.

Some will think the idea that tolerating and tolerated parties must remain in the presence of one another is plausible and shows that there is cultural diversity when one group tolerates another. That seems right. The point here is not that there is no cultural diversity – there obviously is. The point is only that such diversity is not necessary for toleration.

Though toleration does not require cultural diversity, it may seem to require *some* form of diversity. Indeed, as already mentioned, some defend a "diversity" condition for toleration, believing that this follows directly from the opposition condition – if there were no diversity, there would be no differences and if there are no differences there would be nothing to oppose and so nothing to tolerate. Churchill, for example, claims "Toleration arises in 'circumstances of diversity,' i.e., when people are aware of salient differences existing among them" (191). Similarly, Larmore claims it is "because reasonable persons disagree about the value of various conceptions of the good life, [that] we must learn to live with those who do not share our ideals" (Larmore 1987: 23; see also Nicholson 1985: 160; Deveaux 1998: 409; Oberdiek 2001: 38 and 47–48; Rawls 1999b: 11–12 and 131 ff.; and Rawls 1993: 36 and elsewhere).

Despite the above claims, however, the sort of diversity that must be present for toleration may well be trivial. Consider the claim that Mary can tolerate Paul's snoring even if Mary is also a snorer – indeed, even if everyone snores. The lack of diversity here would not make toleration impossible. Of course, someone might claim that when Mary refrains from interfering with Paul's snoring, there is diversity simply because they are two different individuals, in two different spatial locations. This is utterly trivial; as a condition of toleration, diversity is redundant – it adds nothing to the opposition requirement. Mary can tolerate Paul's snoring because Mary opposes things that keep her awake, whether or not they are things she also does.

Diversity as a condition of toleration is at best redundant. Worse though, including it as a necessary condition of toleration might lead some to mistakenly declare an absence of toleration where it is present. Some might think, to continue the example, that Mary cannot tolerate Paul's snoring because they have snoring in common and so there is no diversity. Yet most would likely say that Mary does (or at least can) tolerate Paul's snoring. We should not let this lead us astray. Though diversity is not required for toleration, there is a great deal of diversity and a great deal of opposition to different elements of that diversity – and hence a great deal to be tolerated.

D. Permissiveness, Relativism, Pessimism

Toleration is not mere permissiveness, wherein one cares (having a negative reaction) but is either (i) a relativist who believes that one's view cannot be shown to be better than that of the person potentially interfered with, or (ii) a pessimist about the possibility of (perhaps cross-cultural) dialogue.

As has been frequently noted, the relativist cannot offer any defense of toleration; all he can say is "I approve of it" – and he can only mean this in some emotive sense, not in any way rationally defensible. If it were rationally defensible, it would not be relativist – there would be an objective claim about the value of toleration. The concern here, then, is not "an indiscriminate toleration at times indistinguishable from relativism" (Wolfson 1999, 39). Indeed, toleration *is* a well-defended value. (For arguments in favor of toleration, see Rainer Forst 2013, especially 399–446 and Cohen 2014, 125–150 as well as Chaps. 4 and 5 of Cohen 2018. For arguments that toleration accords better with objectivism than subjectivism, see Graham 1996, esp. 46–48 and 55–58; Williams 1996, esp. 204–8; and Oberdiek 2001: 14–16.) This is important; "toleration does not mean we lack commitment to our own ideals, or are surrendering them. We are enjoined not to suppress ideas of which we disapprove: we are not being asked to like or support or encourage them" (Nicholson 1985: 170). In a nutshell, the relativist seems to think he cannot interfere because he cannot show that his view is better than his opponent's and so merely resigns himself to suffering the disapproved of activity. He is permissive because of that resignation brought on by his relativism.

The situation of the pessimist about dialogue is perhaps less clear than that of the relativist. It may seem that the pessimist thinks her view is objectively valuable but simply does not believe she can convince the other – the one with whom she chooses not to interfere – of that value. Perhaps, then, her noninterference is actually principled so that she is tolerating. If so, she would not be tolerating *because* of her pessimism. Her pessimism might prevent her from engaging in dialogue with the opposed other, but if she tolerates, she does so for some other (principled) reason. Absent a principled reason, she does not tolerate. She likely merely endures, perhaps accepting a modus vivendi as discussed above.

E. Neutrality

Toleration is not the same as neutrality. One can remain neutral between two parties by failing to tolerate either – perhaps even by killing both. Moreover, one can tolerate X – say a disliked religion – while clearly disapproving of it. So too, one may endorse one religion (e.g., a state might give it favorable tax status) while tolerating other religions. All of this should be fairly clear. Say Phillip wholeheartedly endorses and practices Judaism, the religion of his parents. Perhaps Phillip loves Judaism and thinks it vastly superior to all other religions. This would make it impossible for him to tolerate Judaism, but not other religions. Indeed, if he thought Judaism vastly superior to other religions, he would presumably oppose (factors of) those other religions, thus leaving open the possibility of toleration. Still, Phillip might think some of those other religions worse than others. He might think, for example, that Christianity should be tolerated but that Satanism should be suppressed. If that were the case, Phillip would not be neutral toward the three religions; he would endorse one, tolerate another, and advocate suppressing the third.

It is worth noting that neutrality is here used as a form of comparison (perhaps coupled with a resulting behavior). If one is neutral about X and Y, one compares them (either to each other or to a third thing) and acts in the same way toward each of them. Similarly, there can be a neutral comparative attitude where one feels neutral with regard to two or more things – that is, feels the same about both – with or without a negative response to them. One may be indifferent between X and Y, perhaps thinking both heinous. By contrast, having a neutral attitude toward a *single* thing (non-comparatively) implies that there is no negative response; this would rule out the possibility of toleration.

Understanding neutrality as just discussed helps us understand the relationship between toleration and neutrality – or, perhaps better stated, the relationship between toleration and *liberal* neutrality. If, as will be discussed below, an agent tolerates when she intentionally and on principle refrains from interfering with an opposed other (or their behavior, etc.), though she believes she has the power to interfere, a liberal state could only be appropriately neutral if it intentionally and on principle refrains from interfering with any individual or group (or its members, or its or their behavior) even though it (or its agents) believes it has the power to interfere. That is, liberal neutrality can be understood as the liberal state having a policy of *equal toleration.* (For more on this, see Cohen 2004b and Balint 2015, 2017, Chap. 3.) For a contrasting view about this, see, Oberdiek, who claims that a substantive liberalism based on toleration must abandon neutrality (116). In her discussion, Anna Elisabetta Galeotti is concerned with "the acceptance, and hence the inclusion, of a different trait, behavior, practice, or identity in the range of the legitimate, viable, 'normal' options and alternatives of an open society." While this, she says, does not evaluate "the actual content" of the difference, it negates "the majoritarian definition of something as different" (Galeotti 2002: 14–15). She may be right, but this reads like a definition of neutrality, not toleration (she discusses neutrality more extensively on 53–65). Neutrality has been criticized, of course, but a neutrality of procedure with regard to competing individuals, groups, or ways of life is likely as defensible as toleration.

As an aside, it is interesting that some early modern thinkers seem to think a state could reasonably tolerate multiple religions while treating them differently. Pierre Bayle seems to have thought, for example, that religious groups could be differentially taxed and even that a religion could be tolerated while its practitioners were not allowed to *publicly* display their religiosity (see Cohen 2021, forthcoming). Strictly speaking, this latter is correct: the displays of religiosity would not be tolerated though the religion was. Bayle, though, was likely mistaken about differential taxation. Taxation is a form of interference. While one might tax individuals while tolerating their religions, taxing their churches interferes with those churches and thus is not toleration thereof.

F. Tolerance

Finally, it is worth distinguishing toleration and tolerance. It is helpful here to consider the grammatical usage of the terms. While "tolerant" is an adjective, "tolerate" is a verb. "Tolerance" and "toleration," on the other hand, are both

3 Defining Toleration

nouns. As acts of toleration are, it is likely to be thought, tolerant actions, there is certainly a sense of "tolerance" which is synonymous with "toleration." "Tolerance," though, is ambiguous between that sense and (at least) two others. In a second sense, tolerance is simply endurance – this is the sense of the term in the phrase "building one's tolerance" to some drug, to heat, or to an activity. This is sometimes mechanical – as when we talk of the tolerance of a screw, of a type of wood or metal, etc. In the third and more important (for our purposes) sense, tolerance is a moral attitude or virtue. While the first sense – where tolerance and toleration are synonyms – is common, so are the other senses. As such, in the name of clarity, let us reserve "toleration" for the activity, "endurance" for the second sense, and "tolerance" for the attitude (or virtue). Similarly, Walzer (1997) distinguishes between tolerance as an attitude and toleration as behavior (xi) and Oberdiek (2001) distinguishes between toleration as a practice and tolerance as a virtue (vi, 23–24; but see 10, 17, 29–31).

While the attitude of tolerance ("he is so tolerant") and the virtue of tolerance are often treated as equivalent; they are not. Nonetheless, we need not worry here about the difference between attitudes and virtues (or between practices and behaviors). Newey develops what is likely the most sophisticated areteic account related to this discussion (1999: 105; see all of his Chap. 3). His is an analysis of tolerance rather than toleration. He notes that he employs a shift in terminology from toleration to tolerance, but claims that this is "not indicated to align itself with any systematic semantic distinction in ordinary-language uses of the terms" (52, note 35). For an argument that we should not be concerned with the difference between toleration as a virtue and as a practice, see King 1976: 13.

While toleration (the activity) and tolerance (the attitude or virtue) are related, the relation is unclear. One can tolerate another's behavior without at all being tolerant of it. Fletcher points out that some forms of intolerance may be more of a "psychological condition than a moral failing," as, for example, when Kant is intolerant of noise (Fletcher 1996: 231). Perhaps Jane simply cannot stand, but nonetheless values not interfering with, her neighbor's playing rap \ or disco music – and so refrains from interfering. Her increasing aggravation makes clear her lack of tolerance even while she tolerates the music. Toleration and intolerance are compatible. It might seem toleration is also compatible with tolerance – that is, that we can tolerantly tolerate though we cannot indifferently or resignedly tolerate.

Often when people claim to "have tolerance for X" they seem to mean they "do not mind X" (or, even, they "appreciate X"); "intolerance" is akin to dislike in such cases. Used this way, tolerance may not be compatible with toleration. One might have tolerance for ("be tolerant of") a behavior that one does *not* tolerate: one might be tolerant of profanity from neighbors and fail to tolerate it, at least in particular circumstances (when one's child is nearby, for example, one might interfere with the behavior that one does not find particularly offensive). One might lack tolerance and fail to tolerate: one might not tolerate the loud parties of a neighbor (by calling the police) because one is intolerant of such public nuisances. (One might lack tolerance and fail to tolerate for a very different reason: one might not interfere with the behavior of a despised rival whom one is intolerant of just so that rival will face more dire consequences than one can mete out oneself. This is not toleration; see the discussion of the value condition below.) Finally, one might lack tolerance and practice toleration (as with the music tolerating example above): Jane is intolerant of, but tolerates, the music playing. So, we have tolerance without toleration, intolerance without toleration, and intolerance with toleration. Can we have tolerance with toleration? Does one have tolerance, for example, if one is hoping that by tolerating the behavior (the playing of opera, perhaps), one will come to appreciate it? This is unclear, for that may render tolerance mere endurance, or it may too much resemble endorsement of the behavior to be indicative even of toleration.

While the examples thus far discussed might be questioned, they show that tolerance and toleration are distinct. One might think that tolerance is something other than "not minding" – one might, for example, want to define tolerance as an attitude (or virtue) that occurs with toleration. Such issues can be set aside since they are indicative only of the fact that we are not clear about what *tolerance* is. While a conceptual analysis of the attitude would certainly be valuable, that is not the task here, though it is worth noting, with Peter Gardner, a distinction between two different senses of the attitude:

> dispositional tolerance need not involve disapproval or dislike by the person who is dispositionally tolerant, though its objects are what attract, or are likely to attract, dislike or disapproval from some quarters. Deliberative tolerance, however, always seems to involve disapproval or dislike by the person who is deliberatively tolerant, at least initially, for then there is the temptation not to be tolerant and deliberation about whether he should or should not be tolerant. (Gardner 1993: 92)

Deliberative tolerance is often what we think of in discussions of toleration. This explains our unwillingness to say we are being tolerant if we refrain from interfering with someone in order that further harm befall him – as discussed in connection with the value condition (3) below. We would certainly not be displaying *dispositional* tolerance in such a case. Presumably, it is deliberative *intolerance*.

We now have a good idea of what toleration is not. We turn to the definition of toleration, by considering the seven conditions specified above:

1. the presence of an *agent*
2. who *intentionally*
3. and *on principle*
4. *refrains from interfering* with
5. an *opposed*
6. *other* (or their behavior, etc.) though
7. she *believes she has the power to interfere.*

If we adopt all of these conditions, we would say that *an agent tolerates when she intentionally and on principle refrains from interfering with an opposed other (or their behavior, etc.), though she believes she has the power to interfere.* The rest of this chapter provides further discussion of these conditions.

Before moving on, it should be recognized that the division of the conditions is to some extent arbitrary. One could, for example, have one condition combining the "agent" and "object" conditions into a relational factor. There are, moreover, interestingly different approaches to identifying phenomena that are related to, but different from toleration. (See, e.g., King 1976: 54–60 and Creppell 2002: 20–21.) For an entirely different approach, see Fotion and Elfstrom; they discuss toleration as a far broader notion than that considered here, one that includes some of the concepts distinguished from toleration above. Rather than exclude these, Fotion and Elfstrom analyze all the ways *we talk of tolerating*. Galeotti also seeks to broaden our understanding of toleration; she does so in order to argue that when we claim we should tolerate minorities we mean (or should mean) more than that we should allow them freedom to pursue their own conception of the good – we also mean (or should) that we must grant them recognition (i.e., endorsement as morally acceptable; see 10; see also Creppell 2002: 4–6). On the view discussed here, that conflates toleration with endorsement. In contrast to Fotion and Elfstrom, Galeotti, and Creppell, this chapter concerns *the core idea* of toleration; this is consistent with recognizing that people often speak more loosely. (See also Budziszewski 1992.)

The Conditions of Toleration

And now the conditions. Each of the following conditions is likely part of an adequate definition of toleration. There is some debate about each.

1. *Agent ("an agent tolerates when she ...").*

Toleration is practiced by an agent. Importantly, this does not require discussion of the agent's character, attitude, or virtue. Even evil agents can refrain from interference (condition four below) for good principled reasons (condition three below). When Churchill claims that toleration is "an attribute of moral character; it pertains to the attitudes, motives, and behavioral dispositions of those who voluntarily forbear from interference with speech or conduct" (Churchill 1997: 199; see also Oberdiek 2001: 40–41), he conflates tolerance and toleration. Distinguishing them makes clear that it is properly a requirement of the *behavior* of an agent that this condition makes explicit. We could consider that a subcondition:

a. *Behavioral. To tolerate* X is to engage in a particular type of behavior.

Some might prefer to consider this a separate condition, but it need not be as it is also brought out in condition four: *refraining from interfering* is behavioral. Interestingly, the behavior exercised in toleration is negative: one *refrains* from performing a certain action (this may or may not require some performance). This is clear enough, though it is analytically difficult to explain (a thorough explanation would involve intentions – as also with condition two below).

2. *Intentional ("an agent tolerates when she* intentionally . . .")

Acts of toleration must be intended. We do not say of an agent that she tolerates X if she does not interfere with X merely because she never considered doing so. She must intend to refrain from interfering if the noninterference is to count as toleration. Hence, Churchill tells us that toleration requires "voluntary forbearance or voluntary leaving others alone" (Churchill 1997: 192). Inaction is not enough; it must be chosen. One does not tolerate one's child smoking, for example, if one does not know one's child is smoking and for that reason alone forms no intentions regarding the child's smoking. Given this, there is, minimally, one subcondition:

a. *Belief.* One must believe one is not interfering with the doing of X. Toleration "involves awareness; one cannot . . . [tolerate] what one is ignorant of" (Gardner 1993: 85; he uses the term "tolerance").

There is no reason to consider this sort of a belief a separate condition or to spend much time discussing it; no one disputes it. The "belief condition" discussed below is more significant (and somewhat controversial).

That an act of toleration must be intentional might seem to indicate that toleration requires a particular attitude (or one of a limited range of attitudes). This might be a form (or underlying component) of the attitude of tolerance. This attitude (or pro-attitude), however it is fleshed out, is *minimal*, meaning it does not require any positive or negative *emotional* evaluation *of the act of toleration*; that act is positively evaluated (by the actor) only in that it is the result of a commitment to a particular value, as discussed next. (As will be discussed below with condition 5, a less minimal reaction toward *the possible object of toleration* will also be necessary.)

Some – for example, Churchill as quoted above – prefer to say that toleration must be voluntary, rather than intentional. This difference is likely unimportant for the following reason. What is voluntary is necessarily intentional, so those claiming the acts must be voluntary can accept that they must be intentional. What is intentional, though, is not necessarily voluntary. This may cause concern, but the next condition is that toleration requires that one act on principle and if one intentionally acts on (not merely "in accord with") one's principles, one must be doing so voluntarily. Because the next condition is widely accepted, if there is a difference between a Churchillian requirement that toleration be voluntary and the claim that it be intentional, it is merely verbal.

3. *Value ("an agent tolerates when she intentionally* and on principle . . .").

To be tolerating some X requires that one's refraining from interfering is based on principle; put another way, one's noninterference must be due to a good reason. This is not obvious. It is a difficult matter and some may doubt the requirement. To see why it is necessary, consider again the case of tolerating (or not) one's child's smoking.

3 Defining Toleration

Should one learn of the child's smoking, one must decide whether to interfere or not. Most parents would at least try to rationally persuade the child to discontinue the unhealthy habit. Some might go further, but others might not. Why would they not? One reason would be to allow the child to develop into an autonomous adult. That would, presumably, indicate that the parent was tolerating the behavior. By contrast, if the parent decided not to interfere because he thought there was nothing he could do (or because it was not "worth the effort" or because he simply did not care), he would not rightly be said to be tolerating the smoking – he would be resigning himself to enduring it or merely being permissive. The difference is that in the first case the noninterference is principled – based on a value – while in the latter case, it is not.

It is worth noting here that talk about state actions of toleration is likely different than talk of individual actions. Some may think that if a state does not interfere with cigarette smoking because it has determined that its attempted interferences do not work, that it would rightly be said to tolerate smoking even though it does not do so for a principled reason. In the case of states, however, there may be principles behind the policies of toleration, but the state itself does not have intentions. Thus, when we talk of *state toleration,* we are actually talking of state *policies of toleration* (see Cohen 2014: 17–18). In the present case, perhaps the state has a policy of tolerating smoking because it has determined that to be the best way to reduce smoking.

In agreement with the value condition, Jeff Jordan notes that if "S morally tolerates P's doing X" is true, "S believes that she is doing a good [or *right*] thing by doing nothing" (Jordan 1997: 213; see also Galeotti 2002: 22; for our purposes, goodness and rightness are equally values). S believes, that is, that she acts on principle. (A belief subcondition might be added here as it was for the last condition. Again, though, it's not worth further discussion. While some deny toleration must be principled, no one who believes it must be would deny that there must be belief that it be principled.) The reasons S believes that, though, may vary. It may be that toleration (or one of its components) is itself taken as a value, or it may be that the value is autonomy, such that toleration is "a manifestation of respect for persons" (Churchill 1997: 201). More precisely, Churchill tells us, toleration may be a "manifestation of the disposition to subject one's [dislike or] moral disapproval of another's belief or behavior to one's respect for the other's attachment to the belief or behavior in question" (ibid.; see also 193). The point bears repeating: the "decision to tolerate is [or may be] a decision that your respect for the exercise of choice by other people should have priority over your opinion that what they have chosen is bad or wrong" (Raphael 1988: 139; see also Nicholson 1985: 160 and Oberdiek 2001: 24 and 39). The point here is that for it to be an act of toleration, one's noninterference must be based either on respect for the other tolerated (or their autonomy or rights) or on a principled belief that toleration (or one of its components) is a value.

It might be thought that the value could be the attitude of tolerance. As the attitude of tolerance may itself be based on evil (dis)values, thereby inviting, at a different level, the conundrum that follows, this is likely mistaken. (For related discussions, see Horton 1996, 31–32 and 38–41 and Joseph Raz 1988, 162. For a contrast, see Barbara Herman 1996: 6.)

If the principle or value that satisfies this condition did not have to be either respect for the other or the value of toleration itself (or one of its components) and could be anything the agent chooses, there would be a conundrum that can be seen by considering an example provided by Gardner. In his example, "I do not stop a person from doing something I regard as wicked precisely because I believe far harsher treatment than I could ever mete out, awaits that person if he carries on what he is doing . . . [or] because I recognise that it would be disadvantageous to me to do so" (Gardner 1993: 90). If any value will do, either of these reasons would provide an example of toleration. Yet, surely, they do not. The reason, it seems, is that in Gardner's example, the restraint is due to improper reasons – perhaps because the agent values pain in others (see Newey 1999: 20). Such conundrums do not arise with the current formulation: not interfering because pain is valued is not refraining from interference because one respects the other or because of a principled belief that toleration (or one of its conditions) is a value.

Some may worry that there is a circularity in the idea that toleration requires taking as a value toleration (or one of its conditions) such that toleration seems to be analyzed, in part, with reference to values, one of which might be toleration. If this is circular, it is not viciously so. This is because "my valuing X" might be analyzed without analysis of X. Hence, it is reasonable to say "when I tolerate, I may be acting on a principle such that 'I will tolerate'." If that is viciously circular, the solution is likely to define the value condition as satisfied either by the value of the other – that is, respect – or any of the *other* conditions of toleration. The value could not, then, be toleration or (obviously) the value condition, but could be any of the remaining conditions. Several of my examples below are cases where noninterference is the value.

It may be asked why we cannot simply say that toleration requires respect for the other(s) tolerated – full stop. Some do take that view. David Heyd suggests that "to be tolerant one must be able to suspend one's judgment of the object, to turn one's view away from it, to treat it as irrelevant, for the sake of a generically different perspective . . . [It] require[s] an impersonal judgment of beliefs and practices, that is, in abstraction from the person holding them" (Heyd 1996: 11; see also Creppell 2002: 29). "Toleration is," he claims, "thus a sub-category of respect" (Heyd 1996: 12; see also Scanlon 1996: 235). Notice, though, that because Heyd believes the value endorsed when tolerating must be that of the other and that persons are the only beings due such respect, he concludes that only persons can be the objects of toleration (14). There is, though, good reason to believe that other sorts of things can be the objects of toleration, as we will see in the discussion of the object condition (#6), below. That is one clear reason to think other values must be capable of satisfying the value condition.

So, why insist that this condition can also be met by a principled belief that toleration (or one of its components) is a value? The answer is simply that there are times when it seems entirely appropriate to claim to tolerate the behavior of X when X is not a being we respect – or, in any case, when such respect does not explain our toleration. X may be a small child whose constant demands irritate or X may be a pack of wild animals whose behavior is destructive of one's property. We do not, though, respect such beings (certainly not as equals) even if we do (at least, *may*) value their being able to do as they are doing – that is, we value tolerating them or the noninterference. Our refusal to interfere with them likely counts as toleration, in part, because we *value* the noninterference.

Further discussion is required regarding this difficult condition. Imagine that you cultivate a garden for aesthetic reasons and a deer comes in and eats at it, detracting from its aesthetic value. You deplore this loss of aesthetic value, but you choose not to interfere – perhaps because you think the deer is due respect, but perhaps not. If you do think the deer is due respect, it may be that your refraining from interfering is toleration. Importantly, though, even if you do *not* think the deer is due respect, it may be a case of toleration.

If you are to be tolerating the deer, the value preventing you from interfering with it cannot be mere aesthetic appreciation of it (or the scene with it, or all of nature). If you refrain from interfering because you aesthetically value the deer (or the scene, or all of nature) more than keeping the garden, you are not tolerating the deer, because you do not oppose it or its activity, as required by condition 5 (below). It would, in fact, seem that you *endorse* the deer or its activity. However, your opposition to the loss of the aesthetic value of your garden may allow that you tolerate *that loss*, which is conceptually distinct from tolerating *the deer*.

Toleration of the loss of the aesthetic value of your garden may be based on the value of (or inherent in) the deer. Toleration of the deer itself or its activity is also plausibly based on the value of (or inherent in) the deer – we can distinguish a value inherent in X or Xness while opposing X or this particular X – but it need not be. (For our purposes, the related values of the other, respect, and autonomy (or some other value inherent in the other) can be treated the same way though they are different.) One might not value the deer at all and still tolerate it if one refrains from interfering because one values not interfering (we will see much the same about people as objects of toleration in the discussion of condition #6 below).

Some may find it implausible to think noninterference can be valued for its own sake and insist that it can only be valued instrumentally as a means of showing respect or preserving aesthetic value. That the latter is mistaken can be seen by considering Stoicism (in the classic sense, not what is discussed in A above; for related discussion, see Newey 1999, Chap. 3). The Stoic refrains from interfering as a means of achieving *eudaimonia*. Noninterference in such cases is valued instrumentally on that ground alone and not as a means of showing respect or preserving aesthetic value. To see that the value might not be instrumental at all, another example will be helpful.

In cases of extremely ravaging animals (e.g., elephants in southern Africa), we may well want to refrain from interfering with their behavior though the resulting devastation would not be considered a positive aesthetic value and though we do not think it will aid our achieving eudaimonia. While some may grant respect to the animals, even those who do not might think we should refrain from interfering – the *should* suggesting it is not mere endurance. They might simply value, for example, not poisoning (or trapping, or what have you) the animal in question (deer, elephant, or other); this is decidedly different from thinking one should not poison the animal because of *its* value (or because of one's pursuit of eudaimonia, or because of some aesthetic value). Though autonomy may be the more canonical value in cases of toleration (demanding toleration as respect; see Creppell 2002: 21), so long as either of these values – of the other or of toleration (or one of its components) – provides the basis for noninterference, we would have a case of toleration (assuming the other conditions are also satisfied). Newey (1999) comes close to this point when he says "non-prevention [may] be regarded as an end in itself" (158–59), but he backs off when he says the nonprevention "might be counted as an instance of respecting" autonomy (159). The important point, again, is that if it is not respect that is satisfying the value condition, it seems that it must be toleration itself or one of its components – perhaps noninterference.

One further point should be recognized here. Including "value" as a condition of toleration may seem to make toleration ineliminably normative. This is true, but may be misunderstood. There *is* an ineliminably normative component of the definition. The value behind the principled noninterference, like any value, is normative. That value, though, is prespecified: it is either respect of the other or toleration (or one of its components) itself. While there might be a question as to whether these are genuinely values, that question is separate from an analysis of toleration. To know whether an act counts as an act of toleration, one needs to know if the actor acted according to one of these values, not whether or not *we should consider them values* and not whether or not *we should act according to them*. Put another way, if it turned out that these values were not genuine values, it would make no difference – toleration would still be acting in accord with them. After all, an individual might act in a principled fashion, believing a value is present, even when it is not. Or the individual may act mistakenly believing that value is weighty enough in a specific case when it is not. For example, Joe might refrain from interfering with his neighbor Herman who is throwing rocks at passersby because Joe takes Herman to be a rights bearer (or autonomous subject). In such a case, Joe might accurately be described as tolerating Herman *even though he morally ought not*. This is enough to show that the normative element of the concept does not settle any moral issues. The normativity of any given case of toleration is distinct from the normativity of the value condition of toleration.

We should note that one may value noninterference as instrumental to the attainment of a variety of goods and still satisfy the value condition. If this were not the case – if, for example, one would not be tolerating if one refrained from interfering in order to promote peace – then some views usually considered liberal (perhaps Judith N. Shklar's "liberalism of fear" or any view relying on a modus vivendi) would not be liberal since liberalism requires toleration. It is more plausible that noninterference may be valued instrumentally for some goods, but not others. The aesthetic value one gets from not interfering with the deer, for example, seems not to allow for toleration. On the other hand, the Stoic does seem to tolerate when he refrains from interfering in order to attain eudaimonia and most would likely say that when one refrains from interfering to promote peace, one is tolerating. The range of

3 Defining Toleration 41

values for the sake of which one might instrumentally value noninterference and be tolerating properly speaking is not one that can be fully specified here. Likely, guidance to do so can be derived from consideration of what toleration is not, as discussed above.

4. Noninterference ("an agent tolerates when she intentionally and on principle refrains from interfering . . .")

This is the condition at the heart of toleration. Questions about whether someone is or is not properly said to be tolerating another usually arise only when the person is not interfering and claims to be tolerant or tolerating. Philosophically, this is where things get interesting and we begin to ask questions like "Did she mean not to interfere? If so, did she mean to tolerate when she refrained from interfering? Were her reasons appropriate to toleration?" If, by contrast, you interfere in my behavior, you clearly fail to tolerate it and these sorts of questions do not arise (though we may ask if you should have refrained from interfering, we will not ask if your action counts as an act of toleration). If "S morally tolerates P's doing X" is true, then "S takes no steps to interfere with P's doing of X" (Jordan 1997: 213; see also Churchill 1997: 191; Horton 1993: 4; Horton and Nicholson 1992: 3; Nicholson 1985: 160; Oberdiek 2001: 66; Raphael 1988: 139; and Rawls 1999b: 59). Put simply, toleration requires that there be no interference – there must be no action aimed at preventing the behavior in question.

Despite the wide agreement about this condition, some might claim that it is not quite right and that *condemning* a behavior even without interfering with it would be to fail to tolerate it. Gardner, for example, claims that "not condemning something as disgusting and corrupting, despite one's inclination to do so, may be a matter of being tolerant" (Gardner 1993: 85; see also Fotion and Elfstrom 1992: 5) or, someone (perhaps not Gardner) may add, a matter of toleration. Depending on what is meant by "condemnation," this view may be mistaken.

It seems clear that Maria can express her dissatisfaction to Tina with the latter's lateness to work and yet tolerate the behavior – by, for example, not firing her. Condemnation, there, is a matter of dialogue aimed, presumably, at persuasion (not to repeat the behavior). As others have noted, people can tolerate when they "condemn and then stay their intervention" (Fletcher 1996: 237); "I may tolerate someone's behavior while expressing disapproval of it" (Webb 1997: 415–416). Toleration does not rule out rational persuasion. If, however, condemnation means something more powerful, such as coercion, it would be incompatible with toleration – because it would be interference.

Perhaps this is too quick. Gardner's point, after all, is about one's behavior when one refrains from condemning – not about what happens when one *does* condemn. Presumably, he does not mean to be discussing occasions where one simply refrains from voicing one's condemnation (which may itself be seen as a behavioral form of noninterference). His point, rather, is that despite having a negative *emotional* response to some activity – the homosexual behavior of Jack and Jim, for example – George might recognize that his feelings are not sufficient reason even for condemning the activity, much less legally or physically interfering with it, so that the question of whether to interfere is never raised (even to himself). George does not allow himself to make an intellectual judgment based on his purely emotional response – he intentionally and on principle refrains from forming the condemnatory judgment (assume, for the sake of argument, that such is psychologically possible). That sounds at least superficially like toleration and some may think such restraint is a way of tolerating even though it is nonbehavioral. This is better understood, though, as the cultivation of the virtue of tolerance or perhaps merely the "building of one's tolerance" – that is, endurance level – as discussed earlier. It may well be a valuable character-building activity, but it is not then toleration (of course, practicing toleration may also sometimes serve as an aid in character-building).

The cultivation of virtue that we talk of when we speak of "building tolerance" is where the analogy to mechanical tolerance comes in: it is a matter of variation that can be accepted. The more variation one can "tolerate," the more tolerant one is; the more variation a mechanical apparatus can "tolerate" in its component parts, the greater its degree of tolerance (e.g., if it requires a 5 mm screw but can tolerate a 4 mm or 6 mm screw, it has greater tolerance than if it can only tolerate a screw as small as 4.5 mm or as large as 5.5 mm).

Return to George's resisting making a judgment about Jack and Jim. The issue is not simply a question of how to properly describe George's nonbehavioral (purely psychological) activity – as if offering a better description would show it to be (or not to be) properly called an example of toleration. If, in this example, George *is* tolerating, it would mean that the "refraining from interfering" condition can be no part of toleration. Who, after all, is it that George is refraining from interfering with? Not Jack and Jim – ex hypothesi, the question of doing so is not even raised (that there is no interference does not mean there is *refraining from interfering*). Is it George himself? Apparently not – indeed, he seems to be clearly interfering with his own mental life (stopping himself from forming the condemnatory judgment). It might even be accurate to say that George *fails to tolerate* his own otherwise natural response (though for good reason). While there is no need to deny that George's nonbehavioral activity is *related* to toleration, we must recognize that either it is not toleration or toleration is here (and by most theorists) radically misconceived – because conceived of as involving behavior that is refraining from interfering. The former seems more plausible.

Tolerance (the attitude or virtue), the activity of developing such tolerance, and toleration – as well as other concepts – are part of a cluster of related notions. Someone who, like George, works to cultivate tolerance (or any virtue) is surely different from (and perhaps better than) the person who simply does not care at all about his negative responses to others. He is also different from (and perhaps better than) the agent who tolerates without trying to change his views.

Again, toleration is a behavioral matter (condition 1a) requiring that one not interfere. "To tolerate an action or behavior is to permit it to take place, to take no steps to stop it" (Webb 1997: 415).

Horton claims that because there may be a lack of clarity regarding whether a particular act counts as interfering, "toleration is often a matter of degree" (1996: 28;

see also Horton 1985). Though there can be a lack of clarity in this regard, the conclusion is not warranted: in the relevant sort of cases, it might be better for us to simply admit we are *unsure* if there is toleration, rather than saying there is "more or less" toleration. Consider this further.

"Interference" can be understood to be any act that has the effect of impeding or preventing – even partially – an agent from doing as they wish, intend, or will. That is, it is a hindrance or obstruction. That an interference may only partially prevent an agent from doing as they wish is important as it allows us to say that toleration is a binary matter – one either tolerates or one does not. One may decide not to tolerate another's act and *fail* to stop them from doing as they wish. This would nonetheless be a case where one does not tolerate even though one might have acted more aggressively or forcefully in not tolerating. If one decides not to tolerate another but is then overpowered by that other while interfering with them, we do not say that one tolerated the other "but to a lower degree or extent than one might have." We simply note it as a failed attempt at interference (non-toleration). Take a simple case: Jerry decides not to tolerate Tom walking across his yard, but Tom is too quick and simply rushes past Jerry across the yard. Jerry did not tolerate Tom's action – to any degree.

Perhaps this will seem counterintuitive because it is the case that people can be *more or less tolerant*. Consider that three people, X, Y, and Z, may all disapprove of pornography and yet disagree about what should be done. X may think she has no moral right to interfere with its sale or consumption, Y may think that its sale can be restricted to licensed purveyors (and so not strictly prohibited), and Z may think its production and sale ought to both be illegal. X seems more tolerant than Y and Z and Z seems the least tolerant, but if X *tolerates* more it is solely because more acts (and/or kinds of acts) are tolerated on her legal scheme than on Y's or Z's. There is no real question of "degrees of toleration" where this means a particular act may be more (or less) an act of toleration than another act, vis-à-vis the same object. One either tolerates an object or not. While there may be a question of degree of tolerance, there can only be questions of scope of toleration.

One more example might be useful: if one uses an only partially effective spray ("Deer-Off") to prevent deer from eating at one's garden, one may realize that one will fail to interfere effectively with as many deer as one would interfere with using an electric fence (perhaps costs make the latter less feasible). Again, though, one can try to *not tolerate* and fail; this seems to be the case here: the person is not tolerating the deer when he uses the Deer-Off, but he is unsuccessful (or partly unsuccessful). Given the second condition (intentional), *unsuccessfully not tolerating* is not the same as *successfully tolerating*. Again, though, the Deer-Off user may be more tolerant than the user of an electric fence.

5. Opposition ("an agent tolerates when she intentionally and on principle refrains from interfering with an opposed . . .").

Toleration requires that what is tolerated is, in some sense, opposed by the one tolerating it. There is a great deal of disagreement about whether that opposition must be moral opposition or if it can be mere dislike. A few reject the requirement entirely. Creppell seems to reject it as making toleration less (or ir-)relevant to political discourse since much of what we talk about is not interfering when we merely have differences, some of which are not opposed (2002: 3–4). While it is true that we are concerned not to have interference in situations where there is no real opposition, whether that is weighty enough of a consideration is an open question. We have, after all, a related concept about state interference that does not require opposition: neutrality (see earlier discussion). In his 2017, Balint claims that opposition is not always necessary for toleration, but only after explaining that there is both a narrow and a broader, more general, notion of toleration and that opposition *is* required for the former. In other words, Balint recognizes that opposition is a necessary component of toleration in the strict sense and then notes that we sometimes use the word more loosely. Creppell's notion fits with that broader understanding of the term. This chapter is about the narrower use of the term.

The more inclusive way to define toleration given the opposition condition is to allow the opposition to be moral *or* mere dislike, so that "there must be some conduct which is disapproved of (*or at least disliked*)" (Horton 1993: 4, emphasis added; see also Mendus, 15; Newey, 42; Deveaux, 409; Oberdiek, 38, 48–51; and Galeotti 2002: 20–22; see Galeotti 2002: 50–51 for the claim that only moral disapproval results in "an intriguing moral puzzle"). Ordinary language seems to agree that there must be a "dislike or antagonism to the behavior, character, or some feature of the existence of its object" (Raz 1988: 163; see also Raz 1986: 40). Still, several authors take moral disapprobation to be necessary, claiming that mere dislike is not enough.

Jordan claims that if "S morally tolerates P's doing X" is true, "S believes that the doing of X is morally wrong" (Jordan 1997: 213; see also Raphael 1988: 139). What is necessary, Churchill also claims, is "moral disapproval, that is, disapproval based on reasons rather than on simple dislikes, negative feelings, or biases" (Churchill 1997: 199; see also Raphael 1988: 139, 142; Horton and Nicholson 1992: 3; Nicholson 1985: 160). Regarding the sort of opposition involved in toleration, these authors have a restrictive view.

On the broader understanding of toleration, one can tolerate another's behavior (say listening to or playing rap music) that one dislikes, though one recognizes that there is nothing morally wrong with it. Surely, this is the way we ordinarily speak – we do claim to tolerate things like rap music that are clearly not immoral. It is important, though, that it is not enough that one merely *not like* the behavior not interfered with – for one may be merely indifferent to X when one does not like X, and one does not tolerate what one is merely indifferent to (as discussed earlier). Still, dislike seems sufficient for the opposition condition.

Warnock claims that the distinction "between the moral and the non-moral" cannot be maintained (Warnock 1987: 126; but see also King 1976: 41–43). Langerak says: "I agree with those who argue that we probably cannot draw a line between what we dislike and what we disapprove and that, in any case, the issue of toleration can arise whenever there is disagreement about any matter regarded as important, be they mores or morals" (Langerak 1997: 111). We can remain agnostic about whether the distinction can be maintained. If Warnock is correct, the broader understanding discussed in the text is given further support – if there is no way to maintain the distinction between nonmoral dislike and moral opposition, than opposition based on one makes room for opposition based on the other.

What is indicated on either the narrow or broad formulation is that difference or diversity alone is not enough, for there can be differences without any toleration in a utopian state where all individuals are either indifferent to one another or love one another and embrace one another's differences (again, as discussed earlier). "The point to notice is that everyone in this debate agrees that toleration is to be sharply distinguished both from indifference toward diversity and from broadminded celebration of it" (Langerak 1997: 111). It is necessary that the behavior tolerated be *opposed* by the tolerating agent – whether that opposition be dislike (in contrast to mere "not liking") or moral disapprobation. There must be "objection to the item said to be tolerated" (King 1976: 25–26; see also 44–51).

In an interesting discussion, Gardner suggests that claiming the Dutch are tolerant (dispositionally) does not necessarily mean they disapprove of many things, adding that we "might think that one of the reasons for the Dutch being so tolerant is that they disapprove of so little" (Gardner 1993: 86; see also Newey 1999: 180). If, though, the Dutch act as they do because they are *indifferent* to so much, it hardly seems appropriate to say they frequently tolerate. They must at least dislike what they tolerate. But Gardner also claims: "People can be tolerant where they dislike or disapprove, but they can also be tolerant where others, but not they themselves, do, would, or would be likely to, dislike or disapprove. In fact, people may be tolerant about what they, but not others, like or approve ... People can be tolerant without realizing it" (Gardner, 87). It hardly seems appropriate, though, to say that one rap musician *tolerates* another rap musician's making rap music that the first likes just because others dislike it. "Whether a person is tolerant or not depends on his reasons for action. Himmler did not tolerate Hitler when he did not kill him" (Raz 1986: 402 and 1988: 162). Gardner, however, is talking of tolerance rather than toleration and this may be one way the attitude and behavior differ.

Joseph Raz adds a condition such that "the intolerant inclination is in itself [at least in the eyes of the person experiencing it] worthwhile or desirable" (1988: 163 and 1986: 403; bracketed material in the latter; see also Newey 1999: 21–24, on his condition T1). This may indicate that he accepts the narrower opposition requirement, as it seems to demand a principled opposition; it may indicate that the opposition must also be valued in some way. He also offers two additional "features" that are worth brief consideration here: "First, only behavior which is either unwelcome to the person towards whom it is addressed or behavior which is normally seen as unwelcome is intolerant behavior. Secondly, one is tolerant only if one inclines or is tempted not to be" (Raz 1988: 163 and 1986: 403). He is discussing tolerance, but there is reason to doubt that the behavior one refrains from when one tolerates need be behavior that would be unwelcome or normally seen as unwelcome: I can fail to tolerate Cindy's continuous self-deprecation and she may well appreciate my non-tolerating response (she may, in fact, not welcome toleration thereof). The second idea, that one cannot be tolerant if one is not tempted not to be, accords both with the opposition condition (in either its narrow or broad interpretation) and with deliberative tolerance (as discussed earlier).

Finally, it is worth noting that this condition – that one can only tolerate X if one opposes X – stalls any argument against toleration of a particular behavior that claims such toleration involves endorsement (e.g., claims that we should not have laws tolerating homosexuality, abortion, or condom usage because we do not endorse those behaviors). If we can only tolerate X when we oppose X, we cannot be endorsing X when we tolerate it (see Webb 1997: 422). Should it be suggested that one can be opposed to something and not be aware of that opposition, it should be admitted that toleration requires such awareness. (This is made explicit in subcondition 2a.)

6. Object ("an agent tolerates when she intentionally and on principle refrains from interfering with an opposed other (or their behavior, etc.) . . .").

This condition is obvious: there must be something tolerated. What is less obvious is what sorts of things can be included in the class of objects one can tolerate. One can at least be said to tolerate persons, beliefs, behavior, and practices. This list is not likely exhaustive; we have seen that a great number of things can be tolerated.

Churchill claims that the "objects of toleration . . . are not persons per se, but beliefs, attitudes, behavior (including verbal), and practices subject to change or alteration by the persons who hold these beliefs and attitudes or exhibit or participate in the behaviors in question" (Churchill 1997: 201; see also Mendus 1989: 16 and Oberdiek 2001: 40–46; this view is in direct opposition to Heyd's view, discussed above, according to which *only* human beings can be the objects of toleration). If this is correct, when we speak as if we tolerate a person or a group, we are elliptically indicating that there is something about the person or group or what they are doing that we are tolerating. On this view, properly speaking we do not tolerate *John*, but *something John does* – perhaps his loud music playing. If that is right, toleration is "quite compatible with full respect for those with whom we disagree" (Scanlon 1996: 226). On its face, this sort of claim seems plausible. However, as Mendus notes, this means that strictly speaking, talk of "racial toleration" is misleading: what is involved is not so much tolerating a racial group, but tolerating certain behavior or activity of (or believed to be of) the group. She endorses this view (Mendus 1989: 17).

Consider further racial toleration. There likely are racists who are racists because they falsely associate a particular set of behaviors with people from the racial group they hate. Perhaps they hate black people because they think black people and only black people create and listen to rap music. In such cases, Mendus's (et al.) view seems plausible. But there are also racists who would recognize the mistake of these naïve views – they recognize, for example, that some white people make and listen to rap music as well so that this fails to distinguish whom they hate from whom they do not hate. Such racists simply hate a class of people, where that class is typically determined by some factor members of the class cannot change (black people, e.g., cannot ordinarily change their skin color). Such racists might, despite their racism, be able to tolerate those they hate. They may choose not to stand near such people, but they may be prepared, for good principled reasons (perhaps the value of noninterference), not to interfere with those people nonetheless (e.g., they might not try to interfere with the other's riding the bus with them). They might, then, be tolerating the people they hate and not merely the behavior those people manifest.

We can tolerate people. Examples will be enough to indicate other things we can tolerate. We can tolerate behavior, as we have seen in various examples (we tolerate the playing of rap music, smoking, etc.). We can tolerate beliefs (some people apparently sincerely believe that Donald Trump was a good president, for example, and we tolerate those beliefs – and a person's having of those beliefs). We can tolerate practices (e.g., we might tolerate male circumcision though the evidence for its costs and benefits is unclear). Let us continue.

It is often suggested that toleration is an unfortunate behavior which we would do better without if only we could get ourselves to lose irrational dislikes and disapprobations – racial prejudice, for example (see, e.g., Cranston 1987: 101 and Fotion and Elfstrom 1992: 129; the claim is generally framed, though, in terms of tolerance as a virtue). Given how many sorts of things we can tolerate, there must be a limit to this thinking. There are objects we do not like (rap music, for example) that we should tolerate and for which there is no good reason to think we should work to lose our opposition (condition five).

Of course, there may be things – even things generally and rightly associated with particular groups – that we should not tolerate (female circumcision may be in this category). It may be that one cannot conceptually tolerate oneself. This is plausible, but will hinge on one's conception of the self (since a homuncular view of the self would allow that one part of the self can tolerate another). It may also be that one could be *tolerant* with oneself.

7. Believed Power ("an agent tolerates when she intentionally and on principle refrains from interfering with an opposed other (or their behavior, etc.), though she believes she has the power to interfere").

In order for an act of noninterference to count as an act of toleration, the agent who refrains from interfering must believe she has the power to interfere. In one sense this is obvious: if the refraining from interfering must be intentional (as required by condition two; note that subcondition 2a requires only belief that one is not interfering – not belief that one could interfere), surely the agent must have to think about her not interfering and that suggests that she thinks she could interfere. There is, though, some debate about how this condition should be formulated. Some think it must be possible for the tolerator to interfere, not merely that they believe it be possible.

It has been claimed that a person who tolerates "must be in a position to be able to interfere with the behavior of the tolerated; that is she has the ability to suppress, disrupt, or censure the offending speech or behavior, but refrains from doing so" (Churchill 1997: 192; see also Raphael 1988: 139–41; and Oberdiek 2001: 51–52). According to this, a person is not tolerating the opposed behavior if her refraining from interfering is, for example, due to state (police or military) prohibition – if S is physically or coercively prevented from interfering with P's doing X, but absent that prohibition S would interfere (here, the law is assumed to be disabling), then S cannot be said to be tolerating X when S does not interfere. Still, there may be other sorts of cases where one cannot interfere and where we would nonetheless say one does tolerate.

If someone voluntarily refrains from interfering, on a principled basis, with opposed behavior that she *believes* she has the power to interfere with, though she does not have such power, it seems that she is properly described as tolerating the said behavior – actual power to interfere may be unnecessary. If Maria believes she can fire Tina for showing up late to work (and is opposed to the lateness) but refrains from doing so, we can rightly say that Maria tolerates Tina's lateness – even if, as it turns out, only Helen has the authority to fire Tina. If, on the other hand, Maria knows that only Helen can fire Tina, then her lack of interference seems not to be toleration, but endurance – she "puts up" with Tina's lateness because she has no choice (alternatively, Maria may have a tolerant disposition). In short then, this condition requires that if "S morally tolerates P's doing X" is true, then "S *believes* that she has it within her power to interfere with P's doing of X" (Jordan 1997: 213; emphasis added). This accords with what we saw earlier, that "refusal to interfere must be more than mere acquiescence or resignation" (Horton 1993: 4; see also Horton and Nicholson 1992: 3; Nicholson 1985: 160; and Deveaux 1998: 409).

It is worth noting that if what has been said is correct, S may believe she has the power to interfere when she does not and she may have the power to interfere and not believe it. One result of this is that Maria may be tolerating Tina's behavior at 11 am, when Tina shows up late and Maria refrains from firing her though she believes she can, but *not* tolerating Tina's behavior at noon, when she learns that only Helen can fire Tina.

It is also worth noting that the *believed power* does not have to be legitimate authority. In the example just used, Maria at first believes she has such, but it seems clear, to use a different example, that two prison inmates can tolerate each other's activities, even though it is understood that neither has any right to continue those activities, nor to prevent the other from doing so. They each may believe they have the physical power to prevent the other from continuing the opposed activity, though they clearly do not have legitimate authority to do so (and, perhaps, they know this). That would nonetheless be enough to allow that they can tolerate each other.

One final worry about this condition is that while it allows for a broader array of activities to count as toleration than does a condition that one have the actual power to interfere, it may nonetheless be too narrow. Some would say that a counterfactual belief account of the power to interfere would suffice such that if one intentionally and on principle refrains from interfering (etc.), recognizing that one does not have the power to interfere, but one believes that they would not even if they did have the power, that one would be tolerating. This may be correct, but would require an even

3 Defining Toleration

murkier intentionality than is normally involved in the refraining from interfering. In the normal case, the intention is not to interfere. Absent an intention, though, one cannot tolerate – that is the second condition. Yet if one knows one cannot interfere, it seems unlikely that one can intend to not interfere, even if one could do so in some counterfactual situation. By comparison, it seems unlikely that one could intend to jump 30 feet high or to walk through a solid wall (it can be interesting to try developing such intentions). Perhaps it will be suggested that there is nothing very odd in the thought that "I wouldn't interfere even if I could." For reasons just discussed, though, explaining the statement turns out to be far more difficult than making it. In any case, such occurrences might be better described as the agent being dispositionally tolerant rather than tolerating.

Summary and Future Directions

To summarize: if we accept all of the conditions discussed here, an act of toleration is (1) an agent's (2) intentional and (3) principled (4) refraining from interfering with (5) an opposed (6) other (or their behavior, etc.), where (7) the agent believes she has the power to interfere. These conditions, jointly, would be both necessary and sufficient for toleration. Given the discussion throughout, some might argue, though, that some subset of these conditions is what would be necessary and sufficient. We cannot examine all of the possibilities.

To be clear, there are thinkers who prefer a broader understanding of toleration. Anna Elisabetta Galeotti, for example, notes that while "in the literal sense, contemporary toleration consists of an extension of personal liberty from the private to the public sphere … this literal meaning … by no means exhausts the meanings of toleration" (11). She is concerned with the "symbolic meaning" of toleration (for one helpful explanation, see Galeotti 2002: 100–101; for some defense of that approach, see 87–95). Ingrid Creppell also thinks we need a "broader language of toleration" (xii), and in his recent book, Peter Balint distinguishes between toleration narrowly understood (comparable to what is discussed above) and toleration in a broader sense that "involves general permissiveness and need not involve objection or disapproval at all but simply not negatively interfering" (2017: 24).

By contrast to these thinkers, this chapter has been examining the literal and narrow meaning. The purpose is conceptual clarity only, not what might be called "linguistic legislation." People often use the term "toleration" to mean something broader than what is analyzed above and there is certainly something valuable going on when we refrain from interfering with others and their behavior though we do not oppose them and cannot, in the strict sense, be said to tolerating them.

As already noted, it is important that the above presents no normative claims about when toleration is called for – that is, about what is to be tolerated. As King notes, toleration in its definitional "*logical* form is value-free; which is to say that the substantive instances which the form will embrace are not converted by that embrace into acts of restraint which will necessarily be adjudged right or good." Toleration "is in itself neither good nor bad" (King 1976: 37 and 39). Noticing this wards off the claim that toleration is paradoxical as we can be required to tolerate what we think is wrong, and hence what should not be tolerated (see Mendus 1989: 18–19; and Williams 1996). One *can* tolerate what is morally wrong, but it is not necessarily the case that one *should*.

Of course, this is not true of moral or political toleration, which will specifically incorporate limits to what *should* be tolerated so that any act of toleration will be either good or bad. "Toleration as a moral ideal cannot be value-neutral, and for this reason too it must be distinguished from the descriptive concept of toleration which can and should be value-neutral" (Nicholson 1985: 161).

Determining what that moral ideal is – that is, determining the proper moral limits of toleration – is, perhaps, the most important project in contemporary moral, political, and legal philosophy. There are questions regarding what individuals should tolerate, what private institutions like churches and businesses should tolerate, and what government should tolerate. These questions apply at local, national, and international levels. The questions are ubiquitous.

One might ask what should be tolerated regarding how individuals treat animals, whether we should tolerate businesses using animals (whether for research, labor, or agriculture) and various ways those businesses treat employees. We might also ask what a parent should tolerate of a child, what the community or state ought to tolerate of a parent with regard to her child, what the state ought to tolerate of cultural groups (and what those groups ought to tolerate of subgroups or individuals within them), what one state ought to tolerate of another state, what international institutions ought to tolerate, etc.

The questions of toleration apply to all manner of behaviors – presumably we ought not tolerate murder, rape, or theft – but ought we tolerate pornography, hate speech, anti-religious speech, anarchist speech? Ought we tolerate deplatforming of speakers or cancelling of entertainers who have been involved with some transgression of morality (or merely etiquette)? Should we tolerate those speakers or entertainers? On both the national and international levels, we might also ask whether we ought tolerate poverty, inequality, monopolizing activity in business, monopolies (which may not arise because of monopolizing activity)? Of course, most of us insist we ought not tolerate racism or sexism, but some may wonder if we ought to tolerate behaviors rooted in them – for example, circumcision of females (or, differently, of males).

One way to approach all of the "applied" sorts of questions is to seek out principles of toleration (discussed previously). Many have been offered, including the harm principle, the offense principle, legal moralism, legal paternalism, and the benefit-to-others principle (see Cohen 2014). Determining which of these, if any, ought to be adopted – or if there is some other principle that ought to be adopted – to allow us a systematic understanding of what should be tolerated and what should not, is of paramount importance.

In addition to the moral and political limits of toleration, one might be interested in a variety of puzzles toleration raises. For example, ought one tolerate someone who does not tolerate something one thinks should be tolerated? (This is the paradox of toleration.) For another example, ought the tolerating state tolerate those who would seek to limit or undermine its toleration? (This is the paradox of liberalism.)

3 Defining Toleration

Areas of concern related to toleration, it should be clear, are as extensive as they are important. This chapter does not touch on the normative questions, the questions of systematizing the normative, nor of the paradoxes that are of concern. Hopefully, by understanding toleration as an agent's intentional and principled refraining from interfering with an opposed other (or their behavior, etc.), where the agent believes she has the power to interfere (or some variation of that), we are better prepared to address these vexing issues.

References

Balint P (2015) Identity claims: why Liberal neutrality is the solution, not the problem. Polit Stud 63:495–509

Balint P (2017) Respecting toleration: traditional liberalism and contemporary diversity. Oxford University Press, Oxford

Budziszewski J (1992) True tolerance: liberalism and the necessity of judgment. Transaction, New Brunswick

Churchill RP (1997) On the difference between non-moral and moral conceptions of toleration: the case for toleration as an individual virtue. In: Razavi MA, Ambuel D (eds) Philosophy, religion, and the question of intolerance. State University of New York Press, Albany, pp 189–211

Cohen AJ (2004a) What toleration is. Ethics 115:68–95

Cohen AJ (2004b) Defending liberalism against the anomie challenge. Soc Theory Pract 30:391–427

Cohen AJ (2014) Toleration. Polity Press, Cambridge, UK

Cohen AJ (2018) Toleration and freedom from harm. Routledge, London and NY

Cohen AJ (2021) The harms of silence: from Pierre Bayle to Deplatforming. Soc Philos Policy. forthcoming

Cranston M (1987) John Locke and the case for toleration. In: Mendus S, Edwards D (eds) On toleration. Clarendon Press, Oxford, pp 101–121

Creppell I (2002) Toleration and identity: foundations in early modern thought. Routledge, New York

Deveaux M (1998) Toleration and respect. Public Aff Q 12:407–427

Fletcher G (1996) The case for tolerance. Soc Philos Policy 13:229–239

Forst R (2013) Toleration in Conflict (Cambridge University Press, 2013)

Fotion N, Elfstrom G (1992) Toleration. University of Alabama Press, Tuscaloosa

Galeotti AE (2002) Toleration as recognition. Cambridge University Press, Cambridge

Gardner P (1993) Tolerance and education. In: Horton J (ed) Liberalism, multiculturalism and toleration. St. Martin's, New York, pp 83–103

Graham G (1996) Tolerance, pluralism, and relativism. In: Heyd D (ed) Toleration: an elusive virtue. Princeton University Press, Princeton, pp 44–59

Hampton J (1989) Should political philosophy be done without metaphysics? Ethics 99:791–814

Herman B (1996) Pluralism and the community of moral judgment. In: Heyd D (ed) Toleration: an elusive virtue. Princeton University Press, Princeton, pp 60–80

Heyd D (1996) Introduction. In: Heyd D (ed) Toleration: an elusive virtue. Princeton University Press, Princeton, pp 3–17

Horton J (1985) Toleration, morality and harm. In: Horton J, Mendus S (eds) Aspects of toleration: philosophical studies. Methuen, London, pp 113–135

Horton J (1993) Liberalism, multiculturalism and toleration. In: Horton J (ed) Liberalism, multiculturalism and toleration. St. Martin's, New York, pp 1–17

Horton J (1994) Three [apparent] paradoxes of toleration. Synth Philos 9:1–18

Horton J (1996) Toleration as a virtue. In: Heyd D (ed) Toleration: an elusive virtue. Princeton University Press, Princeton, pp 28–43

Horton J, Nicholson P (1992) Philosophy and the practice of toleration. In: Horton J, Nicholson P (eds) Toleration: philosophy and practice. Avebury, Brookfield, pp 1–13

Jordan J (1997) Concerning moral toleration. In: Razavi MA, Ambuel D (eds) Philosophy, religion, and the question of intolerance. State University of New York Press, Albany, pp 212–229

King P (1976) Toleration. St. Martin's, New York

Langerak E (1997) Disagreement: appreciating the dark side of tolerance. In: Razavi MA, Ambuel D (eds) Philosophy, religion, and the question of intolerance. State University of New York Press, Albany, pp 111–124

Larmore C (1987) Patterns of moral complexity. Cambridge University Press, Cambridge

Mendus S (1989) Toleration and the limits of liberalism. Humanities Press International, Atlantic Highlands

Newey G (1999) Virtue, reason and toleration: the place of toleration in ethical and political philosophy. Edinburgh University Press, Edinburgh

Nicholson P (1985) Toleration as a moral ideal. In: Horton J, Mendus S (eds) Aspects of toleration: philosophical studies. Methuen, London, pp 158–173

Oberdiek H (2001) Tolerance: between forbearance and acceptance. Rowman & Littlefield, Lanham

Okin SM (1999) Is multiculturalism bad for women? Princeton University Press, Princeton

Raphael DD (1988) The intolerable. In: Mendus S (ed) Justifying toleration: conceptual and historical perspectives. Cambridge University Press, Cambridge, pp 137–153

Rawls J (1993) Political liberalism. Columbia University Press, New York

Rawls J (1999a) Collected papers. Harvard University Press, Cambridge, MA

Rawls J (1999b) The law of peoples. Harvard University Press, Cambridge, MA

Raz J (1986) The morality of freedom. Oxford University Press, Oxford

Raz J (1988) Autonomy, toleration, and the harm principle. In: Mendus S (ed) Justifying toleration: conceptual and historical perspectives. Cambridge University Press, Cambridge, pp 155–175

Scanlon TM (1996) The difficulty of tolerance. In: Heyd D (ed) Toleration: an elusive virtue. Princeton University Press, Princeton, pp 226–239

Walzer M (1997) On toleration. Yale University Press, New Haven

Warnock M (1987) The limits of toleration. In: Mendus S, Edwards D (eds) On toleration. Clarendon Press, Oxford, pp 123–140

Webb MO (1997) Trust, tolerance, and the concept of a person. Public Aff Q 11:415–429

Williams B (1996) Toleration: An Impossible Virtue? In: Heyd D (ed) Toleration: an elusive virtue. Princeton University Press, Princeton, pp 19–27

Wolfson A (1999) What remains of toleration? Public Interest 134:37–51

What Toleration Is Not

4

David Heyd

Omnis determinatio est negatio
Spinoza

Contents

Introduction 54
Thin and Thick Concepts 55
Mapping What Toleration Is Not 56
The Formal Components of Toleration 59
None of the Cognate Concepts Satisfy the Formal Conditions of Toleration 62
What's Left of Toleration? 66
References 69

Abstract

One of the reasons for the lack of agreement about the normative justification of toleration is the unclarity of the concept of toleration itself. The aim of this chapter is to try to distinguish it from its many cognate concepts with which it is often associated. Some of them are cognitive in character (skepticism, relativism); some are pragmatic (coexistence, compromise); and others are psychological (restraint, indulgence), moral (charity, considerateness), or political (state neutrality, value pluralism). Subjecting these closely associated concepts to the formal conditions of toleration (objection, power to intervene, accommodation, reason for restraint, suffering) demonstrates that none of these cognate concepts can be distinctly identified as toleration. This leaves us with a very restricted concept of toleration which is more moral than political, personal rather than impersonal, and supererogatory rather than a duty or a right.

D. Heyd (✉)
The Hebrew University of Jerusalem, Jerusalem, Israel
e-mail: david.heyd@mail.huji.ac.il

© The Author(s), under exclusive licence to Springer Nature Switzerland AG 2022   53
M. Sardoč (ed.), *The Palgrave Handbook of Toleration*,
https://doi.org/10.1007/978-3-030-42121-2_6

54 D. Heyd

> **Keywords**

Toleration · Skepticism · Accommodation · Respect for rights · Supererogation

Introduction

Thomas Paine has put it in a brilliant way already in 1791:

> Toleration is not the *opposite* of intoleration, but is the *counterfeit* of it. Both are despotisms. The one assumes to itself the right of withholding liberty of conscience, and the other of granting it (Paine 1954, 65).

Rights are natural and universal and hence can be neither restricted by the state (or the church) nor *conferred* by it as a matter of favor or charity. Toleration is a form of despotism because it assumes that the source of the normative force of the rights of individuals lies in the hands of the government. Paine's insight succinctly captures the transition from the old tradition of toleration as grace to the modern, enlightened, liberal conception that rights and their recognition are the moral and political duty of both the state towards its citizens (the so-called vertical axis) and the citizens to their fellows (the so-called horizontal axis). The precarious status of toleration in liberal theory and practice is due to its double nature: it is definitely superior to intolerance as a form of persecution but it shares with intolerance the negative attitude towards the beliefs and practices of minorities, "heretics" and all kinds of "others." This double nature is what makes it "counterfeit" for Paine. Toleration *looks like* acceptance, but it is not really so.

Even if we do not agree that toleration is a masked form of intolerance, we must admit that it is a highly contested concept. The reason for its shaky status has to do with the history of the idea of toleration which served different purposes and was justified by diverse political views. It was at some early point considered loathsome, a sign of moral laxity, then often treated as a practical necessity; some time later it was regarded as an intrinsic value; nowadays some view it as an "interim virtue," having only a transitional value which eventually will become redundant or even judged as a negative attitude as it was in its early origins. The history of the concept may turn full circle in the future.

The aim of this chapter is to focus on the *concept* of toleration rather than on its normative justification. But the conceptual examination of the idea of toleration cannot be independent of its historical development and of our current political views, which of course introduces a normative dimension into the discussion. The study of the idea of toleration in contemporary liberal cultures cannot ignore the decline in its appeal and the rise of two (opposite) alternatives – intolerance, on the one hand, and the full recognition of rights, on the other. The first is illustrated in our time by the persistent (regressive) phenomenon of intolerance of religious and ethnic minorities, which we thought we had overcome, and the latter by the growing (progressive) recognition of the equal rights of sexual minorities, which now demand more than just being tolerated. This dichotomy of intolerance and respect for rights seems to leave little room for toleration.

Thin and Thick Concepts

Toleration is a typically thick concept, to use the term created by Gilbert Ryle and later developed by the anthropologist Clifford Geertz. The concepts of good, right, duty, and justice are thin (although their thinness is a matter of degree). They are stable in the sense that they maintain their basic meaning and context of application throughout the ages and across different ethical theories. Even if the content of the good life or the conception of what is just is widely debated and undergoes significant transformations throughout history, the concept that is the object of these changes remains more or less the same. Thus, we share the concept of retributive justice with the ancient Greeks although we have very different criteria of just retribution or even prefer to justify punishment in non-retributive ways. The historical stability and cross-cultural understanding of thin concepts explain their universality: every human society has some concept of good and bad, duty and obligation, and distributive and retributive justice.

Thick concepts, in contrast, are concepts which contain richer descriptive content and accordingly are used not only to guide action or judge it (as do the concepts of "good" and "right") but to characterize the kind of action in question. Cruelty, saintly and heroic action, tact, and authenticity – are all typical thick concepts which obviously compose a much larger list than that of thin concepts. In contrast to the universality of thin concepts, which fill a normative role that exists in any human society (favorable or unfavorable judgment, permission, or prohibition), thick concepts are value-dependent and accordingly more local.

The concept of toleration is not only thick but also *parochial*. It has been around only for the last 400 years and exclusively in the Western political culture. And from its beginning, it has been highly contested – not only regarding the conditions of its application but also regarding its very coherence and value. We can debate whether the justification of moral duty lies in the consequences of the obligatory act or rather in the law under which the act is performed; but no one doubts the usefulness, indeed necessity, of the concept of duty in any moral theory. This is not the case regarding toleration, which from certain moral and political points of view looks repugnant or at least redundant. Biblical ethics, Plato's republic, the Catholic Church and the Soviet constitution could (and did) dispense with the idea of toleration.

The difficulty in the idea of toleration is usually associated with its inherent paradoxical nature: how can the forbearance from interfering with wrong beliefs and bad practices be considered valuable or virtuous? The paradox has been widely discussed (Horton 1994; Williams 1996; Forst 2017) and different solutions to it proposed, including my own (Benbaji and Heyd 2001). But since the issue belongs to the normative justification of toleration, it will not be discussed here. The focus will rather be on the prior conceptual issue of what toleration is and whether it can be articulated as a distinct concept not reducible to other, thinner (and less controversial) concepts. As the title of this chapter announces, the method deployed here will be the *via negativa*, and the question asked will be what toleration is *not*. This method, which was deployed only by a few scholars (Cohen 2004; MacKinnon 2006), may prove useful in understanding the concept of toleration which is not only thick but also partly invented – the product of political thought rather than ordinary language. Being partly a theoretical construct, the concept of toleration is the object of philosophical reflection, but having been integrated into ordinary language, its uses are broad and call for specification. In thin concepts we are not interested in definitions but rather in the way the different uses and applications of the concepts can be justified. In thicker concepts we search for the characterization of the concept itself before theorizing about its uses. The problem is not only conceptual clarity but a normative necessity, since the way to justify the practice of toleration has proven to be varied and typically dependent on the way we understand the concept. If, as the argument will show, the space for the concept of toleration has significantly narrowed down in liberal theory, its value as a virtue will have to be based on more restricted grounds.

Mapping What Toleration Is Not

The negative way focuses on the very wide variety of *cognate* concepts from which we want to distinguish the concept of toleration in its singularity or uniqueness. The cognate concepts have either been conflated with the idea of toleration or served as the kind (in the sense "genus") of the attitude or practice that toleration is. I suggest mapping them into five categories: cognitive, pragmatic, psychological, moral, and political.

Take the cognitive category first. It is often said that toleration is an expression of the lack of epistemological certainty or commitment. This lack of commitment can be principled, as is the case in Pierre Bayle's skepticism (Bayle 2003, 55–58). Bayle distinguishes between "absolute truth," which due to human infirmity is not accessible to us, and the sincere adoption of a belief in what seems to us to be true. This distinction makes Bayle one of the most important precursors of the liberal attitude in the face of religious pluralism. Epistemological uncertainty may simply be a matter of fact, as in the case of John Locke's agnosticism (Locke 2003, 225). It may carry the form of relativism, that is to say, a philosophical view that all value judgments are dependent on some local moral system of values which cannot be criticized from any universal vantage point, as proposed by Isaiah Berlin (1969, 172). Close to relativism is the belief in the incommensurability of values which undermines the ability to argue for the superiority of one set of beliefs and practices over another. Another form of epistemological laxity is, according to Allan Bloom (1987, 25–43), open-mindedness, that willingness to be exposed to other points of view, cultures, and values in a way that constantly casts doubt on the validity or superiority of one's own values. A weaker form of epistemological commitment is manifested in Rawls' idea of the *reasonableness* of moral views which can apply

4 What Toleration Is Not

even to conflicting and incompatible value systems (Rawls 1993, 58–65). Thus, although I firmly stick to my own opinion, my attitude to your conflicting opinion is different if I believe yours is reasonable than if I believe that it has no basis whatsoever. It merits a more understanding and lenient response. Finally, the cognitive category of concepts with which toleration is associated consists of the proposition that even if I am absolutely certain about the wrongness of your belief, there is no way I can *force* you to change your belief. Although this claim has been challenged by Locke's adversary, Jonas Proast (1690), and in our time by Jeremey Waldron (1988), it has had a long tradition running from the young Augustine to our own time. For Locke, this proposition served as one of the strongest arguments for religious toleration and the absurdity of efforts to use force in matters of faith. And for a protestant coercing people to act in line with certain rituals has no religious meaning when not accompanied by a change of heart.

Toleration based on the futility of coercing beliefs partly belongs to the cognitive semantic field of toleration and partly to the pragmatic, to which we move now. Even before the use of the term "toleration," the sixteenth-century humanist philosopher Erasmus of Rotterdam made pleas for *pax* and *concordia*, peace and harmony. His idea was that by distinguishing between the hard core of the Christian faith and the less significant, peripheral matters of ritual (to which he referred as *adiaphora*), the unity of the Church can be preserved and spared from the religious sectarian wars. This is a pragmatic strategy to save the ultimate value of religious unity in circumstances of deep divides, but it still relies on principled theological reasoning. But toleration has often been associated with sheer coexistence, peace, and social stability. Even at the price of accommodation to wrong-headed beliefs and conduct, toleration is a practical or political *necessity* which calls for compromise. Compromise is a pure form of pragmatic consideration. It represents a balance of power which is achieved not by force but rather by ad hoc agreement in which the two sides give up some of their aims in order to maintain a higher value, that of peace or unity. In its very nature, compromise is contingent and hence unstable, but it is nevertheless a very effective means of ultimately maximizing the interests of all parties concerned.

Note that the term *zero tolerance* (not "zero toleration") is the antonym of compromise – not of toleration. Most scholars use "tolerance" and "toleration" as synonyms, and in most contexts this is indeed acceptable. But there are contexts in which the two vary in interesting ways. Unlike toleration, tolerance in those contexts is involuntary or at least a normative necessity – not a matter of choice or preference. Thus, a patient's tolerance (not toleration!) of antibiotics is not a matter of will. Tolerance is endurance, the capacity not to be broken or harmed rather than a choice for a reason. Similarly, zero tolerance of petty crime by the police is not so much a matter of policy choice but a declaration that society can no more endure the damage caused by such crime. But the individual citizen may choose to show toleration (rather than tolerance) to a person breaking his window by not reporting it to the police.

The third cluster of concepts bordering toleration is psychological: restraint, patience, shyness, and endurance. These are character traits or psychological dispositions – either innate or acquired – that are often the sign of a tolerant person. The inherent tension in the tolerating attitude between the wish to intervene and the decision not to do so requires some measure of these qualities. They are definitely facilitators of tolerant behavior. But then there are the psychological states of indulgence, indifference, and condonation, which are more complex combinations of psychological dispositions and cognitive or moral attitudes. Indifference is lack of concern for what others do; indulgence and condonation are forms of a choice either to forgive or to ignore what is considered wrongful behavior. Indifference is the absence of a judgmental attitude which may be motivated by an exclusive egocentric concern with one's own life ("I couldn't care less"). Indulgence and condonation are not merely facilitators of toleration but share with it some concern for the other or an attempt to see her beliefs and behavior from her point of view (closing one's eyes to wrongful behavior so as to avoid embarrassing the wrongdoer or having to censure the act). Aristotelian magnanimity is also closely related to a tolerant attitude, usually shown by the more powerful to the weaker party. These are all character traits or reactive attitudes that enable people to show restraint in their urge to interfere in other people's lives when these are judged to be wrong or objectionable. Magnanimity is of partly psychological, partly moral nature, which naturally leads us to the fourth category.

The moral category of concepts that are tangential to toleration consists of charity and grace. Toleration in the premodern period was the prerogative of kings and other powerful authorities who could "afford" allowing practices of individuals and minority groups even when those were not fully in line with official theology or moral code. A charitable attitude is a form of "largesse" which serves to demonstrate the power but also the generosity of the tolerator. But it also functions as a pragmatic means to achieve peace and social stability. Thus, as Michael Walzer (1997, 14–19) shows, the Roman Empire had a tolerant attitude to different religious groups, and the Ottoman Empire was willing to tolerate non-Muslim minorities and grant them a measure of autonomy in running their internal affairs. These examples can still be classified as "moral" since beyond the pragmatic considerations of the tolerant ruler lay a pluralist moral and religious view which legitimized diversity. However, in early modern Europe, toleration was also often judged to be a sign of moral softness and laxity, on the one hand, or of a morally offensive attitude of condescension, on the other. In modern times the category of moral concepts turned back to the Roman recognition of value pluralism (Rawls 1993), the recognition of the irreconcilable heterogeneity of valuable ways of life (Berlin 1969) and the value of personal autonomy (Raz 1988). Toleration has now become the proper response to the challenge of the irreducible plurality of ways of life in multicultural society.

Considerateness is a quasi-moral attitude which is closely related to toleration. Both consist of an altruistic motive and the ability to put the interests and feelings of others before one's own. Finally, another quasi-moral concept of toleration is exemplified in norms of politeness, civility, and etiquette. Mary Warnock famously focuses on restraint in judging others on matters of taste and style as central cases of toleration (Warnock 1987).

Last but of course not least is the political category of cognates of the concept of toleration. From Locke and Mill, toleration has often been regarded in terms of state neutrality. Toleration is accordingly not an attitude shown by individuals or groups of individuals towards each other but as the virtue of the state as an institution; and it is an attitude which is devoid of any commitment to a particular set of values – either religious or moral. Thus, from the point of view of the state or its constitution, all religious faiths and conceptions of the good life are equally acceptable at least in the negative sense of not being the object of legitimate interference. The role of the morally neutral state is limited to the protection of citizens' rights; it exercises its power of intervention only when an individual violates the rights of a fellow citizen. Rights are protections from interference by others exactly in cases in which the right holder's behavior is opposed by either individuals or the (non-neutral) state. In that sense respect for rights calls for restraint from intervening in the life of others which without that protection would have been morally justified. The restraint from acting on the basis of a moral objection makes the respect for rights very similar to toleration. The principles of neutrality and respect for rights should be understood here as political in the non-pragmatic sense. Unlike the search for peace and compromise, they are not contingent but derive their authority from general independent principles. Contemporary theory casts doubt on the ideal of state neutrality, suggesting that the state is not completely indifferent between ways of life. It should actively support and promote only valuable ways of life (Raz 1988). But in such a case, the state will still need to exercise toleration towards those citizens who choose to lead non-valuable lifestyles (which is within their rights as long as they do not harm others).

This mapping of the semantic field of toleration is of course inevitably rough. It is probably not exhaustive and surely not exclusive; that is to say, some of the cognate concepts discussed above belong to more than one category. But it does reflect the wide plurality of concepts associated or even conflated with the idea of toleration in its history and theory. Obviously, toleration cannot be defined through all these closely associated concepts because they are often mutually exclusive. This is why the attempt to try to distill a singular concept of toleration by the elimination of what it cannot be may be a fruitful project. The aim is to find the *differentia specifica* of toleration. But for that we will need at least some basic structural conditions, the necessary *formal* components which characterize what we refer to as "toleration," since radically different meanings of the term would make it inaccessible to a theoretically useful articulation and to critical analysis.

The Formal Components of Toleration

There is no agreement about some of the basic characteristics of toleration: who is the tolerating party – an individual, a group, and institution, the law? What kind of beliefs and practices are the objects of toleration – opinions, manners, moral behavior, or aesthetic values? What are the limits of toleration – the object of toleration being tolerant? What is the deontological status of toleration – is it obligatory or just permissible and recommended? How do we justify the tolerant attitude – on a principled basis or on pragmatic ad hoc grounds? These are all contested issues which relate to different *conceptions* of toleration. But we are trying here to delineate the *concept* of toleration, that which underlies all competing conceptions. It seems that there is a wide consensus on the following five fundamental *formal* elements in the concept of toleration: objection, accommodation, power, suffering, and principle (reason).

Here is a short explanation of these five conditions. Toleration is not merely a half-hearted acceptance; it is the readiness to live up with something we find plainly wrong or repugnant, something we disagree with or strongly dislike. The opposition is objectively grounded although some hold that it can also be merely subjective or misguided, like prejudice or other immoral objections. But, as many philosophers have shown (e.g., Horton 1994), the restraint of a racist from persecuting his hated ethnic group can hardly be regarded as tolerant since the initial disapproval is not based on valid reasons. The objectivity condition fits the typically moral cases of toleration but casts doubt on the very possibility of toleration in the aesthetic context or when matters of taste are concerned. Tolerating the squeaky noise of a friend, which one finds unpleasant, is closer to the concept of *tolerance* than to that of toleration.

Accommodation comes under different guises: it may be simple forbearance from interference as a behavioral matter (although the forbearance must be intentional to count as toleration); it may also include a change of attitude, like some measure of understanding of the tolerated party. The choice of noninterference may be accompanied by anger or contempt, but it may alternatively be motivated by good will, social solidarity, or a wish to maintain personal relationship. Accommodation may be expressed by refraining from action, but it may involve only the avoidance of expressing judgment. In any case, the tension between the component of objection and that of nonintervention is inherent to the concept of toleration.

Different conceptions of toleration solve this tension in different ways. One solution is to distinguish between reasons of different orders, such as having objective first-order reasons to oppose one's religious ritual yet simultaneously having a second-order reason to respect the religious freedom of co-citizens. Another solution is to separate between the moral and the political and argue that although the disapproval of the tolerated party's behavior is morally justified, there are principled political reasons for not interfering in it – reasons having to do with the social contract or the recognition of the separation of state and morality (or religion). A third solution to the seeming contradiction between objection and accommodation is the distinction between judging the act or the belief and judging their agent or subject, that is to say, condemning the action but refraining from rejecting the agent. But all these solutions imply, as we shall see, some constraints on the concept of toleration which in its broader meaning still consists of that apparent contradiction between the reason to oppose and the reason to permit, condone, or accept.

The condition of objection (or disapproval) explains why toleration always involves suffering as its etymology connotes (*tolerare* meaning in Latin to suffer).

4 What Toleration Is Not

Not acting on one's objection comes with a price and calls for restraining the initial urge to interfere or criticize. Toleration is burdensome. It is displayed only when the objection to the practice is more than trivial in its meaning for the tolerator. One does not show toleration with joy or enthusiasm. Suffering requires restraint, the ability (and will) to carry the burden of inaction. Children are usually intolerant since they find it hard to restrain themselves from acting to prevent what they dislike in other children's behavior. Children are less capable of toleration also because they find it hard to distinguish between judgment of an act and judgment of its agent. This is interestingly similar to their inclination to "arguments from authority" which is also associated with the difficulty of distinguishing between the authoritative person and the value of her belief (Heyd 2003, 202–203).

All theorists of toleration agree that the power to intervene is a formal condition of toleration. The slave cannot tolerate the master; the subject does not tolerate the king. Power can be physical, legal, or psychological. But we should distinguish between power relations of two kinds – the "vertical" and the "horizontal." In the former, the relations are fairly constant and encompass many spheres of human action. The typical example is of course the sovereign state whose power makes it immune from being tolerated. But so are the relations between boss and employee or between parent and child. This is why in those contexts, toleration is not symmetrical: parents can tolerate their children's rudeness, but children cannot be said to tolerate their parents' antics, since they cannot act on their disapproval. Yet, in interpersonal relations among equal citizens or among friends, toleration may easily be exercised in a mutual or reciprocal way. Generally, people have the power to intervene in each other's lives. An analogy from concepts closely related to toleration may be of help: pardon (in the legal sense) typically belongs to the vertical axis; forgiveness is usually displayed in relations that are mutual and hence belongs to the horizontal axis.

There is an interesting limiting case in which the power condition applies only counterfactually (Newey 2017, 429). I cannot be said to tolerate someone when I lack the power to interfere with her life if I chose to; but I can say that even if I had such power, I would not have used it; that is to say, I would have shown toleration. Although I now refrain from acting on my objection due to fear of the more powerful other, I can form a hypothetical attitude of recognizing that such a person should be tolerated.

Finally, there is the component of principle or reason which is constitutive of the concept of toleration. Toleration (again, as against tolerance in the medical sense) is a matter of choice. And the choice is not capricious or automatic. There is some principle or reason behind the decision to tolerate an objectionable action. It is a reactive attitude that is not purely emotional. In that sense toleration cannot be just a psychological inclination or an unconscious response. Since the forbearance from intervening takes its toll, it must be supported by a good reason. What kind of reason is of course a matter of debate. But it seems to be agreed by all that for an attitude to be described as tolerant, there must be *some* reason having to do with the specific value of forbearance.

None of the Cognate Concepts Satisfy the Formal Conditions of Toleration

It seems that we have now the basic tools for trying to uncover the singular, well-differentiated concept of toleration. We should examine these cognate concepts which we have mapped into categories in the light of the formal components which constitute the concept of toleration. Before doing so it should be noted that the aim is to articulate a theoretically distinct concept rather than to describe the ways in which the term "toleration" has been used in the last four centuries or the way we understand it in contemporary ordinary language. The very broad and under-determined meaning of the concept is the product of its long history in which it was put to use by a whole variety of political aims and systems of values. The "distilled" concept we want to capture here is a concept that fits a liberal political culture which is committed to the rights of individuals, the rule of law, citizens' equality, and human respect. Admittedly, this introduces some normative constraints into the conceptual analysis of toleration, but these constraints are fairly uncontroversial. They definitely reflect the nature of the current political culture which is acceptable to everyone who is nowadays interested in toleration.

To start with the cognitive category: toleration cannot be identified as mere lack of epistemological commitment, since the objection component must be straightforward and even objectively justified. The objection must also be strong, since otherwise noninterference would not involve any element of suffering calling for endurance. Epistemological uncertainty may lead to forbearance from judgment and interference, but that forbearance cannot be regarded as tolerant. It is rather an expression of justified caution: if you are not sure that the other person is wrong, don't interfere. Open-mindedness is, unlike toleration, an attempt to learn, understand, and sometimes even accept new ideas and practices. It is often accompanied by enthusiasm rather than pain. But excessive open-mindedness is a sign of lack of epistemological commitment which again is incompatible with the disapproval condition of toleration. Locke's epistemological argument about the futility of the attempt to *force* people to hold certain beliefs as the basis of toleration is no more in vogue (Locke 2003, 218–219). It made sense in the days of the wars of religion; but today no one would argue that the reason for tolerating Muslims in a liberal society is that there is just no chance to compel them to adopt different beliefs. It may be, as Locke's critics claimed, empirically false that one cannot force beliefs on people yet it would still be considered morally wrong. And anyway Locke's argument applies only to beliefs and not to behavior (which of course can be forced).

Unlike skepticism and agnosticism, pragmatic considerations for refraining from trying to stop others from acting upon their wrong beliefs share with toleration the element of genuine objection. The willingness to compromise does not detract from the firmness of one's epistemic commitments. But then, the effort to maintain coexistence and peace is determined by *contingent* circumstances rather than by principled reasoning which is one of the formal conditions of toleration. Furthermore, and more importantly, toleration, as we have shown, is exercised in circumstances of asymmetrical power: the tolerator is by definition stronger than the tolerated. But compromise is by definition the outcome of the exercise of the relative power of *both* sides. There is no reason to compromise with someone who is completely helpless; but there might still be a reason to tolerate her. Compromise is typically achieved through negotiation and bargaining; toleration is never the product of such a mutual process of converging on an agreed-upon end but a unidirectional and unconditional accommodation by the tolerant party. Compromise aims at the best possible resolution of a conflict to all parties concerned. Toleration does not necessarily secure the best interest of the parties, and its justification does not lie in the interest of the tolerated side as overriding the suffering of the tolerating agent. So although peace and stability were the historical precursors of modern toleration and served as fundamental motives in adopting a forthcoming attitude towards various sorts of dissenters, the principle of toleration we are seeking goes beyond them.

Regarding the psychological cluster of the cognates of toleration, we do indeed associate tolerant people with those who are patient, restrained, and capable of controlling their anger and hostility. These traits are compatible with a principled choice to refrain from intervening in the wrongful action of others; but though they are helpful dispositions in adopting a tolerant attitude, they are not the mark of toleration. For example, kind and lenient people may tend to avoid interference also in *intolerable* practices exactly because their forbearance is not based on reason or principle but rather reflect an independent psychological disposition. As Kant has famously noted, self-control may serve the cold blooded criminal no less than the virtuous saint. Indifference, which is not a purely psychological character trait, has never been recognized as an attitude of toleration, but it is often hard to decide whether the motive behind the forbearance from intervention is a positive recognition of the value of toleration or just total lack of care. Tolerating involves moral care for the right and the good without which there would be no initial urge to interfere with the conduct of others. Accordingly, the proto-toleration of local religions and cultures in the Roman Empire is closer to Rome's indifference regarding the beliefs and practices of the communities under its rule (as long as they paid their taxes and did not rebel) than to what we would call today a policy of religious toleration. Such indifference was no longer a theological option for a Catholic or Protestant ruler in sixteenth-century Europe, and toleration had to be framed in terms of accommodating genuine disapprobation of the tolerated practices.

The last two categories of cognate concepts – the moral and the political – are the most interesting, but the attempt to resist their conflation with toleration is contested in contemporary analyses of the concept. The moral concepts of charity and considerateness do not fit the formal conditions of toleration. They do not involve the elements of objection and accommodation and even not those of power and suffering. Considerateness and charity are forms of doing good to someone else; toleration is restraining oneself from offending or harming another person. Charity is usually exercised with pleasure; considerateness is shown with no objection to the other's situation that calls for sympathy or help, neither does it assume a hierarchy of power; neither does it consist of an inner conflict; and consequently neither does it give rise to a paradox of the kind ascribed to toleration. This is not to deny that a charitable character and a considerate sensitivity may be psychologically instrumental in the development of a tolerant attitude.

Kant and Goethe sharply criticized toleration because they associated it with a condescending attitude of the ruler. In "What is Enlightenment," considered to contain Kant's progressive ideas about the tolerant society, the term "toleration" itself is used pejoratively:

> A prince who does not find it unworthy of himself today that he holds it to be his duty to prescribe nothing to men in religious matters, but to give them complete freedom while renouncing the haughty name of *tolerance*, is himself enlightened. (Kant 1963, 9)

We may follow Kant in that critique of toleration and extrapolate it from its limited use in religious affairs to the general principles of refraining from intervention in the affairs of others. Kant speaks of the "freedom to make use of one's reason in matters of conscience." But we may equally refer to these principles in terms of the recognition of the *rights* of individuals to manage their lives as they wish.

Take a typical definition of toleration in contemporary political theory. According to A. J. Cohen, toleration is "an agent's intentional and principled refraining from interfering with an opposed other (or their behavior, etc.) in situations of diversity, where the agent believes she has the power to interfere" (Cohen 2004, 69). This seems to capture the gist of toleration. Does this definition apply also to the respect of the rights of others? Rights are needed as protections of individual freedom just because people's beliefs and practices are often opposed by others or objected to, particularly in what Cohen calls diverse societies, and respecting them means refraining from intervening in the right holders' lives. Still rights and toleration should not be conflated. Respecting the rights of others is a strict duty, often of juridical nature, which does not seem to be the case in toleration. For example, avoiding the unconsented use of your property, even when I have good reasons to object to the way you acquired it or are using it, is *not* an act of toleration. Nor is the intentional and principled avoidance of interfering with the repugnant way you raise up your children a matter of toleration. Or take *competitive* activities: it is not an act of toleration that I refrain from obstructing your activity as my rival in business, in sports, or in running for a Parliament seat.

Furthermore, and this is crucial for the distinction between respect for rights and toleration, the recognition of rights does not presuppose the element of *power*, the ability to interfere. Remember that power is not only physical; it may be normative. The fact that you have a property right makes me powerless regarding the use of that which belongs to you. Similarly, the government in a constitutional democracy simply *cannot*, does not have the legal power, to put you in jail without due process or to persecute you because of your religious faith. Hence, all these sorts of abstentions from intervention, both by individuals and by the government, are not expressions of toleration.

There is another difference between the two: respect for rights does not necessarily involve suffering. This is by definition the case in the relations of the state to its citizens. Governments do not suffer and cannot said to "restrain themselves" in the psychological sense that applies to the individual attitude of toleration. They do not have their own beliefs to which they are committed. Governments ought to act according to impersonal rules, laws, procedures and rights – whether in a neutral way or in the light of some perfectionist ideal. This applies also to other institutions and public officials on the "vertical" axis. The police, the court judge, the mayor, or the minister is not expected to demonstrate toleration to their respective "clients" but rather act exclusively according to the rule of law and the universal impersonal standards defining their authority and powers. This is exactly what Kant meant in his praise for the enlightened prince.

Joseph Raz (1988) grounds toleration in the value of personal autonomy, the liberty of people to follow their own fundamental choices in life. Toleration is the duty of the state not to interfere with the lives of its citizens (as long as they do not harm others) even when from the perfectionist point of view, the lives chosen by some citizens have little value. But is it a case of toleration in the strict sense? The liberal state does not *object* to non-harmful though value-less practices; it just does not actively support and advance them. The question of state interference does not arise regarding such practices to begin with. Even on the horizontal, interpersonal level, the fact that an act is the expression of *your* choice and makes sense as part of your chosen way of life makes it less objectionable even if it is judged as having little worth. According to the principle of personal autonomy, some beliefs and practices are valuable, *independently* of their content; they have value in being genuinely adopted by an individual as part of her preferred way of life, often even constitutive of her identity.

Rawls is an interesting case for our discussion. Within the political system, there is no need to tolerate since society is run by the principles of justice and based on the idea of respect for persons as free and equal agents. The question of forbearance from intervention rises in the moral sphere which is typically pluralistic and conflictual. The reason to tolerate opposing values may be either the need to cooperate in a political community or some basic respect for persons which Rawls assumes is part of every comprehensive moral system and hence belongs to the so-called overlapping consensus. In a way, toleration is a bridge between the moral and the political belonging to neither. We must tolerate the objectionable aspects of other people's comprehensive moral set of values in order to be able to cooperate with them on the political level according to the agreed-upon principles of justice.

Finally, Galeotti (2002, Introduction) identifies toleration with the recognition of minority groups. Liberal theory should be reframed because minority rights proved to be insufficient to overcome stereotypical and prejudiced attitudes towards racial, ethnic, and gender communities. Beyond recognizing their rights, they should be accorded with respect as groups which have their own identity. I agree that recognition in a pluralist society involves more than just respect for rights and just distribution; but it seems that toleration is exactly an attitude that will *not* create that extra dimension of such positive esteem and full social acceptance Galeotti is seeking due to the objection component which is inherent to it. Toleration is based on the distinction between agent and act and accordingly calls for respect for the agent *despite* having no respect for the act (its content). But Galeotti looks for recognition of the value also of the content of the minority cultures. Furthermore, recognition and respect do not involve the pain of restraint from nonintervention.

What's Left of Toleration?

The outcome of the attempt to distill a distinct concept of toleration from all its traditional cognate concepts seems to have left little room for its application. It is not clear what remains of toleration as a specifically differentiated idea. Has toleration become redundant through some Hegelian process of *Aufhebung* (toleration as the negation of intolerance but then preserved on the higher level of pluralism and rights)? In a way the answer is positive. As Bernard Williams has persuasively argued, toleration is an important and effective means of overcoming persecution and intolerance. But once this goal is achieved, it is not considered good enough. The ideal of toleration should be surpassed. The tolerated wish to be fully recognized, respected, and accepted. This is exactly what happened with sexual minorities in the past few decades. After years of legal and social persecution and intimidation, homosexuals have gradually become tolerated by society. They were left alone, and laws against their practices ceased to be enforced and later completely abolished. But in a "second wave" of social change, sexual minorities have forcefully claimed their full rights and demanded that their way of life be recognized as legitimate and valuable. This change is gradually taking place in many societies in the world. The same social transformation is now expected also by religious minorities, by groups of handicapped people and immigrant communities.

Another way to describe this process is that once the awareness and recognition of value pluralism become universal, opposing values will no more create objection and the urge to intervene; people will accept that others lead ways of life different from their own. Indeed, there will remain some element which Raz refers to as competitive, but it will be more about state priorities in the allocation of resources according to some perfectionist conception than about the desire to block, ban, or constrain others from pursuing their practices.

If indeed the attempt to test all the cognate concepts (with which toleration is associated) according to the five formal conditions of toleration does not yield a single differentiated concept, then toleration cannot serve as a fundamental principle of liberalism as it is often held to be. More significantly, toleration turns out, surprisingly, to be *in*compatible with liberalism, despite much of the theoretical and political rhetoric binding them together. This was exactly Thomas Paine's point with which we started. Paine takes the French Revolution as being (already) the end of the age of toleration:

> The French constitution hath abolished or denounced *toleration*, and *intoleration* also, and hath established *universal right of conscience*. (Paine 1954, 65)

The language of rights, autonomy, value pluralism, and the separation of the political from the moral leave little space for toleration. In pluralist societies there is often no justification for the initial objection to what seems to be a wrong way of life, but even when there is, refraining from intervention is neither a virtue nor an indication of some generous attitude of the powerful towards the weaker party. Like in toleration, the motive of restraint and noninterference is principled, but now the principle is different – respect for rights and for the autonomy of others. And although respect for rights may involve some pain and suffering, these are not constitutive of respect as they are in the case of toleration. At least contingently liberal culture is supposed to reduce the painful cost of accommodating differences in religious, sexual, aesthetic, and even moral views and conduct. Paradoxically, toleration thrives on, or at least presupposes, conflicts of value; liberalism celebrates value diversity.

However, although the space for toleration has narrowed down considerably, it still has a specific meaning which highlights its unique value – both moral and political. This distinctive character of toleration has been characterized as consisting of the three following propositions (Heyd 2008):

- Toleration is a moral – rather than political – attitude.
- Toleration is a personal – rather than impersonal – relation.
- Toleration is a supererogatory – rather than obligatory – practice (meaning that there is neither a duty to tolerate nor a right to be tolerated, which is again a major difference from the deontic status of respecting rights).

If Paine is right and the constitution should be based on human, civil, and legal rights, then toleration has no place in the way the state relates to its citizens. In that sense toleration is not a political ideal. The state and its organs owe duties to its citizens and should be fair and just in its dealings with them. Tolerant attitudes of citizens may lead to changes in the law allowing for certain practices despite their being unpopular or opposed by the majority of the citizens; but once enacted, these laws, rather than any attitude of toleration, should guide state action.

However, although toleration in a liberal society does not operate on the vertical axis of politics, it is a valuable attitude on the horizontal axis, namely, on the interpersonal level. It involves discretion of the individual who chooses to exercise toleration, and it is directed at individuals or groups of individuals for reasons that are not universalizable. In that personal nature, toleration is similar to forgiveness and charity although motivated by different kinds of reasons. Typically, choosing to tolerate is based on the recognition of the dignity of the tolerated person, whereas forgiveness and charity are motivated by empathy or by an effort to restore personal relationships.

The formal condition of power as necessary for the exercise of a tolerant attitude still applies in this case of "horizontal" relationships in a democratic and egalitarian society, since my right to act in a way which is offensive to you gives me an advantage over you in that particular context. I have power over you, although this power is not structural or applying across the board as is the case in the vertical relation between king and subject or parent and child. But just because the power relations of the tolerator and the tolerated are not structurally permanent, forgoing the exercise of rights is potentially mutual. Like giving and forgiving which often trigger reciprocal response from the beneficiary, being tolerated may trigger a reciprocal tolerating attitude, ultimately to the benefit of all.

The first two characterizations of toleration – being moral rather than political and being personal rather than impersonal – lead us directly to the third feature, its supererogatory nature (Newey 1997; Heyd 2003). Individuals may exercise toleration in their interpersonal relationships, but they are under no duty to do so. In liberal regime noninterference in the affairs of others is either required by law, in which case it is obligatory, or a matter for personal discretion, in which case it is supererogatory. The supererogatory nature of toleration is exactly the factor which lends it with a special value. Toleration is not the recognition of rights but rather the willingness *not to insist* on one's rights. This non-insistence on rights as a typical characteristic of toleration is naturally expressed in interpersonal relations. For example, I avoid calling the police when angry demonstrators block my street in an illegal sit-in. Their behavior is wrong, it causes me some suffering, I have the power to stop it, yet I refrain from interfering with it because I recognize the sincerity of their ill feelings. This abstention from interference is supererogatory. I was under no duty to tolerate their deeds. It would have been within my rights if I called the police.

The ultimate basis of the tolerant attitude is the distinction between the agent and the act (or in Augustine's terms, between the sinner and the sin) and the human capacity to change perspectives from judging the act (or belief) to respecting the agent (or individual holding the belief). I judge the action as plainly wrong, but I understand and respect the person behind it. This proposition is consistent with the formal condition of accommodation (or noninterference), since we renounce interference with human agents rather than with abstractly identified acts, with people holding beliefs rather than with the beliefs themselves. Hence, when we say that we tolerate behavior, we strictly speaking mean that we tolerate people. The question of showing toleration (or intolerance) to the practice of cannibalism does not arise in our society since there is no one engaged in the practice.

Admittedly, the concept of toleration suggested here does not do justice to the rich way in which we use the term in ordinary language. However, the theoretically restricted concept is methodologically superior to the overly *broad* interpretations of the concept which are common in the philosophical literature on toleration. For instance, the two agenda-setting examples which Catriona MacKinnon offers in her book on toleration (2006) are the murder of the Dutch filmmaker Theo van Gogh by a Muslim fundamentalist together with the tough intolerant response by right-wing politicians and the Marriage Amendment in the United States which bans gay marriages. These examples are confusing and might lead us to miss the unique meaning of toleration. The error lies in the assumption that toleration is the only opposite of intolerance and its only remedy. But neither Theo van Gogh nor the Dutch Muslim citizens wish to be tolerated. They claim, respectively, freedom of artistic expression and freedom of religion. The same applies to LGBT groups who fight for the legal recognition of their personal status. This is not to judge the substantive merits of any of those debates but only to argue that they are to be discussed as matters of rights and the criminal law (murder being a gross violation of the law rather than an act of intolerance) and not as cases calling for toleration. MacKinnon herself cites the gay people's claim that the amendment violates their "constitutional rights," but does not address the theoretical risk of conflating toleration with rights. Naturally, when analyzing the historical development of the language of toleration, theorists should adopt a broad, nonrestricted concept of toleration (Creppell 2003, Chap. 2); but a theoretically useful concept must be restricted by conceptual and normative considerations.

Nevertheless, even under the restricted personal and supererogatory meaning suggested here, toleration still plays an important, even vital, role in political life. Although it applies only on the horizontal level of interpersonal and intercommunal relations, the liberal state should encourage and inculcate it in its citizens, even if it cannot do it by law (Jones 2013, 635–636). The state and its officials ought not to act supererogatorily because of their commitment to the universal application of the principles of justice and equality. But tolerant attitudes of groups of individuals (or communities) to each other are definitely a significant *political* virtue in which the state has a stake. It is a major benefit to both the tolerated minority and to society as a whole if members of the majority group do not always insist on their rights to behave publicly in ways which they know are regarded as offensive to members of a minority.

Toleration, like other forms of supererogatory behavior (charity and forgiveness), is shown to people to whom we feel close in some way, and the tolerant act itself reinforces social solidarity. Therefore, although the impersonal rule of law, the system of constitutional rights and the principles of justice remain the normative pillars of the liberal state, and although pragmatic considerations are inescapable and valuable in the management of the political sphere and in maintaining social stability, toleration – as an interpersonal and intercommunal attitude – is an important complementary value. It contributes to social cohesion or – in the more traditional terminology – to fraternity, that sentiment which liberal democracy is accused of having lost.

References

Bayle P (2003, first published 1686 as "De la tolérance") The great contest of faith and reason, Sandberg K (ed). Frederick Ungar, New York
Benbaji H, Heyd D (2001) The charitable perspective: forgiveness and toleration as supererogatory. Can J Philos 31:567–586
Berlin I (1969) Two concepts of liberty. In: Four essays on liberty. Oxford University Press, Oxford
Bloom A (1987) The closing of the American mind. Chicago University Press, Chicago
Cohen AJ (2004) What toleration is? Ethics 15:68–95
Creppell I (2003) Toleration and identity. Routledge, New York
Forst R (2017) Toleration and its paradoxes. Philosophia 45:415–424
Galeotti AE (2002) Toleration as recognition. Cambridge University Press, Cambridge
Heyd D (2003) Education to toleration: some philosophical obstacles and their resolution. In: McKinnon C, Castiglione D (eds) The culture of toleration in diverse societies. Manchester University Press, Manchester

Heyd D (2008) Is toleration as political virtue? In: Williams M, Waldron J (eds) Toleration and its limits. New York University Press, New York, pp 171–194

Horton J (1994) Three (apparent) paradoxes of toleration. Synth Philos 17:7–20

Jones P (2013) Toleration. In: Gaus G, D'Agostino F (eds) The Routledge companion to social and political philosophy. Routledge, New York

Kant I (1963) Immanuel Kant, what is enlightenment? In: Beck LW (trans) Kant on history. Bobbs-Merrill, Indianapolis

Locke J (2003) A letter concerning toleration. In: Shapiro I (ed) John Locke. Yale University Press, New Haven

MacKinnon C (2006) Toleration: a critical introduction. Routledge, London

Newey G (1997) Against thin-property reductivism: toleration as supererogatory. J Value Inq 31:231–249

Newey G (2017) Modus vivendi, toleration and power. Philosophia 45:425–442

Paine T (1954) The rights of man. Dent, London

Proast J (2010 [1690]) The argument of the letter concerning toleration briefly considered and answered, Vernon P (ed). Cambridge University Press, Cambridge

Rawls J (1993) Political liberalism. Columbia University Press, New York

Raz J (1988) Autonomy, toleration, and the harm principle. In: Mendus S (ed) Justifying toleration. Cambridge University Press, Cambridge, pp 155–175

Waldron J (1988) Locke, toleration and the rationality of persecution. In: Mendus S (ed) Justifying toleration. Cambridge University Press, Cambridge, pp 61–86

Walzer M (1997) On toleration. Yale University Press, New Haven

Warnock M (1987) The limits of toleration. In: Mendus S, Edwards D (eds) On toleration. Oxford University Press, Oxford

Williams B (1996) Toleration: an impossible virtue? In: Heyd D (ed) Toleration: an elusive virtue. Princeton University Press, Princeton, pp 18–27

Toleration

5

Anna Elisabetta Galeotti

Contents

Introductory Notes 72
The Origin of the Doctrine of Toleration 73
Toleration: Concept, Reasons, and Related Concepts 75
  The Concept 75
  Reasons 77
  Intolerable, Intolerance 78
Conceptions of Toleration 81
  The Social Virtue of Toleration 81
  The Liberal Model of Toleration 83
  Toleration as Recognition 84
Toleration and Cultural Conflicts 86
  Social Standards: Vertical and Horizontal Issues of Toleration 86
  A Vertical Issue: Muslims' Place of Worship 88
  Hate Speech 89
Summary and Future Directions 90
References 91

Abstract

Toleration represents the solution to disagreement whenever contrasting views and actions can coexist peacefully within the same society. While the social value of toleration for the promotion of a peaceful, free, and diverse society is widely acknowledged, many authors question that toleration is a sufficient response to the issues arising from contemporary pluralism. This has led to a wide discussion on the concept, on the justification, on the application, and to the provision of different conceptions of toleration. The first section of this chapter will briefly rehearse the history of doctrine of toleration; the second section will take up first the analysis of the concept, then will consider the reasons for toleration, and lastly

---

A. E. Galeotti (✉)
Università del Piemonte Orientale, Vercelli, Italy
e-mail: elisabetta.galeotti@uniupo.it

© The Author(s), under exclusive licence to Springer Nature Switzerland AG 2022   71
M. Sardoč (ed.), *The Palgrave Handbook of Toleration*,
https://doi.org/10.1007/978-3-030-42121-2_5

will examine some related concepts such as intolerance and intolerable. The third section will deal with the three most common conceptions of toleration, namely, the social virtue, liberal toleration, and toleration as recognition. Finally, the fourth section will focus on the application of the different conceptions and will show that toleration as recognition best addresses the cases arising from cultural conflicts.

Keywords

Toleration · Dislike · Disapproval · Noninterference · Objection component · Acceptance component · Power condition · Intolerable · Intolerance · Recognition

---

Introductory Notes

Toleration is the traditional response to potentially conflicting religious and moral doctrines, practices, and ways of life that do not directly affect the third party. Toleration represents the solution to disagreement whenever contrasting views and actions can coexist peacefully within the same society. More precisely, toleration recommends people to suspend the interference with the object of their disagreement and let others free to behave as they think best. The crucial circumstance for toleration is then pluralism, that is, the presence of conflicting differences, viewpoints, and practices within the same society: were there no differences or only harmoniously combined differences there would be nothing to tolerate. Given pluralism, we have toleration whenever an agent disapproves or dislikes some behavior or practice of some other agent, has some power to suppress or obstruct the disliked behavior, and nevertheless chooses to withhold her power. Reasons for toleration can be prudential, such as preference for peace over conflict; moral, such as respect for other's liberty and autonomy; epistemic, such as the fallibility of human reasoning; and finally political when related to the maximization of liberty and equal respect for all citizens.

This very sketchy presentation makes it clear the *social value* of toleration for the promotion of a peaceful, free, and diverse society. It is more problematic, though, that toleration represents a value as well for both the tolerator and the tolerated. From the tolerator's perspective, it is not immediately clear that accepting or in any case letting go a behavior or a practice that one finds contrary to one's convictions is a good thing. In this respect, toleration seems to be more a disposition resulting from a compromise than a principled choice. From the viewpoint of the tolerated, then, being tolerated is better than being repressed or obstructed, but it is far from being a desirable condition since toleration brings along an aftertaste of condescension. In this light, it seems that toleration may at most be a second best for the tolerated. Yet, despite toleration's ambivalent nature in moral and epistemic terms, there is a general agreement that a tolerant society is a worthwhile ideal and that contemporary pluralism requires more rather than less toleration in social intercourses.

The general acknowledgment of the importance of toleration at the social and political level, coupled with its theoretical and moral difficulty, has caused toleration to return to the front line of philosophy and political theory in the last three decades or so, after a long period of neglect. The discussion has been focused on how to interpret toleration properly so that it can work as both an individual disposition and a social and political ideal to address the issues raising from contemporary pluralism and cultural differences. From a philosophical perspective, the analysis has been concerned with the proper rendering of the concept and on its justification. Toleration can actually be understood in negative terms, as putting up and letting go, hence as a contingent accommodation between two conflicting parties, and also in positive terms, as acceptance, which avoids the tone of moral condescension implicit in the purely negative view of toleration. As to the reasons, the justification of the disposition to let go or to accept what is disapproved represents an intriguing challenge for the philosophy of toleration. Is toleration a necessity or a virtue, and, in the latter case, is it only prudential or is it also moral? Can we reconcile the moral value of toleration with the disapproval of the behavior that is the object of toleration, and if yes, how? The philosophical debate on toleration has been working on these questions proposing varied sophisticated solutions to the puzzle of toleration.

Moving into politics, political issues of toleration often concern where to trace the limits of the intolerable, that is, the limits beyond which toleration turns into a culpable indulgence. In this respect, the discussion is focused on whether contemporary democracy can or cannot afford to tolerate certain practices or, to put it differently, whether too much toleration can expose the liberal society to the risk of being overcome by intolerance. At the same time, if the limits of toleration are too strict, then the liberal society may adopt illiberal measures that might involve the curtailment of liberty rights. To sum up, the philosophical analysis has been mainly concerned with the issue of the justification of toleration in order to overcome the apparent moral paradox ("how can I accept what I disapprove?"). The political analysis has instead taken up the so-called pragmatic paradox that is the "toleration of the intolerant" issue and hence has especially been focused on the limits of toleration and on preserving the liberal society from the intolerants, on the one hand, and from turning illiberal, on the other hand. Some authors have questioned whether the liberal conception of toleration is sufficient to deal with the conflicts induced by contemporary pluralism and, accordingly, have proposed a revised view of toleration as recognition which seems more appropriate to face the issue of the visibility of differences linked to minority groups.

The Origin of the Doctrine of Toleration

Historically, the doctrine of toleration emerged as the solution to the challenge posed by the religious wars that devastated early modern Europe after the Protestant Reformation. The Reformation broke the religious unity of European states under the Church of Rome, and the different creeds advanced intractable and nonnegotiable claims about the true faith and the path to save one's soul. Violent conflicts followed throughout Europe in the sixteenth century but also in the seventeenth and early eighteenth centuries, and no contending party succeeded in winning the contest and imposing itself as the unique representative of the true faith, suppressing all others as the Catholic Church suppressed "heretics" during the Middle Ages.

The idea of toleration emerged slowly from the convergence of several lines of thought. A first pragmatic solution to the wars was represented by the doctrine of *territorialism*, summarized by the dictum "cuius regio, eius religio." Territorialism stated that the religion in any given country should conform to that of the sovereign. The Church of Rome's monopoly over matter of faith was thus broken, and in some areas of Europe (the territories of the Sacred Roman Empire), a partial religious pluralism was legally acknowledged. This solution, however, implied that religious groups had to emigrate into countries where the official religion corresponded to their faith. Territorialism was not toleration but only a first compromise to promote internal peace over religious matters; it was moreover an unstable solution if the area contained religious minorities, excluded from the legal recognition. Lastly, it could not provide reason why conformity to the country's official religion could secure the salvation of one's soul. Meanwhile, many thinkers in different countries advanced various arguments contributing to the idea of toleration. Such arguments ranged from human skepticism, well represented by Erasmus ([1511] 1970), to the folly of persecution, as advanced by Sebastian Castellion ([1553] 1935) to the impossibility of forcing people to embrace the true faith, as defended by John Milton ([1644] 1973) first and by John Locke later ([1667] 1950). In the end, toleration finally won, though in a limited way, because the war could not be stopped and toleration appeared as the only political solution that would lead to a stable peace. Thus, victorious was an idea of toleration patterned after the doctrine of the French "politiques" during the sixteenth century that affirmed that religion should be politically neutralized as the only way to maintain peaceful coexistence in a religiously divided society.

In the troubled period from the sixteenth to eighteenth century, many theories of toleration were proposed. Among the most renowned thinkers of toleration let us mention John Milton, Pierre Bayle ([1688] 2005), Baruch Spinoza ([1670] 2007), John Locke, and Voltaire ([1767] 1961). Their arguments in favor of toleration varied and included (a) *political arguments* in favor of peace over conflict; (b) *epistemological arguments*, concerning (i) human fallibility, (ii) the difficulty of a final access to truth, (iii) the distinction between knowledge and faith, and (iv) the imposition of religious beliefs as groundless; and (c) *moral arguments*, related to the wrong of using coercion in matter of faith.

However justified, toleration's way of working for peace and civil coexistence exhibited a common pattern. It basically consisted in making a strict demarcation between matters pertaining to the political order and public affairs, on the one hand, and matters unrelated to the political order, among which primary were religious convictions. This demarcation divided the society into two areas. The political sphere, on the one hand, was defined around matters that were relevant to peace and order, hence subject to political authorities and to binding regulations for all. The private realm, on the other hand, was instead concerned with matters irrelevant for peace and order, where the state had no business, hence no reason to intervene with coercive action. This protected area, where political interference was to be suspended, constituted the proper object of toleration. The principle of toleration thus relied on and worked through the public/private divide and, as a result, had a double effect: it created protection against state intervention in matters of faith, and it circumscribed religion within a politically neutralized area, the private realm of conscience, hence preventing churches and religious movements from interfering with political decision. Toleration thus engendered a lengthy and highly contested process by which church and state became increasingly autonomous in their respective spheres. Despite the variety of arguments justifying toleration epistemically and morally, ultimately toleration recommended itself to the absolute kings or queens because it was politically more convenient than persecution and also because persecution was shown to be useless in saving souls: not only beliefs cannot be forced but also faith must be reached in the right way to grant salvation.

In this respect, the absolute monarchies of the seventeenth and eighteenth century, granting toleration to some dissenting creeds within their kingdom territories, acted out of grace and reasonableness, not out of justice, in order to neutralize the disruptive effects of religious zeal. Toleration was left to the sovereign's discretion, and the acts of toleration proceeded from the absolute will of the monarch so that toleration appeared to be entangled with absolutism, as vividly remarked by Thomas Paine ([1791] 1989). According to Paine, with the demise of absolutism and the establishment of liberal state, there would be no need for toleration any more. After the American and French Revolution, the inclusion of the ideal of toleration in constitutional rights as a means of protecting individual freedom of conscience, expression, and association seems to render the very notion of toleration superfluous.

While some thinkers follow Paine in holding the notion of toleration at odds with liberal politics, others maintain that liberalism did not do away with toleration but, rather, transformed it from an act of grace of an enlightened king into the universal right to free conscience of all citizens. At this point, though, the political principle and the social virtue of toleration parted ways and became embodied in different conceptions of toleration, which will be properly considered in the third section of this chapter.

Toleration: Concept, Reasons, and Related Concepts

The Concept

Toleration is a concept articulated in different conceptions and theories. While there is an ongoing debate about which conception is the most suitable for addressing certain issues, there is basic agreement on the concept of toleration, despite the fact that it is spelled out differently by different authors (King 1976; Cohen 2004; Forst 2013).

Briefly, the core features of the concept of toleration are:

1. Agent A's dislike or disapproval of agent B's views, codes, or convictions
2. A's wielding of some power of interference with the difference in question
3. A's withholding of such power in favor of leaving B free to live by and pursue her ideals
4. Within the limits of self-defense and of harming others

The first feature, also called the "objection component," specifies a necessary condition for toleration to be the case. In a pluralist society, some differences are matters of disagreement but not all. One can be indifferent to certain different views or lifestyles or can even welcome the diversity. In either case, there is nothing to tolerate. The original objection is instead required for toleration, since in its absence toleration is beside the point.

As to the second feature, the power condition, it is required to mark toleration from acquiescence, for one can put up with something she dislikes merely because of any lack of power to interfere. This condition seems to make toleration an unequivocally asymmetrical disposition, going one-way from the tolerator to the tolerated (King 1976). For this reason, this condition has been debated, since it seems to imply that powerless groups and people cannot by definition be tolerant but only tolerated, on the one hand, and acquiescent, on the other hand (Jones 2007). Yet, even a powerless agent, when confronted with behavior or practices she dislikes, can display a tolerant disposition and not just acquiesce with the object of dislike, even though she lacks the means to obstruct the behavior or the practice. In other terms, the power condition can be interpreted not only as the actual obstructive power blocking certain behavior or practice but also as the normative power to suspend one's objection for higher or more relevant reasons (Forst 2013). In this sense, the power refers to the moral capability to withhold one's objection and to embrace the disposition of being tolerant, even if, in any case, the agent has no actual capacity of interference. So understood, the power condition does not imply that toleration cannot be reciprocal and that powerless people cannot but being tolerated, on the one hand, and acquiescent concerning disliked objects, on the other hand.

The third feature, also called the acceptance component, precisely describes what toleration consists in, namely, the suspension of the original dislike in favor of noninterference. Such component obviously raises the question of the reason why one should accept what she dislikes or disapproves. This question concerns the issue of the justification of toleration which constitutes the main focus of different theories and conceptions of toleration. Whatever the reasons, toleration always implies the choice to withhold the power of interference in favor of letting the other agent free to express and behave as she likes.

Finally, the fourth condition establishes that toleration is limited for unrestrained toleration that can turn into something deplorable. The limits to toleration have been traced from the very beginning. More precisely, John Locke firmly stated that toleration should stop short of intolerant people to prevent the disruption of law and order. To his mind, intolerant were atheists, because their oath could not be trusted, and Catholics, for their primary loyalty was to the foreign power of Rome. In other words, in his *Letter Concerning Toleration*, Locke traced the limit to toleration in the principle of self-defense of the liberal order against potential disruptive forces. Besides the self-defense principle, toleration should also be limited by considerations of harm to others. It was John Stuart Mill who theorized the harm principle as a necessary limit to toleration if it is to stand as a liberal value (Mill [1859] 1972). We shall come back to these two principles, while at present let us focus on whether the concept of toleration should comprise its own limits.

Whether the limits should be included in the conditions of toleration is indeed a matter of controversy. The disagreement concerns whether the concept of toleration should be purely descriptive or whether it should include normative conditions as well (Balint 2017). The limits, in fact, introduce normative boundaries to the concept that go beyond the description of a tolerant disposition and act but define whether an act and a disposition of a certain nature can be qualified as tolerant or as culpably indulgent. According to some thinkers, the introduction of normative conditions, such as the limits of toleration, makes the concept unduly moralized. In general, the concept of toleration is considered moralized if either or both the objection and the acceptance components are sustained by moral reasons, so as to grant the moral quality of toleration as a virtue. A problem with the moralized version is that toleration turns out too restricted since it does not include objects of mere dislike, such as cultural differences, and carries an unpleasant tone of moral condescension toward the tolerated. Nevertheless, the alternative to a moralized concept is not necessarily a purely descriptive account. We can have a normative account, which makes sense of toleration *as a valuable thing* and sets it apart from forbearance of what cannot be tolerated, without relying on an unduly restricted moral view. For, toleration is an ideal and an undisputed social and political value in democratic society, though the reasons why it is a value vary and there is no agreement about that. Under this light, the definition should include the (normative) conditions under which toleration *as valuable* is the case, keeping agnostic concerning the reasons why it is a value. Putting up with murder, for example, is not an instance of toleration. Yet, under a purely descriptive definition, there is no way to set apart toleration of the hijab, for example, and connivance with crime. Therefore, the definition of toleration should not only specify what toleration consists in, in terms of attitudes and actions, but also circumscribe the area within which toleration is a value, for outside that area, the same kind of attitude and action is no more "tolerant" in a proper sense but just "permissive" and more precisely culpably indulgent. If we do not want to equate toleration with permissiveness or forbearance in general, then the limits for toleration to be a value are constitutive of the concept, which has a descriptive content but which is also inherently normative, though not moralized for neither the objects nor the reasons of toleration need to be of moral nature.

Reasons

The reason for toleration represents a puzzle for moral and political theory, given that toleration recommends to accept something for which one has reason to object in the first place. Toleration seems to depend on an internal division of the agent between the objection and the acceptance component. The conundrum can be solved if the reasons for toleration are thought of as second-order reasons with reference to the first-order reasons for objection. In turn, the second-order reasons can either exclude to factor the objection component on grounds of different kind of considerations, and in that case they are exclusionary reasons (Raz 1990), or they can override the objection component with stronger reasons. The exclusionary reasons bracket the objection component in favor of different considerations; in that sense, they recommend toleration for extrinsic reasons, that is, reasons that do not engage with the objection directly. The overriding reasons instead overcome the objection because of higher and stronger reasons; in that respect, they are intrinsic reasons. As to their content, reasons for toleration can be classified as follows:

(a) *Instrumental or strategic reasons*. Instrumental reasons are extrinsic reasons derived from self-interested, prudential motivations.
(b) *Pragmatic reasons*. Agents may have pragmatic reasons to be tolerant, such as a preference for social peace or the value of pluralism. These are typical cases of exclusionary, extrinsic reasons, recommending to put aside the objection and to act on different kinds of considerations.
(c) *Moral reasons*. Agents can then choose toleration because of the value of autonomy or the value of equal respect deemed of a higher order than the reasons for objection (Mendus 1988; Forst 2013) or by a moral disposition to be open toward other people and their difference (Newey 2013). In this case, the reasons for toleration are not exclusionary but rather overriding the reasons for the disapproval of the other side; in this respect, they are intrinsic reasons for toleration.
(d) *Epistemic reasons*. This last kind of reasons is grounded on a fallibilist view of truth and on an attitude of epistemic modesty that considers the possibility that one's first-order reasons, given the limits of human reason and of the available evidence, may turn out to be wrong (Tate 2016). Hence, it is reasonable to refrain to impose them on others, as well as to expect a reciprocal attitude by others. Epistemic reasons are intrinsic reasons as well, in so far as they engage directly with the reasons for objection. I like to stress that epistemic modesty and fallibilism are not to be equated with skepticism. From skepticism, in fact, not toleration but rather the dissolution of the objection component follows, since anyone's opinion is as good as anyone else's (Tuck 1988).

Whatever the justifying reasons for toleration, the objection component is not cancelled, for in that case toleration would be superfluous. Even though both extrinsic and intrinsic reasons grant toleration, intrinsic reasons are more stable and likely to promote a more open society sustained by civic friendship among its members.

Intolerable, Intolerance

As said, toleration is a value only within limits, for "toleration" of murder or rape is certainly not a value. Beyond its limits, toleration turns into culpable indulgence of

5 Toleration

conducts and practices that are "intolerable" (Raphael 1988). In the doctrine of toleration, the self-defense of the social and political order and the harm principle represent the two widely shared boundaries separating objects for toleration from what is intolerable. While the two principles are uncontentious, what counts as a threat to the social and political order, as well as what counts as harm, is a matter of ongoing controversy (Raz 1988; Forst 2013: 369–7; Cohen 2014: 36–54). For example, how far can self-defense trump the freedom of other individuals and groups? Can self-defense be invoked in favor of keeping the cultural landscape intact? And does only bodily and material harm count or also psychological and symbolical (Galeotti 2007)? And what about self-harm? Without getting now into this controversy, let us assume the two limits in their bottom-line definition, which no one can reasonably reject. That is to say, let us take that harm is any violation of other people's bodily integrity, their liberty, and their property. Similarly, let us take that self-defense kicks in when actual threats to law and order are the case, such as terrorist attacks. The two limits of self-defense and harm to others qualify acts trespassing on them as "intolerable." Consequently, the response to the intolerable should be non-toleration of those very acts. The non-toleration of murder or rape, however, is not "intolerant," for the prosecution of crime is mandated by the rule of law and not ascribed to disapproval or disagreement between social parties. The response to the "intolerable," to whatever has infringed the limits of toleration, is therefore not an intolerant act even though it implies the non-toleration of the "intolerable."

Let us move now to intolerance. First, intolerance properly applies to the same domain of objects for which toleration is in order. Intolerance is to be detected within the scope of what can be tolerated, and it is a value to tolerate. It does not apply to what trespasses on the limits of toleration: thus, one can be tolerant or intolerant of vegetarianism, but she cannot be said to be tolerant or intolerant of rape. Imposing a meat-based menu in a cafeteria is an intolerant act toward vegetarians, while prosecuting rape is the proper response to the intolerable. In this way, we have in principle drawn a clear line between intolerant acts and what properly are responses to intolerable acts. This distinction is important descriptively, but it has also very important political implications. Since in liberal democracy, being tolerant is generally considered a value, while being intolerant is generally disapproved, then agents tend to present their intolerant attitudes as responses to the intolerable, for in that case they would be justified and not at all intolerant. The public debate over toleration issues has thus been inflated with the discussion over its limits that, depending on the viewpoints, are judged either too restricted or overstretched. That is why a clear definition of intolerance is in order.

What constitutes an intolerant act within the boundaries of the tolerable? The answer is not obvious for lack of toleration may depend on indifference or acquiescence and requires going back to the concept of toleration. The core concept of toleration comprises both an *original objection* by a social agent with some power of interference and the *suspension of that objection*. If there is no original objection, there is no case for either toleration or intolerance. Intolerance follows from the original objection. More precisely, intolerance is the case when social party A, endowed with some power of interference, objects to some difference x of party B and, instead of suspending the objection in favor of toleration, *chooses to act on that very objection,* even if x does not infringe the limits of toleration. In this way, attitudes and behavior that are intolerant, implying the *non-suspension* of the *original objection*, can be set apart from attitudes and behavior that are *responses to intolerance*, that is, acts of resistance to the interference with one's convictions and lifestyles by another party. If the KKK, out of its dislike of nonwhite people, organizes a racist demonstration, displaying all the symbols of white supremacy and exercising its power of intimidation, this is a display of intolerance, of a dislike openly exhibited with the purpose of intimidating. If African-Americans protest against such a demonstration, which targets them as a racial group, their claim to stop such racist displays is not intolerant but, more properly, is their response to intolerance. Similarly, those who object to the construction of mosques, and pour pig's blood on the building site, are acting intolerantly, whereas Muslims protesting against such behavior are resisting the intolerance directed at them. The line between intolerance and response to intolerance divides (a) the decision to act on the original objection instead of withholding it from the response to the interference with one's convictions and customs and (b) the objection concerning the convictions, ways of life, and customs of the other party from the rebuttal of the attack on *one's own* convictions, customs, and way of life.

Resistance to the attack and defense of one's convictions and lifestyle cannot be equated with the intolerance of those who, disliking those convictions and lifestyle, act in order to penalize them. For example, the aggressive display of homophobic attitudes is intolerant of the sexual orientation of gays and lesbians; in contrast, the gay pride parade is an affirmation of the legitimacy of homosexual orientation and not an attack on the heterosexual lifestyle. Those who protest against the gay pride in fact claim that the gay display in the parade offends, hence harms, their convictions and pollutes the moral fabric of society; hence, it is *intolerable* (Devlin 1959; Hart 1962). Yet, if we allow such a stretching of the limits of toleration, the room for personal liberty of minority groups would be unduly reduced and equal liberty of all would be undermined. Therefore, heterosexuals would be free not only to follow their sexual orientation but also to limit the correlative freedom, and hence the public consideration, of homosexuals. In summary, there seem to be two conditions for intolerance: (a) the original and non-suspended objection and (b) the other-regarding nature of the objection. By contrast, the response to intolerance is characterized by (a) being the counter-objection to a previous objection targeting the respondents and (b) being self-regarding.

In sum, when we are confronting acts harming other people or threatening the security of the political order, we are confronting the "intolerable," and toleration and intolerance are likewise beside the point. If we consider instead practices, conducts, and convictions, which are not violating any right but are the object of moral and social disagreement, this is the area where indifference, acquiescence, toleration, intolerance, and, lastly, response to intolerance are all possible attitudes and types of conduct. If no clear distinction between intolerant acts, intolerable acts, and responses to intolerance and to the intolerable is drawn, then the public discussion over issues of toleration is pervaded by reciprocal accusations of intolerance, making the debate muddy and the reference to toleration problematic. Before discarding toleration from political language though, some conceptual clarification can help to break down such circular accusations.

Conceptions of Toleration

The Social Virtue of Toleration

The concept of toleration is articulated in different conceptions. The different conceptions organize, and partly readjust, the core features of the concept according to two criteria. The first criterion pertains to the reasons justifying toleration, which can vary from strategic, pragmatic, to moral and epistemic. The second concerns whether toleration applies horizontally, among individuals and groups, or vertically, directed by the state or political institutions at certain groups of citizens. While the concept of toleration spells out the general features that any instantiation should have in order to be recognized as toleration, set apart from indifference, acquiescence, and culpable indulgence, the conceptions of toleration specify why toleration is a value, for what reasons, and in what setting. We are going to consider three conceptions of toleration which have been widely discussed in the last decades among philosophers and political thinkers, namely, the social virtue of toleration, the liberal model of toleration, and toleration as recognition. Each of them illustrates how the varying justifying reasons and the horizontal or vertical dimension affect the resulting conception (Galeotti 2015).

The conception of toleration as a *social virtue* articulates the core concept in the horizontal relationship of two social parties, one of which objects to the other's conduct (or convictions, or lifestyle) but withholds the possibility of interfering, choosing to tolerate the disapproved or disliked conduct. Within this conception, positions are divided between a moralized and a non-moralized account of toleration. The disagreement concerns the objects of toleration as well as its justification. For toleration to be a moral value and a virtue, the disapproval must concern, on the one hand, objects that one is morally free to disapprove (Nicholson 1985; Raphael 1988; Mendus 1988; Horton 1996) and, on the other hand, objects that are not categorically wrong. First, if the disapproval concerns, for example, someone's race, ethnicity, or sexual orientation, that is, traits that are received and cannot be changed, overcoming one's distaste for, say, Asians or gays is not an exercise of toleration, because there are good moral reasons to think that disapproval in this case is unjustified. Disapproval is appropriate for actions and dispositions but not for ascriptive characters. In this case, the right thing to do is reviewing the racist or homophobic attitude and not being a tolerant racist (Williams 1996). Second, if the object of disapproval belongs to the class of what is universally condemned and categorically wrong, such as homicide, torture, sadistic actions, and so on, then toleration is turned into culpable indulgence, for in this case being tolerant would infringe on the harm principle and the rights of others. In sum, when we are confronting cases of rights violations and harm to third parties, the correct response is non-toleration of the intolerable. When we are confronting arbitrary and prejudiced disapproval, the correct response is modifying disapproval into indifference and respect. Lastly, when we are confronting a nonarbitrary disapproval, yet lacking universal condemnation, then toleration is the principled response. In this moralized account, the moral quality of toleration depends on reasons: both on the reasons for disapproving x, which should not be arbitrary and unjustified, and on the reasons for suspending the disapproval and letting go x, which, however, should stop short of a categorical wrong. The first set of reasons pertains to the conditions for toleration, and the second set to the justification of toleration. As much as the reasons for disapproval, the reasons for toleration should be moral as the value of autonomy and respect for others or as having the virtue in character of being open to other people.

If however the social virtue of toleration dispenses with a moralized account, then both the objects and the reasons for toleration need not be of moral nature (Warnock 1987; Balint 2017). Not only disapproval but also dislike may constitute the objection condition. Under this light, ascriptive characters, such as ethnicity, gender, and sex orientation, may represent objects of toleration. Similarly, the reasons for toleration can be anything from strategic and prudential to pragmatic, epistemic, and moral. In this case, the value of toleration does not consist in the sacrifice of one's ethical code for higher moral principles such as autonomy or respect or in the aretaic virtue of openness to other; rather it would consist in the social value of respectful social intercourses and civility among social partners.

Before considering the reasons for the social virtue of toleration, let us focus on the power condition. It would seem that in a liberal democratic society no social agent is endowed with an actual power of obstructing others' behavior, for only the political authority has the monopoly of coercion. In this respect, it would seem that no one could be socially tolerant (or intolerant). However, social agents can be economically powerful, or they can have power of influence so that they can make life heavier to people displaying differences they dislike. They can marginalize such people or intimidate them or humiliate them by showing them disrespect. There is a whole range of social sanctions that put a burden on the targeted people. The tolerant agent precisely withholds the sanctions at his disposal and lets others behave and live their life as they prefer. Hence, at the level of the social virtue, the power of interference should be understood as the social power to put a burden on others and not literally as obstructing or suppressing certain kind of behavior. Under this interpretation, the social power can apply not just to actions and practices but also to ascriptive traits, which may be made into a burden for their bearers (King 1976). In light of this more hospitable interpretation, the power condition can as well be understood as the moral capability to withhold one's objection and embrace a tolerant attitude toward differences one dislikes or disapproves.

The different reasons why the tolerator decides to withhold his power of interference characterize the social virtue of toleration either as negative or positive. On this issue, some clarification is in order. In the discussion on toleration, negative tolerance, or forbearance, has often been opposed to positive tolerance, as acceptance (Apel 1997; Zolo 1997). In fact, the negative/positive distinction needs to be reset. Toleration in any versions means noninterference with someone's liberty;

whether noninterference requires omission or commission of the tolerator depends on the context. For example, toleration of a foreign dress code implies the omission of any interference, but toleration of dietary requirements implies changing the menu options in cafeterias; hence, a positive action aimed at setting people free to follow their dietary requirements. Despite the original reasons of objection, noninterference with people's liberty is what toleration always consists in, and in this respect, toleration would appear to have a negative connotation. However, the tone of noninterference may sound differently according to the different reasons for sustaining toleration. If the reasons are just prudential or pragmatic, then the value of toleration is only instrumental and the original disapproval negatively affects the tolerated. If, by contrast, the reasons are intrinsic and lie either in respect for persons, in autonomy, or in epistemic reasons, the meaning of toleration and its scope change from negative to positive. The principle of respect, for example, belongs to a higher order than the reasons for disapproval and hence trumps the latter making them inappropriate for interpersonal exchange, and, moreover, it makes reciprocal toleration not contingently possible. Hence, toleration loses the negative overtone that is present when it is embraced on the basis of extrinsic reasons. In sum, the negative/positive distinction does not pertain to the *what* of toleration, which is always noninterference (either by omission or by commission), but to the *why* toleration ought to be chosen over the original disapproval. The original objection is not canceled by intrinsic reasons but is excluded as an appropriate consideration for interpersonal relationships with persons who are our (moral and epistemic) peers.

The Liberal Model of Toleration

The social virtue of toleration has been elaborated from the traditional doctrine of toleration, which in turn was patterned after the circumstances of the absolute state confronting with religious dissent. The conception of the social virtue was thus originally political. On the one hand, there was the king or the queen – the potential tolerator. On the other hand, there were the dissenters. The former judged the different creed as false and heretical and was endowed with the power of might to suppress it; in such circumstances, toleration was precisely the suspension of the repressive power of the state by the absolute sovereign for the sake of peace. It was properly a case of negative toleration for prudential reasons: the tolerance of the absolute monarch toward religious dissenters is precisely described by the social virtue of toleration. Within liberalism, however, vertical toleration can no more be captured by the conception of the social virtue that applies only horizontally, for the liberal authorities are not supposed to disapprove or to dislike anything within the bound of law. Thus, the move from the horizontal to the vertical dimension changes the structure of the problem and implies a readjustment of the core features: the problem still originates in the dislike between different social parties, but, in this case, the decision to intervene or tolerate the object of dislike resides with the political authority, which has the monopoly of coercion. Hence, a horizontal dislike between two social parties gives rise to a vertical decision for or against toleration. In this way, the parties involved are at least three: the objecting party, the objected party, and the political authority, which has the power and will settle the question in favor or against toleration. The core features – dislike, power to interfere, and suspension of interference, within the limits of toleration – are all in place, but it is the state which has the capacity to intervene or not on the ground of agent A's dislike. More precisely when a toleration issue erupts and becomes political, it means that the issue is not settled between the two social parties, and it implies that the political authorities have to examine the problem and decide whether the contested practice or behavior can or cannot be tolerated.

Such political decision is guided by the principle of political toleration recommending political noninterference with religious and moral convictions of people, if there is no disruption for law and order, principle that within liberalism is generalized in equal liberty rights. If before liberalism, toleration consisted in the king's good reasons for noninterference with religious dissent, within the normative framework of liberalism, the state has a duty of toleration, corresponding to the right of conscience of citizens. Accordingly, liberal toleration is justified by the principle of liberal neutrality. The ideal of neutrality addresses disagreement and dislike over religious, moral, and cultural differences by granting equal liberty to all, without judging the content of the dispute, as long as the harm principle is not violated. Thus, when the political authority has to judge a dispute over toleration, it has to evaluate whether the contested practice infringes on the harm principle, for only infringements on the harm principle can be publicly declared intolerable and hence prohibited. If the practice in question is not prohibited, then the state requires toleration of its citizens in their reciprocal relations, that is, it requires that citizens respect each other's liberty, notwithstanding their disagreement. The political duty to tolerate each other can be supplemented by social tolerance, if citizens adjust their internal dispositions with the civic duty to tolerate disliked practices, but can also be compatible with social intolerance, if some citizens decide to use their social power by marginalizing, intimidating, and ridiculing people behaving in ways they dislike.

Some authors contend that neutrality cannot ground toleration, because the condition of dislike is precisely absent in the neutral attitude of the liberal state (Horton, 1996: 36; Newey 1999: 123–127). However, they do not consider that state neutrality is the response to the conflict among social differences and to the dislike of one group toward another. In the circumstances of political toleration, the disapproving agent is not the agent choosing noninterference, because only political authority possesses the power to prohibit any practice. Neutrality is rather the reason backing political toleration in the form of equal liberty rights. Political toleration implies precisely that a *social* dislike is dealt with by a *political* decision to withhold the dislike, within the boundary of the harm principle, because of the principle of neutrality.

Toleration as Recognition

Toleration as recognition relates to the vertical dimension as well and is meant to supplement liberal toleration in the circumstances of contemporary pluralism

5 Toleration

(Galeotti 2002). In contemporary democracy, where liberty rights are enshrined in constitutions, it would seem that significant questions of toleration were preempted. Yet they still arise, from veil wearing to places of worship, from gay marriage to religiously dietary restrictions. These contemporary issues are special because (a) they explicitly concern *public* toleration and (b) they imply a claim to recognition of the contested differences. The standoff is usually produced by social majorities demanding that practices perceived as being at odds with the host society's principles and customs be restricted, contained, and rendered invisible and, symmetrically, by minorities claiming public toleration of their practices and political protection against offenses, humiliation, and discrimination. There is more than equal freedom at stake: there are asymmetries of power deriving from the social standing of different groups and defining inclusion in, or exclusion from, society, with significant political implications. The principle of neutrality is not sufficiently sensitive to perceive the struggle over exclusion/inclusion underlying issues of toleration. Neutrality does not see that the public space is not difference-free but populated by the majority's customs and conventions and that difference-blind politics runs the risk of reproducing existing exclusion, for not all members of society enjoy the same freedom to follow their convictions and lifestyles, and such asymmetries in freedom correspond to asymmetries in inclusion. Beyond toleration in the sense of equal liberty for minorities, here at stake there is the recognition of minority members, with their different practices and customs, as equal members of the polity worthy of the same respect as members of the majority. In this sense, it is important that the difference in question not only is not prohibited but also receives *public* toleration, and for the *right reasons*, meaning the recognition of its legitimate presence in the public space. Liberal neutrality tends to bracket all social differences together as equally irrelevant politically, thus obscuring the asymmetries among social differences and their implications in terms of inclusion in the polity. Toleration as recognition intends to overcome this specific blindness, by making room for all social differences (within the bounds of the harm principle) while yet reaffirming the principles underlying liberal neutrality, that is, non-perfectionism and impartiality. For the public recognition of a social difference implies its recognition as *a legitimate option* of the pluralist society, but it does not imply a substantive evaluation of that difference as good and worthwhile. Liberal institutions must not abdicate from their nonjudgmental, nonevaluative, impartial stance: toleration as recognition does not imply taking sides. In this respect, toleration as recognition is neither *permission* nor *acceptance*, since liberal institutions are not entitled to forbid or accept, let alone embrace, anything within the bounds of the law, but *legitimization*: a public declaration that a given practice, if it does not infringe any right, is a legitimate option among others. The literal meaning of toleration does not change from liberal toleration to toleration as recognition, but the symbolic meaning does, for the reasons in favor of toleration are not negative but positive. The difference in question is tolerated not just because it does not infringe the harm principle but because it contributes to fully include the bearers of that difference. The legitimization of the public presence of a difference then brings along an accommodation in the social practices and a revision in social standards so as to make room for the difference in question and for its bearers (Galeotti 2008). Some might object that toleration as recognition is in fact referring to a principle different from toleration, such as respect (Newey 2013). Yet, social conflicts over disagreement are what characterize issues of political toleration, and if the political decision is for noninterference, whatever the backing reasons are – equal liberty, equal respect, public recognition of differences, or prudential motivations – then we are confronting a case of political toleration.

To sum up, the three conceptions of toleration supplement each other, depending on the circumstances of their application and the issue at hand. The social virtue of toleration applies horizontally among social agents, and according to the reasons backing the choice for toleration may mean either "putting up" or "accept out of respect." This conception however is inadequate as a political principle because in politics while the primary condition of dislike or disapproval pertains to a social party, the decision to refrain from interference or not is up to democratic authority. In other words, political toleration, either according to the traditional liberal model or to toleration as recognition, resolves a social conflict engendered by the objection of one social group toward the difference of another. The two vertical conceptions differ concerning their backing reasons and their symbolic meaning. In the circumstances of contemporary pluralism, most issues of political toleration have to do not simply with equal liberty but especially with the recognition of equal respect of minority groups whose differences are perceived at odds with the society and hence are contested as legitimate presence in the public sight. In that respect, the liberal model does not address properly what is at stake, while toleration as recognition proves to be a more adequate conception.

Political toleration may then be supplemented by the social virtue of toleration, for the party that raised the objection may internalize the civic duty to toleration with the correspondent attitude, which in turn may be grounded on extrinsic or intrinsic reasons. Thus, vertical toleration can be patterned after the liberal conception, if backed by neutrality and equal liberty, or after toleration as recognition, if backed by equal respect. Either way, vertical toleration can correspond to either acquiescence or social toleration, which, in turn, may mean "putting up" if backed by strategic or prudential reasons or "accepting" out of respect or autonomy.

Toleration and Cultural Conflicts

Social Standards: Vertical and Horizontal Issues of Toleration

Within contemporary pluralistic democracy, most issues of toleration concern cultural conflicts, both at the horizontal and at the vertical levels. By cultural conflicts, I mean the problems emerging from social diversity, where distribution is not the main issue and where some contested practices, customs, or ways of life, maybe with some distributive implications, are claimed either to be intolerable by some sectors of the majority or to be publicly recognized by those who identify with them. Sometimes cultural conflicts erupt in relation to the alleged incompatibility between a given practice and the principles of liberal democracy, as in the case of genital mutilations or forced marriages. Quite often though, the contest concerns not the incompatibility of principles but rather the control over social standards, that is, the web of rules governing daily social life and promoting basic social coordination, for example, in street encounters and casual gatherings in public space (Galeotti 2017). In either case, the conflict may become political and require vertical decision either for or against toleration of the practice. Often, however, in the case of social standards, they remain frictions in daily interactions between the society's majority and minority groups, especially migrants of immigrant origin, engendering issues of horizontal toleration. Such frictions have to do with the arrival in a given community, regulated by given social standards and correlative civil dispositions, of people belonging to other communities, bringing along their different customs, traditions, and conventional codes. If the number of newcomers is significant, at least in certain areas, then migrants affect the hosting society by upsetting the established network of social norms and conventions, the corresponding expectations, and the embedded idea of civility. Since social standards are a necessary instrument of social coordination, and their control represents the specific power of society's majority, conflicts easily break up in front of unfamiliar customs and conventions. Such conflicts generally require time to process what seems threatening into something familiar. Yet, responses at the institutional and at the social level are required as well. The most significant institutional contribution to the solution of cultural conflicts over social standards is the adoption of a steady policy of public toleration making cultural differences visible in the public sphere, at all pertinent levels of institutional action. This policy has the crucial effect of legitimizing the presence of differences in the public space. By making them more visible on a daily basis, toleration as recognition indirectly makes them also more familiar and less threatening. At the horizontal level, how can citizens deal with different customs that look strange and unfamiliar? How can they face the spontaneous dislike toward such novelty upsetting the orderly process of daily life? In such cases, agents ought to recur to the virtue of tolerance: the spontaneous reaction of disapproval one feels toward infringements of one's social standards should be critically suspended in favor of tolerance. In turn, such tolerance can be backed by purely instrumental reasons and hence be an instance of negative toleration as forbearance, or it can be backed by respect, acquiring a positive meaning for strange patterns of social behavior should not be regarded as signs of disrespect of one's expectations but of different traditions. Newcomers are accustomed with different social standards and do not master the ones of the hosting society. Local standards should become common knowledge for newcomers too, yet not through an arrogant imposition, but via a considerate process of familiarization with the hosting society. Neither majority nor minorities should be forced to give up one's norms and conventions abruptly, and that is possible if a much broader tolerance than that required in a culturally uniform society is adopted. In the due course of time, different standards will merge and produce a new and richer network of social norms and conventions, making the toleration unnecessary.

A Vertical Issue: Muslims' Place of Worship

The growth of Muslim communities in European countries in the last decades has brought to the front the issue of appropriate place of worship for them. Despite religious freedom being a constitutional right in all European countries, the resistance over the opening of places of worship and the construction of purpose-built mosques has been widespread and has produced harsh political conflicts in many European cities, often becoming a national issue (Galeotti 2014). This is a case where vertical toleration is in order and where toleration as recognition can supplement the liberal model for the solution of the conflict. Places of worship are a matter of religious freedom, and religious freedom is a fundamental right for anyone. In this respect, political authorities of democratic state should grant this right, implementing liberal toleration without much ado. However, the party opposing mosque building have argued that their position is not intolerant. They maintain that Muslims are free to pray Allah, yet within the boundary of our laws and customary practices without creating problems of public order and security. In other words, building mosques in the public squares of European cities is alleged to violate the limits of toleration on the grounds that (a) it is an invasion of religion in the secular space; (b) it constitutes a threat to public order as secluded places for Islamic propaganda; (c) it represents a sign of Muslim unwillingness to integrate into European society; and (d) it is an unacceptable Islamization of the traditional landscapes of European cities. Thus, according to this view, purpose-built mosques would represent an instance of the *intolerable*. On the other hand, Muslims and people who support the building of mosques maintain that these arguments are specimens of *intolerance*. Political authorities are then called in to settle the issue and to decide whether mosque building may actually be considered a case of trespassing on the limits of toleration. From this example, one can appreciate the distance between traditional and contemporary issues of toleration: in our time, the issue is no more the persecution, suppression, and forced conversion of the infidels but rather the public visibility, and hence, ultimately, the social legitimation, of Muslims' places of worship. That is why it is an issue best addressed by toleration as recognition. Muslims' right to religious freedom is not questioned in general, but it is claimed that purpose-built mosques exceed the limits of toleration in a pluralist, democratic society. In this way, we can explain why some actors and commentators hold that such controversy is not a question of toleration and of religious freedom but rather of concern about public order, architectural fitness, the risk of nurturing terrorism, and so on.

In this controversy, the liberal model of toleration is put under pressure given that it admits of interpretation according to which the claim to prohibit proper mosque building is not intolerant. In fact, those who oppose mosque building refer to the Lockean divide between the private area of conscience, representing the proper object of toleration, and the public arena, where liberty may legitimately be restricted. Using the public/private divide, which was so crucial in the early doctrine of toleration, the building of a mosque is claimed to represent a trespass in the public secularized sphere. In this sense, the prohibition of mosque building would be in line with the liberal model of toleration. This interpretation of liberal toleration, however, is subject to contestations from many different points of view, starting with the public/private divide up to the legitimate limits to toleration. As a rule, no religion is totally confined in private and hidden from public sight. "Public" may in fact mean either "political" or "nonpersonal": public visibility need not be understood in terms of trespassing in the political and secular space but rather in terms of being openly present in civil society instead of hidden in ghettos. As to the expansion of the limits of toleration, it is actually the task of liberal toleration to assess the perimeter of the intolerable and to declare tolerable all that does not infringe on the harm principle or on the self-defense. Actually all the reasons provided by those opposing mosque building are easily contested, for they are vitiated by double standards. At the end, what is left is the claim that mosques upset social standards and the established identity of public space in European society. As seen before, the arrival of immigrants in hosting society causes an upsetting of social standards and the related feeling of displacement. This fact, however, cannot ground the claim that the building of mosque, given that it changes the familiar public space, is to be declared intolerable. For public space, as well as social standards, are as a rule subject to social evolution and always changing: malls, skyscrapers, financial districts, and parking lots, all this has changed the public space of European cities. Hence, claiming to stop just the purpose-built mosques would be again a case of double standards.

This claim, however, leads to consider that the liberal model should, in this instance, be substituted by toleration as recognition. Religious disagreement is not the real point of those opposing the building of proper mosques; the real point is the contest over the control of social standards and the identity of public space, which would be upset by the public visibility of Muslim identity. Toleration as recognition specifically understands the standoff as caused by the unequal standing of groups in contemporary pluralism and that toleration must signify the recognition of the legitimate presence of different identities and a wider and more diverse public space.

Hate Speech

Many other examples of toleration issues arising in contemporary pluralism – from dress codes in public place and/or by public officials, to gay marriage, to circumcision, to requests of censoring hate speech, to dietary restrictions – show a similar pattern as the issue of mosque just considered. That is to say, if examined by the liberal model, all such cases are framed in terms of where to trace the limits of the intolerable. If instead they are considered by the conception of toleration as recognition, the cases are framed as a contest over the public visibility of certain minority differences which sectors of the society's majority dislike. Under this interpretation, it turns out that it is not the disliked differences that are intolerable, but it is the claim to stop or hide them from the public sight that is intolerant, for in general the reasons the limits to toleration are not acceptable. With the due exceptions, toleration as recognition seems to be a more appropriate conception for dealing with contemporary issue of toleration.

A special difficulty is represented by the claims to limit offensive freedom of expression. In hate speech cases, we are actually confronting a very peculiar puzzle, given that, on the one hand, freedom of expression has typically been considered the proper object of toleration and, on the other hand, those invoking the restriction of free speech are claiming that certain forms of speech (hate speech) are hurtful to certain vulnerable groups and hence are intolerable. To this the supporters of free speech respond that in fact it is the request of policing speech to be intolerant for it implies the want to suppress what is disapproved. That offenses can be acknowledged as violating the harm principle is in general doubtful; hence, according to the liberal model of toleration, political toleration of hate speech would seem to follow. Yet, even though political authorities are better to refrain from censoring free speech and to stick to the principle of liberal toleration, the issue of hate speech can and should be reframed at the horizontal level of social relations. Here the conception of the social virtue of toleration properly applies. In this light, those who use hate speech are intolerant, for they do not suspend the dislike toward the targeted group (be it immigrants, gays, women, or others) but rather act out of it to intimidate, marginalize, and demean the members of the group. Social toleration in fact recommends refraining to acting out of one's dislike for the sake of respect of others or even just for social peace. The level of public discussion is the right one to face the issue of hate speech, and the social virtue of toleration is the right normative tool to find a solution.

In sum, we can conclude that toleration is not superfluous in contemporary democracy and that the social virtue of toleration is especially in demand, for it may prevent many issues from becoming a political question. When, however, political controversies arise, then, toleration as recognition is more apt than liberal toleration. The political response should in fact take into account the problem of the unequal social standing of groups beyond the problem of a contested difference and be sensitive to the quest for equality of respect besides that of equal liberty. Public toleration of a contested difference is the symbolic recognition that the bearers of that difference are equal peers and treated with the same consideration and respect than majority's citizens.

Summary and Future Directions

In this chapter, I have reviewed the current discussion on toleration after a brief summary of the traditional doctrine. The current philosophical discussion is mainly focused on conceptual analysis, for there is no agreement on how toleration should be understood. I have proposed to draw a line between the concept and the conceptions of toleration, given that there is a convergence on the former, but not on the latter. I have also taken up the analysis of the correlate concepts of intolerance and intolerable that in my argument are not simply the opposite of toleration. This analysis may help to make sense of issues where all parties involved claim toleration, and refer to the opposite party as intolerant. Among the conceptions of toleration, I have picked up three especially relevant in contemporary society, namely the social virtue of toleration, the liberal model, and toleration as recognition. I have argued that all three are necessary and supplement each other and that toleration is much in demand both as a social virtue and as the political principle dealing with a highly diverse society. Future research should focus in making use of the highly sophisticated discussion developed in the last decades, and apply it to understand conflicts of toleration not only in the domestic arena but also in the international context.

References

Apel KO (1997) Plurality of the good? The problem of affirmative tolerance in a multicultural society from an ethical point of view. Ratio Juris 10:199–212

Balint P (2017) Respecting toleration. Oxford University Press, Oxford

Bayle P [1688] (2005) Philosophical commentary (ed: Kilcullen J, Kukathas C). Liberty Fund, Indianapolis

Castellion S [1553] (1935) Concerning heretics: whether they are to be persecuted and how they are to be treated. Columbia University Press, New York

Cohen AJ (2004) What toleration is. Ethics 115:68–95

Cohen AJ (2014) Toleration. Polity Press, Cambridge

Devlin P (1959) The enforcement of morals. Oxford University Press, Oxford

Erasmus D [1511] (1970) In Praise of Folly, Princeton, Princeton University Press

Forst R (2013) Toleration in conflict. Cambridge University Press, Cambridge

Galeotti AE (2002) Toleration as recognition. Cambridge University Press, Cambridge

Galeotti AE (2007) Relativism, universalism and applied ethics: the case of female circumcision. Constellations 14:91–111

Galeotti AE (2008) Toleration as recognition: the case of same sex marriage. In: Creppell I, Hardin R, Macedo S (eds) Toleration on trial. Lexington Books, Lanham, pp 111–129

Galeotti AE (2014) Toleration and purpose-built mosques: contestations in contemporary Europe. In: Bessone M, Calder G, Zuolo F (eds) How groups matter. Routledge, London, pp 125–144

Galeotti AE (2015) The range of toleration: from toleration as recognition back to disrespectful tolerance. Philos Soc Criticism 41:93–110

Galeotti AE (2017) Cultural conflicts: a deflationary approach. Crit Rev Int Soc Pol Phil 20:537–555

Hart HH (1962) Law, liberty and morality. Oxford University Press, Oxford

Horton J (1996) Toleration as a virtue. In: Heyd D (ed) Toleration: an elusive virtue. Princeton University Press, Princeton, pp 28–43

Horton J, Mendus S (eds) (1985) Aspects of toleration: philosophical studies. Methuen, London

Jones P (2007) Making sense of political toleration. Br J Polit Sci 37:383–402

King P (1976) Toleration. Allen & Unwin, London

Locke J [1667] (1950) John Locke's political philosophy. Oxford University Press, Oxford

Mendus S (ed) (1988) Justifying toleration: conceptual and historical perspectives. Cambridge University Press, Cambridge

Mill JS (1972) [1859] On liberty. Dent, London

Milton J [16] (1973) Areopagitica (ed: Lea RM). Clarendon, Oxford

Newey G (1999) Virtue, reason and toleration. Edinburgh University Press, Edinburgh

Newey G (2013) Toleration in political conflict. Cambridge University Press, Cambridge

Nicholson P (1985) Toleration as a moral ideal. In: Mendus S, Horton J (eds) Aspects of toleration. Methuen, London, pp 158–173

Paine T [1791] (1989) The rights of man, part 1. In: Kuklick B (ed) Political writings. Cambridge University Press, Cambridge

Raphael DD (1988) The intolerable. In: Mendus S (ed) Justifying toleration. Cambridge University Press, Cambridge, pp 137–153

Raz J (1988) Autonomy, toleration and the harm principle. In: Mendus S (ed) Justifying toleration. Cambridge University Press, Cambridge, pp 155–175

Raz J (1990) Practical reason and norms. Princeton University Press, Princeton

Spinoza B [1670] (2007) Theological-political treatise (ed: Israel J). Cambridge University Press, Cambridge

Tate J (2016) Toleration, skepticism and blasphemy: John Locke, Jonas Proast and *Charlie Hebdo*. Am J Polit Sci 60:664–675

Tuck R (1988) Scepticism and toleration in the seventeenth century. In: Mendus S (ed) Justifying toleration. Cambridge University Press, Cambridge, pp 21–35

Voltaire [1763] (1961) Traité sur la tolerance. In: Mélanges (ed) A l'occasion de la mort de Jean Calais. Gallimard, Paris

Warnock M (1987) The limits to toleration. In: Edwards D, Mendus S (eds) On toleration. Clarendon Press, Oxford, pp 123–139

Williams B (1996) Toleration: an impossible virtue? In: Heyd D (ed) Toleration: an elusive virtue. Princeton University Press, Princeton, pp 18–27

Zolo D (1997) Positive tolerance: an oxymoron. Ratio Juris 10:247–251

Paradoxes of Toleration

6

Peter Königs

Contents

Introduction 94
The Paradox of Moral Toleration 95
The Paradox of Self-Destruction 100
The Paradox of Drawing the Limits 102
The Paradox of the Tolerant Racist 104
Summary and Future Directions 106
References 107

> **Abstract**
>
> Although one of the fundamental pillars of liberalism, toleration has come to be seen as a paradoxical value. This chapter explores four paradoxes surrounding toleration and discusses the solutions put forth by toleration theorists. The paradox of moral toleration arises from the conflict between the objection component and the acceptance component of toleration. Toleration requires us to accept beliefs or practices that we find objectionable. But it may seem paradoxical that the acceptance of what we consider wrong should be virtuous. The paradox of self-destruction refers to the fact that unlimited toleration is bound to lead to the destruction of toleration. Paradoxically, for a liberal society to survive, it must itself be intolerant towards some groups, namely those that seek to subvert liberal society. The paradox of drawing the limits concerns the demarcation of the boundaries of toleration. Skeptics have claimed that there is no neutral or universally acceptable way of drawing the limits of toleration, which would mean that any way of drawing the limits would itself be an arbitrary act of intolerance. Finally, the paradox of the tolerant racist points to an oddity of the standard account of toleration. If to tolerate is to accept what one finds objectionable, it seems to follow that a racist who accepts people of other races qualifies as

P. Königs (✉)
Human Technology Center, Applied Ethics, RWTH Aachen University, Aachen, Germany
e-mail: peter.koenigs@rwth-aachen.de

© The Author(s), under exclusive licence to Springer Nature Switzerland AG 2022   93
M. Sardoč (ed.), *The Palgrave Handbook of Toleration*,
https://doi.org/10.1007/978-3-030-42121-2_13

tolerant. But the idea that a racist deserves to be praised as tolerant is counterintuitive.

Keywords

Toleration · Paradoxes · Liberalism · Justification

Introduction

Liberalism is, essentially, about getting along with people with whom one disagrees about how one ought to live one's life. The principle of toleration has therefore rightly been called the "substantive heart" of liberalism (Hampton 1989, p. 802). Many of the most influential figures in the liberal tradition − John Locke, John Stuart Mill, Isaiah Berlin, Karl Popper, John Rawls, Jürgen Habermas, Martha Nussbaum, among others − have written dedicated treatises on toleration or can be read as toleration theorists. Few political ideas have gained such widespread approval as the idea of toleration.

At the same time, one can sense a distinct unease among toleration theorists. Tolerance has been perceived as a "paradoxical," "elusive," and "difficult" virtue, as a quick glance at titles of books and articles on toleration reveals (Forst 2017; Heyd 1996; Horton 1994; Scanlon 2003; see also Churchill 2015, pp. 141–142; Overdiek 2001, pp. 9–22; Scheffler 2010, pp. 312–313). A considerable portion of the literature on toleration is devoted to identifying, describing, and dispelling puzzles and paradoxes that beset the idea of toleration. Thus, despite the broad support for the principle of toleration, political thinking about toleration has also been shaped by the threat of skepticism about the coherence and moral value of toleration.

This chapter explores the principal paradoxes surrounding toleration and discusses the solutions that toleration theorists have put forth. I will consider four such paradoxes in detail: the paradox of moral toleration, the paradox of self-destruction, the paradox of drawing the limits, and the paradox of the tolerant racist. (The names of the paradoxes are due to Forst (2013).)

Before doing so, it is worth saying a little more about the concept of toleration. Most toleration theorists agree that toleration involves a combination of two components, which seemingly pull in opposite directions. First, toleration involves an acceptance component. Toleration is, evidently, about accepting or putting up with other people's views and practices, for instance, with their religious beliefs. Acceptance is what toleration is first and foremost about. But, second, toleration also involves an objection component. For one cannot tolerate that which one does not object to or disapprove of. Some people devote their lives to art, give generously to charity, exercise on a daily basis, or strive to spend as much time as possible with friends and family. These are life choices that we can be said to "accept" but which we cannot be said to "tolerate," because they do not strike us as objectionable. As Bernard Williams observes, perhaps somewhat hyperbolically, toleration is needed when one group of people believes that another group of people is "blasphemously, disastrously, obscenely wrong" (1996, p. 18). Many of the paradoxes discussed in this chapter concern, in some way or other, these two components of tolerance and their interplay.

The Paradox of Moral Toleration

The paradox of moral toleration is the most intensely discussed paradox of toleration, and it is arguably the one that possesses the greatest philosophical significance. This paradox is directly linked to the fact that tolerance involves a combination of acceptance and objection. What has struck many as paradoxical is that tolerance is considered a moral virtue rather than a vice, given that tolerance requires us to accept what we deem objectionable. If we are confident that some view or practice is wrong or harmful, should we not prevent or oppose it rather than accept it? Why, indeed, be tolerant? Here are three typical statements of this paradox:

> Toleration is the practice of deliberately allowing or permitting a thing of which one disapproves. [...] But if your disapproval is reasonably grounded, why should you go against it at all? Why should you tolerate? Why, in other words, is toleration a virtue or a duty? (Raphael 1988, p. 136)
>
> On the one hand, an unwillingness to interfere with the beliefs and practices of others will not count as tolerant at all unless it is accompanied by disapproval of those beliefs and practices. [...] On the other hand, if we restrict ourselves to cases in which the agent deeply disapproves of the practices that are candidates for toleration, then it is unclear why it should be a virtue to tolerate them. (Scheffler 2010, pp. 316–317)
>
> [I]f the reasons for objection as well as those for acceptance are identified as moral, the paradox is exacerbated into the question of *how it can be morally right or even obligatory to tolerate what is morally wrong or bad.* (Forst 2013, p. 21)

It is generally assumed that toleration is a virtue or that we have a duty to be tolerant. But when one reflects about what tolerance is – namely, the acceptance of what one deems objectionable – it is puzzling why tolerance should be virtuous. On the face of it, the case *against* toleration initially appears much more compelling. After all, interfering with others' ways of life can be a way of helping them to lead a good life. This quite intuitive rationale underlying the case against toleration was well stated by Augustine in his letter to Vincent, which would later inspire Pierre Bayle to write his famous defense of toleration: "Not everyone who is merciful is a friend; nor is everyone who scourges an enemy. Better are the wounds from a friend than the spontaneous kisses of an enemy" (Augustinus 2001, p. 379). If you are convinced that someone's way of life is fundamentally wrong, the charitable thing to do is to interfere rather than to tolerate, or so the intuitive reasoning goes.

There may, of course, be pragmatic reasons for accepting worldviews and ways of life that one is confident are mistaken. If you do not possess the means or the power to change people's mistaken beliefs and practices, or if they are likely to get back at you in the future, it would be unwise to attempt to interfere with them. But these are prudential reasons for toleration. What we are trying to understand is, as Rainer Forst rightly emphasizes, why it should "be morally right or even obligatory" to tolerate what one deems objectionable. We are looking for a principled moral rationale why it is good to accept what is bad. This is why it is called the paradox of *moral* toleration.

Three of the most popular responses to this challenge converge on the idea that understanding why one should be tolerant involves adopting an antidogmatic stance towards questions about the good life. They differ, though, in how they spell out this antidogmatic stance. The skeptical argument for toleration holds that we should be, at least moderate, skeptics with regard to questions about the good life. The value-pluralist theory suggests that we should be tolerant because there exists a plurality of valuable ways of living. The Rawlsian approach is premised on the notion that questions about the good life are subject to reasonable disagreement.

According to the skeptical argument, we should not impose our own conception of the good upon others because we cannot be sufficiently certain that our beliefs are actually correct. The skeptical argument has a long and rich tradition, with influential versions of it having been put forth by John Milton (2014), Mill (2003), and Popper (2008). One modern restatement of the skeptical argument is due to Brian Barry. The reason why we ought to be tolerant is, according to Barry, that "no conception of the good can justifiably be held with a degree of certainty that warrants its imposition on those who reject it" (1995, p. 169). His argument rests on the contractualist assumption that citizens seek to reach agreement with others on terms that they cannot reasonably reject. But this assumption on its own does not yet entail toleration. A dogmatist who accepts the requirement of public justifiability could still claim that her conception of the good cannot be reasonably doubted and that its forcible imposition is therefore legitimate. This is why an additional skeptical premise is needed. Noting the persistent disagreement about questions regarding the good life, Barry maintains that no conception of the good, not even his own one, is so compelling as to be beyond reasonable doubt. The skeptical and the contractualist assumption jointly explain why we ought to tolerate what we deem wrong: because our own convictions about these matters are reasonably disputable, which means that we cannot justifiably impose them upon others.

Skeptical arguments for toleration are popular and intuitively appealing, but problematic upon closer inspection. While Barry's line of reasoning disallows the imposition of any particular conception of the good, it does not seem to rule out the suppression of clearly irrational but relatively harmless conceptions of the good. If we can be certain that an irrational but harmless conception of the good is wrong, its suppression would not be reasonably rejectable. And while some skepticism about the good seems sensible, it is implausible that we are never justified in dismissing a conception of the good as clearly irrational. Intuitively, however, it would be immoral to suppress relatively harmless conceptions of the good, even when we can be certain that they are wrong. The scope of toleration that Barry's argument would establish is therefore too restricted.

Another issue with Barry's argument is that it is difficult to see how skepticism can be a reason to tolerate other conceptions of the good without at the same time eroding the objection component. In order to establish genuine toleration, the argument must show that individuals may be perfectly rational to embrace one

6 Paradoxes of Toleration

conception the good and reject all others *despite* skeptical worries (objection component), but also that they would be unreasonable to impose a conception of the good on others *because* of the skeptical worries (acceptance component). But this is puzzling. If they can be confident enough to embrace a particular conception of the good for themselves, should they then not also be confident enough to impose it on others? Or, put the other way around, if no conception of the good can be held with a degree of certainty that warrants its imposition on others, does this not mean that individuals would not be reasonable to adopt a conception of the good for themselves, either? The skeptical considerations do not, it seems, explain why one ought to tolerate what one deems wrong. Rather, they suggest that one ought not have strong convictions about such matters in the first place. Skepticism of this sort would eliminate the objection component.

Finally, many toleration theorists have found skeptical arguments unsatisfactory for another reason. The problem, according to them, is not so much that these arguments are inherently flawed but that they fail to appeal to people with strong convictions. As Thomas Nagel observes, "liberalism purports to be a view that justifies religious toleration not only to religious skeptics but to the devout" (1987, p. 217). A skeptical argument for toleration is seen, in a sense, as question-begging in that it presupposes a doctrine – skepticism – that many of those who need to be convinced do not share.

A prominent proponent of the value-pluralist answer to the "why be tolerant?" question is Joseph Raz (1988). Raz, stressing the value of personal autonomy, argues that we can only be truly autonomous in our life choices if there is a plurality of options to choose from. Following in the footsteps of eminent value-pluralist Berlin (1969), Raz suggests that we adopt a pluralist account of what the good life may consist in. The ideal of autonomy commits one to holding that there is a plurality of valuable but incompatible ways of life, each exemplifying some virtues at the expense of others. The inevitable absence of at least some virtues allows Raz to accommodate the objection component of toleration. Even though alternative forms of life must be recognized as valuable, too, we object to the absence of some virtues that any form of life inevitably includes.

This value-pluralist explanation of why we must be tolerant may be found unsatisfactory on the grounds that it accommodates only very slight forms of objection. Raz writes that "what is tolerated is neither wrong nor necessarily bad. It is the absence of a certain accomplishment" (1988, p. 162). Toleration according to Raz involves awareness that what we tolerate is merely the inevitable side-effect of other strengths and virtues. But toleration thus conceived is not puzzling. There is nothing paradoxical about the idea that we must tolerate inevitable negative side-effects. The question at issue is why we should tolerate what we wholeheartedly disapprove of. And Raz is explicit that "the principle [of autonomy] does not protect repugnant activities or forms of life" (1988, p. 174), because autonomous choices are not valuable unless they are made in pursuit of the good. This value-pluralist approach thus fails to explain why we should tolerate even repugnant ways of life, or, put less harshly, ways of life that fail to exemplify a sufficient range of virtues. Indeed, governments are encouraged to "eliminate" repugnant ways of life (1988,

p. 173). Interestingly, however, Raz eventually provides a different line of argument against coercing people into abandoning repugnant ways of life. Coercion as such is bound to reduce the autonomy of the coerced person, and *this* is why even repugnant ways of life must be tolerated (1988, pp. 173–175). Much of the argumentative heavy lifting is thus done by the appeal to autonomy alone, with value-pluralism playing only a secondary role (see also McKinnon 2006, pp. 63–66).

Controversial is also the unabashedly perfectionist nature of Raz' appeal to the value of autonomy. Some toleration theorists have taken issue with such perfectionist approaches for similar reasons as they have rejected skeptical arguments. A theory that invokes a controversial conception of human flourishing, such as that the good life centrally involves autonomy, will be unacceptable to the large group of people who do not share this conception. If liberal toleration is justified by appeal to such a controversial value as personal autonomy, liberalism risks being "but another sectarian doctrine." (Rawls 1985, p. 246)

The most popular approach among toleration theorists is the one most prominently championed by Rawls and which can be traced back to Pierre Bayle (2005; see Forst 2008; Königs 2015). Its proponents are adamant that their approach rests neither on skepticism nor on any partisan conception of the good, thus differing in important respects from the two previous approaches.

First, the assumption is made that political legitimacy is about reasonable acceptability. Rawls submits that "[o]ur exercise of political power is proper only when we sincerely believe that the reasons we would offer for our political actions [...] are sufficient, and we also reasonably think that other citizens might also reasonably accept those reasons" (1997, p. 771; see also 2005, p. 217). This means that no beliefs or practices may be forcibly imposed on others if doing so can only be justified in ways that can be reasonably rejected. As we have seen above, a version of this contractualist premise was adopted by Barry for his skeptical argument.

Second, and in contrast to Barry's approach, the reason why we must not impose our conception of the good is not that we should be skeptics about questions about the good life but because these questions are subject to reasonable disagreement. Liberal societies are not only marked by a diversity of competing moral and religious doctrines, but by a diversity of *reasonable* moral and religious doctrines. What Rawlsians call "reasonable pluralism" or "reasonable disagreement" differs crucially from value pluralism, as championed, for example, by Berlin and Raz. Accepting the fact of reasonable pluralism does not require one to accept that there is a plurality of valuable and possibly incompatible comprehensive doctrines. Reasonable pluralism is compatible with believing that one's own conception of the good is the one and only true one and that all competing conceptions are flawed. But it requires one to accept that they may nonetheless be reasonable and that they can be espoused by reasonable people. Rawls explains the existence of reasonable disagreement by appeal to what he calls the burdens of judgment. The burdens of judgment are cognitive constraints that even reasonable people have to grapple with. They include, for instance, the complexity of the empirical and scientific evidence, the vagueness of our moral and political concepts, the impact of our personal experience on our evaluations, and the difficulty of making an overall assessment when a plurality of competing normative considerations apply. These sources of reasonable disagreement differ from biases, prejudices, self-interest, or ignorance, which are sources of nonreasonable disagreement. The burdens of judgment explain why reasonable people affirm different conceptions of the good. And it is precisely because rival theories of the good must be acknowledged to be reasonable that we cannot justifiably impose our own conception of the good upon others. The appeal to the truth of one's own view would be reasonably rejectable. Given that political legitimacy is a function of reasonable acceptability, "[i]t is unreasonable for us to use political power, should we possess it, or share it with others, to repress comprehensive doctrines that are not unreasonable" (Rawls 2005, p. 61).

Variations of the Rawlsian approach have been defended by Forst (2013), Charles Larmore (1994), Nagel (1987, 1991) and Jonathan Quong (2007), to name but a few. But whether this approach is successful in formulating a nonskeptical rationale for toleration can be doubted. To begin with, the factors that explain the fact of reasonable pluralism, the burdens of judgment, seem to call for at least moderate skepticism about issues affected by these burdens of judgment. When the empirical and normative considerations bearing on a question are extremely complex, we should arguably be somewhat uncertain about the truth of our commitments. Moreover, it is difficult to see how someone who takes herself to know what the good life consists in can acknowledge the reasonableness of competing visions of the good life, which she believes are wrong. If a given conception of the good is best supported by reason, then alternative conceptions of the good cannot be recognized as equally reasonable. If, by contrast, one concedes that competing conceptions of the good are equally reasonable, then one should be skeptical that one's own conception of the good is really true (McCabe 2000; see also Königs 2013).

Also, like Barry's account, the Rawlsian approach seems overly restrictive, as it only protects doctrines whose validity is subject to reasonable disagreement. It does not, it seems, protect doctrines that are harmless but that no reasonable person could believe to be true. This is an illiberal and counterintuitive implication of this approach, which casts doubt on the underlying assumption that the standard of political legitimacy is reasonable acceptability.

While the most influential attempts to make sense of the moral value of toleration run into problems, it is conceivable that the solution to the paradox of moral toleration is more straightforward than initially thought. The reason why one ought to tolerate what one considers wrong is often simply that there is something intrinsically abhorrent about the kind of interference that is characteristic of intolerance. Not to tolerate a belief or practice is not just to interfere with it but to interfere with it in particularly vicious ways, for example, by using force. And there is nothing paradoxical about the idea that one typically must not use force, or other vicious means, to achieve one's ends, even when the ends are desirable. Sometimes the ends do not justify the means. Looked at in this way, there might not be anything paradoxical to begin with about the idea that one ought to be tolerant of views and practices that one considers wrong (Königs 2021).

The Paradox of Self-Destruction

The paradox of self-destruction arises from the fact that there can be no such thing as limitless toleration. Some beliefs or practices have to be rejected and suppressed, in particular those that threaten to subvert the principle of toleration itself. A tolerant society can only survive if forces that seek to subvert it are not tolerated. Universal toleration would eventually lead to the destruction of liberal society itself. An influential formulation of this conundrum is due to Popper:

> Unlimited tolerance must lead to the disappearance of tolerance. If we extend unlimited tolerance even to those who are intolerant, if we are not prepared to defend a tolerant society against the onslaught of the intolerant, then the tolerant will be destroyed, and tolerance with them. (Popper 1945, p. 265)

A more recent statement of this problem has been offered by international relations theorist John Mearsheimer:

> It would make little sense [. . .] for liberals to practice toleration towards their enemies, since a live-and-let-live approach would destroy the regime. Liberals, of course, are aware of this danger, which means that liberalism has a sense of vulnerability at its core that naturally provokes a tendency toward intolerance among liberals. (Mearsheimer 2018, p. 53)

Toleration without limits would be self-destructive. Some commentators have even suggested that universal toleration would be self-contradictory or incoherent. Peter Nicholson thinks that the "suggestion that one ought to tolerate the destruction of toleration is, quite simply, self-contradictory" (1985, p. 169). Similarly, John Horton suggests that "the very idea of tolerating everything is incoherent," for "[t]olerating something must imply intolerance towards its negation" (1994, p. 16; see also Forst 2013, p. 23; Nehushtan 2007, p. 239). While this is probably an overstatement, it is true that universal tolerance would be unwise, since it is bound to lead to the destruction of the liberal order. There are thus compelling pragmatic reasons to limit the scope of toleration. Unlimited tolerance would be pragmatically self-defeating.

In what sense, however, this is "paradoxical" needs to be explained. It sometimes seems that scholars who find it paradoxical that tolerance requires intolerance mean by this merely that there is something surprising or perplexing about this aspect of toleration. But they do not mean "paradoxical" to imply that there is a philosophical problem to be solved. What the paradox demonstrates is, quite simply, that liberal democracies must suppress particularly aggressive intolerant tendencies in order to secure their own survival. Popper can sometimes be read as conceiving of the paradox along these lines. For him, what the paradox goes to show is simply that "[w]e should [. . .] claim, in the name of tolerance, the right not to tolerate the intolerant" (1945, p. 265).

But the paradox of self-destruction might also be paradoxical in a more troubling way by implying that there is something incoherent about the idea of toleration. For instance, at one point Popper observes that by refusing to tolerate

6 Paradoxes of Toleration

the intolerant, we will invite the allegation that "our tolerance is just a sham, and that it is we, the allegedly tolerant, who were the first to use violence, and who are using violence all the time" (2008, p. 316). Similarly, A.C. Grayling notes that it is often claimed that toleration is "in breach of itself" if the intolerant are not tolerated (2009, p. 77).

More seriously, then, the paradox of self-destruction would imply that true tolerance is unachievable. Either a society fails to be tolerant because it suppresses intolerant groups, or it will eventually cease to be a tolerant society because it fails to prevent intolerant groups from subverting the liberal order. This worry about the achievability of true tolerance is a familiar trope in popular debates about toleration. Whenever it is suggested that even a liberal society must suppress some views, practices, or political movements, someone is always quick to point out that this society thereby becomes intolerant itself.

The claim that a liberal society ceases to be truly tolerant the moment it seeks to suppress intolerant views can be understood in two different ways. First, it can be understood to mean that the ideal of tolerance can only be partially realized, but never fully. While liberal societies, in which many cultures are allowed to coexist, can be credited with being more tolerant than authoritarian regimes, they are still not fully tolerant, because some worldviews are not tolerated. Second, it might be held that a regime that does not tolerate its enemies is not tolerant at all, because tolerating one's enemies is what tolerance is essentially about. Failure to tolerate one's enemies does not just render one less tolerant. It shows that one is not committed to the ideal of tolerance at all.

One way of responding to this paradox is to insist that it is perfectly justifiable, indeed, a duty, to suppress intolerant movements, at least when they pose a realistic risk to the integrity of liberal society. As already mentioned, Popper is adamant that liberal democracies must defend themselves "against the onslaught of the intolerant." Many scholars have concurred that tolerant societies have the right to be intolerant towards the intolerant. Toleration, it is often argued, is about reciprocity, which means that those who refuse to be tolerant forfeit the right to be tolerated themselves (Forst 2013, p. 23; Nehushtan 2007; Popper 2008, pp. 319–320; Rawls 1999, pp. 190–192). This is not to say that it is always permissible to be intolerant towards the intolerant. Rawls, for instance, like many, holds that "when the constitution itself is secure, there is no reason to deny freedom to the intolerant" (1999, p. 192). But when an intolerant movement does pose a serious threat, its freedom may justly be restricted.

The view that societies may or must, at least on occasion, be intolerant towards aggressive intolerant movements is difficult to argue with. Popper came to accept this view when we witnessed Hitler's rise to power in Weimar Germany (2008, p. 316). But one need not invoke such extreme examples to recognize that it must be true. Still, this way dealing with the paradox of self-destruction may leave some skeptics unconvinced. For the rejoinder that it can be justifiable to be intolerant towards the intolerant does not directly address the worry that true tolerance is unachievable. Even if the intolerant do not have the right to be tolerated, would it not still be *intolerant* to not tolerate them?

We can avoid this conclusion by denying the underlying premise that true tolerance really requires universal tolerance. In other words, one might deny that not to tolerate the intolerant even constitutes a (full or partial) violation of the ideal of tolerance. The argument goes that the assumption that true tolerance requires universal tolerance rests on a conceptual confusion. It is natural to think that failure to tolerate some view or practice means that one is not fully tolerant. What else could it mean to "tolerate" and to be "tolerant"? But this intuitive thought seems to rest on a conflation of two different meanings of "tolerance" and its cognates. Often, when we talk about "tolerance," we want to make a purely descriptive, non-normative observation. Tolerance in this non-normative sense means simply that one refrains from interfering in hostile ways with views or practices one disapproves of. Likewise, one can 'tolerate' or be 'tolerant' in this descriptive, non-normative sense. But sometimes, we use these terms to denote a virtue, that is, a normative attribute. When we praise people as tolerant or denounce people as intolerant, or when we speak approvingly of the tolerance of a culture or society, we are not merely describing behavior but making a normative claim. As moral and political philosophers, we are mostly interested in the nature and significance of tolerance in this normative sense (though see Balint 2014).

Distinguishing these two meanings of "tolerance" is helpful because it allows us to see why, perhaps surprisingly, being intolerant towards some people need not necessarily render one less tolerant (Königs 2021; see also Jansen 2006, pp. 26–27). To be sure, to be intolerant in the descriptive sense of the term towards a group of people necessarily means that one does not exhibit full tolerance in the descriptive sense of the term. But it does not mean that one lacks tolerance in the normative sense, that is, that one lacks the virtue of tolerance. This is because the virtue of tolerance does not require one to tolerate everything, just as the virtue of, say, generosity does not require one to randomly give away all one's money to random strangers. The generous person gives the right amount to the right people for the right purpose. Likewise, to have the virtue of tolerance is to tolerate not just anything but those beliefs and practices that ought to be tolerated or that are worthy of tolerance.

This view is confirmed by our pretheoretic intuitions. Intuitively, it seems odd to praise someone who puts up with, say, militant racism as more tolerant (in the normative sense) than someone who refuses to do so, although this person is tolerant of militant racism (in the descriptive sense). Likewise, we would not, and should not, regard someone's refusal to tolerate militant racism (in the descriptive sense) as a sign of intolerance (in the normative sense).

The Paradox of Drawing the Limits

As we have seen, many liberals assume that a theory of toleration must itself be "tolerant" in the sense that it must not rely on values that are specific to a particular conception of the good. Why we ought to tolerate others' views and lifestyles and where the limits of toleration ought to be drawn must be decided in a way that is acceptable to all members of society, or at least to all reasonable ones. Any liberal theory of toleration that fails to meet this requirement would be "just another sectarian doctrine." In the same vein, Habermas contends that "[f]or toleration to extricate itself from the suspicion that it is intolerant, the rules of tolerant behavior must be rationally acceptable for both, indeed, for all sides" (2003, p. 5; see also 2004, pp. 6–7).

This requirement, being difficult to satisfy, creates another paradox, the paradox of drawing the limits. According to Forst's characterization of this paradox,

> there simply is no such thing as toleration if it always implies a drawing of the limits against the intolerant and intolerable; since every such drawing of a limit is itself a more or less intolerant, arbitrary act, and since there is no higher level of morality to draw such limits, toleration ends as soon it begins: as soon as it is defined by an arbitrary boundary between 'us' and the 'intolerant' and 'intolerable.' (2001, p. 195; see also 2013, p. 24)

Similarly, Samuel Scheffler observes:

> On the one hand, it is hard to see how a regime of toleration can be given a principled justification without appealing to some principle. Yet, on the other hand, any particular principle to which one might appeal is likely to be contested in a pluralistic society. If one appeals to such a principle, then partisans of opposing principles are likely to claim that a regime of toleration that is justified in this way is a sham. (2010, p. 318)

This paradox is related to the previous paradox, the paradox of self-destruction. It is the fact that tolerance has to be limited that gives rise to the problem of finding an acceptable way of drawing the limits in the first place. But the two paradoxes are clearly distinct, and it is important to tease them apart. According to the paradox of self-destruction, there might be no such thing as true tolerance because the tolerance of any stable regime of toleration must be limited to exclude particularly aggressive antitolerant groups. By contrast, according to the paradox of drawing the limits, there might be no such thing as true tolerance because true tolerance would require providing a neutral or uncontested justification of tolerance and of its limits.

Three responses to the paradox of drawing the limits are conceivable.

First, one might conclude that true tolerance *is* a chimera. This view has been held by postmodernist critics of liberalism, most notably Stanley Fish. Any attempt to base liberal toleration on impartial common ground and to draw the limits of toleration in an impartial way, he argues, is really just an ad hoc act of arbitrary exclusion. He boldly asserts that the "incoherence of toleration, both as an ideal and as a basis for a politics, seems obvious even on a moment's reflection" (1997, p. 2256). Indeed, as liberalism fails to live up to its own promise of transcending sectarian identities, it is not relevantly different from fundamentalism (Fish 1987).

Williams, although certainly less defeatist than Fish, is also skeptical that an argument for toleration in its "purest and strongest" sense can be found (Williams 1996, p. 24). He takes it that such an argument would have to explain the value of tolerance without appeal to skepticism or controversial values such as autonomy. But finding such an argument is impossible or at least extremely difficult. This does not mean that the mere *practice* of tolerance is unachievable, as it can be based on skepticism, indifference or a Hobbesian balance of power. But the *value* of tolerance cannot be made sense of without appeal to controversial conceptions about human flourishing, which is precisely what liberals have been anxious to avoid.

A second, more optimistic approach is to prove the skeptic wrong by showing that there *is* a nonpartisan theory of liberal toleration that is beyond reasonable contestation. Different versions of this approach, which we already considered above, have been developed by the likes of Rawls, Nagel, Larmore, Forst, and Habermas, among others. At the heart of this approach is the notion that political legitimacy is a function of reasonable acceptability (or nonrejectablity). And since appeals to the truth of some conception of the good are reasonably rejectable, the imposition of such a conception upon others is deemed illegitimate. Of these theorists, Rawls has arguably gone to the greatest length to demonstrate that providing a nonpartisan account of toleration and liberalism is possible. As part of this project, he has suggested that the principle of toleration is the focus of an overlapping consensus, that is, that it can be endorsed from within different, conflicting comprehensive doctrines, provided they are "reasonable" (Rawls 1985, 1996). This approach purports to rest neither on skepticism nor on a contested conception of the good, and to be therefore acceptable to all "reasonable" people. But as we have seen, the feasibility of this approach has been disputed, with critics claiming that the appeal to a neutral account of reasonableness is a sham.

The third approach, which is also optimistic about the coherence of the idea toleration, neither affirms nor denies the availability of a neutral justification of toleration and of its proper limits. Instead, it challenges the underlying notion that there is something intolerant or flawed about a regime of toleration that invokes principles that are contested in a pluralistic society. To be sure, it is true that partisans of opposing doctrines will denounce such a regime of toleration as unjust or erroneous. But this does not mean that it *is* unjust or erroneous. If some account of toleration is correct and if it is implemented in a society, then this society is truly tolerant, even when this regime of toleration rests on contested and partisan principles. The notion that the justification of toleration and of its limits itself has to be "tolerant" – that we must "apply the principle of toleration to philosophy itself" (Rawls 1987, p. 13) – rests on a level confusion (Königs 2021). Thus, even if doubts about the feasibility of a nonpartisan regime of toleration should be warranted, this would not necessarily warrant skepticism about the coherence of liberal toleration.

The Paradox of the Tolerant Racist

The fourth and last paradox, that of the tolerant racist, points to a difficulty with the objection component of toleration. If a person qualifies as tolerant if she puts up with what she disapproves of, it seems to follow that a racist who puts up with people she despises on racist grounds should be praised as tolerant. But to credit a racist with the virtue of tolerance must strike one as perverse. Moreover, it seems to follow that the

6 Paradoxes of Toleration

more racist she is and the more she is inclined to act out her prejudices, the more she deserves to be called tolerant if she manages to keep her racist impulses in check. This, too, is a highly counterintuitive implication. When we encounter a racist, we would not urge her to be tolerant but rather to abandon her racist prejudices altogether. The notion that she might qualify as tolerant or that we should encourage her to be more 'tolerant' of other races seems confused (Forst 2013, p. 19; Horton 1996, p. 31; McKinnon 2006, ch. 2; Newey 2013, p. 9).

We can distinguish between an "exclusive" and an "accommodating" approach to defusing this puzzle (Bessone 2013). The exclusive approach denies that racists could possibly qualify as tolerant in the strict sense of the term. According to the exclusive approach, there is no paradox because there are no tolerant racists. The accommodating approach accepts the existence of tolerant racists and seeks to solve the paradox by mitigating its counterintuitive implications.

One exclusive solution is to dismiss the paradox on the grounds that one cannot tolerate or fail to tolerate traits that people have no control over. Talk of racial toleration is, as one commentator has claimed, "as non-sensical as saying that one tolerates that the sun rises in the morning and sets at night" (Bellamy 1997, p. 177; see also Churchill 2015, pp. 141–142). Proper objects of toleration are only attributes of a person that can be changed. But this response has limited force. The paradox of the tolerant racist is not peculiar to the problem of racism but to any instance of "toleration" that involves a morally inacceptable objection component. And when this objection refers to a trait that is alterable, the above response does not work. It also fails because racists are, I presume, not upset about people belonging to a certain race or having a certain skin color, but about them being full members of society. While attempts to change people's ethnicity may be futile, it is of course possible to forcibly expel an ethnic group or to relegate their members to a lower social status. Their presence or status in society, that is, *can* be altered.

A more promising and rather straightforward exclusive strategy, followed by several toleration theorists, is to qualify the objection component. In its simplest formulation, the objection component states that the tolerating person must hold a negative attitude towards the object of toleration. In view of the paradox of the tolerant racist, one can qualify the objection component, requiring additionally that the objection must also be minimally reasonable. This is the most popular response to the paradox. Forst, for instance, maintains that the reasons for objection "must not fall below a certain moral threshold below which one cannot speak of tolerance as a virtue" (2013, p. 20). On this view, the allegedly "tolerant" racist does not in fact qualify as tolerant for the simple reason that her reasons for objection are not morally defensible. In a similar vein, Horton has suggested that tolerance is incompatible with harboring bigoted objections: "The virtue of tolerance should include more than forbearance in not acting restrictively toward those who act objectionably; it should also include not having an excessive and inappropriate range of objections." (Horton 1996, p. 38; see also Churchill 2015, p. 141; Habermas 2004, p. 10)

This way of dissolving the paradox is straightforward and effective. In fact, given this simple solution, one is led to wonder why one should be puzzled by the paradox of the tolerant racist in the first place. We ordinarily do not call people "tolerant" whose objections are based on particularly obnoxious prejudices or dislikes. Since this is just not how the term "tolerant" is ordinarily used, no paradox arises.

Yet, Ian Carter has criticized this solution as too ad hoc, opting instead for an intermediate – partly exclusive, partly accommodating – position according to which some but not all racists may qualify as genuinely tolerant, depending on the nature of the racist objection (2013). A racist would have no chance of passing off as tolerant if her objection is based on a negative evaluation of the basic agential capacities of members of other races. For such an evaluation is incompatible with the recognition of others as equals, on which the acceptance component of liberal toleration depends. But should the racist's objection be of a different kind, she might, according to Carter, qualify as genuinely tolerant, provided her acceptance is informed by the recognition of others as equals and provided she does not act on her racist beliefs.

A thoroughgoingly accommodating approach has been taken by Peter Balint. He has advocated a purely descriptive concept of toleration that does not include any normative criteria regarding the nature of the objection component. An objection need not be minimally acceptable in order to serve as the objection component of tolerance. And this means that the paradox dissipates because the "racist *is* more tolerant" (2014, p. 277). This does not mean that there is nothing objectionable about the racist's objection, nor that the tolerant racist is a good person. And Balint maintains that a purely descriptive account of tolerance has other advantages, such as being more suitable for use in the political context. Still, to call a racist tolerant is to bite a very hard bullet, which many will feel we need not bite given the availability of a plausible exclusive response.

Summary and Future Directions

Some of the toleration theorists who have contributed the most to the identification and analysis of the paradoxes surrounding toleration have characterized them as apparent or solvable paradoxes (Forst 2013; Horton 1994). This discussion of the four most well-known paradoxes of toleration tends to confirm their optimism. Despite persistent disagreement, and although not all solutions on offer are equally compelling, there seems relatively little reason to conclude that there really is something inherently paradoxical or contradictory about the ideal of toleration. The study of the paradoxes of toleration will continue, contributing an important and unique perspective on toleration and its place in society. It appears that we can be confident that the study of these paradoxes will provide further support for rather than erode the principle of toleration.

Acknowledgments Peter Königs is funded by the Deutsche Forschungsgemeinschaft (DFG, German Research Foundation) under Germany´s Excellence Strategy – EXC-2023 Internet of Production – 390621612

References

Augustinus A (2001) The works of Saint Augustine: a translation for the 21st century (trans: and notes by Teske R; editor Rotelle JE). New City Press, New York

Balint P (2014) Acts of tolerance. A political and descriptive account. Eur J Polit Theo 13(3):264–281

Barry B (1995) A treatise on social justice volume II: justice as impartiality. Clarendon Press, Oxford

Bayle P (2005) A philosophical commentary on these words of the Gospel, Luke 14.2 "Compel them to come in, that My house may be full" (edited, with an introduction, by Kilcullen J and Kukathas Ch). Liberty Fund, Indianapolis

Bellamy R (1997) Toleration, liberalism, and democracy: a comment on leader and Garzón Valdés. Ratio Juris 10(2):177–186

Berlin I (1969) Two concepts of liberty. In: Berlin I (ed) Four essays on liberty. Oxford University Press, London, pp 118–172

Bessone M (2013) Will the real tolerant racist please stand up? J Appl Philos 30(3):209–223

Carter I (2013) Are toleration and respect compatible? J Appl Philos 30(3):196–208

Churchill RP (2015) Liberal toleration. In: Fiala A (ed) The bloomsbury companion to political philosophy. Bloomsbury, London, pp 139–152

Fish S (1987) Liberalism doesn't exist. Duke Law J 36(6):997–1001

Fish S (1997) Mission impossible: settling the just bounds between church and state. Columbia Law Rev 97(8):2255–2333

Forst R (2001) Tolerance as a virtue of justice. Philos Explor 4(3):193–206

Forst R (2008) Pierre Bayle's reflexive theory of toleration. In: Williams MS, Waldron J (eds) Toleration and its limits. New York University Press, New York, pp 78–113

Forst R (2013) Toleration in conflict: past and present. Cambridge University Press, Cambridge, MA

Forst R (2017) Toleration and its paradoxes: a tribute to John Horton. Philosophia 45(2):415–424

Grayling AC (2009) Liberty in the age of terror: a defence of civil liberties and enlightenment values. Bloomsbury, London

Habermas J (2003) Intolerance and discrimination. Int J Constit Law 1(1):2–12

Habermas J (2004) Religious tolerance: the pacemaker for cultural rights. Philosophy 79(1):5–18

Hampton J (1989) Should political philosophy be done without metaphysics? Ethics 99(4):791–814

Heyd D (ed) (1996) Toleration: an elusive virtue. Princeton University Press, Princeton

Horton J (1994) Three (apparent) paradoxes of toleration. Synth Philos 17(1):7–20

Horton J (1996) Toleration as a virtue. In: Heyd D (ed) Toleration: an elusive virtue. Princeton University Press, Princeton, pp 28–43

Jansen L (2006) Staatliche Toleranz und staatliche Wertorientierung. In: Starck C (ed) Wo hört die Toleranz auf? Wallstein, Göttingen, pp 20–62

Königs, P (2013) Was Toleranz ist, was sie nicht ist, und wie man sie nicht rechtfertigen kann. Eine Replik auf Lohmar. ZPhF 67(3):473–490

Königs, P (2015) Pierre Bayles Verteidigung des irrenden Gewissens und das Paradox der Toleranz. ARSP 101(1):16–31

Königs P (2021) The simplicity of toleration. Crit Rev Int Soc Pol Phil 24(1):5–24

Larmore C (1994) Pluralism and reasonable disagreement. Soc Philos Policy 11(1):61–79

McCabe D (2000) Knowing about the good: a problem with antiperfectionism. Ethics 110(2):311–338

McKinnon C (2006) Toleration: a critical introduction. Routledge, London/New York

Mearsheimer JJ (2018) The great delusion: liberal dreams and international relations. Yale University Press, New Haven

Mill JS (2003) On liberty. Yale University Press, New Haven

Milton J (2014) Areopagitica and other writings. Penguin, London

Nagel T (1987) Moral conflict and political legitimacy. Philos Public Aff 16(3):215–240

Nagel T (1991) Equality and partiality. Oxford University Press, New York

Nehushtan Y (2007) The limits of liberal tolerance: a substantive-liberal perspective. Ratio Juris 20(2):230–257

Newey G (2013) Toleration in political conflict. Cambridge Unitversity Press, Cambridge, MA

Nicholson P (1985) Toleration as a moral ideal. In: Horton JP, Mendus S (eds) Aspects of toleration. Methuen, London, pp 158–173

Overdiek H (2001) Tolerance: between forbearance and acceptance. Rowman & Littlefield, Lanham

Popper KR (1945) The open society and its enemies: volume 1. The spell of Plato. Routledge and Kegan Paul, London

Popper KR (2008) On toleration. In: Shearmur J, Turner PN (eds) After the open society: selected social and political writings. Routledge, Abingdon, pp 313–328

Quong J (2007) Political liberalism without scepticism. Ratio 20(3):320–340

Raphael DD (1988) The intolerable. In: Mendus S (ed) Justifying toleration: conceptual and historical conceptions. Cambridge University Press, Cambridge, MA, pp 137–154

Rawls J (1985) Justice as fairness: political not metaphysical. Philos Public Aff 14(3):223–251

Rawls J (1987) The idea of an overlapping consensus. Oxf J Leg Stud 7(1):1–25

Rawls J (1996) Political liberalism. Columbia University Press, New York

Rawls J (1997) The idea of public reason revisited. Univ Chic Law Rev 64(3):765–807

Rawls J (1999) A theory of justice, rev edn. Harvard University Press, Cambridge, MA

Rawls J (2005) Political liberalism, exp edn. Columbia University Press, New York

Raz J (1988) Autonomy, toleration, and the harm principle. In: Mendus S (ed) Justifying toleration: conceptual and historical perspectives. Cambridge University Press, Cambridge, MA, pp 155–175

Scanlon TM (2003) The difficulty of tolerance. In: Scanlon TM (ed) The difficulty of tolerance. Cambridge University Press, Cambridge, MA, pp 187–201

Scheffler S (2010) The good of toleration. In: Scheffler S (ed) Equality and tradition: questions of value in moral and political theory. Oxford University Press, Oxford, pp 312–336

Williams B (1996) Toleration: an impossible virtue? In: Heyd D (ed) Toleration: an elusive virtue. Princeton University Press, Princeton, pp 18–27

The Epistemic Justification for Tolerance

7

Joshua C. Thurow

Contents

Introduction 110
A Taxonomy of Epistemic Arguments for Tolerance 112
Mill's Argument 113
Rauch's Argument from the Success of Liberal Science 118
Objections 120
Summary and Future Directions 125
References 127

Abstract

Epistemic arguments for tolerance aim to show that intolerance has various bad epistemic consequences, whereas tolerance enables various positive epistemic consequences. The epistemic consequences at stake here are epistemic values – things or states that are valuable from an epistemic perspective, a perspective having to do with knowledge, truth, understanding, and the like. John Stuart Mill's defense of free speech in *On Liberty* is a paradigm example of an epistemic argument and his argument is still widely accepted and defended today. He argues that intolerance prevents us from discovering our errors, decreases understanding, and discourages intellectual curiosity, courage, and boldness. More recently, Jonathan Rauch defends an epistemic argument according to which tolerance is a necessary ingredient of liberal science, which is our most successful method for finding truth. However, detractors have argued that often tolerance itself either does not produce epistemic value or has negative epistemic consequences. People sometimes irrationally inflate the evidence, producers and consumers of informa-

J. C. Thurow (✉)
University of Texas at San Antonio, San Antonio, TX, USA
e-mail: joshua.thurow@utsa.edu

© The Author(s), under exclusive licence to Springer Nature Switzerland AG 2022
M. Sardoč (ed.), *The Palgrave Handbook of Toleration*,
https://doi.org/10.1007/978-3-030-42121-2_10

tion often have other than epistemic goals that can encourage the spread of false beliefs, and the structure of networks of testifiers can be exploited to spread false beliefs. Some measure of intolerance – such as what Goldman calls content-related restrictions – might have positive epistemic consequences for society. The extent and effectiveness of such restrictions, as well as how they would relate to the full range of epistemic values both individual and collective, remains an underexplored topic.

Keywords

John Stuart Mill · Epistemic argument for tolerance · Veritistic social epistemology · Epistemic value · Epistemic virtue · Virtue of tolerance · Marketplace of ideas · Fake news · Understanding · Liberal science · Free speech

Introduction

Social and political tolerance of dissenting, novel, unorthodox, or distasteful views is a hallmark of the enlightenment and western democratic societies. Many justifications for the value of such tolerance have been given, including moral, pragmatic, and religious justification of various sorts. Perhaps the most famous defense of tolerance comes from John Stuart Mill's defense of the liberty of thought and discussion in Chap. 2 of his *On Liberty*. Therein Mill argues that neither individuals nor collectives (including governments) should coerce or silence opinion or expression of opinion about any matter because such coercion and silencing hinders our ability to find or understand the truth. His argument – which retains its widespread appeal and has inspired various similar arguments – is an epistemic argument. That is, the argument aims to show that liberty of thought and discussion has epistemic value, that is, value stemming from states like knowledge, truth, understanding, and the like. Mill argues, in short, that liberty of thought and discussion produces states of epistemic value, namely true beliefs and understanding. However, in principle other sorts of epistemic arguments could be given connecting tolerance with epistemic value.

This goal of this chapter is to summarize the current state of play concerning epistemic arguments for tolerance. After some preliminary clarifications in the introduction a taxonomy of epistemic arguments will be presented, followed by a presentation of two popular such arguments – Mill's and an argument from Jonathan Rauch – and some challenges facing those arguments. The chapter concludes with a summary of the discussion and some suggestions of promising avenues of future research on epistemic arguments for tolerance.

First, some clarifications. This chapter examines arguments that tolerance is epistemically valuable. None of these arguments take a further step to the conclusion that tolerance is overall good or valuable or that human societies ought to protect tolerance. There are many other possible ways to evaluate tolerance – its other social effects on, say, political stability, its moral aspects such as whether it is an element of

7 The Epistemic Justification for Tolerance

respect for persons or of justice, or the positive and negative effects of tolerance of widespread activities. Weighing all of these evaluations is beyond the scope of this chapter. This chapter merely examines whether the epistemic value of tolerance should be placed on the scale.

The notion of tolerance that will be employed in this chapter is broader than the liberty of thought and expression. "Tolerance" is used in a couple different ways. Sometimes we say a person is tolerant – here tolerance is a disposition or a character trait (some would go further and say it is a virtue). Sometimes we say that an action is or is not tolerant. Tolerance the disposition, as it shall be understood in this chapter, is a disposition to patiently endure what one takes to be an objectionable state or act or person (this notion is inspired by, but distinct from Bowlin's (2016) conception). A tolerant act is an act of patiently enduring what one takes to be objectionable. These definitions stay neutral about whether tolerance is a virtue and about when and in what ways tolerance is appropriate or inappropriate. "Patient endurance" is of course somewhat vague, but it involves enduring something objectionable rather than attempting to eliminate, accept, ignore, or treat with indifference what is objectionable. Tolerating something is thus different from accepting or endorsing it. Tolerance is patient – the endurance must be done patiently rather than impatiently; impatient endurance is either short-lived, or lasts only while one is in a good mood, or is granted only in certain fragile conditions. Tolerance is more stable than that.

These definitions strictly apply to persons, but they could easily be rephrased and extended to apply to collectives. We can speak of institutions, organizations, and governments being tolerant or intolerant; of laws and policies (which we can treat as actions of collectives) being tolerant or intolerant. Laws protecting liberty of opinion and expression of opinion are examples of tolerant laws.

Tolerating something objectionable is incompatible with coercing that thing to change its objectionable features. Coercion can be direct – such as by outlawing the objectionable behavior – or indirect – such as by refusing to help or cooperate with those who do what is objectionable. Tolerance is, however, consistent with some other attempts to change a thing's objectionable features. For instance, I can tolerate a person's objectionable attitude while also attempting to persuade the person by giving them reasons to abandon the attitude (indeed, as we shall see Mill's argument depends crucially on the idea that people will attempt to persuade each other).

The sorts of potentially tolerated acts that are most relevant to the epistemic argument for tolerance are acts of expressing, discussing, and disseminating beliefs, viewpoints, and attitudes. Following or living out beliefs, viewpoints, and attitudes is also relevant. Some beliefs are so connected with action and how one lives one's life (e.g., religious beliefs) that it would be a very thin sort of tolerance that tolerates the former but not the latter. If there are epistemic benefits to tolerating these sorts of beliefs and the expression thereof, there may often be epistemic benefits to tolerating many actions intimately connected with those beliefs, for one way of evaluating a belief is by its fruit.

A Taxonomy of Epistemic Arguments for Tolerance

Epistemic arguments for tolerance argue that there is some sort of epistemic value connected with acts of tolerance (either in general or with respect to certain sorts of acts). These arguments vary depending on a) which epistemic values are connected with tolerance, and b) the manner of the connection between tolerance and epistemic value.

The manner of the connection could be one of two broad sorts: tolerance could be an intrinsic or extrinsic epistemic good. There are two ways something could be an intrinsic good – it could be a fundamental intrinsic good or a constituent of a fundamental intrinsic good. Several fundamental epistemic goods have been suggested: having true belief, avoiding false belief, having knowledge, understanding, having coherent beliefs (Riggs 2008). Epistemic value monists say that one of these is the fundamental epistemic value and the others are valuable either as constituents of or through being extrinsically connected to the fundamental epistemic value. Some monists say having true belief is the fundamental epistemic value (David 2014). On this view, knowledge can be intrinsically valuable, even if it is not of fundamental value, because it is composed of what has fundamental value (i.e., true belief). Other monists reverse things and say knowledge is of fundamental value (Williamson 2014) and that true belief is intrinsically (but not fundamentally) valuable in virtue of being a constituent of the final epistemic value. Pluralists say that several things can all be fundamental, nonreducible, epistemic goods (Kvanvig 2014).

Being tolerant of beliefs and their expression seems plainly not to be of fundamental epistemic value. Imagine a situation in which each member of a group has a different belief – each false – about a certain subject matter. Imagine the people in this scenario, with respect to these beliefs, lack all of the other candidate fundamental epistemic goods. And yet they tolerate each other's beliefs. There does not seem to be anything of fundamental epistemic good in this scenario. Tolerance might be epistemically helpful because it sets them up, perhaps, to discuss the matter and come to a more accurate view. Perhaps there are other reasons tolerance is epistemically valuable, but it seems we would articulate those reasons in terms of the relations of tolerance to some other value; tolerance itself seems not to be of fundamental value. But perhaps it could be argued that tolerance is sometimes intrinsically but not fundamentally valuable.

Typically tolerance is assigned extrinsic epistemic value. Riggs (2008) notes four kinds of extrinsic value: instrumental, teleological, contributory, and indicative. Tolerance would be instrumentally valuable if it brought about some other distinct state – fundamental or not – of epistemic value (or prevented epistemically worse states). It would be teleologically valuable if tolerant acts were aimed at producing some state of epistemic value. Tolerance would have contributory value if it were a necessary part of a great whole that has epistemic value. Finally, it would have indicative value if it were an indication of something of epistemic value, as smoke is an indication of fire.

Besides the fundamental epistemic values, there are other epistemic values. One interesting set of values would be epistemic virtues such as love of knowledge,

7 The Epistemic Justification for Tolerance

firmness or steadfastness, courage, caution, humility, autonomy, open-mindedness (Roberts and Wood 2007; Baehr 2011). Some epistemologists might categorize some epistemic virtues as fundamental epistemic goods. However, some are not fundamental. Some might even be contingently epistemically valuable. Tolerance might count as extrinsically valuable with respect to its connection with the epistemic virtues.

In the end, for the purposes of the epistemic argument for tolerance, it does not much matter how various epistemic values are categorized. The key point is to see that there are many sorts of epistemic values, including the ones that have already been mentioned, and epistemic arguments from tolerance might in principle be built to connect tolerance with any number of them.

Mill's Argument

John Stuart Mill developed the most influential defense of free speech in the western philosophical/political tradition in his essay, *On Liberty*. Most notably, for our purposes, it is primarily an epistemic argument that tolerance is instrumentally and sometimes teleologically epistemically valuable. In this section we shall unpack Mill's argument, generalizing it a bit to argue for tolerance in the sense mentioned above.

Mill is concerned about collectives – whether they be governments or non-governmental groups, or just the general public – imposing or coercing their views on individuals. He recognizes that this sort of coercion can happen in a variety of ways, not just through government restrictions or dictates, but also through various sorts of social stigma (Mill 1859/1989, 34). He argues that neither collectives nor individuals should impose their views on individuals; in other words, individuals and collectives should tolerate the public expression of opposing views. Mill offers a four-fold argument for this conclusion, which amounts to an argument that a variety of epistemic goods are obtained, instrumentally or teleologically, through tolerance. The argument can be summarized as follows:

> M1. Intolerance hinders us from identifying our mistaken beliefs and encourages cowardice and timidity of thought.
> M2. Intolerance causes people to accept beliefs (even when true) simply because of social pressure, hindering them from coming to a good understanding of the reasons in favor of those beliefs.
> M3. When people accept beliefs as described in (2), their meaning and significance, including their implications, become less well recognized.
> M4. Many disputes are such that both sides have some measure of truth to them. Intolerance hinders us from obtaining the truth that may be present in the views that are not tolerated.
> M5. Tolerance does not have the above-mentioned problems. Indeed, tolerance opens up the possibility of obtaining true knowledge.
> MC. Therefore, tolerance encourages or brings about various epistemic goods and intolerance hinders the acquisition of such goods.

Mill plainly thinks that the epistemic goods at stake here are of great importance for individuals and for societies, and so we have here (according to him) a strong argument for valuing and practicing tolerance.

Mill justifies M1 based on human fallibility. Our beliefs are fallible; even our most confident beliefs, apparently supported by strong evidence, sometimes turn out to be mistaken. If we were to not tolerate beliefs opposed to our beliefs – even our most confident beliefs – we would prevent ourselves from being able to detect mistakes that we will inevitably make. Perhaps worse, such intolerance, should it become common, would encourage intellectual cowardice and timidity. People would be hesitant to explore and defend new and uncommon views, for fear of ending up on the wrong side of intolerance. People generally avoid social stigma when they can. So, according to Mill, not only would intolerance prevent us from detecting our present errors, it would also hinder us from finding future truths and perhaps encourage us to slide into intellectual grooves that are ultimately dead ends. Notice that in M1 Mill connects tolerance to a couple different epistemic goods: a) tolerance encourages the avoidance of error and b) tolerance is a part of (or a means to) the intellectual virtues of intellectual courage and boldness.

With M2 and M3 Mill points out a couple of epistemic costs of intolerance even if the beliefs being reinforced by intolerance are true (and the beliefs not tolerated are false). First, with M2, beliefs that are propped up by intolerance towards opposing beliefs will come to be accepted largely because society has deemed objection to them beyond the pale. When that is the case – when people accept a belief merely on the basis of testimony that the belief is true backed by social pressure against questioning the belief – people will be hindered from understanding the full range of reasons justifying the belief. Mill here treats an understanding of the reasons – something beyond the mere possession of good reasons – as an epistemic value.

Furthermore, with M3, views accepted in this way become "dead beliefs" (Mill 1859/1989, 42). That is, we tend not to grasp the meaning of the views and their significance for our lives. Social pressure to accept a belief tends to also produce pressure not to think too hard about the belief because doing so might produce an account of the belief or a set of implications that might themselves be regarded as improper, thus inviting further social stigma. As a result, the content of the belief is left somewhat vague and imprecise, making it hard to see the meaning and implications of the belief. Mill eloquently describes the result: "the creed remains as it were outside the mind, incrusting and petrifying it against all other influences addressed to the higher parts of our nature; manifesting its power by not suffering any fresh or living conviction to get in, but itself doing nothing for the mind or heart, except standing sentinel over them to keep them vacant" (42). This result surely involves a variety of possible non-epistemic costs, but there are epistemic costs too – as one's beliefs become more vague and indeterminate, one loses out on having true beliefs about more specific and precise propositions. So there is a loss of true belief. And if these beliefs are significant, then there is a loss of significant true belief. Significance may be a further epistemic value if significant beliefs are beliefs that have inferential power and offer explanations. Such features seem deeply connected with understanding, and thus significant beliefs would be valuable as components of understanding.

With M4 Mill draws attention to an important feature of the disputes concerning which intolerance might feel tempting – they are typically disputes about packages of propositions rather than over a single proposition. Or if a single proposition is the focus of dispute, those on different sides of the dispute assess that proposition from quite different viewpoints which are themselves composed of packages of propositions. In such disputes there is a substantial chance of truth on both sides of the issue. One side might be correct about some relevant set of propositions while the other is correct about others. Mill refers to another possibility when he writes, "truth, in the great practical concerns of life, is so much a question of the reconciling and combining of opposites, that very few have minds sufficiently capacious and impartial to make the adjustment with an approach to correctness, and it has to be made by the rough process of a struggle between combatants fighting under hostile banners" (49). In contentious practical decision-making, typically there are considerations that point in different directions. Weighing those considerations and keeping proper sight of all the considerations can be quite difficult. Even if I am correct, say, about what should be done in a given case, I might still be able to learn from the opposing position that I have not fully taken into consideration a relevant factor. Even if that factor would not, on proper consideration, change my view about what to be done in this case, it might affect what I think about other cases or even amend in certain ways what I think about this case. If I were to treat opposing positions with intolerance I would be denied an opportunity to learn about this relevant factor and come to further true beliefs as well as great understanding of the broader issue. Both are significant epistemic costs.

We have seen that, according to Mill, intolerance has various epistemic costs. But this amounts to an argument for tolerance only if tolerance does not also share the same costs – thus, M5 is a crucial premise. Mill does not himself say much to defend the claim that tolerance does not share the same costs. And some have argued that tolerance in itself can also produce some of the same epistemic costs as intolerance. George Fletcher (1996) argues that tolerance is unstable. The mental act involved in disapproving something while also patiently enduring it is quite challenging to sustain, and so tolerance will tend to devolve into a ceasing of patient endurance (i.e., intolerance) or a ceasing of disapproval (e.g., acceptance, skepticism, or a "who cares" attitude). John Bowlin articulates (but, to be fair, does not endorse) the consequences of Fletcher's argument well:

> we will live and let live, but not because we have managed to combine objection and restraint, but rather because we believe nothing with conviction, or failing that, because we accept uncritically what our recent ancestors, courageous and upright, would have found abominable, intolerable. Either way, the tolerance we are encouraged to exercise in practice conspires with our meager virtue and lands us in a contemptible nihilism, a traitorous moral flabbiness. (Bowlin 2016, 30)

In short, to maintain a semblance of tolerance many folks will rescind in some way from their former judgment that the opposition is incorrect. Our conviction will flag. This brings epistemic costs that are similar to those Mill attributes to intolerance: a loss of true belief, a loss of understanding, and an encouragement of cowardice and timidity of thought. If Fletcher is correct, then it appears tolerance and intolerance are both fraught with epistemic danger.

Perhaps the reason Mill is not sensitive to this worry is that he contrasts intolerance with the pursuit of true knowledge. There are lots of ways to be tolerant, including the ways indicated by Fletcher and Bowlin, and surely some of those ways are not any (or much) epistemically better than intolerance. But Mill envisions a particular way of being tolerant in which one seeks true knowledge, which he takes to be of great value. Regarding the nature of true knowledge, he writes, "nor is it ever really known, but to those who have attended equally and impartially to both sides, and endeavored to see the reasons of both in the strongest light," (39) and doing this well requires one to actively endeavor to seek out objections to one's views, indeed to hear the objections from adversaries who actually affirm opposing views and arguments (38–9). True knowledge requires tolerance and so tolerance is valuable not because it in itself is more likely to produce epistemic goods, but because it is a prerequisite of a great epistemic good – namely, true knowledge.

Mill anticipates a natural objection to this argument: not everyone is capable of or interested in achieving the high goals of true knowledge. This requires skills and time that few possess. Mill even grants that "ninety-nine in a hundred of what are called educated men" (39) do not meet the standards for true knowledge. Perhaps it is enough if just some people can achieve this kind of knowledge so that there are people who can respond to all the objections and considerations adequately. Mill replies: "the argument for free discussion is in no way weakened. For even this doctrine acknowledges that mankind ought to have rational assurance that all objections have been satisfactorily answered; and how are they to be answered if that which requires to be answered is not spoken?" (40). In short, yes true knowledge is rare, but it is still quite valuable and we want there to be some people in our community who have it. And tolerance is necessary for there to be such people. Furthermore, according to Mill, there is no practical way to allow intolerance of a view amongst ordinary folks while allowing tolerance of the same view among the privileged few who can obtain true knowledge (not that he would endorse this option even if it were practical).

Akeel Bilgrami (2015) has recently criticized Mill's argument on two further grounds. First, he suggests that it is close to self-undermining. The conclusion of the argument says we should tolerate other views and take heart that even our best arguments may be flawed. But of course Mill's argument itself could be, and is, opposed and we should take to heart the possibility that it is mistaken. So Mill's argument seems to entail that we should be hesitant in endorsing his argument.

It should be clear, however, from Mill's discussion of true knowledge that he is not opposed in general to confident belief. Confident belief is warranted when one has competently carried out the procedures of aiming at true knowledge (Mill 1859/1989, 23). In principle, one could have carried out such procedures with respect to Mill's argument itself, and thus be confident in it. But even if one has not yet done so, one might still have some confidence in the argument and so be fairly confident of its conclusion. And of course Mill would endorse the conclusion that we should be tolerant of those who would oppose Mill's argument; on his view such tolerance is necessary for acquiring knowledge that Mill's argument is a good argument! So Bilgrami's first objection appears toothless.

Second, Bilgrami argues that Mill (i) assumes that the pursuit of truth is an epistemic value while (ii) regarding the attainment of truth as a goal we can never know we have achieved. No matter how confident we are, how good our reasons are, or how many objections we have considered, there is still a chance we are wrong and so we should always be on the lookout for our error. He says Mill's argument in some ways resembles the paradox of the preface: "the author's declaration of impending falsity in the pages to come is idle, because it gives him or her no instruction about what to do to remedy things" and "as pragmatists say, something that makes no difference to practice makes no difference to inquiry and epistemology at all" (Bilgrami 2015, 15–16).

One might think that Bilgrami wants something from Mill that just cannot usually be had – an infallible grasp that the reasons we have for p, when we know that p, guarantee that p. One lesson to be learned from Descartes is that this is very hard to come by. We should not expect this kind of grasp of our reasons and so we should endorse a view of knowledge that is less stringent. But a more satisfying response than this is available. Mill grants that we can have knowledge; it is just that true knowledge is hard to obtain. We could even, on Mill's view, know that we knew p, although that would also be hard to obtain. And we can tell whether we know something by looking to see whether we have carried out the procedures of obtaining true knowledge. True, there will inevitably be claims that we think we know – even after carrying out the procedures of obtaining true knowledge – and yet fail to know. But we have a procedure for finding those claims: look at the objections more carefully. At some point we may become relatively satisfied that we have true knowledge of something and spend our time investigating other claims. Nothing about this would be unreasonable for anything Mill has said. So, contrary to Bilgrami, it appears that Mill can grant that we have knowledge and that we can know that we know, while at the same time accepting that we will make mistakes. And we do have a method for finding our error – doing a more thorough job of following the procedures for obtaining true knowledge.

To summarize, Mill argues that intolerance brings about a variety of epistemic costs, whereas tolerance opens up the possibility for obtaining many epistemic goods including true belief, avoidance of error, understanding, a better grasp of reasons, intellectual courage and boldness, and true knowledge. Thus there are substantial epistemic reasons to favor tolerance (both individual and social) of beliefs we not just oppose but confidently reject. Bilgrami's objections seemed to have little force. But Fletcher's objection and Mill's anticipated objection raise a possibility that others have explored in more detail: that sometimes there might be substantial epistemic costs to policies of tolerance. We shall explore this possibility in greater detail later on and discuss whether it presents a more serious objection than Mill himself thought.

Rauch's Argument from the Success of Liberal Science

Journalist Jonathan Rauch published a lively defense of free thought and speech – tolerance more generally – in his 1993 book, *Kindly Inquisitors* (expanded edition published in 2013) which, given his prominence as a social commentator in America, has received considerable attention. Drawing on a conception of science inspired primarily by Karl Popper, Rauch argues for the benefits of what he calls "liberal science." Liberal science is the scientific culture that developed in the western world and began flourishing in the seventeenth century. Rauch argues that liberal science is a powerful tool for rooting out truth about the world and we need such tools because humans make wise and beneficial decisions based on a grasp of the truth. Furthermore, liberal science works as well as it does precisely because it operates according to a variety of principles that require tolerance of dissent. Rauch thus presents us with another epistemic argument for tolerance: tolerance is necessary for the proper function of liberal science, which when done well, is one of our most reliable methods for obtaining the truth. On this argument, tolerance is of contributory epistemic value. In the expanded edition Rauch extends the argument; he suggests that moral reasoning in a society is best done by following something like a liberal scientific method. Thus we should tolerate dissenting opinions on moral matters because the process of society working through disagreements on moral matters produces, in the long run, true moral beliefs.

Rauch's Popperian-inspired picture of liberal science is evolutionary. Science makes progress through a process of selection. The things selected for are ideas, or hypotheses. Hypotheses go through an extensive period of criticism, which function as selection pressures. Scientists form a critical society – "a community of people looking for each other's mistakes" (Rauch 2013, 63). They look for evidence for and against hypotheses, doing their best to put them to the test. The hypotheses that best survive this criticism spread among the community of scientists and typically attract further testing. Eventually, over time, the hypotheses that best survive this criticism become widely accepted. And we can be fairly confident of the hypotheses accepted by the scientific community that have been subject to this process and have survived and spread because the selection pressures were pressures precisely against false hypotheses. False hypotheses will make false predictions, which will be discovered and outed by the critical society (given enough time and effort).

Evolutionary processes act on variation, so for there to be any selection pressures in favor of some hypotheses over others there needs to be variation in hypotheses. And in order for selection to direct the community of scientists toward the truth, selection pressures have to come in the form of positive and negative evidence bearing on the hypotheses. Both of these aspects of the evolutionary process require tolerance – tolerance for hypotheses alternative to those that are already accepted and tolerance for the raising of objections. So tolerance is an integral part of the process that the scientific community practices in order to find the truth.

Rauch points out that individual scientists do not need to be personally interested in finding the truth. In fact, they could be biased in their acceptance of their favored hypotheses. So long as the community functions as we described above, we can expect that the community will get closer to – and with sufficient time, find – the truth. Philip Kitcher's (1990) work on the division of cognitive labor supports this point. He argues that there are many situations in which it is better for the community of scientists – better, that is, with respect to their epistemic goals – to have a subcommunity of scientists develop and test hypotheses that everyone regards as less probable than some other theory regarding the phenomena at issue. Dissenting opinions should not only be tolerated, but they should be supported so that, collectively, the community of scientists comes closer to achieving their epistemic goals. Furthermore, to encourage some individuals and subcommunities of scientists to pursue the less likely hypotheses, it would help for the community to offer incentives such as prizes to those who solved the problem or answered the question at issue. Thus, as Rauch claims, individual scientists can be motivated by concerns other than epistemic value and, indeed, such motivation may help the community to achieve its epistemic ends.

In an afterward to the 2013 edition of *Kindly Inquisitors*, Rauch broadens the scope of his argument. Not only do scientific communities that respect tolerance acquire (over time) knowledge about the universe and its operations, but human communities that respect tolerance acquire (over time) moral knowledge. Although the critical tools we can use differ for evaluating moral claims as compared to scientific claims, "from the standpoint of social epistemology and the public quest for knowledge, ethical propositions are like any other kind," says Rauch (2013, 173). The same evolutionary selection mechanisms can operate, and tolerance will be just as useful a tool for acquiring moral truth within those mechanisms. As an illustration, he suggests the American struggle with the acceptance of homosexuality. As a gay person himself, Rauch is quite familiar with all the ways in which America has not been tolerant of the acceptance of homosexuality and he describes several of those ways. However, he thinks that American society was tolerant enough to allow some brave people to air and defend acceptance of homosexuality and once "gay people stepped forward, liberal science engaged" (Rauch 2013, 177) and began questioning various assumptions of opposition toward homosexuality. That process of questioning – some carried out in academic contexts, some carried out in everyday life through increased familiarity with homosexual people and how they lived, felt, and loved – enabled society to come to accept homosexuality.

Rauch appears to accept an evolutionary version of the "marketplace of ideas" defense of tolerance. Justice Holmes famously described this defense in a 1919 dissenting opinion: "the best test of truth is the power of the thought to get itself accepted in the competition of the market" (quoted in Goldman 1999, 192). This epistemic argument is narrower than Mill's in that it focuses on just two epistemic goods – the acquisition of truth and the avoidance/elimination of error. Societies that are broadly structured to function like Rauch's vision of liberal science are bound, over time, to achieve more of these goods. That is, society as a whole as well as individuals within the society will acquire more true beliefs and avoid/eliminate false beliefs. And tolerance is part of the engine that drives liberal science toward these ends. Therefore to achieve these ends, so goes the argument, we should be tolerant.

How strong of a case have Mill and Rauch together made for tolerance? In the next section we will discuss various objections to their arguments that, if correct, indicate that intolerance of various sorts may well be neutral or positive with respect to epistemic values.

Objections

It is widely accepted that intolerance in many circumstances hinders people and communities from achieving epistemic goods and that tolerance conveys, generally speaking, an epistemic benefit. Objections to these arguments mostly claim either (i) that the arguments support at best a more restricted epistemic benefit and that in many cases there are no or little epistemic costs to a measure of intolerance, or (ii) there are cases in which intolerance can have epistemic benefits. Of course there are also arguments that attempt to override the force of the epistemic arguments by claiming that reasons of justice or beneficence sometimes require that we should be intolerant and justice and benevolence often should override epistemic benefits. We will not discuss these latter sorts of arguments here, as these arguments do not find a limitation in the epistemic arguments per se. They rather suggest that other reasons are more forceful.

The first objection we will examine argues that complete tolerance of dissent does not generate much in the way of epistemic benefits in certain kinds of cases, namely, when we have extremely strong evidence for a proposition. For example, we have extremely strong evidence that the earth is round, and yet a small minority of people dispute this claim. The epistemic benefits of tolerance in this case seem minimal. We already almost assuredly have the truth about this matter, so tolerance is not going to give us more truth or help us to avoid error. Probably no amount of discussion is going to convince the minority who believe the earth is flat. So there would not be much to lose epistemically if we were to decide to be intolerant of flat earthers, say, by refusing to allow them to publicize their views in certain forums or to require their publications to display a disclaimer stating that the scientific community believes that an enormous body of evidence supports the claim that the earth is round. So maybe with more controversial issues tolerance promises substantial epistemic benefits, but with issues like these there is little epistemic reason to favor tolerance.

Both Mill and Rauch anticipate this kind of argument. We have already seen Mill's response: there are epistemic benefits to be had other than getting truth and avoiding error, including understanding and having opportunities to exhibit epistemic courage. Flat earth defenders could well help the general community come to a better understanding of the earth. The dispute can clarify matters, exhibit connections between different bodies of evidence, and help people see the implications of the spherical earth hypothesis more clearly. Flat earthers do not have to be correct in order to have a positive epistemic effect on the community; the discussion and interaction with their views can produce understanding. Furthermore, allowing varieties of intolerance regarding not-p whenever the evidence is overwhelmingly in favor of p might well produce epistemic costs. Odds are that over time there will be a case in which p is false and so intolerance of not-p will hinder us from discovering p's falsity. As Mill argues, such a policy would likely lead to intellectual cowardice – a fear of being or ending up on a socially stigmatized position. So even if the epistemic costs of intolerance in any given case of this sort are low, over time the policy of being intolerant in these sorts of cases will produce substantial costs.

Rauch and Kitcher mention another possible epistemic cost of intolerance in such cases: epistemic backfire. When government or a sense of what "enlightened" people are supposed to say regulates expression, people who espouse or are attracted to a proscribed belief "are reinforced by the idea that official ideology has stepped in to conceal an uncomfortable truth" (Kitcher 2001, 105). They may become more confident in their belief, suspect that others are conspiring against them, and work even harder to defend and spread their belief.

Furthermore, it is worth remembering that neither Mill nor Rauch think that tolerance of a view requires giving that view air time, or interacting with it in a public forum, or giving it any kind of professional recognition or respect. They both think of tolerance as a component of a broader process: for Mill, a search for true knowledge; for Rauch, submission to the process of liberal science. For both, the community might judge that a view has so much evidence going against it, or has been tested often enough and found wanting, that it largely decides not to discuss the view or give it much airtime in publications or public forums. For Rauch this is a legitimate by-product of the evolutionary selection process that liberal science thrives on; some views die and the community makes little to no effort to resurrect them. So if a community is committed to seeking true knowledge or employing liberal science, false views over time will wither and die out in the community. Intolerance is not required. Now this point raises a further question: what if neither our communities nor citizens are much interested in, or competent with, true knowledge or liberal science? Would this affect the epistemic argument?

Philip Kitcher provides an interesting variant of this first sort of objection. Kitcher argues that there are conditions in which scientists should not pursue a line of inquiry (2001, 93–108). Those conditions are when (i) the inquiry is likely to produce evidence that is roughly indecisive with respect to the hypothesis in question, (ii) many people in the community will, perhaps due to a bias, assign a probability to the proposition that is higher than what the inquiry supports, and (iii) an increased confidence in the hypothesis in the community will result in a reduced quality of life for some disadvantaged people in the community. In this sort of situation, the epistemic benefits of the inquiry are mixed at best. Researchers will have a more accurate assessment of the hypothesis and their understanding of the phenomena in question will probably increase, but many people in the community will come to a less accurate assessment of the hypothesis. When biases and other epistemic vices or shortcomings are widely present in a community, more inquiry, discussion, and evidence will not always produce a net epistemic benefit. In fact, Kitcher argues that Mill's fundamental concern for liberty of thought supports his claim that scientists should not pursue a line of inquiry in the above circumstances, for inquiry would harm the already disadvantaged, which hinders their ability to enjoy the benefits of liberty of thought.

Alvin Goldman has developed several arguments of the second sort for speech regulation – arguments that indicate that speech regulation (intolerance of some sort) can sometimes have positive epistemic effects (Goldman 1999, 189–217). His arguments are given from within a veritistic social epistemology framework – that is, an epistemology that evaluates social practices based on their impact on true belief, error, and ignorance. He argues that the marketplace of ideas defense of tolerance fails. First, he points out that a market does not inevitably produce better products. The economic theory of markets predicts that "the levels of output for each type of good will reach efficient levels, relative to the production possibilities facing producers and the preferences of consumers" (Goldman 1999, 197). The market might end up producing mostly cheap short-lasting rather than expensive durable toothbrushes. Similarly, a marketplace for ideas is not guaranteed to produce true beliefs, particularly if the consumers do not have a strong preference for the truth as compared to other features of beliefs. How many people in our communities really care about having Mill's real knowledge? How many people in society want to play a role in something analogous to Rauch's critical society, testing claims and raising objections to beliefs that float through the public consciousness? Although humans perhaps are not as gullible as has previously been thought (Mercier 2020), most average people do not have the time to evaluate most of the claims that come their way in the public forum and are subject to various cognitive biases such as confirmation bias (Nickerson 1998). And average people will have difficulties evaluating many of the claims they will hear about, such as claims about whether a product is safe, or whether a certain nationwide policy is better than an alternative policy. If most average people are like this, there is little reason to think that they are interested in pursuing true knowledge or that Rauch's evolutionary mechanisms will play out in the general public arena.

Goldman points to two features of our modern societies that raise particular problems for the marketplace of ideas defense. First, there is an information glut. On any given day we are overwhelmed with far more information than we could possibly process. And we are all aware that there is even more information available online. We might have time to carefully evaluate a small number of claims, but lots of claims will slide through relaxed critical filters. And given the glut of information, we get to select what we pay attention to and we probably select sources and content that tends to fit pretty well with what we already believe (Lynch 2016). Second, for many statements, speakers and hearers have divergent interests that do not combine to make it likely that hearers come to truth and avoid error (Goldman 1999, 212). Companies have incentive to say wonderful things about their products and to avoid speaking about their limitations – it makes them money. People who do not like the product or find problems with the product have less incentive to air their opinions – it takes time and, unless they work for Consumer Reports, they do not make money. Divergent incentives like this will result in a glut of positive, well-designed, statements about the product and a comparative lack of critical statements, even if there are grounds for criticism. Divergent incentives can produce a biased evidence sample which can suppress the spread of truth and sow error.

7 The Epistemic Justification for Tolerance

Goldman goes on to argue that, in addition, various speech regulation policies plausibly have or would have positive veritistic effects (Goldman 1999, 205–8). Libel laws plausibly provide an incentive against the spread of false personal information. Various US government regulations originating in the New Deal, such as SEC restrictions on what people can say when they sell stocks and bonds and FDA food labeling requirements, plausibly prohibit the spread of false information (which in these contexts would be especially tempting for sellers to spread) and encourage the spread of true information. Requirement of cigarette labels warning of the harms of smoking, the freedom of information act, and courtroom practices about what can and cannot be said in a trial also all probably have positive veritistic outcomes.

Although he thinks these arguments give us reasons to explore whether some speech restrictions might be veritistically positive, Goldman does not favor content-specific government regulation – that is, restriction of the espousal of certain contents. Governments have non-veritistic interests in restricting speech, especially speech that criticizes the government and its allies and agents, and so governments probably cannot be trusted to reliably establish veritistically positive content-specific regulations. However, content-neutral regulations, such as time, place, and manner restrictions, may well not hinder veritistic outcomes. Although some such regulations might severely reduce the quantity of speech on an issue, which in some cases might have negative veritistic outcomes. Content-related regulations, such as "requiring revelation of a speaker's identity and financial interests in the content of the message," could increase the spread of truth and avoidance of error (Goldman 1999, 217). Such regulations are intolerant in a certain sense – they are intolerant of speech acts advocating a message while hiding one's identity and interests.

In their book, *The Misinformation Age: How False Beliefs Spread*, philosophers of science Cailin O'Connor and James Owen Weatherall conclude that "we should stop thinking that the 'marketplace of ideas' can effectively sort fact from fiction" (O'Connor and Weatherall 2019, 179). They develop mathematical models of how scientists alter their beliefs over time in response to data they receive within a network of other scientists. They can use these models to estimate how effective people in the models would be at coming to the truth about a given issue. The models can vary in the shape of the connections between scientists and in how the scientists respond to evidence they receive from their connections in the network. These models indicate that over time scientific communities tend to converge towards a consensus on the truth. Initially one might think this result favors Mill and Rauch – communities of scientists doing experiments, testing various hypotheses on an issue tend to converge toward the truth. This whole picture requires scientists to be tolerant of diverse views. However, O'Connor and Weatherall develop various models of circumstances in which communities of people that include scientists do not converge towards a consensus on the truth. These models illuminate various real-world case studies and suggest that some widespread practices and conditions actually hinder communities from converging on the truth. Furthermore, these models can also be used to model how beliefs spread in ordinary communities containing ordinary citizens, where various practices and conditions – where they obtain – make it even less likely that people in the community converge to the truth. Crucially, false beliefs can spread even when every person in the community is responding to the evidence available to them in a rational way.

Here are several situations in which, according to their models, false beliefs are prone to spread within a community:

> (Bad Data) An influential member or set of members receives a string of bad data.
> (Polarization) Two groups of researchers produce different data and each scientist adjusts his degree of belief in the other's data based in part on how closely the other's belief about the matter at hand matches their own.
> (Conformity) When people want to conform to the dominant view of their group.
> (Biased Research Production) When an industry directly funds research on a given issue, has an interest in a certain action, A, being taken, and selectively publishes the studies that support A or support neither A nor B (a competing action). A propogandist presents all of these studies to policy makers.
> (Selective Sharing) A propogandist culls the literature for studies that support A, or are ambiguous, or that suggest other possible explanations for the phenomena in question. These and quotations that express caution and uncertainty are presented to policy makers.
> (Industrial selection) Industry funds various methods for investigating an issue, finds out which ones produce desirable results, then selectively funds those methods in the future. Funding increases productivity, which can then attract non-industry funding and more researchers, lending the method respectability in the community.
> (Authority) Using an audience's trust of certain authority figures to spread a message.

Several of these situations are prone to allow false belief to spread because evidence is probabilistic – that is, if p is true and p predicts q, it will still often be the case that when you test for p by checking for q, you will sometimes find not-q. So there will inevitably be studies and methods that will not find what a true claim predicts, or that will find results contrary to what a true claim predicts. This is why a string of bad data can occur and lead a community astray. It is why industry can fund research and not in any way taint or influence the work of the researchers they fund and still end up with studies that either support their view or are ambiguous. And the lower the sample size used in a given experiment, the more likely it is that an experiment will produce results that do not fit with the truth; so a company could fund tons of small sample-size experiments and feel confident that some of those studies will have results favorable to their view, which they can turn around and selectively publicize, thus influencing their audience toward their view even if their view is false (O'Connor and Weatherall 2019, 114–15).

O'Connor and Weatherall suggest that their models of how false belief spreads in these situations can explain how fake news spreads and influences people through social media (O'Connor and Weatherall 2019, 170–3). Polarization, selective sharing, and authority explain why Russian methods have been effective. They rely on an already somewhat polarized society, in which people adjust their trust in what another person says based on whether that person agrees with them about related issues. The Russians set up Facebook pages and groups (and other social media groups) united around some common characteristic, acquired followers, and thus gained a measure of trust. A social media group functions like a central hub in a star-shaped network structure and so, according to O'Conner and Weatherall's models, can have an outsized effect on the beliefs of people within their network. The trust people place in the social media group can then be used to mold beliefs within the group by selectively sharing stories that push the members of the group to more extreme versions of views they are already somewhat inclined toward. The Russians did this for both conservative and liberal groups, thus enhancing the effect of polarization and creating even more distrust between members of these groups. And given that social media sites are designed to selectively share with you items that you are more likely to look at, people in groups different from your own can receive very different messages in their feeds, pushing them towards more extreme views without you even knowing about those messages. Fake news can spread in a group and affect its members' beliefs before other groups know about it and have an opportunity to respond. And once they are able to respond, increased polarization makes it less likely that those who have consumed the fake news will take the responses seriously.

Completely open tolerance of speech and the way information is produced can thus, according to these models, make communities vulnerable to the above sorts of situations in which false beliefs spread. The more common these situations are, the weaker is the epistemic argument for tolerance.

O'Connor and Weatherall make a number of suggestions about how to improve our societies to make us less vulnerable to these situations. Many of their suggestions are entirely consistent with tolerance in the sense at issue, such as urging people to be more concerned about local politics, relying more on human editorial discretion, and funding armies of fact checkers. Others are intolerant to some degree, such as abandoning reliance on industry funding of research, modifying journalistic standards to require sharing an unbiased sample of relevant evidence, and broadening legislative frameworks to restrict and punish the spread of misinformation. Using Goldman's terminology, these are examples of content-related, but not content-specific, regulation.

Summary and Future Directions

It is widely accepted that arguments like Mill's and Rauch's establish that tolerance in general increases epistemic value. Content-specific regulation of the expression of views is likely to have worse epistemic consequences than tolerance. But we have seen that there are substantial disputes about how much epistemic value is generated by tolerance, and about the prevalence of situations in which tolerance has poor epistemic consequences and intolerance of various sorts might have better results. Kitcher points to situations in which humans are prone to inflate or deflate the degree of evidential support for a proposition and further research is unlikely to point decisively in any direction. Goldman draws attention to the fact that humans often have various interests related to their beliefs – some nonepistemic – and those interests, together with varied interests of message-conveyers can lead to situations where the incentives favor the spread of false information. And he describes a few regulations that have plausibly had positive epistemic effects despite some measure of intolerance. Finally, O'Connor and Weatherall developed models of communities in which false beliefs are prone to spread, even if individual persons in the communities each respond to their evidence rationally. The structure of testimonial networks and natural human proclivities regarding trust and conformity together make our communities vulnerable to the spread of false belief when agents in the community support and selectively spread information that they want, for nonepistemic reasons, an audience to hear.

These challenges to epistemic arguments for tolerance all assume that the epistemic values at issue are veritistic – that is, they have to do with the production of true belief and the reduction of error and ignorance. Rauch's evolutionary marketplace of ideas argument plainly shares this assumption, but interestingly Mill's argument draws on a much broader range of epistemic values. He is concerned with veritistic values, but he also is concerned about understanding, true knowledge, intellectual courage, and intellectual boldness. These latter values are not taken into account in the above challenges. Furthermore, Mill is interested in both collective and individual epistemic virtues, as he speaks not only of individuals gaining true knowledge, but also of mankind having rational assurance and understanding. In contrast the above challenges focus on the epistemic effects on individuals.

These differences between Mill's argument and its challengers suggest a number of interesting and relatively under-explored future lines of research:

- Whether the challenges to epistemic arguments for tolerance are weaker once non-veritistic epistemic values are taken into account.
- How tolerance relates to collective epistemic values. Would there be a collective epistemic cost to restricting tolerance in ways suggested by the challengers? Or might some restrictions enhance and support collective epistemic value?
- How much does tolerance support epistemic values like curiosity, intellectual courage, and intellectual boldness – both in individuals and at the collective, cultural level?

In addition, the challenges themselves raise further issues:

- How adequate is mathematical modeling as a tool for describing the spread of beliefs? Can we accurately model other situations and analyze other mechanisms for the spread of false belief and other epistemically bad states?
- Can we model or test for the epistemic consequences on a society of the various suggested interventions that manifest some measure of intolerance? If so, what are the short and long term consequences?
- Most of the challenges to the epistemic argument for tolerance suggest governmental and other group-level policies and regulations. Are there other forms of influence that might be equally likely to be effective in avoiding epistemic costs and making epistemic gains?
- The main focus of discussion has been on whether and to what extent governments and societies should be tolerant. But to what extent should individuals be

tolerant? Might the case for social tolerance differ from the case for individual tolerance? And how does individual tolerance relate to open-mindedness and other epistemic virtues?

- Mill's and Rauch's epistemic arguments and the challengers implicitly assume that tolerance, if it is epistemically valuable at all, is valuable instrumentally, teleologically, or contributorily. However, might tolerance have indicative epistemic value – that is, value in virtue of indicating or pointing toward something of epistemic value? For example, perhaps tolerance as a social value has symbolic epistemic value for a community and might certain intolerant policies undermine its symbolic value?

Epistemic arguments are among our most venerable and oft-repeated defenses of tolerance. A clear view of the value of tolerance for society requires a careful examination of a host of epistemic arguments, while accounting for a range of epistemic values. Mill, his successors, and their critics have taken us far, but much remains unexplored.

References

Baehr J (2011) The inquiring mind. Oxford University Press, Oxford
Bilgrami A (2015) Truth, balance, and freedom. In: Bilgrami A, Cole J (eds) Who's afraid of academic freedom? Columbia University Press, New York
Bowlin JR (2016) Tolerance among the virtues. Princeton University Press, Princeton
David M (2014) Truth as the primary epistemic goal: a working hypothesis. In: Steup M, Turri J, Sosa E (eds) Contemporary debates in epistemology, 2nd edn. Wiley-Blackwell, Malden, pp 363–377
Fletcher G (1996) The instability of tolerance. In: Heyd D (ed) Toleration: an elusive virtue. Princeton University Press, Princeton
Goldman A (1999) Knowledge in a social world. Oxford University Press, New York
Kitcher P (1990) The division of cognitive labor. J Philos 87(1):5–22
Kitcher P (2001) Science, truth, and democracy. Oxford University Press, New York
Kvanvig J (2014) Truth is not the primary epistemic goal. In: Steup M, Turri J, Sosa E (eds) Contemporary debates in epistemology, 2nd edn. Wiley-Blackwell, Malden, pp 352–362
Lynch M (2016) The internet of us. Liveright, New York
Mercier H (2020) Not born yesterday. Princeton University Press, Princeton
Mill JS (1859/1989) 'On liberty' and other writings (ed: Collini S). Cambridge University Press, Cambridge
Nickerson RS (1998) Confirmation Bias: a ubiquitous phenomena in many guises. Rev Gen Psychol 2:175–220
O'Connor C, Weatherall JO (2019) The misinformation age: how false beliefs spread. Yale University Press, New Haven
Rauch J (2013) Kindly inquisitors, expanded edition. University of Chicago Press, Chicago
Riggs W (2008) The value turn in epistemology. In: Hendricks V, Pritchard D (eds) New waves in epistemology. Palgrave Macmillan, New York, pp 300–323
Roberts R, Wood WJ (2007) Intellectual virtues. Oxford University Press, Oxford
Williamson T (2014) Knowledge first. In: Steup M, Turri J, Sosa E (eds) Contemporary debates in epistemology, 2nd edn. Wiley-Blackwell, Malden, pp 1–9

Political Toleration Explained

8

Peter Balint

Contents

Introduction	130
The Neutrality Challenge	131
Toleration Without Objection	132
Toleration as a General Political Practice	136
Indifference	136
Forbearance Tolerance	137
Respect	138
The Neutrality Challenge Revisited	138
Three Further Challenges to Political Toleration	140
Understanding State Objection	140
Locating State Power	142
The "Symmetry Thesis"	142
Conclusion	145
References	146

Abstract

Political toleration may initially seem unremarkable. For a long time, debates about toleration were debates about what the state should or should not tolerate. But given rise of the liberal democratic state, especially in political theory, political toleration has faced a number of conceptual challenges. The most prominent of these is "The Neutrality Challenge": if the state is supposed to be neutral, then it cannot have the values on which to object, values which are a necessary feature of orthodox understandings of toleration. This chapter defuses this challenge, by showing how it misunderstands both neutrality and toleration.

P. Balint (✉)
School of Humanities and Social Sciences, UNSW Canberra, Canberra, ACT, Australia
e-mail: p.balint@unsw.edu.au

© The Author(s), under exclusive licence to Springer Nature Switzerland AG 2022
M. Sardoč (ed.), *The Palgrave Handbook of Toleration*,
https://doi.org/10.1007/978-3-030-42121-2_44

129

Both toleration and neutrality only make sense in relation to a specific range. Moreover, toleration has both a general and specific sense, and only the specific sense requires an objection and is necessarily a type of forbearance. States can be generally tolerant and then respect, be indifferent to, or tolerate in an objection sense, the specific differences they have power over. While this explains the general nature of political toleration, three problems remain when this is applied to specific acts of forbearance tolerance: understanding state objection, locating state power, and Glen Newey's "symmetry thesis." These are dealt with in the remainder of the chapter, and political toleration both in its general and more specific forbearance sense is explained.

Keywords

Political toleration · The Neutrality Challenge · Toleration · Tolerance · Respect · Indifference · Forbearance · Symmetry thesis · State neutrality · Intolerance · State power

Introduction

Contemporary diverse societies contain strongly felt, and occasionally violent, tensions. Given this fact, it may seem obvious that toleration is the practice to manage conflict and to help us all live our lives freely together. That is, it may seem self-evident that liberal societies should be guided by the practice of toleration – both between citizens and in the state's relationship to their diverse citizen body. Toleration allows different ways of life to coexist; it is a practice that avoids the imposition of one way of life on others; and it has a long and strong pedigree (Zagorin 2003). Nevertheless, the political practice of toleration faces several important conceptual challenges. These challenges have led to claims that toleration is redundant, nonsensical, or incoherent, at least in contemporary liberal democratic political regimes. This piece explains the main conceptual critiques of toleration as a political practice, before showing how we can make sense of toleration as a political practice. While toleration between citizens is important, the focus here is squarely on the state, as it is here that all the main conceptual challenges arise.

The chapter begins by outlining "The Neutrality Challenge," the most prominent of the conceptual challenges. According to this challenge, if the state is supposed to be neutral, then it cannot have the values on which to object, values which are a necessary feature of toleration. The chapter then turns to the question of the tolerant state and suggests that two senses of toleration are at play – one of which involves objection and power and the other of which only requires power. The Neutrality Challenge is then defused using both this insight and a more sophisticated understanding of state neutrality. Three problems then remain for political toleration: understanding state objection, locating state power, and Glen Newey's "symmetry thesis." These are dealt with in the remainder of the chapter.

The Neutrality Challenge

Toleration has faced several philosophical issues in the mid-late twentieth century, most of which have been presented as "paradoxes." For example, how can someone both object to something and permit it? How can someone with racist views who does not act on them be more tolerant than someone without such views (Horton 1994; Bessone 2013, cf. Balint 2016)? And if a state is tolerant, then this very toleration of opposing views (especially on the question of toleration) will likely lead to a rise of intolerance and undermine toleration altogether (Popper 1945). Despite the interest these issues have led to, none of them challenge toleration's political applicability. In this chapter, which seeks to explain political toleration, it is political applicability that matters. And while there are a number of conceptual challenges, the main conceptual challenge to the political practice of toleration, at least among liberals, is what has be called "The Neutrality Challenge" (Balint 2017). This focusses on the apparent incompatibility between state toleration and state neutrality. This challenge, although expressed in various ways, purports to show an inconsistency in liberal theory. A widely held view is that the contemporary liberal state should be neutral among its citizens' (justice-respecting) ways of life, that is, it should not favor one way of life over any other. This type of state could then be said to place no value at all on particular differences. Such a state should not, for example, have an official line on religion or on a whole host of other "private" matters. A common understanding of toleration is that it involves withholding power despite objection. So if a state is neutral, it would no longer have the sort of values on which it may object and withhold power.

Thus Glen Newey (2013: 42) writes:

> [I]n neutralist theory...political authority is thought of as a normative vacuum. Since toleration requires that the tolerator have reasons for disapproving of the practice, and must nonetheless have reasons for regarding non-intervention as good, the normative vacuum is filled, and neutrality disappears.

While Robert Paul Churchill (2003: 65–76, 65) argues, "..far from being neutral, 'liberal toleration' may paradoxically endorse hostility ('intolerance') towards the persons, values, and beliefs others are said to be tolerating."

Finally, in the words of John Gray (1995: 19):

> Toleration as a political ideal is offensive to the new liberalism – the liberalism of Rawls, Dworkin, Ackerman and suchlike – because it is decidedly non-neutral in respect of the good. For the new liberals, justice – the shibboleth of revisionist liberalism – demands that government, in its institutions and policies, practise neutrality, not toleration, in regard to rival conceptions of the good life.

According to this challenge, of which there are many other proponents (e.g., Horton 1996; Newey 1999, 2001; Meckled-Garcia 2001; Seligman 2003), political toleration is at best redundant and at worst entirely incompatible within liberal neutrality. A state or institution can either be neutral and liberal, or it can be tolerant and not liberal (or at least not neutralist liberal); it cannot be both.

Toleration Without Objection

While those pushing The Neutrality Challenge see no room for toleration in liberal political structures, how much "toleration" really occurs in non-neutral political toleration? Do tolerant political regimes – neutral or otherwise – actually "tolerate" their citizen's diverse ways of life? Or is something quite different going on? The answer to this question depends very much on what is meant by "toleration." According to the current theoretical orthodoxy, toleration must always have three basic components: an objection, the power to negatively act on this objection, and intentionally not acting in this way (Balint 2014). It is, therefore, a type of forbearance. Many views are even stricter, requiring the reasons for the objection and the withholding of negative interference to be of the morally right kind, rather than more pragmatic or less unreflected upon (e.g., Nicholson 1985; Raphael 1988; Meckled-Garcia 2001; Forst 2013; Habermas 2004). In political contexts, the paradigmatic case of this understanding of toleration is taken to be a like traditional ruler who tolerates their subjects practicing religions that rival their own. As the sovereign, there is the power to intervene, as well as clear objection, and moreover in this case, the objection can be seen as morally grounded in rival scriptures.

This view that toleration must always involve an objection, the power to hinder, and intentionally not hindering has, in theoretical circles at least, become the dominant orthodoxy. But it is certainly not the only way to understand the concept. There is a much broader understanding that does not require objection but simply power and intentional non-hindrance. It is this understanding of toleration that is present when somebody or some environment is described as relatively tolerant. When a university, for example, is described as relatively tolerant, this does not mean that this institution has a great many objections which, despite having the power, are not acted upon. What is usually meant is that the institution has few, if any, objections to things that others might find objectionable (as well as having the power to act negatively in these areas if it so wished). This understanding of toleration is general in nature. It applies when we talk in general terms about tolerant political structures.

This broader understanding of toleration is permissive in two crucial ways. First, as stated, it is wider than the narrow and much more moralized view that has come to dominate recent political philosophy. This understanding matches our everyday language. The way certain societies are described as particularly tolerant, for example, does not mean they contain a lot of people and institutions constantly overcoming their deeply grounded moral objections but simply that most people and institutions in such a society do not really care about a great many things others would object to and consequently are relatively permissive. A tolerant society usually involves significantly more indifference than it does forbearance.

Second, toleration is permissive in a more literal sense. The more toleration that is practiced, the more permissive a society is, and with it the more freedom its citizens enjoy (cf De Ceva 2019). This does not mean that toleration should not have limits, but these limits, however, well justified, are restrictions and make such a society less permissive, even if rightly so. Generally speaking we might want to say toleration is better than intolerance. But there will be many occasions – such as when harm is likely to be caused to others – where intolerance is to be preferred. This is to say nothing more than any liberal regime of toleration will have a range. Everything within its range will be permitted – either because there is no objection or any objection is outweighed by another consideration such as freedom of conscience or freedom of association. Beyond this range things will, and should, be subject to intolerance.

None of this is to dismiss the more philosophically orthodox understanding of toleration as forbearance. A full understanding of the liberal practice of political toleration will require both the permissive *and* the forbearance senses of toleration: one certainly does not cancel the other out. If we wish to make sense of toleration *as a political practice*, we need both these senses of toleration. Put simply, the understanding of toleration that does not always require objection describes general political arrangements. In contrast, the objection sense of toleration ("forbearance tolerance") applies in specific cases relating to specific acts of tolerance – acts which may occur under a general regime of toleration. Using this general/specific distinction has important advantages, particularly in a field where the two notions are all too often used interchangeably. And while a distinction between "toleration" and "tolerance" is sometimes made in the literature (e.g., Crick 1971: 144; King 1976: 12–13, 68; Galeotti 2001: 273, n. 1; Forst 2004: 315; and Habermas 2004: 5), it is not the semantic distinction that is important but the general/specific distinction that matters. Applying this distinction to political toleration allows us to understand a general regime of toleration, such as that of a liberal state, as not solely being sustained by specific acts of forbearance tolerance but also by indifference and even potentially by acts of respect for difference.

One way to make the case for toleration not always being about forbearance and negative valuing is to look at our use of the adjective "tolerant." Sometimes it is used in a specific sense, for example, the way we might describe the historic power-sharing deal between Ian Paisley (Democratic Unionist Party) and Gerry Adams (Sinn Fein) in Northern Ireland in 2007. Both men clearly loathed each other yet still agreed to work together. When specific actions are described as tolerant in this sense, this usually means that there is some objection or disapproval that is then overcome for some other reason, in other words, forbearance.

In contrast, when an agent is described as particularly tolerant in the general sense, something quite different is usually meant. Sweden, for example, might be described as having a particularly tolerant society. Here what is normally meant is that a wide range of activities/differences are permitted. Yet importantly, in the general sense, this permissiveness is not the whole picture. Also implied is that this type of person/agent has fewer reasons to forbear in the first place. That is, a generally tolerant agent not only does not intervene particularly often but also, and crucially, has less reason to interfere. As John Horton (1996: 38) writes:

> ...The tolerant person is not a narrow-minded bigot who shows restraint; he or she is not someone with a vast array of prejudices about others' conduct but who nonetheless heroically restrains him- or herself from acting restrictively...[t]he restraint involved in toleration is not exclusively of action but also of judgement.

Horton (1996: 38) continues: "the extension of the concept to include narrowing of the range of what is considered objectionable is no doubt controversial...[y]et it is not altogether incongruent with many ordinary uses of tolerance." This point can also be made conversely. When an agent is described as *intolerant* in the general sense, this usually means that they not only put up with a lesser range of things before intervening but also have narrower and stronger views on what they will permit in the first place. When a person or institution is said to be comparatively intolerant, this does not mean that they simply have the *same* values or types of irritants as a tolerant agent but choose to intervene more often. Rather, it means that the intolerant agent's greater readiness to interfere is a result of their having significantly more potential irritants than a tolerant agent, thereby generating a much wider scope of interference. Many things that may cause others to negatively intervene simply do not affect the generally tolerant agent at all – that is, they are entirely *indifferent* to many things that the intolerant agent associates a strong value and thus reacts to.

It is this sense of being tolerant that is captured in toleration as a general practice. A tolerant liberal state, for example, not only withholds power but also crucially withholds judgment on a very wide range of its citizens' differences. The tolerant liberal state is highly permissive, not because it forbears in relation to the ways of life of its citizens but because, in most cases, it is indifferent to them.

Some readers may still find this unconvincing. They may retort: "when I tolerate my student's lateness, my partner's cooking, or my neighbour's leaf-blower, these are all things I certainly object to." But these are not counterexamples; they are simply *specific* acts of forbearance tolerance which *do* involve objection or disapproval. It is only the general practice of toleration, and not specific acts of tolerance, in which objection is not required.

Another objection may be that this is stretching the concept of toleration too far as we already have suitable concepts to cover this general meaning of "tolerant" in political contexts. Why not, for example, talk about the importance of individual liberty or a liberal approach to diversity? Yet if individual liberty is the concern, then we still need a policy or practice to realize it: toleration is one of the practices that realizes and upholds this value. And while liberalism does justify a particular approach to toleration, a general regime of toleration need not be liberal. There are many examples of tolerant regimes that are justified by non-liberal principles (perhaps the most well-known of which was the Millet system of the Ottoman Empire). As such, the general/specific distinction is intended to make sense of both our ordinary language and our political practices.

8 Political Toleration Explained

Before examining the general nature of political toleration, it is worth noting that the "traditional" objection-type-only conception of tolerance which dominates discussions of toleration in moral philosophy may actually be a quite recent orthodoxy in political philosophy. For example, in his *Second Letter on Toleration*, John Locke ([1690]1824: 62) suggests a wider usage in matters of religious conversion; "[t]oleration is but the removing [of] force." Locke, describing the parliamentary debate over toleration in his letter to Philip van Limborch in 1869, also suggests that toleration can take the form of either "indulgence" – which is an objection-type of toleration – or "comprehension" – which in religious matters involves making the rituals of the church as minimal and accommodating as possible so that many more people can be made to conform (cited in Cranston 1987: 111–112; and Kaplan 2007: 132–133; cf. Tate 2016). Indeed it appears that "comprehension" was his preferred form of toleration (Cranston 1987: 112). Seeing this as far from unique, Perez Zagorin (2003: 7, 199–208, 256–288) in his seminal work on the rise of religious toleration in the West argues that neither Locke, Pierre Bayle, nor Roger Williams distinguished toleration from liberty of conscience. Finally, Sally Jenkinson (1996: 320) argues Bayle goes further, aiming for a form of toleration that was pluralist and an enlightened republic that was "presided over by a confessionally neutral sovereign supported by a civic, not religious, administration."

Much more recently, Preston King states that "toleration is broader than tolerance" with "toleration" consisting of all "negations of intolerance...[including] indifference [and] favouritism, and most particularly...a system of equal rights," while "tolerance" is the "most minimal negation of intolerance" (1976: 12–13, 68; Cf. Newman 1982: 5; Walzer 1997: 2; and Scheffler 2010). Even John Rawls (1999: 188) uses toleration in a general sense as equivalent to liberty of conscience, and this is clearly in a situation without a state religion or similar grounds for objection.

Finally, among historians of Western religious toleration, it is standard to employ the wider sense of concept. The two most prominent recent examples are Zagorin, who describes toleration "in its broadest terms as equivalent to the condition of religious freedom" (2003: 6), and Benjamin J. Kaplan who defines toleration as "the peaceful coexistence of people of different faiths living together in the same village, town, or city" (2007: 8, 11, 162). This view is consistent with the earlier major histories of toleration by W.K. Jordan and Joseph Lecler (both cited in Zagorin 2003: 314). None of this is to say that the narrow objection-type-only conception of tolerance is incorrect, just that it is not the only way we employ the concept, and nor should it be thought of as particularly traditional, orthodox perhaps, but certainly not traditional.

It is not the case that the strict more philosophically orthodox sense of tolerance plays no role, nor that it is somehow morally or politically unimportant, nor even that it is somehow inferior – forbearance tolerance is a crucial minimum in many cases. This distinction between two senses of toleration is conceptual, rather than morally or politically normative. And in making sense of the actual practice of political toleration, we need *both* senses of toleration.

Toleration as a General Political Practice

While we do talk of generally tolerant citizens, the conceptual challenge that most needs addressing is when the state is the agent of toleration, and this will be the primary focus here. In making sense of the general state practice of toleration, it will be shown that it neither reduces to forbearance tolerance nor is wholly independent of it.

In most political regimes of toleration, forbearance tolerance has a marginal role to play. It will be quite uncommon for a state, particularly a liberal state, to perform acts that meet the three conditions for a specific act of forbearance tolerance (an objection, the power to hinder, and intentionally not hindering). Most of the time, despite having the power to hinder, the state will be entirely indifferent to the various ways of life of its citizenry. So while a generally tolerant regime does withhold the power to negatively interfere and is thus accommodating of particular differences, only the conditions of power and non-hindrance need hold.

While historically states engaged in acts of tolerance in relation to deeply held religious views, the contemporary liberal state does not have these grounds for objection. Power, at least in material sense, is withheld for very different reasons; in the vast majority of cases, it is simply not the business of the state to interfere in (most of) the various ways people live their lives. While in some cases a (non-neutral) liberal state may have a view on what is a good life – for example, one that promotes autonomy – and thus will be forbearing in some areas, even here, the state will have no view at all on the vast majority of its citizens' ways of life. This is not to say that such a state is not generally tolerant, just that it does very little forbearing. Acts of forbearance tolerance are just one of the ways – and not a very common way – that a general liberal practice of state toleration will accommodate the various ways of life of its citizens, instead indifference will be the dominant relationship. If the general/specific distinction is accepted, then there is nothing anomalous here.

Indifference

Given the importance of indifference in a general account of political toleration, it is worth discussing it further. "Indifference" can be used in at least two senses, and it may appear to matter which sense is being referred to. The first sense is studied and principled. Here a state is indifferent to a particular way of life or set of beliefs because it fits within certain principled parameters. For example, a secular liberal state should be indifferent to somebody's religion (notwithstanding its practices). The state in this case has a principled reason to associate a value of indifference to all religions within a particular range. The second sense of indifference is something more like apathy. In this case, to be indifferent is to not really have thought about something before. While this is a meaningful distinction, it does not seem to do any work in the case of the tolerant liberal state. The areas in which a liberal state is indifferent *are* principled – the importance of the private sphere, for example, is central to liberalism. This is not to say that all reasons for withholding the power to hinder are principled, just the scope for indifference in a liberal state is. So it is not so much an issue of whether the state has considered this or that way of life or practice, but that for principled reasons, anything within a particular range (such as in the private sphere, however, defined) is treated indifferently.

This discussion might also raise a related concern over describing something that is treated indifferently as being subject to toleration in a general sense. This is the concern that for something to be subject to toleration, even if via indifference, there must at least be the possibility of objection. As discussed earlier, to call Sweden generally tolerant means there is indifference for things that in less tolerant states are commonly either objected to and/or prohibited. In other words, to call Sweden tolerant is to be comparative. On this reading, then, saying the state tolerates basketball or someone's sock color is nonsensical, as these are unlikely grounds for any possible objection. As Newey (2013: 6–7, 30) writes, the "intransitive" use of toleration can only be considered tolerant if there is the possibility of intolerance. This is true, but given the nature of human politics, there is always the possibility of objection and intolerance, a possibility that has all too often been realized, with political authorities caring about almost any aspect of their citizens' lives. What makes a state liberal is almost precisely because it does not object to a range of activities which other political structures either object to or reserve the right to object to. Thus, this distinction also has little application in this domain.

Forbearance Tolerance

While it is mistaken to think that the general liberal practice of toleration reduces to acts of forbearance tolerance, it is also mistaken to think that forbearance tolerance plays *no* role. No liberal state (and presumably no conceivable state) will be entirely indifferent to all of its citizen's ways of life. A liberal state will still have values – most notably those of justice – and some of its citizen's ways of life will conflict with these values, yet perhaps not to such an extent that they are beyond the boundaries of toleration. Examples of things that a liberal state should certainly not be indifferent to include white supremacist groups such as the Aryan Circle in the USA, *Magyar Gárda* in Hungary – neither of which believe in the equal moral worth of all citizens – or a religiously based political party such as the Dutch *Staatkundig Gereformeerde Partij* (SGP or Reformed Political Party) which holds that public roles should not be held by women, and until recently did not allow women to hold positions in its own party (Davies 2006). But the importance of both freedom of conscience and of association would seem to give liberal states good reasons not to interfere, at least initially, with the activities of such groups. Because there is clearly a clash of values here and the state does have the power to hinder – even if because of constitutional provisions not to entirely prevent – the state can be said to be engaging in acts of forbearance tolerance with such groups. A liberal state has reasons for not negatively interfering which may win out and which means there is space between permission and prohibition for state acts of tolerance. (Further challenges to the possibility of state acts of forbearance tolerance are dealt with in the section after next).

Respect

Finally, liberal regimes of toleration can involve acts of respect for difference to varying degrees, as acts of respect for difference also involve power and non-hindrance. At minimum, some differences will, for reasons of justice, need positive support from the state. One example here would be disability. Assuming that justice dictates the need for equality of opportunity, those with particular disabilities may need positive actions taken by the state for them to have equal or sufficient opportunities ("respect" here is in the form of Darwall's (1977) recognition respect, cf. Balint 2013). While a disability is not usually thought of as a way of life (there are notable exceptions such as deafness), the same reasoning could and has been given for *some* identities. Liberal nationalists, for example, argue for state involvement in building and promoting an overarching national identity because of its importance for the success of redistributive justice, among other key social goods (see, e.g., Miller 1995; Tamir 1993; Soutphommasane 2012; Lenard 2012). Thus they call for respect of the national identity and culture. Liberal perfectionists favor respecting some ways of life and not others – generally these are ways of life that are consistent with increased autonomy (most notably, Raz 1986). As such, the liberal perfectionist will advocate *respecting* ways of life that promote a good such as autonomy, being *indifferent* to many other ways of life, and having *forbearance tolerance* toward ways of life that either do not substantiate that good or somehow actively discourage it. Finally, liberal multiculturalists require the state to respect (at least some) minority differences. Thus although indifference will remain the primary value associated with individual differences, forbearance tolerance, and even respect for difference, will still have a role to play: how much of a role will be contingent on one's view of liberalism. These are all possible pathways from a general practice of toleration to the potential accommodation of specific differences.

The Neutrality Challenge Revisited

The Neutrality Challenge was the argument that if the state is supposed to be neutral, then it should have no value associated with its citizens' ways of life, and thus cannot be said to have any of the objection required for "toleration." On this reading, any general notion of liberal toleration is at best irrelevant and at worst incoherent. Either neutrality and toleration are inconsistent or neutrality has simply supplanted toleration. More formally the argument is as follows:

1) Liberal neutrality involves neither interfering with nor judging people's differences, including valuing them negatively.
∴2) Liberal neutral states do not value negatively the differences of their citizens.
3) Toleration involves valuing differences negatively.
∴4) Liberal neutral states do not practice toleration.

Yet the argument that the liberal neutral state practices indifference and not toleration has two main problems. The first is that indifference can never be the whole story, even if indifference is the main attitude associated with differences in a liberal society. As raised already, a liberal state will still have values – including those of justice – which it upholds. There will be practices and beliefs that should be permissible within a liberal society but at the same time will go against these core values. Thus Gray seems to entirely misunderstand contemporary liberalism when he writes, "What neutrality of radical equality mandates is nothing less than *the legal disestablishment of morality*" (1995: 20, emphasis in original). The white supremacist groups that did not believe in the equal moral worth of all citizens are a potential example here; the liberal state should not be indifferent to groups like this. The liberal neutral state is *not* neutral about everything. Neutrality, like toleration, is a range concept: states are neutral about everything within a certain range (typically a justice-respecting range), and things outside this range – for example, violence or theft against others, as well as denials of equal moral worth – are certainly not things the liberal state should be neutral about (Balint 2015). Things outside this range are either negatively interfered with, such as in the case of violence and theft, or at least judged, as in the case of those who deny equal moral worth. Premise 1 in the above argument is therefore false.

The second problem with the argument that neutrality and toleration are inconsistent should hopefully now be evident. Premise 3 has been directly challenged by the argument of the previous section. Toleration need not involve negative valuing and is entirely consistent with indifference. If this is accepted, toleration as a general practice *is* entirely compatible with liberal neutrality. The argument that liberal neutrality and toleration are not compatible thus fails on two counts. First, liberal neutrality is not simply indifference, and second, even if it was, it could still (at least conceptually) be considered tolerant.

Because neutrality and toleration are range concepts, no liberal state will be either neutral *or* tolerant toward everything. There is an ongoing debate over precisely what should be tolerated in a liberal state, that is, about what is inside and what is outside the limits or range of toleration. Nevertheless, there is broad agreement that ways of life that cause nonconsensual harm to others should not be tolerated (e.g., Cohen 2014). There is also, at least within liberal political theory, the argument that the state should be neutral among ways of life, but not among conceptions of justice. This means that, in theory at least, the range of toleration and neutrality may largely coincide. If they coincided completely, then those who say that liberal toleration is nothing more than indifference would be correct, and neutrality (as "hands off") would entail indifference to everything that is within the limits of toleration. Anything beyond these limits would neither be tolerated nor viewed neutrally. Yet even if the state *was* indifferent to all ways of life within its range of toleration, then it would still rightly be described as both tolerant and neutral (though probably not liberal). There is nothing (at least conceptually) in the general practice of toleration that requires anything more than indifference.

Nevertheless, the range of toleration and the range of neutrality in a liberal state will not entirely coincide. The range of liberal neutrality will be narrower than the range of liberal toleration. The liberal state will still tolerate, that is, not negatively interfere with some things that are outside its range of neutrality – these will primarily be things that contradict its conception of justice, but are still not sufficiently powerful to be able to commit acts of injustice. (The earlier example of the Dutch SGP's position on women may fit in here). Thus a liberal neutral regime of toleration will be sustained by acts of indifference *and* acts of tolerance.

A liberal neutral regime of toleration will also involve likely acts including respect for difference. A state could be both tolerant and neutral and respect difference. In relation to the examples discussed earlier, a neutral state should respect disability; may, if the liberal nationalist argument holds, respect national culture and identity; and, finally, may also take a "hands-on" rather than "hands-off" approach to neutrality, whereby the state attempts to actively recognize minority cultures.

This picture of the general practice of toleration, in which people's ways of life can be objects of forbearance tolerance, indifference, or respect for difference, holds irrespective of this discussion of neutrality. There is nothing in this understanding of toleration as a general practice that means this must be the case. This conceptual structure of toleration is entirely consistent with strong multicultural approaches to difference, as well as with liberal perfectionism and other non-neutral positions. This model of toleration simply describes the conditions under which a general practice of toleration can lead to the accommodation of ways of life. It is a separate normative question as to which is the right way to link the general practice of toleration with the accommodation (or not) of a way of life. Indeed this high degree of normative neutrality is one of the significant advantages of this model of toleration.

Three Further Challenges to Political Toleration

Using a general as well as a specific understanding of toleration and highlighting the range aspect of both toleration and neutrality deflate most of the conceptual challenge to political toleration. There are, nevertheless, three remaining issues: understanding state objection, locating state power, and Glen Newey's "symmetry thesis." These relate not to the general practice of toleration but the state's capacity to tolerate in the specific forbearance sense. Because liberal political toleration requires both the general *and* specific senses of toleration, the conceptual issues that apply to the specific sense also need addressing.

Understanding State Objection

David Heyd (2008: 178) and Peter Jones (2007: 387) both suggest that the state may not be the type of agent that can *experience* tolerance, that is, the "suffering" and reconciling of beliefs and practices which are not subscribed to are not something an impersonal institution such as the liberal state can be described as doing. Note though that this "suffering" view of tolerance has the features of a *personal* moral virtue; it requires the moral capacities of individuals, not institutions, and thus it clearly is not something that the state (or state-like institutions) can do, and they are thereby defined away. This seems to demand too much of the concept.

Tolerance as a moral virtue is not the only understanding of forbearance tolerance, and it should not be strange that it does not have institutional applicability. The more basic understanding put forward earlier simply requires grounds for objection and grounds for non-hindrance despite this objection. The idea of suffering is certainly not present in all conceptions of tolerance. Forst (2013), King (1976), and Kuhler (2019), for example, also simply have an "objection" component.

But even if we take toleration to involve objection rather than "suffering," it may not be clear how the state can object to (or for that matter respect or be indifferent to) a way of life. In the words of Heyd (2008: 178), "The law either permits or prohibits certain practices and activities. The prohibited act cannot be tolerated by the law and the permitted practice cannot be said to be endured as a matter of charity or restraint." Jones (2007) also accepts this view of the state but argues that forbearance tolerance is still relevant to liberal democratic political arrangements.

Understanding tolerance as a relationship rather than personal attitude seems a more apt way to think of tolerance in the political domain. In not overextending the use of tolerance as a moral virtue, a relational, rather than attitudinal interpretation of tolerance dissolves this problem. As Sune Lægaard (2015) argues, conceiving of tolerance as a relationship, rather than attitude, makes it entirely applicable to impersonal institutions such as the state. Rather than focus on whether or not an agent has a particular attitude or particular motive – something that would be required for a virtue understanding of tolerance – a relational account focusses on what can be publicly known about the relationship between an agent and a subject of tolerance (Lægaard 2015: 10).

Even so, for a state to be said to be engaging in an act of forbearance tolerance, objection must be present, and the question remains of how it can be said that a state objects to something. To be clear, the question is not whether government or executive members object but whether the state itself objects (Jones 2007: 385–386; and Lægaard 2015: 9). Cohen (2014: 22) suggests that for the state to be engaging in forbearance tolerance, it is enough that it *need not* object and that state officials *might* object. But this solution demonstrates the difficulty of trying to use only the forbearance conception of tolerance to understand political relations. He seems to be grounding all objection on officials rather than states – which misses the point – and also to be using a generally permissive conception of toleration (which he rejects). It might seem that locating objection is a big task, but it does seem possible to know whether or not the state objects to something. Objection might be inferred from its actions (e.g., it has outlawed similar illiberal political parties in the past), be publicly expressed (e.g., a stated position against smoking), or even be written into its constitution. Likewise, reasons for non-interference, which are also required for acts of tolerance, may be either publicly stated or inferred from past actions. It is worth noting that this relational analysis of tolerance can be applied to respect too and thus shows how both concepts can have institutional applicability (Lægaard 2015: 10–12).

Locating State Power

There is a second issue tied up in the quote from Heyd, and this is whether the state actually has the power to negatively interfere – remember power is a necessary condition. On the face of it, and especially if one uses a material sense of power, it seems obvious that the state has a lot of power and could negatively interfere in a whole range of activities. But if one assumes the state is liberal, then it might seem that this sort of power is quickly limited – constitutions and the like are designed to explicitly limit state power. On this understanding, there is no space for forbearance tolerance or indeed any intentional withholding of power – no such power exists.

There are three ways of dealing with this problem. The first is to maintain a material understanding of power: the state could negatively interfere, but does not because of constitutional provisions. The second is to accept such limits on power but look a little deeper at what they might mean. Heyd's challenge is that states do not have *any* power in relation to constitutionally protected freedoms. But this seems a little too quick and relies on intolerance involving complete prevention, rather than negative interference. A liberal state may, because of constitutional provisions for free speech, permit a group whose activities undermine its core values of free and equal citizenship but may still take steps to "talk back" (Brettschneider 2012). Take the case of the Westboro Baptist Church, whose central theological message is "God hates fags." The 2011 Supreme Court decision (*Snyder v Phelps*) upheld their right to picket soldier's funerals (the deaths of US soldiers were seen by the church as God's punishment for permitting homosexuality in the USA). But as Corey Brettschneider argues, the case need not end there. For even if free speech is protected from the coercive power of the state, it need not be protected from its expressive power. Brettschneider argues that the state has a role as an educator, speaker, and spender to promote the counterview of free and equal citizenship and that its demonstration of non-neutrality in these cases can involve not giving subsidies such as tax exemptions and tax deductibility to such groups (Brettschneider 2012: 133–134). This suggests that even if a state cannot outlaw such groups, it can negatively interfere with their practice.

Finally, this discussion of power has avoided all the areas that are not constitutionally protected and which require states to make decisions and trade-offs. Take the case of Hizb ut-Tahrir, for example. The British government had planned to ban the organization following the 2005 London bombings, but decided not to because "driving it underground could backfire" (Morris 2006). Or, as seems to be the case throughout the world, the decision to focus limited resources on religiously motivated terrorism, but not on domestic violence (which has killed many more people). Given the state does object in both cases, and could do something more, but decides not to, it is rightly said to be engaging in forbearance tolerance.

The "Symmetry Thesis"

The third issue that needs addressing if the state is said to be tolerant in both senses is Newey's "symmetry thesis" (Newey 1999, 2001: 325–326, 2010). More recently,

Newey (2013: 51–54) has slightly qualified this view, but it is still held as central to political conflict. Newey argues that where two civil society groups come into conflict, each side can level the charge of intolerance against the other. He uses the example of Northern Ireland Orange Order lodges wanting to march through Catholic neighborhoods and residents of these Catholic neighborhoods not wanting them to do so. As such, there may be no uniquely tolerant action for the state to take (Newey 1999: 161, 2001: 319–321, 2010: 223). If the state is supposed to be a third-party authority in these sorts of disputes, then it is not at all clear which action would be tolerant – both parties to the conflict can claim the other is intolerant, and whichever party the state supports will simply have its intolerance enforced. For Newey, what may appear to be acts of state tolerance are not actually tolerance – to force tolerance for one side is at the same time to be intolerant of the other, and thus the problem of 'tolerating the intolerant" is a central rather than marginal issue for political toleration (Newey 1999: 160–162, 2001: 320–321). What looks like an act of tolerance – for example, allowing the Orange Order lodge to march – is in fact an act of intolerance, and thus in democratic circumstances, democratic toleration is a "rubber duck." In these circumstances, both "democratic" and "rubber" are alienans adjectives; if a duck is made of rubber, it cannot really be a duck, and similarly for Newey, if toleration is democratic, it cannot really be toleration.

There are, however, a number of ways in which Newey's symmetry thesis can be resisted and the coherence of state acts of forbearance tolerance can be maintained. The first is to note that it entails a view of the state as an arbiter of democratic claims. For Newey the political circumstances of toleration occur when a civil society dispute is taken to the state – if one of the parties to such a dispute is willing to forbear, then there is no political question to address (Newey 2001: 319). But note that this view of the state is the same "neutral" view that was rejected in the previous section. Perhaps purely democratic tolerance is not possible, but this does not mean that *liberal* tolerance is not possible.

Second, we can examine the plausibility of the symmetry thesis more directly. According to Newey, both an antiabortion activist who tries to stop a women having an abortion and a woman who goes ahead with an abortion are intolerant; they are both performing actions the other does not want them to (Newey 2010: 224–225, 226). Now the easy way out of this problem is to simply claim some other principle, perhaps a "right to choose" or a "right to life," and ascribe intolerance to the party going against your preferred principle. But this is to unnecessarily, and unhelpfully, moralize tolerance – and Newey rightly avoids this move. Instead the third part of the definition of tolerance, "intentionally not negatively interfering with this thing or its holder" (Balint 2014), offers useful guidance. For what is an act of intolerance but intentionally negatively interfering with a thing or its holder (on the basis of an objection)? The woman who ignores the antiabortion activist on her way into the clinic is not, perhaps despite objection, negatively interfering with the person who wishes to stop her having an abortion. (She may, of course, be acting intolerantly toward the fetus, but this is not the symmetry). For her to be said to be intolerant of the protester, she would have to take some more direct action, such as perhaps confronting the protester and attempting to intimidate him into leaving. Moreover, any action taken would have to be intentional; it is not enough to just happen to go against someone else's wishes. So without invoking further values, we can say that the woman having the abortion is not intolerant in this sense, whereas, at least under certain, but not all conditions, the protester could be said to be acting intolerantly.

If we accept that intolerance is intentional negative inference (on the basis of objection), then we also do not need to follow Peter Jones' suggestion that to resist the symmetry thesis, intolerance should be understood as "curtailing agency." That is, for an act to be one of intolerance and not something else, someone's freedom must be restricted in some way (Jones 2007: 398). On this understanding of intolerance, someone's agency must be curtailed for intolerance to have taken place; simply having your wishes contradicted is not intolerance. Therefore, according to Jones, not all cases of toleration would be symmetrical because not all claims of intolerance actually involve intolerance.

The main problem with using a curtailing agency understanding of an act of intolerance is, as Newey argues, a problem of how to deal with issues of identity (Newey 2010: 225–226). If something is said or done that is offensive to you, you might rightly claim to be wronged, but it seems a stretch to say your agency has been curtailed. Thus Jones, in his defense of a curtailing agency view of intolerance, needs to use a wide view of agency that includes "manifesting a particular identity" (Jones 2007: 398). Without including identity as part of agency, symbolic acts such as desecrating a religious text could not be classified as intolerant acts on this account. But intentional negative interference seems a much more accurate depiction of an act of intolerance and one that usefully avoids issues of agency and identity. Putting a pig's head outside a Mosque or throwing stones at a group holding a funeral procession both involve intentional negative interference and are intolerant acts, whether or not anyone's agency is curtailed. Indeed, a further problem for identity-based agency accounts is that acts such as these, while being intolerant, might inadvertently strengthen rather than curtail the agency of their victims. It is quite likely that the consequences of some acts of intolerance might cause victims to both have their identities strengthened and feel empowered to take action – witness the "rally-round-the-flag" phenomenon.

Returning to the symmetry thesis, then, even in cases where the state is called to arbitrate disputes, it is not necessarily the case that both parties are equally or even symmetrically intolerant. We do not necessarily need a normative principle to adjudicate which party is intolerant; a descriptive understanding of intolerance is sufficient. In many cases we can say that one party wants intolerance and the other liberty. To use an example from Jones (2010: 445–447) that does not play on liberal sympathies when one group wants to practice pedophilia and the other wants to stop them, it is those who wish to stop them who are the intolerant party (and rightly so). Whatever else the wrongs of paedophiles, intolerance of those who wish them to desist is not one of them.

Thus the symmetry thesis does not make political tolerance a conceptual error. Without denying that there may well be cases where the symmetry thesis holds, there are many cases when tolerance is not symmetrical; liberal states are not simply arbiters in civil society disputes but have their own values on which they may also object; and not all civil society disputes involve symmetrical intolerance either. As such, both the general and specific senses of toleration are applicable to liberal states.

8 Political Toleration Explained

Let me conclude this section with a final point of disagreement with Newey's approach – his view of the political. Newey argues that the political involves conflict, writing:

> Suppose that there is some practice, and that it is carried on or supported by one group, while being opposed by another. Of course, the latter may choose to suffer in silence, or adopt low-level methods of expressing disapproval, to which the first group takes no exception. This happens a lot of the time. In this case, it seems, *there is no political question to address*. (Newey 2001: 319, emphasis added)

But we need to be careful about saying political questions only arise when conflict clearly occurs (such as in the Orange Order marching case) and when the state is directly involved in mediation. This view seems too narrow. It first misses the role that political structures and institutions have in avoiding, minimizing, or containing conflict. And second, we need to remember that not all institutions and structures are under the direct control of the state either. Acts of tolerance between citizens that allow individuals to do important public activities (e.g., get a job, housing, etc.) are relevantly political as they also minimize or contain conflict. Newey's focus on whether the state is (or is not) tolerant avoids both these dimensions of political toleration and which a full understanding will need to include.

Part of this problem may stem from Newey's central question of politics – "What do we do?" – and his inclusion of deliberation as a necessary component of the political (2013: 24–27). Newey (2013: 23) also argues that "no prior limits can be placed on the content of politics" and that attempts to define politics are themselves political (see also Newey 2011). It is worth noting that this chapter and Newey have differing positions on "the political," and thus this plays out in the different understandings of political toleration. The chapter has assumed a focus on *liberal* political toleration and has thus used a broadly liberal (though certainly not Rawlsian) understanding of the "political." Newey (2013: 31–32) instead seems to be working with a very permissive democratic understanding of the "political." Newey's deliberative component, though not intended to be normative, leads to a particular understanding of the political – and one where politics is explicit. The liberal understanding is normative, even if broadly so, but allows the political to be about sites of power (and conflict) that may be much less explicit in nature but are within the purview of a broadly liberal approach. It seems this is ultimately a tension between a broadly liberal approach to political toleration and a broadly democratic approach to the same set of issues. And while the two might overlap, there are distinct differences.

Conclusion

When explained, the problem of political toleration may seem to render the concept oxymoronic. But the challenges to political toleration rely on idiosyncratic conceptual understandings. This is certainly the case with The Neutrality Challenge. No state, especially a liberal state, will be neutral toward everything. They have values, particularly those of justice, and will only be neutral within a particular range. This leaves plenty of scope to forbear practices that conflict with its values while still rightly being considered neutral. Moreover, a generally tolerant state need not forbear at all. Toleration as a general political practice is consistent with, and typically involves, respect, indifference, and forbearance tolerance toward the specific differences of the citizenry. To require only forbearance tolerance is to be unnecessarily beholden to a very recent orthodoxy. But while this explains the general nature of political toleration and removes The Neutrality Challenge, political toleration is still vulnerable to critiques in its specific forbearance tolerance form. But both state power and state objection can be made sense of, and while Newey's "symmetry thesis" *may* trouble purely democratic toleration, liberal political toleration still makes sense. Despite the changes since the early modern period in forms of political power, political toleration is still conceptually coherent.

Note: This chapter draws upon Chapter 2 of Peter Balint (2017) *Respecting Toleration: Traditional Liberalism and Contemporary Diversity* (Oxford: Oxford University Press).

References

Balint P (2013) Against respecting each others' differences. J Appl Philos 30:254–267

Balint P (2014) Acts of tolerance: a political and descriptive account. Eur J Polit Theo 13:264–281

Balint P (2015) Identity claims: why liberal neutrality is the solution, not the problem. Polit Stud 63:495–509

Balint P (2016) The importance of racial tolerance for anti-racism. Ethn Racial Stud 39(1):16–32

Balint P (2017) Respecting toleration: traditional liberalism & contemporary diversity. Oxford University Press, Oxford

Bessone M (2013) Will the real tolerant racist please stand up? J Appl Philos 30(3):209–223

Brettschneider C (2012) When the state speaks, what should it say? How democracies can protect expression and promote equality. Princeton University Press, Princeton

Churchill RP (2003) Neutrality and the virtue of toleration. In: Castiglione D, McKinnon C (eds) Toleration, neutrality and democracy. Kluwer, Dordrecht, pp 65–76

Cohen AJ (2014) Toleration. Polity Press, Cambridge

Cranston M (1987) John Locke and the case for toleration. In: Mendus S, Edwards D (eds) On toleration. Oxford University Press, Oxford, pp 99–121

Crick B (1971) Toleration and tolerance in theory and practice. Gov Oppos 6:144–171

Darwall SL (1977) Two kinds of respect. Ethics 88(1):36–49

Davies G (2006) The Netherlands: (thou shalt not discriminate against women: public subsidies to religious parties condemned in *Clara Wichmann foundation* v. *The Dutch State*. Court of first instance, the Hague. Judgment of 7 September 2005). Eur Const Law Rev 2(1):152–166

De Ceva E (2019) The good of toleration: changing social relations or maximising individual freedom? Crit Rev Int Soc Pol Phil. https://doi.org/10.1080/13698230.2019.1609398

Forst R (2004) The limits of toleration. Constellations 11(3):312–325

Forst R (2013) Toleration in conflict. Cambridge University Press, Cambridge

Galeotti AE (2001) Do we need toleration as a moral virtue. Res Publica 7:273–292

Gray J (1995) Enlightenment's wake: politics and culture at the close of the modern age. Routledge, London

Habermas J (2004) Religious tolerance–the pacemaker for cultural rights. Philosophy 79(1):5–18

Heyd D (2008) Is toleration a political virtue? In: Williams MS, Waldron J (eds) Toleration and its limits (NOMOS 48). New York University Press, New York, pp 171–194

8 Political Toleration Explained

Horton J (1994) Three (apparent) paradoxes of toleration. Synth Philos 17:7–20

Horton J (1996) Toleration as a virtue. In: Heyd D (ed) Toleration: an elusive virtue. Princeton University Press, Princeton, pp 28–43

Jenkinson SL (1996) Two concepts of tolerance: or why Bayle is not Locke. J Polit Philos 4(4):302–321

Jones P (2007) Making sense of political toleration. Br J Polit Sci 37(3):383–402

Jones P (2010) Political toleration: a reply to Newey. Br J Polit Sci 41:445–447

Kaplan BJ (2007) Divided by faith: religious conflict and the practice of toleration in early modern Europe. Harvard University Press, Harvard

King P (1976) Toleration. George Allen & Unwin, London

Kühler M (2019) Can a value-neutral liberal state still be tolerant? Crit Rev Int Soc Pol Phil. https://doi.org/10.1080/13698230.2019.1616878

Lægaard S (2015) Attitudinal analyses of toleration and respect and the problem of institutional applicability. Eur J Philos 3(4):1064–1081

Lenard PT (2012) Trust, democracy, and the challenges of multiculturalism. Penn State University Press, University Park

Locke J ([1690] 1824) Second letter on toleration. In: The works of John Locke in nine volumes, 12th edn, vol 5. Rivington, London, pp 59–138

Meckled-Garcia S (2001) Toleration and neutrality: incompatible ideals? Res Publica 7:293–313

Miller D (1995) On nationality. Oxford University Press, Oxford

Morris N (2006) PM forced to shelve Islamist group ban. The Independent, 18 Jul 2006

Newey G (1999) Virtue reason and toleration. Edinburgh University Press, Edinburgh

Newey G (2001) Is democratic toleration a rubber duck? Res Publica 7(3):315–336

Newey G (2010) Political toleration: a reply to Jones. Br J Polit Sci 41(1):223–227

Newey G (2011) Philosophy, politics and contestability. J Polit Ide 6(3):245–261

Newey G (2013) Toleration in political conflict. Cambridge University Press, Cambridge

Newman J (1982) Foundations of religious tolerance. University of Toronto Press, Toronto

Nicholson P (1985) Toleration as a moral ideal. In: Horton J, Mendus S (eds) Aspects of toleration. Methuen, London, pp 158–173

Popper K (1945) The open society and its enemies, Volume 1: the spell of Plato. Routledge, London

Raphael DD (1988) The intolerable. In: Mendus S (ed) Justifying toleration: conceptual and historical perspectives. Cambridge University Press, Cambridge, pp 137–154

Rawls J (1999) A theory of justice. Harvard University Press, Boston

Raz J (1986) The morality of freedom. Oxford University Press, Oxford

Scheffler S (2010) The good of toleration. In: Scheffler S (ed) Equality and tradition: questions of value in moral and political theory. Oxford University Press, Oxford, pp 312–336

Seligman AB (2003) Tolerance, tradition and modernity. Cardozo Law Rev 24(4):1645–1656

Soutphommasane T (2012) The virtuous citizen: patriotism in a multicultural society. Cambridge University Press, Cambridge

Tamir Y (1993) Liberal nationalism. Princeton University Press, Princeton

Tate JW (2016) Liberty, toleration and equality: John Locke, Jonas Proast and the letters concerning toleration. Routledge, New York

Walzer M (1997) On toleration. Yale University Press, London

Zagorin P (2003) How the idea of religious toleration came to the West. Princeton University Press, Princeton

Toleration, Respect for Persons, and the Free Speech Right to Do Moral Wrong

9

Kristian Skagen Ekeli

Contents

Introduction 150
Political Toleration and Viewpoint-Based Restrictions on Extremist Speech 152
Heyman and Quong on Extremist Viewpoints and the Limits of Toleration 153
    Heyman's Argument 153
    Quong's Argument 156
Viewpoint Neutrality, Political Toleration, and the Free Speech Right to Do
Moral Wrong 159
Respect for Persons as Thinking Agents: A Libertarian Status-Based Theory of Rights 161
Do Persons Have a Basic Right to Recognition or Dignity? 166
The Silencing Effects of Extremist Speech 167
Summary and Future Directions 170
References 171

Abstract

The purpose of this chapter is to consider the question of whether respect for persons requires toleration of the expression of *any* extremist political or religious viewpoint within public discourse. The starting point of my discussion is Steven Heyman and Jonathan Quong's interesting defences of a negative answer to this question. They argue that respect for persons requires that liberal democracies should not tolerate the public expression of extremist speech that can be regarded as recognition-denying or respect-denying speech – that is, speech or other expressive conduct that expresses viewpoints that explicitly reject that *all* persons should be regarded and treated as free and equal persons or citizens. According to

---

I would especially like to thank Eric Heinze and Kjartan Koch Mikalsen for valuable comments and discussions. Thanks also go to Steven Heyman and Jonathan Quong for useful comments on earlier drafts of my presentation of their positions and arguments.

K. S. Ekeli (✉)
University of Stavanger, Stavanger, Norway
e-mail: kristian.ekeli@uis.no

© The Author(s), under exclusive licence to Springer Nature Switzerland AG 2022   149
M. Sardoč (ed.), *The Palgrave Handbook of Toleration*,
https://doi.org/10.1007/978-3-030-42121-2_39

Heyman and Quong, recognition-denying speech falls outside the scope of the right to participate in public discourse (i.e., what it is a right *to*). In contrast to Heyman and Quong, one can argue that a strong case can be made for viewpoint neutrality on the basis of what can be called a libertarian or Nozickean status-based theory of rights. According to this theory, toleration in a liberal democracy requires respect for the status of persons as thinking agents, and respect for thinking agents and their sovereignty over their own mind requires viewpoint neutrality – that is, a basic right to participate in public discourse as speakers and listeners free from state-imposed viewpoint-based restrictions. All persons should have a basic right to express, hear, and consider any viewpoint within public discourse. This doctrine of viewpoint neutrality requires that citizens in liberal democracies ought to have a *legal* free speech right to do *moral* wrong – that is, a legal right to express and defend any viewpoint within public discourse, even if it is morally wrong to express, or expose others to, such views.

Keywords

Extremist speech · Freedom of expression · Jonathan Quong · Respect for persons · Robert Nozick · The right to do wrong · Toleration · Steven Heyman · Viewpoint neutrality

Introduction

In the liberal tradition of political philosophy, it is a widely held assumption that political institutions in a liberal democracy should show respect for persons. However, even within the liberal tradition, there is deep disagreement about what respect for persons or the dignity of persons requires. This disagreement is evident in ongoing debates about toleration and the right to freedom of expression – especially in discussions about the extent to which liberal democracies should tolerate or ban the public expression of different forms of extremist political or religious viewpoints, such as hate speech and advocacy of terrorism. Respect for persons is a Janus-faced requirement that can be cited on both sides in these debates about toleration and the scope of the right to participate in public discourse as speakers and listeners. On the one hand, one can argue that respect for persons requires that liberal democracies should tolerate the expression of any political or religious viewpoint within public discourse (see, e.g., Dworkin 1996, 2009; Brettschneider 2012; Ekeli 2020). On the other hand, one can argue that respect for persons or the dignity of persons requires certain viewpoint-based restrictions on extremist speech (see, e.g., Heyman 2008, 2009; Quong 2004, 2011; Waldron 2012).

The purpose of this chapter is to consider the question of whether respect for persons requires toleration of the expression of *any* extremist political or religious viewpoint within public discourse. *Public discourse* can be said to refer to processes of deliberation on matters "concerning the organization and culture of society" or issues of public concern (Barendt 2005: 189. See also Heinze 2016: 27–30). It includes speech or other expressive conduct that is relevant to intrapersonal and interpersonal deliberation on both political and religious questions and issues. Interpersonal deliberation refers to the process of discussion with others or interpersonal communications, such as a debate in a legislative assembly or other public fora. Intrapersonal deliberation refers to an individual's internal reflections (or considerations) on political or religious issues – for example, when we read a newspaper or watch a political discussion on TV and deliberate about the pros and cons of alternative policies (Ekeli 2012: 282).

The starting point of my discussion is Steven Heyman and Jonathan Quong's interesting defenses of a negative answer to the outlined question about toleration of extremist speech. They argue that respect for persons requires that liberal democracies should not tolerate the public expression of extremist speech that can be regarded as recognition-denying or respect-denying speech – that is, speech or other expressive conduct that expresses viewpoints or ideas that explicitly reject that *all* persons should be regarded and treated as free and equal persons or citizens. According to Heyman and Quong, recognition-denying speech falls outside the scope of the right to participate in public discourse (i.e., what it is a right *to*). Both Heyman and Quong reject that citizens in a liberal democracy should have a free speech right to do moral wrong that includes a right to express recognition-denying political and religious viewpoints within public discourse. As Quong points out, the public expression of recognition-denying viewpoints, such as hate speech, is unreasonable, and "there is no right to be unreasonable" (Quong 2011: 309).

In contrast to Heyman and Quong, one can argue that a strong case can be made for viewpoint neutrality on the basis of what can be called a libertarian or Nozickean status-based theory of rights. According to this theory, toleration in a liberal democracy requires respect for the status of persons as thinking agents, and respect for thinking agents and their sovereignty over their own mind requires viewpoint neutrality – that is, a basic right to participate in public discourse as speakers and listeners free from state-imposed viewpoint-based restrictions (Ekeli 2020). All persons – including radical extremists – should have a basic right to express, hear, and consider any political or religious viewpoint within public discourse. This doctrine of viewpoint neutrality requires that citizens in liberal democracies ought to have a *legal* free speech right to do *moral* wrong – that is, a legal right to express and defend any political and religious viewpoint or idea, even if it is morally wrong to express, or expose others to, such views. For example, this means that extremists should have a right to express their viewpoints within public discourse even if these viewpoints cause psychological harms.

This chapter proceeds as follows. Section "Political Toleration and Viewpoint-Based Restrictions on Extremist Speech" gives an account of different kinds of restrictions on speech – especially viewpoint-based restrictions. Section "Heyman and Quong on Extremist Viewpoints and the Limits of Toleration" sets out Heyman and Quong's arguments for the position that respect for persons requires that liberal democracies should not tolerate the public expression of recognition-denying speech. The aim of section "Viewpoint Neutrality, Political Toleration, and the Free Speech Right to Do Moral Wrong" is to present the doctrine of viewpoint neutrality, and explain the way in which this doctrine requires that citizens in a liberal democracy ought to have a legal free speech right to do moral wrong. Section "Respect for Persons as Thinking Agents: A Libertarian Status-Based Theory of Rights" sets out a case for the doctrine of viewpoint neutrality. In sections "Do Persons Have a Basic Right to Recognition or Dignity?" and "The Silencing Effects of Extremist Speech," two problems facing the doctrine of viewpoint neutrality are discussed. The first concerns the issue of whether persons have a basic right to recognition or dignity that outweighs the basic right to express, hear, and consider any viewpoint or idea within public discourse. The second problem concerns the silencing effects of extremist speech.

Political Toleration and Viewpoint-Based Restrictions on Extremist Speech

The liberal ideal of toleration requires A (e.g., an individual, a group, a state, or a majority) to permit B (i.e., individuals or groups) to do X, even when A strongly dislikes or disapproves of X (e.g., B's actions, beliefs, or practices). My discussion of the scope and limits of toleration will primarily focus on what can be called political toleration. Like Peter Jones, my point of departure is that *political toleration* refers to toleration secured through the apparatus of the state (Jones 2007). In a liberal democracy, political toleration is located in the political and legal institutions that regulate and constrain people's conduct in order to protect the freedom of individuals and groups or their choice-protecting rights. A tolerant liberal democracy is a political order in which the state's political and legal institutions secure a state of affairs where B is not prevented from doing X by A – that is, intolerant others (individuals, groups, or a majority of citizens and their elected representatives) who dislike or disapprove of X and who might otherwise impede B from doing X. A central aspect of a liberal democracy is that it is tolerant in virtue of preventing A from using coercive political power to prevent B from doing X.

Even among those who defend a liberal democratic state, there is deep disagreement about the scope and limits of political toleration. One central question about the scope and limits of toleration concerns whether, and to what extent, it is permissible for a majority of citizens and their elected representatives to enact, and authorize the enforcement of, viewpoint-based restrictions on extremist speech – such as hate speech, holocaust denial, blasphemy, or speech that advocate or encourage terrorism.

In order to explain what viewpoint-based restrictions refer to, it can be useful to make a distinction between three kinds of restrictions on speech that play an important role in US constitutional law. *Content-neutral restrictions* limit communication for reasons that are unrelated to the content or message of the expression – such as restrictions on time, place, or manner of the exercise of speech (e.g., political demonstrations). *Content-based restrictions* limit communication because of the content or message of the expression. However, all content-based restrictions are not viewpoint-based. For example, a ban on all political speech in a certain place (e. g., airports or railway stations) is content-based, but viewpoint neutral.

Viewpoint-based restrictions or viewpoint-selective restrictions are a subset of content-based restrictions that restrict the communication of particular ideas or viewpoints. Such restrictions differentiate and discriminate between different political or ideological viewpoints. Typically, viewpoint-based restrictions are *viewpoint discriminatory* in the sense that they grant freedom to express, hear, and consider the state-approved viewpoint in public discourse, but prohibit some forms of expression of a competing viewpoint (Heinze 2016: 20 and 22). In a political context, viewpoint-based restrictions suppress at least some forms of expression of the viewpoints or ideas of one side in a political debate or disagreement.

Heyman and Quong on Extremist Viewpoints and the Limits of Toleration

Both Heyman and Quong argue that respect for persons requires that liberal democracies should not tolerate recognition-denying speech. This refers to speech or other expressive conduct that expresses viewpoints or ideas that fulfill one of the two following related conditions. (1) The viewpoints explicitly reject or deny that all persons should be regarded and treated as free and equal persons. (2) The viewpoints violate the idea or requirement that persons should recognize and respect each other as free and equal persons. According to their theories of toleration and freedom of expression, recognition-denying or respect-denying speech falls outside the *scope* of the right to participate in public discourse.

The starting point of Heyman and Quong's arguments is the abstract liberal idea that citizens should be regarded and treated as free and equal persons or citizens, and that this idea provides the core foundation or justificatory basis of liberal democratic rights. Persons should be regarded as *free* in the sense that they are rational and moral agents with plans and projects for their own life. Persons should be regarded as *equal* in the sense that they have the same fundamental moral status (Quong 2011: 14; Heyman 2008: chs. 1 and 3).

Heyman's Argument

The point of departure of Heyman's argument is that rights are based on respect for the dignity and freedom (i.e., autonomy) of persons (Heyman 2008: 2 and 37–40). For Heyman, dignity refers to the Kantian idea that a person possesses an absolute inner worth that commands respect from others. Proceeding from this idea about respect for the dignity of persons, Heyman claims that all persons have a *right to recognition* – that is, a right to be recognized and respected as a free and equal person. This right has a special status and significance within a framework of rights. According to Heyman, rights are rooted in respect for personhood, and an individual cannot enjoy rights in relation to others unless they recognize him or her as a person. The right to recognition is the most fundamental right that individuals have, and it lies at the basis of all their other rights – including their right to participate in public discourse (Heyman 2008: 171).

Heyman assumes that the outlined dignity-based justification or foundation of the right to participate in public discourse limits the scope of this right. The idea is that recognition-denying speech falls outside the scope of the right to participate in public discourse, because the public expression of recognition-denying viewpoints violate the claim-right to recognition and the correlative *duty of recognition* – that is, the duty of individuals to recognize and respect others as free and equal persons and citizens.

> Although individuals have a right to take part in public discourse, they also have a duty [of recognition] to respect other citizens as equal participants in that discourse. In other words, it is not enough that the *state* should view individuals as free and equal; citizens must also view *one another* in this light. (Heyman 2008: 175)

The duty of recognition can be understood as an integral feature of public discourse itself (Heyman 2008: 176). According to Heyman, this duty is a ground rule – a civility rule – that should govern public discourse, and recognition-denying speech, such as hate speech, violates this ground rule or duty. Heyman's ideas about the connection between public discourse and the duty of recognition also play a central role in his moralized understanding of political speech. "[P]*olitical speech* is best understood as discourse among individuals who recognize one another as free and equal persons and members of the community" (Heyman 2008: 177; italics added). According to Heyman, "the duty to refrain from speech that denies recognition to others is not one that is imposed on public discourse from the outside, but one that is inherent in the concept of political freedom of speech" (Heyman 2008: 179). This means that recognition-denying speech falls outside the scope of the right to freedom of political speech properly understood. There is no right to recognition-denying speech – such as public hate speech. In Heyman's words, "public hate speech does not fall within the ... right to political freedom of speech" (Heyman 2009: 177). In view of this moralized understanding of public discourse and political speech, Heyman assumes that the right to participate in public discourse has an exception clause – i.e., a *recognition or respect clause* – that limits the *scope* of this right. The idea appears to be that P has a right to participate in public discourse except in cases where P uses or exercises this right in a way that violates the moral duty to recognize and respect the dignity of others as free and equal persons.

Heyman's argument from mutual recognition and respect does not only provide a basis for viewpoint-based restrictions on hate speech, but also other forms of recognition-denying speech, such as advocacy of terrorism. Typically, acts of expression that advocate or encourage political violence against innocent civilians are forms of recognition-denying speech, in the sense that such speech denies recognition to others and expresses a lack of respect for the dignity and the moral status of the potential targets of terrorism. For example, direct and indirect encouragements to kill innocent civilians in order to promote political objectives constitute an explicit rejection of the dignity and the equal moral status of persons. Like the

UK's Terrorism Act 2006, one can say that indirect encouragements to terrorism primarily refer to glorification of terrorism – for example, praise or celebration of suicide bombings or holy war (or Jihad).

Heyman seems to distinguish between two aspects of the wrongfulness of recognition-denying speech, and these throw light on why the public expression of such extremist viewpoints should not be tolerated in a liberal democracy. First, both Heyman and Quong seem to regard recognition-denying speech as a *malum in se* – a wrong in itself. The idea is that the public expression of recognition-denying viewpoints is inherently immoral or unjust through the aim or intention to diminish or reject equal respect for all persons or citizens. Recognition-denying speech, such as hate speech, is wrong in itself because it degrades its targets. The expressive act itself inherently denies equal respect for all persons or the equal worth or dignity of all persons or citizens. This provides a strong reason for bans on such speech, regardless of whether any further harmful or detrimental effects can be traced back to it. Thus, hate speech is a *malum in se* that should not be tolerated, irrespective of whether the public expression of hateful viewpoints causes psychological harms, increases the likelihood of violence, or pollutes the social and moral environment of the society.

Second, recognition-denying speech is wrongful and harmful because it undermines or violates the rights of its targets. As we have seen, Heyman claims that recognition-denying speech violates the right to recognition or dignity, and this is a serious matter because he regards this as "the most basic right of all" (Heyman 2008: 183). According to Heyman, recognition-denying speech can also undermine or violate other rights, such as the right to participate in public discourse. Recognition-denying speech does not only violate the ground rules of public discourse (as outlined above). It also has a silencing effect that undermines or violates its targets' right to participate in public discourse. Heyman sets out the following *silencing effect argument* for certain viewpoint-based restrictions on extremist speech, such as hate speech.

> [H]ate speech tends to silence its targets and undermine their right to free expression. Because political discourse involves interaction with others, an individual cannot fully engage in such discourse unless other citizens are willing to interact with her and take her views seriously. By refusing to engage in discourse with their targets and by dissuading other citizens from doing so, hate speakers curtail the ability of target-group members to take part in democratic deliberation. Hate speech can also silence its targets by diminishing their sense of personal security and by attacking their dignity in ways that discourage them from full participation in the life of the community. These considerations suggest that hate speech regulation is justified not only to secure other rights but also to protect freedom of expression itself. (Heyman 2008: 279, note 65)

More recently, Alexander Brown has developed a similar silencing effect argument that also focuses on how certain forms of extremist speech can undermine its targets' opportunity to participate in democratic deliberation or public discourse as "ordinary deliberative democrats" (Brown 2015: 198). Both Heyman and Brown defend certain viewpoint-based restrictions on extremist speech within public discourse the aim of which is to promote the overall freedom or opportunity to participate in public discourse for *all* persons in a democratic society. Since this silencing effect argument can be regarded as an important objection to the doctrine of viewpoint neutrality, it will be discussed in more detail in section "The Silencing Effects of Extremist Speech."

Quong's Argument

In his discussion of the rights of "unreasonable" extremist citizens, Quong also defends the position that respect for persons requires that liberal democracies should not tolerate recognition-denying speech. According to Quong, unreasonable citizens that reject fundamental liberal democratic values have all the normal rights and liberties of citizenship. However, the otherwise valid rights claims of unreasonable citizens cease to be valid when they are used in the pursuit of *unreasonable objectives* or activities – that is, objectives or activities that do not respect the freedom and equality of persons or "activities that are motivated by, or aim at, the rejection of fair cooperation between free and equal citizens" (Quong 2011: 308. See also Quong 2004: 332).

The idea is that unreasonable citizens and groups cannot be denied any of the liberal democratic rights of citizenship just because they reject fundamental liberal democratic values and rights, but they can be prevented from exercising those rights when their aims are explicitly unreasonable. The rights in question cease to be rights when unreasonable citizens or groups exercise or attempt to exercise them in this way. The reason is that unreasonable activities are in clear conflict with the justificatory basis or ground of liberal democratic rights, and such activities "cannot plausibly be protected by liberal [democratic] rights" (Quong 2011: 310). Like Heyman, Quong assumes that there is a close link between the foundation of rights (i.e., the normative idea that citizens should be regarded and treated as free and equal persons) and the specification of the scope of rights.

> Any alleged right must be at least consistent with the ideal of citizens as free and equal. . . . [U]nreasonable activities – activities that are motivated by, or aim at, the rejection of fair cooperation between free and equal citizens – are not protected by standard individual rights and freedoms. Such unreasonable activities are by definition inconsistent with the moral ideal upon which rights are grounded, and so they cannot be protected by such rights. . . . [B]ecause that moral ideal [of citizens as free and equal] is where our reasoning about justice begins, . . . the rights and benefits of citizenship are meant to aid citizens only in the pursuit of those conceptions of the good life that are compatible with that ideal. (Quong 2011: 308–309 and 312)

Choice-protecting (or liberty-protecting) liberal democratic rights, such as freedom of association, only protect *reasonable choices* – that is, choices that "respect the freedom and equality of persons" (Quong 2004: 332). This means that the choice-protecting right to freedom of association does not cover the liberty or freedom to choose to join a racist political or religious organization, or the liberty to establish such organizations. Presumably, this also applies to the right to join or form an Islamophobic organization, the aim of which is to establish a political regime that will deny Muslims political and civil rights – for example, deny Muslims the civil right to equality before the law and political rights to participate in political processes. Quong assumes that choice-protecting liberal democratic rights have an exception clause – i.e., a reasonableness clause – that limits the *scope* of such rights. The idea is that P has a liberal democratic right to X except in circumstances where P uses or attempts to use the right in the pursuit of unreasonable objectives.

Quong's position has important implications with regard to the scope of the right to participate in public discourse and permissible viewpoint-based restrictions on extremist political and religious speech. There is no right to be unreasonable, and the public expression of recognition-denying viewpoints is unreasonable. Thus, Quong claims that there is no right to extremist recognition-denying speech, such as hate speech – that is, "expression whose primary intention is to deny the freedom or equality of persons or citizens" (Quong 2011: 305, note 45). Like Heyman's theory of the limits of toleration and freedom of speech, Quong's theory will open the door to a wide range of viewpoint-based restrictions on extremist political and religious speech that can be regarded as recognition-denying or respect-denying speech. It will, for example, be permissible for a liberal democracy to enact and enforce bans on different forms of advocacy of political violence that amounts to recognition-denying speech. It might not only be permissible to ban direct and indirect encouragements to terrorism, but also others forms of political violence, such as advocacy of war or violent revolution, provided that the advocacy constitutes recognition-denying speech.

Although both Heyman and Quong assume that there is a close link between the justification of rights and their scope, there is a noteworthy difference between their theories of the ground of rights. Heyman defends a version of a liberal *natural rights theory* inspired by John Locke and Immanuel Kant. Like other natural rights theories, Heyman's can be regarded as a form of a status-based theory of rights, in the sense that rights are grounded in the nature of persons or the morally crucial characteristics of persons. (An alternative libertarian or Nozickean version of a status-based theory is presented and defended in section "Respect for Persons as Thinking Agents: A Libertarian Status-Based Theory of Rights.")

Quong defends an *interest-based theory* of the ground of rights that is partly inspired by Joseph Raz. Like Raz, he assumes that P has a right if P's interest is a sufficiently strong reason or ground for holding some other person(s) to be under a duty (Raz 1986: 166; Quong 2011: 306). To say that a person has a right is to say that his or her interest is sufficient to justify the existence of a duty on another person to behave in a way which serves the interests of the right-holder. This raises the question of what sorts of interests are sufficiently strong in order to provide interest-based reasons for rights. Quong's answer is that basic liberal democratic rights are grounded in the fundamental or higher-order interests of persons regarded as free and equal citizens. More precisely, "[b]asic rights and freedoms are meant to protect the especially important interests that citizens have in making (reasonable) choices over certain aspects of their lives such as freedom of association and religious expression" (Quong 2011: 310). Basic rights are only meant to protect the fundamental interests of citizens when they are pursued with reasonable objectives in mind. If fundamental interests are being pursued in order to promote unreasonable political or religious objectives, these interests fail to ground rights, and they should not be protected.

At this point, it should be noted that Quong defends a moralized understanding of interests. Unreasonable interests cannot provide a basis for liberal democratic rights because such interests are at odds with the freedom and equality of persons (Quong 2004: 333). Thus, unreasonable interests cannot ground the choice-protecting right to participate in public discourse, because such interests fail to recognize and respect other citizens as free and equal persons or citizens. According to Quong, this is important when it comes to the question of whether liberal democracies should tolerate recognition-denying speech, such as hate speech. The main reason radical extremists or hate speakers do not have a right to express their recognition-denying viewpoints is not that their views may cause psychological damage to the members of the groups they are attacking. Rather, it is because "hate speech or literature is not a genuine exercise of the right to free speech at all," and this means that there is no strong countervailing reason to weigh against reasons for state interference, the aim of which is to contain the spread of extremist anti-liberal-democratic ideas or values (Quong 2011: 311). In cases of hate speech, "the primary (and possibly only) interest being pursued . . . is unreasonable" (Quong 2011: 311). Thus, there is no valid rights claim to be considered.

Before proceeding, it is worth noting that Quong assumes that the *strength of rights* is relative to the weight or importance of the interests they are meant to protect (Quong 2004: 333, note 54). Quong seems to defend a version of a balancing approach to justifiable infringements of rights. The general idea of a balancing approach is that we need to weigh competing interests against each other and determine the relative strength or importance of the interests at stake. Quong appears to defend a balancing approach that can be described like this. In cases where a right comes into conflict with other moral considerations, one must weigh the importance or strength of the reasonable interests of the right-holder(s) against the competing reasonable interests of other affected parties. In this balancing process, the fundamental reasonable interests of free and equal citizens weigh more than other reasonable interests, whereas unreasonable interests do not count at all – they are irrelevant.

Heyman and Quong's arguments provide an interesting basis for viewpoint-based restrictions on extremist speech. However, even if one accepts the abstract liberal ideas that citizens should be regarded as free and equal persons and that rights are based on respect for persons or the dignity of persons, it is far from clear that recognition-denying or respect-denying speech falls outside the scope of the right to participate in public discourse. The move from these abstract assumptions (or premises) to Heyman and Quong's conclusions is controversial, and a number of prominent liberal and libertarian philosophers would reject it (see, e.g., Dworkin 1996, 2009, 2012; Hospers 1971; Mill 1985/1859; Nagel 2002; Rawls 1993: 336 and 354–55; Rothbard 2006). One can accept the idea that persons should be regarded and treated as free and equal in a liberal democracy, but reject Heyman and Quong's views on the scope of the right to participate in public discourse. In the remaining sections of this chapter, the aim is to elaborate and defend my version of this position. It will be argued that Heyman and Quong's theories of toleration and freedom of expression are overly intolerant, and that respect for the status of persons as thinking agents and their sovereignty over their own mind requires that liberal democracies ought to tolerate the public expression of *any* political and religious viewpoint within public discourse.

Viewpoint Neutrality, Political Toleration, and the Free Speech Right to Do Moral Wrong

The doctrine of viewpoint neutrality requires that *all* persons – including unpopular and radical extremist dissenters – have a right to express, hear, and consider *any* political and religious viewpoint, idea, or doctrine within public discourse. This means that liberal democracies should impose no criminal or civil penalties upon the expression of opinions or ideas that are relevant to intrapersonal and interpersonal deliberation on matters concerning the organization and culture of society or matters of public concern. The doctrine of viewpoint neutrality requires that citizens in a liberal democracy should have a basic right to participate in public discourse as speakers and listeners free from *state*-imposed viewpoint-based restrictions. Democratic majorities or their elected representatives have no moral right to enact and enforce viewpoint-based restrictions on public discourse. This does, however, not mean that liberal democracies should be neutral in the sense that they should grant radical extremist dissenters the right to attain political power to turn their political or religious ideas and objectives into law (Ekeli 2012).

With regard to extremist political and religious speech, the doctrine of viewpoint neutrality has two aspects that correspond to two basic rights. First, radical extremist dissenters (e.g., racists, Islamophobes, or radical imams) have a right to express and defend their political or religious convictions and ideas, however immoral or unreasonable they may be considered – except in cases where their speech acts violate the basic rights of other persons, such as their basic civil or political rights. Thus, *all* citizens have a right to participate in public discourse free from viewpoint-based restrictions, even if they express strongly worded and provocative recognition-denying viewpoints that are intended to stir up hatred, contempt, and hostility. Second, the rest of us – their potential audience – have a right to listen and make up our own minds.

According to the doctrine of viewpoint neutrality, political toleration in a liberal democracy requires a free speech right to do moral wrong that Heyman, Quong, and other defenders of viewpoint-based restrictions reject. The aim of this section is to explain in more detail the way in which this doctrine demands that citizens in a liberal democracy ought to have a *legal* free speech right to do *moral* wrong – including a right to be unreasonable. The argument for this doctrine is set out in section "Respect for Persons as Thinking Agents: A Libertarian Status-Based Theory of Rights."

A right to do moral wrong is a moral or a legal right to do something that is wrong from a moral point of view. P has a right to do moral wrong if P has a right to do something that P ought not to do. To put it differently, a right to do moral wrong is a right to do something one has a moral duty not to do – a right to violate one's own duty. Rights to do moral wrong are *choice-protecting rights*, the aim of which is to protect the choices or the freedom of choice of the right-holder. Examples of choice-protecting rights are freedom of speech, freedom of association, and freedom of religion. A choice-protecting right contains a *claim-right* that imposes a duty on others and the state not to interfere with the choices of the right-holder – that is, a duty of noninterference. Thus, to say that a person has a choice-protecting right to do moral wrong is to say that the state and other persons have a duty not to interfere with the right-holder's moral wrongdoing. As Ori Herstein points out, a right to do wrong "is a right against enforcement of duty, that is a right that others not interfere with one's violation of one's own obligations" (Herstein 2012: 343).

At this point, it should be noted that there is an interesting and important difference between moral duties and choice-protecting rights. *Moral duties* provide reasons for action. If P has a duty to do X, this entails that P has a reason to do X. Thus, if we have a moral duty to respect persons or the dignity of persons in Heyman and Quong's sense, this provides a reason to do so. *Choice-protecting rights* do not provide reasons for action. The function of a choice-protecting right is not to guide choices, but to protect choices. If P has a right to X, this does not entail that P has a reason to do X. Thus, if P has a right to express and defend extremist political viewpoints or ideas, this does not entail that P has a reason to express such views. Choice-protecting rights do not give the right-holder reasons for action, but they give others reasons against interference. This means that a choice-protecting right to do moral wrong provides a reason for other people and the state not to interfere with the right-holder's moral wrongdoing, but it does not give the right-holder a reason to do moral wrong.

If one accepts the doctrine of viewpoint neutrality, political toleration in a liberal democracy requires that citizens ought to have a *legal* free speech right to do *moral* wrong. This right to do moral wrong contains, at least, two important and related elements (Ekeli 2020). First, viewpoint neutrality requires that citizens should have a legally protected *liberty* to express and defend any political and religious viewpoint or idea within public discourse, even if it is morally wrong to express, or expose others to, such views. For example, this right covers the freedom to express racist or Islamophobic views that can cause psychological harms such as humiliation, fear, or anxiety. Even if it is morally wrong for citizens to express recognition-denying viewpoints that attack the dignity of persons and that can cause psychological harms, the doctrine of viewpoint neutrality requires that they should have a choice-protecting legal right to do moral wrong – subject to the *exception clause* that their speech acts do not directly and demonstrably violate the basic rights of other persons. This exception clause limits the scope of the free speech right to do moral wrong. A specification of the exception clause demands an answer to the question of the nature and ground of basic rights. This issue is discussed in more detail in section "Respect for Persons as Thinking Agents: A Libertarian Status-Based Theory of Rights."

Second, the doctrine of viewpoint neutrality requires that citizens ought to have a free speech right to do moral wrong that constitutes a right against legal enforcement of moral duty – that is, a legal *claim-right* against interference with moral wrongdoing. This means that it is not permissible for majorities in a liberal democracy to enact hate speech laws or bans on advocacy of terrorism that legally enforce the moral duty of individuals to respect the dignity of persons, because the state has a duty of noninterference. More generally, the enactment and enforcement of viewpoint-based restrictions on public discourse fall outside the scope of *the legitimate jurisdiction of majorities* – that is, the scope of the majority's moral right to rule. In a liberal democracy, the majority has no moral power-right to enact, and authorize the enforcement of, viewpoint-based restrictions on public discourse. With regard to the duty of noninterference, it is important to note that the doctrine of viewpoint neutrality prohibits *state*-imposed viewpoint-based restrictions on public discourse, but not viewpoint-based restrictions imposed by private citizens on their property. Each individual – including the owners of media platforms such as Google and Facebook – has a right to decide what ideas or worldviews that should be spread or disseminated on their property.

Respect for Persons as Thinking Agents: A Libertarian Status-Based Theory of Rights

Respect for persons or the dignity of persons can be cited on both sides in debates about the right to participate in public discourse and its scope (i.e., what the right is a right to) and strength (i.e., the weight of the right when it comes into conflict with competing ethical considerations). On the one hand, one can, as Heyman and Quong do, argue that respect for persons requires viewpoint-based restrictions on recognition-denying speech. On the other hand, one can argue that respect for persons requires viewpoint neutrality and the associated legal free speech right to do moral wrong (Ekeli 2020).

One way to develop an argument for the doctrine of viewpoint neutrality proceeds from the assumption that political institutions in a liberal democracy should show *respect for persons as thinking agents*. This is a normative idea that political institutions and procedures should instantiate and respect, and it provides the main justificatory basis of the basic rights of persons. The core idea of this status-based theory of rights is that persons, regarded as thinking agents with separate lives, have certain attributes or capacities that warrant or command respect, and these respect-warranting characteristics make it fitting to grant them certain basic rights that limit the scope of the state or the majority's moral right to rule.

The version of a status-based theory of basic rights that will be developed and defended here is crucially different from Heyman's, and it can be called the libertarian or Nozickean status-based theory. *The libertarian status-based theory* of rights provides a basis for a specification of the scope and strength of the right to participate in public discourse as speakers and listeners that supports the doctrine of viewpoint neutrality. This theory has three pivotal aspects. The first is that *the ground of basic rights* is respect for the status of persons regarded as thinking agents. Basic rights are grounded in certain fundamental morally significant characteristics of persons and their existential condition in the world as separate individuals each with their own lives to lead.

1. The worth, inviolability, and separateness of persons: Basic rights reflect the Kantian idea that persons have an unconditional worth (i.e., "a worth that has no price"), and Robert Nozick's idea of the inviolability of persons – that is, basic negative rights express and specify what it is not permissible to do to persons being ends in themselves, who should never be treated merely as means or resources for other persons or collective ends without their consent (Kant 1797/2017: 201 and 225; Nozick 1974: 30–33). According to Nozick, there is a close link between respect for the inviolability of persons and the separateness of persons – that is, the morally significant fact that "[t]here are only individual people, different individual people, with their own individual lives. ... To use a person [for the benefit of others or to serve the interests of others] does not sufficiently respect and take account of the fact that he is a separate person, that his is the only life he has" (Nozick 1974: 33). Respect for the separateness of persons requires that we respect the distinctiveness of individuals who have different and separate lives to lead and their own ends to set in view of what they regard as meaningful and valuable projects to pursue in their own life.

2. A person's sovereignty over himself/herself: Basic rights are a response to, or an expression of, a person's authority over his/her body, mind (i.e., a person's beliefs and values), and separate life or existence. Every individual person has sovereign authority over their own person, and they are entitled to choose which goals and projects they will use their own bodily and cognitive powers or capacities to pursue in their own separate lives – individually or cooperatively – limited only by the basic rights of other persons.

3. The respect-warranting capacities of persons as thinking agents: Basic rights are a response to, or an expression of, the respect-warranting capacities of persons as thinking agents, the most important of which are the following. (i) The deliberative capacity to make up their own mind in matters of politics and faith. (ii) The ability to express their most fundamental moral, political, or religious convictions and defend them against criticism. (iii) The ability to choose how they will live their own separate lives in accordance with their own understanding of what is a meaningful and valuable life. (iv) The capacity to take responsibility for their choices, the personal and political goals they aim for, and the manner in which they pursue them. These respect-warranting capacities of persons regarded as thinking agents and their sovereignty over their own beliefs and values provide the main reason for why it is fitting or appropriate to grant persons certain basic choice-protecting rights – such as the right to freedom of association, the right to freedom of thought, and the right to express, hear, and consider any viewpoint within public discourse.

Before proceeding, it is worth noting that to say that persons are thinking agents who have the deliberative capacity to make up their own mind about what to believe and what reasons to act on does not mean that they always or mostly use this ability in a good or rational way – for example, deliberate thoroughly or rationally about political or religious issues. Rational deliberation and decision-making require both information and the ability to process it rationally. The extent to which thinking agents are informed and rational varies from person to person, and it is a matter of degree. A thinking agent is rarely, if ever, fully informed or fully rational. One important reason for this is that we as thinking agents are subject to cognitive biases that prevent us from believing, thinking, or doing what we ought to believe, think, and do in view of the information we have available.

A core idea of the libertarian status-based theory of rights is that respect for the status of persons as thinking agents with sovereignty over their own body, mind, and separate life has *justificatory priority* over the protection and promotion of interests or the promotion of good consequences. For example, the reason why it is fitting to grant hate speakers and their potential audience (i.e., the rest of us) the right to participate in public discourse as speakers and listeners free from state-imposed viewpoint-based restrictions is not that their fundamental interests as free and equal citizens outweigh the interests of the targets of hate speech. Rather, it is respect for the status of persons as thinking agents and their sovereignty over their own beliefs and values that provide the basis of this right – regardless of the importance or weight of their interests in expressing, hearing, or considering extremist viewpoints. As Warren Quinn points out, "[i]t is not that we think it fitting to ascribe rights because we think it a good thing that rights be respected [or that such an arrangement or political system best promotes overall human welfare or the interests of all affected parties]. Rather, we think respect for rights a good thing precisely because we think people actually have them – and . . . that they have them because it is fitting that they should" (Quinn 1989: 312). This status-based approach to the justification of basic rights is crucially different from Raz' interest-based approach. According to Raz, "rights are based on evaluating the interests not only of their beneficiaries, but also of others who may be affected by respect for them" (Raz 1994: 35–36).

The second aspect of the libertarian status-based theory is that basic rights are *deontological side constraints* that provide a basis for assessing and constraining the actions and decisions of the state or the majority, as well as individuals and groups. Status-based rights impose what Nozick calls "moral side constraints" on the pursuit of the interests and goals of other people and the state. These moral side constraints reflect the limited authority individuals, groups, and states have over persons regarded as thinking agents with sovereignty over their own body, mind, and life. A specification of our basic rights as deontological side constraints is a specification of our rightful freedom and our rightful powers and immunities with respect to one another as thinking agents with separate lives.

The third aspect of the libertarian status-based theory is that *the strength of basic rights* is a reflection of the status of persons as thinking agents. Respect for the status of persons has justificatory priority over the protection and promotion of interests, and this justificatory priority is crucial when considering the strength of basic rights. Although rights typically protect interests directly and indirectly, the strength of a basic right, such as the right to participate in public discourse, can be out of proportion to the interests it protects and promotes. As Frances Kamm points out, "we can recognize that any given person's interest in speaking freely is not great, yet still argue that he has a strong [status-based] right to free speech, even when its strength is independent of serving (directly or indirectly) any other interest of his or anyone else's" (Kamm 2007: 246–247). When we consider whether a basic right should be respected, its strength is not a function of the interests at stake. The issue of justifiable infringements of basic rights is not a matter of balancing competing interests.

Basic rights are trumps in at least two important senses. In the first place, basic rights trump moral considerations of aggregative welfare. The normative force of basic rights places them on a different plane from any aggregative calculus of interests. A basic right is not just another consideration to be weighed and balanced against conflicting interest-based or welfare-based reasons – whatever their strength. Secondly, a basic right expresses the inviolability and separateness of persons, and it is a trump in the sense that the overall promotion of respect for basic rights in a society cannot justify a violation of the right. As Nozick points out, basic rights should not be treated as *goals* to be promoted, but as deontological side *constraints* to be respected – that is, as constraints that reflect respect for the status of persons with sovereignty over their own body, mind, and separate life. Consider the basic right to freedom of religion. It is reasonable to assume that if a state respects the basic right to freedom of religion, this will have the consequence that some citizens form extremist religious communities or sects that provide breeding grounds for violent radicalization, and that some members of these communities or sects will violate the basic rights of persons both within and outside these communities. Nevertheless, the right to freedom of religion is a constraint on the actions of the state that makes opportunistic violations of this right impermissible – even if violations would over time minimize the total amount of violations of basic rights in the society. From the point of view of the Nozickean status-based theory of rights, it is not permissible to violate a person's basic right to freedom of religion as a means to advance the interests or goals of others or even his/her own interests and goals.

The libertarian status-based theory of rights provides a basis for a specification of the scope and strength of the right to participate in public discourse that supports the doctrine of viewpoint neutrality. Respect for the status of persons as thinking agents and their sovereign authority over their own mind requires that they are ascribed a basic right to participate in public discourse as speakers and listeners free from state-imposed viewpoint-based restrictions. A political system that does not respect this basic right as a deontological side constraint fails to respect persons. Persons regarded as thinking agents can complain about the disrespect or indignity of being told by the state or a majority what political or religious views they can express, hear, and consider in processes of public discourse. To subject competent adult citizens to viewpoint-based restrictions is to treat them like children who need protection from being exposed to dangerous, poisonous, or contagious viewpoints.

A democratic state does not respect persons as thinking agents if it functions as a moderator of public debate and deliberation that suppresses or censors the political ideas and viewpoints that they are allowed to express, hear, and consider. Viewpoint-based restrictions on extremist speech within public discourse constitute an indignity and insult to *all* persons who are subject to them – both speakers and their potential audience. This also applies to members of minority groups who are targets of extremist speech, such as hate speech. I will return to this point in section "Do Persons Have a Basic Right to Recognition or Dignity?."

Another argument for the position that respect for the status of persons as thinking agents requires viewpoint neutrality can be called the *argument from freedom of thought*. According to this argument, there is an inseparable link between freedom of thought and viewpoint neutrality, and respect for the status of persons as thinking agents requires both freedom of thought and viewpoint neutrality. One way to develop this argument goes like this. The liberal and democratic idea that political institutions should respect persons as thinking agents requires the protection of free intrapersonal and interpersonal deliberation on matters concerning the organization and culture of society. *The right to freedom of thought* is a precondition for free processes of deliberation. Freedom of thought is a basic right that is a response to, or an expression of, respect for the status of persons as thinking agents with sovereignty over their own mind – that is, their own beliefs and values. This right includes the freedom of belief on all subjects (e.g., religious, political, scientific, philosophical, literary, or artistic), and the liberty to live in accordance with the demands of conscience. For present purposes, the most important dimension of the right to freedom of thought is the right or liberty to make up one's own mind about what to believe, and what is valuable and worth doing. This includes the liberty to develop or form one's own viewpoints or thoughts in processes of deliberation or discussion with others. Thus, the right to freedom of thought protects both inquiry and discussion.

There is an inseparable link between the outlined right to freedom of thought and viewpoint neutrality – that is, the basic right to participate in public discourse as speakers and listeners free from state-imposed viewpoint-based restrictions. According to the doctrine of viewpoint neutrality, this basic right to participate in public discourse has, as we have seen, two aspects: (a) It is a right to *express* and *defend* one's viewpoints or thoughts, even if it is morally wrong to express, or expose others to, such views. (b) It is a right to *hear* and *consider* the viewpoints or thoughts of other persons.

Viewpoint-based restrictions represent a form of state coercion that fails to respect the inviolability and separateness of persons as thinking agents, who have the ability and the right to develop their own political and religious viewpoints or thoughts. First, viewpoint-based restrictions, such as bans on recognition-denying speech, constitute a kind of thought control – the aim of which is usually to prevent citizens from acquiring or developing dangerous or poisonous ideas or viewpoints that can bring about harmful changes in their subsequent behavior. The state attempts to control (1) what particular political and religious ideas or viewpoints people are exposed to; (2) how they should think about certain political or religious issues, ideas, and aims (e.g., to prevent violent radicalization); and (3) what ideas should be allowed to influence processes of democratic deliberation or the society's moral environment in which people form their characters. Second, viewpoint-based restrictions on recognition-denying speech constitute a form of state coercion that is especially problematic with regard to respect for dissenters, who are subject to institutions and laws that they reject, and that are in clear conflict with their fundamental moral, political, or religious convictions.

Do Persons Have a Basic Right to Recognition or Dignity?

In section "Heyman's Argument," we saw that Heyman claims that persons have a basic right to recognition or dignity – that is, a right to be recognized and respected as a free and equal person. Presumably, Quong would also say that persons have a similar basic right to be respected as free and equal persons that is grounded in the fundamental interests of persons regarded as free and equal citizens. On this basis, one can argue that persons have a basic right to recognition or dignity, the aim of which is to protect persons – especially members of minority groups – from the public expression of extremist recognition-denying viewpoints that attack their dignity or their status as free and equal persons and citizens. If one accepts this, the issue of whether the expression of extremist recognition-denying viewpoints should be tolerated in a liberal democracy involves a conflict between two basic rights – the basic right to recognition and the basic right to express, hear, and consider any political or religious viewpoint within public discourse. Moreover, if one accepts Heyman's assumption that the right to recognition is "the most basic right of all," one could argue that the strength of this right outweighs the conflicting basic right to express, hear, and consider any viewpoint within public discourse. This objection to the proposed status-based theory of viewpoint neutrality raises the question of whether persons have a basic right to recognition or dignity.

It is worth considering three responses to this objection. First, political institutions in a liberal democratic state must respect the status of persons as thinking agents and their sovereign authority over their own mind, and this means that I must accept that other persons have a basic right to hold me in contempt, to think that I lack dignity, and to express these beliefs or convictions. This applies to me and all other persons – regardless of whether I belong to a vulnerable minority, or whether I am a communist, a libertarian, a racist, a religious fundamentalist, an Islamophobe, an alcoholic, or a junkie. As Ronald Dworkin points out, no one has a basic right that other individuals, who do believe they lack dignity, not hold or express that conviction (Dworkin 2012: 342). A liberal state should not be in the business of using the coercive apparatus of the state to regulate or control what we think and feel about other persons or citizens, and how we choose to express those thoughts and convictions within public discourse. According to the status-based doctrine of viewpoint neutrality, a majority has no moral right to enact, and authorize the enforcement of, laws that prohibit or penalize recognition-denying viewpoints stating that members of certain groups are inferior beings who have no moral status.

The same applies to viewpoints that express an aspiration or wish to deprive members of certain groups of all or some elements of citizen status. There might be strong reasons for regarding the public expression of such viewpoints as morally wrong, but they should be tolerated in a liberal state.

Second, from the point of view of the Nozickean status-based theory of rights, the viewpoint-based restrictions on recognition-denying speech defended by Quong aim to protect the dignity or status of persons, but fail to respect the dignity of persons as ends in themselves. One important reason for this is that the restrictions fail to respect the inviolability and separateness of persons, in the sense that they use persons as means to advance the interests of others. The point is that the bans violate a person's right to participate in public discourse as a speaker *and* listener as a means or tool to protect and promote the dignity-based interests of other persons – that is, their interest in being protected from attacks on their dignity or their status as free and equal persons or citizens.

Third, political institutions do not show wrongful disrespect for people if they treat them as persons who have the deliberative capacities to evaluate, deal with, and respond to political and religious viewpoints that attack their dignity or their status as free and equal persons or citizens. Rather, respect for the status of persons as thinking agents requires that they are treated as persons who have the ability to deal with such viewpoints, and the ability to defend and stand up for themselves. This applies to all of us when other individuals or groups express viewpoints that deny that we should be regarded or treated as free and equal persons or citizens. To respect the status of adult competent persons as thinking agents is incompatible with treating them as weak and helpless victims who need special state protection from viewpoints attacking their dignity or their social reputation.

In their famous defenses of hate speech laws, Richard Delgado and Jeremy Waldron seem to defend the competing perspective that regards the targets of hate speech as weak and defenseless victims who need special state protection from "words that wound" (Delgado 1982; Delgado and Stefancic 2018; Waldron 2012). In contrast to Delgado and Waldron, one can argue that this form of special state protection of members of certain selected groups undermine their status as thinking agents, in the sense that it is an indignity and insult to suggest that members of certain selected minority groups need special protection from speech that attack their dignity or social reputation and that might cause psychological harm. The African American conservative political activist Alan Keyes makes a similar point: "The. . . protection [of a "hate speech" law] incapacitates. . . . To be told that white folks have the moral character to shrug off insults, and that I do not . . . That is . . . the most racist statement of all!" (Quoted in Strossen 2018: 164).

The Silencing Effects of Extremist Speech

In section "Heyman and Quong on Extremist Viewpoints and the Limits of Toleration," we saw that both Heyman and Brown argue that one important argument for certain viewpoint-based restrictions on extremist speech within public discourse is that such speech can have silencing effects. This argument can provide an objection to the doctrine of viewpoint neutrality that can be called *the silencing effect objection*. One way to develop this objection that is inspired by Brown's silencing effect argument goes like this. If left unchecked, the public expression of certain forms of extremist viewpoints can "deter or inhibit members of targeted groups from functioning as *ordinary deliberative democrats*" – that is, the targets can be prevented "from participating normally or as other citizens in the formation of democratic public opinion" (Brown 2015: 198; italics added).

> What is at stake is a sort of deliberative exclusion in which out of fear for their personal safety or livelihood or as a result of an impaired sense of their status some, perhaps many, victims of hate speech tend to refrain from participating in the formation of public opinion; adapt their expressed preferences in order to fit their reduced circumstances; and/or find that even when they do decide to speak up what they say falls on deaf ears because of the low opinion that others have of them, partly as a consequence of the negative stereotypes carried and reinforced by hate speech. (Brown 2015: 198)

This silencing effect objection raises the following questions. If political institutions should respect the status of persons as thinking agents, why should it not be permissible for a liberal democracy to ban the expression of extremist political and religious viewpoints if the views can have the outlined silencing effects, and the viewpoint-based restrictions will promote the freedom or opportunity to participate in public discourse for people overall in a democratic society? Should citizens in a liberal democracy have a legal free speech right to do moral wrong even if they express extremist viewpoints within public discourse that silence others in the way described by Brown and Heyman?

A defender of viewpoint neutrality grounded in the libertarian status-based theory of rights can give a twofold answer to these questions. First, the libertarian status-based theory regards viewpoint neutrality and the associated free speech right to do moral wrong as a deontological side constraint that prohibits the state from violating this constraint even if a violation would better serve freedom of expression overall in the society. This means that the basic right to participate in public discourse free from viewpoint-based restrictions can be invoked against a liberal democratic state that would ban the extremist political viewpoints of a Neo-Nazi group, even when the group, if allowed to express their hateful viewpoints, is likely to psychologically "deter or inhibit members of targeted groups from functioning as ordinary deliberative democrats" (Brown 2015: 198). If a state is prepared to ban political viewpoints in order to promote the freedom or opportunity to participate in public discourse for people overall, then it does not (as Nozick would have said) endorse the basic right to express, hear, and consider any viewpoint within public discourse as a deontological side *constraint* on its actions that respects the status of persons as thinking agents and their sovereignty over their own mind. Rather, it merely treats this right to participate in public discourse as a *goal* that should be promoted, and this would allow the state or the majority to violate or transgress this basic right when doing so promotes the overall freedom or opportunity to participate in public discourse. To treat viewpoint neutrality and the associated free speech right to do moral wrong as a deontological side constraint means that the state cannot justifiably fail to respect or instantiate this status-based constraint simply because an opportunistic breach or transgression promises to promote the overall realization of the freedom or opportunity to participate in public discourse better than respecting this constraint would do.

Second, the proposed doctrine of viewpoint neutrality and libertarian status-based theory of rights do not imply that it is never permissible for a liberal democracy to ban speech acts that silence or aim to silence other persons. As pointed out in section "Viewpoint Neutrality, Political Toleration, and the Free Speech Right to Do Moral Wrong," the free speech right to do moral wrong does not cover speech acts that directly and demonstrably violate the basic rights of other persons. This exception clause means that if a speech act silences or aims to silence others in a way that constitutes a violation of other persons' basic right to participate in public discourse, then such speech acts fall outside the scope of the free speech right to do moral wrong. One can argue that speech acts that fulfill one of the two following conditions can silence others in a way that amounts to a violation of the right to participate in public discourse (Ekeli 2020). It is important to point out that even though these conditions open the door to prohibit certain speech acts, these prohibitions are not viewpoint-based restrictions on public discourse.

1. *The coercion* via *threat condition*: A speaker A communicates a serious expression of intent to commit an act that will inflict serious harm upon B or other people B cares about in order to obstruct B's freedom to participate in public discourse or prevent B from exercising this right. Typically, the term "an act that will inflict serious harm" refers to acts of severe physical force or violence (e.g., murder, torture, rape, abduction, or enslavement), but it can also refer to acts that cause grave property damage or destruction of valuable property (such as a threat to burn down a person's home). It is irrelevant whether A (or A's associates/co-conspirators) actually intends to carry out the threat, and whether A (or A's associates) has any intention of carrying out the threatened act imminently or not. This coercion via threat condition is fulfilled in situations in which A communicates a serious expression of intent to kill B or his/her children if B participates at a political demonstration, or if B publishes certain political or religious viewpoints. In such cases, A's intention is to coerce B into acting against his/her will – the conditional threat is a form of coercion.

2. *The incitement to imminent violence condition*: A's speech act is intended and likely to incite C to imminent use of severe physical force or violence against B in order to obstruct B's freedom to participate in public discourse or prevent B from exercising this right. This condition is fulfilled if A incites a group of Neo-Nazis to imminent use of violence against B in order to prevent B from participating as a speaker in a public debate, and it is likely that the Neo-Nazis will be persuaded by A to commit imminent violence in the given context. The condition is also fulfilled in a relevantly similar situation in which A incites a group of radical Islamists to start a violent riot in order to prevent B and others from participating at an anti-Islamic political meeting or political demonstration. Although it is outside of A's control whether the Neo-Nazis or the radical Islamists will in fact

be persuaded to use violence to prevent B, it is reasonable to assume that A's act of incitement to imminent violence qualifies as a violation of B's basic right to participate in public discourse. What make the incitements at issue a violation of B's basic right is the combination of the intent with which the words are communicated and the high degree of certainty that the Neo-Nazis or the radical Islamists will act on the incitement.

Summary and Future Directions

This chapter has considered the question of whether respect for persons requires toleration of the expression of *any* extremist political or religious viewpoint within public discourse. On the one hand, we have seen that Heyman and Quong have developed interesting defenses of a negative answer to this question. According to Heyman and Quong, recognition-denying or respect-denying speech falls outside the scope of the right to participate in public discourse, and this means that there is no free speech right to do moral wrong that includes a right to express recognition-denying viewpoints within public discourse. On the other hand, we have seen that a strong case can be made for the competing position that toleration in a liberal democracy requires respect for the status of persons as thinking agents, and that respect for thinking agents and their sovereignty over their own mind demand viewpoint neutrality and an associated free speech right to do moral wrong.

The competing positions that have been discussed in this chapter illustrates that respect for persons is a Janus-faced requirement that can be cited on both sides in debates about toleration and the scope and strength of the right to participate in public discourse. We have also seen that these debates raise a number of interesting and important questions related to political, legal, and moral philosophy. This means that future directions for research in this area are numerous. Here I will just mention one issue or research direction. This concerns the question of whether the expression of viewpoints within public discourse can amount to a "violation" of the basic rights of other persons – that is, basic moral rights that the state should respect and protect. Delgado and Heyman are among the advocates of viewpoint-based restrictions on extremist speech who assume that the answer to this question is positive. In his defense of hate speech bans, Delgado claims that "a racist insult is always a dignitary affront, a direct violation of the victim's right to be treated respectfully. ... [I] ndividuals are entitled to treatment that does not denigrate their humanity through disrespect for their . . . moral worth" (Delgado 1982: 143–144. See also Delgado and Stefancic 2018: 12). The assumption that a person's expression of his or her opinions, ideas, or convictions within public discourse can qualify as a "direct violation" of a basic right can be questioned, and it deserves further analysis and scrutiny.

The expression of political or religious viewpoints within public discourse can, in a number of different ways, have a significant impact on the lives of other people and change the context or environment in which other persons act. First, the public expression and discussion of more or less extreme viewpoints on matters concerning the organization and culture of society can influence how we think about other people and ourselves. Second, the public expression of extremist viewpoints (e.g., racist views or ideologies) can, as Delgado emphasizes, cause psychological harm, such as "emotional distress." Having said that, even Delgado admits that the psychological impact of viewpoints or ideas depends on a number of individual or subjective factors (e.g., an individual's attitudes and personality traits) and situational factors (Delgado 1982: 143; Delgado and Stefancic 2009: 366). Third, the spread of ideas and ideologies can over time lead to conflicts and serve as a source of inspiration for political violence – war, revolution, and terrorism. Although an individual's public expression of his or her opinion or ideology can change the context or environment in which other persons think, feel, and act, it is far from straightforward that the public expression of viewpoints or ideas about the culture and organization of society can amount to a "direct violation" of the basic moral rights of other persons. In this connection, it is worth considering the following questions: Can the expression of viewpoints or ideas within public discourse *violate* the basic rights of other persons? For example, is the public expression of a clearly racist viewpoint or a racist ideology in a debate about immigration or integration a violation of some basic right of the targets? If the answer to the first two related questions is positive, (a) what particular rights can the public expression of viewpoints or ideas violate, (b) what is the normative ground or foundation of the alleged rights (e.g., Delgado's "right to be treated respectfully"), and (c) how does the expression of viewpoints or ideologies within public discourse violate the alleged rights?

References

Barendt E (2005) Freedom of speech. Oxford University Press, Oxford
Brettschneider C (2012) When the state speaks, what should it say? Princeton University Press, Princeton
Brown A (2015) Hate speech law: a philosophical examination. Routledge, New York
Delgado R (1982) Words that wound: a tort action for racial insults, epithets, and name-calling. Harv Civ Rights-Civil Lib Law Rev 17:133–181
Delgado R, Stefancic J (2009) Four observations about hate speech. Wake For Law Rev 44:353–370
Delgado R, Stefancic J (2018) Must we defend Nazis? Why the first amendment should not protect hate speech and white supremacy. New York University Press, New York
Dworkin R (1996) Freedom's law. Harvard University Press, Cambridge, MA
Dworkin R (2009) Foreword. In: Hare I, Weinstein J (eds) Extreme speech and democracy. Oxford University Press, Oxford, pp v–ix
Dworkin R (2012) Reply to Waldron. In: Herz M, Molnar P (eds) The content and context of hate speech. Cambridge University Press, Cambridge
Ekeli KS (2012) The political rights of anti-liberal-democratic groups. Law Philos 31(3):269–297
Ekeli KS (2020) Democratic legitimacy, political speech and viewpoint neutrality. Philos Soc Crit. https://doi.org/10.1177/0191453720931902
Heinze E (2016) Hate speech and democratic citizenship. Oxford University Press, Oxford
Herstein O (2012) Defending the right to do wrong. Law Philos 31(3):343–365
Heyman S (2008) Free speech and human dignity. Yale University Press, New Haven

Heyman S (2009) Hate speech, public discourse, and the first amendment. In: Hare I, Weinstein J (eds) Extreme speech and democracy. Oxford University Press, Oxford, pp 158–181

Hospers J (1971) Libertarianism. Nash Publishing, Los Angeles

Jones P (2007) Making sense of political toleration. Br J Polit Sci 37(3):383–402

Kamm F (2007) Intricate ethics. Rights, responsibilities, and permissible harm. Oxford University Press, Oxford

Kant I (1797/2017) The metaphysics of morals. Cambridge University Press, Cambridge

Mill JS (1985/1859) On liberty. Penguin Books, London

Nagel T (2002) Concealment and exposure. Oxford University Press, Oxford

Nozick R (1974) Anarchy, state, and utopia. Basic Books, New York

Quinn W (1989) Actions, intentions, and consequences: the doctrine of doing and allowing. Philos Rev 98(3):287–312

Quong J (2004) The rights of unreasonable citizens. J Polit Philos 12(3):314–335

Quong J (2011) Liberalism without perfection. Oxford University Press, Oxford

Rawls J (1993) Political Liberalism. Colombia. University Press, New York

Raz J (1986) The morality of freedom. Oxford University Press, Oxford

Raz J (1994) Ethics in the public domain. Oxford University Press, Oxford

Rothbard MN (2006) For a new liberty. Ludwig von Mises Institute, Alabama

Strossen N (2018) Hate. Oxford University Press, Oxford

Waldron J (2012) The harm in hate speech. Harvard University Press, Cambridge, MA

Toleration and Political Change

10

Lucia M. Rafanelli

Contents

Introduction 174
Toleration as an Obstacle to Political Change 175
Toleration as Creating Space for Political Change 181
Toleration as a Spur to Political Change 183
Summary and Future Directions 185
References 187

Abstract

This chapter explores the relationship between toleration and political change. On one understanding, toleration threatens to stifle political change. Not only is toleration often understood as involving reluctance to try to change others' behavior, but several thinkers argue that ideas and practices of toleration can work to prop up entrenched powers and stymie revolutionary change. Similarly, in the international arena, toleration is often invoked to block international actors from opposing (alleged) injustice in foreign societies. However, on another understanding, toleration is not an obstacle to political change, but rather is necessary to create spaces in which political change can be pursued – though it may or may not be pursued successfully. On a third understanding, a closer examination of the moral reasons in favor of toleration, or of toleration itself, may actually support pursuing certain kinds of political change. Given this variation, the chapter raises several questions and sketches some possible avenues of future research. For example, why does toleration appear to have such an ambivalent relationship to political change? Is there a fundamental tension within the ideal of toleration itself between encouraging and discouraging political change, or is the appearance of this tension simply a reflection of differences in

L. M. Rafanelli (✉)
The George Washington University, Washington, DC, USA
e-mail: lmrafanelli@gwu.edu

© The Author(s), under exclusive licence to Springer Nature Switzerland AG 2022
M. Sardoč (ed.), *The Palgrave Handbook of Toleration*,
https://doi.org/10.1007/978-3-030-42121-2_57

173

the other moral commitments of those who write on toleration? If there is such a tension, how should our political and social institutions navigate it?

Keywords

Toleration · Tolerance · Pluralism · Repressive tolerance · Liberating tolerance · Revolution · Identity · International toleration · Lorde · Wolff (RP) · Marcuse · Rawls · Walzer

---

Introduction

In both academic political theory and everyday political discourse, toleration takes on many guises. Sometimes it appears as an essential part of healthy political life, sometimes as a tool that may be wielded both righteously in the name of liberation and unjustly to enable oppression, sometimes as an embodiment of every person's equal claim to autonomy and respect, and sometimes as an atomizing force that precludes genuine cooperation and solidarity. Toleration's chimerical nature reflects and is reflected in its ambivalent relationship to political change, which this chapter explores.

On one understanding, toleration is an obstacle to political change. It encourages people to acquiesce in socio-political arrangements they have legitimate reason to oppose, propping up existing elites and preventing radical departures from the status quo. On a second understanding, toleration's core function is not to obstruct political change, but to create arenas in which diverse people can pursue political change. On this view, toleration helps constitute the communal spaces in which political change happens. On yet a third understanding, toleration can not only enable but also spur political change. Understood and practiced in the right ways, toleration can be an important part of emancipatory political struggles. And, on some views, the same moral commitments that ground our commitment to toleration also ground commitments to pursuing certain reformist – or even revolutionary – political projects.

This chapter elaborates these three understandings of toleration's relationship to political change. It ends with reflections on their significance for our understanding of toleration itself and suggests several directions for future research.

Before proceeding further, a clarification is in order: some authors distinguish among "toleration" and "tolerance." However, this distinction is not always drawn in the same way. (For some examples of different ways to understand these terms and the distinction, or lack thereof, between them, see Blake 2007, 2; Cohen 2004, 76–9; Creppell 2003, 20–1, 26; Marcuse 1965, 85, 92fn; Oberdiek 2001, 5, 23–7; Walzer 1997, 10–2; Wolff 1965, 4, 23.) Moreover, even if not identical, "toleration" and "tolerance" are clearly related to the same core concept. Better understanding one of them will also help us understand the other (even if we can't simply assume what is true about one is also true about the other). Thus, this chapter does not limit itself to discussing authors who (for example) write only about "toleration" as opposed to "tolerance." Rather, it engages with authors who may write with either (or both) of

Toleration as an Obstacle to Political Change

On one understanding, toleration – or at least its valorization – is an obstacle to political change. While it may allow or even encourage small reforms, taking toleration as one of our central political values and understanding its practice or public manifestation as a primary goal of political life precludes truly radical departures from the status quo.

Some build a resistance to pursuing change into the very conceptual structure of toleration. Take, for example, AJ Cohen (2004, 69, emphasis added), who defines an "act of toleration" as "an agent's intentional and principled *refraining from interfering with an opposed other* (or their behavior, etc.) in situations of diversity, where the agent believes she has the power to interfere." Similarly, Godfrey-Smith and Kerr (2019, 405, emphasis original) write, "A person is tolerant with respect to X if they are *disposed not to interfere* with others in ways that would tend to curtail or constrain their choices concerning X."

Others reveal how toleration can – in certain political contexts – play the conservative role of obstructing radical social change and cementing existing privilege. So suggests Audre Lorde (2007, 112) when, writing on women's liberation, she says, "[a]dvocating the mere tolerance of difference between women is the grossest reformism." For Lorde (2007, 111–4), women can only transcend the patriarchal order by embracing their interdependency; and this, in turn, will only happen when they stop simply *tolerating* difference and begin celebrating it and recognizing it as a resource for creative re-making of their social world.

Robert Paul Wolff (1965) similarly questions the compatibility of tolerance – at least as it has manifested itself in modern American pluralist democracy – and revolutionary social change. Though Wolff's (1965) critique of tolerance is contextually specific (it is not meant to show that tolerance *necessarily* or in all contexts stymies radical change), his analysis of its function in American pluralist democracy reveals how it *could* play this conservative role. On his view, tolerance is the principal virtue of modern American pluralist democracy (Wolff 1965, 4). Moreover, in the modern American context, *tolerance* has primarily meant *tolerance of all major social groups,* and the valorization of tolerance has thus meant marginalizing emerging but not-yet-established groups as well as individuals who aren't well represented in any established group (Wolff 1965, 20–3, 40–9). As a result, a social order organized to embody tolerance allows for certain kinds of political change (as when one established group newly succeeds in advancing its interests in the public sphere), but it forecloses other kinds (because individuals whose interests aren't represented by their group's leadership, or who don't belong to an established group, are not recognized as legitimate players in any political contest) (Wolff 1965, 40–9).

For example, Wolff (1965, 41) notes, modern American pluralism and its cardinal virtue, tolerance, may enable (and even celebrate) public recognition of and political contestation among society's major religions, but this marginalizes non-religious individuals. Likewise, pluralism and tolerance may enable (and even celebrate) competition among diverse interest groups – labor and business, say – in civil society, calling upon the government to "referee" this competition (Wolff 1965, 46–7). But if government "referees" recognize and cater to only the leadership of each group (e.g., union bosses) this marginalizes those whose interests the leadership doesn't represent (e.g., dissenting workers within the unions) (Wolff 1965, 46–9). Thus, some political changes are possible: there can be a new "winner" from among the major social groups in each round of competition. This or that religious group may be successful one day and not the next. The leaders of labor and business groups might strike a balance between their interests favoring business leaders for now, only for it to be replaced later by a new balance favoring labor leaders. But other political changes are foreclosed – or at least made much more difficult – by the pluralist frame. The theory and practice of pluralism make little room for challenges to the organization of society around whatever particular social groups have already been identified as the "major" ones or movements that assert the claims of disadvantaged individuals made from outside, or even against, these groups. The "winners" may change from game to game, but the rules and teams are all but set in stone. And tolerance is the virtue that ensures these same teams get to keep playing by these same rules, indefinitely.

In addition to distorting the landscape of political contestation in this way, Wolff (1965, 49–51) argues an over-zealous pluralism (where, again, this centrally involves a commitment to tolerance for all major social groups) forecloses the possibility of certain radical solutions to extant political problems. After all, if the archetypal political question regards how power and influence should be distributed among a number of pre-determined social groups, then the archetypal "social problem" is a flawed distribution, whereby one of these groups doesn't receive its rightful share (Wolff 1965, 49). The archetypal remedy, then, would be to redistribute resources from one recognized social group to another (Wolff 1965, 49).

This kind of flawed distribution may well be a genuine problem, and redistribution among social groups may sometimes be an appropriate remedy. However, Wolff (1965, 49–52) argues, not all social problems, and not all necessary remedies, take these forms. Some social problems can't be explained in terms of the interests of one particular social group as against the interests of others, but instead must be understood in terms of the common good – they represent obstacles to achieving the interests of society *as a whole* (Wolff 1965, 49–52). Wolff (1965, 49–50) cites, for example, declining environmental conservation, decreased support for the arts, and a limited capacity for maintaining public safety. These kinds of problems are not only obscured, but actually rendered unintelligible, by the pluralist frame, since it represents society as a collection of groups with distinct interests rather than as a community in its own right with an overarching common good (Wolff 1965, 49–52). And to put up tolerance as the cardinal political virtue is to say society should be designed to facilitate the equal recognition of established social groups, implying that the ultimate goal should be to attend to the good of each group, rather than the good of society as a whole.

10 Toleration and Political Change

Likewise, solving the problems that plague society-at-large doesn't require (only) redistributing goods or influence from one established social group to another (Wolff 1965, 49–52). It requires both re-conceiving society as suggested above – as a community in its own right with an overarching common good – *and* radically reorganizing it to allow the effective pursuit of the common good (Wolff 1965, 49–52). But again, these solutions are obscured by the pluralist frame, as Wolff (1965, 50–1) notes when he writes that pluralism "simply does not acknowledge the possibility of wholesale reorganization of the society." Thus, the familiar refrain recurs: while a society organized around pluralism (and, by extension, tolerance) allows for certain kinds of political change (e.g., redistributing resources from one social group to another), it precludes other, more "thoroughgoing social revisions" (Wolff 1965, 52).

Organizing a society in pluralist fashion, around the virtue of tolerance, may ensure that all recognized social groups have standing to press their particular interests and to struggle for their fair share of society's resources. Tolerance ensures all recognized groups have equal standing to engage in political struggle so conceived. But in so doing, it also ensures that certain ways of understanding politics and society, and certain approaches to solving major social issues, are off the table. After all, Wolff (1965, 51) notes, pluralism can only understand *society's interest* as the collected interests of its constitutive social groups, and, "One could hardly expect a committee of group representatives to decide that the pluralist system of social groups is an obstacle to the general good!" Hence his concluding call for "a new philosophy of community, beyond pluralism and beyond tolerance" (Wolff 1965, 52).

Perhaps, one could argue, tolerance only becomes the kind of conservative force – the kind of obstacle to radical change – that Wolff envisions in the very particular context about which he writes: modern American pluralist democracy. Perhaps detaching tolerance from the particular form it takes in this context (roughly, equal recognition for all major social groups as legitimate political players) would cure it of its conservatism. However, other treatments of tolerance suggest it may play a similar conservative role even in other contexts: the problem does not begin and end with modern American pluralism.

Take Marcuse's (1965, 1968) treatment, for example. It is certainly not acontextual: its primary focus is tolerance in industrialized democracies (Marcuse 1965, 81, 92). But its conclusion that tolerance has the potential to prop up status quo authorities and power structures is applicable beyond the context of modern American pluralism. For Marcuse (1965), the conservative pull of tolerance arises from the political uses to which it is put and the overall character of the society in which it is practiced. Though Marcuse (1965, 1968) suggests there are emancipatory variants of tolerance, there are also, he says, repressive variants. And the repressive variants can arise even if tolerance doesn't take the specific form Wolff (1965) identifies with modern American pluralism.

In societies of a certain organization – where the class structure works to suppress genuinely autonomous, democratic decision-making on the part of the populace and to establish "rules of the game" that favor the powers that be – tolerance itself can function to prop up those same powers (Marcuse 1965, quote from 83). In Marcuse's (1965, 82) words, the call to *practice tolerance* becomes a call to "laissez-faire the constituted authorities." Marcuse (1965, 1968) has two central insights here. First, when *tolerance* becomes a kind of official neutrality among the political factions those in power countenance (because they don't pose any fundamental challenges to the society's organization), not only is the society "all but closed against qualitative change," but "tolerance itself serves to contain such change rather than promote it" (Marcuse 1965, 116). Second, when *tolerance* takes the form of neutrality between that which serves the cause of repression and that which serves the cause of liberation – between developments that have helped install dominating authorities, presumably like those of the status quo, and those that have resisted their dominating influence – it serves to reconcile people to their ongoing oppression (Marcuse 1965, 113).

Lori G. Beaman (2013) highlights toleration's conservative potential in the context of multicultural societies – especially those built on a history of colonialism, including settler colonialism. Beaman (2013) problematizes what she sees as a common tendency in the theory and practice of multiculturalism to understand the claims of minorities, immigrants, and Indigenous people as claims to "tolerance" and "accommodation." Though Beaman's (2013) focal cases come from contemporary Canada, her theoretical points are more broadly applicable. Beaman (2013) argues that characterizing minorities', immigrants', and Indigenous people's claims in this way establishes them (minorities, immigrants, and Indigenous people) as outsiders to the society from which they seek redress, in search of special treatment (rather than as members of the society, in search of the equal treatment to which all are entitled). Hence her claim that "tolerance and accommodation are vestiges of the empire that conceptually anchor a hierarchy of privilege that works to maintain a boundary of *otherness*" (Beaman 2013, 120–1, emphasis original).

On this view, toleration not only precludes radically re-organizing society around a commitment to the "deep equality" (Beaman 2013, 130–2) of all members – because it offers up the less radical alternative of granting piecemeal accommodations to citizens whose national or cultural identities, or distinctive social practices, make them "outsiders" to the society's "normal" (and presumptively desirable) way of life. Toleration also pre-empts and stifles attempts to contest the hierarchies associated with colonialism and settler colonialism around which the world order and many multicultural societies are built. By reinforcing the idea that the world is divided into "enlightened," "civilized" societies and "unenlightened" or "uncivilized" others – where the former are called upon to generously bestow accommodations on the latter (see Beaman 2013, 120–6) – the ideal of toleration can simultaneously entrench the power of those (colonizing and settler) societies historically seen as the bearers of civilization and entrench the subjugation of those (colonized, immigrant, minority, Indigenous) people(s) historically seen as their antithesis.

In the international context, too, toleration can act as an obstacle to political change. John Rawls (1999) famously makes toleration the crux of his argument against liberalizing interventionism. Rawls (1999) envisions the ideal international

10 Toleration and Political Change

community (the "Society of Peoples") as encompassing two kinds of societies: liberal peoples and "decent" peoples. Decent peoples as Rawls (1999, 62–80) understands them meet several political-moral criteria, including respecting basic human rights, refusing to wage aggressive wars, and granting their members some role in political decision-making. Despite these many virtues, decent peoples need not be liberal. For example, their legal systems may not recognize or treat every individual citizen as a free and equal person; they may attach religious tests to certain political offices; and, while each social group must be represented in political decision-making processes, it's not necessary that each individual have a direct say or vote (Rawls 1999, 65 fn 2, 71–8). In Rawls's (1999, 59–62) eyes, any of these features would make decent peoples genuinely unjust, but he nonetheless argues they deserve equal standing – alongside just, liberal peoples – in the international community.

Decent peoples, Rawls (1999, 59–62, 84–5) argues, deserve toleration, meaning they deserve immunity from external intervention in their affairs – even if that intervention would aim to make them more liberal and, therefore, more just. This is a curious position for Rawls to take. After all, his overarching views on what justice requires seem to entail that a world containing illiberal peoples would contain more injustice than an otherwise identical world made up of only liberal peoples. This implies that we have genuine moral reason to prefer the second (fully liberal) world, and suggests that, if we could make political changes to move from the first to the second world, we would have reason to do so. But in the case of relations between liberal and decent peoples, Rawls (1999 59–62, 84–5) explicitly prohibits this kind of change promotion in the name of toleration.

Rawls (1999, 62) argues that there are "strong reasons" to allow decent peoples to continue committing injustice rather than hold them to liberal standards, the chief such reason being the need to preserve "mutual respect among peoples." And this mutual respect is only preserved when liberal peoples practice toleration toward decent peoples; refusing to tolerate decent peoples and instead requiring them to liberalize would deny them "a due measure of respect" (Rawls 1999, 61). This mutual respect among peoples is a central feature of the ideal international community as Rawls envisions it, and he considers the reasons for achieving this vision "as overriding the lack of liberal justice in decent societies" (Rawls 1999, 62). One reason Rawls (1999, 62) gives for the great importance he assigns to preserving mutual respect among peoples is pragmatic – actively intervening to liberalize non-liberal peoples would likely cause backlash and resentment, and would ultimately lower the odds that the latter would liberalize. But Rawls (1999, 59–62) clearly thinks there are also principled reasons – grounded in a principled commitment to toleration – for liberal peoples to respect, grant equal standing to, and therefore not intervene in the affairs of non-liberal but decent peoples. These reasons have to do with the moral merits of decent peoples' internal organization. So, Rawls (1999, 83) writes that a decent people "meets moral and legal requirements sufficient to override the political reasons we might have for" intervening to liberalize them. One reason against intervention is the pragmatic one that interveners may exhibit "error, miscalculation, and also arrogance" (Rawls 1999, 83). But the other main reason is principled – that, regardless of the likely (good or bad) consequences of a proposed intervention, decent peoples "have certain institutional features that deserve respect" (Rawls 1999, 83–4). The way for liberal peoples to express this respect, on Rawls's (1999, 59–62) view, is by practicing toleration toward decent peoples; and this, in turn, means refraining from liberalizing intervention even when its outcome would serve the cause of justice.

In sum, imagine a liberal people had the opportunity to promote liberalizing political change within a "decent" but illiberal people. Assume, for the sake of argument, the liberal people could do this successfully and without causing backlash. Its main choice, then, is between producing a liberalizing change and accepting (or at least not challenging) the status quo. Rawls's view that the decent people is genuinely unjust implies the liberal people has genuine reason to produce this liberalizing change. But Rawls explicitly argues the liberal people has even stronger reason not to try. What is their reason not to try? It is that decent peoples deserve toleration – which means they deserve (1) freedom from "political sanctions – military, economic, or diplomatic" designed to make them more liberal, (2) recognition as "equal participating members in good standing" in the international community, and (3) to be treated in ways justifiable in terms of reasons all liberal and decent peoples could accept (where *that treating them a certain way would make them more liberal* is not a reason decent non-liberal peoples could accept) (Rawls 199, 59).

Walzer's views on international toleration can be read in a similar way – to present toleration as an obstacle (in his view, an often-necessary one) to certain political changes that the international community might otherwise (that is, in the absence of toleration) pursue. Walzer (1997, 19–22) characterizes the international community as one in which all recognized states are "tolerated" as long as they don't transgress certain (relatively permissive) limits. For Walzer (1997 19–22), international toleration is closely intertwined with state sovereignty. In fact, he writes it is an "essential feature of sovereignty" (Walzer 1997, 19). Sovereignty, in turn, "guarantees that no one on *that* side of the border can interfere with what is done on *this* side" (Walzer 1997, 19, emphasis original).

And this is not only *descriptively* true of the international community; Walzer also presents toleration so understood as a morally desirable feature of international society. He acknowledges that what international actors in fact do or don't tolerate often doesn't align with what is genuinely tolerable or intolerable (i.e., what does or doesn't deserve to be tolerated) (Walzer 1997, 21). But he also offers a vision of a world divided into distinct sovereign states, each allowed to conduct its own affairs as it sees fit – as long as it refrains from the gravest abuses, like genocide, massacre, enslavement, mass expulsion, and other forms of oppression so egregious that even those with vastly divergent ideas about justice would condemn them – and he offers this vision not merely as a description but as a normative ideal (Walzer 1980, 1994, 2011, 2015). Toleration, on Walzer's view, is the practice of leaving these many states to pursue their distinctive projects and goals in whatever ways they choose. It is the practice that makes his normative ideal possible.

10 Toleration and Political Change 181

Thus, for Walzer, like for Rawls, that a certain group (such as a sovereign state) deserves toleration means international actors shouldn't interfere with its domestic political processes – even if by doing so they could promote political change for which there are genuine moral reasons. Though such interference may sometimes be all-things-considered justified, Walzer (1997, 21–2) characterizes it as "intolerance." Toleration, then, requires international actors to leave other states to their own affairs. Hence Walzer's (1994, 79) pronouncement, "Every tribe within its own modest bounds: this is the political equivalent of toleration for every church and sect." On this understanding, toleration once again appears as an obstacle to certain kinds of potential political change – namely, those changes that could be brought about by international actors involving themselves in the domestic affairs of sovereign states.

There is, however, another way to interpret the relationship between toleration and political change in Walzer's view. Examining this interpretation reveals a second way of understanding the relationship between toleration and political change more generally.

Toleration as Creating Space for Political Change

On this second understanding, toleration is not an obstacle to political change, but is rather a set of beliefs and practices that helps constitute the spaces in which political change can be pursued. Walzer (2015, 89) suggests this understanding when he says states – the integrity of which toleration supposedly protects – are the only "arena within which freedom can be fought for and (sometimes) won." Similarly, Walzer (2011, 46) identifies states as "the crucial agent of self-help" – the only vehicle through which people and political communities can "help themselves" by protecting their interests and achieving their goals (including explicitly political goals, like achieving justice, whatever that means for them).

For Walzer, the state is the main arena in which politics happens. Political activity, in his view, constitutively involves people creating and negotiating the terms of a "common life," and it is this "common life" that states house and protect (see Walzer 2015, 54). While defending his (relatively restrictive) view about when states are liable to external intervention against his more interventionist critics, Walzer (1980) even more explicitly establishes the state as the home of politics. To those who would argue he should give state sovereignty less moral weight and permit a wider range of interventions meant to protect individual rights, Walzer (1980, 228) replies that his statist view represents "a defense of politics" against his critics' "philosophical dislike for politics." On this view, the problem with over-zealous interventionists is not exactly that they want political change (in targeted states) when there should be none. Rather, it is that the interventions they justify and the interveners they call upon to carry them out are in an important sense apolitical. They are neither part of the "political arena" of the targeted state, nor do their actions (unlike the actions of that state's officials) result from the internal political processes of that state (Walzer 1980, 228; 2015, 54). When interveners protect the rights of a state's citizens, they do so not as a part of that state's political processes, but rather as a force that cuts off those processes, decimates their ability to shape the local conditions, and replaces them with something else entirely (perhaps "bureaucratic" rule, or pure violent imposition (Walzer 1980, 229)).

What does all this have to do with toleration? The connection is this: for Walzer (1994, 79; 1997, 19–22), a major function of toleration in the international sphere is to preserve the integrity of separate states. And he indicates, in turn, that these states are (for the most part) where political struggle can happen. This suggests we should preserve their integrity (by practicing toleration) not in order to oppose (or support) political change, but in order to preserve politics itself – to preserve the arena in which political change can be pursued, though it may or may not be achieved in any given case. So, Walzer (1980, 229) writes that the difference between him and his more-interventionist critics "has to do with the respect we are prepared to accord and the room we are prepared to yield to the political process itself. . ..It has to do with the range of outcomes we are prepared to tolerate. . .."

Creppell (2003) offers another account of toleration that suggests its purpose is not to stymie or spur political change, but rather to inaugurate the conditions under which politics can happen. For Creppell (2003), norms, practices, and ideas of toleration emerge among people with unreconciled differences who nonetheless want to maintain relations with one another: toleration is what allows them to do so on mutually agreeable terms. Thus, not only does toleration make community among such people possible – this community is distinctively *political* (Creppell 2003, 28). Without recourse to a shared faith or vision of the morally good life, for example, people who wish to forge community must also forge new *explicitly political* identities, ideas about their common good, and norms to govern their relations (Creppell 2003, 28). These identities, ideas, and norms are explicitly political in that they are distinct from purely moral or religious commitments. They are derived instead from a commitment to construct and maintain a shared communal life in the presence of differences that might ordinarily make such community impossible (by inspiring "practices of domination and coercion" (Creppell 2003, 28)). As Creppell (2003, 28) writes, "a conscious coming to terms with differences creates uniquely political identities and identifications. . .."

Once a political community is formed, its governing norms can – and should – be continually re-negotiated, ultimately yielding communal standards of justice that are the "outcome of engagement and interaction across differences" and that are themselves dynamic and contestable (Creppell 2003, 155). For Creppell (2003, 155), we can facilitate this process by recognizing toleration for what it is – a tool for enabling continued engagement and close co-existence among diverse individuals whose differences may well translate into different ideas about what norms should govern their shared life – and then adopting it (toleration) as a social ideal. Thus, on her view, we should not understand toleration as an obstacle to political change. Rather, it lays the groundwork for and enables political contestation – in any given iteration of which the proponents of political change may either succeed or fail.

Toleration as a Spur to Political Change

On yet a third understanding of toleration's relationship to political change, toleration does not obstruct, nor merely create space for, political change. On this understanding, it serves to spur political change – either because of the role toleration itself is made to play in society, or because the same values that ground a commitment to toleration also ground commitments to pursuing certain kinds of political change.

For a depiction of toleration as a potential tool of emancipatory political struggle, and therefore as a harbinger of radical departures from an oppressive status quo, we can turn again to Marcuse (1965, 1968). Though he sees in modern industrialized society a perverse, repressive version of tolerance, he also sees the possibility to practice an alternative, productive, liberating version (Marcuse 1965, 1968). The emancipatory variant of tolerance is distinctively asymmetric – "partisan," or "discriminating," in Marcuse's (1965, 85; 1968, 123) words. Repressive tolerance encourages impartiality between ideas, words, and actions that serve the causes of repression, domination, and violence (on the one hand) and ideas, words, and actions that serve the causes of emancipation, democracy, and humanity (on the other hand) (Marcuse 1965, 82, 85, 88, 94, 98–9, 109–13, 115–6; 1968, 120). It represents a "spurious neutrality" (Marcuse 1965, 113) on issues about which people should never be neutral (Marcuse 1965, 82, 88, 94, 98–9, 113; 1968, 120).

Conversely, "liberating tolerance" (Marcuse 1965, 109) amounts to intolerance toward whatever serves the cause of repression, domination, and violence – toward the conservative political movements that work to maintain the oppressive status quo and their associated propaganda – and tolerance toward whatever serves the cause of emancipation, democracy, and humanity – toward the leftist political movements that seek to upturn the status quo power relations (Marcuse 1965, 82, 85, 88, 98–9, 109–13, 116; 1968, 122–3). This, Marcuse (1968, 123) says, is the kind of tolerance that marks – and makes – a "free society," and it must be fought for by the oppressed themselves. This kind of tolerance not only brings liberation; it is borne of emancipatory struggle.

Michael Blake (2007) also suggests a more amenable relationship between toleration and political change. Like Rawls and Walzer, Blake (2007) is interested in how tolerance should manifest itself in international affairs – and more specifically in to what extent liberal states ought to show tolerance toward non-liberal states. According to Blake (2007, 2–3), tolerance involves showing "principled respect" for another party one believes to have committed some moral error and, in virtue of that respect, refraining from interfering to correct the error. Blake (like many whose views present toleration as an obstacle to political change) holds that tolerance involves refraining from promoting certain behavioral changes on the part of the "tolerated" party. But Blake's (2007, 2–3, 9–15) view is distinctive in that he argues the very moral commitments that (ought to) underlie a liberal's commitment to tolerance also require that liberals refuse tolerance toward states whose organizing principles are decidedly antithetical to liberalism. More specifically, Blake argues that, in the interpersonal case, liberals should *tolerate* those who endorse religious or moral beliefs they (the liberals) think mistaken for two reasons: first, there is value in each person working out the answers to life's deep theological and moral questions on their own; and, second, there are many different plausible sets of answers to such questions (even if only one set of answers is true) (Blake 2007, 9–11).

For similar reasons, Blake (2007, 11–15) proposes that liberal states, in conducting their international affairs, should *tolerate* other states that adopt policies they disagree with. After all, a state's core mission (from a liberal perspective) should be to govern so as to recognize "the equal moral worth of individual humans," and it is presumably morally valuable when states endeavor to do so (Blake 2007, 11). Moreover, that states should govern in accordance with the moral equality of persons is an abstract standard, whose concrete requirements may be understood in many different ways that are all plausible (even if only one is correct) (Blake 2007, 11). People who try to answer life's deep theological and moral questions for themselves deserve principled respect even if they end up endorsing answers we think are wrong; similarly, states that govern in line with some plausible interpretation of what it means to recognize persons' moral equality deserve principled respect even if they don't govern in line with the particular interpretation we think is correct (Blake 2007, 9–15).

Notice, though, that on this account the same values that give liberal states reason to tolerate states that govern in line with some plausible interpretation of what it means to recognize persons' moral equality also give liberal states reason to refuse to tolerate states that *don't* govern in line with any such plausible interpretation (Blake 2007, 11–15). Blake (2007, 15) even depicts this reason to refuse tolerance to certain parties as a part of his understanding of tolerance itself, writing, "To insist upon th[e] value [of equality] – and to be intolerant towards those who deny it – is in the end, the best understanding of tolerance we have." Thus, when liberal states encounter other states whose governing principles plainly reject the moral equality of persons, toleration doesn't recommend restraint in favor of maintaining the status quo. Instead, the values that should underpin liberals' commitment to tolerance – and, indeed, tolerance itself, properly understood – seem to recommend pursuing political change to bring the offending states' government in line with some plausible interpretation of what it means to recognize and treat all persons as equals.

Tan (2000, 50–1) puts forward a similar view – that liberals' fundamental moral commitment should be to individual autonomy, and that toleration is only valuable insofar as it helps protect and preserve individual autonomy. On this view, as with Blake's (2007), the same moral values that underlie a proper moral commitment to toleration may give us reason to refrain from promoting change in certain political contexts (for Tan (2000), when existing political arrangements protect individual autonomy), but they also give us reason to promote change in other political contexts (for Tan (2000), when existing political arrangements undermine individual autonomy). In Tan's (2000, 51) words, "cultures whose practices violate this more fundamental liberal value [of individual autonomy] defeat the very moral reason for tolerating them."

Finally, Rafanelli (2019, 6–8) argues, again in the international context, that some attempts to promote political change in a society other than one's own in fact treat the people there with toleration. In particular, attempts to promote change in another society that leave the people there sufficient freedom to decide for themselves whether or not they will adopt the proposed change treat them with toleration (Rafanelli 2019, 6–8). Rafanelli (2019, 6–8) argues that this means attempts to promote change by persuading or incentivizing (as opposed to coercing or forcing) people in another society to adopt some reform treat those people with toleration – at least as long as the reforms they encourage don't themselves promote intolerant behavior. Toleration, on this view, seems to give us reason to promote whatever political change there is independent moral reason to promote *in certain ways* – namely, those that leave the people whose behavior is to be changed sufficient freedom to decide for themselves whether they will adopt the proposed changes.

As understood by the views above, then, toleration itself – or at least the moral values that should underlie our commitment to it – may function to encourage certain kinds of political change. The range of possible relationships between toleration and political change, then, is strikingly wide. Toleration sometimes appears as an obstacle to political change; sometimes as neither an obstacle nor a spur to political change, but rather as a precondition for political contestation; and sometimes as a spur to political change.

Summary and Future Directions

That political theory scholarship casts toleration in so many different – and seemingly inconsistent – lights raises several questions and suggests some possible directions for future research. First, why does toleration take so many different forms? Why does it sometimes appear as an obstacle to political change, sometimes as a tool for facilitating politics (though neutral with respect to the promotion of political change per se), and sometimes as a spur to political change? One hypothesis is that toleration takes on different forms in virtue of the different background assumptions or value commitments of the different thinkers who write about it. Perhaps, for example, left critical theorists are likely to see toleration as a tool of the powers that be, whereas devout liberals are more likely to see it as a founding virtue of ideal political life. On this view, toleration's chimerical nature is not really a feature of toleration itself, but a reflection of other differences in the worldviews of these different thinkers.

That Marcuse (1965, 1968) sees both oppressive and emancipatory potential in tolerance, and that Walzer (1980, 1994, 1997, 2011, 2015) could plausibly be read to depict toleration *either* as an obstacle to political change *or* as a tool for facilitating politics, casts some amount of doubt on this hypothesis. Presumably, Marcuse's background moral commitments are self-identical. But, still, he sees tolerance as sometimes repressive (inimical to political change) and sometimes liberating (a spur to political change). Similarly, it's safe to assume Walzer's background moral commitments (even over the decades his cited work spans) are self-identical. But, even so, his work illustrates how toleration can work to obstruct certain kinds of political change *and* how it can help facilitate politics by protecting the common spaces in which it's practiced.

If we can't trace toleration's apparently ambivalent relationship to political change to the differing background commitments of the relevant thinkers, from where does it come? An alternate hypothesis is that toleration is simply a tool that can be used for whatever purposes those who utilize it want to further. On this view, it is unsurprising that toleration sometimes appears as an obstacle to political change, sometimes as a spur to it, and sometimes as a facilitator of political activity (whether it pulls in the direction of entrenching the status quo or changing it). Ideas, language, and norms of toleration in the hands of a state official may be used to entrench state power; whereas the same ideas, language, and norms in the hands of a revolutionary may be used to upturn status quo institutions and power relationships. This, notice, has virtually nothing to do with the *content* of the ideas, language, and norms of toleration. The claim is not that there is something unique or distinctive about toleration that gives it this ambivalent relationship to political change. Rather, the claim is more generally that any concept or set of ideas can be utilized to serve different – even contradictory – ends. That toleration can be utilized to serve ends that are unfriendly, friendly, or neutral toward political change is simply one instantiation of this more general rule. Presumably, the same could be said about other concepts as well, like fairness, equality, liberty, and recognition.

A third hypothesis is that there *is* something unique or distinctive about toleration that generates its ambivalent relationship to political change. The root cause, on this view, is an ambivalence within the concept of toleration itself. Perhaps it is the way that toleration is designed to reconcile diverse people and groups to living with their differences without eliminating them or even necessarily resolving the conflicts they inspire. Thus, Creppell (2003, 16–7) describes the distinguishing feature of "the project of toleration" as "its efforts to pursue unity and diversity at the same time." Yet, though toleration seems to recommend against eliminating difference, it doesn't necessarily involve *endorsing* beliefs or practices different from one's own, *celebrating* difference, or *utilizing* difference as a resource to promote social transformation (see Lorde 2007, 111–4; Oberdiek 2001, 5; Walzer 1997, 10–2). So, Oberdiek (2001 4, emphasis original) notes that tolerance and toleration appear to possess an "inherent *instability*," inhabiting "a no-man's-land between intolerance. . .and complete acceptance."

One direction for future research, then, is to further investigate what generates toleration's chimerical nature – in particular, what makes it have, or appear to have, such an ambivalent relationship to political change. If this investigation discovers that the ambivalence is the result of an ambivalence or tension within the concept of toleration itself, this opens up more questions. For example, if there is a fundamental tension within toleration itself between encouraging and discouraging political change, how should political and social institutions navigate this tension? Could institutions be designed so as to promote or instantiate toleration without raising objectionably high obstacles to political change, entrenching existing power structures? Perhaps one could avoid this danger by designing institutions to reflect a commitment to toleration that emphasized its more change-friendly elements or that heightened its revolutionary potential. How could such a thing be done? Is enabling or encouraging revolutionary change even the job of established social institutions? Or must this, as Marcuse (1965, 116–7; 1968, 123) suggests, be the task of individuals and communities acting outside or on the margins of such institutions?

References

Beaman LG (2013) Tolerance and accommodation as vestiges of the empire. In: Berman BJ, Bhargava R, Laliberté A (eds) Secular states and religious diversity. UBC Press, Vancouver

Blake M (2007) Tolerance and theocracy: how liberal states should think of religious states. J Int Aff 61(1):1–17

Cohen AJ (2004) What toleration is. Ethics 115(1):68–95

Creppell I (2003) Toleration and identity: foundations in early modern thought. Routledge, New York

Godfrey-Smith P, Kerr B (2019) Tolerance: a hierarchical analysis. J Polit Philos 27(4):403–421

Lorde A (2007) The master's tools will never dismantle the master's house. In: Sister outsider: essays and speeches by Audre Lorde. Crossing Press, Berkeley

Marcuse H (1965) Repressive tolerance. In: A critique of pure tolerance. Beacon Press, Boston

Marcuse H (1968) Postscript 1968. In: A critique of pure tolerance. Beacon Press, Boston

Oberdiek H (2001) Tolerance: between forbearance and acceptance. Rowman and Littlefield Publishers, Lanham

Rafanelli LM (2019) Promoting justice across borders. Political Studies 0, 0:1–20. https://doi.org/10.1177/0032321719875402

Rawls J (1999) The law of peoples with "the idea of public reason revisited". Harvard University Press, Cambridge

Tan K-C (2000) Toleration, diversity, and global justice. The Pennsylvania State University Press, University Park

Walzer M (1980) The moral standing of states: a response to four critics. Philos Public Aff 9(3):209–229

Walzer M (1994) Thick and thin: moral argument at home and abroad. University of Notre Dame Press, Notre Dame

Walzer M (1997) On toleration. Yale University Press, New Haven

Walzer M (2011) Achieving global and local justice. Dissent 58(3):42–48

Walzer M (2015) Just and unjust wars: a moral argument with historical illustrations, 5th edn. Basic Books, New York

Wolff RP (1965) Beyond tolerance. In: A critique of pure tolerance. Beacon Press, Boston

Toleration and the Law 11

Stijn Smet

Contents

Introduction 190
Toleration and Tolerance in the Law 190
    Conceptualizations of Toleration/Tolerance by Apex Courts 191
Toleration and Neutrality in the Law 195
    Categories of Legal Toleration 197
    Pragmatic Justifications for Legal Toleration 199
    Implications of Legal Toleration 200
Toleration and Respect in the Law 201
    Alternative Constitutional Understandings of Toleration and Respect 202
    Toleration, Respect, and Religious Exemptions 204
Summary and Future Directions 206
References 208

Abstract

The merits, drawbacks, and paradoxes of toleration have been studied extensively in political theory. By contrast, we know comparatively little about the salience of toleration to the law. This chapter aims to address this gap in our knowledge by mapping what we do know about "legal toleration," examining how the law relates to three central dichotomies: toleration/tolerance, toleration/neutrality, and toleration/respect. Throughout the chapter, two descriptive claims are made. First, the conceptualization of toleration is (even) murkier – and certainly looser – in law than it is in political theory. Second, the more pragmatic approach of the law enables state practices of toleration to persist in practice, even in the face of conceptually more coherent and normatively more desirable ideals such as neutrality and respect.

S. Smet (✉)
Faculty of Law, Hasselt University, Hasselt, Belgium
e-mail: stijn.smet@uhasselt.be

© The Author(s), under exclusive licence to Springer Nature Switzerland AG 2022
M. Sardoč (ed.), *The Palgrave Handbook of Toleration*,
https://doi.org/10.1007/978-3-030-42121-2_56

> **Keywords**
>
> Toleration · Neutrality · Respect · Constitutional law · Legal toleration · Vertical toleration · Horizontal tolerance · Religious freedom · Religious exemptions · Pragmatic reasons · Deontological reasons

Introduction

Toleration occurs when an agent deliberately refrains from interfering with persons or their beliefs, opinions, behavior, and practices of which the agent disapproves, because they believe there are good reasons not to act on their disapproval (▶ Chaps. 3, "Defining Toleration," and ▶ 2, "Toleration: Concept and Conceptions"). The merits, drawbacks, and paradoxes of toleration have been studied extensively in political theory and political philosophy (see most chapters in this volume). By contrast, we know comparatively little about the salience of toleration to the law (but see Berger 2008; Nehushtan 2013; Fredman 2020; Smet 2019a, 2020).

Unsurprisingly, the questions David Heyd raises in his chapter also inform the relationship between toleration and the law:

> who is the tolerating party – an individual, a group, an institution, the law? What kind of beliefs and practices are the objects of toleration – opinions, manners, moral behaviour, or aesthetic values? What are the limits of toleration [...]? [And h]ow do we justify the tolerant attitude – on a principled basis or on pragmatic *ad hoc* grounds? (▶ Chap. 4, "What Toleration Is Not")

This chapter aims to map our understanding of the role of toleration in the law by providing initial answers to at least some of these questions. Throughout the chapter, two descriptive claims are made. First, the conceptualization of toleration in law is (even) murkier – and certainly looser – than it is in political theory. Second, the more pragmatic approach of the law enables state practices of toleration to persist in practice, even in the face of conceptually more coherent and normatively more desirable ideals such as neutrality and respect. The chapter is structured around three central dichotomies and examines how the law relates to each of these: toleration/tolerance (section "Toleration and Tolerance in the Law"), toleration/neutrality (section "Toleration and Neutrality in the Law"), and toleration/respect (section "Toleration and Respect in the Law"). The chapter concludes by summarizing the main findings and providing avenues for further reflection and future research.

Toleration and Tolerance in the Law

In political theory, toleration is commonly distinguished from tolerance, whereby the former refers to activities or practices and the latter to an attitude or moral virtue (▶ Chaps. 3, "Defining Toleration," and ▶ 2, "Toleration: Concept and

Conceptions"). An additional distinction is often made between vertical forms of toleration/tolerance that occur in the arena of politics between the state and its citizens, and horizontal forms that shape interpersonal relationships between citizens (▶ Chap. 4, "What Toleration Is Not"). Combining both axes – toleration/tolerance and vertical/horizontal – gives us four central concepts to map onto the law. Certain nuances are packed into the terms used in the rough definitions that follow. The pertinence and accuracy of these nuances cannot be entered into here, but most are discussed elsewhere in this volume (e.g., ▶ Chaps. 8, "Political Toleration Explained," ▶ 3, "Defining Toleration," ▶ 2, "Toleration: Concept and Conceptions," ▶ 4, "What Toleration Is Not," and ▶ 41, "Toleration and Religious Discrimination").

- *Vertical tolerance* is an attitude of tolerance held by the state toward its citizens.
- *Vertical toleration* refers to state practices of toleration, that is, acts by which the state tolerates citizens' beliefs, opinions, behavior, and/or practices of which it disapproves.
- *Horizontal tolerance* is an attitude or moral virtue of tolerances held by citizens in their interpersonal relationships.
- *Horizontal toleration* refers to acts by which citizens tolerate one another and/or each other's beliefs, opinions, behavior, and/or practices of which they disapprove.

The central aim of this section is to map these varying conceptions of toleration and tolerance onto the law.

Conceptualizations of Toleration/Tolerance by Apex Courts

Conceptual and normative arguments to the contrary (see sections "Toleration and Neutrality in the Law" and "Toleration and Respect in the Law"), in practice the law continues to both promote horizontal tolerance *and* engage in vertical toleration. For instance, when the Supreme Court of Israel holds that "[m]utual tolerance among persons of different [. . .] faiths is a fundamental precondition for the existence of a free, democratic society" (*Universal City Studios v. Films and Plays Censorship Board* 1989), it aims to promote horizontal tolerance as a moral virtue among citizens with competing conceptions of the good. Conversely, when the United States Supreme Court rules that "[t]he Free Exercise Clause [which guarantees freedom of religion] commits government itself to religious tolerance" (*Church of the Lukumi Babalu Aye v. Hialeah* 1993), it indicates that the state ought to engage, in at least some circumstances, in vertical toleration.

In what follows, four examples are discussed to illustrate how apex courts (i.e., the highest court in a given jurisdiction) conceptualize and understand the role of toleration and tolerance in law. Judicial understandings of toleration/tolerance, as reflected in these examples, moreover align with Rainer Forst's four conceptions of toleration: the permission, coexistence, respect, and esteem conceptions of toleration (▶ Chap. 2, "Toleration: Concept and Conceptions").

When reviewing the French ban on full-face veils, the European Court of Human Rights found that as "[p]luralism, tolerance and broadmindedness are hallmarks of a 'democratic society'," the state is under a duty "to ensure mutual tolerance between opposing groups" (*S.A.S. v. France* 2012). In other words, the European Court imposed a legal obligation upon states to promote horizontal tolerance among their citizens (cf. Jones 2007). On the face of it, the Court's approach seems to draw on either Forst's coexistence conception or his respect conception of horizontal tolerance (both of which are discussed below).

In operationalizing the cited principles, however, the European Court ultimately endorsed France's reliance on the *permission conception* of tolerance. As Forst (▶ Chap. 2, "Toleration: Concept and Conceptions") explains, on the permission conception "toleration designates the relation between an authority or majority and a minority which does not subscribe to the dominant system of values," whereby "the authority (or majority) grants the minority the permission to live in accordance with its convictions" provided these remain a private matter. This implies that "the authority or majority [. . .] has the power [. . .] to intervene and to coerce the minority into (at least external) conformity" (ibid.), but chooses not to use that power and tolerate the minority instead.

In passing a ban on the wearing of full-face veils, France *did* decide to use its power – by deploying the force of the criminal law – to coerce a visible minority into external conformity with the majority's conception of "living together." Put differently, France *withdrew* permission toleration vis-a-vis the minority religious practice of concealing the face. In its ruling, the European Court of Human Rights endorsed, as a choice of society, France's decision to enforce "the requirements of 'living together'" by promulgating a blanket ban on full-face veils in order to "protect a principle of interaction between individuals" (*S.A.S. v. France* 2012). Ironically, the European Court thereby inscribed the French ban in the logics of the permission conception of vertical toleration and its limits, contrary to the Court's own established principle "that democracy does not mean that the views of a majority must always prevail over those of a minority" (ibid.).

A more steadfast commitment to the *coexistence conception* of horizontal tolerance can be discerned in Israeli constitutional law. In Forst's terms, coexistence tolerance "counts as an appropriate means of avoiding conflict" by which "groups of approximately equal strengths [. . .] recognise that they must exercise tolerance for the sake of social peace" and forge mutual compromises to that end (▶ Chap. 2, "Toleration: Concept and Conceptions"). In Israeli constitutional law, tolerance is deployed precisely in those terms: as a tool to navigate tensions that pit equally powerful groups of (ultra) orthodox Jews and secular Jews against one another. Within this divisive context, a primary function of tolerance is to enable compromise solutions between the opposing groups (Smet 2020). As the Supreme Court of Israel puts it, "[s]ocial consensus, based on compromise, is by far preferable to an imposed judicial decision," for in stepping back the judiciary enables social solutions "based on mutual tolerance" (*Horev v. Minster of Transportation* 1996). The idea, in other words, is that the moral virtue of horizontal tolerance will propel parties to a religious

11 Toleration and the Law

dispute toward a compromise that allows them to coexist, thereby avoiding the need for constitutional litigation.

But even when mutual tolerance fails and the Court is compelled to truncate religious disputes itself, it often settles on a compromise solution in the name of toleration, since "[i]t is appropriate that the legal ruling should reflect [. . .] the spirit of compromise and tolerance" (*Shavit v. Rishon Lezion Jewish Burial Society* 1999). Consider, for instance, the Court's response to practices of coerced gender segregation on *mehadrin* (meticulous) bus lines. In *Ragen v. Ministry of Transport* (2011), the Supreme Court of Israel ruled that such coercive segregation was unconstitutional, while simultaneously indicating that there was no legal impediment to allowing *voluntary* gender segregation on buses. "[I]t is even possible," the Court noted, "that we must try to help" those who wish to voluntarily practice gender segregation, out of "consideration [for their] religious needs and beliefs" (ibid.). Although the latter claim could also be read in terms of Forst's respect or even esteem conception of tolerance, the *Ragen* judgment is best understood as indicating a compromise solution on the boundaries of coexistence tolerance in Israeli society: coercive gender segregation on buses is outside those boundaries, whereas voluntary segregation remains within them.

Moving on to Forst's *respect conception* of tolerance, under which "[t]he tolerating parties respect one another as autonomous persons or as equally entitled members of a political community constituted under the rule of law" (▶ Chap. 2, "Toleration: Concept and Conceptions"), this conception of tolerance arguably undergirds the United States Supreme Court's ruling in *Masterpiece Cakeshop v. Colorado Civil Rights Commission* (2018). Although an altogether different register of language – that of neutrality, coercion, separation, endorsement and accommodation – guides constitutional discourse on religion in the United States, toleration arguably remains foundational to a nuanced understanding of the First Amendment to the Constitution of the United States (Smet 2020).

This is evident from the *Masterpiece Cakeshop* case, which involved a Christian baker who had refused to make a wedding cake for a same-sex couple and was subsequently found in breach of antidiscrimination legislation by the Colorado Civil Rights Commission. In reviewing the baker's case, the Supreme Court of the United States held that the Commission's treatment thereof disclosed constitutionally impermissible hostility toward religion. How the baker was treated, the Court found, "was neither tolerant nor respectful of [his] religious beliefs" (*Masterpiece Cakeshop v. Colorado Civil Rights Commission* 2018). Derogatory statements about the baker's religious beliefs by one of the commissioners, in particular, indicated hostility to the Supreme Court. In future, the Court concluded, "these [kinds of] disputes must be resolved with tolerance, without undue disrespect to sincere religious beliefs, and without subjecting gay persons to indignities when they seek goods and services in an open market" (ibid.).

The last passage is reminiscent of the Israeli Supreme Court's emphasis on compromise solutions that enable opposing groups to coexist. Yet the primary concern of the United States Supreme Court in *Masterpiece Cakeshop* was arguably not with ensuring "mere" peaceful coexistence. Instead, the Court indicated that groups with incompatible conceptions of the good should tolerate each other's beliefs and practices, *while* fully respecting each other as autonomous persons or as equally entitled members of a political community. In other words, the Court aimed to promote the respect conception of tolerance in how citizens and legal actors (e.g., civil rights commissions) resolve religious disputes like the one at the heart of *Masterpiece Cakeshop*.

Canadian constitutional law, finally, approximates – and seemingly informs – the *esteem conception* of toleration, which "involves a more demanding form of recognition than the respect conception for [it] also [requires] esteeming [persons'] convictions and practices as ethically valuable" (▶ Chap. 2, "Toleration: Concept and Conceptions"). This esteem conception of toleration undergirds, for instance, a Canadian case concerning the construction of sukkahs by Jewish condominium co-owners in violation of the condominium's by-laws (Kislowicz 2017: 224). In balancing the Jewish co-owners' religious freedom against the right to property of the other co-owners, the Supreme Court of Canada held:

> In a multiethnic and multicultural country such as ours, which accentuates and advertises its modern record of respecting cultural diversity and human rights and of promoting tolerance of religious and ethnic minorities – and is in many ways an example thereof for other societies –, the argument of the [other co-owners] that nominal, minimally intruded-upon aesthetic interests should outweigh the exercise of [...] religious freedom is unacceptable. (*Syndicat Northcrest v. Amselem* 2004)

The Canadian example confirms Forst's doubts as to whether the esteem conception of toleration can still be classified as toleration, properly understood, since the element of disapproval (or rejection) can be difficult to identify (▶ Chap. 2, "Toleration: Concept and Conceptions"). Indeed, it is far from obvious that the Supreme Court of Canada somehow disapproved of the religious practice of constructing sukkahs (or acknowledged disapproval thereof in society). In that sense, the Court's emphasis on "promoting tolerance of religious and ethnic minorities" in *Amselem* could also be interpreted in terms of what Peter Balint calls *general* toleration (▶ Chap. 8, "Political Toleration Explained"). The salience to the law of Balint's argument on general toleration is discussed in some detail in subsequent sections of this chapter.

This section has intended to illustrate how apex courts conceptualize the role of toleration in law. The limited examples given do not – and cannot – do justice to the complexity and nuances present in the wider case law, nor to how other legal actors than courts understand and deploy toleration. At the same time, the four examples do reveal a murky patchwork of understandings and conceptions of toleration operating in the law, across jurisdictions. At times, the same apex court even relies on diverging conceptions of toleration within a single ruling (e.g., the European Court of Human Right in *S.A.S. v. France*).

In most of the discussed examples, however, apex courts prioritize promoting a conception of horizontal tolerance rather than extending (or withholding) vertical toleration themselves. As such, the above examples also provide some support for Jones's (2007) understanding of political toleration in the liberal state: the idea that the liberal state should not engage in practices of toleration itself, but can and should actively promote tolerance and toleration among citizens. In the remainder of this chapter, by contrast, the focus shifts from horizontal tolerance to vertical toleration in and by the law (henceforth referred to as "legal toleration"). The discussion is structured around the core arguments *against* vertical toleration, to wit arguments drawing on neutrality (section "Toleration and Neutrality in the Law") and on respect (section "Toleration and Respect in the Law").

Toleration and Neutrality in the Law

Legal toleration, that is vertical toleration in and by the law, generates conceptual problems, including the possibility that, like all forms of vertical toleration, it may well be an oxymoron (Gray 2000; Heyd 2008). In this volume, Heyd (▶ Chap. 4, "What Toleration Is Not") argues forcefully that "toleration has no place in the way the state relates to its citizens," since all laws enacted by the state must comply with the human/civil rights guaranteed by the constitution. "Tolerant attitudes of citizens may lead to changes in the law allowing for certain practices despite their being unpopular or opposed by the majority of the citizens," Heyd (ibid.) continues, "but once enacted, these laws, rather than any attitude of toleration, should guide state action." In other words, "[t]he law either permits or prohibits certain practices and activities [but t]he prohibited act cannot be tolerated by the law and the permitted practice cannot be said to be endured the state" (Heyd 2008: 178). Therefore, the state – and the law with it – is said to be incapable of embodying vertical toleration.

A central challenge to legal toleration concerns the relationship between vertical toleration and neutrality (▶ Chap. 8, "Political Toleration Explained"). This relationship can be conceptualized in at least three ways.

First, in terms of incompatibility. Incompatibility between vertical toleration and neutrality is said to arise from the fact that toleration entails disapproval whereas neutrality precludes the state from disapproving of its citizens' conceptions of the good (Gray 2000; Heyd 2008). As a result, the neutral state cannot (or ought not to) engage in vertical toleration. It either permits practices or bans them. There is no middle ground in which the state can tolerate its citizens' practices (▶ Chap. 14, "Toleration and State Neutrality: The Case of Symbolic FGM"). Since the argument from incompatibility between vertical toleration and neutrality poses an acute challenge to legal toleration, it needs to be engaged with in this section. The primary aim, however, is not to dispute or affirm the conceptual validity of the argument from incompatibility. Instead, it is to show that in liberal democracies the law does, as a matter of actual practice, tolerate certain practices *and* does so largely for pragmatic reasons. I call this pragmatic legal toleration (Smet 2019a). Yet before discussing legal toleration in detail, we need to briefly consider two ways in which the relationship between vertical toleration and neutrality can be conceptualized in terms of *compatibility*.

One way to argue for compatibility of vertical toleration and neutrality is to insist that the neutral state cannot possibly be neutral about everything (Moon 2012).

Instead, the neutral state can and does disapprove of certain practices. The state can either ban these disapproved of practices or tolerate them. Either way, the state's duty of neutrality is perfectly compatible with its tolerating specific practices. This way of conceiving of the relationship between neutrality and vertical toleration relies on the alleged impossibility of absolute neutrality, a point frequently made by legal scholars (e.g., Moon 2012). Yet these legal scholars seem to understand neutrality as neutrality of outcome, whereas there is more or less general agreement within liberal political theory that this is an unachievable or impractical aim to strive for (Rawls 1993). As such, the argument for compatibility misunderstands the nature of the argument from *incompatibility*, which draws on understandings of neutrality as justificatory neutrality or neutrality of intent. For that reason, the first argument for compatibility between vertical toleration and neutrality is disregarded in the remainder of this chapter.

A different way to argue for compatibility of vertical toleration and neutrality is not by reinterpreting the requirements of neutrality, but by refining our understanding of toleration. This project is undertaken by Balint in this volume (see also Jones 2007). Balint (► Chap. 8, "Political Toleration Explained") makes sense of toleration as a political practice by distinguishing general toleration from forbearance tolerance. Whereas the latter involves specific acts of tolerance that entail disapproval, the former describes the general approach of the state to issues of difference and, crucially, does not involve negative valuing. Instead, the tolerant liberal state in the general sense "withholds judgement on a very wide range of its citizens' differences [...] because, in most cases, it is indifferent to them" (► Chap. 8, "Political Toleration Explained"). As such, "toleration as a general practice is entirely compatible with liberal neutrality" (ibid.).

Balint's argument for compatibility between vertical toleration and neutrality is, however, best discarded for our current purposes for two reasons. First, it seems to rest on conceptual fudging of toleration and indifference (cf. ► Chap. 3, "Defining Toleration"). Second, and more importantly, this chapter is primarily concerned with how the law engages in toleration with regard to specific practices. In other words, we are not in the domain of Balint's general toleration but of specific instances of forbearance tolerance. In this domain, incompatibility between neutrality and vertical toleration persists, although part of the descriptive account that follows tracks Balint's understanding of forbearance tolerance.

In the remainder of this section, two conceptual claims are made in relation to the (alleged) incompatibility between vertical toleration and neutrality. The first, descriptive claim concerns the actor and object of toleration and is relatively simple: as a matter of practice, vertical toleration of persons' beliefs, practices, behavior, and opinions by the law is not an uncommon occurrence in constitutional democracies. Theoretical arguments about the state's duty of neutrality notwithstanding, the law's response to a broad range of contested issues – prostitution, marijuana consumption, tobacco use, hate speech, conscientious objection – can be subsumed under the analytical structure of toleration (Smet 2019a, *contra* ► Chap. 14, "Toleration and State Neutrality: The Case of Symbolic FGM"). The second claim concerns the justification for vertical toleration in and by the law: such legal toleration is often, though not exclusively, founded on pragmatic reasons (Smet 2019a).

Categories of Legal Toleration

As a matter of practice, legal toleration is not an uncommon occurrence in constitutional democracies (Smet 2019a; ► Chap. 8, "Political Toleration Explained"). But for legal toleration to be characterized as a form of toleration, it must combine two opposing forces: disapproval and permission. When the law tolerates a given practice, it permits that practice despite disapproval thereof. This schizophrenic combination of disapproval and permission means that legal toleration cannot be pervasive. Otherwise legal systems would be plagued by the equivalent of dissociative identity disorder. Nevertheless, a range of legal rules and policies can be subsumed under the analytical structure of toleration. Such legal toleration comes in two categories (Smet 2019a). Although both are instances of vertical toleration, this qualification is (even) more controversial in relation to the second category than the first.

The first, relatively uncontroversial category involves situations in which legal actors *de facto* permit practices that are *de jure* illegal. For instance, prostitution or sex work is often permitted (i.e., not prosecuted) in red light districts, despite criminal provisions that prohibit acts related to prostitution (e.g., procuring, running a brothel, and soliciting outside designated areas). Labeling this and similar cases as instances of legal toleration is relatively uncontroversial, since both components of toleration – disapproval and permission – are clearly present. Prohibitions in criminal law underscore the objectionable nature of a practice, thereby signaling state disapproval in the law on the books (see also ► Chap. 8, "Political Toleration Explained"). Yet, the criminal law is intentionally left unenforced. In other words, the law in action permits the practice. This slippage between the law on the books (disapproval) and the law in action (permission) creates space for legal toleration (Smet 2019a).

Consider, by way of example, the law on marijuana (Smet 2019a). In Uruguay, Canada, and several US states, the production, sale, and consumption of marijuana are legal. At the federal level in the United States, by contrast, marijuana is criminalized and the object of strict enforcement policies under the Trump administration. But in other countries still, the criminal law penalizes the sale and possession of marijuana, thereby expressing disapproval, yet is deliberately left unenforced in practice. In the Netherlands, for instance, the sale and possession of marijuana are illegal, but prosecutorial policies of nonenforcement are in place up to a certain threshold. Marijuana can be sold in dedicated shops and individuals are not prosecuted when found in possession of small quantities of the drug. The law in action thus tolerates the sale and possession of marijuana up to a certain point. At the same time, markers of disapproval are in place. In the law on the books, the sale and possession of marijuana remain criminal offences and possession above the threshold of toleration can thus lead to prosecution. Moreover, the sale of marijuana in coffee shops is subject to strict regulatory conditions, including not selling to minors, bans on advertising and prohibitions on giving access to nonresidents of the Netherlands.

In the second, more difficult category of legal toleration, the converse occurs: the state disapproves of practices that are entirely legal. In this category, the criminal law does not – not even as law on the books – coercively interfere with a given practice. For example, no state has banned tobacco use, even if smoking is increasingly disapproved of due to the third-party harm it causes. At first blush, there are no markers of legal toleration here. Indeed, in the absence of criminal prohibitions the disapproval that distinguishes legal toleration from acceptance or indifference can be difficult to identify. Yet, disapproval can also be discerned in state communicative action, through which lawmakers signal that certain practices are "merely" tolerated and nothing more. In other words, under this category of legal toleration the law on the books permits, while the law in action signals disapproval. In the case of tobacco use, the state communicates disapproval in various ways: by directing manufacturers to display dissuasive labels on tobacco products, by restricting the public spaces in which smoking is allowed, by banning commercial advertising for tobacco products and by increasing taxes on their sale (see also ► Chap. 8, "Political Toleration Explained").

Consider also, by way of a further example, hate speech in the United States (Smet 2019a). Although hate speech is legal in the United States, it is not accepted as inherently valuable speech. Instead, it is the object of legal toleration (Rosenfeld 1996, *contra* ► Chap. 14, "Toleration and State Neutrality: The Case of Symbolic FGM"). Under United States constitutional law, neo-Nazi and white supremacist marches – whether in Skokie in 1978, Charlottesville in 2017, or Washington, DC, in 2020 – cannot be banned on the sole basis of their hateful content (*Village of Skokie v. National Socialist Party of America* 1978). Toleration plays an important role in supporting this – comparatively speaking – extreme take on free speech. As the Supreme Court puts it, "in public debate [we] must tolerate insulting, and even outrageous, speech in order to provide adequate 'breathing space' to the freedoms protected by the First Amendment" (*Snyder v. Phelps* 2011, citing *Boos v. Barry* 1988).

Hate speech is thus legal in the United States. But the law is not indifferent towards it. As the Supreme Court also held in *Snyder* (2011): "[t]he state's protection of these [hateful] viewpoints [. . .] is not equivalent to the state's indifference to them." Instead, hate speech is arguably the object of legal toleration in United States constitutional law. This presupposes, however, that legal actors somehow communicate their stance of toleration, including and especially the disapproval it entails (Brettschneider 2012). If they do not, legal toleration of hate speech is likely to be mistaken for indifference or even acceptance. As noted above, vertical toleration in and by the law depends on legal actors utilizing their communicative power to somehow express disapproval of the tolerated practice (see also ► Chap. 8, "Political Toleration Explained").

This is exactly what courts in the United States have done in prominent hate speech cases. The Supreme Court has for instance ruled that confronting racist beliefs cannot "consist of selective limitations upon speech," *while* taking pains to emphasize its "belief that burning a cross in someone's front yard is reprehensible" (*RAV v. City of St Paul* 1992). Similarly, the Court of Appeals for the Seventh Circuit, reviewing the case of the neo-Nazi march in Skokie, went to great lengths "to express [its] repugnance at the doctrines" of the National Socialist Party of

America (*Collin v. Smith* 1978). The court described those doctrines as "generally unacceptable" and "repugnant to the core values held generally by residents of this country and, indeed, to much of what we cherish in civilization" (ibid.). Nevertheless, the court concluded that the Constitution demanded that the hate speech at issue be tolerated: "if these civil rights are to remain vital for all, they must protect not only those society deems acceptable, but also those whose ideas it quite justifiably rejects and despises" (ibid.).

Pragmatic Justifications for Legal Toleration

Whereas the first claim served to establish the salience of vertical toleration to the law, the second claim locates the justification for legal toleration in pragmatic reasons. Lawmakers and other legal actors often, though not exclusively, support policies of legal toleration on pragmatic grounds (Smet 2019a). This is a good thing, for if and when lawmakers instead regulate moral controversies by balancing the deontological arguments that undergird competing normative viewpoints in society, they are liable to deepen societal divisions rather than alleviate them. From that perspective, *pragmatic* legal toleration provides a useful alternative in that it effectively sidesteps protracted deontological disagreement by supplying less contentious reasons in support of legal policy. This minimizes the risk that state policies of legal toleration (inadvertently) increase polarization in society (Smet 2019a).

Consider, by way of example, conscientious objection to abortion (Smet 2019a). When doctors refuse to perform abortions for reasons of religious conscience, lawmakers can respond in a variety of ways. They can ban conscientious objection to abortion, guided by disapproval of doctors' refusal to perform abortions. They can insert conscience clauses in abortion legislation out of respect for doctors' religious conscience. Or they can permit conscientious objection, despite their disapproval thereof. The latter response is one of legal toleration, which can be based on different kinds of reasons. A possible deontological reason to tolerate doctors' refusal to perform abortions is deference to their personal autonomy. Yet personal autonomy is at the very heart of divisive disagreement over abortion. By explicitly giving more weight to a doctor's right to refuse than a woman's right to choose, lawmakers thus risk intensifying societal division over abortion rather than alleviating it.

Instead, lawmakers can also base legal toleration on pragmatic grounds, which the legislature in the United Kingdom for instance did when it inserted a conscience clause in the Abortion Act 1967 (Smet 2019a). As the Supreme Court of the United Kingdom has indicated, "[t]he conscience clause [of the Abortion Act 1967] was the quid pro quo for a law designed to enable the health care profession to offer a lawful, safe and accessible service to women" (*Greater Glasgow Health Board v. Doogan* 2014). A central pragmatic reason in support of the conscience clause was to ensure the safety of surgical abortions by removing them from the back alley: "the policy of the 1967 Act [was] to ensure that abortion was carried out with all proper skill and in hygienic conditions [whereas before] many women [sought] the services of 'back-street' abortionists, which were often unsafe" (ibid.). Yet this required a concession, in the shape of a conscience clause, to ensure that doctors with conscientious objections would not be forced to proceed with an act they feel incapable of performing, and would presumably perform badly if coerced to do so. Crucially, contestants on both sides of the moral debate can arguably subscribe to the importance of avoiding poorly executed and unsafe surgery, regardless of their deontological position on abortion. As such, the pragmatic reason can engender broad(er) support for legal toleration of conscientious objection to abortion (admittedly, this argument would not hold for medical abortions).

Consider also, once more, hate speech (Smet 2019a). Several rationales have been invoked to justify the ban on most content-based restrictions of speech in United States constitutional law. Some of these justifications, such as the rationale from autonomy (Fried 1992), are deontological and will not be considered here. An influential pragmatic rationale, which "has been dominant" (Rosenfeld 1996) ever since it was first formulated by Justice Holmes, is skeptical of the idea of truth. Commonly known as "the fortress model" (Blasi 1987), the skeptical rationale for broad protection of free speech is based on the notion that any idea can be false and most likely is.

Perhaps somewhat counterintuitively, the skeptical rationale is primarily concerned about the threat of overbreadth (i.e., excessive restrictions of speech) attending government regulation of speech. The Supreme Court of the United States has for instance held that "we think it is largely because governmental officials cannot make principled distinctions in this area [of aspects related to the truth value of speech] that the Constitution leaves [these] matters [. . .] largely to the individual" (*Village of Skokie v. National Socialist Party of America* 1978, citing *Cohen v. California* 1971). In other words, hate speech is tolerated in United States constitutional law to avoid a sliding scale on which the government inevitably ends up restricting valuable speech, however commendable its original intentions are (but see Nehushtan 2007). The antidote of the fortress model is "to overprotect speech" by erecting a "doctrinal buffer zone" (Blasi 1987). Legal toleration of hate speech resides in that buffer zone, where it is supported by pragmatic reasons concerning the negative consequences attending overzealous regulation of speech by the government. Since these negative consequences could in principle impact on everyone, their avoidance is a shared pragmatic reason to which both sides of the hate speech controversy could subscribe.

Implications of Legal Toleration

What follows from the above claims about legal toleration? The primary conclusion we may be tempted to draw is that law and political theory are misaligned on the relationship between vertical toleration and neutrality. If vertical toleration and (justificatory) neutrality truly are incompatible, the law should not (be able to) tolerate certain practices. Yet, that is exactly what it appears to sometimes do in practice.

There are at least two ways to escape the conclusion that law and political theory are misaligned on the question of vertical toleration and neutrality. One way is to reinterpret what is going on in instances of legal toleration. If Jones (2007) is right in arguing that the state cannot engage in vertical toleration itself, but can – and must – promote horizontal tolerance among its citizens, the converse might also occur. That is, the state can also be guided by societal disapproval of certain practices, but decide to permit these practices regardless. This resolves the misalignment problem by separating the locus of the objection component and the permission component of toleration: "the liberal state tolerates what society dislikes" (▶ Chap. 18, "Political Toleration as Substantive Neutrality"). Thus reconstructed, instances of legal toleration need not be incompatible with the state's duty of neutrality.

Another way to avoid the conclusion of misalignment is to insist that the account of legal toleration sketched above does not – or does not only – involve competing conceptions of the good, but a broader range of practices than those to which a duty of justificatory neutrality would ordinarily apply. A different way of putting this is that the above account is not one of toleration at all, but one of the limits of constitutional rights, proportionality, and/or harm analysis (Heyd 2008; Jones 2015; ▶ Chap. 14, "Toleration and State Neutrality: The Case of Symbolic FGM"). Conceptualizing the above examples as instances of legal toleration, however, seems to more accurately reflect what is going on in practice, even if this requires an extended understanding of the kinds of practices that can be the object of (vertical) toleration (see ▶ Chap. 3, "Defining Toleration").

Toleration and Respect in the Law

Toleration not only involves a combination of disapproval and permission, thereby generating a tension with neutrality. It also requires that agents who engage in toleration (believe that they) have the power to interfere with the practices they disapprove of, but opt not to use that power (▶ Chaps. 3, "Defining Toleration," and ▶ 2, "Toleration: Concept and Conceptions"). A state, authority, or majority that engages in toleration disapproves of what members of a minority believe, say or do, but decides not to use its power to interfere with their beliefs, opinions, behavior, or practices.

To the idea that disapproval and power imbalances are inherent to practices of toleration, a relatively straightforward counterargument is often put forward: minorities do not wish to be tolerated, especially not by the state, given the disapproval and subordination this entails. Instead, minorities lay claim to and are said to be deserving of something more: acceptance, respect, and/or recognition (Mendus 1989; Galeotti 2002; Nussbaum 2008; ▶ Chap. 4, "What Toleration Is Not"). This concern with a move beyond toleration echoes the thoughts of several founding figures of the United States Constitution (see also ▶ Chap. 49, "Early Modern Arguments for Toleration"). James Madison, for instance, objected to a reference to toleration in a draft of the Virginia Declaration of Rights – the draft proclaimed that "all men should enjoy the fullest toleration in the exercise of religion" – because it suggested legislative grace, "as if it were by the blessing of the majority that the minority was not persecuted" (McConnell 1990; Nussbaum 2008). As David

Richards (1986: 133) argues, Madison's position was motivated by an ethics of equal respect that is reflected in the contemporary account of Martha Nussbaum (2008). In short, the idea (or value, if it is one) of toleration appears to be in tension with that of (equal) respect.

When we examine how the law deals with this tension, quite a bit of slippage and overlap can be discerned in how the law deploys notions of toleration and respect to respond to religious diversity (Smet 2020). Constitutional courts, for instance, frequently invoke both toleration *and* respect to indicate how the law, society at large, and citizens within it should engage with religious diversity. In doing so, these courts appear to conflate both notions. The Supreme Court of the United States, for instance, has noted that "destroying or defacing [a] Cross that has stood undisturbed for nearly a century would not [...] further the ideals of respect and tolerance embodied in the First Amendment" (*American Legion v. American Humanist Association* 2019). Similarly, the Supreme Court of Canada has stated that "[a]n important feature of [Canadian] constitutional democracy is respect for minorities [...] Indeed, respect for and tolerance of the rights and practices of religious minorities is one of the hallmarks of an enlightened democracy" (*Syndicat Northcrest v. Amselem* 2004).

Since it is impossible to provide a generalized account of how the law understands the relationship between toleration and respect, in what follows this relationship will instead be analyzed from the perspective of two instructive case studies (Smet 2020). First, the conceptualization of toleration and respect in Indian constitutional law indicates that both notions need not be understood in incompatible terms (Sub-section "Alternative Constitutional Understandings of Toleration and Respect"). Second, the response of United States constitutional law to the problem of religious exemptions shows that legal actors can shift back and forth between the lenses of toleration and respect (Sub-section "Toleration, Respect, and Religious Exemptions").

Alternative Constitutional Understandings of Toleration and Respect

Conflation, or what appears to be conflation, of toleration and respect in constitutional discourse is particularly puzzling in light of arguments in the literature that consider respect superior to toleration. Yet, in at least some constitutional settings, such conflation is more apparent than real. Consider, for instance, Indian constitutional law (Smet 2020). The Supreme Court of India has held that "[a]rticles 25 and 26 [of the Constitution, which safeguard religious freedom] embody a tolerance for all religions" (*Hinsa Virodhak Sangh v. Mirzapur Moti Kuresh Jamat* 2008), while also insisting that "the Constitution gives equal respect to all [...] sects" (*Commissioner of Police v. Acharya Jagdishwaranand Avadhuta* 2004). Considered in light of the literature, these seem to be incompatible commitments: a constitution can either tolerate religious practices or respect them, but it cannot do both simultaneously. Yet the Supreme Court of India does not conceive of respect and toleration as incompatible values, but as two sides of the same coin.

The Supreme Court of India has noted that "the Constitution does not display an indifference to issues of religion" (*Abhiram Singh v, CD Commachen* 2017). Instead, the Court reads the Constitution as extending respect to religion, against objections and disapproval in society: "our Constitution is benign and sympathetic of all religious creeds however unacceptable they may be in the eyes of the non-believers" (*Commissioner of Police v. Acharya Jagdishwaranand Avadhuta* 2004). Here, the specter of incompatibility between toleration and respect seems to emerge. As Ian Carter (2013) argues, the kind of respect extended to religion by the Indian Constitution – that is, Stephen Darwall's appraisal respect (Darwall 1977) – is logically incompatible with toleration.

Crucially, however, this conclusion only follows if toleration is understood in its usual "negative" terms, as implying disapproval. The Indian Supreme Court, however, seems to conceptualize toleration differently (Smet 2020). In Indian constitutional law, toleration takes on a distinct meaning, *devoid* of disapproval, which allows it to align with the value of respect to support the Indian conception of "ameliorative" secularism (ibid.). In that sense, the Indian case could well be interpreted as an instantiation of Balint's general toleration (▶ Chap. 8, "Political Toleration Explained").

Yet that does not make it unproblematic. Quite to the contrary, the "benevolent" conception of toleration in Indian constitutional law comes with a catch. To preserve its understanding of the secular constitutional framework, the Indian Supreme Court has become heavily invested in (re)defining religion, contrary to courts in most other constitutional democracies (Smet 2020). Whenever religious practices (appear to) contradict secular values, they cannot – on the Indian Court's understanding of the secular constitutional framework as a harmonious whole – be considered part of religion. The alternative would jeopardize the Court's conception of religion as an unambiguously good thing that aligns entirely with the Constitution's secular values and is therefore meritorious of appraisal respect. In short, the Court's conception of toleration is benevolent, in the sense that it is devoid of disapproval. But it remains marked by the second component of toleration: power. Such power is exercised, through constitutional law, to the benefit of mainstream forms of the majority religion of Hinduism and to the detriment of both minority sects within Hinduism and minority religions (Smet 2020). In Indian constitutional law, benevolent toleration entails that the "older brother" (Hinduism) ought to help his "younger siblings" (especially Islam) to become secular (Bajpai 2008; Adcock 2013).

Ironically, this way of thinking has generated a pattern in constitutional adjudication whereby adherents to minority religions do not always benefit from "benevolent" toleration (Smet 2020). Instead, their religious practices risk being *excluded* from the very scope of religious freedom as being "non-essential" whenever the specter of incompatibility with the secular constitutional framework emerges. Muslim practices, in particular, have suffered from this definitional process (Sen 2010; Smet 2020). To cite just one prominent example, in *Ismail Faruqui* the Supreme Court of India ruled that praying in "[a] mosque is not an essential part of the practice of the religion of Islam and *namaz* (prayer) by Muslims can be offered anywhere" (*Ismail Faruqui v. Union of India* 1994). When, as in *Ismail Faruqui*, minority religious practices are defined away from the very scope of religious freedom, the potential tension between "benevolent" toleration and ameliorative secularism disappears: there is nothing left for the law to extend benevolent toleration to and thus nothing to generate a clash within the secular constitutional framework. But the cost, needless to say, is grave: minority religious practices lose the protection generally provided by the constitutional right to religious freedom.

Toleration, Respect, and Religious Exemptions

In theory, it matters whether constitutional courts view claims for religious exemptions through the lens of toleration or of respect, since both lenses operate differently and can thus generate opposing outcomes (Smet 2020). Toleration arguably operates as a negative lens, to the extent that it entails disapproval by those with power (an authority or a majority) of those without power (generally a minority). In its most pernicious mode – the permission conception – toleration involves drawing boundaries of societal belonging, of in-groups and out-groups. This has led Nussbaum (2008: 24) to reject toleration as "too grudging and weak" an attitude.

Nussbaum argues that issues of religious diversity ought to be considered through the lens of (equal) respect instead. Unlike tolerance, respect does not have a "condescending and superior air" about it (Horton 2011: 290). In its strongest form of appraisal respect, it even equates to esteem or positive regard for difference (Darwall 1977). In other words, respect operates as a positive lens. Yet Brian Leiter (2013) categorically rejects this positive lens as unsuited to resolving religious disputes. Leiter argues that religion is not the sort of thing that warrants respect, at least not in the strong sense intended by Nussbaum. Rather, he submits, toleration is all that is required in the face of religious difference.

The conceptual disagreement between Nussbaum and Leiter has immediate implications for constitutional law (Smet 2020). Given that Nussbaum and Leiter developed their arguments in the context of the United States, it is unsurprising to see their arguments reflected in how the Supreme Court of the United States has interpreted the Free Exercise Clause of the First Amendment. Over time, the Court has undergone a notable evolution – from toleration to respect and back to toleration – in how it evaluates claims for religious exemptions from facially neutral laws, in particular. It is worth tracing that evolution here, since it provides useful insights in the implications for religious freedom of legal actors shifting back and forth between the lenses of toleration and respect (Smet 2020).

Religious exemptions are precluded on the Lockean understanding of toleration, favored by Leiter in contemporary terms and by Thomas Jefferson in historical terms, to the extent that "the private judgment of any person concerning a law enacted in political matters, for the public good, does not take away the obligation of that law, nor deserve a dispensation" (Locke as cited in McConnell 1990: 1434). By contrast, at least some religious exemptions are required under the respect-based interpretation of religious freedom favored by James Madison in historical terms and by Nussbaum (2008) in contemporary terms.

11 Toleration and the Law

In its early case law, the Supreme Court of the United States favored the Jeffersonian/Lockean toleration track. This is evident from the Court's rejection of religious exemptions from criminal law in the polygamy cases *Reynolds* and *Davis*. In both cases, the Supreme Court expressed disapproval of the Mormons' religious practice of polygamy. In *Reynolds*, the Court held that "[p]olygamy has always been odious among the northern and western nations of Europe" (*Reynolds v. United States* 1878). In *Davis*, the Court added that not "everything which may be [. . .] called [religion] can be tolerated. Crime is not the less odious because sanctioned by what any particular sect may designate as 'religion'" (*Davis v. Beason* 1890). As a result, Mormons were denied an exemption from the criminal law on bigamy.

This toleration-based understanding of claims for religious exemptions, under which the Supreme Court of course *withheld* legal toleration, continued at least until *Minersville*, in which the Court refused to grant Jehovah's Witnesses an exemption from reciting the pledge of allegiance to the American flag in school. In its ruling, the Court held fast to its Lockean understanding of toleration: "[c]onscientious scruples have not, in the course of the long struggle for religious toleration, relieved the individual from obedience to a general law not aimed at the promotion or restriction of religious beliefs" (*Minersville School District v. Board of Education* 1940).

Gradually, however, the constitutional pendulum swung away from a toleration-based understanding of free exercise toward respect. The Supreme Court, one could say, moved from a Jeffersonian to a Madisonian interpretation of the Free Exercise Clause (Smet 2020). This process culminated in a couple of landmark cases in which the Court *did* grant religious exemptions from facially neutral laws: *Sherbert* and *Yoder*. These are the judgments on which Nussbaum (2008) relies when she claims that the American constitutional tradition of religious liberty is founded on equal respect (see also ▶ Chap. 49, "Early Modern Arguments for Toleration"). In *Sherbert*, for instance, it was held that "the guarantee of religious liberty embodied in the Free Exercise Clause affirmatively requires government to create an atmosphere of hospitality and accommodation to individual belief or disbelief" (*Sherbert v. Verner* 1963).

Ultimately, however, the Supreme Court shifted back toward a Lockean understanding of toleration. It did so in *Smith* by rejecting the claim for a religious exemption of two Native Americans who had been dismissed for use of peyote (listed as a controlled substance) and were subsequently excluded from unemployment benefits. In its ruling, the majority cited the "conscientious scruples" passage from *Minersville* and borrowed from *Reynolds* the idea that a general system of exemptions would make "each conscience [. . .] a law unto itself," before concluding that religious tolerance under the Free Exercise Clause does not require exemptions from general, facially neutral laws:

> To make an individual's obligation to obey [a general] law contingent upon the law's coincidence with his religious beliefs [. . .] permitting him, by virtue of his beliefs, "to become a law unto himself," – contradicts both constitutional tradition and common sense. (*Employment Division v. Smith* 1990)

As a matter of constitutional law, the *Smith* ruling reinstated the permission conception of toleration, while instantly refusing to extend such toleration to claims for religious exemptions from facially neutral laws. But it was not that the Supreme Court considered such exemptions to be wholly unwarranted. Rather, it did not find them to be constitutionally required. In other words, the Court left the decision to grant religious exemptions squarely in the hands of the legislature. In doing so the Court did anticipate, however, that this would be to the detriment of minority religions, as they were envisaged to struggle to find favor in the arena of majoritarian politics (*Employment Division v. Smith* 1990). In that sense, the *Smith* ruling knowingly and willingly surrendered minority religious practices to the kind of legislative grace that was vigorously opposed by James Madison in his rejection of toleration (Smet 2020).

Yet the United States Congress and state legislatures have taken a different position on the question of religious exemptions to that of the Supreme Court (Smet 2020). Several legislatures in the United States have restored the respect-based, pre-*Smith* case law of the Supreme Court in statutory law. The US Congress has done so by enacting, amongst others, the Religious Freedom Restoration Act, which prohibits the federal government from "substantially burden[ing] a person's exercise of religion even if the burden results from a rule of general applicability," unless a *Sherbert*-style compelling interest test is met. The federal legislature has thereby reinstated a respect-based understanding of religious exemptions in United States law, albeit at the sub-constitutional level. This process is indicative of how different legal actors may favor different lenses through which to consider religious claims: whereas the Supreme Court has adopted the lens of (permission) toleration, the federal legislature favors the lens of (equal) respect.

Summary and Future Directions

This chapter has given a broad overview of the role of toleration in the law. It has done so by examining how the law is positioned in relation to three dichotomies identified in the political theory literature: toleration/tolerance, toleration/neutrality, and toleration/respect. In examining how these dichotomies operate in the law, two descriptive claims were made. First, the conceptualization of toleration is (even) murkier – and certainly looser – in law than it is in political theory. Second, the more pragmatic approach of the law enables state practices of toleration to persist in practice, even in the face of conceptually more coherent and normatively more desirable ideals such as neutrality and respect.

From the descriptive and conceptual points made throughout the chapter, possible insights can be gleaned for different debates about toleration in political theory. Potential avenues for future research can also be identified. These insights and avenues relate to (a) conceptions of toleration, (b) actors and objects of toleration, (c) the analytical structure of toleration, and (d) justifications of toleration.

In terms of conceptions of toleration, the discussion in this chapter has revealed a murky patchwork of diverging conceptualizations of toleration/tolerance operating in the law. Nevertheless, it has also buttressed some claims made in the political theory literature. First, all four conceptions of toleration proposed by Forst (▶ Chap. 2, "Toleration: Concept and Conceptions") continue to inform how the law approaches issues of (religious) diversity. Second, in line with Jones's (2007) conception of political toleration, legal actors – courts in particular – often use the law to promote horizontal tolerance among citizens. Third, there are indications that the law can embody the kind of general toleration, which is devoid of disapproval, proposed by Balint (▶ Chap. 8, "Political Toleration Explained").

In terms of actors and objects of toleration, challenging questions arise in relation to legal toleration, that is, toleration in and by the law of persons' beliefs, practices, behavior, and/or opinions. We have seen that the law's response to a broad range of contested issues – prostitution, marijuana consumption, tobacco use, hate speech, conscientious objection – can be subsumed under the analytical structure of toleration. Yet qua vertical toleration, the existence and persistence of legal toleration is difficult to reconcile with conceptual and normative arguments for neutrality and/or respect. One conclusion we may be tempted to draw is that law and political theory are misaligned on the relationship between vertical toleration and neutrality. In the chapter, two ways to escape this conclusion were put forward. If neither of these avenues proves tenable, law and political theory may really be misaligned on the relationship between vertical toleration and neutrality. Either the legal understanding of toleration or the position in political theory (at least as a matter of nonideal theory) ought then to be revised.

In terms of the analytical structure of toleration, discussion of the Indian case has revealed good reasons for a renewed focus on the power element inherent in toleration. In political theory, disapproval often seems to be taken as the core problem with toleration in liberal democracies (Horton 2011; ▶ Chap. 4, "What Toleration Is Not"). Yet in Indian constitutional law, a disapproval-free conception of toleration has gradually morphed into a majoritarian instrument of power. The Indian Supreme Court's conception of toleration is benevolent, in that it is devoid of disapproval. But its being marked by the second component of toleration – power – has enabled a pattern in constitutional adjudication whereby adherents to minority religions do not always benefit from benevolent toleration. Instead, their religious practices risk being excluded from the very scope of religious freedom. The Indian case thus confirms the importance of evaluating the implications of the power imbalances inherent in toleration (cf. Brown 2006; Berger 2008). It moreover indicates that the salience of power may irrevocably separate toleration from respect, rendering both notions incompatible regardless of which conception one favors (*contra* Carter 2013).

In terms of justifications of toleration, finally, we have seen that legal toleration is often, though not exclusively, supported by pragmatic reasons. Some political theorists, however, argue that toleration ought to be grounded on principled rather than pragmatic reasons (▶ Chap. 3, "Defining Toleration"). Could pragmatic legal toleration, considered in this light, then still be considered an instance of toleration, properly understood? More importantly, are there principled or normative limits to the desirability of pragmatic legal toleration? In other words, when is pragmatic legal toleration an acceptable response to difference and when is it not? The normative question arguably asks us to choose between neutrality, toleration, respect, and prohibition (and the attending stances of indifference, disapproval-overcome, acceptance, and disapproval-followed-through) (Smet 2019a). Although the answer to this normative question is crucial for our understanding of how the law should respond to issues of diversity in a constitutional democracy, it has not been the intention of this chapter to engage with it (for a partial answer, see Smet 2019b).

References

Adcock CS (2013) The limits of tolerance: Indian secularism and the politics of religious freedom. Oxford University Press, Oxford

Bajpai R (2008) Minority representation and the making of the Indian constitution. In: Bhargava R (ed) Politics and ethics of the Indian constitution. Oxford University Press, Oxford, pp 354–391

Berger B (2008) The cultural limits of legal tolerance. Can J Law Jurisprud 21:245–277

Blasi V (1987) The teaching function of the first amendment. Columbia Law Rev 87:387–417

Brettschneider C (2012) When the state speaks, what should it say?: how democracies can protect expression and promote equality. Princeton University Press, Princeton

Brown W (2006) Regulating aversion: tolerance in the age of identity and empire. Princeton University Press, Princeton

Carter I (2013) Are toleration and respect compatible? J Appl Philos 30:195–208

Darwall S (1977) Two kinds of respect. Ethics 88:36–49

Fredman S (2020) Tolerating the intolerant: religious freedom, complicity, and the right to equality. Oxford J Law Relig (advance access). https://doi.org/10.1093/ojlr/rwaa017

Galeotti A (2002) Toleration as recognition. Cambridge University Press, Cambridge, UK

Gray J (2000) Pluralism and toleration in contemporary political philosophy. Polit Stud 48:323–333

Heyd D (2008) Is toleration a political virtue? In: Williams MS, Waldron J (eds) Toleration and its limits. New York University Press, New York, pp 171–194

Horton J (2011) Why the traditional conception of toleration still matters. Crit Rev Int Soc Pol Phil 14:289–305

Jones P (2007) Making sense of political toleration. Br J Polit Sci 37:383–402

Jones P (2015) Toleration, religion and accommodation. Eur J Philos 23:542–563

Kislowicz H (2017) The court and freedom of religion. Supreme Court Law Rev 78:221–233

Leiter B (2013) Why tolerate religion? Princeton University Press, Princeton

McConnell M (1990) The origins and historical understanding of free exercise of religion. Harv Law Rev 103:1409–1517

Mendus S (1989) Toleration and the limits of liberalism. Palgrave Macmillan, London

Moon R (2012) Freedom of religion under the charter of rights: the limits of state neutrality. U.B.C. Law Rev 45:497–549

Nehushtan Y (2007) The limits of tolerance: a substantive-liberal perspective. Ratio Juris 20:230–257

Nehushtan Y (2013) What are conscientious exemptions really about? Oxf J Law Relig 2:393–416

Nussbaum M (2008) Liberty of conscience. In: Defense of America's tradition of religious equality. Basic Books, New York

Rawls J (1993) Political liberalism. Columbia University Press, New York

Richards D (1986) Toleration and the xonstitution. Oxford University Press, Oxford

Rosenfeld M (1996) Pragmatism, pluralism, and legal interpretation: Posner's and Rorty's justice without metaphysics meets hate speech. Cardozo Law Rev 18:97–151

Sen R (2010) Articles of faith: religion, secularism, and the Indian Supreme Court. Oxford University Press, Oxford

Smet S (2019a) The pragmatic case for legal tolerance. Oxf J Leg Stud 39:344–373

Smet S (2019b) Conscientious objection through the contrasting lenses of tolerance and respect. Oxf J Law Relig 8:93–120

Smet S (2020) Comparative constitutional interpretation of religious freedom. Int Comp Law Q 69:611–651

Toleration and Domination

12

Monica Mookherjee

Contents

Introduction 210
Wendy Brown and Internalized Domination: Tolerance as a Discourse of
De-politicization 211
Nondomination as Involvement in the Sphere of Reasons: Resisting Domination Through
Neo-Kantian Respect Toleration 216
Reconsidering Toleration and Nondomination: Securing Tolerance as Active
Nondomination 221
Summary and Future Directions 224
References 226

Abstract

The concept of toleration has received scrutiny in recent years, with concerns raised that pursuing value involves a form of domination, understood as the capacity to exercise of arbitrary power. This chapter aims for critical consideration of concepts of toleration and domination firstly by addressing Wendy Brown's suggestion that current discourses on toleration "governmentalize" social minorities, by subtly controlling their access to the public sphere. On this understanding, toleration dominates in an "internal," psychological sense, by encouraging minorities to interiorize an inferior social status. Domination also has, however, an external dimension, in so far as it is viewed as probable hindrance or obstruction in the external world from acting according to one's own reasons and motives. The chapter considers the relation between toleration and external domination, by critically considering Rainer Forst's neo-Kantian view that a respect-based conception secures the "discursive involvement" of minorities in the justificatory processes involved in decisions to tolerate. Not only does respect-toleration have certain limitations as regards nondomination. Also,

---

M. Mookherjee (✉)
School of Social, Political and Global Studies, Keele University, Stoke-on-Trent, Staffordshire, UK
e-mail: m.mookherjee@keele.ac.uk

© The Author(s), under exclusive licence to Springer Nature Switzerland AG 2022   209
M. Sardoč (ed.), *The Palgrave Handbook of Toleration*,
https://doi.org/10.1007/978-3-030-42121-2_21

Brown's and Forst's approaches to external and internal toleration commonly focus on a passive subject of toleration, or the person who awaits the wider society's tolerance in a way which may fail to equalize opportunities for non-domination. This chapter concludes by outlining a conception of nondominating toleration understood less as a one-off event, and more as a stable subjective attitude of civility. Following Modood, Honohan, and Tonder, this conception depends on the need to establish endurance as a positive, forward-looking mental attitude.

Keywords

Toleration · Domination · Permission · Respect · Subordination · Governmentality · Duality · Coexistence · Esteem · Minorities · Arbitrary power · Endurance · Resilience · Nondomination · Secure toleration

Introduction

While the idea of toleration plays a central role in debates about liberalism as a political discourse, recent years have witnessed the emergence of a vigorous debate surrounding the "darker" aspects of this value. Contemporary tolerance is, it is suggested, something less than a democratic ideal. Despite its egalitarian appearance, it involves the state's exertion of arbitrary power against individuals or groups who are taken to deviate from certain social norms. This predicament has especially concerned writers from a post-Marxist perspective, who suggest that the liberal value of tolerance "de-politicizes" social inequalities, in the sense of presenting tolerance as a means to conflict resolution but in such a way that undermines the role of minority issues on the political agenda. For instance, although Wendy Brown (2006, 2008) does not reject the "elusive virtue" of tolerance (Heyd 1996), by viewing this discourse as a form of Foucauldian governmentality especially in relation to non-Western cultures, she takes toleration to involve a certain "internalized" or psychological domination. It encourages in the minds of minorities and majorities' official acceptance of toleration as a mechanism for equality, while in reality marking a limit to this equality. Meanwhile writers from a neo-Kantian background address the more usual dimension of domination associated with external unfreedom, namely the extent of one's involvement and control over public reasoning which leads to decisions to tolerate. Forst's concept of respect-toleration, for instance, offers minorities a certain resistance to domination in the form of what I call, following Pettit (2010, 2012), "discursive involvement."

However, while Forst and Brown do provide particular insights for this study, by focusing on different dimensions of domination, and while they view the threat of domination differently in toleration practices, their common focus lies in toleration as a passive state. To transcend this passive conception, and to fully theorize the relationship between tolerance and (non)-domination, the chapter lastly aims for reconciliation of the external and the internal dimensions of domination and

12 Toleration and Domination

nondomination by conceiving toleration in terms of an active ethos of civility and decency, or a more active will to renounce domination, arising from the works of Tariq Modood, Iseult Honohan, and Lars Tonder.

Wendy Brown and Internalized Domination: Tolerance as a Discourse of De-politicization

In her influential work *Regulating Aversion*, Wendy Brown takes contemporary toleration to disguise power, domination, and exclusion. While she does not dismiss the value of tolerance, she remains concerned that, in the cultural history of the West, toleration takes on a form of governmentality (Lemke 2002). As will be explained, for Brown toleration subtly consolidates institutional power through the social status internalized in the minds of the tolerator and tolerated. From a Foucauldian perspective, in other words, toleration dominates by affecting a person's self-understanding rather than through an act of external power.

Before providing a detailed analysis, it is worth commenting first on how the idea that toleration expresses a vertical hierarchy or power-relation has been noticed by many writers, not only those inspired by Foucault. It may even be a structural feature of the concept of tolerance that the threshold of interference is not determined by the tolerated. This central feature of toleration has concerned writers from broader theoretical backgrounds. Some claim that contemporary acts of toleration are unable to capture the procedural problems concerning the participation of minorities in society, and that they fail to offer any critical tools to establish what judgments the majority is entitled to consider (see Ceva and Zuolo 2013). Also, Glen Newey (2013) incisively asks whether, given the disagreements arising even between those who are commonly reasonable, toleration comes to seem something less than it presents itself to be – namely an act of reining in one's aversion in favor of an overriding public reason to accept. Rather, because the tolerator does not truly override their reason for aversion, toleration may be understood more simply as an acceptance of coercive state power.

Brown, however, seems to offer a particularly potent diagnosis of this situation. She draws in particular from Foucault to suggest that contemporary acts of toleration reflect the dispersal of modern forms of power, and, consequently a certain psychological work performed on liberal subjects through different levels of social and political life. That is, tolerance today subjugates by maintaining antipathies and aversions towards those who differ socially in the minds of both the tolerator and the tolerated. By drawing on Foucauldian understandings of disciplinary power and biopower, Brown highlights how, in the cultural history of the West, toleration has always involved a form of "enduring," "licensing," and "indulging" (Brown 2006: 12). Because the idea of suffering is central to the idea of tolerance, the tolerator internalizes their contestable judgment that their aversion is understandable and legitimate; and the tolerated person, correlatively, internalizes an abject, inferior status as "merely" tolerated. At least, for Brown, tolerance has taken this form in the civilizational development of the West. For Brown, toleration is akin to Christ's indulgence for a sinful humanity. Whereas the Christian ideal of indulgence of the sinful trades on the possibility of redemption, contemporary toleration is modeled on a version of the religious ideal of *imitatio Christi*, the pursuit of the devotional life as a matter of martyrdom: to tolerate is to reflect Jesus' charitable attitude (Brown 2006). However, divested of the possibility of full social inclusion, the secularized version of redemption, the tolerator's privileged benevolence shores up, Brown fears, "troubled orders," "troubled universalisms," and "provid[es] a cover for imperialism" (2006: 9).

While Brown insists that this critique does not mean that she wishes to reject toleration *tout court*, she is concerned about this socially dominating aspect to contemporary tolerance. Because toleration supplements, by residing outside the realm of, legal equality and freedom, it takes the form less of justice than social identity management (Brown 2008: 9). In this sense, toleration forms a key prop in the wider discourse of liberal individualism, which "depoliticizes" minority identitiesy status, by refusing to view their social status as a question of governmental significance. Although toleration is often held out to be the precursor to full political parity, in fact it depoliticizes minority modes of living "by personalizing, naturalizing, and culturalizing" particular identities rather than viewing them as potentially suffering injustice (2006: 15). Toleration, on this understanding, becomes a second-best substitute for full political equality (2006: 16). To some extent, this phenomenon is the outcome of attempting to mobilize toleration to accommodate ascriptive identities of race and ethnicity, when historically it arose as a political response to controversies over religious belief in Europe. Toleration, on this understanding, arose historically as the behavioral solution to disagreements over personal convictions and doctrinal disputes, to which there was no uncontroversial answer. As such, it provides an ambiguous solution for brokering conflicts pervading late-modern societies, such as disputes concerning race and ethnicity.

Moreover, from Brown's perspective to fail to tolerate or be tolerant is in this discourse branded as a sign of barbarism, but in a way that obscures the historical contingency of the distinctions between the civilized and barbaric. As she explains:

> Tolerance as a de-politicizing discourse gains acceptance and legitimacy by being nestled among other discourses of de-politicization; and it draws on their techniques of analytically disappearing the political constitution of conflicts and subjects. Moreover, as is the case with liberalism, the American culture of individualism, and neoliberal market rationality [. . .] there is no acknowledgement of the norms, the subject construction, the subject positioning *or the civilizational identity* at stake in tolerance discourse; likewise, there is no avowal of the means by which certain peoples, nations and practices or utterances get marked beyond the pale of tolerance. (Brown 2006: 19, emphasis in the original)

Within this liberal genealogy, toleration becomes associated with social benevolence or even *noblesse oblige*. However by masking the relations of power which it embodies, Brown believes toleration to increase a distinctly modern form of power, "biopower," which, following Foucault's insights, involves the subjugation of bodies by controlling the individual's self-conception rather than through the outright threat of death (2006: 26). Toleration, for Brown, also instantiates what

Foucault identifies as "disciplinary" power, or power which encourages individuals to internalize social norms and rules, moulding their characters in particular ways, rendering them docile in relation to those normative requirements. Whether, in the act of toleration, biopower and disciplinary power amount to domination, however, seems to depend on how this latter concept is defined. If domination is defined as the capacity (even if not the actual act of) to exercise arbitrary power in relation to another's will (Pettit 2010; Friedman 2008), one might object that it is exactly the purpose of the Foucauldian perspective to question the extreme conclusion that subjects of power may suffer the extreme interference with their will seemingly implied by radical feminist conceptions of domination (e.g., Preston 2010; MacKinnon 1998; Munro 2003). These radical feminist accounts have deepened the neo-republican conception of domination as the capacity of one party arbitrarily to interfere in the life-choices of another, or to determine the conditions under which these life-choices are made (see Pettit 2012; Lovett 2010a, 2012; McCannon 2015). However, in contrast with these more radical accounts, Brown implicates toleration in a form of domination which is less focused on the external manifestations of arbitrary power, for instance, through the practical implementation a norm, law, or rule. Rather, she focuses on domination as an internalized, self-imposed barrier to freedom. This Foucauldian conception of domination has recently been developed through innovative discussions of the toleration of Muslim veil (Valdez 2017).

On this reading, Brown takes toleration to involve the subtle reinforcement of a person's vulnerability to power in the context of a wider ideological acceptance of liberalism. Toleration might work, for instance, by subtly representing the desire of Muslim women to wear the *hijab* in European states as a sure sign of female oppression rather than as a legitimate cultural option undertaken freely. This internalization process appears to maintain inequality precisely because the act of toleration reinforces existing representations of social difference. This point is borne out, for Brown, by the different ways in which the "Woman Question" and the "Jewish Question" have been conceived historically in Western cultural history. In each case the perceived need for tolerance hinged on the extent to which the identity which deviates from public norms could be addressed by "privatization," or through its accommodation in the domestic sphere. Jews and women, Brown observes, were formally emancipated in the nineteenth and twentieth centuries in Europe, although the emancipation in both cases came at the price of not "fully shedding the stigma of their difference" (2006: 77; also Brown 1994). It was not necessary to tolerate female identity as a specific mode of difference, because their difference could be contained in the domestic sphere. In contrast, for Jews the issue was precisely that, despite political enfranchisement, the racialized form of their identity remained a possible *public* threat to the Euro-Atlantic nation-state norm. In both cases, political rights did not amount to full social equality. While women's equality hinged on being regarded as the "same" as men in the public sphere, and hence on specifically not demanding recognition of their femininity; for the Jewish "Other", tolerance marked the limit of formal equality, in such a way which, for Brown, "veil[ed] its own work of subordination." Toleration, she concludes, is therefore not quite what it claims to be. Presented as a benign strategy for coexistence, it limits social options and opportunities by encouraging subjects of tolerance to view themselves as "merely" tolerated, the recipient of social benevolence rather than substantive political parity.

The question remains, however, as to whether the Foucauldian critique of toleration in terms of biopower and disciplinary power amounts to domination. At first, this conclusion seems doubtful. For, central to the logic of power in modern societies according to Foucault is its dispersal, or its transmission through multiple venues, relationships, and discourses. What is also central is the normality, even the ubiquity, of resistance as the productive force made possible by power (Foucault 1994). However, while these ideas seem to rule out the possibility that power could become so totalizing as to amount to domination, the later Foucault at least seems to maintain this possibility. While standing behind his earlier idea that where there is power there is also resistance, he also concedes that domination may occur where the "pluri-potentiality," fluidity, and productivity of power become "set and congealed" by a particular constellation of power-relations. Domination may occur, then, where specific power-relations render conditions of resistance vastly undermined. In such situations, "the problem is not of trying to dissolve [power-relations] in the utopia of perfectly transparent communication; but to give oneself the rules of law, the techniques of management, and also the ethics, the ethos, the practices of the self, which would allow these games to be played with a minimum of domination" (Foucault 1994: 20). As Munro explains (2003), for Foucault domination is one particularly extreme manifestation of power; and while the possibility of resistance is for Foucault never "conceptually obliterated," the problem is always to dilute the potential of particular constellations of power to congeal into domination, even without hope of radically transcending that power (Munro 2003: 94). In light of Brown's conception of tolerance as a "discourse," as pervading both global and domestic political questions by liberal states, one might suppose that power-relations in specific acts of toleration do risk becoming congealed in Foucault's later sense. This analysis of toleration as internalized domination seems significantly to counter the optimism of liberal writers who link tolerance to increased social equality (Galeotti 1993; Kukathas 1997; Laegaard 2011).

More specifically, Brown's account draws heavily from Foucault's concept of governmentality – a term which, as noted, refers to the rationalized, dispersed nature of modern power, and which applies from individuals to mass populations, from the body and psyche to appetites. While accepting Foucault's major insights, Brown's concern is that Foucault's analysis of the state seems, however, limited to the way in which the organs of government are also governmentalized (Brown 2006: 81; Foucault 1988; Burchell et al. 1991). For Brown, this focus deflects attention from the state itself as a source of power (2006: 82), which, by offering tolerance as a behavioral solution, obscures the geopolitical and economic factors relevant to late modernity which have lessened its own capacity to govern for full equality, and to offer minorities full inclusion. These factors seem to indicate domination in the later Foucault's sense. In this context, resistance to the power of the state is significantly reduced, and the state itself is increasingly shorn of its effective capacity to "control a motley, potentially ungovernable and growing number of transnational affiliations in

12 Toleration and Domination

a time of weakening nation-states, dramatic international migration patterns and erupting fundamentalisms" (Brown 2006: 95). Toleration, on this conception, becomes a peculiarly internalized form of domination, according to which the state not only maintains the appearance of "peace," but also serves more internalized, psychological aims of reigniting its citizens' faith in liberal universalism and in a culturally unified nation at a time at which both are faltering. Hence toleration "performs" domination by instrumentally brokering conflicts which are the results of the end of the Cold War, of mass migration and the forces of economic globalization, while failing to question the inequalities which give rise to the need for toleration itself.

This form of domination works psychologically, through use of public, medical, and other social discourses, to affect the judgments and perceptions of citizens concerning binaries such as tolerable/intolerable, them/us, and civilization/barbarism. Evocative of the classical republican focus on the example of slavery, which reduces people to property and things rather than viewing them as full human beings (see Pettit 2012), Brown refers to the toleration extended to Mexican immigrants or of "law-abiding" Muslims in the USA. Yet for Brown, in contrast with the classical republican idea, the late-modern master–slave relation is more complex: it is in fact entire liberal populations, with their docile acceptance of official distinctions between civilization and barbarism, who are subject to the mastery of a regime of knowledge. For Brown, therefore, the *revenu* of tolerance on both sides of the Atlantic begs many questions concerning the psychological capacity of majorities and minorities to resist domination. In late-modernity, the question liberal subjects should, but frequently do not, pose is what ramifications toleration might have beyond its surface aim of "conflict resolution" (2006: 87).

Brown's concern is that the resort to toleration in the contemporary suggests "fear of the political" and the retrenchment of a more robust democratic politics (2006: 90). The legitimization crises which toleration covertly expresses are exemplified, for Brown, by particular issues in recent US politics such as the debate around same-sex marriage and the Bush administration's "them" and "us" discourse after the September 11 attacks (2006: 90). Specifically, the US government's extension of tolerance to "law-abiding" Muslim citizens was accompanied by an apparent carte blanche for the use of state prerogative powers in relation to "other" Muslims, however extreme or intolerant this appeared (2006: 101).

Brown's focus on the apparent internalization of power and domination through toleration critically adds, then, to the insights of contemporary republicans, who distil the distinction between arbitrary and nonarbitrary power in terms of an external definition of freedom (Valdez 2017). This neo-republican emphasis on external freedom as nondomination will be revisited shortly. Yet, for the moment, one issue which seems to haunt Brown's specific conception of toleration is how far subjects of liberal toleration may act critically and oppositionally. For Gregg (2008), Brown provides no straightforward solution to this issue: although Brown finds in liberal tolerance a value which is less a matter of respect than of managing the other, her seeming focus on the psychological dimension of toleration as domination seems to reach a normative impasse, in recommending only an "unresolved play of ambiguity, relativism and ambivalence" (2008: 320). Not only do there remain substantial questions concerning whether the resistance of the tolerated could ever transform toleration into substantive political equality. Moreover, there remain questions as to whether Brown's reliance on Foucault's writings contains the normative tools to advocate for a more resistant conception of toleration. If tolerance is an ideal which modern societies ultimately cannot renounce, but which also cannot fully broker the conflicts to which it responds, it is worth moving back to the external conceptions of freedom implied usually by republican theorists of nondomination. Does a neo-Kantian perspective suggest a certain form of toleration as nondomination in the form of concrete actions to resist arbitrary power?

Nondomination as Involvement in the Sphere of Reasons: Resisting Domination Through Neo-Kantian Respect Toleration

Equally conscious of the inequalities of modern societies, Rainer Forst draws on neo-Kantian concepts of equality and reciprocity to put forward what he views as an emancipatory concept of toleration, one based on respect. Forst's concept of respect-toleration may be thought to address the external aspect of domination, or domination enacted through arbitrary interference with the concrete activities of others, or their pursuit of a specific conception of the good life. This process promises to build the potential of minorities to achieve what Pettit (2012) calls a form of "discursive control," or autonomy in reasoning towards tolerance. While respect-toleration most likely does not challenge the deeper threat of internalized domination raised by Brown, it challenges the threat of external domination by encouraging the input of all social groups in public decision-making by recommending a process of inclusive justification. To evaluate the potential of this idea, I focus on the distinction between "control" and "involvement" in the republican conception of nondomination (Markell 2008; Pettit 2012). By encouraging only the former, Forst's respect conception, while advantageous in some ways, may, I suggest, inevitably lack full emancipatory potential.

This interpretation of Forst's perspective may be understood firstly by referring back to Pettit's classical republican conception of domination. Pettit (2010, 2012) refers to two central forms of domination, which take their cue from the classical Roman example of slavery, namely *imperium* (which relates to the structures of government power) and *dominium* (which refers to the social or personal exercise of power). While slaves were often inescapably involved in much productive labor, which opened up certain – though obviously limited – possibilities for creative agency, ultimate control lay not in the hands even of specific masters but in Roman *imperium*, which controlled the terms of slaveholding (Pettit 2012; Markell 2008). Although the example of Roman slavery seems obviously remote in the contemporary age, it provides a key analogy through which to suggest that the public reasoning implicated in respect-toleration may offer citizens a certain level of involvement and inclusion, which counters subjectivity to the capricious preferences of dominant groups. It is, however, unlikely that this process guarantees discursive control. While Forst's conception therefore has certain advantages, its potency is unclear.

Specifically, Forst presents respect-toleration in contrast with what he takes to be a more simple form of toleration as a "vertical," top-down expression of government power. As Goethe thought, the latter permission-based concept seems to express a form of contempt (2013: 15). For Forst, all forms of toleration raise the issue of whether the "limit" reason, or the reason for refusing to tolerate, is legitimately imposed. While the permission conception allows for no dialogue with citizens concerning this limit, the coexistence conception of identified by Forst, based on a modus vivendi, seems more promising first of all. However, it is hindered by its pragmatic grounding and thus its moral and political instability (2013: 29). Ultimately, for Forst, while toleration is always both liberatory and potentially repressive, respect-toleration seems most promising. By requiring all to exchange general and shareable reasons for their decisions to tolerate (Forst 2013: 114), it loosens the majority's control over the outcomes of public debate by explicitly obliging them to locate shared justifications for policy decisions.

The respect-conception, specifically, depends on a distinction between faith, which is not amenable to rational justification, and reason. Drawing from Bayle, for Forst a justification based on reason may stem from the desire for social recognition or the insights of natural reason. However, so long as there is no indisputable proof as to the truth of a particular belief-system or conception of the good life, the central idea is that liberal democratic life involves all assuming a duty of mutual justification which is an aspect of one's civic responsibility (Forst 2007: 299). This duty generates particular minorities' rights to inclusion in justificatory processes, in an approach which places faith in the power of reasons and rationality to somewhat equalize competing claims regarding the tolerable and the intolerable. On this account, reason cannot prove faith and thus human reason has to accept its own boundaries. While Forst believes that the right to justification underwriting the respect conception therefore clearly values autonomy, it pursues a public, rather than a perfectionist, conception of this value by requiring the socially privileged to offer a reason which does not depend on the "higher truths" of their own, substantive theory of freedom or the good life. The right to justification therefore potentially frees minorities from the lifestyle dominium of privileged majorities. Dominant groups cannot impose their own conception of the good without sanction, or without being beholden to provide others an acceptable justification for doing so. This conception seems promising, in empowering the underprivileged who might otherwise lack control or involvement in the justification of policies which affect them.

Considerable ambiguities exist, however, in taking up this concept as a means to address external domination. Forst's example of the German Federal Constitutional Court's declaration as unconstitutional the law that ordered crucifixes to hang in Bavarian public schools is relevant to consider. Following intense constitutional debates, one proposed solution which appears consistent with respect-toleration was to disallow all religious symbols by law, even if they stand for the religious beliefs of the majority (2007: 305). Forst takes this solution to exemplify respect for minorities, as it does not support the preferences and lifestyle of the majority. If the Jew cannot wear the *kippah* ostensible signs of Christian belonging should not be tolerated either. An example of respect-toleration may also be found in considering currently fraught debates concerning the accommodation of extremist political parties in modern states. While in practice these groups are often tolerated pragmatically, their disavowal of the value of democratic respect suggests that they should not be permitted according to the "reciprocity of reasons" element in Forst's respect-based concept of toleration (Forst 2013: 453; Etinson 2014).

This controversial second example, however, highlights exactly the ethical ambiguity raised by the respect conception. While the ideal of democratic respect is justly influential, the issue may be how the meta-standard of the right to justification is itself justified; and whether this standard amounts to a form of social control over the terms of dialogue which cannot be opposed or questioned. This is not to suggest that the regulative ought to be questioned; but rather only to observe that taking it as the standard against to judge all questions in social and political life might seem to undermine the participatory equality of whose conception of the good life, while not being overtly harmful, discriminatory, or antidemocratic, includes certain hierarchical and (apparently) inegalitarian beliefs. The questions alluded to previously regarding campaigns around veiling may be considered again. Multicultural and intersectional debates have identified issues regarding whether gender-hierarchical beliefs, such as those which justify women's seclusion in the domestic sphere, should be viewed as unreasonable or irrational (see Werbner 2007). To the extent that groups with seemingly inegalitarian views participate in the exchange of reasons concerning toleration, it is plausible to take them to be discursively involved. However, the likelihood of hierarchical beliefs being accepted as public reasons seems doubtful. Thus, on matters most important from their perspective, these groups' involvement would not amount to control of the public reasoning process. Indeed, the purpose of the democratic justification concerns the sharing of power, in such a way that no party holds ultimate control over outcomes.

Even where the minority's beliefs are not overtly hierarchical, the potential of Forst's respect-conception to encourage the greater discursive control of minorities would often remain ambiguous, as it will often be unclear what counts as a reciprocal or general justification. As Etinson (2014) observes, Forst does not mean that the reason for tolerance need be at present shared. However, it is unclear whether the reason should be assumed to be shareable in the future, and on what basis this assumption could be made. Forst leaves the meanings of the terms generality and shareability open, while insisting the outcome of a question of toleration depends on the "the force of the better argument" (2007: 311). For Forst, to appeal to this argument is to be committed to the norm of reasonableness.

While the reasonableness requirement seems to increase discursive involvement and does seem to protect minorities from arbitrary censure or interference, realistically, however, there is no guarantee that the requirement for other-regarding justification will provide respite from domination. One reason is that often informal domination might prejudice from the outset what are deemed the best arguments. Indeed, the distinction between prejudice and reason is questioned by the recognition that reasons are often constructed by visceral or unconscious reactions, perhaps longstanding political prejudices and hatreds (Allen, cited in Allen et al. 2014: 27). Feminist writer Marilyn Friedman (2003) has drawn attention to the fact that despite formal political equality, unequal sexual divisions of labor within societies are often covertly supported by laws regarding marriage. These laws are often regarded as the building blocks of society even though the informal effect of marital norms may be to involves many women in disproportionate assumptions of caring responsibilities. For Friedman, the emotive efficacy of the reasons given for upholding these norms – namely claims concerning the need for the reproduction of society – explains the distinctive and often unchallenged nature of male dominance. Similar forms of informal domination are likely to affect minority religious and cultural groups.

Forst does concede that reason and feeling overlap to some extent (Forst, cited in Allen et al. 2014: 31). Consequently he is aware that the reasonableness requirement of respect-toleration does not necessarily counter domination. For Forst, toleration always involves a dialectic between moral progress and of domination which attempts to counter this progress, in such a way that is ambiguous with regard to dialogue between diverse people concerning issues such as sexuality, ethnicity, immigration, and other contested matters. Forst suggests that toleration is always normatively dependent on more widely affirmed political values such as equality or unity (Forst 2007; Galeotti 2014). Thus to be respect-tolerant depends on calling on these meta-values to defeat the reason for objecting to what one considers ethically problematic or socially undesirable. Consensus is needed to demonstrate the inadequacy of the reason for exerting power to interfere. Yet this point seems to raise another aspect of the problem confronting minorities: it may be precisely in these contexts that the discursive involvement of different groups is limited to dialogue over the interpretation of public reasons, rather than to a form of power as control which might enable questioning the terms on which the distinction between a public and nonpublic reason is drawn. All things considered, this process seems to provide some respite from dominium, but probably not from imperium in Pettit's sense. Ultimately the commitment to equal respect seems not to be a procedural principle but rather a substantive ethical preference, which appears assumed rather than fully justified. To some extent, this may be inevitable: the presumption for democratic equality could not be questioned as it is a condition of the dialogue itself (Buchanan 1998–1999). However, this may mean that minorities do not participate on equal terms, or what they perceive to be so from their perspective.

The equality promised by discursive involvement is problematic in another sense too. If political respect is a matter of considering others' reasons, although not being obliged to act in accordance with them, the relationship between toleration and the balance of power between social groups becomes even less clear. Even if citizens should rightly be encouraged to shift their reasoning contextually between the public and the nonpublic, the psychological burden and ethical tension involved in having to do so might, for certain groups, reduce "respect" to "gritted teeth" toleration. In these situations, again the discursive involvement of citizens would not be an equal matter, on equal terms.

These ambiguous outcomes may not, moreover, indicate a lack of will to engage inclusively and equally. Rather, they may mostly be a condition of the nature of value pluralism. For Forst, in respect-toleration the second-order (public) reason is supposed to defeat the first-order ethical reason. However, most belief-systems contain multiple intuitions about other-regarding conduct. They are therefore likely to contain different, contradictory public reasons. For instance, reasonable people may be equally committed norms concerning the free marketplace of ideas while also retaining concerns for state security, the weighting of which may be impossible to determine even in particular cases. Taken together, then, the norm of respect-toleration suggests numerous epistemic, practical, and normative difficulties. While the politically privileged would be required to temper their capacity to interfere, the obligation to find true consensus on reasons may always be inconclusive from the perspective of equal participation. And, as suggested by Pettit's central example of Roman slavery, it seems highly possible to be involved, in the sense of participating, while holding no or little control over the terms of engagement. A double-edged picture therefore emerges of respect-toleration as an antidote for external domination. Indeed, the difficulties of bringing about equality through public reasoning may be reflected in the variable potential of subaltern peoples fully to oppose or resist power (Scott 1990).

Finally, taking Forst's and Brown's perspectives on toleration together, it seems clear that, while they analyze toleration in terms of different dimensions of domination, they both remain appear to remain focused on a passive subject of toleration rather than on tolerance as a virtue involving an active capacity and will to resist domination. While, in other words, both writers are sensitive to Marcuse's (1965) seminal critique of repressive tolerance, which claimed that tolerance no longer in modernity encourages truly oppositional conduct, Forst's neo-Kantian conception and Brown's post-Marxist critique commonly seem to focus on a static figure of the "patient" or recipient of toleration (see Tonder 2013b).

For consider: in their shared debate at the Berlin Centre for Cultural Inquiry in 2008, Brown characterizes the difference in their respective positions by casting doubt on the full emancipatory potential of Forst's respect conception. While Forst believes that holding others to a duty to justify their public reaction renders power less arbitrary, Brown's concern is that this perspective presumes rather than enacts social equality. Without this assumption, she argues, it is unclear how the tolerated are "demanding" a mutually acceptable justification. For, in any conditions, it is always, she suggests, the dominant person who always chooses to "hold back their power and soften their dominance" (Brown and Forst 2014). If this is a pure choice on the part of the dominant person, then it is not clear in what sense there is genuinely an *enforceable* duty for mutual justification or reciprocity.

While Brown's point is important, and will be revisited below, a common factor in their approaches to toleration seems to involve their common concentration on toleration as a passive state; or their common characterization of toleration as a question of being tolerated or receiving toleration. Up to a point, the focus is understandable given their common concern with increasing substantive equality and decreasing domination (Tonder 2013b). Although Forst's neo-Kantianism could be construed in terms of conferring on the tolerated more active resistance, ultimately this focus, too, seems passive. That is because even the discursive

12 Toleration and Domination

involvement which seems to boost nondomination does not suggest which transformations of the mind are necessary for both the tolerator and the tolerated, in order to move societies towards a more consistently secure status for minority communities over time.

Reconsidering Toleration and Nondomination: Securing Tolerance as Active Nondomination

While the critiques and proposals of both writers above bear certain advantages, I finally suggest an alternative, or more accurately a combination of alternative approaches, which together seem to address the internal and external dimensions of domination in a different view of toleration. Overall, this conception may be labeled, following Honohan (2013), "secure" toleration, although it reaches beyond her account to address the internalized psychological aspect of toleration as well as its institutional conditions. On this conception, toleration is still viewed in terms of action in the external world; but it also emphasizes the need for the tolerator's deeper internal, mental transformation away from the will to dominate. By combining the insights of recent approaches, this conception of nondominating, secure tolerance speaks to the concerns raised in connection with Brown's and Forst's perspectives earlier regarding internalized domination and discursive involvement. It emphasizes the need securely to increase the social status of different groups in a context where one core change involves the tolerator's active capacity for benevolent endurance.

This rethinking of toleration can be considered first by questioning non-interference as the guiding light of nondomination; and by suggesting *secure expectation* of that noninterference as its important condition (Lovett 2010a). Modood and Dobbernack (2013) are sensitive to this need, especially when the status of vulnerable groups such as Muslims in Europe is considered. From their perspective, the justification of toleration – whether this is to be found in respect, permission, prudence, or skepticism – is less important than the minimal decency toleration brings about. Even gritted-teeth tolerance brings about a level of decorum and peace which is the necessary condition for such a society. Labeling this process "demanding tolerance from below," Modood and Dobbernack view toleration as indispensable for setting the baseline of reasonable behavior without which engaging in projects of civic unity cannot be imagined, and the possibility of an outbreak of more violent forms of conflict would be ever present.

Modood and Dobbernack's concern for an open concept of toleration which will build the social status of minorities is further supported by Iseult Honohan's extended concept of "secure" toleration. Drawing consciously on Pettit (2010) and Lovett's perspectives on domination (2010a), Honohan insists that the state of being tolerated is only empowering, and will only encourage critical and oppositional agency, if viewed in terms of the group's wider social status rather than as a one-off event (2013: 10). Hence, toleration is best conceived as a means of placing social groups on an equal footing in a secure way and over time. Responding to Lovett's (2010a) conception of domination as the condition according to which long-term planning is undermined due to the threat of willful or capricious interventions of others, Honohan specifies that toleration "requires institutional safeguards and takes account not only of public domination by the state but also of areas such as work and the family that have been often understood as private and non-political" (2013: 84). For Honohan, the goal of tolerance is not to enable single policy recommendations, but rather to bring about a society in which "people can look others in the eye as equals." As an aspect of a robust democratic politics, this perspective requires: (a) respect for the rule of law; (b) the contestability of public decisions and deliberatively formed policies; and (c) an attitude of civility. Observing that, while the treatment of other human beings as equals clearly involves respect for their basic rights to bodily integrity, considering them as *citizens* involves giving due weight to their perspectives on political affairs – through the creation and maintenance of an expectation of due consideration over time. Consistent with Pettit's republican conception of domination as a continual state of being, to counter domination through tolerance becomes a question of equalizing social status for a sustained length of time (Honohan 2013: 87).

The risk, of course, is that secure toleration comes to seem something other than toleration, and, indeed, closer to the more ambitious concept of "recognition" (Baumeister 2011), which seems to require active endorsement of differences. However, Honohan, like Laegaard (2010), suggests more overlap between (secure) toleration and recognition than may usually seem evident. The need for a richer conception of toleration is highlighted by the fact that it is possible to be "merely" tolerated but still dominated. Particular groups may be merely tolerated if others simply turn a pragmatic blind eye to their religious or cultural practices, and refuse to view them explicitly as religious and cultural. Alternatively, minorities may be tolerated but still dominated where their practices and symbols are accepted on certain conditions, such as if they are not regarded as "ostentatious"; and if, on this account, minorities choose to remain relatively invisible or to publicly assimilate to avoid arbitrary interference (Honohan 2013:89). Overall, the core question raised by secure toleration is "whether the burdening of a particular social practice would create new opportunities for domination" (Honohan 2013: 94, citing Lovett 2010b: 259–260).

Honohan's perspective on secure toleration speaks to the need, explored through the discussion of Forst's concept of respect-toleration, for minorities to enjoy a secure expectation of discursive involvement, one which is not conditional on ignorance or denial of their cultures in the public sphere. However, from Honohan's account alone, it is less clear how, beyond institutional policy decisions, societies as a whole can secure the civility needed to sustain the chances of equalizing the social status of groups over time. The conception of secure toleration might, thus, be supplemented by a focus on how the internalized will to dominate, on which Brown's incisive critique concentrated attention, may be overcome through a psychologically active conception of toleration. My suggestion is, therefore, that the Spinozan insights of Lars Tønder's (2013a, b) recent approach may be viewed together with Honohan's and Modood's conceptions, in order to suggest the internal and external conditions of secure toleration.

12 Toleration and Domination

Consider that, for Lars Tonder, toleration should be viewed as an "internal," subjective matter first, before offered as a norm regulating social or institutional relations. Spinoza's philosophy of immanence, according to Tonder, depicts the relationship of tolerance and power in such a way that overcomes the focus on the subject of toleration in post-Marxist and republican perspectives, respectively. Importantly, particular psychological orientations hold a certain power which may be mobilized in emancipatory ways. For Tonder, while the approach to toleration grounded in rights to noninterference is clearly important, a more active conception is also required to "inspir[e] contemporary democratic theory" (2013a: 689; see also Tonder 2013b).

Briefly, Spinoza's philosophy of immanence, Tonder claims, directs attention to the affective components of political life. On this account, it is not that there is power *in* tolerating, so much as that tolerance *is* a power. More specifically, in *The Ethics* Spinoza considers the practice of tolerance as a way of entering into more empowering relationships. In this sense, cultivating tolerance in the face of forces that we cannot control in the world around us inculcates a form of resilience which enables us to break out of competing narratives of whether tolerance either represses or liberates from an institutional or policy perspective. These perspectives say little, in themselves, about how the tolerator becomes emancipated within themselves from the will to dominate; and how therefore the will to secure the social status of others securely over time could be realized. In fact, to link toleration to rights too closely may be an aspect of the problem, not least because rights under-describe domination. By viewing tolerance simply as inaction or negative rights, it becomes less clear why privileged individuals should be, or would be, motivationally committed to securing the social status of underprivileged groups in the public sphere.

To further his conception of the active mental attitude of tolerance, Tonder refers to "tolerance" (*tolerantia*) as a way of fostering what Melamed and Rosenthal (2010) call, in interpreting Spinoza, the strength of character needed to act where a person is confronted by "human finitude and worldly pluralism." The idea is not that conceiving toleration as endurance and resilience will always ensure that relations of privilege and domination are overcome. It is, however, reasonable to believe that subjective attitudes of resilience and endurance increase the possibility of a stable, secure expansion of nondomination over time, by increasing expectations of being treated with civility, decency, reasonableness, nonaggression, and respect. In these ways, Tonder's perspective provides the psychological counterpart, I suggest, to the institutional call for secure tolerance advocated by Honohan. Tonder specifically draws from Spinoza's thought the possibility that power resides within tolerance because it modifies bodily vibrations of those practising it. More specifically, Spinoza contends in the *Ethics* that the reason why one would tolerate "vice," what one takes to be ethically problematic, is that it stems from the "freedom to philosophize" (*libertas philosophandi*), which is itself a way of increasing the power to think and act. Tolerantia, then, for Spinoza connotes the human act of endurance, which is linked with the human desire for connectedness (*convenientia*) and tranquility (*ataraxia*), both of which are needed for the stoical stance towards one's own limitations as a human being and the diversity of the world.

While it is unfortunately impossible in one chapter fully to explore the Spinozan background of Tonder's analysis, his perspective does seem to provide the psychological background for the institutional practices of Honohan's "secure" toleration. It therefore seems attractive for societies committed to stable nondomination for all. The stoic ability to "patiently bear" is an inherent part of being human; the external world inevitably causes pain and frustration. Yet, despite this, we still increase our own power to act through confronting and enduring this vulnerability (Tonder 2013a: 697). While these ideas initially seem distant from the political conceptions of toleration surveyed earlier, it seems deeply relevant for marking out the psychological starting point from which to will the secure, undominated status of others. On this conception, it is not that everything is tolerated or tolerable so much as that tolerance is viewed as a long-term achievement supported by the subjective desire of citizens to deepen their connection with the unfamiliar and diverse world. This conception of toleration as an inner acknowledgment of the finitude of oneself and the world might also point to the truth of Brown's suggestion of a certain finitude in the project for equality. It is impossible to know with certainty what will lessen the domination of all minority groups, not least because domination takes different forms. As Tonder says, the concept is "inherently open-ended" but enhances a "shared sense of vulnerability and dependence" in relation to what is perceived to be an objectionable belief or practice (Tonder 2013a: 706).

In fact, Tonder's perspective may seem crucial in circumstances in which the moral reasons to tolerate politically on a particular issue are not conclusive. As Kahmeh describes, the circumstances of political toleration arise in the face not of *familiar* conflicts to which political justice in liberal democracies has a stable response in terms of rights. Rather, these circumstances tend to arise when it is not clear whether to accept or reject, to interfere or not interfere (Khameh 2017: 658). Thus, it is especially when political societies must address newness and the unfamiliar that political tolerance becomes necessary, and when the attitudes of decency and civility which citizens are called on to demonstrate would be enhanced. Securing the status of all is, ultimately, a collective endeavor dependent, not exclusively but importantly, on the psychological will of the less dominated actively to will-to-resist domination, and to reconsider the boundaries of what they consider to be either distasteful, profane, or otherwise contrary to their world view (Gill et al. 2012). If contestation is an ordinary human process, this extended conception of Honohan's secure toleration, addressing the internal and external elements of nondomination, hopefully provides important insights for modern societies today.

Summary and Future Directions

The core aim of this chapter has been to explore the complex and contested relationship between concepts of toleration and domination in contemporary political philosophy. Following the analysis presented of Brown's and Forst's perspectives and the new republican and multiculturalist perspectives defending secure, active toleration, clearly some distinctive avenues for future research come to the fore.

At one level the discussion above suggests the need for further exploration and examination of the active conception of toleration suggested in the final stages of this chapter, one which opposes, and attempts to overcome, the subjective will-to-dominate. New critical perspectives in this area have begun to be initiated on how more active conceptions of toleration may play a significant role in revitalizing democratic politics. Gill et al. (2012), for instance, raise the possibility that some forms of tolerance may productively increase possibilities for minority dissent, by deepening deliberative politics, rather than simply containing conflicts and quelling the possibility of violence. However, the precise ways in which this more active, nondominating conception of toleration may encourage or renew democratic politics remains a subject for future development. The avenue seems vital in view of the ambivalence with which political theorists have regarded the concept of toleration in recent years.

In considering, also, the conditions of securely equalizing the social status of minorities, and thus in considering what is involved in increasing nondomination in the ways suggested above, it remains to be explored, more specifically, how these conceptions might increase the possibilities of "genuine political moments" theorized by Jacques Ranciere (2004). Moreover, how might these moments decrease the political domination of minorities (Gill et al. 2012: 510)? Can distinct forms of toleration be found which increase participation, as well as some which too evidently do not? While it seems true that certain forms of tolerance only barely cover deep-seated political animosities, it remains to be seen how some more active conceptions produce a space for more creative forms of recognition (Gill et al. 2012: 511). It also remains to be explored whether it is true, as Modood and Dobbernack (2013) suggest, that toleration *anticipates* nondomination more frequently than it *instantiates* it.

The debate on this matter has to some extent already been initiated by Zizek (2008), who, like Brown, points to the ways in which some conceptions of toleration foreclose disagreement, while others provide an invitation to further debate. There is also the possibility that active and passive concepts of toleration cannot be fully separated; and that there may be unexplored potential in the negative conception of toleration to secure the status of social groups. Zizek refers, if indirectly, to a more active conception of toleration, as the space in which the otherwise rejected and the "disdained speak." He suggests a "tolerant post-political logic," following Brown, where claims to tolerance are resolved in a case-by-case manner. More specifically, how this conception of toleration may contribute to republican debates concerning nondomination remains a question for further exploration.

It is, secondly, clear that our understanding of the relationship between the respect-based conception of toleration and nondomination has not been exhausted. A number of issues remain worthy of fuller examination and critique. One persistently challenging issue is, as Elisabetta Galeotti (2002) suggests, whether real contemporary issues of toleration necessitate going beyond toleration towards a different conception of value, such as respect, endorsement, or recognition. While

Galeotti has for long synthesized two concepts in terms of the idea of *"toleration as recognition"* (Galeotti 2002, 2015; Laegaard 2008; Baumeister 2011), Ceva (2015) recently contests the utility of respect-based conceptions of tolerance to address the situation of minorities, arguing that this conception will amount to a clearly "inflationary" use of the concept. However, in view of Honohan's idea and the attempt in this chapter to supply the psychological grounding for the institutional requirements of secure tolerance in the form of active, benevolent endurance, future research may lie in discerning in more acute detail the relationship between toleration and concepts ancillary to, and thus separate from, toleration itself. In countering different forms of domination in modern societies, to what extent should toleration be creatively combined with other political values such as equality or community, in order to pursue the theoretical and practical aims of securing the underprivileged from domination?

References

Allen A, Forst R, Haugaard M (2014) Power and reason, justice and domination: a conversation. J Polit Power 7(1):7–33

Baumeister A (2011) Diversity and equality: 'toleration as recognition' reconsidered. In: Mookherjee M (ed) Democracy, religious pluralism and the liberal dilemma of accommodation. Springer, Dordrecht, pp 103–117

Brown W (1994) Toleration and/or equality? The "Jewish question" and the "woman question". differences 15(2):1–31

Brown W (2006) Regulating aversion: tolerance in the age of identity and empire. Princeton University Press, Princeton

Brown W (2008) Tolerance as/in civilisational discourse. Nomos, vol 48. Toleration and its limits, pp 406–441

Brown W, Forst R (2014) The power of tolerance: a debate. Edited by Di Blasi L, Holzhey CFE. University of Columbia Press, Columbia

Buchanan GS (1998–1999) Upping the procedural ante: a study in competing democratic values. Brandeis Law J 37:175

Burchell GD, Gordon C, Miller P (eds) (1991) The Foucault effect: studies in governmentality. University of Chicago Press, Chicago

Ceva E (2015) Why toleration is not the appropriate response to dissenting minorities' claims. Eur J Philos 23(3):633–651

Ceva E, Zuolo F (2013) A matter of respect: on majority-minority relations in a liberal democracy. J Appl Philos 30:239–253

Etinson A (2014) On shareable reasons: a comment on Forst. J Soc Philos 45(1):76–88

Forst R (2007) A critical theory of multicultural toleration. In: Laden AS, Owen D (eds) Multiculturalism and political theory. Cambridge University Press, Cambridge

Forst R (2013) Toleration in conflict: past and present. Cambridge University Press, Cambridge

Foucault M (1988) Technologies of the self: a seminar with Michel Foucault. In: Hutton PH, Gutman H, Martin LH (eds) University of Massachusetts Press, Amherst

Foucault M (1994) The ethics of the self as a practice of freedom. In: Bernauer T, Rasmussen D (eds) The final Foucault. MIT Press, Cambridge, MA, pp 1–21

Friedman M (2003) Autonomy, gender and politics. Oxford University Press, Oxford

Friedman M (2008) Pettit's civic republicanism and male domination. In: Laborde C, Maynor J (eds) Republicanism and political theory. Blackwell Publishing, Malden

Galeotti E (1993) Citizenship and equality: the place for toleration. Political Theory 21(4):585–605

Galeotti E (2002) Toleration as recognition. Cambridge University Press, Cambridge

Galeotti E (2014) Toleration out of conflicts: review article of Rainer Forst's 'Toleration in conflict'. Eur J Polit Theory 14(2):246–255

Galeotti E (2015) The range of toleration: from toleration as recognition back to respectful tolerance. Philosophy and Social Criticism 41(2):93–112

Gill N, Johnstone P, Williams A (2012) Towards a geography of tolerance: post-politics and political forms of toleration. Political Geography 31:509–518

Gregg B (2008) Review of Wendy Brown, Regulating aversion, law and politics book review, pp 318–325

Heyd D (1996) Toleration: an elusive virtue. Princeton University Press, Princeton

Honohan I (2013) Toleration and non-domination. In: Modood T, Dobbernack J (eds) Tolerance, intolerance and respect: hard to accept? Palgrave Macmillan, London, pp 77–102

Khameh A (2017) Political toleration, exclusionary reasoning and the extraordinary politics. Philos Soc Crit 43(6):646–666

Kukathas C (1997) Cultural toleration. NOMOS, vol 39. Ethnicity and group rights, pp 69–104

Laegaard S (2008) Galeotti on recognition and inclusion. Crit Rev Int Soc Polit Philos 11(3):291–343

Laegaard S (2011) A multicultural social ethos: tolerance, respect or civility? In: Calder G, Ceva E (eds) Diversity in Europe: dilemmas of differential treatment in theory and practice. Routledge, London, pp 81–96

Laegaard S (2010) Recognition and toleration: conflicting approaches to diversity in education? In: Sardoc M (ed) Toleration, respect and recognition in education. Wiley Blackwell, Chichester, pp 17–32

Lemke T (2002) Foucault, governmentality and critique. Rethink Marx 4(3):49–64

Lovett F (2010a) A general theory of domination and justice. Oxford University Press, Oxford

Lovett F (2010b) Cultural accommodation and domination. Political Theory 38(2):243–267

Lovett F (2012) What counts as arbitrary power? J Polit Power 5(1):137–152

MacKinnon C (1998) Difference and dominance: on sex discrimination. In: Phillips A (ed) Feminism and politics. Oxford University Press, Oxford

Marcuse H (1965) Repressive tolerance. In: Wolff RP, Moore B Jr, Marcuse H (eds) A critique of pure tolerance. Beacon Press, Boston

Markell P (2008) The insufficiency of non-domination. Political Theory 36(1):9–36

McCannon C (2015) Domination: a rethinking. Ethics 125(4):1028–1052

Melamed YY, Rosenthal MA (2010) Spinoza's theological-political treatise: a critical guide. Cambridge University Press, Cambridge

Modood T, Dobbernack J (2013) Introduction. In: Modood T, Dobbernack J (eds) Tolerance, intolerance and respect: hard to accept? Palgrave Macmillan, Basingstoke

Munro V (2003) On power and domination: feminism and the final Foucault. Eur J Polit Theory 2(1):79–99

Newey G (2013) Toleration in political conflict. Cambridge University Press, Cambridge

Pettit P (2010) The domination complaint. Nomos, vol 46. Political exclusion and domination, pp 87–117

Pettit P (2012) On the people's terms: a republican theory and model of democracy. Cambridge University Press, Cambridge

Preston J (2010) Concrete and abstract racial domination. Power Educ 2(2):115

Ranciere J (2004) Disagreement: politics and philosophy. University of Minnesota Press, Minneapolis

Scott JC (1990) Domination and the arts of resistance. Yale University Press, Yale

Tonder L (2013a) Spinoza and the theory of active tolerance. Political Theory 41(5):687–709

Tonder L (2013b) Tolerance and the sensorial approach to politics. Oxford University Press, Oxford

Valdez I (2017) Non-domination of practices of freedom: French Muslim women, Foucault and the full face-ban. Am Polit Sci Rev 110(1):18–30

Werbner P (2007) Veiled interventions in pure space: honour, shame and embodied struggles among Muslims in Britain and France. Theory Cult Soc 24(2):161–186

Zizek S (2008) Tolerance as an ideological category. Crit Inq 34(4):660–682

State Responses to Incongruence: Toleration and Transformation

13

Paul Billingham

Contents

Introduction	230
Tolerating Incongruence? Three Responses	231
Are Transformative Liberal Interferences Intolerant?	236
State Speech and Toleration	240
Conclusion	244
References	246

Abstract

This chapter focuses on toleration in relation to "incongruent practices," which are in tension with liberal egalitarian norms and principles. It identifies three responses to these practices, two of which deny that the liberal state should tolerate them (but for opposite reasons), but the third of which does claim to tolerate them. This third response can take the form of "transformative liberalism," according to which the state should permit various incongruent practices but should also seek to transform them through the use of its expressive and noncoercive powers. The rest of the chapter explores the relationship between transformative liberalism and toleration in more detail, with the aim of learning about both of them: to see what looking at transformative liberalism through the lens of toleration tells us about that approach and also to see what this can teach us about the nature of toleration itself. It suggests that the forms of interference involved in some transformative liberal policies might be considered intolerant, even if less intolerant than outright prohibition. This might even be the case with respect to state speech, in the light of the particular meaning and force of state condemnation. In considering these issues, the chapter examines several recent debates concerning how toleration is best conceptualized.

P. Billingham (✉)
Department of Politics and International Relations and Magdalen College, University of Oxford, Oxford, UK
e-mail: paul.billingham@politics.ox.ac.uk

© The Author(s), under exclusive licence to Springer Nature Switzerland AG 2022   229
M. Sardoč (ed.), *The Palgrave Handbook of Toleration*,
https://doi.org/10.1007/978-3-030-42121-2_58

Keywords

Transformative liberalism · Incongruent practices · Religion · Conceptual analysis · Degrees of toleration · State speech · Toleration and speech · Neutrality objection · Objection component · Acceptance component

Introduction

Liberalism is closely associated with the idea of toleration, and thus with debates about toleration's definition and proper scope. These debates are the root of various claimed paradoxes of toleration. Can (and should) we tolerate the intolerant? If we cannot tolerate everything, then does this mean that toleration always involves line-drawing that is itself intolerant (Forst 2013, pp. 24–25; ► Chap. 2, "Toleration: Concept and Conceptions"; Königs 2021a)? If the liberal state ought to be neutral concerning conceptions of the good, then does this mean that it is not tolerant after all, since toleration must involve the tolerator objecting to the thing that they are tolerating (Kühler 2021)?

Such questions can be approached both descriptively and normatively: both by seeking to develop a clear and coherent account of what toleration is and by offering an account of what ought and ought not be tolerated. Often these descriptive and normative elements are intertwined. If one believes toleration to be a good thing, a value or virtue, then one will want an account of toleration that produces attractive judgments concerning what does and does not count as an act of toleration. This presumably helps to explain the sense that there is something paradoxical about the idea of a "tolerant racist" (Forst 2013, p. 19; ► Chap. 2, "Toleration: Concept and Conceptions"; ► Chap. 6, "Paradoxes of Toleration"). More generally, the best descriptive account of toleration should help us to explain toleration's relevant moral features, including the fact that toleration is at least sometimes desirable and attractive. The account will thus be normatively informed. Importantly, this does not mean that the account will be fully moralized, such that all acts of toleration are justified and all intolerance is unjustified. The questions of whether X is tolerating Y and of whether X ought to tolerate Y should be distinct, such that there can be cases of unjustified toleration and of justified intolerance. But normative considerations will nonetheless properly shape the descriptive concept.

One of the foci of debates about the scope of toleration concerns groups whose practices appear to be in tension with liberal egalitarian norms and principles, but which do not clearly violate basic rights, by which I mean the set of basic rights familiar from liberal theory and practice. Think here of religious groups who believe that only men can hold certain positions of leadership or who refuse to admit members who do not endorse the group's views on sexual ethics. Such discriminatory leadership and membership policies deviate from liberal egalitarian norms, but do not violate the basic rights of those who are discriminated against, or at least not obviously or uncontroversially. This is also true with respect to associations that are organized in hierarchical, nondemocratic ways, or that require their members to

13 State Responses to Incongruence: Toleration and Transformation

dress in ways that (arguably) reflect patriarchal norms. Such practices seem to be in tension with liberal egalitarian norms of equality and democracy, but again do not uncontroversially violate anyone's basic rights. They are examples of what we can call *incongruent practices*. (For further characterization and discussion of incongruent practices, see Billingham 2019a.) How should the liberal egalitarian state respond to such practices, and the beliefs that motivate them? More specifically, should it tolerate them?

This question is particularly interesting due to the fact that these beliefs and practices seem to fall in a "gray zone." They do not fall into the category of practices that are clearly intolerable and must be prohibited, but they also are not obviously innocuous (although this is not to say that they are necessarily wrongful). This makes them centrally relevant to the question of the scope of toleration.

The next section sketches three possible responses to the question of whether the liberal state should tolerate incongruent practices. The first two of these deny that it should, but for opposite reasons. The first holds that the state should not tolerate these practices because it should not disapprove of them, and thus its noninterference with them does not constitute toleration. The second holds that the state should not tolerate these practices because it should not permit them. In contrast to both of these, the third response does present itself as tolerating incongruence, because it involves both disapproval and permission. Some versions of this response add to this the claim that the state should express its disapproval, in various ways that fall short of prohibition. This view can be called "transformative liberalism," since it seeks to tolerate yet also noncoercively transform incongruent practices.

The subsequent two sections explore the relationship between transformative liberalism and toleration in more detail, with the aim of learning about both of them: to see what looking at transformative liberalism through the lens of toleration tells us about that approach and also to see what this can teach us about the nature of toleration itself.

Tolerating Incongruence? Three Responses

Standard accounts of toleration involve what Rainer Forst (2013, pp. 18–20), following Preston King (1976, pp. 44–51), calls the "objection component": the tolerator disapproves of or dislikes the object of their toleration. This is what distinguishes toleration from indifference or affirmation. There is some debate about exactly what is involved in "objection," for example, whether one must have reasons for objection that are based on moral grounds, or at least meet some minimal moral standards. But what matters for our purposes here is simply that some kind of disapproval is involved. You tolerate me eating a beef burger if you disapprove of it, because you are a vegetarian, but do not interfere. But you do not tolerate me eating a vegetarian burger with my hands rather than cutlery when you don't interfere with this, since you do not disapprove of my eating in this way (let's assume).

This observation generates a first possible response to whether the state ought to tolerate incongruent practices: no, it should not tolerate them, because it should not disapprove of them. Such practices fall within the realm of freedom of expression, religion, and association. They are part of citizens exercising their basic liberal rights to live out their conceptions of the good. As long as freedom of exit from groups that engage in incongruent practices is secured, the state should have no negative attitude toward them. Such practices should not be prohibited, but this lack of prohibition does not constitute toleration. Thus, when liberal states exempt religious groups from certain anti-discrimination laws, they are not "tolerating" the exempted practices, but reflecting an appropriate lack of opposition to them.

This is a version of the "neutrality objection" to liberal toleration. Practices that violate others' rights should be prohibited, while the state should be neutral toward those that do not. There is thus no space for toleration.

This argument crucially depends on viewing objection as an essential component of toleration. Most theorists do so. Indeed, Forst (2013, p. 18) takes it to be uncontroversial and "of primary importance for the concept." Similarly, Peter Königs (2021, p. 6) writes that "as a matter of conceptual necessity, you cannot tolerate what you do not consider wrong." Edward Langerak (1997, p. 111) comments that "everyone in this debate agrees that toleration is to be sharply distinguished both from indifference toward diversity and from broadminded celebration of it."

Langerak's claim that there is universal consensus on this matter is no longer true, however (if it ever was). Peter Balint (2017; ▶ Chap. 8, "Political Toleration Explained") has recently defended a broad view of toleration whereby it simply involves not negatively interfering with something. For Balint, noninterference counts as toleration even when we are indifferent toward, or even positively appraise, the relevant action or practice. Cases where we disapprove of the practice fall into a subcategory of the concept of toleration, which Balint (2017, p. 28) calls "forbearance tolerance." Adopting this view provides a reply to the neutrality objection: even when the liberal state is neutral toward a practice, and refrains from interfering with it for this reason, this lack of interference still counts as toleration (Balint 2017, pp. 32–33). This would thus be one route by which we might conclude that the state should tolerate incongruent practices, even accepting that the state should not disapprove of them.

Balint's view has faced forceful objections, however. Several critics have argued that dropping the objection component deprives toleration of the feature that makes it a distinctive phenomenon. The specificity of relations of toleration is non-interference *despite* grounds for objection, and thus the tolerator having some reasons or desire to interfere (Ceva 2020). "Toleration" carries with it the assumption that the object could well *not* be tolerated. This is why it seems odd to say that "Swedish society tolerates children born with a genetic disease," to borrow an example from Élise Rouméas (2018). Further, the presence of objection is what marks toleration out from mere noninterference, and thus makes it a distinctive concept rather than "pretty much a synonym for freedom" (Horton 2020, p. 193) (or at least negative liberty), as it becomes on Balint's broad account. It is also what makes toleration politically resonant: toleration matters when interference is a live possibility (Rouméas 2018). In sum, then, dropping the objection component from our conceptualization of toleration is certainly one way to dissolve the neutrality objection, but it is one that comes at a high cost with respect to conceptual clarity, normative salience, and political resonance.

As an aside, we should note in passing that the neutrality objection is consistent with the idea that *citizens* within liberal democratic societies practice toleration toward one another, since they can still object to one another's conduct, including in relation to incongruent practices. This leads to a different puzzle, however, which is that citizens might not seem to have the *power* to interfere with those practices. Such power is generally seen as another necessary element in an act of toleration; otherwise interference is again not an option. The precise formulation of this condition is contested, for example, whether actual power is necessary (Balint 2017, pp. 81–83) or it is enough that the agent believes that she has such power (Cohen 2004, pp. 93–94; Langerak 1997, p. 117). Forst (2013, pp. 25–26) endorses a counterfactual power condition, whereby agents who lack power (and know that they lack it) but are of the conviction that they would not interfere even if they did have power can in this way adopt an attitude of tolerance. Even if this is right, however, having this attitude is not the same as actually engaging in acts of toleration (Jones 2007, pp. 384–385). For this, power (or at least believed power, if we follow Cohen) is required.

However, citizens within democracies do have some modicum of political power, since they can seek to effect a change in the law, such that some practice that they object to is legally prohibited. They can do this in various ways, including through voting, lobbying, and protest. When they refrain from doing this, or indeed seek to enact laws that enforce noninterference, we could say that they are acting tolerantly (Jones 2018, p. 214), or at least acting in accordance with the ideal of toleration by seeking to establish rules that instantiate its demands (Jones 2012, p. 268). Further, the law never actually incapacitates; citizens retain the power to interfere with one another in ways that the law prohibits (Jones 2012, p. 269). This is especially the case since the law often "leaves gaps, is too difficult to apply in all but the most egregious cases, or the risk of being caught and severity of punishment is too low to properly constrain choices," as Balint (2017, p. 92) puts it. Willingly following the law could also thus be seen as tolerant (Jones 2007, p. 388). In sum, there are several possible ways that citizens could be conceived as tolerant, although further argument would be needed to establish their ultimate plausibility.

In any case, the focus of this chapter is on toleration of incongruent practices by the state. A first response to this issue, as we have seen, is that the state should not tolerate such practices, because it should not disapprove of them, and thus its noninterference does not qualify as toleration.

A second response to incongruence also rejects toleration, but in the opposite way: it holds that incongruent practices should be legally prohibited. This response reflects what we would more commonly understand by the claim that something should not be tolerated. We might mark this difference by saying that while the first response involves the state "not tolerating" incongruent practices, this second response involves the state being *intolerant* toward them.

Prohibition is clearly the appropriate response to some practices, even ones that are based upon a conception of the good. For example, religious groups should not be permitted to engage in child sacrifice. The easy cases here are ones where basic rights are clearly violated, so that fall outside the definition of incongruent practices above. However, some theorists have defended prohibition for practices that do fall within that definition. For example, Sarah Conly (2016, pp. 34–35) has argued that the Catholic Church should be prosecuted for discrimination in employment on account of its male-only priesthood.

Conly's view remains a minority position. Much more common is the view that purveyors of goods and services should not be permitted to refuse to supply those goods when such supply would conflict with their conscience. This has been at issue in the infamous "gay cake" cases in both the UK (*Lee v. Ashers Baking Company* [2018]) and the USA (*Masterpiece Cakeshop v. Colorado Civil Rights Commission* [2018]), as well as in two of the UK cases that were the subject of a prominent decision at the European Court of Human Rights (*Eweida and others v United Kingdom* [2013]; the relevant cases involved Nancy Eweida and Gary McFarlane). These cases differ in many important respects that are highly relevant to normative evaluation. Nonetheless, a fairly common view of all such cases is that incongruence can be permitted only when it stays within the bounds of civil society associations and only impacts upon a group's own members. It becomes intolerable when it enters the public, including economic, realm in ways that affect other citizens who do not adhere to the relevant comprehensive doctrine. This idea has recently been expressed within the literature on legal accommodations using the notion of "third-party harms." The presence of such harms is said to rule out accommodation, or at least make them much harder to justify (Sepinwall 2015; Tebbe 2017, pp. 49–70; for critique see Esbeck 2017). This leads to complex questions regarding what count as relevant harms. Debates over the public wearing of the burqa, for example, partly center on whether this practice causes genuine third-party harms, as claimed by the French government in its argument that the burqa breaks the social tie and is incompatible with the principle of "living together" (*S.A.S v. France* [2014]).

For my part, I think that the idea that incongruence must be prohibited as soon as it impacts nonmembers is too quick, and there might be scope for accommodations even in cases where we can plausibly identify certain third-party harms. I will not pursue that argument here, however. The key point for our purposes is simply that a second response to incongruence is intolerance. Few, if any, theorists would apply this response to all cases of incongruence, but there are active debates about the merits of its application to various incongruent practices.

Let's now turn to a third response to our question regarding toleration and incongruence. Even in cases where one decides that the second, prohibitionist, response is inappropriate – liberal freedoms make prohibition unjustified – one might feel that the first, neutralist, response is insufficient. Even if the state should not make an incongruent practice illegal, it might seem unsatisfactory for it to be indifferent toward that practice, as the first response assumed. Shouldn't the incongruence count for something? If the practice is in tension with the liberal egalitarian values of the state, then does this not mean that the state should have an attitude other than indifference toward it?

This is where we might find space for toleration. The state might permit a practice but nonetheless disapprove of it. This response to the neutrality objection has recently been offered by Kühler (2021) and Balint (2017, pp. 34–35). In some cases liberal egalitarian values speak against a practice but other such values (or perhaps pragmatic considerations) speak against prohibiting it, with the balance of reasons rendering toleration – permission in the face of disapproval – the appropriate response. Balint calls this the range of state "forbearance tolerance" – his term for noninterference in the face of objection.

To be clear, the claim here is a conceptual one concerning the space for toleration by the liberal state, rather than a normative one that the state should in fact disapprove of incongruent practices. There is a substantive debate to be had about when such disapproval is appropriate. My own view is that in many cases incongruence is not a sufficient reason for state disapproval; the state really should be neutral, that is, indifferent, toward many incongruent practices. We should resist the "logic of congruence": the claim that it is "imperative that the internal life and organization of associations mirror liberal democratic principles and practices" (Rosenblum 1998, p. 36; see also Billingham 2019a; Spinner-Halev 2008). Nonetheless, there might be a class of incongruent practices that the state should indeed disapprove of, but still should not prohibit, and thus can be said to be tolerating. The size of this class is a matter for normative debate.

If the state is tolerating an incongruent practice, then one might think that it should make its disapproval evident. It could do this in various ways. State officials could speak out against the practice; the state could refuse to employ individuals who engage in it and dismiss existing employees who do so; and groups that engage in it could be denied state subsidies or tax-exemptions, have existing tax-exemptions withdrawn, or even have additional taxes applied. According to advocates of such polices, they are ways that the state can display opposition to incongruent practices, and encourage their reform, while nonetheless respecting associational and religious freedom by not prohibiting the practices. Call this approach "transformative liberalism." It is liberal due to its protection of familiar liberal freedoms, but supplements this with an ambition to transform incongruent beliefs and practices when these are deemed to be in sufficient conflict with liberal egalitarian values. (Again, this will likely not be the case for all incongruence, but for some subset of it.)

The idea that liberalism is, or should be, a transformative project, one that ultimately must reshape citizens' attitudes and behaviors so that they conform to liberal values, has been emphasized by theorists such as Stephen Macedo. For him, liberalism protects the freedom "to resist full compliance with liberal and democratic values," but it nonetheless "counts on shaping, to some degree, people's extra-political associations and communities, including families and religious communities" (Macedo 2012, p. 165). Indeed, liberal constitutionalism "is a pervasively educative order" (Macedo 1998, p. 57). For Macedo, then, liberalism is always transformative. This claim is controversial in itself, since it suggests that liberalism interferes with citizens' private lives and conceptions of the good more than is usually thought.

"Transformative liberalism" actively considers what policies the liberal state should adopt in order to achieve its transformative ends. Rather than transformation merely happening as a side effect of the functioning of liberal institutions, the state "should intentionally seek to transform" (Brettschneider 2012, p. 99) some incongruent beliefs and practices. One way to do this is through "positive" policies, such as civic education and various kinds of symbolic expression – public memorials, statues, street names, and so on, that celebrate events or individuals reflecting ideals and principles that the state wishes to promulgate. These policies present the state's values without directly opposing alternatives. But the focus in this chapter is on "negative" policies, which directly target incongruent practices: critical state speech, denial of state subsidies, and so on.

I have criticized transformative liberalism, and especially the version of the view developed by Corey Brettschneider (2012), at length elsewhere (Billingham 2019a, b). The rest of this chapter examines the view further through the lens of toleration.

Are Transformative Liberal Interferences Intolerant?

The previous section introduced transformative liberalism as a view that involves the liberal state in toleration: in permitting incongruent practices that it nonetheless objects to. However, the transformative liberal state also *expresses* this objection in various ways, and uses those means to encourage reform. Does this mean that it is not tolerant of the relevant incongruent practices after all? Or that it is somehow tolerant and intolerant toward them at the same time? Exploring these questions might tell us something about both transformative liberalism and toleration itself.

Our questions here center on what Forst (2013, pp. 20–23) (again following King 1976, pp. 51–54) calls the "acceptance component" of toleration – the not interfering with, or allowing, or putting up with, the objected-to practice. What precisely is required in order for an agent to count as "putting up with" something such that they can be said to tolerate it? Asking this the other way around, what kinds of "not putting up with" count as intolerant? What counts as a relevant form of interference? Whether or not transformative liberalism qualifies as tolerant will turn on our answer to these questions.

One possible answer is that intolerance involves *preventing* a practice. Peter Jones (2007, 2018), for one, uses the language of prevention when defining toleration. If we take this literally, then it suggests that merely discouraging or disincentivizing a practice does not count as intolerance. The transformative liberal state would thus be tolerant toward incongruent practices.

The truth in this thought is that one does not have to be silent about a practice in order to tolerate it. Communicating one's objection, or engaging in dialogue concerning the propriety of a practice, does not generally constitute intolerance (although we will consider this issue in greater detail in the next section). However, there are various forms of interference that lie between prevention and dialogue.

Issuing threats that impose extra costs upon an action or obstacles that make the action more burdensome both surely constitute intolerance, even though they do not necessarily prevent the action and certainly do not make it impossible (Balint 2017, p. 83). Indeed, even legal prohibitions do not make actions impossible or prevent them in a strict sense; they threaten punishment, imposing costs upon the action. It seems clear, then, that "prevention" sets the bar for intolerance too high. Jones (2007, p. 395, fn 21) in fact acknowledges this, noting that while prevention is the paradigm case, intolerance can also take the form of disincentives or disadvantages imposed on conduct.

Nonetheless, one might hold that these various kinds of interference all involve an *intention* to prevent the action, and this is why they are intolerant. Intolerance must involve the intention to prevent, even if the prevention is unsuccessful. Thus, Andrew Cohen (2004, p. 85) writes that toleration requires that there is "no action aimed at preventing the behavior in question." Similarly, Jones (2015, p. 556) emphasizes that it is "intentions rather than consequences that mark people out as tolerant or intolerant."

It is not completely clear where transformative liberalism would stand on this view. There is certainly a sense in which transformative policies aim to prevent incongruent practices; the hope of transformative liberals is that their policies will ultimately lead to reforms that produce congruence. But some might find it odd to speak of the state intending to prevent a practice when it is refraining either from legally prohibiting it or from imposing conditions on it that make it practically impossible or completely unaffordable – acts that are within the state's power. It might seem more natural to say that the state is deterring or discouraging the practice. Now, this could still count as "intending to prevent," since the ultimate aim is that the practice ceases. But the term then risks becoming too broad. After all, even rational persuasion in some sense involves the intention to prevent the action that one objects to, via convincing the other party to cease engaging in it. The term "prevent" would then no longer be doing the limiting work that was its original attraction.

It might thus seem better to think in terms of a range of possible forms of (negative) interference, all of which constitute intolerance except (usually) for mere expression of dislike and engagement in rational dialogue. (Again, this exception still requires further examination and justification, which we will turn to in the next section).

Balint (2017, pp. 83–84) endorses this view, defining toleration in terms of an absence of negative interference or hindrance. In this case, various transformative liberal policies would be intolerant, qua hindering. For example, take the state threatening to withdraw a group's tax-exempt status, or to cease to allow it to provide state-funded services, unless it ceases to engage in some incongruent practice. This threat hinders the continuation of that practice by raising its costs. The same applies to excluding from public employment anyone who engages in an incongruent practice. Such policies can thus be seen as intolerant toward the practice, despite not prohibiting it.

Peter Königs has recently defended a narrower view, however. He argues that intolerance must involve "particularly vile or ruthless means of interference"

(Königs 2021, p. 8), offering coercion (including state coercion), hate campaigns, and public demonization as paradigm cases. "Not to tolerate a practice or worldview is to intervene with it in a particularly cruel and ruthless manner" (Königs 2021, p. 10), whereas interference that exhibits "a certain degree of civility, human decency and benevolence" (p. 8) does not count as intolerant. Transformative liberalism would thus presumably not be intolerant.

One problem with Königs view is that it does not seem right to see all forms of coercion as "cruel and ruthless." If the state prohibits driving above the speed limit and penalizes transgressors with a moderate fine, then this is clearly coercive, and makes the state intolerant of speeding. But this interference doesn't seem "vicious" (Königs 2021, p. 10). Indeed, we might well believe that the liberal state's coercion should never be cruel, vicious, or ruthless. The limits placed on state action by liberal values and norms are meant to ensure this. Königs view thus seems to imply that the liberal state is never (or at least very rarely) intolerant, which does not seem right.

One might wonder if this is simply to quibble over words. Königs could perhaps reformulate his view using some other less severe adjectives that do capture state coercion. This might create other problems for his argument, however, since his account is offered as a way to show why toleration has value, and indeed has value that is obvious, or "readily intelligible" (Königs 2021, p. 9) (thus defusing the "paradox of moral toleration," which questions how it can be morally right or valuable to tolerate what is morally wrong or bad [Forst 2013, pp. 21–22; ▶ Chap. 2, "Toleration: Concept and Conceptions"]). Königs's argument here depends on the fact that it is clearly valuable to avoid interference with others that is cruel, vicious, inhumane, and so on. But if those terms are in fact too strong to properly capture the nature of toleration-relevant interference, then this argument loses its force. And without this normative motivation for adopting Königs narrow view, the broader nonhindrance view seems more plausible.

Even if one adopts this broader view, Königs's argument highlights that some forms of intolerance are more severe than others. This suggests that we need to make distinctions regarding degrees of toleration. More vicious forms of interference do seem more intolerant. More generally, making an action more costly and completely preventing it might both count as intolerance, but they are intolerant to different degrees. The transformative liberal state is surely more tolerant of an incongruent practice than a state that prohibits that practice, even if the former state is still somewhat intolerant toward it.

While rarely discussed in detail, the idea that toleration can come in degrees seems to be fairly widely endorsed (e.g., see King 1976, p. 53; Horton 1996, p. 28; Jones 2007, p. 395, fn. 21). Cohen (2004 pp. 88–89, fn. 21) rejects it, however, arguing that one either tolerates an object or one does not. Cases where we might be tempted to talk about degrees of toleration should instead be conceptualized in terms of scope. More or fewer objects are being tolerated, but for any particular object one is either interfering or not, and thus tolerating or not.

An example using an arguably incongruent practice might help here. No liberal state completely prohibits the wearing of the Islamic veil (the niqab or burqa). But various European countries have banned the wearing of a full-face veil in public places (BBC 2018). Another possible arrangement is to limit a ban to certain settings, such as courts and schools, or to individuals in certain roles, such as judges and teachers. Other states, including the UK and the USA, have imposed no ban at all.

These policies might be seen as involving different degrees of toleration: states tolerate the wearing of the veil to different degrees. Cohen's point is that it is better to see it as a matter of scope: different veil-wearing activities are tolerated or not tolerated in different states. With respect to any particular activity (e.g., "wearing the veil on public transport," "wearing the veil when doing one's job as a teacher") the veil is either tolerated or not tolerated. The differences between states concern the scope of veil-wearing activities that are or are not tolerated.

There can be cases, however, where one can engage in different levels of interference with the same act or object. One state might prohibit male-only priesthoods, while another permits them but withdraws tax-exempt status (which would otherwise have been available) from religions that practice it. The latter, transformative liberal, policy is intolerant of the practice, but to a lesser degree than the former, prohibitionist, policy. To give a more abstract example, I might interfere with your ϕ-ing by wrestling you to the ground, throwing rocks at you from a distance, or threatening to harm your pet dog. These different forms of interference hinder your action to a greater or lesser degree. Even if we cannot precisely measure the different levels of hindrance, it seems to make sense to see them as different degrees of toleration.

In other words, we might want to talk about the scope of toleration when the same form of interference is being imposed on different actions (even if those actions are all manifestations of the same general practice, such as veil-wearing), but the degree of toleration when different levels of interference are imposed on the same action.

Some cases involve a combination of these things. Take sin taxes, for example, which are taxes imposed on specific goods based on the judgment that they are harmful to their consumers. Compare a state that prohibits smoking with one that imposes a sin tax on tobacco. There is a difference in scope here, in that certain actions are interfered with in the former state but not the latter, for example, producing and selling cigarettes. But there is also a difference in degree, with respect to the same act: buying cigarettes. In the former state, this act is illegal, while in the latter it has a cost imposed upon it on the grounds of the state's disapproval.

It is possible to collapse this distinction and only recognize differences in scope, by more finely individuating the objects of toleration. Wrestling you to the ground means not tolerating your ϕ-ing. Throwing rocks at you tolerates you ϕ-ing, but does not tolerate you "ϕ-ing without risk of harm." Threatening to harm your dog tolerates both of those things, but does not tolerate you "ϕ-ing while protecting your dog from harm." If we precisely individuate acts in this kind of way, then we can always say that different acts are being tolerated rather than the same act being tolerated to different degrees. Such an individuation (in this context at least) seems highly artificial, however. It seems much more natural to distinguish degrees of interference with, and thus toleration of, the same act.

Indeed, if anything, it might be better to collapse the distinction between degree and scope in the other direction and make all the differences about degree, even if this involves identifying the objects of toleration slightly more loosely. For example, as an example of different degrees of toleration, Jones (2007, p. 395, fn. 21) writes that a society that imposes sin taxes on tobacco is more tolerant "of smoking" than one that prohibits smoking. Similarly, it seems natural to say that states that ban the veil only in certain public buildings are more tolerant "of veil-wearing" than those who ban it in all public places.

A different objection to this talk of degrees of toleration, which might be motivating Cohen, holds that while there can be various forms of interference, the most normatively salient fact is that they all constitute intolerance. I am interfering with you φ-ing, and thus intolerant of it, and there is nothing to be gained by distinguishing degrees of intolerance. Saying that I am more tolerant of your φ-ing when I throw rocks than when I wrestle, or (even worse) that in the former case I am both tolerant and intolerant of you φ-ing (since I interfere, but to a lesser degree than I could), is misleading. What matters is that I interfere with you, and so am not tolerant of your φ-ing. There might be distinctions to be drawn here with respect to interference, freedom, and justification; but it is all simply intolerance.

There is some attraction to this view. If you accuse me of being intolerant and I respond by saying that I am being more tolerant than I could have been, then this does seem to somewhat miss the point. Nonetheless, there also does seem to be something important about being able to recognize that the transformative liberal state is more tolerant than the prohibitionist state. Many transformative liberal policies hinder incongruent practices, and are thus acts of intolerance. The transformative liberal state is not fully tolerant toward those incongruent practices; we can rightly call it intolerant of them. But we also want to recognize that it is less intolerant than the prohibitionist state. Speaking of degrees of toleration is a helpful way to do this.

Further, when we turn to the normative question of what we *ought* to tolerate, this approach allows us to ask this question both in terms of scope (which practices ought the state interfere with?) and degree (what degree of interference is warranted with any particular practice?). This is an important advantage.

The more basic idea that we have explored in this section, however, is that the transformative liberal state might plausibly be said to display some intolerance through its negative interference with intolerant practices, even though that interference falls short of prohibition.

State Speech and Toleration

As noted above, the mere expression of disapproval, or engagement in rational persuasion, is not usually taken to constitute intolerance (e.g., see Cohen 2004, pp. 85–86). Mark Webb (1997, p. 416) writes that one "certainly" may tolerate another's religion even while trying to convert her. Forst (2008, p. 289) goes so far as to claim that mutual toleration "presuppose[s] that one knows the other's point of view and argues against it."

Some transformative liberal policies take this kind of form. State officials such as judges and executive office-holders express disapproval of some belief or practice and explain why (they believe) it is incompatible with the liberal egalitarian values endorsed by the state. Brettschneider (2012, pp. 156–157) gives the example of New York's Mayor Bloomberg rebuking opponents of plans to build an Islamic center near the former site of the World Trade Center for displaying anti-Muslim animus. Do the claims in the previous paragraph show that such speech is undoubtedly tolerant? Or is there more to say about it from the perspective of toleration? Might this kind of expression constitute intolerance when it comes from the "mouth" of the state?

Balint (2017, p. 117) suggests that "speaking back" against practices that one disapproves of can be a form of intolerance, since it is intended to hinder the performance of the criticized acts. This would certainly apply to speech-based transformative liberal policies. Balint's claim here risks being too broad, however, since it seems to apply to all forms of critical speech, including all cases of rational dialogue. Rational dialogue seeks to persuade the other party to change their beliefs and behavior, and is in that sense intended to hinder their performance of the objected-to act. Balint's argument would thus seem to categorize all such speech as intolerant, in contrast to the standard view.

Perhaps this simply shows that the standard view is mistaken, and we should categorize all oppositional speech as intolerant after all, viewing its usual exclusion from the category of toleration-relevant interference as arbitrary. Ben Cross (2019) has recently defended this claim, at least in relation to "unwilling hearers," who wish to avoid exposure to the arguments. Unwilling hearers have their choices and options limited against their will, by being made to hear arguments against their beliefs and practices that they wish to avoid. This diminishes their freedom (Cross 2019, p. 333) and autonomy (p. 346). We can generally assume that those who engage in incongruent practices do not want to hear those practices being criticized or argued against by state officials. So if Cross is right, then speech-based transformative liberal policies would be intolerant, along with large swathes of argument-expression, including most proselytism.

Cross's argument faces two significant objections, however. First, even with respect to unwilling hearers, argument expression does not usually constrain agency in a way that makes an accusation of intolerance plausible. Hearers of arguments can generally exercise their own reason and judgment in determining what to believe and how to act. The arguments might affect that process, but do not constrain or undermine it. Cross is right that presenting arguments to unwilling hearers limits their choices, in the sense that it removes the option not to be exposed to those arguments. But this is not enough to say that their agency is curtailed. After all, all actions that others dislike limit their choices in this sense: the option for those actions not to occur is removed. But, as Jones (2007, pp. 394–396, 2018, pp. 210–211) emphasizes, merely acting in a way that another person dislikes does not make one intolerant.

Second, we want a concept of toleration where it is possible, and not unreasonably demanding, to tolerate. We want toleration to be an attainable ideal. Cross

(2019, pp. 335–336) acknowledges that it might often be unreasonable to insist that people do not express their disapproval, but holds that this simply means that we should often permit this form of intolerance; when we call for toleration, we should instead be understood to be objecting to certain kinds of intolerance (such as threats, intimidation, and harassment). But while this is a conceptually viable move, it means that the concept of toleration loses its distinctive use, applicability, and normative appeal. It seems better to recognize considerations concerning reasonable expectations as playing a role in shaping our conceptualization of toleration itself.

This also relates to an argument that Königs (2021, pp. 11–12) makes concerning the political resonance of toleration. Toleration has positive valence, and the charge of intolerance is a serious one. This normative consideration should constrain the kinds of negative interferences that we label intolerant. While this argument is not sufficient to justify Königs's narrow definition of intolerance, discussed above, it does give further reason not to see all argument expression aimed at unwilling hearers as intolerant. This is an example of the way that normative considerations properly shape the descriptive concept of toleration, such that disputes over conceptualization are not merely terminological.

In sum, Cross's view would see speech-based transformative liberal policies as intolerant, but that view faces some important challenges. Those who reject it will hold the conventional view holds that expressing opposition to a belief and practice, and seeking to persuade practitioners to change their views, is generally compatible with toleration. But this does not mean that speech can never be intolerant (Jones 2018). The question for us is whether condemnatory state speech might be.

There does seem to be something distinctive about opposition to a belief or practice being expressed in the name of the state, as opposed to by a private citizen. Consider the controversy over the racist comments made by Donald Sterling, the owner of the LA Clippers basketball franchise, in April 2014. Many people rightly condemned these comments, but there was arguably something distinct about the condemnation delivered by President Barack Obama. He could be understood as speaking on behalf of the state, of "we the people," when expressing the fact that Sterling's comments were unacceptable, even if they were constitutionally protected free speech. Obama stated that the comments were "incredibly offensive" and ignorant, and that "we just have to be clear and steady in denouncing" such racism. He also noted that the fact these statements stood out so much was in itself a reason for hope, since it showed that "there has been this shift in how we view ourselves" (Chappel 2014). The difference between Obama's speech and that of others is not simply that he was a high-profile figure or particularly influential; many prominent people, such as former players, spoke out against the comments. The difference is that Obama's speech communicates that the comments are ones that "we around here," the collective of citizens, consider unacceptable, incompatible with "how we view ourselves," even if we have reasons to stop short of legally prosecuting them. The condemnatory speech of other individuals, in contrast, even if those others are rich, famous, and/or powerful, can only communicate that they, or perhaps a group that they represent, disapprove. (Although the NBA authorities did also display intolerance toward Sterling's comments: they forced him to sell the Clippers and banned him from the NBA for life.)

The example of Obama's response to Sterling might suggest that the state is able to communicate something in its speech that private citizens cannot: the censure of the community as a whole. Of course, this censure will likely be contested within the community, not least by those who endorse the condemned belief or practice. Nonetheless, when the state expresses condemnation of incongruence it is claiming that a belief or practice is incompatible with the values on which society is based and ought to be viewed as beyond the pale by society at large. The practice is officially declared to be incompatible with good citizenship. This distinctive kind of communication could plausibly be said to make such speech intolerant, even accepting the conventional view that not all oppositional speech is intolerant. The transformative liberal state tolerates the condemned practice in terms of refraining from prohibiting it, but the communication of society's official opposition to it can plausibly be construed as itself a form of intolerance.

Jones (2018, p. 214) notes, drawing on Mill, that there is a kind of social disapproval that can be an instrument of intolerance, due to the pressure it places upon its targets. Such disapproval can sometimes interfere with agency in a way that normal kinds of expressions of opposition or persuasive argument do not. Arguably, state speech could constitute this kind of intolerant social disapproval, precisely due to the way that it involves speaking in the name of the people.

One way to capture this idea would be to say that condemnatory state speech is coercive, in a way that private persuasion usually is not. Cohen (2004, p. 86) and Jones (2018, p. 214) both suggest that condemnation that has a force amounting to coercion should count as intolerant and Webb (1997, p. 416) notes that significant power differences between parties can give speech such force. This could well apply to state speech.

Brettschneider (2012, p. 152) denies that state speech is coercive, as long as its voice is one among many. Others have suggested that this underestimates the distinctiveness of state speech. Jacob Rowbottom (2017, p. 45) writes that "treating certain views as officially disfavored and subject to government-sponsored opposition in the field of political debate is a significant step and should not be underestimated." Such government speech "is itself a vertical intervention into the horizontal competition of ideas among citizens, which openly treats some ideas as officially having lower status and necessitating official opposition." This does not in itself mean that oppositional state speech is coercive, of course. There might be other reasons not to appeal to that concept. For example, if coercion must involve threats or the use of sanctions to foreclose some options, then perhaps oppositional state speech does not count as coercive. For our purposes, the key point is that state speech imposes an important kind of pressure on its targets, through the distinctive message that it can send, such that the label of "intolerance" does seem appropriate, whatever verdict we reach regarding "coercion."

Another way to approach this is to revisit what toleration is centrally about: being willing to live with differences that we object to (Kühler 2021, p. 26; Horton 2020, p. 191). The expression of official state censure toward a practice communicates a clear desire that as a society we would not have to live with this difference. This seems different to merely holding that this practice would not exist in an ideally just or moral society; it involves actively seeking to move toward a society free of this practice, by pressuring its adherents to abandon it. One might say that the same is true of all forms of rational persuasion and dialogue. These too seek to change the difference that they are targeted at, rather than simply to live with it. But, again, the use of the state's capacities seems to make a difference to the character of the expression here. Seeking to change people's minds through persuasion does not impose the same pressure upon the practice's adherents as that practice being officially held up as incompatible with society's values. Preferring a world where everyone agreed with me and seeking to bring about that world through the force of my arguments is not the same as declaring that world to be required by the core principles of society, while speaking on behalf of society as a whole. The latter arguably involves a kind of intolerance lacking from the former.

If this is right, then it means that while transformative liberalism tolerates incongruent practices in the sense of permitting them, it also acts intolerantly toward them through the various means that it employs to express state censure, from literal speech to educational practices to the use of the state's spending power. Importantly, the argument in this section applies to all of these policies, since all of them express state opposition to the targeted beliefs and practices. Thus, even if one is unconvinced by the suggestion in the previous section that policies such as withdrawing (or threatening to withdraw) tax-exempt status are intolerant qua hindering, one might still accept that they are intolerant through the way that they express state censure, on the basis of the discussion in this section. Even if transformative liberal policies are noncoercive, or at least less coercive than prohibition, they exert significant pressure upon their targets through their intolerance. The state's expressive and spending capacities are powerful tools. This is part of what makes them attractive to transformative liberals, but it is also a reason for caution.

Conclusion

This chapter has considered transformative liberalism through the lens of toleration in order to learn about both of them: both to examine whether transformative liberalism should be categorized as tolerant or intolerant and to consider interesting questions that this raises concerning the conceptualization of toleration. In particular, it has explored the way in which toleration might come in degrees and whether speech can count as intolerant.

What normative implications, if any, follow from this discussion? Certainly we cannot simply infer from the fact that transformative liberalism is not maximally tolerant that it is normatively unattractive or objectionable. Even if our concept of toleration is normatively informed, such that normative considerations affect the choices that we make within our conceptualization, this does not mean that toleration is always a good thing. For example, some of the arguments considered in this chapter relied on the idea that our conceptualization should capture the fact that toleration generally has positive valence. But this is consistent with holding that some things should not be tolerated; there can be justified intolerance. We thus still face the central normative question of what we (including the state) ought and ought not be intolerant toward, and in what ways that intolerance ought to be manifested. As Jones (2018, p. 219) puts it, "the ideal of toleration requires more than the idea of toleration."

Nonetheless, as Jones also emphasizes, our ideal of toleration will certainly be influenced by the concept: we need to know what counts as tolerant and intolerant in order to identify what ought and ought not be tolerated, and those normative judgments will themselves be informed and clarified by our understanding of the concept.

Further, if transformative liberalism is intolerant then this does highlight a reason that liberals might be hesitant of it (Spinner-Halev 2008). I have argued elsewhere that the use of transformative liberal policies should be much more limited than their advocates tend to claim (Billingham 2019a, b). There are several reasons for this: the tendency toward defining the liberal democratic values on which these policies are based in increasingly expansive ways, the difficulties of interpreting the meaning of associations' practices and evaluating them against liberal values, the need to maintain limits on the state's authority over civic society, troubling implications for associational freedom, and the risk of alienating good-willed citizens who should be allies of liberal democracy. Many of these concerns can be captured by highlighting, or framed as pointing toward, the intolerance of transformative liberalism. Future debates concerning the justifiability of transformative liberal policies might thus be partly framed in terms of toleration.

The discussion in this chapter also points to more general lessons regarding our theorizing about toleration, which suggest avenues for further research. One lesson is that we should think about both the degree and scope of toleration. Different actions can be tolerated, and each action can be tolerated to different degrees. If this is right, then we might want to think more about how to conceptualize these different degrees and to measure the level of intolerance of different forms of interference, including different kinds of transformative liberal policy. One possibility is that the degree of intolerance is defined by the extent of the restriction on freedom; but perhaps this relationship is not so straightforward. We might also consider to what extent, if at all, the degree of intolerance is determined by the subjective perceptions of its targets, as compared to how hindering the interference is in more objective terms.

Beyond these conceptual questions, normative arguments for toleration or intolerance should also speak to the questions of both scope and degree. Some disputes will be about what precise actions or practices should (not) be tolerated (scope), while others will be about what kinds of interference are appropriate (degree). This will certainly be true with respect to debates about the state's response to incongruent practices, given both the diversity of such practices and the range of different policies available – whether permissive, prohibitionist, or transformative – and their different degrees of intolerance.

A second lesson is that we can hold to the idea that not all oppositional speech is intolerant while also recognizing that some can be, and in particular that state speech might be in this category. Future work might further distinguish different kinds of state speech and the way that they relate to toleration. Differences might arise based both on precisely who the speaker is and the content of their speech. We might also consider further whether nonstate speech can sometimes be intolerant, and the conditions under which this could be the case. Again, there are also normative questions to ask here, such as what intolerant speech is justified, and indeed whether intolerant speech is generally easier to justify than intolerant action. This might be true, for example, if we think that speech involves a lesser degree of hindrance, or in the light of the central importance of freedom of speech within liberal societies.

More broadly, this chapter has shown how considering the example of the state's response to incongruence raises interesting questions about both the theory and practice of toleration. No doubt there are many other such examples that raise similarly important questions.

Acknowledgments I owe thanks to Tom Parr, Élise Rouméas, Mitja Sardoč, and Anthony Taylor for helpful comments on an earlier draft of this chapter.

References

Balint P (2017) Respecting toleration: traditional liberalism and contemporary diversity. Oxford University Press, Oxford

BBC News (2018) The Islamic veil across Europe, 31 May 2018. http://www.bbc.co.uk/news/world-europe-13038095

Billingham P (2019a) Shaping religion: the limits of transformative liberalism. In: Seglow J, Shorten A (eds) Religion and political theory: secularism, accommodation and the new challenges of religious diversity. ECPR Press/Rowman & Littlefield International, London, pp 57–77

Billingham P (2019b) State speech as a response to hate speech: assessing 'transformative liberalism'. Ethical Theory Moral Pract 22(3):639–655

Brettschneider C (2012) When the state speaks, what should it say?: how democracies can protect expression and promote equality. Princeton University Press, Princeton

Ceva E (2020) The good of toleration: changing social relations or maximising individual freedom? Crit Rev Int Soc Pol Phil 23(2):197–202

Chappel B (2014) Obama discusses racist comments attributed to clippers owner. NPR, 27 Apr 2014. https://www.npr.org/sections/thetwo-way/2014/04/27/307346184/obama-discusses-racist-comments-attributed-to-clippers-owner. Accessed 27 Jan 2021

Cohen AJ (2004) What toleration is. Ethics 115(1):68–95

Conly S (2016) In defense of the (somewhat more) invasive state. Philos Public Issues New Ser 6 (1):25–37

Cross B (2019) Intolerance and argument expression. Soc Theory Pract 45(3):329–352

Esbeck CH (2017) When religious exemptions cause third-party harms: is the establishment clause violated? J Church State 59(3):357–376

Forst R (2008) Toleration and truth: comments on Steven D. Smith. In: Williams MS, Waldron J (eds) Toleration and its limits. New York University Press, New York, pp 281–292

Forst R (2013) Toleration in conflict: past and present. Cambridge University Press, Cambridge

Horton J (1996) Toleration as a virtue. In: Heyd D (ed) Toleration: an elusive virtue. Princeton University Press, Princeton, pp 28–43

Horton J (2020) Conceptualising toleration. Crit Rev Int Soc Pol Phil 23(2):191–196

Jones P (2007) Making sense of political toleration. Br J Polit Sci 37(3):383–402

Jones P (2012) Legalising toleration: a reply to Balint. Res Publica 18(3):265–270

Jones P (2015) Toleration, religion and accommodation: toleration, religion and accommodation. Eur J Philos 23(3):542–563

Jones P (2018) Can speech be intolerant? In: Essays on toleration. ECPR Press/Rowman & Littlefield International, London, pp 203–222

King P (1976) Toleration. St. Martin's Press, New York

Königs P (2021) The simplicity of toleration. Crit Rev Int Soc Pol Phil 24(1):5–24

Kühler M (2021) Can a value-neutral liberal state still be tolerant? Crit Rev Int Soc Pol Phil 24(1): 25–44

Langerak E (1997) Disagreement: appreciating the dark side of tolerance. In: Razavi MA, Ambuel D (eds) Philosophy, religion, and the question of intolerance. State University of New York Press, Albany, pp 111–124

Macedo S (1998) Transformative constitutionalism and the case of religion: defending the moderate hegemony of liberalism. Political Theory 26(1):56–80

Macedo S (2012) Hauerwas, liberalism, and public reason: terms of engagement? Law Contemp Probl 75(4):161–180

Rosenblum NL (1998) Membership and morals: the personal uses of pluralism in America. Princeton University Press, Princeton

Rouméas É (2018) Review of Peter Balint: respecting toleration: traditional liberalism and contemporary diversity. Ethical Theory Moral Pract 21(5):1255–1257

Rowbottom J (2017) Government speech and public opinion: democracy by the bootstraps. J Polit Philos 25(1):22–47

Sepinwall A (2015) Conscience and complicity: assessing pleas for religious exemptions in Hobby Lobby's Wake. Univ Chic Law Rev 82(4):1897–1980

Spinner-Halev J (2008) Liberalism and religion: against congruence. Theor Inq Law 9(2):553–572

Tebbe N (2017) Religious freedom in an egalitarian age. Harvard University Press, Cambridge, MA

Webb MO (1997) Trust, tolerance, and the concept of a person. Public Aff Q 11(4):415–429

Court Cases

Eweida and others v United Kingdom [2013] ECtHR 37
Lee v. Ashers Baking Company Ltd and others [2018] UKSC 49
Masterpiece Cakeshop v. Colorado Civil Rights Commission 584 U.S. __ (2018)
S.A.S. v. France [2014] ECHR 695

Toleration and State Neutrality: The Case of Symbolic FGM

14

Federico Zuolo

Contents

Introduction 250
Impossible Toleration? 251
The Case: Female Circumcision 253
Reasons for Objecting and for Accepting 255
Female Circumcision and Its (Surprising?) Cognate Practices 257
Should Liberal States Tolerate Female Circumcision? 259
Summary and Future Directions 261
References 261

Abstract

Traditional theories of toleration have to face the well-known problem of pre-emption of toleration. A liberal state should maximize individual liberties and be neutral with respect to diverse religions and theories of the good. In this scenario, the state cannot tolerate a certain practice because for toleration to obtain the state should object to a practice, while accepting it for some other reason. However, if the state is neutral, there should be no reason to object to a given practice, while allowing it. Hence, either the state allows a certain practice, without objecting to

---

Federico Zuolo is Associate Professor in Political Philosophy at the University of Genoa (Italy). Before joining the University of Genoa he held positions in Pavia, Berlin, and Hamburg, and was Alexander von Humboldt Foundation Senior Research Fellow. His main interests include animal ethics, public reason, toleration, respect, and the basis of equality. He has published papers on animal ethics (*Utilitas, Social Theory and Practice, Ethical Theory and Moral Practice, International Journal of Philosophical Studies, Journal of Value Inquiry*) and on issues of pluralism, toleration, and respect (*Journal of Applied Philosophy, Journal of Social Philosophy, European Journal of Political Theory*). He has published a book on animal politics, *Animals, Political Liberalism and Public Reason* (Palgrave 2020).

F. Zuolo (✉)
Department of Classics, Philosophy and History, University of Genova, Genova, Italy
e-mail: federico.zuolo@unige.it

© The Author(s), under exclusive licence to Springer Nature Switzerland AG 2022   249
M. Sardoč (ed.), *The Palgrave Handbook of Toleration*,
https://doi.org/10.1007/978-3-030-42121-2_15

it, or such a practice should be banned. Then, toleration in a liberal state seems pre-empted by state neutrality and individual liberties.

Within this traditional understanding of toleration, the case of symbolic genital cutting might represent a genuine case of toleration insofar as a liberal state might have reasons to accept it, while still having reasons of objection. The reasons for accepting this symbolic practice include the principle of harm reduction and the idea that a symbolic formulation of this practice might contribute to an evolution of the practice that does not harm women. However, the conditions for these reasons to apply are hard to obtain. Hence, the case for toleration in a liberal state, although possible in theory for symbolic genital cutting, might not easily be translated into practice.

Keywords

Toleration · Female genital mutilation (FGM) · Symbolic genital cutting · Ritual circumcision · Neutrality · Cosmetic genital surgery · Double standards · Pre-emption of toleration

Introduction

The debate on toleration is typically torn by two opposing tendencies. In public discourse, people praise toleration as one of the founding principles of liberal democracies, whereas academic disputes have variously gleaned the troubles that lie within this notion. If in the former case toleration amounts to respecting people's differences and is the adequate response to the fact of diversity, in the second case many critics have pointed out the defects of toleration in comparison to other principles such as respect and neutrality. Within this overall dispute, many theorists have held that toleration may be pre-empted by neutrality because toleration requires an objection that a neutralist state cannot have without relinquishing its neutrality. Another chapter has focused on this issue in a general manner (▶ Chap. 17, "Toleration and Neutrality"). This chapter addresses this problem by asking whether there can be a specific issue that could be the object of toleration by the institutions of a liberal (and neutralist) state. If there is such an issue, which meets the condition for toleration in a liberal state, that is female circumcision.

Given certain conditions, female circumcision can be a genuine case of toleration in a liberal state. However, after establishing that this is the case, the substantive case for the state to tolerate such actions remains to be discussed. Indeed, even though we admit that female circumcision is a genuine issue of toleration, it is quite another question as to whether liberal states should actually tolerate such a practice. Only given certain conditions – that might not easily obtain – there could be such a duty. Hence, the case of female circumcision may represent a solution to the old paradox of the impossibility of toleration in a liberal and neutralist state. However, this victory in theory may not be easily translated into practice.

Impossible Toleration?

Following Cohen's (2004, p. 94) standard definition,

> an act of toleration is (1) an agent's (2) intentional and (3) principled (4) refraining from interfering with (5) an opposed (6) other (or their behavior, etc.) (7) in situations of diversity, where (8) the agent believes she has the power to interfere.

For the purposes of this chapter, the sixth component of this definition (the *objection component*) should be emphasized. This component is fundamental to distinguish toleration from another seemingly similar notion. If there were no objection, one would not tolerate something but merely be indifferent toward it.

According to many theorists (the most forceful formulation of this idea has been presented by Newey 2001; Heyd 2008; Meckled-Garcia 2001), in a liberal state committed to the ideal of neutrality there cannot be space for toleration. This impossibility depends on the objection component. A liberal state should be committed to being neutral toward a range of admissible worldviews, religions, ideologies, etc. Of course, a state cannot be absolutely neutral with respect to all possibilities and it must rule out some options as unacceptable. But within the admissible space, the neutralist state should not favor any of them or should not justify a policy on the basis of a controversial reason. Although the difference between neutrality as a property of outcomes and neutrality of justification is relevant in this discussion, this chapter is particularly focused on the idea of neutrality of justification. Indeed, a neutralist state is committed not to grounding its policies upon personal preferences, ideologies, religions, and so on. The commitment to neutrality implies either that the state should ban a certain practice because it is outside the domain of acceptability, or that, if it is inside this domain, the state cannot object to it. The state should either ban a practice or accept it without assessing its merits, thus without either praising or criticizing it.

> For the same reasons, toleration is not an attitude that can be shown by any state *organ* or institution. The court operates on the basis of the law and has no values of its own which can be overcome or restrained. On the one hand, it is the duty of judges to *ignore* their personal moral views rather than to manifest toleration of other, incompatible views. On the other hand, the court should not tolerate violations of the law, even if the judge personally feels she could tolerate the offensive act. The same applies to political authorities, officials, and institutions. (Heyd 2008, p. 179)

Hence, either the state may legitimately object to something which, then, should not be tolerated, or the state is not allowed to object to something. In sum, toleration, in the proper sense, seems impossible in a liberal state insofar as the state is committed to neutrality.

Elisabetta Galeotti and Peter Jones have proposed two accounts of toleration in which the problem of the impossibility of toleration seems not to arise. Briefly reviewing these alternative accounts will clarify why analyzing the traditional problem of impossibility of toleration in a liberal state is still an interesting issue.

As is known, Galeotti (2002) has argued that contemporary states should in many cases adopt a different type of toleration, one that consists in recognizing contested practices of minority groups with a view to promoting their full inclusion in a democratic polity. In this sense, toleration is a set of actions and attitudes by the state, which does not shrink into what is already due by the state's commitment to neutrality. With respect to the issue at stake here, toleration as recognition may dissolve the problem of the impossibility of toleration insofar as it moves the content and boundary of toleration, thus causing the objection to miss its critical target. In a different manner, Peter Jones's attempt to make room for toleration in a liberal state may be a response to the problem I am addressing. His proposal (Jones 2007) somewhat rests on the idea of a division of labor: if institutions and laws cannot be tolerant but only neutral, toleration may still be found in the attitudes and practices of the citizenry because people do not have a duty to remain neutral and may object to something while still having reasons to accept it (Balint 2012). It is worth remarking that the core of Jones's proposal is not rejected by the standard way of formulating the argument of the impossibility of toleration in a liberal state. "States or nations, then, can be tolerant only in the derivative sense, namely in consisting of tolerant individuals (or communities of individuals). States can only indirectly promote moral norms that encourage tolerant attitudes in interpersonal relations. Cultures may be described as generous, forgiving or tolerant, but states or institutions as such cannot" (Heyd 2008, p. 183). Despite its overall interest, Jones's proposal is not relevant here insofar as Jones asks whether there is space for toleration in a liberal polity, a question he answers positively by locating toleration in the domain of the citizenry. This chapter, instead, focuses on whether there can be at least a single case in which a state, as a set of institutions, bodies, and laws, can and should tolerate a specific practice. Accordingly, this chapter will not discuss other related issues, such as whether toleration is the best response to the treatment of minority groups (Ceva and Zuolo 2013) or whether groups are agents of toleration (Zuolo 2013).

Setting aside these alternative reformulations, the question is whether the thesis of the impossibility of toleration holds true in all cases. One may ask this question from a conceptual point of view (Kühler 2019). But, one may also point out that even though neutrality *usually* pre-empts toleration on the part of institutions, there might be some borderline cases in which neutralist institutions could tolerate a certain practice. This means that neutralist institutions could legitimately object to these practices without violating their commitment to neutrality, while still having second-order reasons not to intervene and suppress them. The main question is then: what can a neutralist state legitimately object to, while still having some more important reason to not interfere with it? Here we should focus on the *type of objection* that is specific to toleration. Indeed, a state may object to a number of practices while still allowing them in practice, at least to a certain extent. Many states, indeed, tolerate things they have reason to object to, such as the consumption of drugs. But are cases such as tolerance to drugs genuine cases of toleration in the sense in which we understand toleration here?

The case of drugs and other similar cases are different because they pose a challenge to states' (legitimate?) paternalism, not to states' neutrality. Indeed, as clearly argued by Galeotti (2007, p. 100), a state can justify paternalistic interventions in adults' lives without violating its commitment to neutrality on the grounds of prudence or matters of cost. Similarly, requiring that people use motorcycle helmets or seat belts may be considered paternalistic but on grounds that are not based on controversial conceptions of the good or religion.

Then, we should look to other cases of possible genuine toleration. An interesting one is that of tolerating white supremacism. In this case liberal institutions may have reasons to object without violating the commitment to neutrality because the affirmation of white supremacism clearly runs counter to some of the most important principles of a liberal polity: equality and nondiscrimination. Hence, liberal institutions may not tolerate it. The reasons in favor of not repressing the manifestations of white supremacism are grounded on the right to freedom of speech and/or on the ineffectiveness of repressing one's thought, whatever it is, because a repressed voice may gain further strength by presenting itself as unjustly victimized. Moreover, in a Millian vein, one may say that false views must continuously be presented in the public debate and be overcome discursively. Hence, for reasons of prudence or as a matter of principle a state may decide not to interfere with such ideas. As is known, the issue is quite intricate with regard to the question of freedom of speech. But in principle it is usually taken for granted that in liberal states the possible limits to free speech are established by the harm principle: once the expression of white supremacism becomes a harm to somebody or is a tangible risk, the state should use coercive means to suppress it. When it comes to hate speech there is a practical and conceptual controversy about what kind of harm, if any, hate speech exerts on its addressees. Therefore, although this case too might be a case of toleration in a liberal state, it should be better framed, as it is usually done, in terms of the limits of free speech. In other words, framing this issue as a question of toleration, although not inappropriate, may be less illuminating than understanding it in terms of a special case of limits to free speech and harm done with discourses (and symbols). Hence, the case of female circumcision seems more interesting from the point of view of toleration than the case of white supremacism.

The Case: Female Circumcision

The first problem of this case concerns its name. There are diverse practices that are brought together under a single umbrella term, as we will see below. The standard way of naming this set of practices is *female genital mutilation* (FGM). I prefer not to use this expression because the type of practice that I will discuss does not constitute a mutilation in the proper sense. *Female circumcision* is a suitable term because it is a neutral expression that characterizes a practice which is more similar to male circumcision than to other, more invasive and harmful practices done to girls and women. An analogous alternative could be *female genital cutting* which is equally free from moral condemnation. However, female circumcision is preferable because it is reminiscent of the cultural grounds that are sometimes appealed to (circumcision as a rite of passage that justifies both the female and male versions). Instead, FGM will be used to indicate the more harmful practices that consist in removing parts of or permanently modifying females' genitalia. However, this terminological choice should not give the impression that female circumcision is unproblematic or even commendable.

The World Health Organization (WHO) classification includes four main types of FGM according to the level of harm they cause. The first three types consist in a removal of the clitoris and/or the labia, and/or in a narrowing of the vaginal opening. Type IV, instead, is comprehensive of a variety of less harmful practices, including "pricking": "Pricking, piercing and incision can be defined as procedures in which the skin is pierced with a sharp object; blood may be let, but no tissue is removed" (WHO 2008, p. 32). Although some have objected to the inclusion of this practice in the catalog of FGMs because it involves no anatomical changes, the WHO statement still includes it because it may be used as a strategic form: "there are strong indications that pricking described as a replacement often involves a change in terminology rather than a change in the actual practice of cutting" (WHO 2008, p. 32). Here is not the place to discuss the merits and limits of this classification. Others have shown its inconsistencies (Arora and Jacobs 2016; Shahvisi and Earp 2019).

If it is indisputable that the first types of FGM are unacceptable practices that any state should prohibit, some specific forms of the last type of FGM (so-called "nicking" or "pricking") that it would be more apt to call female circumcision, or female genital cutting, are not evidently so. There have been and still are a number of local and global debates about this (Johnsdotter and Mestre i Mestre 2017), but for the sake of brevity we may recall two particular cases. The first took place in 1995 in Seattle where a doctor proposed practicing the "pricking" or "nicking" of girls' clitorises as a symbolic practice to replace more invasive ones, as a standard rite to be performed on females alongside the performance of male circumcision of male brothers of the same family. After a fierce campaign against it, the proposal was dismissed.

The second took place in Italy, in the early 2000s in a hospital in Florence. A doctor of Somalian origin proposed to the hospital the possibility of practicing a form of mild "pricking" as in the previous case. The hospital interrogated the regional bioethical committee which produced an advisory statement in which the proposed practice was considered admissible, as a form of harm reduction. This document maintained the overall negative judgment about interventions on female bodies and genitals in particular, both for their physical harms and symbolic meaning. But it accepted the proposed practice as an effective measure to prevent more serious harms performed in private houses or abroad, and as an intervention that merely "alludes" to more intrusive practices. After the release of this document, a heated national debate took place. Many feminists took the lead to oppose the practice. As a result of this initiative, the Italian Parliament passed a law (9 January 2006, no. 7) that forbids any kind of FGM, including the symbolic and mildest instances, and makes no distinction between adult females and girls.

There have been other cases and debates in other countries, but this case is more relevant here because it represents a (failed) attempt at toleration. Indeed, the bioethical committee's statement was a proposal of tolerating female circumcision because it included both reasons to object and reasons to accept the practice.

Reasons for Objecting and for Accepting

After this empirical reconstruction, we can now seek to assess female circumcision from a normative point of view by analyzing the reasons in favor of and against tolerating symbolic forms of female circumcision. Of course, the assessment may vary depending on the specific form it takes. But for the sake of simplicity let us consider only the one (namely pricking or nicking) that consists in a sort of bloodletting with no permanent damage or mutilation. If this mildest form proves unacceptable, other, more harmful forms will do too. In assessing the case we should at least use two distinctions: the one between voluntary and non-voluntary interventions, and that between first- and second-level reasons.

First, we should consider whether the persons who undergo this practice are adults or minors, namely we should introduce the criterion of voluntary consent. The distinction between adults and minors is a shorthand for saying that we should presume that the former can choose in a voluntary, free, and informed manner, while the latter cannot. This does not mean that in any case the adults meet the condition of autonomous choice. It just means that we should presume that the adults are capable of such choices because we cannot assume that adult women who choose to undergo this intervention are per force subjugated to their culture and unable to act freely. This would amount to alleging an unacceptable cultural incapacity of women. (See below.)

Second, we can distinguish between first- and second-level kinds of reasons: the first level is comprised of reasons that apply to each singular case, and the second level of reasons applies at a general level. Let us now see the reasons in favor of and against female circumcision, starting with the latter.

As to the reasons for objecting to this practice, at the first level, there is the harm that nevertheless takes place. Some might claim that this pricking, if performed in a proper manner with anesthesia, does not constitute a real harm insofar as it does not cause permanent damage and is far less harmful than other things that people ordinarily experience in everyday life. In reply, following Earp (2016, p. 127), we should admit that, even if this were true, it could constitute at least a psychological harm for somebody. Whether and how it can be a psychological harm depends on the technical condition of its performance (whether it is done in a sanitized manner, by reassuring and competent professionals and by supporting parents, in case of minors) and its cultural meaning. In sum, its being a psychological harm depends on concrete circumstances that we cannot address here. But it is plausible to say that tolerating symbolic female circumcision may diminish the occurrence of psychological harm, although it does not make it necessarily harmless. However, a full assessment of the pricking's harm should include proper consideration of the use of pain control, the child's age, the psychological context, whether there is a ritual, the absence or presence of complications, and the cultural (and parental) motivations (for a full list see Earp and Steinfeld 2018, p. 12).

Furthermore, the other reason for objecting to this practice is that in case of minors there is the lack of consent to a practice that in future they might regret having undergone. To be sure, pricking does not cause modifications to the body. Yet it is a form of invasion in one's body that needs to be either consented to appropriately or justified on medical grounds, both of which are absent in this case.

At the second level, the practice is objectionable because it seems to legitimize, albeit in a very mild form, a practice that we all consider objectionable in its more invasive forms (FGM). Related to this, there is the issue of symbolic harm. It has been claimed that allowing female circumcision, albeit in a very mild form, constitutes a sort of harm because it is a way of repeating a practice that has been and is harmful to many women. By reaffirming it, female circumcision expresses the reason behind FGM, namely the subjugation of women, and, as it were, validates such reasons. In this sense, even in a mild form, it may constitute an offense to every woman. However, as pointed out by Galeotti (2007, pp. 95–7), tolerating a practice does not necessarily mean legitimizing it because for toleration to occur, there should be the objection component. We cannot address here the issue of how, in practice, a state can at the same time allow and object to a practice. But we can think of a public statement that allows the practice, while explicitly saying that such an admission is a step toward the overcoming of the practice by the interested social groups. The Italian case and the bioethical committee's statement (see above) may be an example of this option.

Now we can discuss the reasons for accepting this practice. At the first level, there is the argument from harm reduction. Unlike FGM, female circumcision does not cause a mutilation or a permanent modification of women's and girls' genitalia. However, harm reduction should be factored in as a reason in favor only if we assume as constant the number of people who would have undergone (autonomously or because of their parent's initiative) the practice irrespective of whether or not it is legally admissible. In other words, this argument does not count the possible discouraging motivation that the legal prohibition may have. That there would be harm reduction is probably the only indisputable fact. However, it is difficult to assess the extent of this harm reduction vis-à-vis the alternative of prohibiting this practice altogether because we do not know, if the practice were banned, how many would be discouraged and how many would perform it in private houses or abroad. This points to an indeterminacy at the societal level which calls for an analysis of the second-level reasons.

At the second level, allowing the practice may have the positive consequence of transforming its cultural meaning. This applies in particular to the performance of female circumcision on minors. Although there are cases of adult women who choose to undergo this intervention, the relevance of the practice's cultural meaning is particularly significant when it is a reason to request female circumcision for young girls. Irrespective of whether in the original culture it is a rite of passage or a form of women's subjugation, making this practice a controlled, sanitized, and publicly recognized performance would at least partially neutralize its cultural meaning. This is a second-level reason because it obtains (or fails to obtain) for the whole phenomenon. However, it is difficult to assess whether this will be the case. There are good reasons to think that it will because in some cases (e.g., Seattle) the symbolic practice of female circumcision is requested by parents who have migrated to Western countries who want to comply with the cultural group requirements, but who are also not willing to cause harm to their daughters. In light of this, it is reasonable to expect that parents and girls of those groups would continue to practice this rite while girls would live it in a non-harmful manner. But this argument is dependent upon contexts. Hence, it is difficult to use it in general and must be updated to specific requests and circumstances. Wahlberg et al. (2017) have shown that female circumcision (or "pricking" as they call it in their research) has considerable support from migrant communities (in Sweden). However, different people of the same community give different meanings to this intervention and associate it with variable values. Hence, although research like this can increase the confidence that we have in terms of how a group may perceive the meaning of female circumcision as a transformative practice, its contested and variable nature renders this inquiry conjectural.

In this reconstruction, second-level reasons play an important role. However, they are hardly conclusive insofar as they are conjectural. Hence, given the inconclusiveness of the reasons at the second level and the fluidity of the cultural meaning, it may be helpful to compare this practice with other practices that are surprisingly similar at the anatomical level but that have different cultural meanings.

Female Circumcision and Its (Surprising?) Cognate Practices

Different theorists have highlighted the physical similarities between symbolic forms of FGM, or as we call it here female circumcision, and other practices, such as male circumcision and aesthetic vagina surgical interventions (Earp 2016; Galeotti 2007). But, before proceeding, we should bear in mind that these sorts of comparisons are not meant to underplay or allay the nature of female circumcision in Western countries or in other countries that traditionally practice FGM. Rather, the point is that of showing how we assess differently and give diverse cultural meanings to practices that may be more intrusive and damaging than some forms of female circumcision.

Let us start with the obvious comparison with male circumcision. We are accustomed to considering it a non-maleficent or beneficent practice that may be performed for medical reasons. However, it also is frequently performed on very young babies without medical reasons. It has traditionally been considered a healthy and prophylactic intervention that fosters personal hygiene and presents no counterindications. However, it is still a permanent removal of healthy tissue which changes at least in part the tissue's sensitivity thus affecting one's sexual experience. But since male circumcision has been considered part of Western cultural practices, its psychological and physical costs have been underplayed.

Similar considerations have been appealed to by the Italian Bioethical Committee concerning the practice of Jewish male circumcision. The Committee stated that this is a non-damaging intervention whose traditional meaning has no psychological and physical drawbacks, despite the fact that this is still a removal of healthy bodily tissue which unnecessarily violates the child's bodily integrity. Italian Bioethical Committee, *La circoncisione: profili etici*, 25 settembre 1998. However, some circumcised adults and some courts' decisions are looking to the cultural perception of this practice by pointing out that it is unnecessary and constitutes a permanent modification of one's body without one's consent.

The other more surprising similarities may be found in the growing and varied set of interventions to female genitalia. These interventions are requested by Western girls or women to pursue certain ideals of beauty or remove perceived imperfections (Shahvisi and Earp 2019). The authors of this paper emphasize the biased double standard according to which similar practices are banned if categorized as traditional practices of FGM, while being admitted if considered as forms of plastic surgery. The latter, unlike the former, are seen as voluntary interventions of improvement, while the former are always considered an expression of the subjugation of women.

Whether these practices are admissible or should be rejected cannot be adjudicated here. Rather, we should ask what we should do in case we attribute to similar interventions – such as the ones involving the reduction of labia – two culturally different, or even opposed, meanings. This is particularly problematic if we stick to the assumption we have made, namely that of having a neutralist state.

If what matters for a state is the harm perpetrated to individuals, as it should be in a liberal state, we face an uneasy situation: we should either explain why we consider female circumcision differently from other forms of intervention on genitalia, or treat all the mentioned practices – female circumcision, male circumcision, and vaginoplasty – alike. The first route would be that of appealing to the cultural meaning of the practice to justify the differential treatment. This is cumbersome because a liberal state should rely on non-controversial issues, while the meaning of a practice, such as pricking, male circumcision, and vaginoplasty, is subject to disagreement: given that its meaning evolves and depends on the role one plays in the debate, its perception may change. Moreover, allowing female circumcision also has the aim of changing its meaning. Therefore, it seems that the state cannot justify the different treatment on the basis of a diverse cultural meaning. Hence, the three practices should be treated in the same manner. This would mean either allowing or banning all. Forbidding all of them would perhaps be paternalistic but coherent. And, if allowed, all three may be allowed without being negatively judged (hands-off permission) or tolerated (thus also negatively judged).

A neutral state committed to passing and enforcing laws that are based on no controversial doctrine is usually a non-perfectionist state. Such a state cannot sanction actions that go against one's best interest to the extent that one does so voluntarily. Leaving aside such complicated and borderline cases of voluntary enslavement, and focusing only on actions that pertain to the intervention on one's body, there are a number of actions that are legal (and should be so), which people do against their (supposed) best interest and against what people would choose were they in a condition of calm reflection.

Should Liberal States Tolerate Female Circumcision?

So far, we have asked whether female circumcision can be a genuine case of toleration in a liberal state. The answer is affirmative because female circumcision meets the conditions for toleration in a liberal state: the state may have reasons to object to this practice while also having countervailing reasons to accept it. However, it is quite another question as to whether liberal states *should* tolerate this practice and/or perform it in public hospitals, for instance covered as part of a public health service. Answering all these issues cannot be done here. For the purposes of this chapter, it will be sufficient to cast some doubts on the all-things-considered reasons for liberal states to tolerate female circumcision.

To establish whether a liberal state should admit and tolerate female circumcision, we should distinguish between people who choose to undergo this intervention autonomously and people who cannot choose autonomously, namely between adults and minors. Focusing first on adults, it is difficult to understand how a liberal state may prohibit this practice. Catriona McKinnon (2006, p. 111) argues in a similar vein, although she has some reservations. But, she concludes, states should not issue a blanket prohibition on consensual acts or should not presume that women cannot really consent to these actions and are by default subjugated by their culture (McKinnon 2006, p. 112). This argument is strengthened by the comparative considerations. If a liberal state allows aesthetic surgery on vaginas, it can hardly ban female circumcision by adult women. It could do so only if it presupposes that women undergoing aesthetic surgery freely choose this intervention, while women who undergo female circumcision do not act voluntarily. Which is patently discriminatory on cultural grounds. Of course, a state may not cover the costs of these interventions, but it cannot discriminate between them if it is committed to neutrality and non-perfectionism.

Now we can focus on female circumcision performed on minors. As we have seen above, it can be a genuine case of toleration. However, I contend, liberal states should tolerate female circumcision only if the following two conditions are met. First, there should be a clear case of harm reduction. Harm reduction obtains when the people who perform female circumcision in a symbolic manner outnumber those who would not perform any action were any kind of intervention legally banned. If so, we may suppose that there actually is harm reduction if the parents who are committed to perpetuate this practice explicitly request to have the symbolic procedure. If that is the case, the merely symbolic act would significantly reduce the harm traditionally perpetrated against young women. If this condition does not apply, there may be reasons to ban the practice and seek to discourage its continuation by enforcing the law.

Second, it should be likely that the legal admission of female circumcision could transform the cultural meaning of the practice, thus making it a ritual and harmless practice without implying women's subjugation. Establishing how this condition could be met and ascertained in practice is an issue that we cannot discuss here. Be it sufficient to think that it is possible to satisfy this condition. Then, it is interesting to remark that if this condition is met, it is likely that the need for performing and maintaining this practice would tend to disappear. If the cultural meaning of female circumcision would tend to change – from a passively received cultural practice to a freely chosen cultural tradition which does not subjugate women – then the objection component for the toleration of this practice would tend to disappear. This would be so for two different reasons: either fewer and fewer people would choose to undergo this practice, because the transformation of the practice has made people freer to accept it or not; or the cultural meaning of the practice would be less and less objectionable thus making it a practice toward which liberal institutions should be indifferent and not properly tolerant. In sum, in case of successful transformation, the practical consequences would lessen the impact of female circumcision and the symbolic effect would make it appear less harmful.

This is mostly a hypothetical conjecture. But it highlights a peculiar feature of toleration. Even though we can show that toleration is not impossible in liberal states because there is at least a practice that can and should be tolerated by the state under certain conditions, it is likely to be the case that the satisfaction of these conditions tends to make room for the overcoming of the need to tolerate the practice. In other words, even when toleration is required, it is an unstable situation that creates the conditions in which it is no longer necessary. Either the situation does not meet the condition that tolerating the practice would prompt a transformation of female circumcision; but, then, that practice should not be admitted. Or a successful toleration of that practice would tend to change the meaning of female circumcision. If so, then, toleration would be instable because, if successful, there would no longer be the need to tolerate the practice. Indeed, female circumcision would either tend to disappear as a practice or it would become a non-objectionable tradition.

At this point it is helpful to compare this reconstruction of toleration of female circumcision with Galeotti's take on this. She writes:

> I do not see why the toleration of female circumcision should worsen her prospects. Indeed, the availability of the revised [viz. of symbolic female circumcision] procedure could work the other way in the community: it can be used by women to negotiate a reinterpretation of traditional ways more in line with their interests, and can be seen by the community as a reasonable middle ground for accommodating to Western society. Obviously such considerations are only conjectural, female circumcision having been criminalized and the girls' fates now being completely hidden from public scrutiny. But the idea that toleration of female circumcision would increase women's submission is likewise conjectural. (Galeotti 2007, p. 104)

Galeotti plausibly argues that the probabilities of both outcomes – that of the revised procedure producing better outcomes or the criminalization decreasing the number of FGM – are uncertain. However, it is also plausible to be less optimistic about toleration's capacity to change the situation and the possibility of meeting the conditions of toleration.

In sum, although female circumcision is a genuine case of toleration in liberal states, its prospects are not straightforward. On the one hand, we do not know how likely it could be that there is harm reduction and that the toleration of female circumcision could transform the cultural meaning of such a practice. On the other, even if such conditions were to obtain and the practice were actually tolerated, it might be the case that the toleration of female circumcision would be unstable and tend to dissolve.

Summary and Future Directions

The case of female circumcision has the features that make it a candidate for being a case of toleration by institutions in a liberal state. However, it is not clear whether liberal states should tolerate this practice. First of all, its scope would be narrower than it is usually thought because we should not include the permissibility of adult women requesting female circumcision as a genuine case of toleration. As far as adults are concerned, a truly neutralist state should have no reasons against it to the extent that the state accepts other, less invasive practices and it cannot assume that all women requesting it are incapable of acting autonomously.

Second, the case of symbolic circumcision of girls is different because it affects individuals who – we presume – cannot freely and autonomously choose such an intervention. In this case the decision would be taken by their parents or legal guardians. Given the legitimate worry for their best interest, this case raises concern and therefore reasons for objection properly apply. However, there might be reasons for acceptance (harm reduction and promotion of a change in this practice). Hence, the case of symbolic circumcision of minors is a genuine case of toleration in a neutralist state. However, even though it can certainly be conceived of in this way, it does not necessarily mean that the institutions should tolerate this practice. Indeed, even though the preliminary conditions for toleration apply, it is not clear whether the (second-order) reasons in favor of tolerating this practice are stronger. They can be so, but not necessarily. It is not necessarily the case that admitting this practice could prompt a positive transformation in the meaning of the cultural practice in that society. Finally, we have seen that in case the state admitted symbolic female circumcision, and such a practice were to change its cultural meaning, the need for tolerating it would tend to disappear. Even a successful case of liberal toleration might be unstable.

References

Arora KS, Jacobs AJ (2016) Female genital alteration: a compromise solution. J Med Ethics 42:148–154

Balint P (2012) Not yet making sense of political toleration. Res Publica 18:259–264

Ceva E, Zuolo F (2013) A matter of respect. On the relation between majority and minorities in a liberal democracy. J Appl Philos 30(3):239–253

Cohen AJ (2004) What toleration is. Ethics 115(1):68–95

Earp BD (2016) Between moral relativism and moral hypocrisy: reframing the debate on FGM. Kennedy Inst Ethics J 26(2):105–144

Earp BD, Steinfeld R (2018) Genital autonomy and sexual well-being. Curr Sex Health Rep 10:7–17

Galeotti AE (2002) Toleration as recognition. Cambridge University Press, Cambridge

Galeotti AE (2007) Relativism, universalism, and applied ethics: the case of female circumcision. Constellations 14(1):91–111

Heyd D (2008) Is toleration a political virtue? In: Williams M, Waldron J (eds) Toleration and its limits. Nomos XLVIII. New York University Press, New York/London, pp 171–194

Italian Bioethical Committee (1998) La circoncisione: profili etici. Presidenza del Consiglio dei ministri, Dipartimento per l'informazione e l'editoria, Roma. 25 settembre

Johnsdotter S, Mestre i Mestre RM (2017) 'Female genital mutilation' in Europe: public discourse versus empirical evidence. Int J Law Crime Justice 51:14–23

Jones P (2007) Making sense of political toleration. Br J Polit Sci 37(3):383–402

Kühler M (2019) Can a value-neutral liberal state still be tolerant? Crit Rev Int Soc Polit Philos, online first: pp 1–20

McKinnon C (2006) Toleration: a critical introduction. Routledge, New York

Meckled-Garcia S (2001) Toleration and neutrality: incompatible ideals? Res Publica 7:293–313

Newey G (2001) Is democratic toleration a rubber duck? Res Publica 7:315–336

Shahvisi A, Earp BD (2019) The laws and ethics of female genital cutting. In: Creighton SM, Liao L-M (eds) Female genital cosmetic surgery: solution to what problem? Cambridge University Press, Cambridge, pp 58–71

Wahlberg A, Johnsdotter S, Ekholm Selling K, Källestål C, Essén B (2017) Factors associated with the support of pricking (female genital cutting type IV) among Somali immigrants – a cross-sectional study in Sweden. Reprod Health 14(92):1–10

WHO (2008) Eliminating female genital mutilation: an interagency statement (Ohchr, Unaids, Undp, Uneca, Unesco, Unfpa, Unhcr, Unicef, Unifem, Who). https://apps.who.int/iris/bitstream/handle/10665/43839/9789241596442_eng.pdf;jsessionid=F7A7B008C0AE205 9BA93AB98FC05E444?sequence=1. Last accessed Apr 2019

Zuolo F (2013) Toleration and informal groups. How does the formal dimension affect groups' capacity to tolerate? Eur J Polit Theo 12(3):288–305

Toleration of Moral Offense

15

Thomas E. Hill Jr

Contents

Introduction 264
Offenses 265
Moral Offenses 266
Professional Offenses and Moral Offenses 268
Toleration and Respect 269
Basic and Earned Respect for Persons 270
Self-respect as a Reason Not to Tolerate Moral Offenses 272
Respect for Others as a Reason to Tolerate Moral Offenses 274
Concluding Remarks 274
References 275

Abstract

The focus of this chapter is on offensive words and implications in interpersonal exchanges, specifically false and baseless attacks on a person's behavior, character, and dignity as a human being. The idea of moral offenses is explained by analogy with what is offensive under codes of honor. Four kinds of moral offense are distinguished, and two kinds of respect for persons are explained. To illustrate, it is argued that self-respect gives us reason not to tolerate moral offenses while respect for others gives us reason sometimes to tolerate them. Hard cases call for judgment and more attention to *how* resist moral offenses, when we should, and *how* to tolerate them, when we must, with due respect for humanity.

Keywords

Toleration · Offenses · Moral · Respect · Self-Respect · Character · Kantian · Dignity · Honor · Humanity · Status · Standing · Resistance

---

T. E. Hill Jr (✉)
Department of Philosophy, University of North Carolina, Chapel Hill, NC, USA
e-mail: thill@email.unc.edu

© The Author(s), under exclusive licence to Springer Nature Switzerland AG 2022
M. Sardoĉ (ed.), *The Palgrave Handbook of Toleration*,
https://doi.org/10.1007/978-3-030-42121-2_47

Introduction

We can be offended personally, as officers, as professionals, as proud members of groups with whom we identify, or as loyal defenders of our local system of etiquette, but we can also be offended morally. What does it mean to be offended, for example, as opposed to being annoyed or harmed? And what is distinctive about moral offenses? Are there not different kinds of moral offense, some more gravely offensive than others? These conceptual questions lead to practical questions. When and why, if ever, should one tolerate moral offenses? When and why should one refuse to tolerate them? And *how*, if at all, should we push back against what is intolerable, and *in what manner* should we tolerate offenses when we must? Although many factors may be relevant, considerations of self-respect and respect for others are especially salient in this context. My focus will be on close encounters between individuals, but thinking specifically about moral offenses in this context may be suggestive with respect to larger (even political) contexts.

Many moral considerations may be relevant, but respect for persons is especially important we consider how to respond to serious moral offenses. Kantian ethics, broadly viewed, points to considerations of respect that that may be neglected in familiar consequentialist thinking, even though it offers no quick and easy solutions to all hard cases. What respect requires specifically in particular cases may be debatable, but respect for persons is not the same as concern for their welfare. Respect for oneself is no less important than respect for others. Without self-respect, our respect for others degenerates into servility, but also without respect for others our self-respect degenerates into arrogance and false pride. Recognition of the requirements of both self-respect and respect for others alerts us against over-simple solutions to complex moral problems. What it calls for is not an unworthy compromise of principles but rather sensitivity to context and search for innovative ways to honor both in an imperfect world.

The plan is as follows: *first*, the idea of an *offense to a person* is distinguished from injuries, deprivations, and other wrongs. Of course, in many contexts, what is offensive may also be damaging and what unjustly injures or deprives a person may also be offensive; but the concepts here are not the same. *Second*, a *moral* offense to a person is distinguished from other kinds of offense. The explanation here relies on an analogy between morality and honor cultures. Both assign to persons an honorable status and standing, but the criteria on which they rely are importantly different. Moral offenses, at least of the deepest sort, are challenges to a person's honorable *standing* as a good and decent human being, or, worse, challenges to a person's basic *status* as a human being, an honorable status that is not earned and can never be forfeited. *Third*, to illustrate, moral offenses are contrasted with what offends us as professionals. In both cases, the presupposed background treats offenses as challenges to a person's honorable standing or status in a system of norms. *Fourth*, the discussion turns to what it means to tolerate moral offenses and how considerations of respect are important when we ask when we should tolerate moral offenses and when we should not. *Fifth*, a brief summary of the basic requirements of *respect for persons* is given. The conception presented here is broadly Kantian but is probably

15 Toleration of Moral Offense

widely shared. In any case, what matters here is not the ancestry of ideas but the values that they invoke and how they apply to the problems that we face. *Fifth,* to illustrate, the chapter explains how self-respect gives us reasons not to tolerate what offends against either our moral status as human beings or our standing as decent and good people. *Sixth,* nevertheless, the chapter also explains how respect for others may give us reason to tolerate some moral offenses. Since there are potentially respect-based reasons both for and against toleration of a given moral offense, much depends on what tolerating and refusing to tolerate would be like in the particular case. Finally, the discussion concludes by calling attention to the need to explore *how* we can *respectfully* tolerate moral offenses when we must and *respectfully* resist them when they are intolerable. The relevant moral considerations should become clear, but sensitivity to context, innovative thinking, reasonable flexibility, and good judgment are needed for practical solutions.

Offenses

The first task is to clarify what is meant here by "offense". In a minimal sense, an offense is a violation of a norm in some recognized system of rules. Consider various kinds of offenses. We can be *offended personally* when others' words or actions express attitudes that we take to be unfairly disparaging of us as individuals, for example, falsely implying that we are failures by our various nonmoral standards that we happen to care about (such as our table manners, athletic skills, or academic achievements). We can also be *offended as members of groups* that we value. For example, we can be deeply offended as citizens, alumni, teachers, doctors, judges, veterans, Muslims, Christians, Jews, and so on, when someone's words or practices unjustly challenge our rightful claim ("pretention") to membership, charge that our conduct makes us unworthy of membership, or insinuates that the valued group itself is worthless or even contemptible.

We can also be offended as members of a group that we value when, without necessarily denying that one is a worthy member or that one's group is valuable, someone violates the normative expectations regarding how our group members are to be treated. For example, to be a university teacher and scholar is to belong to a valued group that has high standards for membership, for the professional conduct of members, and for treatment that members can expect from students, university administrators, and colleagues. I would have been offended as a university teacher and scholar, for example, if my students had never listened to me, if my employer had fired me without cause, or if a professional colleague had plagiarized my work. Similarly, legal systems set out criteria for who can be a judge in criminal proceedings, standards for a judge's conduct in trials, and norms for the behavior of defendants, lawyers, and observers in the courtroom. What is offensive to a judge and other participants in their official capacities is largely determined by these background conventions. For example, a judge in a criminal case might be offended as a judge if a juror slept through the trial, the defense attorney came to court as if dressed for a party, or anyone blatantly refused to be silent when so ordered.

Independently of our moral judgments, we can see that what is *offensive* in a courtroom is dependent on a complex background of conventions that define the role of participants and determine what is honorable and what is dishonorable conduct.

A common presupposition for these nonmoral offenses is membership in a group (such as teachers and judges) with a set of norms that include *a code of honor*, prescribing not only who can be a member and how members deserve to be treated but also how members must act towards one another in order to be worthy of their honorable status (Darwall 2015). Besides the norms for judges and teachers, another paradigm might be the social orders adopted by sword-carrying military officers in eighteenth-century Europe. These codes of honor set the standards for membership, what counts as offensive, and how an honorable member must respond to an offense. What was offensive to an officer often led to duels, and refusal to duel when challenged showed that one was unworthy of one's position. Systems of norms that include codes of honor can be explicit or vaguely defined, firmly entrenched or fragile, and morally admirable or deplorable. Despite the variations, they say who can be a member, how one must act to be in good standing, what is offensive to someone as a member, and how members should respond to an offense.

Moral Offenses

When a person does something morally wrong to another (such as stealing the person's watch, betraying the person's confidence, or lying to damage the person's reputation), we may speak of the wrongful acts as "moral offenses" in a loose sense analogous to "legal offenses." That is, an act is a legal offense because it violates valid laws, and so in a loose sense an act may be regarded a moral offense just because it violates moral principles. Likewise, we speak of a legal offense *against* another person when it violates that person's *rights* under the law, and so we may be tempted to say that, in a loose sense, an act is a *moral* offense against a person when it violates that person's moral rights. This is apparently a common way of speaking, and there is nothing wrong with it. What we need to identify, however, is a more specific and deeper sense of moral offense that draws on a conception of morality that incorporates ideas of an honorable status and standing in an ideal community.

So what is a *moral offense* in this more specific and deeper sense? For present purposes, we can assume here that all such moral offenses are serious but baseless and false charges or insinuations made by one morally competent person to another. We can distinguish several related kinds or levels of moral offense.

First, specific moral criticisms are morally offensive when false and made without factual grounds. For example, "You cheated" or "Your behavior last night was mean and selfish." Such false and baseless criticisms can, of course, be *hurtful* and *damaging* to a person's reputation, but they are also *offensive* insofar as they attack the recipients' reputation with themselves, challenging their right to a clear conscience and a sense that they are behaving as good persons. In effect, they charge, "Your *behavior* is dishonorable from a moral point of view."

For simplicity let us suppose that the offensive charge was false and knowingly made without evidence in the absence of excusing or justifying conditions for the lack of evidence. A typical case might be a malicious lie with a "made up" story, but the focus here is not on malice but on the assertion of critical and demeaning falsehoods about another's moral behavior and character without evidence, independently of the accuser's bad or innocent motives. In a sense, the baseless charge itself is offensive and so deserving of an acknowledgment and apology. Even if the accuser had some good excuse or justification for making a baseless charge, the accuser needs to cancel its false message when the situation allows.

Specific moral criticisms of behavior are often used as evidence for negative judgments of a person's character, and when these judgments are expressed without evidence, they are more deeply offensive (the second type of moral offense, below).

Second, as noted, such specific moral criticisms can be distinguished from more general false and baseless attacks *on a person's character*. For example, "You are a selfish, arrogant, mean, and untrustworthy coward." Again, when false and made without evidence, such attacks are morally offensive as well as hurtful, but they cut even more deeply because they do not merely criticize particular behaviors but directly attack a person's (presumably valued) sense of being a morally good person. They say, in effect, "You are in significant ways *a bad person*, not in *good standing* as an honorable human being."

Third, the most profound moral offenses, going beyond specific moral criticisms and beyond general condemnations of a person's character, are unwarranted dismissals of person's *status* as a human being with moral rights and due consideration from every other human being.

The message here is often expressed as "You are a dog (pig, snake, dirt, scum, excrement)." Though sometimes said in jest, the message all too often reveals a serious readiness to discount or altogether deny that a person has a place in the moral community of responsible human beings who are worthy of respect and consideration. Such expressions are most deeply offensive morally because they not only attack one's self-regard as a decent and good person who is behaving well, but when serious, they convey the *degrading* implication that one lacks the capacity or worth to engage with others and be treated as a person.

The moral offense here is an affront to what many call *human dignity*, which is an irrevocable, nonforfeitable status that is not earned by special merit or lost by bad conduct or character (Dillon 1995; Hill 1997, 2014a, b, 2020; Duewell et al. 2014; McCrudden 2014; Wood 2008).

Fourth, sometimes the degrading message is not totally dismissive but is demeaning by implying, insinuating, or presupposing that one belongs to a lower rank, class, or caste. The offender may express the demeaning message in the haughty manner of an arrogant snob or, more commonly, in the thoughtless manner of those who take their superior entitlements for granted. The implication is not that those offended are without moral rights altogether but that they belong to a class whose given role is to serve their superiors, to stand aside for them, and to agreeably accept that their betters naturally deserve the lion's share of public goods. Consider, for example, how Native Americans were portrayed in American "Western" films – as "savages" but not always as contemptible snakes, worthless toads, or pieces of excrement. Again, during the Second World War, films and street talk often referred to Japanese soldiers as "Japs" (said with contempt) and pictured them as wild, mean, and ugly but still as human. (No doubt the sentiment was reciprocated.) Now the "Black Lives Matter" movement demands full recognition of the humanity of people of color, rightly insisting that partial recognition as second class citizens is not enough.

The type of moral offense matters when we consider how and why we should respond. In the next section, I briefly contrast being offended as a professional with being offended as a human being (a moral offense). The comparison underscores the difference between specific criticisms of a person's behavior and offensive challenges to one's honorable status and standing in a valued community.

Professional Offenses and Moral Offenses

To offend someone is often to harm them, not just by causing discomfort but by threatening to undermine their self-esteem and standing with others. Some offenses may turn out ultimately to be beneficial to the recipients, and in any case to offend someone is not merely to cause them discomfort or to set back their interests (Feinberg 1985). For present purposes, let us assume that in general *offenses* are challenges to one's *honorable status* and *standing* in some community. Typically, we value having a respectable place in our communities, a good opinion of ourselves, and the esteem of our colleagues and associates. So we are generally hurt by accusations and insinuations that threaten to diminish our self-esteem and honorable status and standing in our communities, but to be offended is not simply to be hurt. Being offended may be experienced as hurtful and painful but, even so, our reasons to stand up to offenders and to avoid offending others are not simply to make their lives or our own more comfortable.

The kind of offense depends on the kind of community in which we have and value an honorable status. For example, suppose a colleague not merely criticizes our work (as a scholar, a doctor, or social worker, etc.) on professional grounds but implies sarcastically, without an adequate basis, that we are bad at our profession, or worse, that we are unfit to be to be in it. Typically, we value our good standing in such professions when we maintain our membership in them and try to uphold their standards, and so we would naturally be offended by *baseless* claims by a colleague that we are bad as professionals or, worse, that we are utterly unworthy of being a member of the profession. However, we can expect and should accept without offense honest professional criticism of our work. Specific criticisms of our work may annoy us, but even if they were dishonest and meanly motivated, they may not go so far as to impugn our professional standing. Such specific criticisms may imply that we are not the best possible scholar, doctor, social worker, etc., but not necessarily that we are bad at our jobs and even so bad as to be altogether unfit. Consider the differences between "You failed to check your references," "You are a careless scholar," and "You are no scholar!" Those who value their place in a community of scholars and believe the charges are unwarranted would likely find the first to be annoying, the second to be an offensive attack on one's *good* standing as a scholar, and the third to be an offensive and degrading dismissal of one's status as a scholar altogether.

Examples of offenses that are not necessarily moral offenses are not restricted to the professions that have established standards. Consider teams and families. Teammates in football can give and take harsh criticism without anyone necessarily being offended. Even if what is said critically is false, it could be well intended, and even if it is meanly motivated and false, it may not impugn one's good standing as a team member. One can be a member in good standing who is playing badly. If accused of bad play, one can respond by denying the charge of bad performance and even by criticizing the motives of the fault-finder, but to do so is not yet to defend one's standing as a team-member (which was not in question). Similar remarks apply, I think, to family relations. When criticized for her parenting, a woman may or may not be offended, depending on whether or not she understood what was said as implying falsely that she is a bad mother or, worse, utterly unworthy be a mother. In all these examples, whether regarding professional, team, or family relationships, there may be criticism without offense and offense that is not yet what I call a moral offense. We may be offended as a doctor, as a team-mate, as a parent, and so on, but not necessarily offended as a human being.

By contrast to such professional or social offenses, moral offenses challenge a person's honor as someone with an irrevocable moral status who is also in good standing in the moral community. If a person falsely and maliciously accuses another of moral wrong-doing, the accused may rightly take offense and defend his or her honorable standing *as a decent, morally upright, conscientious person,* just as professionals under false accusations may defend their honor as decent, upright, conscientious professionals. Consider, for example, professionals defending their honor as loyal soldiers, good doctors, careful scholars, or competent lawyers. All the more, if a person falsely and without evidence accuses someone of being a bad person or a nonperson, then the accused may rightly see this as morally offensive and so want to defend his or her honor as a responsible human being with a good moral record.

Toleration and Respect

To tolerate something is to "put up with it," accept it conditionally, see it as wrong or undesirable but as not as something to be constrained, prohibited, or coercively interfered with. There can be many reasons for tolerating behavior and practices that we dislike. For example, in many cases, prudence may dictate that we should put up with disliked behavior and practices because of the negative consequences of refusing to tolerate them. You may tolerate the baby's noisy chatter but put up with it because you prefer it to the baby's crying. Political leaders may tolerate religious practices that are alien to them in order to win votes or avoid violent confrontations. Here, however, we are looking for *moral* reasons for toleration, in fact *moral* reasons for tolerating moral offenses. The questions are these: From a moral point of view, when and why should we tolerate behavior and practices that we consider to be moral offenses of the types described earlier? When and why should we refuse to tolerate such offenses? Or are those subject to moral offenses free to tolerate the offenses or not as they please (a matter of moral indifference)?

Obviously the relevant contexts of the offenses can be quite different, and several different moral principles and values may prove relevant to a case. For example, suppose someone falsely and without evidence calls you "a racist bigot." This aspersion on your character is morally offensive to you, but you might see yourself as morally obliged to tolerate the moral offense by remaining silent because you foresee that any retaliation would likely pull you into a dangerous fight, breaking your promise to your spouse, causing harm, and showing ingratitude to your host, the offender's mother. Such considerations of promise-keeping, gratitude, and avoiding harm are often relevant but are not likely to be sufficient by themselves to settle in all cases whether or not the moral offense should be tolerated. In fact, this list of moral considerations leaves out the one most obviously and generally relevant in cases of moral offense, namely, *respect*. Especially if (as argued here) moral offenses are challenges to one's honorable status or standing as a human being, we must consider the basic requirements of respect for persons, which for Kantians (and perhaps many others) are among the highest priority (if not dominant) moral requirements. In any case, let us explore briefly the reasons for and against toleration that derive from *respect for persons*. The moral questions, of course, are not just about *whether or not* to tolerate, but about *how* to tolerate what we must and *how* to resist what is intolerable. Respect is important here as well.

Basic and Earned Respect for Persons

Everyone agrees that we should have a proper respect for others and for ourselves. But what are the requirements of "proper respect"? It is uncontroversial that we should have and express respect for people of extraordinary talent, accomplishment, and willingness to serve worthy causes, but many believe that in addition we should respect humanity and each individual person independently of their special merits (Darwall 1977). The latter is a core tenet of Kantian ethics, but the aim here is not to interpret Kant's texts but to articulate some of the respect-based claims, values, and ideals that would be generally acknowledged by common sense moralists and theorists regardless of their special commitments.

As often noted, we may respect a particular person in two ways. *First*, we may respect the person for his or her individual merits, and insofar as the respect is the moral kind considered here, the relevant merits are good character traits and morally worthy actions. Following Darwall, we may call this *moral appraisal respect*. Obviously, this kind of respect is not due towards all human beings. Not everyone deserves it, and those who have earned our respect may also lose it. *Second*, we may and should respect the particular person and every other as a human being, a moral agent with basic rights and responsibilities that are not just reserved for the virtuous. These fundamental rights and responsibilities are core aspects of human dignity, and as such they are neither earned by morally admirable behavior nor lost by reprehensible behavior. Following Darwall, we may call this *recognition respect*. The two kinds of respect are related because basic respect for humanity (recognition respect) sets standards for the conduct and character that is worthy of respect as morally commendable (moral appraisal respect) (Hill 2012b, pp. 296–319; 2012c, pp. 320–342; Wood 2008, pp. 85–105).

These general remarks require further explanation. At least some further specification is needed for the main points here about respect and toleration of moral offenses. Interpretations will vary, but from a broadly Kantian perspective respect for persons as human beings requires recognition and appreciation of their humanity, which can be understood as a cluster of capacities and dispositions needed for moral agency and assumed for practical purposes to be possessed, at least latently, by all human beings. These include natural enabling capacities such as conceptual understanding, memory, foresight, and communication as well as developed dispositions to self-governance, which presuppose having preferences, seeing options for choice, setting oneself ends, and recognizing the need to take means necessary to one's ends. Insofar as respect for persons is a moral respect for their humanity, we must think of humanity as including also specifically moral capacities and dispositions, such as a rational and reasonable desire to live with others on mutually agreeable terms (Rawls 2005, pp. 45–58), to persuade others and be moved by reasons ("guiding" and not "goading" Falk 1953), and to give priority in deliberation to principles that one judges all rational and reasonable persons would accept when thinking from a moral point of view. To respect persons as rational and (potentially) reasonable, we must *respect facts* because among the characteristics involved in being rational and reasonable are not only an ability to calculate, draw logical inferences, and coordinate one's means and ends, but also an ability to use one's epistemic powers to judge realistically the circumstances that one faces.

Respect for individual persons is based on respect for humanity, which includes the wish and practical concern that humanity will survive, thrive, and improve as a global moral community whose members' interactions are based on facts, reason, and regard for common moral principles. This moral ideal, for Kantians a "kingdom of ends," draws from honor cultures but makes the basic *status* for human beings all-inclusive, nonoptional, and irrevocable. It takes the standards for good *standing* as a member to be, in large part, commitment and conformity to moral principles derived from basic respect for humanity. Arguably among the requirements for good standing, which everyone should strive for, is a serious commitment and effort to support, maintain, and restore when lost our communities of mutual respect.

Suppose a manipulative, deceitful, and insulting person, who is not in good standing in the moral community, is disrespectful to us. Imagine that he accuses us of serious wrongdoing falsely without evidence, thereby morally offending us as individuals, and imagine that he also mocks and demeans groups of us as inherently second class, thereby morally offending us as human beings. Understandably, we may conclude that respect for ourselves and for humanity calls for us to protest to counter his insulting message. It is not always enough, however, to call out the offender or even to demand retribution of some kind. The moral ideal of respect for persons calls for serious attempts to improve the situation, to move closer to the ideal community of mutual respect if possible.

Self-respect as a Reason Not to Tolerate Moral Offenses

Recalling the distinction between two kinds of respect for persons mentioned earlier, we can distinguish at least two kinds of *self*-respect.

First, consider moral *appraisal self-respect*. In this sense, self-respecting persons are those who respect themselves for their individual merits, and insofar as respect is the moral kind considered here the relevant merits are good character traits and morally worthy actions (Darwall 1977). This is *earned* self-respect that individuals deserve to different degrees. Surely, no one behaves well all of the time, and no one is perfectly virtuous. But if it is evident that certain people are conscientious, regularly do what is morally required, avoid serious wrong-doing, have developed good character, and strive continually to improve, then they are people whom others should respect as decent, good, and virtuous individuals. For the same reasons, arguably, such people should respect *themselves* as decent, good, and virtuous individuals. Realistic self-appraisal, if not humility, sets limits to how much self-respect of this kind we can have. If we are immoral, we cannot deserve it. We should, however, see being fully self-respecting in this sense as a goal towards which we aspire, even if we can never reach it fully and never know ourselves well enough to judge how far we have come.

Still focusing on this first kind of "appraisal" self-respect, let us consider its implications regarding whether or not we ought to tolerate what we take to be false and baseless moral offenses to us as individuals. Let us take the perspective of ordinary imperfect and fallible people, such as we are, rather than omniscient observers who understand and appreciate all relevant facts fully. We are looking for *guiding* principles for the real world and cannot assume that we know all the facts about ourselves, those who offend us, or the context. From this perspective, we can perhaps see that the value or ideal of respecting oneself as a morally good individual provides a *defeasible reason not to tolerate* false and baseless accusations that one's behavior and character are immoral. Why? To aspire and try to earn one's respect for oneself as a morally good person is what anyone should do, for to earn one's self-respect in this sense is just to become a morally good person so far as one can. False and baseless attacks on one's moral character and behavior disrespect and threaten to undermine one's good moral aspirations and efforts. Becoming a morally good, or just a better, person is psychologically difficult and requires some cooperation and support of others, and insofar as false baseless attacks on a person show disregard for the person's good efforts at moral self-improvement, such attacks might well tend to *undermine* the person's efforts. Regardless of these causal effects, the false baseless accusations show *disrespect* for the accused moral aspirations and efforts, which are worthy of respect from everyone. If so, those who aspire to respect themselves as morally decent and good people have reasons not to tolerate false baseless attacks on their moral behavior or character.

It may seem that that the considerations offered here only give reason to think that *good people* who are being falsely accused should refuse to tolerate it, but those with bad character *should* become morally self-respecting and to do so they must earn their (moral appraisal) self-respect, and they can do so only by aspiring and trying to improve themselves morally. Even though they are bad people, they still may be subject to false baseless charges of moral vices and wrongdoing – they are not bad in the ways charged. These, I suggest, are still moral offenses that they have reason (stemming from the moral value of being self-respecting) to refuse to tolerate. The offensive accusations disrespect and tend to hinder the aspirations and efforts that they should be making towards moral self-improvement. Those who value self-interest over morality may not care much, of course, but arguably anyone with moral interests has reason to care.

Second, consider *recognition self-respect*. In the last section, we considered moral offenses that call into question an individuals' moral *standing* as a good person, but let us turn now to the deeper offenses of denying or demeaning a person's *status* as a human being.

In these cases, all the more, self-respect gives us reason not tolerate moral offenses. Now the relevant moral offenses are to *deny* people their due status as human beings, by treating them as subhuman, or to *demean* them, by relegating them to an inherently inferior status. Examples of these moral offenses abound in the mistreatment of slaves from Africa, Blacks in the "Jim Crow" era and under South African apartheid, the "untouchables" in India, and women throughout history. Besides systematic injustice, cruelty, and exploitation, cultures have encouraged and set the stage for the morally offensive interchanges between individuals – boss and employee, citizen and citizen, neighbor and neighbor, even husband and wife. Some of these moral offenses are made in a blatant, deliberate, haughty, and arrogant manner, but perhaps even more often they are softened, sweetened, and hidden in subtle ways so that even the offender fails to see the offense.

Those who are subjected to these moral offenses have many reasons to object, but the reason to be highlighted here is that self-respect demands a proper response. That is, as Kantians affirm, all morally capable human beings should have basic recognition respect for themselves (and all others) as human beings with dignity. This is an honorable moral status that cannot be taken away or forfeited, and should be respected by all. It is not earned or lost by one's level of intelligence, race, place of origin, or individual talents or accomplishments. The moral offenses considered here deny this, excluding people in certain groups, in effect denying their humanity. Everyone, however, should respect humanity in every person, which implies that they have reason to refuse to accept and to push back against whatever denies, threatens, or demeans their own or anyone else's full status as a human being. Ideally, in a moral community we are "all for one and one for all." Of course, responsibility for moral ends, including resisting moral offenses, is distributed for practical reasons, and it makes sense that a greater share falls to those who were directly offended and by those who have more power. In short, at least from this Kantian perspective, those subjected to moral offenses that deny or demean their humanity have a strong reason not to tolerate them. Even in these cases, however, the case against toleration is not absolute. The next section suggests ways in which proper respect for persons may sometimes call for toleration.

Respect for Others as a Reason to Tolerate Moral Offenses

Although there are reasons of self-respect not to tolerate moral offenses, respect for ourselves as human beings sometimes also gives us reasons to tolerate moral offenses. The same general remarks apply whether we are considering tolerating false and baseless attacks on our character or more deeply dismissive and demeaning offenses against our humanity. We need to take into account self-respect but also respect for the people who made the insulting charges. They too are human beings, and at least from the broadly Kantian perspective taken here, respect for our own humanity is respect for our place in an ideal community in which every human being must be so respected. We are all fallible and particularly liable to have a distorted view of our own exceptional merit, what others owe us, the purity of our motives, and the offensiveness of others. Arguably our respect for humanity, including our self-respect, requires us to maintain some reasonable doubts about the merits of our own moral judgments relative to others' and to cut some slack for the apparent errors of others. Due respect for our accuser should lead us to acknowledge there may be a grain of truth in their charges, and we should not completely "write them off" as totally lacking in moral judgment. When we respect ourselves as human beings, members of a global moral community in which both we and our offenders are imperfect members, our ultimate aim should be to move towards a more ideal community of mutual respect. Sometimes tolerating another's offensive words and conduct is the best step towards that end, especially when we can work towards the goal in other ways than what would be involved in refusing to tolerate. Responding to insults in kind rarely works, and violence can eliminate offenders but not make them better people. Much depends on the gravity and persistence of the offenses that would have to tolerate, but also on the moral costs of nontoleration.

Concluding Remarks

The value of respect for persons pulls two ways, then, regarding toleration of moral offenses. Often self-respect provides strong and compelling reasons to protest, push back, and stand up for oneself as good and respect-worthy person, but respect for others also gives us reason to be cautious in our moral judgments and find acceptable ways to put up with offenses while we work towards a mutually respectful community. What is especially needed now is exploration of *how* we can push back against what is intolerable and *how* we can tolerate what is morally offensive when necessary *with due respect* for all human beings, so that we can advance towards a community of mutual respect.

References

Darwall S (1977) Two kinds of respect. Ethics 88:36–49

Darwall S (2015) Respect as honor and as accountability. In: Timmons M, Johnson R (eds) Reason, value, and respect. Oxford University Press, Oxford, pp 70–88

Dillon R (ed) (1995) Dignity, character, and self-respect. Routledge, New York/London

Duewell M, Braavig J, Brownsword R, Mieth D (eds) (2014) The Cambridge handbook of human dignity. Cambridge University Press, Cambridge

Falk D (1953) Guiding and goading. Mind 62:145–189

Feinberg J (1985) Offenses to others. Oxford University Press, Oxford

Hill R Jr (1992) Dignity and practical reason in Kant's moral theory. Cornell University Press, Ithaca

Hill T Jr (1997) Must respect be earned? In: Peterson G (ed) The Tanner lectures on human values. University of Utah Press, Salt Lake City, pp 37–76

Hill T Jr (2012a) Virtue, rules, and justice: Kantian aspirations. Oxford University Press, Oxford

Hill T Jr (2012b) Treating criminals as ends in themselves. In: Hill TE Jr (ed) Virtue, rules, and justice. Oxford University Press, Oxford

Hill T Jr (2012c) Kant and humanitarian interventions. In: Hill TE Jr (ed) Virtue, rules, and justice. Oxford University Press, Oxford

Hill T Jr (2014a) In defense of human dignity: comments on Kant and Rosen. In: McCrudden C (ed) Understanding human dignity, proceedings of the British Academy, vol 192. Oxford University Press, Oxford, pp 313–327

Hill T Jr (2014b) Kantian perspectives on the rational basis of human dignity. In: Düewell M, Braarvig J, Brownsword R, Mieth D (eds) The Cambridge handbook of human dignity. Cambridge University Press, Cambridge, pp 215–221

Hill T Jr (2020) The kingdom of ends as an ideal and constraint on legislation. In: Kato Y, Schönrich G (eds) Kant's concept of dignity. De Gruyter, Berlin, pp 177–194

McCrudden C (ed) (2014) Understanding human dignity. Proceedings of the British Academy, vol 195. Oxford University Press, Oxford

Rawls J (2005) Political liberalism. Columbia University Press, New York

Wood A (2008) Kantian ethics. Cambridge University Press, Cambridge, UK/New York

Moralism and Anti-Moralism in Theories of Toleration

16

John Christian Laursen and Zachary Dorson

Contents

Introduction	278
Moralism and Anti-Moralism	279
Basic Approaches to Tolerance	282
Modes of Moralism in Theories of Toleration	282
Intolerance of the Intolerant	282
Excluding the Intolerant from Politics	284
Changing the Meaning of Toleration	285
Subordinating Free Speech to Respect: A Case Study	287
Theories of Toleration that Accuse Other Theories of Moralism	289
Idealism Versus Realism	289
The Critique of Changing the Meaning of Toleration	293
Is Negative Toleration Irrational?	295
Summary and Future Directions	297
References	297

Abstract

This chapter is about moralism and antimoralism in theories of tolerance or toleration. Broadly speaking, moralism is the taking of morality to an extreme, such as making everything a moral issue that calls for decisive measures, or assuming that many people are on the wrong side of any issue and need correcting. Antimoralism is the critique of this excessive moralism. Toleration has been the subject of debate for hundreds of years, and there are many possible connections between tolerance and moralism. A tolerant person or a tolerant community might be moralistic, or might reject moralism. An intolerant person or community, similarly, might be moralistic, or might reject moralism. A moralistic person might be tolerant or intolerant, and an antimoralist might be either

---

J. C. Laursen (✉) · Z. Dorson
University of California, Riverside, Riverside, CA, USA
e-mail: johnl@ucr.edu

© The Author(s), under exclusive licence to Springer Nature Switzerland AG 2022
M. Sardoĉ (ed.), *The Palgrave Handbook of Toleration*,
https://doi.org/10.1007/978-3-030-42121-2_26

of the two. Our purpose here is the identification and evaluation elements of moralism or antimoralism in theories of tolerance or toleration.

Keywords

Tolerance · Toleration · Intolerance · Negative tolerance · Moralism · Antimoralism · Liberalism · Autonomy · Liberty · Realism · Respect

---

Introduction

This chapter is about moralism and antimoralism in theories of tolerance or toleration. Broadly speaking, moralism is the taking of morality to an extreme, such as making everything a moral issue that calls for decisive measures, or assuming that many people are on the wrong side of any issue and need correcting. Antimoralism is the critique of this excessive moralism. Toleration has been the subject of debate for hundreds of years, and there are many possible connections between tolerance and moralism. A tolerant person or a tolerant community might be moralistic, or might reject moralism. An intolerant person or community, similarly, might be moralistic or might reject moralism. A moralistic person might be tolerant or intolerant, and an anti-moralist might be either of the two. The issue becomes more complicated when we limit our focus to theories of toleration. Our purpose here is the identification and evaluation elements of moralism or anti-moralism in theories of tolerance or toleration. We are interested in the elements of such theories that might be considered moralistic or anti-moralistic.

This chapter is about moralism or its absence in theories of toleration. We will not be making a distinction here between "tolerance" and "toleration," but rather use the words interchangeably as seems natural in ordinary language. Many theories and many definitions of toleration are offered in this volume, and we will try to be precise about the meanings that we are using. But some readers may not be very familiar with the term "moralism" and its family of terms such as "moralistic" and "moralizing," so we will start with a general definition. Broadly speaking, moralism is the taking of morality to an extreme, such as making everything a moral issue that calls for decisive measures, or assuming that many people are on the wrong side of any issue and need correcting. More definitions are presented below.

Toleration has been the subject of arguments and theories for hundreds of years. We will limit ourselves here to selected theories of the last half-century. Surely some of the theorists and theories of toleration of the previous centuries were moralistic or charged others with moralism as well, but we do not have the space to explore all of history.

There are many possible connections between tolerance and moralism. A tolerant person or a tolerant community might be moralistic, or might reject moralism. An intolerant person or community, similarly, might be moralistic or might reject moralism. A moralistic person might be tolerant or intolerant, and an anti-moralist might be either of the two. Although one might be tempted to think that a moralistic person is likely to be intolerant, it is not necessarily the case. One could be excessively moralistic about oneself but leave others alone, or one could be moralistic about insisting on the value of toleration. This is not quite the same as the first- and second-order tolerance (that is, for example, one is tolerant of X and intolerant of those who are intolerant of X) that have been discussed recently by Godfrey-Smith and Kerr (2019), but there are similarities. Distinct levels of psychological, social, or political tolerance could very much complicate the story. But our purpose here is the limited one of identifying and evaluating elements of moralism or anti-moralism in theories of tolerance or toleration.

After some preliminary analysis of the meaning of moralism and anti-moralism, and of the basic approaches to toleration, our chapter is divided into two parts. One surveys some of the prominent ways in which theories of toleration can be moralistic, and the other surveys some of the charges of moralism that some theorists of toleration bring against other theorists.

A key point for all of our discussion is that what counts as tolerance or intolerance, or moralism or anti-moralism, will always be debatable. There was a time when one could describe oneself as healthily intolerant of a wide range of ideas and behaviors, but now it is much more common to take pride in a certain tolerance, even though it has its limits. One describes others as intolerant. Similarly, people are much more likely to describe the ideas and behavior of others as moralistic, and their own ideas and behavior as appropriately moral and anti-moralistic. So, for example, people on the left will have a tendency to describe people on the right as moralists, but maintain that they themselves are just being moral, and people on the right will reflect a mirror image of this, describing themselves as properly moral but the left as moralistic. Whether or not it is possible to have a neutral or objective view of moralism is a question. Before proceeding further, we shall attempt to describe moralism and anti-moralism.

Moralism and Anti-Moralism

It has been observed that the term moralism does not have a widely accepted definition (Coady 2005, 101). The term is usually used in a pejorative sense for something to be avoided, but beyond that it is difficult to pin down the exact characteristics of moralistic behavior. Nevertheless, people often recognize it when they see it in political discourse and political theory, so we ought to be able to come up with some working definitions. Robert K. Fullinwider says that the term "moralist" is used to describe a person with a collection of vices and uses a character from Dickens, Mr. Pecksniff, to illustrate what a moralistic person is and to showcase the core vices of moralism (2005, 109). Fullinwider also provides a catalog of synonyms from ordinary language that everyone should be able to understand: "swollen with self-importance," "pompous," "busybodies and meddlers," and "sanctimonious, holier-than-thou prigs" (2005, 106). Other terms we use for this phenomenon include "fanatics" and "extremists."

Fullinwider concludes that moralism is the proclivity "to judge others uncharitably" in public (2005, 109). His definition therefore equates moralism with a kind of unjustified and excessive judgmentalism. Having respect for others makes one less inclined to be judgmental, says Fullinwider. While he seems to be in favor of nonjudgmentalism, he recognizes that it can become problematic as well. Taken to the extreme, nonjudgmentalism causes a "critical flabbiness" or "mindlessness" where one cannot critically assess the conduct of others at all (Fullinwider 2005, 113). Fullinwider calls this extreme nonjudgmentalism an "indiscriminate tolerance" (2005, 113). This would imply that healthy nonjudgmentalism is a selective tolerance of others. According to Fullinwider, moralism and morality are opposites; one is a vice while the other is a virtue. Fullinwider then asks whether one can truly separate moralism from morality and be a genuinely moral person. Perhaps a foolproof distinction cannot be made, he concludes (2005, 115).

Anti-moralists or critics of moralism go far back in the history of philosophy, arguably starting with the ancient skeptics. In the twentieth century, George Santayana was a strong opponent of moralism (Román and Laursen 2016). In his novel, *The Last Puritan,* he created a character, Oliver Alden, who was very moralistic. Oliver's mother and father were also moralistic, which harmed themselves and others around them, but Oliver's moralism was so subtle and ran so deep that he could not escape it and enjoy life. Santayana thought that the purpose of philosophy was to combat philosophies infected with moralism that prevent one from living a natural life. He advised being peacefully detached from intense feelings, and did not think in terms of good or bad, saying that it is unclear how to make moral judgments in nature. Fundamentally, Santayana appreciated variety in ideas and views, and demanded tolerance of new ideas. Santayana's critique of liberalism was part of his critique of moralism because he saw many moralistic judgments being made by liberal societies.

It may be very difficult to completely avoid being moralistic at all times. Yet there have been important anti-moralists who have tried to show us how to avoid it if possible. Anti-moralists can be found across the political spectrum and often use similar arguments. An example is Michael Oakeshott, who identified two types of morality: a habit-based morality that comes from tradition and culture, and a rules-based morality that comes from philosophizing and organized religion (Oakeshott 1991). Contrary to what some people would expect, he argued that traditional morality is constantly changing while philosophical morality resists change (Laursen 2013). Oakeshott thought that a habits-based morality is something you do intuitively, so there is no need to learn rules to be good. This notion surely draws on Aristotle's virtue ethics which says morality is achieved through practice rather than following rules (Aristotle 1971). Basically, one should go with what "feels right" because of your education and habits rather than trying to apply and follow a moral rule.

Scholars have also accused Oakeshott of being moralistic in his political views, sometimes because they see him as conservative. But Oakeshott held views that are not typically conservative, and these critics may misinterpret Oakeshott's writings as moralistic simply because they assume he is conservative (Laursen 2013).

Nonetheless, it would not be surprising that even powerful anti-moralists, such as Oakeshott, occasionally fall into moralistic thinking.

A recent scholar who has grappled with definitions of moralism is Shalini Satkunanandan, who claims that being moralistic is a way of evading genuine responsibility (Satkunanandan 2015). People naturally gravitate toward calculable responsibility (CR) in how they view morality, she says, which is highly prone to becoming moralistic. She explained that CR "is a particular way of approaching human responsibility... [as] something amenable to calculation – as a series of debts that can be identified in advance, reckoned up, negotiated, balanced out, and discharged" (2015, 2). CR is associated with debt justice, a conception of justice where one engages in morally good acts to "pay off the debt" incurred by the morally bad acts one has committed. Her main criticism of debt justice is that "paying off debts" does not make us ask questions about our behavior; there is no impetus to change for the better, only a motivation to justify our current and inadequate behavior. For us to make ourselves genuinely better people we must reconceptualize justice, which requires us to abandon the CR view in many situations (2015). But CR is not all bad, and Satkunanandan argues that this way of thinking is part of human nature. In certain cases, CR and debt justice are useful in resolving problems. However, there are many situations where CR and debt justice do not seem appropriate. And Satkunanandan wrote that "morality's calculable view of responsibility is at the heart of that perversion of morality called "moralism": a petty, vengeful, simplifying, overly inflexible approach to responsibility" (2015, 2–3).

Satkunanandan observed that "the 'self-certainty' of moralizers is often connected to the belief that what one should do is more or less knowable and specifiable in advance" (2015, 11–12). Moralism is thus "a thoughtless, simplifying, petty or punitive concern with following and enforcing moral rules" (Satkunanandan 2015, 12). CR "keeps us so narrowly focused on moral concerns – we carefully bookkeep our duties – that we can be recklessly unresponsive to the details and larger contexts of our unfolding world" (Satkunanandan 2015, 13). Believing that for some purposes morals and politics can be separated, Satkunanandan defined "moralized politics [as encompassing] any politics that appears to give moral standards some kind of authoritative say on how politics should be conducted" (2015, 15). As we will see, a number of political philosophers promote some form of moralized politics in their theories of toleration.

There is a common assumption that moral absolutism gives rise to moralism while moral relativism implies anti-moralism. Fullinwider claims that Nietzsche and Derrida articulated this view (2005). But it can be challenged (Laursen and Morales 2020). It is more likely that these four notions can be combined in opposite ways. There can be relativist moralists and relativist anti-moralists. One could say that in the absence of fixed morals one could either adopt a strong moral position on impulse or for emotional reasons, or one could reject all such moral positions on impulse or for emotional reasons. Similarly, there can be absolutist moralists and absolutist anti-moralists. Belief in absolute morals certainly could lead to moralistic excesses. However, one could believe that an objective truth about what is morally right exists, but feel uncertain that one knows what that truth is, and thus have a feeling of humbleness that enables one to avoid moralism.

Moralism is perhaps best defined as one end of a spectrum of morality: an excessive and extreme form of morality that is psychologically and socially unhealthy. The other end of the spectrum is amorality or immorality, and in the middle of the spectrum is normal healthy morality. Since healthy morality should oppose the extremes of moralism, it is an anti-moralism. We shall now see how this distinction maps onto theories of toleration.

Basic Approaches to Tolerance

In recent decades, scholars have conceptualized tolerance in different ways and have provided different theories of toleration in society. Some people see toleration as a way of "putting up with" disagreeable behavior in order to maintain peace. For example, one definition of tolerance is the acceptance of the existence of beliefs and practices that one dislikes rather than attempting to suppress or eliminate those beliefs and practices. As an end state, this tolerance is believed to be "good enough" for society. Since this toleration entails a negative freedom, a freedom from harmful interference, we will call this negative toleration.

Others see tolerance as a way to bring about a just society. Either negative tolerance is not seen as an end state, but only a temporary truce or ceasefire, or the definition of toleration is changed so that it is a desirable and just end state. In this analysis, toleration is considered a path towards an ideal society. In other words, negative toleration is a phase we must move beyond. In this version, toleration includes mutual respect and equality among everyone in society. This toleration involves a positive freedom, the freedom to participate as equal and respected members of society, and so we will call it positive toleration.

What separates these two camps may be the degree to which they are moralistic. Some people might feel that those who are dissatisfied with negative toleration and who prefer positive toleration are more moralistic than those satisfied with negative toleration, since they may push for an excessively high moral standard for toleration rather than accepting that it is no more than a modus vivendi. We shall proceed to explore some examples of what is arguably moralism in theories of toleration.

Modes of Moralism in Theories of Toleration

Intolerance of the Intolerant

One well-known scholar who can be accused of moralism was Herbert Marcuse. In a classic essay titled "Repressive Tolerance," Marcuse asked whether intolerant people should be tolerated (1965). His answer was no. Tolerating the intolerant enables them to carry out their programs. Their intolerance of other ideas and beliefs is a trait of people with evil intentions, according to Marcuse. Therefore, a policy of tolerating the intolerant only serves to protect evil (Marcuse 1965). If we are to prevent the implementation of policies that bring evil to society, we must eliminate the ideas and beliefs that give rise to such policies. And toleration should not be afforded to views we want to eliminate. There may be some difficulty here in avoiding the problem of self-reference: if Marcuse is promoting intolerance, does it not follow under his own theory that his own intolerance reveals evil intentions? Presumably, his answer would be that he is not intolerant in the first instance, but only intolerant of the intolerant, and thus, his intolerance is not evil.

For Marcuse, it is very easy to identify where intolerance is found: it is always found on the political right (1965). He did not find any on the left. He wrote that "the Chinese and the Cuban Revolutions" achieved "an increase in the scope of freedom and justice" in their respective societies (1965, 107–108). Now, if at the time one accepted this view of the facts and Marcuse's general Marxist ideology, one would presumably have concluded that Marcuse was being properly moral, and not moralistic. But if one had a different view of the facts and believed that violent purges and imprisonment of dissidents in those countries were followed by famines and widespread poverty, and also had a different political ideology, Marcuse's dismissal of only the ideas and beliefs of conservatives as intolerant may have been considered a judgmental and moralistic stance. Marcuse also might have been considered blind to the intolerance found on the political left, and thus moralistic. Similarly, if today one agrees with his view of the facts and his ideology, one might see him as properly moral, but if one disagrees with his facts and his ideology, one might find him to be moralistic.

Marcuse asserted that there is an objective truth and that we can ascertain it (1965). This is a dogmatic position, which he uses to advance his theory of toleration. Progress towards this truth has been made by leftist movements throughout history, he argued. Therefore, it is justifiable to censor and be intolerant of the "regressive" right. Marcuse challenged the argument made by John Stuart Mill that the best ideas will win out in the marketplace of ideas. He contended that most people are indoctrinated to support the status quo and are incapable of the critical deliberation needed in the marketplace of ideas. Taken together, this means the majority of people in society cannot be trusted to distinguish good ideas from detrimental ones. Only those few who are truly rational, Marcuse argued, can make the distinction and teach people the right ideas (1965). This is an elitist position and seems contradictory to his claims of promoting an egalitarian society, and some would see it as moralism.

One interesting criticism of toleration that Marcuse provides is that it could lead to stagnation in society. If people tolerate the current political regime, they may not be inclined to challenge and change the status quo, even if the status quo is one of oppression (1965). Other scholars have taken up a similar line of reasoning. This may sound plausible at first, but it may not be true. Toleration does not necessarily equal approval, and in fact one of the factors often used to define toleration is disapproval. One can argue against certain beliefs and practices, trying to persuade people to abandon them, while also tolerating their existence. For example, one might oppose abortion and attempt to persuade people to not get abortions, while at the same time opposing laws that ban the practice of abortion. Change is possible in many regimes of tolerance. Change may occur as more people are persuaded by argument or as economic and social conditions change.

Excluding the Intolerant from Politics

Michael Walzer thought that while there are limits to toleration, we can tolerate the intolerant so long as we are participating in a democracy (1997). Walzer defined toleration as "the peaceful coexistence of groups of people with different histories, cultures, and identities" (1997, 2). There are many kinds: peaceful coexistence "can take very different political forms, with different implications for everyday moral life" (Walzer 1997, 2). He presented five possibilities, or attitudes, laid out on a spectrum: resignation, indifference, stoical acceptance, curiosity, and enthusiasm. That last attitude might fall outside toleration, Walzer said, because enthusiasm for differences does not seem to fit the core meaning of tolerance, i.e., putting up with disliked behavior (1997, 11). Resignation, indifference, and stoical acceptance probably fall under negative conceptions of toleration, while curiosity and enthusiasm likely fall under positive toleration. He wrote that "comparisons across [toleration] arrangements are morally and politically helpful in thinking about where we are and what alternatives might be available to us" (1997, 4).

There are limits to what Walzer thought should be tolerated. He valued democracy and therefore asserted that anti-democratic movements should not be tolerated in politics, saying that "it is merely prudent" to deny them participation in politics (1997, 9). This may be a moralistic stance, although it is not as harsh as Marcuse's. Antidemocratic parties should be denied political power, he said, separated from power but not violently persecuted. "What separation means in their case is that they are confined to civil society: they can preach and write and meet; they are permitted only a sectarian existence," he wrote (Walzer 1997, 82). This is the same reasoning behind the separation of church and state, but that doctrine does not usually go as far as to say that members of certain social or religious groups may not participate in politics. It seems likely that members of such movements that are denied political participation would feel that they were missing something important, and might feel it as intolerance. They will also most likely deny that they are anti-democratic, and accuse those who deny them political rights of being anti-democratic. Excluding some groups from political power may be prudent, but it may well be a moralistic stance and would certainly be resented, perhaps enough to destabilize a country.

Godfrey-Smith and Kerr also recommended that the intolerant be restrained to a certain degree (2019). As mentioned previously, they want to frame the debate about tolerance, and its paradoxes, using a hierarchical model. This hierarchy, starting with first-order tolerance, contains ever higher orders of tolerance. First-order tolerance consists of tolerance of disliked private behaviors, and second-order tolerance concerns tolerance of other people's intolerance of these behaviors. Godfrey-Smith and Kerr claimed that we can use this hierarchical model to find logical consistencies and inconsistencies within questions of tolerance and intolerance. They asserted that "[a] person is tolerant with respect to X if they are disposed not to interfere with others in ways that would tend to curtail or constrain their choices concerning X" (2019, 405). They explained that interference includes "physically harming, impeding, or threatening a person, or bringing the forces of law to bear on them" (2019, 405–6). This is a negative conception of toleration.

According to Godfrey-Smith and Kerr, the "familiar liberal combination" is first-order tolerance, where individuals are free to live the lifestyle they want, and second-order intolerance of intolerance, where people with controversial lifestyles are protected from interference by intolerant people who oppose them by intolerance of those people (2019, 420). Some scholars, such as Rawls and Popper, saw this combination as a compromise: "They did seem to see intolerance of the intolerant as regrettable," as "a falling away from an ideal of wholesale tolerance" (Godfrey-Smith and Kerr 2019, 421). But this is because they did not have this hierarchical model of tolerance, Godfrey-Smith and Kerr explain. The hierarchy model "does not represent a trade-off between competing values, but may represent a whole-hearted endorsement and defense of base-level autonomy—of autonomy restricted only by the effects of one's choices on others" (Godfrey-Smith and Kerr 2019, 421). They concluded that preservation of toleration does not entail a paradox.

Godfrey-Smith and Kerr wrote:

> When this [liberal] combination is in place, and a response to first-order intolerance becomes necessary, that response need not be violent, and should not target behaviors by the intolerant that would otherwise receive protection under first-order tolerance. A response of this kind is not an expression of a 'tit-for-tat' policy. The aim instead will be to protect, using the most restrained means available, a regime of first-order tolerance. (2019, 420)

Walzer seems to have a policy similar to what Godfrey-Smith and Kerr recommend here, a nonviolent interference that preserves the regime of tolerance. But it denies participation in politics to those who it convicts of intolerance, and that will surely be felt as intolerance. Will this non-violent interference also be considered moralistic? Again, this will depend on the observer's point of view and judgment.

Changing the Meaning of Toleration

Anna Elisabetta Galeotti analyzed both negative and positive conceptions of toleration. These conceptions are taken up by, respectively, what she called liberal neutralists and liberal perfectionists (2004). Galeotti argued that the liberal neutralist's theory of toleration is inadequate for resolving the political issues facing society. This is because it allows individuals to choose to be different without interference. However, like Walzer, Galeotti claimed that contemporary issues are about differences between groups, not individuals (2004). And the main political issue in Western countries is the struggle for recognition by minority groups who differ meaningfully from the majority. She did not mean to discuss tolerance or intolerance of mass murderers, Nazis, religious fanatics, or other possible targets of intolerance, but only of minority groups.

Galeotti defined recognition "as acknowledging, or even endorsing, the intrinsic value of the differences in question" (2004, 14–15). This could roughly correspond with the attitudes of curiosity and enthusiasm toward differences described by Walzer. Galeotti endorsed a politics of recognition, which she wanted toleration to be a part of. The politics of recognition, or identity politics, "groups together a cluster of claims and demands aimed at the public assertion of the collective identities of oppressed and excluded groups and at securing public protection and support for them" (2004, 18). She thought that pursuing such politics would help create social justice in society. But some people will see this as moralism on the ground that it requires too much supervision and control over people.

In liberal democratic regimes, there is a problem in working out how to create consensus in governing. Galeotti said there are two solutions to this problem: one is to exclude everyone's conception of the good in political deliberation, while the other is to bring these conceptions of the good together to integrate them in political deliberation. The former is endorsed by liberal neutralists who are only concerned with creating legitimacy for the regime. The latter was supported by Galeotti, who wanted to create social justice in society. Galeotti said she would "defend toleration of differences in the public sphere not on the grounds of an argument showing the compatibility of the recognition of differences with neutrality, but on the grounds of justice" (2004, 10). Giving recognition to minority groups is how social justice can be achieved. Oakeshott identified a possible danger here: letting the value of justice override other values (1991, 476).

In Galeotti's view, what we have been calling negative toleration is incapable of addressing the disadvantages minorities face. Features of the neutralist liberal theory of toleration "induce a basic insensitivity to social differences, which are consequently considered either as publicly irrelevant and as not pertaining to the public sphere or, at best, as disadvantages to be compensated, in order to be justly dismissed in the political domain" (Galeotti 2004, 52). Neutralists are insensitive because they see social differences as a problem, the solution to which is to ignore the differences by treating all citizens equally. Galeotti rejected this solution because it ignores the social stigmas that members of minority groups have: they are seen as deviating from what is normal and are treated as outsiders.

Like Marcuse, Galeotti thought we must be intolerant of certain behaviors in order to be truly tolerant of vulnerable minorities. This intolerance would be "the second step in the process of inclusion" after official recognition is given (Galeotti 2004, 13). The public presence of minorities needs to be protected and stabilized because it will initially be weak. According to Galeotti, minorities would still be "targets of prejudice, stereotyping, and discrimination" by the majority (2004, 13). Therefore, the behavior of members of the majority must be policed and restricted. This may require what others would describe as moralistic policies.

Galeotti wrote that "[i]n order to become tolerant [one] first needs to dislike or disapprove of the different practices which are at odds with their own, and then to overcome such feelings, giving way to toleration" (2004, 20–21). This is not how negative tolerationists conceptualize tolerance. They think one can disapprove of practices *and* tolerate them. Toleration is not about overcoming the feelings of dislike, but overcoming the urge to violently suppress the disliked behavior. But Galeotti asked, "how can toleration be good if it involves putting up with what is disliked or disapproved of? In this light, toleration seems to be more a disposition that results from a compromise than one which could count as having *positive ethical and political value in its own right*" (2004, 21, emphasis added). This is an example of the moralistic language Galeotti used. She wanted toleration to be a force for good rather than just a way of living or custom or habit. Toleration, in her view, must be a conscious practice aimed towards a righteous goal.

Galeotti complained that "[t]he merely negative meaning would imply that being tolerated is better than being coerced into or prevented from doing something, but it is far from being an *ideal* condition of social and political life, and this looks more like a modus vivendi than a principled solution to the conflicts of pluralism" (2004, 21, emphasis added). The use of the term "ideal" is another indicator of moralistic thinking. Galeotti wants an "active acceptance" of differences, not a modus vivendi. How is such active acceptance to be cultivated in people? Her answer is the implementation of a discriminatory intolerance of bigotry and prejudice, but of course the important question will be who gets to decide who is bigoted and prejudiced, and this will not be a neutral question. Most people will only see bigotry and prejudice on the other side of any political or social divide. And what if intolerance of alleged bigotry does not work and some people simply never embrace an active acceptance of others? Must they be coercively repressed? What if intolerance of bigotry provokes a significant reactionary movement vindicating that bigotry?

If Galeotti gets her way and toleration is redefined as acceptance and respect, such that the minority groups she is worried about are treated better than under negative tolerance, it may still be the case that other people and their ideas and actions, such as nonviolent Nazis or religious fanatics, are not respected and not accepted. If their ideas and behavior are not illegal, there may be a case for letting them alone and not persecuting them. Then there will still be a use for the term and the theory and practice of negative toleration.

Subordinating Free Speech to Respect: A Case Study

John William Tate observed that debates about the meaning of toleration center on the tension between free speech and equal respect (2016). These two concepts are integral to liberalism. Tate says that there are two types of liberalism: Enlightenment and Reformation liberalism. Enlightenment liberalism, also known as classical liberalism, "is concerned, above all, to advance the value of individual autonomy within the polity" (Tate 2016, 37). For classical liberal scholars, wrote Tate, "freedom of expression, either in terms of speech or religion, was inextricably linked with individual liberty" (2016, 35). Tate explained that "Enlightenment liberals are likely to perceive a tolerant society as one where the principle of free speech is advanced" (2016, 37).

Reformation liberalism, on the other hand, "is primarily concerned with ensuring peaceful coexistence between diverse (and often conflicting) cultures and practices," Tate said (2016, 37). Equal respect, coming out of natural rights theory, was also important to classical liberal philosophers, and sometimes overrides freedom of expression (Tate 2016). For Reformation liberals, "the peaceful maintenance of diversity may require a limit on the principle of free speech, particularly when such speech precludes treating other cultures with 'equal respect'" (Tate 2016, 37). This inevitably clashes with the advancement of free speech promoted by Enlightenment liberals.

Tate reported on a case of the clash of these values. In 1995, the Australian Parliament added a section, called §18C, to a law that forbids public speech that creates "offence, insult, humiliation, or intimidation" of racial minorities to an anti-racial discrimination law (Tate 2016, 38). If it meant to allow such speech against the racial majority such differential treatment might be considered moralistic by some, exaggerating the moral implications of speech against minorities and minimizing the implications of the same speech against the majority. The goal of this legislation was to "promote racial tolerance" (Tate 2016, 38). Tate wrote that "Parliament evidently understood toleration, in this context, to require not free speech, but rather the maintenance of 'equal respect' for those of diverse racial, national or ethnic origins" (2016, 38).

The section was challenged in court for violating the principle of free speech. When Tony Abbott became Prime Minister of Australia, he proposed repealing this section of the law. Tate cited a lawyer, Mariam Veiszadeh, who opposed the repeal of §18C. "She acknowledged that [free] speech was 'the cornerstone of our democratic rights and freedoms'," wrote Tate, "but she said it also allowed 'those who spew hateful and misleading vitriol' to 'thrive from the protection it offers'" (2016, 45). This may be understood by some as moralistic language that sounds like that of Marcuse. Veiszadeh also espoused views similar to Galeotti, saying that vulnerable and marginalized minorities must have protection from bigotry by repressive legislation (Tate 2016). Some would see such repressive legislation as moralistic, but others will say that it is not moralistic at all but strikes the right balance.

The equal respect camp ultimately won and §18C was retained in the law. Australians were afraid that "free speech, unrestricted by the limits of §18C, might threaten the peaceful maintenance of [the racial and ethnic] diversity [in their country]. In other words, liberalism's "Reformation" concerns were, for these individuals, paramount," Tate explained (2016, 45).

Tate cited an Australian politician named Barry O'Farrell, who said:

[W]e must not lower our defences against the evil of race and religious intolerance. Bigotry should never be sanctioned... Vilifications on the grounds of race or religion, is always wrong. There's no place for inciting hatreds within our Australian society... No government, no organisation, no citizen, can afford to be less than vigilant, in combating bigotry, intolerance, and hatred, and frankly, our way of life depends on that vigilance. (2016, 46)

To some, this will sound moralistic. It raises an interesting question: can legitimate criticism of a religion or a racial group be distinguished from "bigotry" or "vilification"? There may be no room for people to voice negative opinions of others in this view, which would abolish free speech. If free speech is a "cornerstone" of democracy, as Veiszadeh claimed, how will Reformation liberals preserve it? Perhaps a balance should be found between Reformation liberalism and Enlightenment liberalism, rather than pursuing the extreme of one of them. In the meantime, the Australian government made a "decision to place a greater priority upon maintaining conciliatory relations between the government and specific ethnic and religious communities, rather than on free speech concerns" (Tate 2016, 47). Defenders of free speech might see this as moralism in politics.

Theories of Toleration that Accuse Other Theories of Moralism

Idealism Versus Realism

One of the most important debates in political theory in the last several decades has been labeled the "Ideal versus realist (or nonideal)" debate. "Ideal" can mean theories that are perfectionist, in reality impossible to achieve, or simply a very high evaluative standard (Stemplowska and Swift 2012). John Rawls is often cited for his definition of an ideal theory as a political theory that assumes full compliance of everyone in society in following these ideals and favorable circumstances for these ideals to be realized (Stemplowska and Swift 2012). In contrast, nonideal theory takes into account "obstacles to a well-ordered society due to injustice (partial compliance) and due to socioeconomic limitations (unfavorable circumstances)" (Stemplowska and Swift 2012, 375). Ideal theory sets the standard: "the task of ideal theory is to identify requirements that people can comply with given 'merely' their sense of justice, not their capacity for moral heroism" (Stemplowska and Swift 2012, 376). Ideal theory can be used "to find out what perfect justice requires" (Stemplowska and Swift 2012, 376). Ideal theory plays two roles, according to Rawls. One is the target role in which it provides "nonideal theory an ultimate target" to pursue, while the second is the urgency role in which "ideal theory helps us assess the urgency of injustice we face" in the real world (Stemplowska and Swift 2012, 376).

The realist camp of political theory accuses those from the idealist camp of moralism. One such scholar was Bernard Williams: "for Williams, [Rawls's] 'political liberalism' is itself grounded in an overambitiously moralized, and ideal-ized, conception of political relationships" (Stemplowska and Swift 2012, 382). Williams thought most political theories prioritize "the moral over the political" and act "like applied morality" (2005, 2). These theories he categorized as *political moralism*, a term that Satkunanandan used as well (2015, 15). Williams contrasted political moralism with *political realism*, a group of theories which prioritizes the political over the moral in decisions about politics and society. He cited Rawls for arguing that the stability of pluralistic society depends on the "moral psychology of citizens" (2005, 2). This sounds like something Marcuse or Galeotti would say. The conditions for a liberal society to exist cannot be "a mere modus vivendi," as Williams cited Rawls (Williams, 2005, 2), a sentiment explicitly shared by Galeotti (2004, 21). Williams disagreed with Rawls's view that moral questions must be addressed before political ones. "A very important reason for thinking in terms of the political," Williams wrote, "is that a political decision... does not in itself announce that the other party was morally wrong [but rather] announces that *they have lost*" (2005, 13). Being accused of being morally wrong elicits a visceral reaction, one that can easily lead to violence. Simply failing to persuade people to take a certain course of political action may not create such strong emotions among them as accusing them of evil. In a pluralistic society, it is prudent and safer to avoid political moralism and adhere to political realism, Williams argued (2005, 13).

Toleration should be treated as a political matter, rather than a moral one, Williams thought. He relied on Thomas Scanlon's definition of toleration, which is a form of negative toleration (2005, 128). Williams did not consider the attitudes of skepticism or indifference to be forms of toleration. Like Walzer, Williams discussed the issue of power and the asymmetrical relationship between tolerator and tolerated. "It is the practice of toleration or intolerance as a *political undertaking* that introduces the asymmetry associated with the concept, and not the underlying attitudes," Williams wrote (2005, 129). It is only when people express their tolerance or intolerance in the political sphere that power becomes relevant.

According to Williams, toleration depends on the right to be left alone. Scholars see this right as either a moral right or a political right (Williams 2005, 130). The moral right is grounded in the principle of moral autonomy: someone should not interfere with the lifestyle of another because each person's morality should be in his or her own hands. Williams used "interference" quite broadly to include even efforts to persuade or non-violently pressure others to change (2005, 132). Assuming that attempts should not be made to change anyone's morals, this view of toleration as a moral right might sound like a strict form of anti-moralism. But a paradox emerges in the sense that saying that it is morally wrong to criticize the morals of others actually imperils free speech, he argued (2005, 132–133). And then a further paradox emerges to the effect that his argument against moralism also may be a form of moralism. David Estlund has recently argued that Williams's anti-moralism may be a form of moralism in its own right that exaggerates the moral dangers of ideal theory (2017). He argues for "anti-anti-moralism" on the ground that none of the relevant arguments actually succeed in undermining the effort to evaluate political arrangements in accordance with moral standards (2017, 399). It may be the case that moral and political arguments are always intertwined and interdependent and cannot be separated from each other, and thus that we will always evaluate political arrangements from a moral point of view.

Estlund had previously argued against what he labeled "utopophobia," "the unreasonable fear of utopianism," but even his theory might be classified as a moralistic anti-moralism (2014, 116). He asserted that even "hopeless aspirations" have their place in morals and politics (2014, 118). He recognized that hopelessly high aspirations can be dangerous, but so can low expectations (2014, 120). The realists can be accused of complacency and acceptance of injustice. Sometimes what has been previously thought to be absurdly unrealistic has come to pass (2014, 133). One example might be religious toleration as practiced in multicultural societies.

Shortly thereafter Michael Frazer answered Estlund by arguing that "a moderate form of... 'utopophobia' is actually an integral element of a proper professional ethic for political philosophers" (2019, 3). He asserted that "if the community of academic political theorists and philosophers cannot help us navigate the problems we face in actual political life, they have not lived up to the moral demands of their vocation" (2019, 3). In fact, "the system of incentives that structure our profession" is "dangerously inclined" to "encourage only utopian theorizing" (2019, 3). So he, too, insisted on limits: "utopianism is defensible only insofar as it can reasonably be expected to help inform or improve nonutopian political thinking" (2019, 3). But how will we know this before we have done the utopian thinking? One person's "reasonable expectations" may differ from another's. It begins to look like one person's useless utopian thinking will be another person's helpful utopian thinking, and vice-versa.

Seen as a political right, toleration means people can attempt to change others' morals but cannot use force or the law to do so. Williams thought this is much more practical than attempting to prohibit efforts to persuade others because people inevitably want to influence others' behavior. Liberalism values individual autonomy, but Williams asked ideal theorists where liberalism should draw the line for determining what is interference. He wrote that "[t]he case of toleration is... a central one for distinguishing between a strongly moralized conception of liberalism as based on ideals of individual autonomy, and a more skeptical... politically direct conception of it as the best hope for humanly acceptable legitimate government" (2005, 138). The liberal practice of toleration cannot be grounded in the value of individual autonomy, Williams argued, and therefore this pure individual autonomy is an impractical ideal.

Gerald Gaus also criticized ideal theory and made a case for pursuing an Open Society rather than an ideal society (2016). He borrowed the term "Open Society" from Karl Popper. Gaus wrote that he was setting aside "ideal theory as mere dreaming; whether or not achieving the ideal is itself hopeless, my concern is the type of political theorizing in which the ideal is not useless—in which the ideal serves as a criterion that assists in regulating, directing, or facilitating less-than-ideal judgments of comparative justice" (2016, 16). He argued that "an Open Society will not be characterized by a shared ideal" but by deep diversity (2016, 147). This was because in an Open Society everyone "is free to pursue his or her own inquiry into justice, exploring the terrain of justice as he or she sees it, using the methods he or she thinks most fit" (Gaus 2016, 149). This meant that "we must choose between full normalization, which yields a definite theory of justice but makes it most unlikely that we can find the ideal, and relaxing normalization, which improves the chances that many will find better alternatives, but which yields disagreement about what ideal justice is" (Gaus 2016, 150).

Gaus asserted that "liberty is fundamental to the moral constitution of the Open Society" (2016, 187). The *principle of natural liberty* states that whatever is not prohibited is permitted, while its opposite, the *residual prohibition principle*, states that whatever is not permitted is prohibited (Gaus 2016). Whichever principle a society adopts shapes its political system as well as the form of toleration that is adopted. Gaus explained that:

> In a natural liberty system, if a moral innovator does not conclude that the analogy holds, he will conclude that morality allows his innovative activity; in a residual prohibition system, unless the innovator concludes that a relevant analogy holds—that the new action type is analogous to a permitted type—he will desist. It is in this sense that a natural liberty system encourages experimentation and discovery. (2016, 196)

Gaus thinks that one is likely to be less moralistic in a natural liberty system than in a residual prohibition system because the latter requires moral judgments to justify something new where the former does not.

The Open Society is essentially a tolerant society, Gaus argued, and toleration frustrates utopian aspirations. This is because "[t]he very aim that the ideal theorist cherished, to know justice and just social states as well as possible," Gaus wrote, "requires an open, diverse society, in which innumerable perspectives simultaneously cooperate and compete, share and conflict" (2016, 246). No uniformity is possible. If we are to pursue an ideal society and ideal justice, we will have to abandon toleration of diverse perspectives and be united around this one perfect perspective on society and justice. Gaus tried to show that "such an ideal is ultimately a mirage, yet one that tyrannizes over our thinking and encourages us to turn our backs on pressing problems of justice in our own neighborhood" (2016, 246).

One of the elements of moralism that appears in the work of ideal theorists, according to Gaus, is arrogance:

> When one thinks one has hit upon a standard of justice, and finds again and again that attempts to construct 'rules of regulation' to implement it have repeatedly led to disaster, the proper response is not to shake one's head sadly that the children are not yet up to Justice. Rather, the embarrassing fact for the philosopher is he is the one who has erred. He got justice wrong. (2016, 249–250)

There is a moral component to Gaus's arguments – he is saying that an Open Society is a good and valuable society. Marcuse and Galeotti might argue that he drifts into moralism because he is using morality to criticize their kind of theory of tolerance. By his own lights, he is surely making a strong anti-moralism argument.

Finally, Andrew Sabl has pointed out that the merits of toleration were not so much the product of a philosophical discovery as an empirical finding based on the practice, before the theory, of toleration (2017). Thus, Sabl's argument counts as a charge of moralism against those who think that morals and politics derive from high-minded moral and philosophical thinking. The anti-moralistic lesson that he derives from this is that "no political theory should imagine itself indispensable" (2017, 375).

The Critique of Changing the Meaning of Toleration

Peter Balint defended the neutralist conception of toleration by addressing three challenges to it: the multicultural, despotism, and neutrality challenges. He wanted "to defend both the ideal and the practice of political toleration in response to issues raised by the diversity that exists in contemporary liberal democracies" (2017, 2) He defined a neutralist as someone whose "intention is to be neutral between mere preferences and deeply held beliefs, and not try to dig too deep or use some criteria as to why some people's differences may matter more than others" (2017, 72). His premise was that the "state's primary role is not to make us better persons, or fulfil some metaphysical or aesthetic ideal, but to give us the space and security to live our lives as we see fit" (2017, 12). To some, this is an anti-moralistic argument, although Marcuse and Galeotti might think it is moralistic, giving too much weight to people's own decisions when we know they are often wrong.

Balint summed up the recent debate by stating that:

> [T]he link between toleration and neutrality has not been well understood, and political toleration is too commonly conflated with the moral virtue of tolerance. As a result, it has been too easy to critique traditional liberalism as not being able to accommodate diversity adequately or fairly; with toleration as something we need to 'move beyond'. These concerns and misunderstandings have opened up the space for proposing replacements or major modification to traditional liberal principles. (2017, 14)

But one should resist these changes, as Balint explained:

> A proper understanding of toleration and neutrality, the link between them, and their subsequent application, is what is required... If one cares, as we should, about people living their lives as they see fit, then, as I will argue, it is toleration and neutrality that should be recognized and respected, and interventionist policies and laws that try to target and help particular citizens to achieve this good should be strongly resisted. (2017, 15)

Here Balint expressed his moral principle, and we can ask if it is properly moral or moralistic. Should we care about people living their lives as they see fit? Different people will give different answers to this question. Those who think they know how people should live their lives, and that it is not up to them, will find Balint moralistic, taking his own morality too far.

Balint's definition of tolerance comprised three elements: "(1) objecting to some thing; (2) the power to interfere negatively with the thing or its holder; and (3) intentionally not negatively interfering with the thing or its holder" (2017, 28). Balint identified three challenges to this liberal tolerance. One is the multicultural challenge, which argues that "the contemporary liberal state inevitably privileges some ways of life, generally those of the majority of citizens, over others, usually those of minorities" (2017, 52). As we have seen, Galeotti was one such multiculturalist. Another is the despotism challenge made by those "who see 'neutrality' as simply masking and preserving the power of a dominant culture; that what is claimed as 'neutral' or 'indifferent' is in fact a status quo that seriously favors those with power and disadvantages minorities" (Balint 2017, 52).

The third is the neutrality challenge which argues that a truly neutral state would "place no value at all on particular differences," but then paradoxically "it would no longer have the sort of values on which it may object and withhold power" (Balint 2017, 4). Toleration, therefore, is superseded by neutrality and "is at best redundant, and at worst incompatible with liberal neutrality, and cannot describe the actions of contemporary liberal democracies" (Balint 2017, 4). One cannot be considered tolerant if one has no opinions at all on something, such that one is not putting up with anything, nor refraining from suppressing it. But if the state does have some values and makes some judgments, then it can be tolerant.

Balint attempted to refute all three of these challenges. He wanted "to make the case for... a conception of tolerance where the reasons for objection and the reasons for non-hindrance do not need to conform to any moralized criteria" (2017, 77). He tried to avoid moralism in his defense of toleration. He argued that "use-value, and with it the protection of individual freedom, can best be achieved by a descriptive rather than moralized conception of forbearance tolerance" (2017, 93). He clarified that "[t]his is not an argument against the moral virtue of tolerance, but simply against its application in political contexts" (2017, 97).

Balint made a distinction between *appraisal respect* and *recognition respect*. The former "is essentially a merit based way of respecting. It involves respecting something as a 'good' thing" (2017, 103). The latter "is for roles or status... It is respect for the particular status, and involves taking that status into consideration when deciding how to act" (Balint 2017, 103). For scholars like Galeotti, the status of minorities should always be considered when interacting with them. Can we demand that people be always cognizant of this status? Balint wrote:

> For respect for difference among citizens to be a legitimate demand there must exist an appropriate way of respecting. As I have argued, using appraisal and recognition respect, no such way exists; it is either too demanding from a liberal point of view, or unnecessary for accommodation, or both. If accommodation is the goal, then citizens need not respect difference but may simply engage in forbearance tolerance or indifference. (2017, 115)

According to George Sher, it would be too demanding to determine an "appropriate" way of respecting others (2018). This is because it amounts to knowing what people really feel about others and changing their minds if these feelings are inappropriate. Attempting to control one's own mind is just as futile as attempting to control other people's minds. Sher argued that "the realm of the purely mental is best regarded as a morality-free zone" (2018, 2). This is one of the elements of the reasoning behind tolerating inappropriate thoughts as long as people behave within the limits of the law.

There are many scholars who say that "even purely private mental states are fair game for moral assessment," Sher observed (2018, 3). He questioned this view by asking: What are the justifications for trying to police the thoughts of others? One potential justification is that the boundary between the internal and external is very permeable; one who thinks bigoted thoughts is highly likely to act bigoted, so these thoughts are "morally hazardous" (Sher 2018, 5). Marcuse seems to have relied on this justification. Sher countered this argument by observing that there are numerous instances where one thinks bad thoughts of others, yet one does nothing (2018, 6). Most people have enough self-control to not act on problematic thoughts, and so it does not matter by-and-large that they have them.

Another possible justification is based on the claim that to interact with each other in a mutually beneficial way requires a mutual sense of good will. A person can be criticized for lacking feelings of good will toward others. Galeotti seems to rely on this justification. Sher counters that many people are able to get along with each other despite knowing the other side does not like them. "As long as strangers treat me right, I don't need their good will," Sher wrote (2018, 8).

Sher provides two arguments against attempts to constrain thought. One is that there is a lack of clear boundaries in the mind. Trying to avoid one thought entails trying to prevent many other thoughts from occurring at the same time or *before* the forbidden thought has a chance to occur. His second argument is based on the fact that there is a lack of correspondence between what one is imagining and what they are actually engaged in at the moment. The subjective mind is independent of the objective world. The "people" we imagine in our minds are not real people, and we do not have moral obligations to imagined people.

As we have seen, Galeotti criticizes the "benign neglect" policies of neutralists. Balint advocates an "active indifference" approach instead. He wrote that:

Neutrality of intent can and should be active rather than entirely passive. Contemporary diversity is ever-changing, and striving to be neutral in this fluid landscape is very difficult. Rather than taking a 'set and forget' approach, liberal states should be willing to change and adapt policies, laws, and institutions to the range of diversity that presents itself. (2017, 146)

Balint explained:

On this "hands off", yet still active, understanding of neutrality, no ways of life need to be recognized or respected, all that needs to happen is that unjustified restrictions and unjustified privileges are removed, and thus there is little need to distinguish between preferences and deeply held beliefs. (2017, 146)

Balint's argument may be described as an effort to avoid moralism.

His response to the multicultural challenge is that "it is liberal toleration that should be respected by legislators and policy-makers, and not people's differences—whether they be minority *or* majority" (2017, 147). His response to the despotism challenge is that "toleration often does not have the features this challenge describes, and when it does, it may actually be normatively preferable" (2017, 147–148). His response to the neutrality challenge is that "Both [toleration and neutrality] are range concepts, and no state will ever be neutral or tolerant to all possible forms of diversity" (2017, 148).

Is Negative Toleration Irrational?

Ryan W. Davis argued there are two accounts of toleration: one based on diversity, and the other based on autonomy (2017). He asserted that the autonomy account of toleration is more helpful for society because it "provides the better foundation for a valuable political relationship partly constituted by an attitude we might call toleration" (2017, 94). Davis draws upon Samuel Scheffler, who identified a potential problem in toleration, the paradox of suppressed disapproval: "if one does not share some set of values, what reason could there be to accommodate them, or lend them authority in one's life?" (Davis 2017, 93). Another way of describing this paradox is: "[I]f there are good reasons for tolerating [something], these reasons will also tend to undermine one's objection to the thing being tolerated" (Davis 2017, 97). This seems to indicate that toleration is irrational behavior.

Davis provides two responses to this paradox: the diversity and autonomy accounts of toleration. He wrote that the diversity account states that "[i]t is sometimes rational to defer to a value to which one objects, because doing so can make possible significant goods associated with life in a diverse society, and these goods can justify the cost incurred by toleration" (2017, 93). The autonomy account says that "[i]t is sometimes rational to defer to a value to which one objects, because the goods associated with another agent's minimally autonomous pursuit of this value justifies the cost incurred by toleration" (Davis 2017, 93). Deferring to a value can mean not interfering with those who hold that value, or it can mean the more positive toleration of "engaging in actions or adopting attitudes that appreciate or promote the value" (Davis 2017, 94).

If we want to live in a society with diverse values, Davis argued, "a society that includes some values we disapprove of. . ., then we have reason to support the maintenance and continuity of values we disapprove of," which may seem puzzling (2017, 99). But Davis says that these attitudes are coherent, explaining that "[t]here can be reasons for tolerating a practice that do not count as reasons for endorsing the practice" (2017, 100).

The diversity account is said to be justified by three versions: pluralist, relationship, and fraternity (Davis 2017). Davis tests these versions of the diversity account and finds that these versions are inadequate in defending the value of diversity as morally good. "In many cases, political disagreement supervenes on moral disagreement. When citizens oppose the political projects of others, this is frequently because they judge that there are moral reasons against those projects" (Davis 2017, 109). Davis wrote that "moralized conflicts tend to undermine opportunities for deference to the values of others" (2017, 109). The diversity account "might recommend a spirit of toleration appealing to those citizens who already find toleration appealing, but one that will stoke latent antagonisms in exactly those citizens it seeks to persuade," Davis asserted (2017, 110). In other words, the diversity account appeals to those who already value diversity, but it cannot effectively persuade other people to accept diversity.

The autonomy account, Davis explained, is where "I might regard it as good that others pursue values of their own choosing, even if I do not regard the values they choose as correct" (2017, 110). He argued that "treating autonomy as the motivating value for toleration can avoid the paradox of suppressed disagreement" (2017, 110). The key is that "the autonomy account takes no stand on whether normative diversity is desirable" (Davis 2017, 110). Thus, "your choice, or exercise of autonomy, is both a response to the balance of reasons that you face and a transformation of the balance of reasons that you face. This is why I can advise you to do one thing, but sincerely support your decision not to take my advice" (Davis 2017, 111). Toleration, according to Davis, involves mutually seeing each other's control over their choices in life as good, which allows to people "to maintain a social world" (2017, 112). Davis defines moralism as when one's "moral thinking is more rigid" (2017, 112). Moralistic people are concerned about having to share values with "their cultural antagonists," but Davis argues that the autonomy account of tolerance can alleviate these concerns (2017, 113). Davis concludes that "[a]ppealing as the value of diversity is, the aim of this article has been to suggest that it cannot provide a general basis for mutually valuable relationships of toleration" (2017, 113). The value of diversity is a moralism, he thinks, in that it takes morality too far.

Summary and Future Directions

We have reviewed a number of ways in which theories of toleration can be accused of moralism, and also a number of scholars who have in effect or explicitly accused other theories of moralism. Judgments about moralism will depend in part on the observer's perspective. If toleration is understood as it often has been in history, as a minimalist mode of putting up with objectionable ideas, practices, or people, then any theory that tries to make the concept do something more positive may be interpreted as moralistic. If toleration is much more than that, overlapping with respect and good will, then demands for such respect and appreciation of the tolerated may seem excessively moralistic to those who do not want to commit themselves to more than putting up with something or someone. And if toleration is absorbed into a constellation of values such as respect and approval, we will probably need another term to describe the bare putting up with of the traditional meaning of toleration.

References

Aristotle (1971) The Nicomachean Ethics of Aristotle (trans: David Ross). Oxford University Press, London

Balint P (2017) Respecting toleration: traditional liberalism & contemporary diversity. Oxford University Press, Oxford

Coady CAJ (2005) Preface. J Appl Philos 22:101–104

Davis RW (2017) Autonomy and toleration as a moral attitude. J Soc Philos 48:92–116

Estlund D (2014) Utopophobia. Philos Public Aff, 42:113–134

Estlund D (2017) Methodological moralism in political philosophy. Crit Rev Int Soc Pol Phil 20:385–402

Frazer M (2019) Utopohobia as a vocation: the professional ethics of ideal and nonideal political theory. Soc Philos Policy 33:175–192

Fullinwider RK (2005) On moralism. J Appl Philos 22:105–120

Galeotti AE (2004) Toleration as recognition. Cambridge University Press, New York

Gaus G (2016) The tyranny of the ideal: justice in a diverse society. Princeton University Press, Princeton

Godfrey-Smith P, Kerr B (2019) Tolerance: a hierarchical analysis. J Polit Philos 27:403–421

Laursen JC (2013) Michael Oakeshott, Wendy Brown, and the paradoxes of anti-moralism. Ágora 32:67–80

Laursen JC, Morales V (2020) Relativism and moralism. In: Kusch M (ed) Routledge handbook to the philosophy of relativism. Routledge, London, pp 174–181

Marcuse H (1965) Repressive tolerance. In: A critique of pure tolerance. Beacon Press, Boston

Oakeshott M (1991) Rationalism in politics and other essays. Liberty Fund, Indianapolis

Román R, Laursen JC (2016) Santayana's critique of moralism. Limbo 36:5–39

Sabl A (2017) Realist liberalism: an agenda. Crit Rev Int Soc Pol Phil 20:366–384

Satkunanandan S (2015) Extraordinary responsibility. Politics beyond the moral calculus. Cambridge University Press, Cambridge

Sher G (2018) A wild west of the mind. Australas J Philos 97:483–496

Stemplowska Z, Swift A (2012) Ideal and nonideal theory. In: Estlund D (ed) The Oxford handbook of political philosophy. Oxford University Press, Oxford

Tate JW (2016) Free speech, toleration and equal respect: the Bolt affair in context. Aust J Polit Sci 51:34–50

Walzer M (1997) On toleration. Yale University Press, New Haven

Williams B (2005) In the beginning was the deed: realism and moralism in political argument. Princeton University Press, Princeton

Toleration and Neutrality

17

Peter Jones

Contents

Introduction	300
John Rawls and the Idea of State Neutrality	302
Neutrality and Toleration	304
Types of Neutrality	307
Neutrality and Distributive Justice	308
Neutrality and Public Policy	310
Balint and Patten on Neutrality	312
Justifying Neutrality	314
The Limits of Neutrality	317
Summary and Future Directions	319
References	322

Abstract

In liberal thinking, a neutral state is one that takes no position on the ends its citizens should pursue in their lives. It establishes the ground rules within which they are to live but refrains from steering them either toward or away from any conception of the good life. The idea that toleration requires the state to remain neutral on differences of religion is widely accepted. Recent liberal thinking has sought to generalize that idea: a society should not use political power of any sort either to favor or disfavor a particular conception of the good life, be it religious or nonreligious. The idea of the neutral state is therefore an attempt to realize political toleration in a thorough-going fashion. This chapter locates neutralist thinking in the work of contemporary liberal philosophers, particularly that of John Rawls. It examines how the ideas of toleration and neutrality are related and how the toleration secured by a neutral state differs from that exhibited by the pre-democratic regimes of earlier ages. It explains different ways in which state

---

P. Jones (✉)
Newcastle University, Newcastle upon Tyne, UK
e-mail: peter.jones@ncl.ac.uk

© The Author(s), under exclusive licence to Springer Nature Switzerland AG 2022
M. Sardoĉ (ed.), *The Palgrave Handbook of Toleration*,
https://doi.org/10.1007/978-3-030-42121-2_7

299

neutrality can be understood and how different understandings of neutrality bear on issues of distributive justice and public policy. It then turns to the question of how state neutrality might be justified. Finally, it considers how extensive the liberal state's neutrality might be and whether there can be a rapprochement between neutralism and its opposite, perfectionism (the belief that the state should be guided by a conception of the good).

Keywords

Comprehensive doctrine · Conception of the good · Justice · Liberalism · Neutralism · Neutrality · Perfectionism · Political neutrality · Rawls · State neutrality · Toleration

---

Introduction

In liberal political philosophy, a neutral state is one that remains neutral with respect to the ends its citizens should pursue in their lives. It establishes the ground rules within which citizens are to live but allows them to decide for themselves what sort of lives they will lead within those rules.

Most contemporary societies are "plural" in that their populations possess different and conflicting conceptions of what a good life is. Neutralism is a response to that social fact. It is a position most favored by "deontological" or "political" liberals, who distinguish between "the right" and "the good." The state should not, they believe, become a party to disputes about the nature of the good life or use its power either to compel or to cajole citizens into pursuing a particular form of life. Its proper concern is with the right rather than the good: it should establish and maintain a just framework of rules and arrangements within which its citizens are to live but leave them free to pursue, within that framework, whatever sorts of life they reckon to be good. The neutral state, so understood, is usually contrasted with the "perfectionist" state – a state that is committed to and strives to realize a particular conception of the good life.

The liberal idea of the neutral state is often conceived as an attempt to develop and expand the idea of religious toleration (e.g., Arneson 1990a, 216; Rawls 1993, 9–10, 154). Differences of religious belief are paradigm instances of the differences upon which a neutral state should remain neutral, but the liberal neutralist believes the state should be similarly neutral with respect to nonreligious doctrines, philosophical or moral, that prescribe how people should live. Nor need its neutralism be limited to doctrinal differences. It can also encompass the more mundane wishes that shape people's lives. The citizens of a plural society are free to judge the merit of one another's lives, and they may have good reason for judging as they do, but state neutrality debars them from using political power either to suppress or discourage forms of life of which they disapprove or to promote the forms of life they favor. Neutralism therefore seeks to extend the idea of toleration from the historically dominant case of religion to the many different forms of life that people may opt to live and the many different reasons that they may have for living in a particular way.

How then should we formulate what the neutral state is neutral about? The standard answer is as "conceptions of the good" or "conceptions of the good life." That is the answer of John Rawls, with whom neutralism is most associated. He describes a conception of the good as "an ordered family of final ends and aims which specifies a person's conception of what is of value in human life, or alternatively, of what is regarded as a fully worthwhile life" (2001, 19). Thus, he takes seriously the "conception" in "conceptions of the good" and models them as views grounded in religious, philosophical, or moral doctrines. Frequently, however, the phrase is used more generously so that it includes less cerebral notions of the good life. The liberal neutralist, Ronald Dworkin (1986, 191), famously observed that "the scholar who values a life of contemplation has such a conception; so does the television-watching, beer-drinking citizen who is fond of saying 'This is the life', though he has thought less about the issue and is less able to defend his conception." Another term sometimes used is "preference." In the context of liberal neutrality, that term has a more generous sense than in ordinary language so that it encompasses all forms of positive valuing, including religious and ethical commitments as well as simple desire-based preferences.

Since "conception of the good" is the most commonly used term, it will be used here. As already indicated, it is an umbrella term which, as well as including what it literally describes, might include tastes and desires that incorporate little by way of "conceptions" and broad-ranging ways of life grounded in societal cultures or comprehensive systems of belief, such as religions, which for their adherents prescribe the right way as well as the good way to live. The critical consideration is that each individual has a preferred form of life which he or she wishes to live and, in the eyes of the neutral state, each preferred form, whether it manifests a mere desire or a complex set of beliefs, matters, and matters equally as the form preferred by a citizen of equal status.

Two other features of liberal neutrality are worth stressing at the outset. First, insofar as the state's neutrality is conceived as a requirement of fairness, that fairness is owed not to conceptions of the good but to the individuals who possess them. For the neutralist, a state in remaining neutral between different conceptions of the good treats fairly those whose conceptions they are.

Second, liberal neutrality is a *political* principle. It restricts the use that can be legitimately made of political power. It does not require individuals to be neutral with respect to conceptions of the good in their ordinary lives, either singly or in association with others. It would be absurd if it did. More particularly, within liberal neutralism, the priority of the right over the good is a principle of political morality rather than of morality in general. Liberal neutrality in its full form does, however, apply to ordinary citizens insofar as they exercise political power, for example, as voters or political campaigners. A fully neutral society would refrain from using political power of any sort, whether by politicians, state officials, or ordinary citizens, to favor or disfavor any particular conception of the good.

The liberal idea of neutrality is, then, an idea of how the ideal of toleration should be realized in the political domain. The association of religious toleration with political neutrality is not new. Locke asserted a version of it in his *Letter on Toleration*, first published in 1689, and the US Constitution of 1789 made it a political reality in providing that "Congress shall make no law respecting an establishment of religion, or prohibiting the free exercise thereof." But the more wide-ranging liberal idea of political neutrality is historically recent. It has its origins in Rawls's *A Theory of Justice* (1971). The term "neutral state" does not appear in that text, though it does in Rawls's subsequent writings, but the idea of political neutrality was clearly present in his theory of a just society.

Section "John Rawls and the Idea of State Neutrality" briefly sketches Rawls's thinking to indicate how and why he thought a just state would remain neutral among conceptions of the good. Section "Neutrality and Toleration" turns to the question of what precisely the relationship between toleration and political neutrality is and considers why some commentators reckon neutrality to be not only different from, but also incompatible with, toleration. Section "Types of Neutrality" examines different ways of understanding neutrality and the different demands they make. Section "Justifying Neutrality" reviews a variety of justifications that have been given for the neutral state. Section "The Limits of Neutrality" considers how far the state's neutrality should extend, and section "Summary and Future Directions" discusses the possibility of a rapprochement between neutralism and perfectionism.

John Rawls and the Idea of State Neutrality

The aim of Rawls's *Theory of Justice* was to set out arrangements that would provide justly for a society whose citizens possessed different and conflicting conceptions of the good. The neutralist nature of his endeavor was apparent in the thought experiment he used to work out what those arrangements should be. Citizens, or their representatives, were placed in an "original position" in which they had to agree upon the principles that would structure the society in which they were to live. But they had to reach agreement behind a "veil of ignorance." That "veil" deprived them of information about themselves that might otherwise lead them to favor their own interests and disfavor the interests of others. In other words, it obliged them to decide impartially because it rendered them ignorant of information about themselves they would need if they were to be partial. They did not know whether they would turn out to be rich or poor, more or less talented, male or female, black or white, and so on. They were also ignorant of their conceptions of the good. That ignorance ensured that they would not select principles that favored their own conception or disfavored the different conceptions of others. If they opted to favor some conceptions over others, their own conception might turn out to be among the disfavored set, and that was a possibility, Rawls assumed, they would not risk.

Rawls's theory of justice was distributive. It aimed to distribute freedoms and resources fairly among citizens whatever their conceptions of the good. That meant that the goods his theory distributed had themselves to be neutral with respect to conceptions of the good. Rawls characterized those neutral goods as "primary goods." Primary goods were all-purpose means that enabled citizens to pursue their conceptions of the good whatever those happened to be. They included rights and liberties, opportunities and powers, income and wealth, and the social bases of self-respect. Thus, in the original position, individuals had to agree on principles governing how primary goods should be distributed among themselves. Two basic principles of justice, Rawls argued, would emerge (1971, 302–303). First, each citizen would have an equal right to the most extensive total system of equal basic liberties compatible with a similar system of liberty for all. Second, social and economic inequalities would be arranged so that they were (a) to the greatest benefit of the least advantaged and (b) attached to offices and positions open to all under conditions of fair equality of opportunity. His theory also provided that the first principle should take priority over the second, so that liberty could be restricted only for the sake of liberty, and that the second part of the second principle (fair opportunity) should take priority over the first part (the "difference" principle). Those principles set the just terms upon which people would be able to pursue their conceptions of the good.

Rawls's theory of justice is about much more than state neutrality, and much of its substance is inessential to that idea. Other theorists have used other thought experiments to work out just arrangements of which state neutrality should be a part and have taken different views of what those arrangements should be (e.g., Ackerman 1980; Dworkin 2000). It is difficult to imagine a liberal theory of state neutrality that was not committed to something like Rawls's first principle of justice, but state neutrality could be and has been a part of theories of socioeconomic justice quite different from that incorporated in Rawls's second principle (e.g., Nozick 1974). Rawls's *Theory of Justice* is therefore but one example, if the most influential example, of a theory of justice that has incorporated the idea of state neutrality.

Rawls subsequently became dissatisfied with his theory as he had presented it in *Theory of Justice* for reasons directly related to neutrality. The conceptions of the good that most preoccupied him, and for which he aimed to provide, were conceptions grounded in "comprehensive doctrines." He used that term to describe religious, philosophical, or moral doctrines that presented accounts of what was of value in human life generally and of how it should be lived. A doctrine might be "partially comprehensive" in that it did not address every aspect of human life, but it remained "comprehensive" in character insofar as it addressed human living in general rather than only political life in particular.

Rawls came to think that his theory as presented in *Theory of Justice* was unsatisfactory because it was itself "comprehensive" in character. It therefore stood alongside and rivaled other comprehensive doctrines to which citizens were committed and from which they would draw their conceptions of the goods. He therefore recast the foundations of his theory (his thinking on the content of justice remained largely unchanged) so that it assumed a specifically "political" character.

His revised theory was "political" in that it was not an offshoot of a more general moral theory, such as Kantianism or utilitarianism, but a theory of justice designed solely for a society's "basic structure" – its main political, economic, and social institutions. It remained a moral theory but one addressed only to that subject. Instead of finding its foundations in a comprehensive doctrine, it drew on certain fundamental ideas "implicit in the public political culture of a democratic society" (1993, 13), particularly the ideas of society conceived as a fair system of cooperation and of citizens conceived as free and equal persons. Most significantly, it was "political" in that it was "freestanding." Its foundations and content "stood free" from comprehensive doctrines and their associated conceptions of the good and free therefore from the conflicts and controversies in which they were embroiled.

In shifting to a specifically "political" conception of justice, Rawls made neutrality a much more imposing feature of his theory. His theory became even more conspicuously one that removed comprehensive doctrines and conceptions of the good from the foundations and jurisdiction of political institutions and which concerned itself instead with what constituted just political arrangements for citizens of equal status who were wedded to different and conflicting conceptions of the good.

Two further features of Rawls's thinking are worth noting. First, he distinguished the "fact" of pluralism as a mere state of affairs from "reasonable" pluralism. It was the reasonableness of pluralism rather than its mere existence that made it an appropriate subject for justice. The plurality of doctrines and conceptions that characterized modern liberal societies should be seen not as unfortunate but as "the inevitable long-run result of the powers of human reason at work within the background of enduring free institution" (1993, 4, 36–37). That is why it should be provided for justly rather than merely managed.

Second, the reasonableness of pluralism did not make it other than something that called for toleration. Disagreement among citizens might be reasonable, but each citizen, as the bearer of a particular comprehensive doctrine, still had reason to regard the conflicting doctrines of others and their associated ways of life as misconceived and unfortunate. Hence, each still had reason to regard as "tolerant" political arrangements that required all citizens to respect others' freedom to embrace whatever comprehensive doctrine they saw fit and to live whatever form of life it prescribed.

Neutrality and Toleration

How are toleration and neutrality related? In examining that question, I shall, for the moment, use a simple and traditional definition of toleration. We tolerate x when we (a) disapprove of or dislike x and (b) possess the power to impede x if we choose but (c) refrain from impeding, or trying to impede, x in spite of (a) and (b).

Toleration so understood need not be associated with neutrality, including when it is shown by those who wield political power. Typically, it was not in the case of religiously tolerant monarchs of the sixteenth- and seventeenth-century Europe. Those monarchs embraced a particular version of Christianity and made that version the official religion of their realm. They were not religiously neutral even though they might tolerate the practice of faiths other than their own. Moreover, their toleration was an act of grace; they tolerated what they had no obligation to. In addition, the freedom of religion they extended to their dissenting subjects was often far more limited than that enjoyed by those who subscribed to the ruler's officially approved faith. Thus, religious toleration during the early modern era, and for long afterward, was a one-sided affair. Nothing in the traditional idea of toleration required that it should be otherwise.

If toleration need not be associated with neutrality, must neutrality be associated with toleration? Not necessarily. Toleration, as defined above, must be toleration of something that the tolerator appraises negatively; otherwise, he or she has nothing to tolerate. But the differences to which a state responds neutrally might be entirely free of negative appraisal. The members of a population may, for example, possess different likes and dislikes and be entirely indifferent to the fact that others' tastes differ from their own. In that case, their differences will make no call upon their toleration. Yet each may still press for his or her desires to be satisfied which may, in turn, generate competing demands for limited resources. In that event, it can still be right that a state should respond neutrally to competing demands for desire-satisfaction: it should neither favor nor disfavor the desires of any particular individual or desires of any particular sort. Not every instance of state neutrality need therefore be an exercise in toleration.

Toleration and neutrality are not then coextensive, and neither wholly subsumes the other. Some commentators go further and deny that the two share anything in common. They make a simple analytical point. Negative appraisal is a defining feature of toleration. But a state's neutrality consists not merely in its not impeding conceptions of the good of which it disapproves. It consists in its not making any appraisal, negative or positive, of the conceptions to which its citizens adhere. But a state that does not appraise negatively is a state that cannot tolerate. Hence, neutrality precludes toleration (e.g., Churchill 2003, 72; Horton 1996, 36; Meckled-Garcia 2003; Newey 1999, 123–124, 128–130).

That summary dismissal mistakes the relationship between neutrality and toleration as liberal thinkers such as Rawls conceive it. For them toleration is the parent, not the child, of neutrality. It is a commitment to toleration that makes the case for state neutrality. Rawls's model citizens commit to mutual toleration as an essential component of a fair system of cooperation among free and equal citizens. They tolerate in resolving not to use *any* of the instruments of political power either to promote their own conception of the good or to disadvantage the different conceptions of others. Thus, so far from sidelining or displacing toleration, the neutrality of Rawls's state manifests a peculiarly strong and thorough-going commitment to it (Jones 2018, 43–59).

The idea of the neutral state does, however, require political toleration to be conceived rather differently from its past instantiations. We must, in particular, set aside the model of the early modern monarch. His or her toleration was "vertical" in nature. The toleration secured by the neutral state is "horizontal." It is toleration among citizens. It is important, therefore, not to think of the neutrality of the neutral state as the neutrality of a government that stands over, above, and apart from its population. Typically, the democracy of the neutral state will, of course, be indirect, even if not exclusively so, and the majority of day-to-day decisions will be made by officeholders who will be bound by the same rules of neutrality as ordinary citizens. But those officeholders will act on behalf of citizens. The liberal state is fundamentally a state of its citizens, and the toleration secured by its neutrality is toleration among its citizens.

That is not to say that political toleration in a democratic society must be horizontal in form. An elected government may assume the role of master and tolerate those it governs, even though that inverts the democratic idea that a government should stand to its people as servant to master. More simply, a majority, or a government acting on its behalf, might tolerate a minority in the same spirit of condescension as an early modern monarch. In that case, its toleration will be no less vertical for being democratic. Majoritarian toleration of that sort clearly differs from the even-handed toleration of liberal neutralism.

That neutralism departs from toleration, as commonly conceived, in another respect. Typically, we think of toleration as something that one person or party extends to another. Thus, it might be extended by a monarch to his dissenting subjects, or by a majority to a minority, or by individuals to one another. In the case of the neutral state, however, toleration resides primarily in the character of its rules and arrangements rather than in acts of toleration that citizens perform to one another. Its laws and institutions establish an order of things that enable citizens to live their lives as they see fit, unimpeded by disapproving others. Its toleration therefore resides in the political condition it establishes rather than in tolerant acts that citizens gift to one another.

That, in turn, raises a question about how we should conceive toleration in liberal-democratic circumstances. We might follow Rawls in modeling a tolerant society as one in which prospective citizens embrace the principle of toleration, embed it in the institutions they create, and honor it in the lives they go on to lead. But consider the individual who is a citizen of an already-existing neutral state. She finds herself subject to laws and institutions she has had no hand in constructing which require her not to impede conceptions of the good with which she disagrees. If she complies with them, does she tolerate? Not, it would seem, according to the traditional definition cited above, since that definition stipulates that she tolerates only if she has the power to do otherwise. Yet there is something odd about that power condition. It implies that toleration is possible in a society only as long as its citizens remain at the mercy of one another's intolerance. If the society puts in place measures designed to safeguard its citizens from one another's intolerance, it eliminates toleration.

How can we resist that bizarre implication? We might insist that a liberal regime *can* satisfy the power condition: rather than rendering citizens incapable of doing what it prohibits, it assigns them a legal obligation not to do what they remain capable of doing. But that claim remains tied to the person-to-person model and may fail to convince. A more compelling answer lies in what matters about toleration. The important thing about a tolerant liberal-democratic regime is not that it should afford its citizens opportunities to perform acts of toleration but that it should protect them from one another's potential intolerance. It is in that form that a neutral state secures toleration. (See further Jones 2018, 17–26, 61–68.)

Finally, some commentators allege that toleration and neutrality cannot be conjoined because they belong to different moralities. The neutral state figures most commonly in theories of justice (although it does not have to). Toleration, by contrast, is sometimes said to be supererogatory (e.g., Benbaji and Heyd 2001; Heyd 2008; Newey 1999). Supererogatory acts are good to do but not wrong not to do or, conversely, good not to do but not wrong to do. They exceed the demands of duty. Acts of mercy, generosity, and charity are classic examples. They would not be the kinds of acts they are if they did not exceed the demands of duty. In like manner, if toleration is supererogatory, it will belong to a moral realm quite different from that inhabited by duties, rights, and justice.

Why might we think it does? The answer seems to lie in an elision of moral liberty with power conceived as a possibility-condition of toleration. As we have just seen, the power condition holds that we tolerate only if we have power to do otherwise. We might hold similarly that we tolerate only if we are morally at liberty to do otherwise. If we have a moral duty not to impede, we have no moral option but to refrain from impeding, and because we have no other option, we cannot be said to "tolerate" when we do not impede. Thus, duty preempts toleration; toleration can be toleration only if it is supererogatory.

The supererogatory view obviously presupposes a person-to-person model of toleration. It maps onto the toleration of the early modern monarch but not onto that of a liberal-democratic political order. That is why its proponents reckon toleration to be of only minor significance for contemporary liberal-democratic politics. Opponents of the supererogatory view might object that conceptualizing toleration so that it has no relevance for contemporary liberal democracies, the plurality of whose populations evidently makes political toleration both possible and desirable, is unnecessarily perverse. The supererogatory view implies that if there is compelling moral reason for toleration and if that compelling reason generates a duty, its being a duty must transform it into something other than a duty of toleration. That too might seem perverse. Nowadays, it has become the norm rather than the exception to couch issues of political toleration in the language of duty, rights, and justice, and liberal neutralists, such as Rawls, have done their best to vindicate that norm.

Types of Neutrality

What is it for a society's public rules and arrangements to be neutral, or to function neutrally, with respect to different conception of the goods? For Alan Montefiore (1975, 5), to be neutral is "to do one's best to help or hinder the various parties concerned in an equal degree." That definition implies that a society deals neutrally with its citizens' conceptions of the good only if it helps or hinders their pursuit in equal measure. Neutrality so understood is usually described as neutrality of effect (or consequence or outcome). A quite different view holds that a society's rules and arrangements are neutral provided only that they are not grounded in any particular conception of the good or not designed to help or hinder any particular conception. On this view, a society's arrangements may impact differently upon different conceptions, but provided those arrangements are genuinely neutral in foundation or purpose, they can still claim to be neutral. Neutrality so understood is usually labeled either neutrality of justification (or ground) or neutrality of aim (or intention).

These rival understandings of neutrality relate to two aspects of the liberal state: its underlying conception of distributive justice and the character of its public policies. Each of those needs separate consideration.

Neutrality and Distributive Justice

Suppose a society has to distribute means among its population, the sort of means that Rawls describes as "primary goods": rights and liberties, opportunities and powers, income and wealth. Let's describe those as "resources." How should those resources be distributed? Should they be distributed without reference to individuals' different ends, or should the distribution take account of the different demands of different individuals' ends? Suppose, for example, that some individuals have more costly ambitions than others. Should they receive the same resources as others, or should they receive more so that they can fulfill their ambitions to the same degree as others? Or suppose that, with one exception, two faiths make similar demands upon their followers. The exception is that one faith requires its followers to undertake a pilgrimage (which for most of them entails travelling to a foreign land); the other does not. Should the two groups of followers receive the same resources, or should one receive more than the other to compensate for its having to undertake a pilgrimage?

The competing conceptions of distributive justice implicit in these questions are commonly labeled "resourcism" and "welfarism." For simplicity's sake, let's suppose that a just distribution would be an equal distribution. The question is then: what is it that we should distribute equally? Is it resources themselves or the welfare that people derive from them? Resourcists answer the first and welfarists the second. Resourcism is associated with neutrality of justification or aim and welfarism with neutrality of effect, but those labels provide little indication of the competing forms of neutrality at issue in distributive justice.

Liberal neutralists, such as Rawls (1971, 1993) and Dworkin (2000), are resourcists. Why? Principally because they hold that individuals should take responsibility for their ends. Individuals are at liberty to embrace whatever ends – whatever conceptions of the good – they deem fit, but they must take responsibility for the ends they embrace. They are entitled to their fair share of resources, but none is entitled to more than others just because they have more expensive or more demanding conceptions of the good. If those with modest ends received less so that those with more extravagant ends could receive more, that would be unfair. That is why a just distribution would take no account of the different demands of different conceptions of the good. Indeed, ideally a distribution of resources should precede citizens' adoption of ends, so that, in deciding upon ends, citizens can take account of the resources justly available for their pursuit.

The main objection brought against resourcism is that identical resources can be of different value to different people. If two individuals receive the same quantum of resources but one is physically handicapped and the other not, their identical resources will not translate into identical levels of welfare. Physical handicap is a special case, but it conveys graphically the more general point that those with different preferences, commitments, and makeups are likely to derive different amounts of value from a given quantum of resources. Thus, welfarists conclude that the distribuend of distributive justice should be not resources themselves but the relative welfare people gain from them.

What is "welfare"? We might understand it in a standard utilitarian sense. If we do, we shall run into the objection that we have abandoned neutrality, since we have adopted a controversial conception of the good – the conception that utility, understood in something like its Benthamite sense, is the ultimate good which subsumes everything else we have reason to deem good. If we are to avoid that objection, we must understand "welfare" in a less sectarian and more portmanteau sense. We might, for example, interpret "welfare" as an individual's success in attaining whatever good that individual reckons his or her good to be. We can then characterize equal welfare as "equal fulfillment": individuals achieve equal fulfillment when they realize in equal measure the good, as they themselves understand it (religious, hedonic, aesthetic, self-abnegating, etc.).

Equal fulfillment so understood encounters a formidable array of difficulties. (For an extended critique, see Dworkin 2000, 11–64.) Can there be a metric that measures degrees of fulfillment across qualitatively different conceptions of the good? Suppose some individuals willfully set challenging goals for themselves which they have little chance of attaining, while others opt for more attainable goals because they are more attainable; how then should we interpret "equal" fulfillment? The goods that individuals reckon to be constituents of a good life are likely to be various and incommensurable rather than singular; how are we to assess each individual's aggregate quantum of fulfillment? Are individuals to be equally fulfilled at every moment or only over the course of their lives as a whole, and, if the latter, how is that an outcome we can contrive? We can also question, with the resourcists, whether we should to take seriously aims and aspirations that people adopt with no regard for their impact upon the resources available to others.

Welfarism can, however, be modified to take account of personal responsibility and to present a more serious challenge to resourcism. Richard Arneson (1989, 1990a, b), for example, has argued that the goal of distributive justice should be equal *opportunity* for welfare rather than equal welfare as such. Insofar as people's different welfare levels are consequences of their own choices, justice does not require they be equalized. But, insofar as their different welfare levels result from unchosen circumstances, including unchosen preferences and what is needed to satisfy them, ideally they would be equalized. Arneson understands "welfare" as preference-satisfaction, but he equates "preference-satisfaction" with "fulfillment" as described above. Hence, he describes his position as "distributive subjectivism" (1990b, 159) (a position he abandoned for perfectionism in his later work).

G. A. Cohen (1989) argued similarly that distributive justice should aim for "equal access to advantage," which requires eliminating the effects of involuntary disadvantage. People have no claim in justice to be compensated for disadvantages resulting from their choices, but the division between the chosen and the unchosen does not coincide with that between preferences and circumstances. Insofar as people are relatively disadvantaged by their unchosen preferences and the costs of satisfying them, justice dictates they should receive whatever resources are necessary to remove that disadvantage.

Arneson's and Cohen's modified welfarism confronts many of the practical difficulties that afflict the idea of equal fulfillment, as they concede. Even so, the possibility that people's ends and the costliness of realizing them can be consequences of chance rather than choice presents a significant "in principle" challenge to resourcism. That issue is, however, far from simple. The critical question concerns what we may reasonably hold people responsible for, consequentially if not causally, and the simple idea of choice is not equal to the complexities of that question (cf. Cohen 2004; Dworkin 2000, 285–303, and 2004, 339–350; Rawls 1993, 185–190; Scanlon 1986, 2006).

The debate between resourcists and welfarists has been conducted mainly with reference to "tastes" and the relative expense of satisfying them. Traditionally, toleration has been more concerned with beliefs and the demands they make of their holders. Switching from tastes to beliefs may be thought immaterial (cf. Arneson 1989, 80–81; Cohen 1989, 935–939), but that switch does indicate how the debate turns on more than "choice" ordinarily understood. Believers may reasonably insist that they do not choose their beliefs; they can believe only what seems to them to be the case. Holding or coming to hold a religious belief is usually, for example, quite unlike choosing a career or a holiday destination. Yet, it is still reasonable to hold religious believers responsible for believing what they do and to resist demands that they should receive more resources than others so that they can meet their religious obligations and ideals. Even if they were socialized into their faith as children, they can be held responsible for persisting with it as adults. Thus, even if unchosen tastes prove troublesome for resourcism, conceptions of the good grounded in Rawls's "comprehensive doctrines" need not (see further Jones 2020, Chaps. 5 and 6).

Neutrality and Public Policy

Societies do not use their public power only to distribute primary goods. They pursue a myriad of other policies, and it is with respect to those policies that the terms "neutrality of justification," "neutrality of aim," and "neutrality of effect" are more readily intelligible.

Neutrality of justification deems a law or policy neutral provided that its justification is independent of any particular conception of the good. The test of neutral justification can be either subjective or objective. It is subjective if it concerns the considerations that motivate the policy's sponsors. It is objective if it concerns whether the policy can be justified neutrally. If we are assessing a policy's acceptability, the objective test would seem more pertinent: it is the policy itself that matters rather than the motives of those who sponsor it. On the other hand, it can also matter that a government's commitment to neutrality should be genuine rather than feigned. It is all too easy for a government to claim neutral justification when its real purpose lies elsewhere. A government may, for example, justify a ban on the public wearing of religious face coverings by appealing to the threat they pose to public security. That appeal may express the government's real concern, but it may also be a ruse that hides a different motive, such as its hostility to a minority's religion or its desire to appease public hostility to that minority.

We might therefore insist that a government's policy should be neutral in aim rather than in justification. Neutrality of justification and neutrality of aim are frequently conflated, but they can be prized apart. A policy may be neutral in justification but not in aim. A government may, for example, aim to achieve more widespread devotion to its society's dominant religion, not because it believes that religion to be true but only because it believes that greater religious uniformity will make for greater civic unity (cf. Arneson 1990a, 218–219; Patten 2014, 110–111, 113). Similarly, a policy may be neutral in aim but not in justification. A government might, for example, aim to maximize and equalize its citizen's freedom of religion, not because it is committed to neutrality but because it wishes to promote individual autonomy as a perfectionist ideal. However, those who commit to neutrality of justification or neutrality of aim generally intend to commit to both; they understand a neutral policy to be one that is neither grounded in a particular conception of the good nor designed to help or hinder any such conception. Henceforth, I shall use the term "neutrality of justification" to include neutrality of aim.

Neutrality of effect deems a law or policy neutral only if it helps or hinders the pursuit of conceptions of the good in equal measure. In liberal thinking, neutrality of that sort is usually posited only to be rejected. (For a qualified defense of neutrality of effect, see Wall 2001.) It encounters the same difficulties as the ideas of equal welfare and equal fulfillment. We may hold the state responsible for equalizing only the effects of its own measures, rather than every circumstance that affects individuals' ability to realize their conceptions, but that will not remove those difficulties. Moreover, if public policies can be adopted only if they affect either no conception of the good or all conceptions equally, few will survive. Neutrality of effect also promises to stimulate rather than sidestep conflicts over the merits of different conceptions of the good since, no matter how beneficial a policy, neutrality of effect allows it to be vetoed by those whose conceptions it inconveniences.

Liberal neutrality most commonly, therefore, takes the form of neutrality of justification. But is that the only sort of justification the liberal should demand? If a policy is capable of neutral justification, should that justification routinely trump any negative impact the policy has, no matter how great, upon people's ability to live their preferred way of life? That would be difficult to defend. A policy can be justified pro tanto without being justified all things considered. Neutral justification may be necessary if a policy is to be justified at all, but that justification may not suffice all things considered. Arguably, then, the complete assessment of a policy should take some account of its impact upon the ways of life of those it affects. That does not entail abandoning neutrality or substituting neutrality of effect for neutrality of justification. It means only that, in assessing the case for a policy, account should be taken of all of its consequences and of how responsibility should be apportioned for them.

A law or policy can avoid disadvantaging a particular good-based practice by excluding the practice from its demands. Thus, turban-wearing Sikhs who work in the construction industry can be exempted from hard-hat laws so that they are not obliged to choose between keeping their jobs and observing their faith. Muslims and Orthodox Jews can be exempted from animal welfare legislation so that they can practice ritual slaughter in accordance with the demands of their faiths. Exemptions of that sort are controversial (see, e.g., Jones 2020; Laborde 2017; Vallier and Weber 2018). Are they consistent with liberal neutrality?

They are insofar as they seek not to privilege the exemptees but only to avoid their being burdened in ways that others are not. Moreover, exemptions, like policies, should be subject to all-things-considered assessment, including the costs they displace onto others. Sometimes (so-called) exemptions are matters of constitutional right, rather than legislative concession. If a constitution recognizes the right of freedom of religion, for example, the issue of exemption can turn on the scope that right has. If a law burdens a religious practice, even though incidentally, a court may deem it unconstitutional. In such cases, exemption relates to the state's architecture rather than only to its piecemeal decision-making.

There is, however, one respect in which the exemptions typically granted in contemporary liberal societies are not neutral. Practices grounded in religious or conscientious belief are commonly candidates for exemption, as sometimes are practices identified as "cultural"; those that are matters of taste or "mere" preference are not. Thus, Sikh motorcyclists who wear turbans are candidates for exemption from safety-helmet legislation, while bikers who enjoy the thrill of riding bareheaded are not. Those who believe that eating meat is religiously or morally wrong, or whose form of dress is "cultural," may be candidates for exemption; those who find eating animals simply repulsive or who dress according to individual taste will not. There may be good reason for treating different *types* of conception of the good differently in that fashion, but whatever that reason is, it has to justify a significant departure from full liberal neutrality. (For different views on that issue, see Balint 2017; Barry 2001; Bou-Habib 2006; Kelly 2002; Laborde 2017; Leiter 2012.)

Balint and Patten on Neutrality

Finally, two recent reinterpretations of liberal neutrality are worthy of note.

For Peter Balint (2017), the neutrality that should guide the tolerant state is neither justificatory neutrality nor neutrality of effect but "neutrality of intent": "a neutral institution or policy should not intend to favor (or hinder) any particular way of life" (56). That may sound like neutrality of aim, but Balint understands it more ambitiously. A neutral state should be "difference-sensitive" rather than "difference-blind": it should endeavor, actively and deliberately, not to advantage or disadvantage any way of life. In particular, with the emergence of ways of life new to a society, arrangements that were once neutral may become non-neutral, in which case they should be amended or replaced so that neutrality is restored. That makes Balint's neutrality of intent more akin to neutrality of effect, but he radically tempers its demands by arguing that it is best secured by government's adopting a "hands-off" approach to diversity. The less a government intervenes in its citizens' lives, the less it will become entangled with and affect unequally their different ways of life.

In arguing for active hands-off neutrality, Balint means to argue for a tolerant society: a society that accommodates as broad a range of ways of life as it reasonably can, so maximizing its citizens' negative freedom to live as they wish. (For a similar view, but without the language of neutrality, see Cohen 2015.) Unlike many neutralists, he conceives state neutrality not as an inviolable principle but as an action-guiding ideal; neutrality cannot and should not be realized fully, since it competes with, and should sometimes yield to, other values. For example, societies increasingly have populations that speak a multiplicity of languages, but the cost and inconvenience of having more than a single language as an official language makes linguistic neutrality unfeasible. Thus, neutrality should function as a pro tanto consideration rather than an absolute requirement, and that also tempers the demands of Balint's neutrality of intent.

Alan Patten (2014) reformulates liberal neutrality, correctly understood as "neutrality of treatment." The policies of a neutral state should be "equally accommodating of rival conceptions of the good" (115). If a state accommodates, or fails to accommodate, a particular conception of the good, it should afford the same degree of assistance, or hindrance, to other conceptions. That may sound like neutrality of effect, but Patten's neutrality relates to inputs rather than outputs. In the argument over "responsibility for ends," he sides with Rawls and Dworkin rather than Arneson and Cohen and so embraces resourcism rather than welfarism (139–48, 161–162). His neutrality of treatment aims to secure fair opportunity for self-determination among a society's citizens, not to realize their conceptions of the good in equal measure. It does, however, apply across the entire range of public policies, and its test of "equal accommodation" is more exacting than the test set by neutrality of justification. (For critical discussion of Patten's neutrality of treatment, see Cordelli 2017; Laborde 2018; Lippert-Rasmussen 2017.)

Patten aims to apply the idea of liberal neutrality to cultural diversity, particularly to societies whose populations are divided between majority and minority cultures. Almost inevitably, minority cultures will find themselves disadvantaged relative to majority cultures. To correct that disadvantage, a society must do more than provide all of its citizens with a uniform set of liberal rights. It must also give cultural minorities special rights, such as language rights, self-government rights, and others' rights needed for their equal recognition. Only then will it accommodate cultures equally and afford them neutral treatment; only then will individuals enjoy fair opportunities for self-determination whatever their culture.

Extending the idea of liberal neutrality from Rawlsian conceptions of the good to societal cultures is challenging. For one thing, it is not easy to maintain the means/end distinction that resourcist neutralism presupposes – a distinction between culture as a resource for the pursuit of conceptions of the good and culture as something that figures in those conceptions. For another, so many different cultures are now present, and unequally present, in the populations of many societies, that the goal of representing them equally in all aspects of a society's public life is hard to justify, normatively as well as practically. Patten recognizes that and so, like Balint, argues that neutrality should function in public policy-making not as an inviolable principle but as a significant pro tanto consideration (28, 106, 111). In addition and unlike Balint, he argues that neutrality should weigh more heavily for some conceptions of the good – those that are "identity-related," such as religious and cultural conceptions – than for others (158–159, 168–169).

Justifying Neutrality

What might justify a commitment to state neutrality, whether as an inviolable principle or a guiding ideal? Political neutrality demands that the state should not deliberately favor or disfavor any particular conception of the good, but it might still be a conception of the good that justifies that demand. If we hold, for example, that a life can be good only if it is lived freely, that provides reason for the state not to compel its citizens to pursue a particular form of life. If we follow Kant in holding that the morally good life is a life that individuals should themselves recognize as good, a coerced form of life will not rank as good. Similarly, if, like J S Mill, we believe that human beings can achieve the highest form of utility of which they are capable only if they can freely pursue their own good in their own way, we again find reason why the state should allow them to do just that. Historically, this sort of good-based argument for states respecting their citizens' freedom has figured prominently in the liberal tradition and still does.

Its drawback is that it remains mired in disputes about the good. Not everyone will accept that the good life has the character that Kant or Mill claims for it. The religious devotee may hold, for example, that the good life consists in submission to the will of God and compliance with the form of life He has prescribed for us. We might insist, with John Locke (1968), that a life lived in conformity with a religious faith will be of no value to God if it does not manifest the sincere belief of those who live it. But that view is itself theologically controversial so that, once again, a good-based justification remains entangled in the very disputes from which neutrality seeks an escape.

That is why liberal neutralists who take the idea of political neutrality most seriously distinguish between the right and the good and justify neutrality by appealing to the right rather than the good. Liberalism, as its name indicates, gives especial value to freedom, but contemporary liberalism gives no less value to equality, understood as the equal moral status of persons and the equal political status of citizens. Persons and citizens, in virtue of their equal status, owe equal

17 Toleration and Neutrality

respect to one another, including respect for one another's capacity to form, revise, and pursue a conception of the good which, in turn, means recognizing their right to exercise that capacity and respecting their freedom to pursue their conception of the good. That freedom is an equal freedom which will be violated if some citizens use political power to promote their conception of the good at the expense of others. The state's neutrality is therefore a requirement of justice. Because that is its justification, it can be embraced by citizens in spite of their different and conflicting conceptions of the good. It does not require citizens to row back from their conceptions or to accept that other's conceptions are of equal value with their own. It requires them to recognize only that other citizens are of equal status with themselves and are entitled to the same freedoms and opportunities to pursue their conceptions of the good whatever those happens to be.

We might question, even so, whether this sort of justification is modest enough. If neutrality aims to stand clear of conflict and controversy, should it not avoid morality altogether? Should we not justify it amorally? We might, for example, conceive political neutrality as no more than a modus vivendi: an arrangement that enables people to live together in peace in spite of their differences (cf. Gray 2000). A modus vivendi will be amoral insofar as it is founded only upon mutual advantage – the interest each individual has in living in peace with others and in enjoying the many goods that peace makes possible. Will then self-interest suffice to justify state neutrality? Fairly obviously, it will not since it will sustain neutrality only so long as the balance of forces in a society makes neutrality everyone's best option. If that balance shifts so that one faction can capture political power and impose its vision of the good upon others, self-interest will provide it with no reason not to (cf. Barry 1995, 31–46).

Another possible amoral foundation for neutrality is skepticism. If disagreement about the good is an enduring feature of contemporary plural societies and if there is no prospect of that disagreement being resolved, we might conclude that no conception of the good can plausibly claim to be true or right. If we do, we can go on to hold that the state should abstain from taking any position on the good because there can be no epistemic justification for its doing otherwise. The fact of disagreement figures importantly in liberal neutralist thinking, as does the idea of reasonable disagreement. Reasonable people will recognize that they can disagree reasonably about the good – a proposition that is more plausible if what makes their disagreement reasonable is its being disagreement among reasonable people rather than disagreement among beliefs each of which is reasonable as a belief. Some neutralists link the reasonableness of disagreement to skepticism. Brian Barry (1995, 168–188) argues "there is no conception of the good that nobody could reasonably reject." Bruce Ackerman (1980, 365–369) cites skepticism as one of "four highways" that can take us to liberal neutrality. Most neutralists, however, abjure skepticism (e.g., Larmore 1996, 126–127, 171–174; Rawls 1993, 58–63), not because they find it mistaken but because it is a controversial philosophical position of the sort they believe neutralism should avoid and because they want a justification that citizens can accept while remaining firmly committed to their conceptions of the good.

Another form of justification that is nonmoral in the first instance appeals to rational dialogue. If people disagree over conceptions of the good, they must find terms of political association on which they can agree in spite of their disagreement. The only instrument through which they can do that is rational dialogue, and we can anticipate that, through dialogue, they will settle upon a political arrangement that remains neutral with respect to their different conceptions. Rational dialogue unaided, however, cannot guarantee that outcome. Why should a stronger party not turn to force and coercively impose its preferred position upon others? We need therefore to explain why the parties *ought* to settle their differences through rational dialogue, and that is why theorists, such as Ackerman (1980) and Larmore (1987, 1996), incorporate the moral norm of equal respect in their dialogical justifications of neutrality.

Unsurprisingly therefore, a satisfactory justification for political neutrality has to be a moral justification. The liberal neutralists' hope is that reasonable people can and will embrace a justification that appeals to the right in spite of their disagreements about the good. It must pass that test if neutral political arrangements are to solve the problem posed by the pluralism of contemporary societies. But liberal neutralists aim for more than mere efficacy. They want a solution that can claim to be just and that can deliver political legitimacy since it can be recognized as just by the citizens whose lives it regulates. "The governing idea is that people should not be subject to state coercion unless there are good reasons for it, reasons that should be convincing to *them*" (Klosko 2003, 168). They can find such reasons only if they are not drawn from conceptions of the good they reject. (See, e.g., Barry 1995, 164–168; Bird 1996; Larmore 1996; Lecce 2003; Nagel 1991, 154–168; Rawls 1993.)

The merit and plausibility of right-based justifications remain matters of dispute among political philosophers, and we should not lose sight of the possibility with which we began this section: that state neutrality might be grounded in a conception of the good. How so? How can a conception of the good argue for anything other than its own promotion by the state? The answer might be pragmatic. Given the limitations of politicians and bureaucrats, pursuit of the good may be best left to individuals and civil society associations. State interventions may be clumsy and inept and do more to hinder than promote good lives.

A more interesting answer is that a conception of the good can be "second-order" in character, such that it can accommodate a variety of "first-order" conceptions (Barry 1995, 129). The obvious example is autonomy. Suppose we hold that a life can be good only if it is autonomously chosen by the person who lives it. That conception leaves unspecified the substantive first-order forms of life that individuals are to lead; those can be determined variously by the individuals who go on to live them. The state then has reason to remain neutral on the forms of life citizens have chosen for themselves. Toleration can be part of that story. Individuals may have – justifiably as well as empirically – different views on the first-order goods to which their fellow citizens have committed their lives, but the good of autonomy will give them reason to tolerate, especially politically, forms of life to which they take exception.

That is not to say that the path from autonomy to political neutrality is altogether smooth. The state may be able to do non-neutral things that will enhance its citizens' capacities and opportunities for autonomy, but it can be non-neutral on those matters while still being neutral on the first-order conceptions its citizens autonomously choose. The notion that the good of autonomy will always outweigh the bad of the lives that individuals might choose for themselves is, by contrast, both contestable and contested (e.g., Hurka 1993, 148–160; Sher 1997, 45–71; Wall 1998). Autonomy may be reckoned valuable only insofar as it is used to pursue forms of life that are themselves valuable (Raz 1986, 369–399). If the state has to weigh the good of autonomy against other goods or bads and to discriminate between valuable and valueless uses of autonomy, little scope may remain for its neutrality.

Other second-order good-based justifications for neutrality are possible. Steven Wall (2010) has argued that perfectionism is compatible with value pluralism, the view that lives can be differently but equally or incommensurably good. Those lives will constitute a limited set, but, insofar as none of them can be deemed better than others, the state has reason to remain neutral among them; it would act arbitrarily if it did not. Value pluralism is itself, however, a controversial moral theory, and, even if it does provide a case for neutrality, arguably it provides none for toleration, since we should have no need to "tolerate" forms of life that are of equal or incommensurable value with our own (Jones 2018, 177–202). Ronald Dworkin, despite being a celebrated deontological proponent of neutrality, has proposed a second-order conception of the good life, "the model of challenge," which should lead us to endorse liberal equality and political neutrality (2000, 237–284). He, however, intends his second-order model to supplement rather than replace the justice-based case for neutrality (Dworkin 2000, 241; for discussion and criticism of Dworkin's model, see Clayton 2004, Dworkin's reply 2004, 357–358, and Rawls's comment 1993, 211).

The Limits of Neutrality

If state neutrality is based on a conception of the good, its scope will be circumscribed by that conception. If it is based on a conception of the right, its scope can be more generous. Should it be unlimited?

Liberal neutralists agree that a just society need not accommodate conceptions of the good that conflict with justice itself. The right must have priority over the good. A just society is not obliged, for example, to accommodate conceptions of the good that deem manifestations of religious belief, or unbelief, intolerable. Citizens have no right to pursue conceptions that violate the rights of others; such conceptions are excluded not because they mistake the good but because their pursuit would be unjust.

That does not mean that non-state associations, such as organized religions or private clubs, must exhibit the same values of freedom and equality as the state. If an organized religion, for example, prescribes that its internal affairs should be conducted undemocratically or that men and women should perform roles of unequal spiritual significance, its adherents should be free to comply with them.

Voluntary associations, because they are voluntary, are not bound by the same rules of justice as the state, but they must respect the rights people possess as citizens. A church should be free, for example, to excommunicate those who break its rules but not free to compel its members to remain members.

Liberal neutralists also accept that the conceptions of the good that citizens come to hold are likely to be influenced by the liberal nature of the society to which they belong. That is another respect in which they do not claim neutrality of effect. Indeed, Rawls (1993) expects his citizens to be ready to adjust or modify their conceptions if they should conflict with the demands of political justice. He hopes that, ultimately, the different comprehensive doctrines to which citizens subscribe will come to "overlap" in supporting his political conception of justice.

A more contentious question concerns the range of matters, within the limits set by justice, on which a state should be neutral. Given the sharp distinction political liberals draw between the "political" and the "nonpolitical," we might expect them to insist that no political decision should be grounded in a comprehensive doctrine or conception of the good. Yet Rawls draws back from that position (1993, 214–215, 230), as do some others including Barry (1995, 143–145, 160–161) and Larmore (1996, 126). Here I focus on Rawls, since he is more explicit than others on this issue.

For Rawls, a liberal society's basic structure must be characterized by neutrality. In other words, on "constitutional essentials and matters of basic justice" (1993, 214), the state must remain neutral with respect to conceptions of the good. By "constitutional essentials," he means the structure and powers of its main political institutions and the basic rights and liberties its citizens possess in conformity with his first principle of justice (5–7, 227–228). By "matters of basic justice," he means matters concerning the just distribution of opportunities and resources, matters that are covered for the most part by his second principle of justice, such as equality of opportunity and the permissible range of social and economic inequalities (6–7, 228).

The principles of political justice need to be interpreted and applied, and that task should fall to "public reason." Public reason is the reason that citizens share as citizens. It draws on the values of political justice and other "political" values, such as reasonableness and fair-mindedness. It also employs the normal rules of judgment, inference, and evidence and appeals to "general beliefs and forms of reasoning found in common sense, and the methods and conclusions of science when these are not controversial" (224, 225). It contrasts with "nonpublic reason," the non-neutral reason of comprehensive doctrines. In their nonpolitical lives, citizens can be guided by nonpublic reason, but when they address public questions relating to constitutional essentials or matters of basic justice and whether they do so as public officeholders or as ordinary citizens, they should be governed by public reason alone. Public reason will not always yield clear and uncontestable answers. Different political values can be weighed and balanced differently so that citizens might reasonably disagree over what their decision should be, but both their disagreement and its resolution should remain within the limits of public reason (240–241).

What, then, of "ordinary" political decisions? Rawls observes that "citizens and legislators may properly vote their more comprehensive views when constitutional essentials and basic justice are not at stake; they need not justify by public reason why they vote as they do" (235). That concession would seem radically to diminish the scope and significance of neutrality, especially as an instantiation of liberal-democratic toleration. Is ordinary political decision-making to be nothing more than a power struggle in which citizens compete to impose their conceptions of the good upon one another?

Rawls's few remarks on this question leave the answer unclear (1993, 215; 2001, 91). He gives the following as examples of nonbasic matters that need not be settled by public reason: "much tax legislation and many laws regulating property; statutes protecting the environment and controlling pollution; establishing national parks and preserving wilderness areas and animal and plant species; and laying aside funds for museums and the arts" (214). It is not clear why tax legislation and property laws should not be matters for public reason. His other examples clearly concern "goods." Indeed, they would normally be characterized as "public goods" – goods that are shared by, or available to, citizens at large and whose description as "goods" would be widely accepted. The disagreements they occasion are more likely to concern why they are valuable and how their value compares with that of other goods, public or private, with which they may compete for resources. Rawlsians, unlike Rawls himself, might still hold that public reason can contribute to the resolution of those disagreements (e.g., Quong 2011, 283–287).

If we value political neutrality as an instrument of toleration, should we be troubled by its stretching no further than Rawls's constitutional essentials and matters of basic justice? Those "essentials" and "matters" range over an extensive area of political life, and the cause of toleration would seem well served by them. Freedom of thought, religion and conscience, freedom of expression and association, and rights of political participation all rank, for Rawls, as "essentials" which legislative majorities must respect (1993, 227–228). Moreover, in putting those essentials to work, public reason will have to address complex questions that will take it far from the remote heights of the constitutional and into the foothills of ordinary legislation and public policy. But, even if we can say that much on Rawls's behalf, many other liberals would expect there to be a larger role for neutrality in everyday political decision-making than Rawls seems willing to contemplate.

Summary and Future Directions

The ideal of state neutrality has received much critical attention, both from liberal and non-liberal political philosophers. Some doubt that political arrangements that claim to be neutral really are, or ever can be (e.g., MacIntyre 1988; Sandel 1998). Some question whether the right can be separated from the good and, if it can, whether it need prove any less controversial than the good (e.g., Caney 1995, 1998; Clarke 1999; Gray 2000). The most complete assault upon neutralism comes from its polar opposite, perfectionism, which rejects it as normatively misconceived. Even if a state could be neutral, it should not be. It is responsible for the wellbeing of its citizens, and it fails in its duty to them if it makes the goodness or badness of their lives none of its business (e.g., Hurka 1993; Raz 1986; Wall 1998; Sher 1997).

Is there scope for a rapprochement between neutralism and perfectionism? After all, most actual states that think of themselves as liberal democracies do promote some things as goods (e.g., the arts, learning) and deter other things as bads (e.g., drug dependency) while remaining neutral on the merit of still others. Clearly, there can be no rapprochement if perfectionism requires the state to adopt and impose the one true religion or a similarly doctrinaire nonreligious conception of the good life. But contemporary forms of perfectionism are often more modest and liberal in their ambitions. Joseph Chan (2000), for example, distinguishes between extreme and moderate perfectionism. Extreme perfectionism presents a comprehensive doctrine as the proper basis of state policy and legal coercion as the appropriate instrument for its realization. The same two features drive neutralist opposition to perfectionism. But, Chan suggests, moderate perfectionism need propose only that the state should promote non-comprehensive goods and do so, as far as possible, by way of non-coercive means.

Those means can include education and publicly funded campaigns along with measures designed to encourage or discourage, such as penal taxes or subsidies. Insofar as they promote without compelling, noncoercive means might be characterized as exercises in "liberal tolerance" (Macleod 1997) though, since they aim to deter the bad as well as promote the good, they might equally be described as instances of "liberal intolerance." Their use still needs justification which will be yielded, or not, by the ends they are used to pursue, which returns us to the question of what sorts of good, if any, the state should promote. That question breaks down into several others, and here we can do no more than indicate what they are.

Moderate perfectionism does not claim that the state should promote or impede goods whose characterization as goods depends on comprehensive doctrines. It does not, in other words, propose that the state should promote or impede conceptions of the good as they are modeled by Rawls. It limits its advocacy to the non-doctrinal goods which other liberals, such as Dworkin, include in their more generous notion of "conceptions of the good." That more modest ambition implies a rationale for curbing the state's neutrality that differs from Rawls's (although his narrow definition of "conceptions of the good" may hint at it) – a rationale that turns not on whether a matter relates to a society's basic structure but on what sort of good is at stake.

The most obvious question raised by the possibility of combining moderate perfectionism with neutralism is whether we can distinguish between different sorts of good in the way it requires. If we can deal with that question satisfactorily, we face another: why should doctrinal conceptions enjoy a status and immunity that non-doctrinal conceptions do not? Why should one sort of conception be off-limits to state power, while the other remains subordinate to it?

A feature of conceptions grounded in comprehensive doctrines, which both Rawls and Chan emphasize, is their conflictual nature; they are matters of deep disagreement. Therein may lie an answer. The state should promote goods if their goodness is not a matter of dispute among citizens. But if that is the perfectionist's answer, the neutralist can agree with it. Certainly, a strict neutralist might insist that the state should in no circumstances either make or act on a judgment of the good, but if neutrality is a device for securing toleration among citizens and if citizens agree that a particular good is indeed a good, neither toleration nor neutrality will veto the state's promoting it (cf. Larmore 1996, 125).

The debate must therefore focus on non-comprehensive putative goods about whose goodness citizens disagree. Given their disagreement, citizens, or their representatives, may try to resolve it through deliberation, but experience shows that while deliberation may reduce disagreement, it rarely eliminates it. In that case, the disputants may settle on a compromise or turn to a decision procedure, such as majority voting. If they use a decision procedure, they may, if they are disciples of Rousseau, believe that it will reveal the correct conception of the good, in which case those who previously thought differently will change their minds and all citizens will embrace the same conception of the good. More credibly, those who voted against the decision will continue to doubt its correctness but find reason to accept it in the legitimacy of the procedure itself, a procedure whose legitimacy lies in part in its neutrality – in its not being skewed as a procedure either for or against any particular conception of the good or any particular person. Even dissenters, however, can accept that the ultimate point of the exercise, and others like it, is that there are goods that the state should endeavor to promote.

What sort of goods are they? They will be particular and piecemeal rather than comprehensive in nature. Chan (2000, 11) suggests they will include virtues and dispositions conducive to a good life, such as wisdom and temperance, and goods that contribute to it substantively, such as aesthetic experiences, family relationships, knowledge, and amusement. We shall not need to dig very deeply into those goods before we encounter disagreement, but it may be better that goods are promoted in some form than not at all. Many considerations will bear on the question of whether the state should be the agent of an alleged good, such as the depth and breadth of the disagreement it evokes, the scope it leaves citizens for living their preferred lives, the case for its being promoted by the state rather than civil society, and the extent to which it competes with values of other sorts. Chan identifies a willingness to adopt that sort of "mixed" or "impure" approach to public policy as another feature that distinguishes moderate from extreme perfectionism.

It may be that neutralists should also accept that mixed approach. There will be differences of view about the good on which the state should remain steadfastly neutral because they are differences that merit full political toleration, and there will be goods about which there is so little controversy that the state can pursue them with little inhibition. But, in the intermediate terrain, perhaps the right course will be to follow Patten (2014) and Balint (2017) and think of toleration and neutrality as values to which we should give significant weight rather than principles that we should never violate.

References

Ackerman B (1980) Social justice in the liberal state. Yale University Press, New Haven

Arneson R (1989) Equality and equal opportunity for welfare. Philos Stud 56:77–93

Arneson R (1990a) Neutrality and utility. Can J Philos 20:215–240

Arneson R (1990b) Liberalism, distributive subjectivism and equal opportunity for welfare. Philos Public Aff 19:158–194

Balint P (2017) Respecting toleration. Oxford University Press, Oxford

Barry B (1995) Justice as impartiality. Clarendon Press, Oxford

Barry B (2001) Culture and equality. Polity, Cambridge

Benbaji H, Heyd D (2001) The charitable perspective: forgiveness and toleration as supererogatory. Can J Philos 31:567–586

Bird C (1996) Mutual respect and neutral justification. Ethics 107:62–96

Bou-Habib P (2006) A theory of religious accommodation. J Appl Philos 23:109–126

Caney S (1995) Anti-perfectionism and Rawlsian liberalism. Polit Stud 43:248–264

Caney S (1998) Impartiality and liberal neutrality. In: Kelly P (ed) Impartiality, neutrality and justice: re-reading Brian Barry's justice as impartiality. Edinburgh University Press, Edinburgh

Chan J (2000) Legitimacy, unanimity and perfectionism. Philos Public Aff 29:5–42

Churchill RP (2003) Neutrality and the virtue of toleration. In: Castiglione D, McKinnon C (eds) Toleration, neutrality and democracy. Kluwer, Dordrecht

Clarke S (1999) Contractarianism, liberal neutrality and epistemology. Polit Stud 47:627–642

Clayton M (2004) A puzzle about ethics, justice, and the sacred. In: Burley J (ed) Dworkin and his critics. Blackwell, Oxford

Cohen GA (1989) On the currency of egalitarian justice. Ethics 99:904–944

Cohen GA (2004) Expensive tastes ride again. In: Burley J (ed) Dworkin and his critics. Blackwell, Oxford

Cohen AJ (2015) Contemporary liberalism and toleration. In: Wall S (ed) The Cambridge companion to liberalism. Cambridge University Press, Cambridge

Cordelli C (2017) Neutrality of what? Crit Rev Int Soc Pol Phil 20:36–48

Dworkin R (1986) A matter of principle. Oxford University Press, Oxford

Dworkin R (2000) Sovereign virtue: the theory and practice of equality. Harvard University Press, Cambridge, MA

Dworkin R (2004) Ronald Dworkin replies. In: Burley J (ed) Dworkin and his critics. Blackwell, Oxford

Gray J (2000) Two faces of liberalism. Polity, Cambridge

Heyd D (2008) Is toleration a political virtue? In: Williams MS, Waldron J (eds) Toleration and its limits. New York University Press, New York

Horton J (1996) Toleration as a virtue. In: Heyd D (ed) Toleration: an elusive virtue. Princeton University Press, Princeton

Hurka T (1993) Perfectionism. Oxford University Press, Oxford

Jones P (2018) Essays on toleration. ECPR Press/Rowman & Littlefield, London

Jones P (2020) Essays on culture, religion and rights. ECPR Press/Rowman & Littlefield, London

Kelly P (ed) (2002) Multiculturalism reconsidered. Polity, Cambridge

Klosko G (2003) Reasonable rejection and neutrality of justification. In: Steven W, Klosko G (eds) Perfectionism and neutrality: essays in liberal political theory. Rowman & Littlefield, Lanham

Laborde C (2017) Liberalism's religion. Harvard University Press, Cambridge, MA

Laborde C (2018) The evanescence of neutrality. Political Theory 46:99–105

Larmore C (1987) Patterns of moral complexity. Cambridge University Press, Cambridge

Larmore C (1996) The morals of modernity. Cambridge University Press, Cambridge

Lecce SA (2003) Contractualism and neutrality: a defence. Polit Stud 51:524–541

Leiter B (2012) Why tolerate religion? Princeton University Press, Princeton

Lippert-Rasmussen K (2017) Dispositional neutrality and minority rights. Crit Rev Int Soc Pol Phil 20:49–62

17 Toleration and Neutrality

Locke J (1968) A letter on toleration (ed: Klibansky R). Clarendon Press, Oxford

MacIntyre A (1988) Whose justice? Which rationality? Duckworth, London

Macleod CM (1997) Liberal neutrality or liberal tolerance? Law Philos 16:529–559

Meckled-Garcia S (2003) Toleration and neutrality: incompatible ideals? In: Castiglione D, McKinnon C (eds) Toleration, neutrality and democracy. Kluwer, Dordrecht

Montefiore A (1975) Neutrality and impartiality. Cambridge University Press, Cambridge

Nagel T (1991) Equality and partiality. Oxford University Press, New York

Newey G (1999) Virtue, reason and toleration. Edinburgh University Press, Edinburgh

Nozick R (1974) Anarchy, state and utopia. Blackwell, Oxford

Patten A (2014) Equal recognition: the moral foundations of minority rights. Princeton University Press, Princeton

Quong J (2011) Liberalism without perfection. Oxford University Press, Oxford

Rawls J (1971) A theory of justice. Oxford University Press, Oxford

Rawls J (1993) Political liberalism. Columbia University Press, New York

Rawls J (2001) Justice as fairness: a restatement. Belknap Press, Cambridge, MA

Raz J (1986) The morality of freedom. Clarendon Press, Oxford

Sandel M (1998) Liberalism and the limits of justice. Cambridge University Press, Cambridge

Scanlon TM (1986) Equality of resources and equality of welfare: a forced marriage? Ethics 97:111–118

Scanlon TM (2006) Justice, responsibility, and the demands of equality. In: Sypnowich C (ed) The egalitarian conscience: essays in honour of G. A. Cohen. Oxford University Press, Oxford

Sher G (1997) Beyond neutrality. Cambridge University Press, Cambridge

Vallier K, Weber M (eds) (2018) Religious exemptions. Oxford University Press, Oxford

Wall S (1998) Liberalism, perfectionism and restraint. Cambridge University Press, Cambridge

Wall S (2001) Neutrality and responsibility. J Philos 98:389–410

Wall S (2010) Neutralism for perfectionists: the case of restricted state neutrality. Ethics 120:232–256

Political Toleration as Substantive Neutrality

18

Bryan T. McGraw

Contents

Introduction 326
Toleration and Moral Judgment 326
Political Toleration as Substantive Neutrality 331
Conclusion 337
References 338

Abstract

The nature and scope of political toleration is a matter of much controversy within liberal democratic politics. This chapter suggests that toleration itself should be understood as emerging from the practice of adjudicating likely irreconcilable goods with an eye toward individual agency. Further, it shows that political toleration is best understood as what a number of scholars have described as "substantive neutrality," where the liberal state aspires to remain neutral among different ways of life and is committed to redressing inequities arising from that effort to remain neutral.

Keywords

Toleration · Liberalism · Democracy · Pluralism · Neutrality · Recognition · Autonomy · Freedom

B. T. McGraw (✉)
Wheaton College, Wheaton, IL, USA
e-mail: Bryan.McGraw@wheaton.edu

© The Author(s), under exclusive licence to Springer Nature Switzerland AG 2022
M. Sardoč (ed.), *The Palgrave Handbook of Toleration*,
https://doi.org/10.1007/978-3-030-42121-2_42

Introduction

Toleration has long been something of a moral and philosophical puzzle. What could it mean to "tolerate" morally actions or beliefs that are themselves immoral? What are toleration's limits, if any? Extended beyond the interpersonal, the puzzles multiply, to the point that many have come to doubt the coherence and utility of toleration itself and especially its application to political institutions and practices. This chapter explains both the coherence and utility of toleration and shows that under conditions of wide and widely reasonable moral pluralism, what scholars call "substantive neutrality" is a plausible way of making toleration politically effective.

This chapter begins by describing the debates around the nature of toleration itself, settling on the view that toleration emerges out of the practice of moral judgment in which persons adjudicate among competing and irreconcilable goods with a sharp eye on how those judgments engage others' individual agency. It then shows that this means that a liberal polity should not only aspire to be generally neutral – not favoring one way of life over another – but also to try and ameliorate the negative effects of its always only aspirationally "neutral" institutions, what it calls "substantive neutrality." The upshot is that properly effecting political toleration in pluralist liberal democratic orders is a difficult and politically controversial issue, one whose always partial resolution relies on fallible, limited, moral judgments involving important goods in serious and persistent conflict. Taking refuge in the notion that it is possible to resolve these conflicts without remainder by just getting our moral principles right is not just a philosophical mistake; it is, more importantly, a foolish impulse that makes the pluralist democratic order less just and less stable.

Toleration and Moral Judgment

The first thing to do is to get a clear fix on what toleration means, for its meaning appears both intuitively obvious and also widely disputed. Generally speaking, when talking about toleration people tend to have in mind the idea of putting up with some practice or belief that they find morally objectionable or inappropriate. This suggests why toleration often gets tied to individual autonomy, since to object morally to others' actions or beliefs is to focus inevitably on their capacity to act on their own accord, out of their individual agency and autonomy. For some, autonomy is entirely the point. Hans Oberdiek (2001, 120) argues that toleration is necessary so that men and women can pursue their "self-directed li[ves]," updating John Stuart Mill's justly famous argument in *On Liberty*, where he looks to maximize political *and* social toleration as a means of protecting and encouraging human individuality. One way of characterizing toleration, then, is as a way of simply protecting individual autonomy.

Individuality is an important good (especially in the context of modern liberal societies) but making toleration the handmaiden of autonomy ultimately relies on the unpersuasive claim that a comprehensive, maximal autonomy limns the edges of what should count as a reasonable and flourishing human life. As Susan Mendus (1999, 65–66) has pointed out, this might require some rather unsavory and illiberal practices to make those who are incapable of exercising their individuality or for some reason refuse to do so become capable or willing (Cf. Hamburger 1999, 2016; Gill 2001). Overemphasizing autonomy could also so narrow toleration's scope that it undermines its practical defensibility. In the course of criticizing Will Kymlicka's autonomy-based claim for group rights, Moshe Halbertal (1996, 109–10) argues that focusing on what is "important and central in…life" better describes the harm that befalls the objects of (unjustified) intolerance than a focus on what it is putatively "chosen" does. On his account intolerance harms us by "robbing [us] of the possibility of continuing a way of life that harbors great meaning for [us] as individuals" rather than just undermining our ability to *choose* some way of life. If the toleration-for-autonomy argument is correct, the many aspects of people's lives that are often unchosen – family, religion, language, etc. – might not actually generate plausible toleration claims.

This does *not* mean that autonomy is unimportant. Halbertal cites the story of Paul's conversion to Christianity on the road to Damascus (as related in the book of Acts, Chap. 9) and points out that Paul's conversion was not simply the product of rational reflection—to "tolerate" such a conversion simply in terms of autonomy misdescribes what is being tolerated. But that does not mean that Paul had no choice in the matter, a point that Halbertal seems to miss. After his vision on the Damascus road, after all, Paul traveled on to Damascus, joined the Christians there, and eventually began preaching, putting his own life in danger. At each point along the way, he had and made a choice (and if tradition is to be believed, paid for those choices with a martyr's death). We "tolerate" conversions because they attach to something in human beings that is amenable to change, even if "choice" does not exhaust what happens with conversion in particular. Toleration is indeed inextricably tied to moral evaluation and individual autonomy, even if the latter does not exhaust what is at stake in toleration.

Toleration is *unnecessary* in two sorts of situations: (a) where everyone agrees on what is moral and immoral, and (b) if everyone agrees that *nothing* is moral or immoral. If (b) is true, there is no need to even talk about tolerance, for there is nothing that can be the object of moral opprobrium (Williams 1999). But that is also the case if (a) is true, for if everyone actually agrees on what is moral, then no one can rightly object to being coerced on those moral grounds. Some seem to anticipate just that situation, suggesting that toleration is an inherently paradoxical and incoherent concept, less a virtue and more a relic of outmoded moral judgmentalism (Heyd 2008). Bernard Williams (1999, 65), for one, has famously noted,

> The difficulty with toleration is that it seems to be at once necessary and impossible. It is necessary where different groups have conflicting beliefs – moral, political, or religious – and realise that there is no alternative to their living together. [It is impossible] because people find others' beliefs or ways of life deeply unacceptable. In matters of religion, for instance…, the need for toleration arises because one of the groups, at least, thinks that the other is blasphemously, disastrously, obscenely wrong…It is because the disagreement goes this deep that the parties to it think that they cannot accept the existence of the other.

We need to tolerate other people and their ways of life only in situations that make it very difficult to do so. Toleration, we may say, is required only for the intolerable. That is its basic problem.

Toleration thus seems, even at its best, a puzzling conjunction of claims. People are asked to tolerate what is "intolerable," to allow that which they find immoral and wrong to persist or even thrive. If something is truly wrong, then how can they be asked to tolerate it? They might accept toleration for now on prudential grounds but it is always only temporary until the question about what is *actually* the correct answer morally is resolved (Cf. Forst 2014). And then we no longer need to tolerate.

The claim that toleration is paradoxical rests on the conjunction that toleration means tolerating the "intolerable," and put that way, it does seem like a paradox. But the conjunction looks that way only because it elides the distinction between what is 'wrong' and what is 'intolerable.' The two are not the same thing. At least, as Williams himself notes, they need not be the same thing. Toleration makes sense in that it is precisely about understanding when, if ever, the two ought to be separated. A decision to tolerate (or not) does not emerge straightaway from the judgment as to whether some practice is right or wrong. Rather, toleration emerges from it being right or wrong in a certain way or in a certain context. Consider adultery, which most still consider morally wrong. We tolerate it legally (and to a lesser degree culturally) except in the military, where service-members can be prosecuted if a commanding officer judges that adulterous relations have harmed unit effectiveness. The willingness to let adultery slide in everyday legal proceedings is not premised on adultery's moral acceptance; neither is its legal prohibition in the military a sign that they are more morally attuned than the rest to adultery's wrongness. Rather, the distinction reflects a contextual judgment about the circumstances in which a particular wrong ought to be deemed intolerable. If toleration is indeed conceptually incoherent or paradoxical, then it has to be shown – not assumed – that the everyday distinctions most make between 'intolerable' and 'wrong' do not in fact make sense.

Preston King (1998) seems right, then, when he suggests that practicing toleration means, in fact, balancing a set of "competing objections." People may, for example, object to someone's religious beliefs, either because they think them wrong or morally noxious, but they tolerate them – when they do – because they think that the objection to denying someone her religious liberty is stronger. If those beliefs include something entirely unacceptable – say, sacrificing infants – then the religious liberty claim loses out and people will think ourselves justified in practicing *intolerance*. As William Galston has quipped, there is no religious liberty for the (human sacrificing) Aztec. The "difficulty" with tolerance lies not in some set of internal contradictions or incoherence but more simply in the kind of judgments necessarily implicated in the very possibility of toleration (and its denial).

Consider that any activity is oriented toward some good (or end), and that some of those goods conflict: choosing to pursue one good may foreclose the possibility of achieving another. Attending to a friendship may require neglecting study or exercise. When reflecting on whether to tolerate some practice or belief, central among the competing claims inevitably to be considered is the already implicit commitment to respecting another person's agency and autonomy. Again, in even contemplating the possibility of toleration, one's attention is inevitably drawn to the fact that those participating in that purportedly noxious practice have a kind of freedom to order their affairs as they see fit, within limits that are themselves, of course, framed by the boundaries of toleration. People need not be full-blooded Kantians or Millians in their views of human autonomy but in even considering the possibility of toleration one is already implicitly embracing (or at least taking seriously) a central feature of modern liberalism – namely, that in deciding whether to tolerate or not, the decision inherently involves taking serious consideration of others' capacity to make their own decisions and be responsible for them (Cf. Eberle 2002).

Toleration is best understood, then, as the emerging from the practice of adjudicating among competing and apparently incompatible goods in the context of behaviors or views that some find morally objectionable where individuals keep a sharp eye on how their judgments takes account of others' individual agency. But note something important here. It is not toleration itself that, strictly speaking, interests. What interests, rather, is the practice of moral judgment, in the adjudication of "competing objections" or competing goods. Heyd (2008) is right in some sense, then, to say that toleration is not really a virtue—or, at best, it is merely a second-order one. Unlike being courageous, deciding to tolerate someone or something is not always appropriate. Similarly, when Oberdiek (2001) complains that toleration is inherently unstable, the instability does not come from toleration per se but from the difficulty in getting moral judgments right. The fact that so few, if any, have explicitly grasped this fact about toleration perhaps explains why so many seem so perplexed about it. Getting toleration right means getting the practices of moral judgment right.

That is, it hardly needs saying, a condition that makes getting toleration right very difficult indeed. Not only is it intrinsically difficult to collect and evaluate all the information relevant to any particular case, but it is also implausible to expect that one could articulate reasonably straightforward, clear arguments that can achieve even a broad consensus on contentious moral issues. These difficulties might, as some would have it, be partially solved by erecting and enforcing deliberative rules ala Rawls' "public reason." But such rules, as Rawls himself discovered, are notoriously difficult to police and often end up tying their proponents into argumentative knots. Steven Smith (2010) has nicely shown how even those committed in principle to these kinds of rules all too often end up "smuggling" in controversial moral claims that violate the rules in practice. (Cf. McGraw 2010; Bowlin 2016) Public reason (or similar kinds of schemes) cannot rescue from the difficulties attendant to public moral judgments and get to the sort of consensus that would make toleration unproblematic.

So what to do? There is hardly the space to offer anything but the barest sketch of what the practice of moral judgment consists in. But consider how people negotiate these sorts of issues in their common conversations. Ordinary persons do often make principled, even philosophical, arguments in the context of moral disagreement, even if those arguments are not as coherent or tightly constructed as might sometimes be hoped. But these often tend to run out in the sense that they do not definitively settle the issue philosophically and sometimes do not seem to wield much in the way of persuasive power even if they do. People deliberate and would like to persuade, but it is not uncommon to find that they simply fail to do so. So they make recourse to a different set of resources: stories and examples (hypothetical and otherwise), and not just in common conversations. Even in the context of the most rigorous and abstract moral argumentation, scholars also almost always turn to stories and examples as a means of persuading others. Charles Larmore (1987) points out that even Kant did this, suggesting that even at the most philosophical and abstract humans are, for better or worse, just simply the sorts of creatures whose moral judgments are tied in some important way to stories and examples (Hauerwas 1981; MacIntyre 1980). Moral reasoning is not *just* stories and examples, but it cannot seemingly do without them. This is perhaps especially true when it comes to public political deliberations.

Why might individuals be so inclined to argue in this way? Partly, it emerges out of an interest in how abstract principles might work out in practice. What makes sense in the abstract can show itself absurd or unpalatable in the particular. But another part of the answer, and this is the part that Alasdair MacIntyre and Charles Taylor have been so influential in developing, is also that the moral claims invoked in our deliberations and the ways in which these are adjudicated (or even judged as a moral claim) are themselves embedded in particular communities with particular histories. There is no need to avert to some crude historicism to recognize that moral judgments rely in important ways on the histories within which the actors doing the judging find themselves. Nor is there a need to avert to some crude Whig view of those histories to recognize how they can serve to improve our moral judgments. Most expect, as a general rule, that individuals with more experience, more history under their belts, will have better judgment. Everyone can relate to the frustration in dealing with someone who cannot seem to learn from his mistakes – experience *should* lead to better judgment. So perhaps individuals tell stories and use examples in deliberating about and making moral judgments not just as a way of seeing how preferred principles might apply practically but just as importantly because they offer a sort of "moral shortcut" to the benefits history and experience otherwise can offer. Insofar as hypotheticals and stories help flesh out the practices of moral reasoning they can function in much the same way that experience can in improving moral judgments. And, of course, when moral judgments go wrong it is often possible to show how their embeddedness in a particular history or set of stories made it possible for them to go wrong.

Suppose this is right and that the use of stories and examples reflects an intuitive sense that history matters, both as a relevant set of facts and as an inevitable (and potentially salutary) condition of moral reasoning. If toleration does, as argued, reflect the practice of judgment about competing and likely incompatible moral goods, then it too is thus tied inevitably to stories and examples – and to history. There just is no way to reduce a practice of toleration to some easy or straightforward formula. It becomes clear why it is so difficult, impossible really, to draw a bright line between, say, "self-regarding" and "other-regarding" actions or between acts that cause "harm" and those that do not. Simply invoking "autonomy" or "liberty" or some-such value cannot solve the problem of toleration, for the choice to tolerate (or not) depends profoundly on contexts that incline people to value one good over another. And it becomes clear why it is that individuals so often get moral judgments wrong, deciding to tolerate things that should not be tolerated and not tolerating things that should be. Toleration's critics are right, then, to be suspicious, but they should be suspicious for the very reasons they should tolerate: human beings are fallible, limited creatures who inevitably engage in moral judgments about competing and likely irreconcilable goods, judgments that are embedded in historical moments and thoroughly suffused with examples and stories meant to enrich those judgments without any sure expectation that they will always get them right. To refuse toleration is to either ignore the conflict among goods or pretend that one has finally, unlike everyone else, unlocked the key to seeing their ranking without error. The correct word for that would be hubris, not wisdom.

Political Toleration as Substantive Neutrality

What does this imply for *political* toleration? Or, how are political institutions and practices to be structured so that they make the sorts of moral judgments described above well, and reliably so? It is not just a question of "scaling up" from individual practices, since whatever judgments get made by states come with the promise (or threat) of coercive force, get written into law, and are typically "stickier" than individual judgments. So it seems reasonable to suppose that political communities should take correlatively *more* care in thinking about how to make these judgments: getting individual moral judgments wrong might have some worrisome consequences but getting political judgments wrong is likely to be comparatively much worse. The breaking of friendships versus spending time in prison on account of moral judgments would seem to make that distinction clear.

Liberal societies give a great deal of deference to individual freedom. It was suggested earlier that making individual autonomy a trump for deciding matters of toleration is a mistake, since to do so erroneously relies on the idea that the fully autonomous life is the singular measure of human flourishing i.e., all human lives worth our respect, on this account, must be characterized by autonomy, even if they differ in other ways. If it is reasonable to think that the range of good human lives includes those that are *not* fully autonomous, and it is reasonable, then human agency and autonomy stand as an important, but not dispositive good. But it does stand as an important good and liberal societies should be reluctant to coerce. This reluctance and the demand for good moral justifications for coercion stand at the heart of the liberal order, and help show why liberal theorists have long argued that political toleration requires what they typically call neutrality, the idea that the liberal state should not favor one way of life over another, insofar as such favoring is not required by the demands of the liberal polity itself (Cf. Sher 1997; Koppelman 2004, 2013). To take seriously the idea that individuals (and groups, for that matter) will work out what counts as a good life differently and do so reasonably places a significant moral constraint on state actions that promote one conception of the good life over another.

There are (broadly speaking) two sorts of liberal neutrality, the "neutrality of effect" and "neutrality of intent." The former argues that state action can be considered properly neutral provided that it has an equal impact on those affected. "Disparate impact" arguments in legal scholarship more or less embody this sort of neutrality. Rawls (1996, 193–200) argues that a neutrality of effect is "impracticable" as a matter of "commonsense political sociology," noting that it is very difficult – he says it is "futile" – to figure out exactly how basic political institutions affect the long-term fortunes of distinct ways of life and that in any case every sort of society involves "social loss." Instead, he offers that neutrality is violated only when "the well-ordered society of political liberalism fails to establish, in ways that existing circumstances allow – circumstances that include the fact of reasonable pluralism – a just basic structure within which permissible forms of life have a fair opportunity to maintain themselves and to gain adherents over generations." The state is properly neutral, and thus gives practical effect to political toleration, when it does not as a matter of course *intend* to disadvantage any particular way of life, at least among those deemed permissible (or "reasonable") within liberal democratic societies. Liberal political toleration in this sense requires that the liberal state avoid importuning those ways of life compatible with a just and stable liberal democratic political order.

The very fact that Rawls distinguishes his version of neutrality from a neutrality of effect tells the reader that some ways of life will inevitably do better than others. He suggests that ways of life permissible under a liberal polity may still "fail to gain adherents" and perhaps even disappear, but that such an outcome, while it might be lamentable, does not necessarily rise to the level of injustice. As long as a liberal society's basic institutions are not "arbitrarily biased" against those ways of life and that the conditions leading to their decline or demise are not themselves unjust, there is little more to be said. Others have not been quite as sanguine, suggesting that this sort of benign neglect often amount to an injustice. Instead, they argue that a liberal state has the responsibility to ensure that groups of citizens, especially those who have historically been the object of injustice, feel properly included in the wider political community. Rather than neutrality, or toleration more broadly, the state should pursue what they call *recognition*.

Recall that one of the things essential for the practice of toleration was critical moral evaluation. In order to say that a person tolerates something, she needs to think it morally objectionable. So to the degree that liberal neutrality is meant to instantiate a regime of political toleration, it suggests (even if only implicitly) to those whom it "tolerates" that their acts or views are thought by the state (or perhaps just by most of the citizens at large) to be morally problematic in some respect: the liberal state tolerates what society dislikes. Since those being "tolerated" in a liberal democratic society are likely also to be largely excluded from significant social or political influence – otherwise, they would hardly need political toleration – they are likely to find themselves doubly marginalized. This, as Anna Galeotti (2002, 12) points out, has the practical effect of undermining their civic standing. Being the object of political condescension makes it difficult to develop the kind of self-respect neces-sary for the effective exercise of civic duties and even for pursuing human flourishing. Rather than simply encouraging mutual toleration, the state should, she says, "make all citizens feel positively at ease with their full-blown identities in public as well as private" (Galeotti 2002, 105). It should extend, through subsi-dies, legal protection, or some sort of affirmative cultural policy, *political recogni-tion*: state action designed to provide material and psychological support for the disparate and competing religious, ethnic, or cultural identities that inhabit modern democratic life.

Recognition has the real virtue of taking account of the ways in which an ostensibly neutral set of political institutions can serve to reinforce or even create social inequalities that can then have pernicious political consequences. But it has real problems as well. It oversimplifies the connection between civic capacities and cultural esteem and neglects the ways in which mediating institutions like families, churches, and parties can themselves create and sustain cultural identity, making state action less necessary and more problematic (Rosenblum 1998, 329–31). It can very quickly, as both Taylor (1992) and Galeotti recognize, run afoul of even the most basic liberal commitments. Arguments in favor of recognition also seem to ignore or (at best elide) the zero-sum quality of some political conflicts: extending recognition to one group sometimes means de-recognizing another. Consider some-thing as relatively innocuous as public holidays. In deciding who or what gets honored with holidays, the state goes some way toward "recognizing" one element of a pluralistic culture over another. To the degree that the state decides to adjust those holidays to shift its recognition, it is likely that some groups will feel slighted as they "lose" their holiday.

Perhaps most importantly, the argument for recognition founders on a tension that stands at the heart of its claims. It claims that in modern democratic societies there exist diverse and contesting ways of life on whose fortunes purportedly neutral laws will have disparate – and thus unjust – effects. But it then argues that to compensate for (or to avoid) such injustices, laws should be altered and public resources committed to ameliorating those effects. What is lacking is any real argument as to *why* or *how* those laws will be altered or resources committed. Why will the members of these diverse and contesting cultures agree to extend to one another these sorts of resources if, in fact, they are as diverse and contesting as the recognition argument suggests? If the marginalized cultures are really as marginal-ized and despised as advertised, it is hard to see how a practical program of recognition gets off the ground at all, except to the degree that these diverse and contesting ways of life are actually not all that diverse or contested. If, as Galeotti put it, the goal of recognition is to "make all citizens feel positively at ease with their full-blown identities in public as well as private," that can only happen so long as those identities are relatively easily compatible with one another. Recognition tends to involve the extension of public benefits (money, employment set-asides, legal exemptions, and so on) to minority groups that have historically been the object of social marginalization and ostracism. These benefits must garner, I take it, some reasonably significant levels of political support. It must be the case that some large (or at least politically potent) portion of the population clearly accepts the necessity of extending recognition and most citizens must already view minority groups at least somewhat positively, meaning in effect that problem for which recognition is meant to be a solution is pretty marginal itself. After all, if some group is so widely despised that they would qualify for recognition, it is hard to see how they would get it, and if they get it, do they really need it?

So recognition looks to be unpersuasive as a full-blown alternative to neutrality or political toleration. Thinking through the recognition claim does, however, point up something important. The arguments for recognition are rooted in the commonplace observation that institutions can systematically and predictably disadvantage groups of people even if they are not meant to do so. The claim for recognition takes that to mean that the whole edifice of neutrality ought to be overthrown. Rawls (among others) argues, alternatively, that the neutrality of intent is the right way to make toleration politically effective because it fulfills what justice requires and is, unlike the neutrality of effect *and* recognition, practical. The neutrality of intent fulfills the requirements of justice because it treats various ways of life fairly. The fact that some ways of life prosper and others fall into desuetude is not, on this account, in itself a problem with a neutrality of intent. As long as the institutions do not aim at promoting one way of life over another, no one is done an injustice, even if her way of life does not prosper.

Suppose, though, that some people find it systematically more difficult than others to pursue their way of life because liberalism's political institutions exact what John Tomasi (2001, 35) has called an "unequal psychological tax." That is, even though their political views qualify them as citizens in good standing, these citizens find themselves persistently frustrated in pursuing their nonpolitical ends. As Rawls (1996, 196) points out, ways of life might do poorly under political liberalism for one of two reasons. First, they might be "in direct conflict with the principles of justice." Slaveholders will find their lives frustrated in liberal societies, but, of course, that is nothing to be concerned about; the fact that ways of life dependent on injustices incompatible with any reasonable sort of liberal politics will not do well under liberal institutions is part of reason for upholding those institutions in the first place. Second, some ways of life "may be admissible but fail to gain adherents under the political and social conditions of a just constitutional regime." Examples of this type include "certain types of religion" that "can survive only if [they control] the machinery of state and [are] able to practice effective intolerance." Since this sort of religion could only survive provided that the state violates a central liberal claim – religious liberty – its passing (or radical change) might be lamented, but cannot be considered unjust.

Rawls' second example here is a strange one, for it does not differ in principle from the first. In both cases, a way of life or comprehensive view can only be sustained through a political injustice that any liberal democratic regime is fundamentally committed to preventing. As Alfred Stepan (2000) has pointed out, an established church is not in itself incompatible with liberal democratic government. But a *coercive* establishment, where membership is compulsory, is another matter altogether. So what does Rawls mean by saying that the coercive religion is

18 Political Toleration as Substantive Neutrality   335

"admissible" under a liberal regime? Perhaps he means that a liberal state need not outlaw such a religion, as opposed to its duty to outlaw slaveholding, but in the context of trying to understand whether political liberalism is fair to different ways of life, it is an unhelpful example, to say the least. The question that needs addressing revolves around when political institutions systematically disadvantage some people over others and whether they do so for good reasons. So if the establishmentarian religion does poorly, then *by definition* there is not a problem, but that does not mean much more than saying that political institutions animated by liberal principles are unfavorable to those who oppose them. It says nothing about believers whose beliefs and practices are broadly compatible with liberal politics.

This brings the argument to a quite important question: should there be anything be done if liberalism systematically disadvantages ways of life that *are compatible* with liberalism properly understood? Is the neutrality of intent truly fair if it has predictably and persistently disparate effects? Liberalism seems committed to being fair to the different ways of life within its borders and if it looks like some of those ways of life do poorly *because* of liberalism's institutions, then it seems quite plausible to at least explore ways to make liberalism's requirements less burdensome or more equitable.

Rawls declaims any such attempt. He notes that any set of social institutions will necessarily favor some ways of life and disfavor others. No one could reasonably expect to achieve a full "neutrality of effect," even if that were desirable. But Rawls (1996, 193) goes further, and suggests that it "is futile to try to counteract these effects and influences, or even to ascertain for political purposes how deep and pervasive they are. We must accept the facts of commonsense political sociology." This is a strange conjunction of claims. We must, Rawls tells us, "accept the facts of commonsense political sociology," which would apparently require all to (a) believe (and rely on the idea) that the effects of political institutions are deep and pervasive and (b) accept that it is futile to try and counteract such effects when their unintended consequences are unfortunate in some respect. If one takes Rawls at his word here, then what is left is the rather puzzling idea that political institutions have lots of non-political effects, but that really knowing what those effects are – or, at least, how "deep and pervasive" they are – is itself unknowable and no one certainly can do much of anything about them, except, it seems, rely on them to underpin their liberal political institutions.

It is almost certainly true that to discern *precisely* how political institutions affect social and private life is quite difficult, and it is also true that the ability to design political institutions to effect particular goals is always only partial, but there is still a great deal to say about how institutions do in fact have their effects. If all shops are closed on Sundays, Christians probably have a comparative advantage over religions that have their worship services on other days. If all children are forced to go to secular schools, probably fewer of them will be religious than if some had gone to the religious schools of their (religious) parents' choice. More to the point, even if no one intended for a particular set of institutions to be unequal in their effects, once such effects are evident, refusing to adjust those institutions to account for those effects clearly then becomes part of "intent." "Commonsense political sociology" can tell a great deal about how institutions shape social life, and even if it is far from perfect, a set of institutions whose design turns out to favor one way of life over another cannot really be called neutral, even if they are not at first intended to act in that manner. And to the degree that the possible adjustments are themselves compatible with liberal principles and not productive of greater problems, political institutions absent those adjustments cannot be considered properly neutral or fair.

So it seems that Tomasi (2001, 43–56) is right to suggest that once liberals have committed themselves to a neutrality of intent as a means of making toleration politically effective, they are then in turn committed to ensuring that such neutrality is truly as neutral as it can be; they must be concerned with political institutions' nonpolitical effects. But Rawls and others might complain that this simply leads us back to some kind of neutrality of effect, a standard that he plausibly claimed was "impracticable." It is quite difficult to delineate with sufficient clarity whether some people's lives go well and others go poorly due to political institutions, technological shifts, cultural trends, or any of the other bewilderingly myriad ways that societies change. Moreover, it is not even often clear whether people's lives *are* going well, going poorly, or simply changing. Multiplying these uncertainties across groups of people produces some real sympathy for Rawls' (and others') unwillingness to tread in such territory.

Nonetheless, it is not so obvious what sort of force the "practicability" objection should have, especially when we are considering disparate effects on ways of life politically compatible with liberalism. *If*, for instance, political institutions *could* be arranged so as to have perfectly equal effects on the various ways of life compatible with political liberalism, what reason could there be for not doing so? What is striking about Rawls' discussion of the neutrality of effect is the absence of a moral argument: the critique is entirely practical. There is nothing in Rawls' argument to suggest he thinks there is anything *morally* wrong with thinking about neutrality this way, it is just too hard to make it work. If that is right, then perhaps practicability ought to be understood as little more than a prudential warning against expecting too much out of a system of political neutrality; it is not a knock-down argument against attempting to mitigate political institutions' disparate effects on people's ways of life. It is perhaps unavoidable that political institutions will unfairly advantage some ways of life over others, while it is just as unavoidable that a liberalism properly understood will understand itself as at least having a moral obligation to assuage that unfairness as a means of making toleration politically effective.

Rather than a neutrality of intent, liberal states seeking to make toleration politically effective could commit to something analogous to what Stephen Monsma (2000) and Douglas Laycock (1990), among a number of others, have called (in the context of discussions of how to interpret the First Amendment) "substantive neutrality" (Cf. McConnell 2000). In this view of neutrality, the liberal state should take care that its actions do not, at first pass, intend to advantage or disadvantage any particular way of life, insofar as that way of life looks to be compatible with liberal order. It should then take further action, or reconstruct its first action, to try and mitigate the disadvantages that might emerge on account of that first action. In other words, the liberal state should act fairly with respect to most of the diverse ways of life within its borders and look to correct itself if and when any unfairness becomes evident.

It might be easy to suppose that this substantive neutrality runs into many of the same problems suggested above for recognition, and it is true that both can get themselves entangled in any number of practical problems such that might tempt some to abandon this amended view of neutrality as well. Two things distinguish substantive neutrality, though, and suggest why it might be reasonable to endorse one but not the other. First, recognition requires (or assumes) that citizens possess a kind of positive regard for one another, while substantive neutrality more plausibly merely asks individuals to be attentive to the ways in which state actions put some citizens at a disadvantage and see if there are ways to mitigate that disadvantage. That is, substantive neutrality does not ask citizens to forego their critical views of others' lives or beliefs but instead to construct political institutions such that they are reasonably likely to be properly *tolerant* of those whose views do not in the main shape policy outcomes.

Second, note how substantive neutrality, unlike recognition, is an inherently corrective process; it takes for granted that even well-meaning policymakers will act in ways that substantially favor some groups over others. One way to think about this is that substantive neutrality calls for liberal states as a first-order effort to be evenhanded when it comes to distributing their benefits and burdens and then to try and correct that evenhandedness as a second-order effort when it becomes clear that the first-order evenhandedness carried with it some inequitable distributions. Recognition hopes for the establishment of a social order in which are equally valorized by the state and equally (or at least reasonably) valorize one another. Substantive neutrality has much more modest hopes: we might be able to correct some inequities, but it is unreasonable to suppose that we can correct them all. Even when political actors act in good faith this is true because sometimes politics really is a zero-sum game. When we secure one good, we sometimes must sacrifice another.

Conclusion

Substantive neutrality thus seems to make the most sense in regard to how to make toleration politically effective in democracy under conditions moral and religious pluralism. Toleration emerges from the practice of moral judgment in which we make choices regarding apparently irreconcilable goods with an eye on individual agency. In pressing on this second-order effort of substantive neutrality, liberal orders can genuinely look to redress inequities precisely because they have a serious commitment to treating citizens fairly with regard to their own agency and independence. But those orders cannot expect to do so without remainder: in securing one set of goods they (nearly always) inevitably forfeit or neglect others. Such efforts are quite likely to be messy, imperfect and even on occasion issue in real injustices, but none of the alternatives—recognition or neutrality of intent—are as morally attractive. Indeed, it might very well be the case that embracing those alternatives, either in the name of practicality or moral integrity, could do real damage to the stability and decency of the liberal democratic orders they are meant to support. There are any number of sources for the populist discontent roiling democracies across the globe, but a moment's reflection suggests that democratic orders' ham-handedness at managing and redressing slights and injustices endemic to the difficulties of pluralist societies is a contributing factor. Scholars and policymakers might do well, then, to consider more deeply a number of important questions around political toleration.

What are, first, the proper bounds of entirely unacceptable moral views in pluralist democracies? We saw above that the fact that liberal orders stand foursquare against some ways of live – the life of the slaveholder – is no moral problem; the same goes for the religious tradition that requires human sacrifice. As societies' moral intuitions have shifted rapidly on issues like race and sexuality, have our hard lines of unacceptability shifted as well?

Second, how should substantive neutrality play out institutionally? It is tempting to simply throw everything over to the court systems and rely on judges to act as our chief moral balancers, but that strategy is fraught with all sorts of difficulties, perhaps most acutely that it is not always true that judges are in a good position to recognize or act on situations where groups are suffering the iniquitous effects of some policy or institutional arrangement. What's more, it would be helpful to think much more deeply about how federalized or subsidiary political arrangements can (or cannot) help to mitigate our moral and cultural conflicts. In the American context, what might be a good solution for California might not be right for Arkansas, and vice-versa.

Finally, how do modes and means of communication affect our ability to tolerate one another, both interpersonally and politically? The internet and in particular social media have opened up a world of information and communication that, despite its tremendous promise, has been implicated the growth intolerance and hatred. Can we learn to live with one another as digital neighbors in ways that give due regard for our real and enduring differences? The answer is decidedly unclear, and it may be the case that the future of pluralist, politically tolerant liberal democratic orders depends on the answer.

References

Bowlin, John R (2016) Tolerance among the Virtues. Princeton, N.J.: Princeton University Press
Eberle, CJ (2002) "Religion and liberal democracy." In The Blackwell Guide to Social and Political Philosophy, edited by R.L. Simon. New York: Blackwell
Forst, Rainer (2014) "Toleration and Democracy." Journal of Social Philosophy 45(1):65–75
Galeotti, AE (2002) Toleration as Recognition. New York: Cambridge University Press
Gill ER (2001) Becoming Free: Autonomy and Diversity in the Liberal Polity. Lawrence: University Press of Kansas
Halbertal M (1996) "Autonomy, Toleration, and Group Rights." In Toleration : An Elusive Virtue, edited by D. Heyd, 242. Princeton, NJ: Princeton University Press
Hamburger J (1999) John Stuart Mill On Liberty and Control. Princeton: Princeton University Press
Hauerwas S (1981) A Community of Character: Toward a Constructive Christian Social Ethic. Notre Dame, IN: University of Notre Dame Press

18 Political Toleration as Substantive Neutrality

Heyd D (2008) "Is Toleration A Political Virtue?" In Toleration and Its Limits, edited by M. Williams, 171–94. New York: New York University Press

King PT (1998) Toleration. London: Frank Cass

Koppelman, Andrew (2004) "The Fluidity of Neutrality." Review of Politics 66(4):633–48

———. (2013) Defending American Religious Neutrality. Harvard University Press

Larmore CE (1987) Patterns of Moral Complexity. New York: Cambridge University Press

Laycock D (1990) "Formal, Substantive, and Disaggregated Neutrality Toward Religion." Depaul Law Review 39:993–1018

MacIntyre AC (1980) After Virtue: A Study in Moral Theory. Notre Dame, IN: University of Notre Dame Press

McConnell MW (2000) "Believers as Equal Citizens." In Obligations of Citizenship and Demands of Faith, edited by N.L. Rosenblum. Princeton: Princeton University Press

McGraw BT (2010) Faith in Politics: Religion and Liberal Democracy. New York: Cambridge University Press

Mendus S (1999) The Politics of Toleration : Tolerance and Intolerance in Modern Life. Edinburgh: Edinburgh University Press

Monsma S (2000) "Substantive Neutrality as a Basis for Free Exercise-No Establishment Common Ground." Journal of Church and State 42(1):13–35

Oberdiek H (2001) Tolerance: Between Forbearance and Acceptance. Lanham, MD: Rowman & Littlefield Publishers

Rawls John (1996) Political Liberalism. New York: Columbia University Press

Rosenblum NL (1998) Membership and Morals: The Personal Uses of Pluralism in America. Princeton: Princeton University Press

Sher, G. 1997. Beyond Neutrality : Perfectionism and Politics. Cambridge; New York: Cambridge University Press

Smith, Steven (2010) The Disenchantment of Secular Discourse. Cambridge, MA: Harvard University Press

Stepan A (2000) "Religion, Democracy, and the 'Twin Tolerations.'" Journal of Democracy 11(4): 37–58

Taylor C and A Gutmann (1992) Multiculturalism and "The Politics of Recognition" : An Essay. Princeton: Princeton University Press

Tomasi J (2001) Liberalism Beyond Justice. Princeton: Princeton University Press

Williams B (1999) "Tolerating the Intolerable." In The Politics of Toleration: Tolerance and Intolerance in Modern Life, edited by S. Mendus. Edinburgh: Edinburgh University Press

Conscientious Exemptions: Between Toleration, Neutrality, and Respect

19

Yossi Nehushtan

Contents

Introduction	342
The Descriptive Aspect of Toleration – and Its Nonexistent Normative Aspect	343
Granting Conscientious Exemptions as an Expression of Toleration	345
Granting Conscientious Exemptions as Toleration: Reply to Possible Objections	347
Confusing Between Toleration and Its Justifications	347
Mistakenly Perceiving Toleration as a Justification	349
When the Legislature Speaks – What Does it Say?	352
Granting Conscientious Exemptions and Neutrality	353
Can there Be a Neutral State?	354
Can the State Be Neutral when it Grants Conscientious Exemptions?	355
Neutrality and Judicial Integrity	357
Neutrality and Toleration	359
Summary and Future Directions	360
References	361

Abstract

This chapter explains why granting conscientious exemptions is almost always the outcome of toleration – and always the outcome of toleration – in cases where the exemption is granted from a law that reflects or enforces moral values. The chapter explains why the principle of toleration better explains both the practice of granting conscientious exemptions and the attitude of those who grant the exemptions.

Much of the discomfort that this argument causes and much of the criticism of it, result from confusing the dominant descriptive aspect of toleration with its

Y. Nehushtan (✉)
Keele University, Newcastle-Under-Lyme, UK
e-mail: y.nehushtan@keele.ac.uk

© The Author(s), under exclusive licence to Springer Nature Switzerland AG 2022
M. Sardoč (ed.), *The Palgrave Handbook of Toleration*,
https://doi.org/10.1007/978-3-030-42121-2_54

non-existent normative aspect; from mistakenly seeing toleration as a reason or justification; and from mistakenly perceiving it as a political or moral virtue. The chapter explains why toleration is a descriptive concept and never a reason or justification to act in a certain way, and why toleration is not a political or moral virtue, but rather either morally good, morally allowed, morally prohibited or a lesser evil – all according to the circumstances.

The chapter then continues to explain why the concepts of neutrality and respect fail to accurately describe the practice of granting conscientious exemptions and the attitude of those who grant the exemptions. As to neutrality, it fails to describe the practice of granting conscientious exemptions, both because the state is not and can never be neutral, and because the argument that granting conscientious exemptions results from state's neutrality can never be coherent. As to respect, it either misses the nature of conscientious exemptions – or collapses into the definition of toleration. The chapter concludes with a conceptual note according to which the concepts of neutrality and toleration have some overlooked similarities, generally, and also within the context of granting conscientious exemptions.

Keywords

Conscientious exemptions · Toleration · Neutrality · Respect · Moral virtue

---

Introduction

The purpose of this chapter is to explain why granting conscientious exemptions is almost always the outcome of toleration and why the principle of toleration better explains both the practice of granting conscientious exemptions and the attitude of those who grant the exemptions. Before doing so, a brief explanation of the concepts of "conscientious exemption" and "toleration" is needed.

A conscientious exemption is called for when deeply held moral values of a group or an individual runs into the demands or determinations of the law. In other words, the conscientious objector seeks an exemption from the law because she holds an alternative set of basic values or an alternative way of balancing basic values – which are all part of her conscience, or the result of it – that conflicts with the ends, the means or the values of a specific law, and, ultimately, contradicts the demands or the determinations of that law (Nehushtan 2015).

As to toleration, it is here understood as refraining from harming the "other" although the tolerant person has good reasons (in her opinion) to harm that "other." The tolerant person makes an adverse judgment about another person (or about her views or behavior), the adverse judgment provides the tolerant person with reasons to harm the other, but the tolerant person restrains herself and avoids harming the other. These three elements of (a) adverse judgment, (b) reasons for causing harm, and (c) restraint – differentiate the concept of toleration and the attitude of toleration from concepts such as respect, neutrality, acceptance, or indifference.

The Descriptive Aspect of Toleration – and Its Nonexistent Normative Aspect

Following the above definition of toleration, it is clear why the concept of toleration and even more so – an attitude of toleration – cause discomfort to some. In an era of multiculturalism, moral relativism and censorious politically correctness, making adverse judgments about others may be perceived as impolite, disrespectful, perhaps even intolerant, or indeed - intolerable. Having this adverse judgment as a reason to harm others sounds even worse. The eventual restraint, that results in not harming the other after all, is of little comfort to those who see toleration as a negative attitude. From the tolerable person's point of view, and if it is clear to her that she is being merely tolerated, the tolerator's decision not to harm her may be perceived as less valuable compared to the very same behavior (not harming), if that resulted from respect, acceptance, indifference or neutrality. Being tolerated while knowing that, can at times be offensive and even insulting.

Yet toleration is here to stay, because of two main reasons. First, the concept of toleration merely describes things as they are, and it does it in a way that no other concept does. There is no other concept that describes the common case where we do make an adverse judgment about others, that adverse judgment provides us with reasons to harm them, yet we restrain ourselves and avoid harming them. And there is no other concept but intolerance, that accurately describes the case where we do act on the adverse judgment that we make about others – and therefore decide to harm them. Second, and in some cases, the principle of toleration, despite the discomfort it causes to some, describes the way in which we *should* behave or the attitude that we should have. Accordingly, and in other cases, it is the concept of intolerance that will describe the way in which we should behave.

Toleration, therefore, has two aspects to it. The descriptive aspect – that merely describes things as they are – i.e., that describes a certain behavior as tolerant (or intolerant); and the (allegedly) normative-guiding aspect – that describe things as they should be – i.e., that describes a desirable, morally justified attitude. This normative aspect of toleration is perhaps not normative at all, but rather still descriptive. This is so because even though the principle of toleration can be used in order to normatively evaluate a certain behavior, toleration itself – and that is a point that is often misunderstood – is never a reason or a justification for a certain behavior. The concept itself does not have this normative aspect to it.

The argument that granting conscientious exemptions from general laws or policies is almost always the outcome of toleration – and always the outcome of toleration when the law or policy reflects or enforces moral values – is a descriptive, analytical argument. Much of the discomfort that this argument causes and much of the criticism of it, result from confusing the descriptive aspect of toleration with its non-existent normative aspect – and also from mistakenly seeing toleration as a political or moral virtue.

It is important therefore to clarify why toleration is never a reason or a justification, i.e., why it is not a normative-guiding principle. Seeing toleration as a justification is quite common. Misguided arguments along this line are that "toleration means that we should not harm others even though we disagree with them or making adverse judgments about them"; or that "toleration is a political or moral virtue, therefore being tolerant is preferable to being intolerant," or that "the principle of toleration provides a strong (or weak) reason for the state to grant conscientious exemptions."

As a reminder, toleration means not harming others, even though an adverse judgment that we make about them, their views or behavior, gives us reasons to harm them. Toleration, understood in this way, merely describes either an existing attitude or a desirable one – but there is nothing in that definition of toleration or in the concept of toleration that provides reasons to be tolerant (or intolerant) – or to act in a certain way. These reasons are external to the concept of toleration. These external reasons may be the justifications or motives for toleration – but they are not part of the concept itself. Put simply, toleration is an attitude, a mindset combined with an omission or an act. It is not, in and of itself, a reason to act in a certain way, or any way.

There can be many reasons, motives or justifications for toleration – yet without toleration itself being a reason to act in a certain way. We may tolerate others because we respect their right to personal autonomy – so their right to be wrong; because we pity them or empathize with them; or because of various pragmatic-utilitarian reasons. These reasons for toleration, these justifications of toleration, are in fact the reasons for not harming others. Toleration is merely the result of acting on these reasons – and not the reason itself.

Toleration is the outcome of acting on reasons, whatever reasons, for not harming others. That is the descriptive aspect of the concept. Sometimes we also use the concepts of toleration and intolerance not just to describe a certain behavior but also to argue for or against that behavior. Even then, toleration does not lose its descriptive nature. A certain tolerant or intolerant behavior will be either morally right or wrong, not because toleration and intolerance are inherently morally good or bad, or because they provide us reasons to act in a certain way. A certain tolerant or intolerant behavior will be either morally right or wrong, because of reasons that are external to these concepts.

That insight runs against the common view that there is an inherent moral value to the principle of toleration. Toleration is not a moral virtue, nor is intolerance a moral vice (▶ Chap. 39, "Toleration and Compassion: A Conceptual Comparison"). Toleration (and intolerance) are not end-points on a spectrum of good and bad. A tolerant behavior will be morally wrong if it is a response to things that should not be tolerated, and an intolerant behavior will be morally right if it is a response to things that should not be tolerated.

Classifying toleration as a moral virtue, as an interim virtue or as a lesser evil, cannot be part of the concept of toleration itself. At most, we can classify certain tolerant behaviors as morally necessary, morally allowed, lesser evils or morally wrong. The question of how we should decide which tolerant behavior falls into which category is a normative and complex question, that is external to the definition of what toleration is, and that will not be discussed in more detail here.

Toleration is not a justification or reason for action, but not just because it does not have inherent value. There are other principles that do not have inherent value, yet they can be used as justifications.

Autonomy, for example, is also not inherently valuable. Autonomy is valuable only when it is being exercised in pursuit of making valuable decisions (Raz 1988). It loses its value when it is being exercised in pursuit of making morally repugnant decisions and it has limited value when it is being exercised in pursuit of making morally misguided decisions or non-valuable ones. Yet unlike toleration, autonomy is a reason for action. It is a justification for treating people in a certain way, including in a tolerant way.

Toleration, therefore, is not a reason or justification, mostly because its dominant aspect is descriptive: it describes a certain attitude, that may or may not be desirable, but it does not provide reasons for this attitude or for any other attitude.

It is this nature of the concept of toleration that informs the argument about seeing granting conscientious exemptions as an expression of toleration; and it is a misunderstanding of this nature of the concept of toleration that leads to some of the criticism of the view that conscientious exemptions are almost always an expression of toleration.

In the next section, the argument that conscientious exemptions are almost always the result of toleration will be explained. In the following sections, criticism and counterarguments will be presented and ultimately refuted, also by bearing in mind the descriptive aspect of toleration and it not being a moral or political virtue.

Granting Conscientious Exemptions as an Expression of Toleration

Accommodating conscientious objection, typically by granting conscientious exemptions from the application of the law or administrative policies, is almost always the outcome of toleration (Jones 2012; Nehushtan 2013, 2015). It is always the outcome of toleration in cases where the general law or policy reflects or enforces certain moral values (Nehushtan 2019).

Typically, granting conscientious exemptions from a legal rule which is not morally neutral, presupposes that the state does not share the conscientious objector's values or his way of balancing between values, or believes it would be unbearable and indeed intolerable if everyone shared the objector's kind of conscience and reasoning. Otherwise, the exemption would have been the general rule rather than the exception to it.

If granting conscientious exemptions is in most cases the outcome of toleration, then the practice of granting conscientious exemptions is closely related to the complex question of the limits of toleration. And if the state is a liberal state, the exact question will be that of the limits of liberal toleration – a question that will not be discussed here. Suffice it to say that these limits can be decided by applying one of two possible theories: neutral liberalism or perfectionist liberalism. The former requires that the state will not take a moral stand regarding the content of the objector's conscience – or that it will not act on this moral stand – when it decides whether to grant conscientious exemptions. The latter allows the state to take such moral stand and act on it.

The argument that granting conscientious exemptions is an expression of toleration, is a descriptive argument. It does not say that the legislature *should* take a moral stand regarding the content of the objector's conscience when deciding whether to accommodate conscientious objections. Rather, it says that the legislature *does* take this moral stand.

Think about cases where the state exempts pacifists from compulsory enlistment to the army; religious groups from compulsory education laws; or physicians from performing abortions. If the state morally approved these types of conscience, it would not have enacted compulsory enlistment laws, compulsory education laws and permissive abortion laws to begin with.

When the state enacts laws that reflect or enforce moral values, the state takes a moral stand on the relevant issues. When people conscientiously object to these laws, the state must make some kind of an adverse judgment about these conscientious objectors' values or their way of balancing between values. This judgment gives the state reasons not to grant the conscientious objector an exemption from the legal rule, thereby harming the objector. If the state decides to grant the exemption after all, it can be seen as tolerant. The state may tolerate conscientious objections for pragmatic reasons – and that would be an expression of pragmatic toleration; or for principled reasons – and that would be a case of principled toleration where the state acknowledges the conscientious objector's right to be tolerated.

When the state, for example, grants exemptions from equality laws to religious organizations, the state, if it is a liberal state, morally disapproves the religious conscience that prescribes discrimination against protected groups (most commonly – on the basis of sex, sexual orientation and religion) (Jones 2012). If the state perceived the religious discriminatory conscience or practice as morally desirable, it would not have enacted equality laws to begin with. Exemptions from equality laws are often granted only to religious organizations. This may lead to perceiving these exemptions as an expression of favoritism rather than toleration. This perception is only partly true. Religious organizations do get special, positive treatment within the context of equality laws, as non-religious organizations will almost never be allowed to discriminate against others on the grounds of sex, sexual orientation or religion, but the true meaning of this favoritism is that religious organizations are the only ones that are being tolerated by the state. This unique mixture of favoritism and toleration does not contradict the argument that granting conscientious exemptions is almost always an expression of toleration – and always the outcome of toleration in cases where the relevant general rule is not morally neutral, i.e., in cases where the general rule reflects or enforces a moral view.

As to laws that do not reflect or enforce moral values, when the state does grant conscientious exemptions from such laws, its attitude will not always be that of toleration, but quite often – it is. Laws that do not reflect or enforce moral values are, for example, laws that focus on health and safety or on coordinating behavior. Such laws may, for example, enforce wearing safety helmets, decide on one designated day of rest, enforce a certain dress code, and so on.

Although these laws might contradict the conscience of some, the fact that these laws do not reflect any significant moral decision made by the legislature means that granting a conscientious exemption from them can – but does not have to – entail a negative judgment about the objector's conscience. The legislature, or the court, may or may not make an adverse judgment about those who conscientiously object to certain morally neutral laws, precisely because these laws are morally neutral. The legislature, or the court, may think, for example, that an objection to obeying a safety law because of religious reasons is silly, and that it results from conducting distorted balance between competing reasons, but they do not have to make this judgment. Having said that, and as will be elaborated below, some kind of an adverse judgment will normally be made in these cases as well.

Cases where laws do not reflect moral values, yet they still result in conscientious objections, with the latter being accommodated without making any adverse judgment about the objectors, are uncommon. These cases would be an exception to the general argument about seeing conscientious exemptions as an expression of toleration. That exception, therefore, does not affect the strength of the general argument. Morally neutral laws are unlikely to be objected on the ground of conscience, and when they are, that normally do not raise important moral or policy issues. These laws present no more than a peripheral case that should not affect the general way of understanding the practice of granting conscientious exemptions.

This section explained why granting conscientious exemptions is almost always an expression of toleration. The next section presents possible objections to this argument – and replies to them. The following section presents a more specific reply to those who think that the concept of neutrality better explains this practice.

Granting Conscientious Exemptions as Toleration: Reply to Possible Objections

The general criticism against the view that granting conscientious exemptions is almost always an expression of toleration, results from three fallacies: confusing between toleration and its justifications; perceiving toleration itself as a justification; and failing to identify the attitude of the legislature when it enacts laws and grants exemptions from them.

Confusing Between Toleration and Its Justifications

One possible objection is that instead of seeing conscientious exemptions as an expression of toleration, we should make recourse to a cluster of moral principles which explain and guide that practice (Adenitire 2017, 2020). The suggested cluster contains various principles, including respect for state neutrality, autonomy, freedom of conscience, and well-being. Except for neutrality (that will be discussed in the next section), these principles are in fact reasons for toleration. These moral principles do not replace the principle of toleration as an *explanation* of the practice of granting conscientious exemptions, but rather *justify* an attitude of toleration when exemptions are granted. Unlike toleration, these principles do not *describe* the nature of the practice of granting conscientious exemptions, but rather *justify* this practice – while this practice still remains that of toleration.

When the state enacts a law that reflects or enforces moral values, the state takes a stand for these moral values. A conscientious objector to such law, by definition, thinks that the moral values that are reflected in the law are misguided. The state, of course, does not and cannot share this view. The state therefore makes an adverse judgment about the conscientious objector's values or his way of balancing between competing values. This adverse judgment always gives the state a reason to harm the objector by not granting him an exemption. If the state refrains from acting on that reason and decides to grant the exemption after all, the state is being tolerant toward the objector. The state can decide to tolerate the objector for various reasons, one of which can be respecting the objector's autonomy, freedom of conscience or well-being. The state, and that should be clear, does not necessarily respect the *content* of the objector's conscience. In almost all cases, the state will not and cannot think that the content of the objector's conscience is valuable or admirable. Rather, the state may respect the fact that the objector is acting on her conscience and will acknowledge the objector's autonomy, by respecting the objector's right to be wrong, and acknowledging that her well-being requires that this right will be respected. When that is the state's attitude, the state acknowledges that the objector's autonomy, freedom of conscience and well-being result in the objector's having a right to be tolerated. Both autonomy and freedom of conscience are particularly important here as both entail the right to do wrong – the legal right to act in a way that is being perceived as wrong, either morally or otherwise, by the public, the state or both. Having a legal right to do wrong, is having a legal right to be tolerated, rather than having a right that the objector's values or way of life will not be judged, or be "respected," i.e., be seen as valuable.

This is the right context within which we should understand arguments such as "when the state grants a conscientious exemption it is usually also paying respect to an aspect of the objector's well-being" (Adenitire 2017). The fact that not granting an exemption harms the well-being of the conscientious objector, does not necessarily mean that granting an exemption results from paying respect to the objector's well-being. "Respect" is a too powerful concept that implies approval, acceptance, admiration, etc., and in any event – it entails a positive attitude toward people's decisions, acts or lifestyle. But the state does not need to respect any of these in order not to harm the conscientious objector's well-being. The state may simply decide that the objector has a right to be wrong, while showing no respect to the *content* of the conscientious objector's decisions, acts or lifestyle.

When the principle of autonomy is being used to justify the practice of granting conscientious exemptions, it becomes even clearer that autonomy does not replace toleration as an *explanation* of that practice but rather *justifies* tolerating conscientious objectors by granting them exemptions. The idea of personal autonomy "is that

19 Conscientious Exemptions: Between Toleration, Neutrality, and Respect

people should make their own lives. The autonomous person is a (part) author of his own life. The ideal of personal autonomy is the vision of people controlling, to some degree, their own destiny, fashioning it through successive decisions throughout their lives" (Raz 1988).

Personal autonomy is the main justification for liberal toleration. If there is a non-absolute right to be granted conscientious exemptions, it will be justified by the principle of autonomy, that in turn justifies the principle of toleration – and the practice of tolerating conscientious objectors by granting them conscientious exemptions.

Mistakenly Perceiving Toleration as a Justification

wSome argue against perceiving the practice of granting conscientious exemptions as an expression of toleration, as it may result in granting exemptions in the wrong cases. Adenitire gives the (real) example of claimants who claim conscientious exemption from an online tax filing requirement, and says that if granting conscientious exemptions is an expression of toleration, then "... we would have had a prima facie reason to entertain the claims of the two claimants who seek an exemption from online tax filing: they have a right to be tolerated" (Adenitire 2017). This argument is misguided for three reasons. First, Adenitire argues that instead of seeing the practice of granting conscientious exemptions through the lens of toleration, we should see it through the lens of respecting the conscientious objector's autonomy, freedom of conscience, and well-being. It is not at all clear how these principles lead to a *weaker* prima-facie reason for granting exemptions – compare with the principle of toleration (assuming, as Adenitire does, that toleration is a reason for granting exemptions). Respect for the conscientious objector's autonomy, freedom of conscience, and well-being, is probably the most powerful prima-facie reason to grant an exemption. Even if toleration is a reason for granting exemptions, and it is not, surely it cannot be a stronger reason than respecting personal autonomy, freedom of conscience and people's well-being.

Second, even if toleration is a reason for granting exemptions (and it is not), and even if an exemption is granted, it does not have to result from the conscientious objector having a right to be tolerated. Conscientious objectors can be granted exemptions, and therefore be tolerated, for pragmatic-utilitarian reasons, without the state acknowledging their right to be exempted.

Third, and more importantly, Adenitire's argument misses the analytical-descriptive nature of toleration – and misinterprets it as a normative-guiding principle. He sees toleration as a justification instead of mere description. As was explained above, toleration is not a justification. It describes a certain attitude. It does not give reasons for this attitude. Toleration, therefore, is not a reason for granting conscientious exemptions. If the state decides to tolerate conscientious objectors by exempting them from the application of the law, the state does that because of reasons that are external to the concept of toleration.

Adenitire then adds that "... on the assumption that toleration is a political virtue, we may have had a normative reason to exempt the objectors: we want the state to act virtuously and we thereby grant a right to exemption" (Adenitire 2017). That is a good observation and it does indeed depend on toleration being a political virtue. However, toleration is neither a political virtue nor a moral one. Therefore, it cannot, in and of itself, provide reasons to do anything, including granting conscientious exemptions. As was explained above, toleration and intolerance are not end-points on a spectrum of good and bad but can be either morally good or morally bad according to the circumstances. Toleration can be either morally necessary, morally allowed, a lesser evil or morally wrong (for example, when we tolerate things that should not be tolerated). Toleration, therefore, does not provide prima-facie reasons for granting exemptions, or any kind of reasons for granting exemptions. It merely describes what the state does when it decides to grant exemptions – for whatever reason.

Adenitire's mistake is perceiving toleration as a reason at all – and as a strong reason for granting exemptions. Interestingly, Smet made a similar mistake to that of Adenitire's by seeing toleration as a reason, but then he continued to argue that viewing the practice of granting conscientious exemptions through the lens of toleration, will lead to granting *less* exemptions than if we view it through the lens of respect for the objector's autonomy or for the objector as such (Smet 2019. Smet does distinguish between "recognition respect" and "appraisal respect," but this distinction is of little importance here).

For Smet, toleration is indeed a reason, but a reason for *not* granting an exemption. Smet argues that we should differentiate between two categories of conscientious objection: claims of conscience that do not infringe the legal rights of others – and those that do. He then continues to say that the former should be viewed through the more permissive lens of respect, whereas the latter "should be evaluated through the more restrictive lens of tolerance."

For Smet, "through the lens of respect, conscientious objection is viewed in a positive light. As a result, a presumption operates in favor of protection and against restriction. By contrast. . . through the lens of tolerance, conscientious objections are regarded with suspicion and disapproval." It is true that through the lens of toleration, conscientious objections are regarded with suspicion and disapproval. After all, toleration does entail making an adverse judgment about the conscientious objector's values or her way of balancing between values. However, it will be wrong to argue that the lens of respect is suitable to cases where the claims of conscience do not infringe the legal rights of others – where exemptions should be positively considered; and that the lens of toleration is suitable to cases where claims of conscience do infringe the legal rights of others – where exemptions should normally not be granted. This is so for four reasons.

First, and as explained above, toleration is not a justification or reason that should be added to the balance of reasons for and against granting an exemption. Toleration merely describes the practice of granting exemptions.

Second, precisely because toleration is not a reason, yet respect for autonomy is, they are interrelated. As noted above, respect for the autonomy of the conscientious objector can be a reason for tolerating her, also by exempting her from the application of the law. It is wrong to perceive toleration as a one-dimensional attitude that only entails "suspicion and disapproval." When the tolerant state makes an adverse judgment about the conscientious objector's values, it does disapprove those values. But if the state decides to grant an exemption after all, it may do so because it respects the objector's autonomy and her right to be wrong.

Third, it is wrong to argue that through the lens of respect, conscientious objection is viewed in a positive light, because – and for all the reasons mentioned above – conscientious objection is almost never perceived in a positive light by the legislature. The legislature almost always disagrees with the conscientious objector's values. The lens of respect, if it is understood as respect regarding the content of the objector's conscience, almost never exists.

Fourth, Smet argues that toleration entails disapproval – and that is true. However, Smet implies that that disapproval is a reason for not granting an exemption, and that that attitude should be applied in cases where claims of conscience infringe the legal rights of others. It was explained above why toleration is generally not a reason or justification – but rather a description. But more should be said here about why the "negative" aspect of toleration – and here, disapproving the objector's conscience – should not be perceived as a weighty reason *against* granting conscientious exemptions, even if we mistakenly think that toleration is a reason to be added to the balance of reasons. If the view that toleration better describes the practice of granting conscientious exemptions is true, that means that the state almost always disapproves the content of the objector's conscience. And precisely because of that, that disapproval should not be a weighty reason for not granting an exemption. If mere disapproval of the objector's conscience is a weighty reason for not granting an exemption, it may lead to not taking the objector's autonomy, freedom of conscience and well-being seriously, and ultimately to not granting exemptions in cases where they should be granted. If the starting point of every claim of conscience is a dispute between the state and the individual regarding the weight that should be accorded to competing values, or even regarding the legitimacy of certain values, then the state must find a reason on top of the mere disapproval of the objector's conscience, in order to refuse granting an exemption. Without elaborating on that point, that reason can be one of two kinds: it can relate to the content of the objector's conscience or it can be content-neutral. As to the former – a weighty reason for not granting an exemption could be that the content of the objector's conscience reflects not merely misguided values with which the state disagrees, but rather illegitimate and morally repugnant values that should not be tolerated in a tolerant-liberal state. As to the latter – the list of possible neutral-content considerations is too long to be mentioned here, but they can all be potential reasons for not tolerating the conscientious objector by not granting them an exemption.

When the Legislature Speaks – What Does it Say?

The argument that toleration better explains the practice of granting conscientious exemptions applies most strongly to cases where the state enacts laws that reflect or enforce moral values. The argument here is that any exemption to such laws, whether a statutory exemption or one that is being granted as judicial remedy, results from the legislature making an adverse judgment about the content of the conscientious objector's conscience, followed by either the legislature or the court not acting on this judgment. This description assumes a certain legislative intention while enacting the law (reflecting or enforcing certain moral values) – and a certain attitude while granting a statutory exemption from it (making an adverse judgment about the conscientious objectors, but not acting on it).

But how can such intentions and attitudes be identified? It can be argued that the attitude of the legislature is an empirical question (Adenitire 2017). Adenitire gives the example of the discussion in the UK Parliament about exempting Sikhs from the requirement to wear safety helmets during employment in any workplace. Given the positive tone of most of the speakers in the discussion, Adenitire wonders whether we should conclude that the exemption was not granted out of toleration but rather out of admiration for the Sikh community. Adenitire is too quick here to use empirical evidence to refute the argument according to which it is very likely that in this case, the attitude of the legislature was that of toleration after all. The reasons for that are threefold.

First, there is no reason to assume that Members of Parliament say what they really think. They, like most politicians, have good reasons to conceal their real views. Empirical data about views of legislatures that were expressed during the legislative process, merely proves that these views were expressed, not that they were sincerely held by those who expressed them.

Second, we can build on Jones' accurate observation that "toleration is a feature of the exemptions themselves rather than an expression of any particular person's or party's toleration" (Jones 2012). Put differently, and as argued above, creating a general norm that reflects certain moral values that the creator of the norm wishes to protect or enforce – and then exempting those who conscientiously object to such values, must reflect, almost as a matter of logic, an attitude of toleration. That attitude is expressed by "the law," regardless of what the lawmakers actually said during the legislative process.

Third, and if we go back to Adenitire's attempt to identify the actual intention of the legislature, it seems that Adenitire's impliedly subscribes to a subjective-intentional method of legislative interpretation, where the aim is to find the meaning of the text according to the "actual" intention of the legislature. Without elaborating on the subject of legislative interpretation, this method has significant methodological shortcomings regarding the ability to identify the genuine intention of dozens, at times hundreds of individuals who form the legislative body. A sounder method would be that of "purposive interpretation." Here, and in order to find the law's purpose, one should turn simultaneously to the subjective and objective purpose of the law. The subjective purpose is the genuine purpose of the legislature, if there is any, and that purpose can be expressed in different levels of abstraction. The objective purpose is the hypothetical purpose of a reasonable legislator, and always – a purpose that coincides with the long-term and basic values of the legal system.

But we do not have to explore methods of legislative interpretation to make the case for seeing granting conscientious exemptions as a reflection of toleration. Common sense will do – and here the "helmets case" can be used an example. In the "helmets case," the purpose of the law that compels workers to wear helmets in certain workplaces, is to protect workers from their own stupidity. It is mostly a paternalistic law that compels workers to make the reasonable decision for them – and to prioritize safety over comfort and most other considerations. And then a special case arises: that of religious people who prioritize a certain dress-code over safety. If the law-makers are not Sikhs themselves, and even more so – if they are not religious, and if they support the paternalistic safety law, how can they possibly not make an adverse judgment about a person who prioritizes a certain dress-code to safety, especially when this dress-code is being perceived as sacred because of religious reasons with which the law-makers utterly disagree. There are many good reasons why a lawmaker should not openly *say* that prioritizing a religious dress-code over safety is silly. Showing respect to a fellow citizen is one of these reasons. But there is no reason why a lawmaker should not *think* that this behavior is silly. That is the adverse judgment that is surely being made in this case. This adverse judgment gives a reason for the legislature not to exempt Sikhs from the law. Yet there are also good reasons not to act on that adverse judgment and to grant the exemption after all – as was done in our case. That is in fact an attitude of toleration.

That is also an example of what was described above as an attitude that mixes toleration and favoritism. A secular worker with a strong objection to wearing helmets, would probably not be accommodated. It was the religious nature of the Sikhs' claim that gave it its political strength. Religious people do sometimes get special, positive treatment when they seek conscientious exemptions, but the true meaning of this favoritism is that in these cases, religious people are the only ones that are being tolerated by the state. This mixture of favoritism and toleration is quite common – and coincides with the argument that granting conscientious exemptions is almost always an expression of toleration.

Granting Conscientious Exemptions and Neutrality

Neutrality is an elusive concept. Neutral liberalism requires the state to pay equal respect to competing moral claims and ways of life. It requires that the state should not endorse, promote or restrict any value or way of life, despite the fact that the state's authorities may believe that some values and ways of life are worth pursuing whereas others are not. According to any perception of neutral liberalism, when the state decides whether to restrict people's freedom – it should ignore the moral content of the values on which the claim for "freedom" is based, and can only take into account content-neutral considerations.

Adenitire (2017) uses this perception of neutrality, and at times adds to that the concept of pluralism, to *justify* having a non-absolute right to be granted conscientious exemptions. He argues, for example, that "... the argument from pluralism is essentially an argument for state neutrality. In imposing a particular rule which creates a barrier to the pursuit of a particular lifestyle, the state may be portrayed as violating its duty of neutrality: the state makes certain lifestyles less accessible and thereby incentivizes individuals to choose other lifestyles... If the state is to remain neutral among competing lifestyles it should, therefore, grant an exemption to alleviate the barrier it has created." Whether the state *should* be neutral – is a question which is beyond the scope of this chapter. The focus of the following discussion will be on two other issues. The first is the question of whether the state *can* be neutral – mostly within the context of granting conscientious exemptions. The second is the relation between neutrality and toleration – and yet again, mostly within the context of granting conscientious exemptions.

Can there Be a Neutral State?

When the state enacts laws, especially laws that are likely to be objected on conscientious grounds, the state must make value judgments about conflicting conceptions of the good and about many aspects of its citizens' lives. Many of these judgments reflect moral choices and preferences of one set of values over another. Such is the case, for example, with regard to legal decisions about the mere existence of income tax and its rate; the existence of national health insurance and its extent; privatization; abortions; euthanasia; criminalizing hate speech; polygamy; anti-discrimination laws; sexual harassment laws; same-sex marriage laws; subsidizing primary and higher education; subsidizing cultural institutions and so on. Any legal or political decision regarding these issues is in fact a moral decision, at least in part. In order to make these decisions, the state has to embrace some values and reject others, or to accord greater weight to some values and less weight to others. Almost any meaningful political or legal decision distributes rights, duties, benefits, responsibilities and goods. Therefore, all states have to make moral decisions about how to apply a chosen version of distributive justice – and to justify that chosen version, that in turn may be objected by some, also because of conscientious reasons. Even Adenitire, who subscribes to neutral-liberalism, admits that "the state cannot permit all expressions of every lifestyle. Some will collude with fundamental public interests and/or the rights of others" (Adenitire 2017). However, the mere existence of "fundamental" public interest, and even more so – rights, their meaning, and the weight that should be accorded to them, cannot be decided by applying purely neutral criteria, and without making any moral judgment regarding competing lifestyles.

If the state must and does express moral judgment every time it enacts a law that reflects or enforces moral values, and if every modern state does enact laws that reflect or enforce moral values, then it will be odd to argue that the state cannot be neutral when it enacts its laws, but must be neutral when it decides whether to grant conscientious exemptions from such laws.

Even if the general argument about the impossibility of a neutral state is rejected, a stronger argument can be made about the impossibility of neutrality within the context of granting conscientious exemptions.

Can the State Be Neutral when it Grants Conscientious Exemptions?

Adenitire offers a neutral-liberal model for granting conscientious exemptions. One of its propositions is that "the liberal state should generally refrain from passing moral judgement on the content of the beliefs which give rise to a claim for conscientious exemption." (Adenitire 2020). This view coincides with his previous writing where he stated that "the state has no place in expressing negative (or positive) moral judgments about the content of conscientious objectors' beliefs, i. e., it has a duty of neutrality" (Adenitire 2017).

The question of whether the state *should* generally be neutral is misleading, because no modern state that is not a Hobbesian, radically libertarian state can be neutral. Within the more specific context of granting conscientious exemptions, an approach of state neutrality is impossible because it can never be coherent. Here, Adenitire's argument is that by enacting laws that reflect and enforce certain moral values, the state is violating its duty of neutrality. In order to remedy said violation, the state should grant exemptions from such laws to those who conscientiously object to them. A coherent argument for state neutrality would be that the state should never enact laws that reflect or enforce certain moral values to begin with. But Adenitire does not make that argument. His argument is that the state is allowed to enact such laws – but then to quickly remedy their non-neutral nature by granting exemptions to those who object to these laws because of conscientious reasons. Thus, the general non-neutral law should be upheld, while exemptions should be granted from it – while adhering to liberal-neutrality.

Using the case of anti-discrimination laws will help in explaining the incoherence of this approach. Anti-discrimination laws are not and cannot be neutral (Nehushtan 2019). They take a moral stand that clashes with many lifestyles and ideologies, both religious and secular. It will seem a bit odd criticizing anti-discrimination laws for not being neutral, i.e., for denying the right to act upon certain moral positions – as this is the exact purpose of such laws. It is, in fact, their nature. When such laws include protected characteristics, such as sexual orientation, they take a moral view on this issue, which almost always contradicts other moral views that some people hold. The prohibition on discriminating against others on the ground of their sexual orientation is not aimed at enlightened people who would never consider discriminating against lesbian, gay, bisexual and transgender (LGBT) people, nor is it mainly aimed at those who discriminate against LGBTs because of mere preferences or interests. It is aimed at homophobes and those who have moral reasons for discriminating against LGBTs. From the liberal state's point of view, it makes no sense to exempt from equality laws the same people who are the reason for enacting such laws. Put simply, granting exemptions from laws that reflect and enforce moral values – to those who conscientiously object to these moral values – will make these law, and therefore core liberal values – redundant. The argument from neutrality can be coherent (yet utterly non-persuasive) if it is aimed against anti-discrimination laws as such. It cannot be coherent if it justifies anti-discrimination laws and at the same time argues for exemptions from such laws to those who really, truly, strongly, and conscientiously wish to discriminate against others.

Adenitire makes two further arguments against toleration and for state's neutrality, within the context of granting conscientious exemptions. He argues that "it is futile for the state to express a view on the merits of the content of the beliefs of the objector for two reasons. First, such moral judgment is unlikely to lead the objector to change his beliefs. Second, the moral judgment is totally unnecessary for the more important task of safeguarding the public interest or the rights of others which the acts of the objector may undermine" (Adenitire 2017, 2020).

The first argument, about the futility of making an adverse judgment about the content of the objector's conscience, is attacking a scarecrow. This is so because of two reasons. First, even if making an adverse moral judgment about the content of the conscientious objector's conscience is not inevitable (yet it is), the purpose of making such judgment is not to make the objector change her belief or conscience. These are not likely to change just because an adverse moral judgment has been made about them, or indeed at all. The reason for making such moral judgment, in cases where that reason exists, is for the liberal state to fulfil its duty to promote and defend liberal values and condemn anti-liberal, unjustly intolerant ones. The purpose is to allow the tolerant-liberal state to properly and proportionally not tolerate unjustified intolerance. Assume that a powerful minority religious group seeks an exemption from an anti-discrimination law that prohibits discrimination on the ground of sexual orientation while hiring school teachers. Assume that the religious group wishes to discriminate on that ground while hiring teachers to their religious yet state-funded schools. Also assume that granting this exemption may be justified because of pragmatic-utilitarian reasons, for example the wish to avoid a violent response from members of that powerful minority group, or an on-going social unrest, or merely because enforcing the law is very unlikely to succeed. What should a tolerant-liberal state do in this case? the state can – and should – grant the exemption, while possibly also to deny state funding to those who will use the exemption, and in any event – to condemn the religious intolerance in this case and allow the public to freely and harshly criticize it. That is the tolerant-liberal state's duty to its gay citizens. This is an important message the state sends to the homophobes, and that must be clear: "we think you are unjustly intolerant and the only reason we do not take the necessary steps to eliminate your intolerance is not because we respect your values or way of life, but because we are unable to enforce the law or because we do not want to expose society to your even more intolerant response, should we not grant the exemption."

Second, Adenitire finds it troubling that the tolerant-liberal state, through its agents, expresses a negative view on the merits of the conscientious objector's conscience when it grants an exemption from the law. This, he argues, violates the state's duty to be neutral. Adenitire, however, is wrong to assume that the tolerant-liberal state must or will always openly express a negative view on the merits of the conscientious objector's conscience.

The argument presented in this chapter is that when the state does grant conscientious exemptions, the state's attitude is that of toleration. The state, however, does not have to publicly and openly express the adverse judgment that it makes about the content of the conscientious objector's conscience. The state, for various good reasons, may decide to be silent about it. Its attitude will still be that of toleration, for all the reasons mentioned in this chapter, but not every person who is being tolerated must know that they are being tolerated rather than "respected," "accepted," and so on. Toleration can and sometimes should be exercised unnoticeably.

Adenitire's second argument was that there is no need for the state to make an adverse moral judgment about the content of the conscientious objector's conscience, because neutral liberalism can properly protect core liberal values and safeguard the public interest or the rights of others which the acts of the objector may undermine. The neutral-liberal state can do that, presumably through its courts, by applying "content-neutral balancing tests." This point leads to the next section.

Neutrality and Judicial Integrity

When judges decide the limits of toleration towards conscientious objectors, they can apply one of two possible approaches: taking into account content-neutral considerations or taking into account content-based considerations (or a combination of both).

It has been argued that the distinction between content-based and content-neutral considerations is ambiguous; that it has its limitations; that it is incorrectly applied by the courts; and that it lacks merit (Wright 2006; Stone 1983; Schultz 1999; Chemerinsky 1994, 2000; Ammori 2009). The following discussion will not present a detailed case against such a neutral approach. It will be limited to only one point.

That point is that applying different neutral balancing tests to one case may lead to different results, and there is nothing in neutral liberalism that can guide the court regarding which tests to prioritize. Take the example of a service-provider who refuses to provide a service, because providing the service entails supporting gay marriage, either directly or indirectly. The service-provider wishes, therefore, to discriminate against certain customers, because her conscience prevents her from taking any part in enabling or supporting gay marriage. The question the court now faces is whether to exempt the objector from the application of an anti-discrimination law. According to any perception of neutral liberalism, when the state decides whether to restrict people's freedom – and in our case, the freedom to treat others differently – it should ignore the moral content of the values (here, the homophobic values) on which the claim for the "freedom to discriminate" is based. The state can only take into account content-neutral considerations, such as (1) who will be harmed more – those who discriminate against others if they are not allowed to discriminate – or those who will be discriminated against if the discrimination against them is allowed; (2) whether there are alternative service providers; (3) is the service provider or the service itself public or private; (4) the sincerity of the values held by the discriminator; (5) the centrality or importance of these values to the objector's holistic way of life; (6) whether the service is offered to the general public; (7) whether the service-provider started the business before the "no-discrimination" legal duty was introduced; etc.

We can easily envisage a case where applying some of the above content-neutral criteria will support granting an exemption, while applying other criteria will support the opposite decision. What should a judge do in such a case? Which criteria should be accorded more weight? Are some of them decisive? Neutral liberalism does not and cannot answer any of these questions. The result of said incompetence of neutral liberalism is obvious and inevitable: judges will pick and choose from the above criteria the ones that will lead to the decision they perceive as morally desirable – or will accord more weight to certain criteria and less weight to others, in order to achieve that morally desirable result. Judges will therefore apply content-based considerations but will hide them behind a neutral reasoning.

Adenitire argues that "judges considering conscientious exemptions are, for doctrinal reasons which reflect valid moral reasons, more than hesitant to express a negative moral judgment about the beliefs of conscientious objectors. If this is true, then judges cannot be engaging in the practice of toleration when engaged in the practice of considering whether to grant conscientious exemptions" (Adenitire 2017). Adenitire is right to argue that judges are hesitant to express a negative moral judgment about the beliefs of conscientious objectors. Yet he is wrong to conclude that because of that, judges do not or cannot be engaging in the practice of toleration when they decide whether to grant conscientious exemptions. Precisely because judges are hesitant, for whatever reason, to openly express a negative moral judgment about the objector's conscience, they find recourse in picking and choosing the neutral tests that will allow them to express either toleration or intolerance toward the conscientious objector, but without exposing their content-based attitude. This approach may have merits, as it may, for example, sustain public trust in courts, but it does not coincide with judicial integrity, it makes it difficult for stakeholders to predict judicial decisions in similar cases, and is certainly not "neutral."

Even if we accept Adenitere's argument that "not only do judges not normally engage in evaluating or condemning the moral beliefs of conscientious objectors; but prevailing doctrines prohibit them from doing so" (Adenitire 2017), we must not be naïve and should therefore revise the argument a bit and say that *because* prevailing doctrines prevent judges from considering the content of conscientious objectors' moral beliefs, judges will not normally *openly* engage in evaluating or condemning

19 Conscientious Exemptions: Between Toleration, Neutrality, and Respect

these beliefs. Instead, they will do it discreetly, while using neutral balancing tests as a red herring.

Neutrality and Toleration

Neutrality can mean either not making adverse judgments about others – or not acting on these judgments. In both cases, the result of neutrality can be identical to that of toleration – not harming the other. The attitudes, however, will still differ.

If neutrality means not making adverse judgments about others based on the values they hold, i.e., if neutrality is equated with moral relativism, then even if its result may be identical to that of toleration, it will have very little to do with the concept of toleration that entails making adverse moral judgment about others.

However, if neutrality means not acting on adverse judgments that we do make about others, then the difference between toleration and neutrality becomes quite blurred. It seems that when Adenitire argues for state neutrality within the context of conscientious exemptions, he does not argue that the legislature or the courts should refrain from *making* adverse judgments about the content of the conscientious objector's conscience. That will go against human nature of people who actually have opinions and take their moral values seriously. Rather, Adenitire probably argues that when the state (the legislature, or the courts) decides whether to grant conscientious exemptions, they should ignore the content of the conscientious objector's conscience and not *act* on the moral judgment they make about it. That is, in fact, an attitude that is very close to that of toleration. Whether the state should or should not ignore the content of the conscientious objector's conscience, is a completely different question that will not be answered here. The point made here is twofold: first, when the state does make an adverse judgment about the content of conscientious objectors' conscience, yet decides not to act on it because of its (alleged) duty to be neutral, the state is very close to being tolerant. Second, and as was argued above, when the state enacts laws the reflect and enforce moral values, and even neutral-liberal states do that, it must and does make an adverse judgment about the content of the values of the those who object to these laws for conscientious reasons. The neutral-liberal state is then being neutral by not acting on this judgment, much like the tolerant-liberal state is being tolerant by not acting on such judgment.

There is, however, one important difference between neutrality as an explanatory-descriptive concept regarding the practice of granting conscientious exemptions – and that of toleration. The neutral state may make an adverse judgment about the content of the objector's conscience – and it must make such judgment when it enacts laws that protect or enforce morality. However, the neutrality of that state means that for it, the adverse judgment that is made about the content of the objector's conscience must be completely ignored. It does not provide any reason, not even a prima-facie reason, let alone a weighty reason, for not granting the exemption. The adverse judgment that is being made about the content of the objector's conscience is in fact excluded from the balance of reasons. The only reasons that can be found against granting the exemption must be content-neutral.

In sharp contradiction to that approach, the tolerant-liberal state does not ignore the content of the objector's conscience. For the tolerant-liberal state, that is a relevant consideration that is added to the balance of reasons. And since the tolerant-liberal state always makes an adverse judgment about the content of objectors' conscience when they object to laws that reflect or enforce moral views, that judgment will always be a reason against granting an exemption. The question of when this reason may be outweighed by competing reasons, is beyond the scope of this chapter. The important point here is that unlike the neutral-state, that does not take the adverse judgment that it makes about the content of the objector's conscience into account, the tolerant-state does do so – and therefore must balance this reason against granting an exemption with the reasons for granting it. These reasons will in fact be the reasons for tolerating the conscientious objector.

Summary and Future Directions

The principle of toleration is a complex one. Its "negative" components that entail making an adverse judgement about others and having this judgment as a reason to harm others, cause discomfort to many, especially liberals, and even more so – neutral liberals. This discomfort, however, should not lead us to ignore how important the principle of toleration is within any meaningful political theory – and especially theories of human rights.

A good understanding of the principle of toleration is fundamental in comprehending the notion of human rights and the related issue of the limits of toleration. The human rights regime is based, inter alia, on the assumption that people have rights to engage in actions that others may consider wrong. In other words, people have a right to toleration. In addition, we must fully understand what toleration means in order to address the critical question of the limits of toleration, which implicates political, moral and legal issues alike. Issues pertaining to human rights can often be dealt with as part of the issue of the limits of toleration, as the limits of toleration often describe the limits of human rights or the limits of the protection granted to them.

This chapter explained why the practice of granting conscientious exemptions is better understood as an expression of toleration, whether the conscientious objector has a right to be tolerated or not. If there is a right to be granted conscientious exemptions, that right will be a specific application of the general right of freedom of conscience, one of the most important yet controversial human rights. This understanding will help us to place the complex question of when conscientious exemptions should be granted – and when freedom of conscience should be protected – within the right context, that is, within the context of the broader question about the limits of toleration.

19 Conscientious Exemptions: Between Toleration, Neutrality, and Respect

Within this context, two of the most important questions that will need to be answered by the liberal state are: (a) is religion special, and (b) should the state apply content-neutral considerations, content-based, or both.

The first question asks whether religious claims to be granted conscientious exemptions should be treated positively or negatively just because of the religious content of said claims, or whether that religious content of these claims is an irrelevant consideration. Put differently, the question is whether, all other things being equal, the religious content of claims to be granted conscientious exemptions should be a reason for tolerating these claims, not tolerating them, or an irrelevant consideration altogether.

The second question is part of a more general question, and indeed a more general clash between perfectionist-liberalism and neutral-liberalism. Within the context of toleration, the question is whether the limits of toleration, also toward conscientious objectors, should be decided according to content-neutral considerations, content-based, or both.

These questions may never be decided, as the disputes about their right answers is not likely to be resolved, but placing the dispute within the context of the principle of toleration will help in describing the nature of the dispute in the most accurate way.

Acknowledgments My thanks are due to my muse who enabled me to complete writing this chapter simply by being my muse.

References

Adenitire J (2017) Conscientious exemptions: from toleration to neutrality; from neutrality to respect. Oxf J Law Relig 6(2):268–292

Adenitire J (2020) A general right to conscientious exemption: beyond religious privilege. Cambridge University Press, Cambridge

Ammori M (2009) Beyond content neutrality: understanding content-based promotion of democratic speech. Fed Commun Law J 61:273–324

Chemerinsky E (1994) The first amendment: when the government must make content-based choices. Cleve State Law Rev 42:199–214

Chemerinsky E (2000) Content neutrality as a central problem of freedom of speech: problems in the Supreme Court's application. South Calif Law Rev 74:49–64

Jones P (2012) Toleration, religion and accommodation. Eur J Philos 23(3):542–563

Nehushtan Y (2013) What are conscientious exemptions really about? Oxf J Law Relig 2:393–416

Nehushtan Y (2015) Intolerant religion in a tolerant-liberal state. Hart Publishing, Oxford

Nehushtan Y (2019) Conscientious objection and equality laws: why the content of the conscience matters. Law Philos 38(3):227–266

Raz J (1988) The morality of freedom. Oxford University Press, Oxford

Schultz C (1999) Therapeutic jurisprudence: content-based restrictions on free expression: re-evaluating the high versus low value speech distinction (symposium). Ariz Law Rev 41:573

Smet S (2019) Conscientious objection through the contrasting lenses of tolerance and respect. Oxf J Law Relig 8(1):93–120

Stone G (1983) Content regulation and the first amendment. William Mary Law Rev 25(2):189–252

Wright RG (2006) Content-based and content-neutral regulation of speech: the limitations of a common distinction. Univ Miami Law Rev 60(3):333–364

Toleration and Its Possibilities: Relativism, Skepticism, and Pluralism

20

John William Tate

Contents

Introduction	364
Relativism and Skepticism I	365
The Conditions of Toleration	366
Toleration and the "Good"	367
"Affirmation" of a "Good"	367
"Orientation" Towards "Goods"	369
Relativism and Skepticism II	370
Skepticism	370
Relativism	371
Toleration, Skepticism, and Relativism	374
Pluralism as an Empirical Reality	376
Pluralism, Relativism, and Skepticism	377
Pluralism as a Normative Ideal	378
"Value Pluralism" and Relativism	379
"Value Pluralism" and Toleration	380
Relativism and Toleration	381
Relativists and Intolerance	384
Skepticism and Toleration	385
Skeptics Versus Relativists	386
"Indifference" and Toleration	388
Toleration as a "Disposition"	389
Toleration as a "Disposition": Relativism, Skepticism, and Pluralism	391
Conclusion	393
Summary and Future Directions	394
References	394

J. W. Tate (✉)
Discipline of Politics and International Relations, Newcastle Business School, College of Human
and Social Futures, University of Newcastle, Newcastle, NSW, Australia
e-mail: john.tate@newcastle.edu.au

© The Author(s), under exclusive licence to Springer Nature Switzerland AG 2022
M. Sardoč (ed.), *The Palgrave Handbook of Toleration*,
https://doi.org/10.1007/978-3-030-42121-2_2

Abstract

Does a situation of "relativism," wherein we lack the normative resources to make categorical distinctions and objective evaluations between competing moral values, practices, or ways of life, affirm or undermine our capacity to engage in toleration? The following chapter seeks to address this question but, in order to do so, finds it necessary to compare the position of "relativism," in this respect, with that of "pluralism," "skepticism," and "indifference." Relativism, pluralism, and skepticism are widely perceived by many as indelible features of our moral universe. But do they inevitably produce a situation in which toleration is endorsed as the preferred means to respond to competing and conflicting beliefs, practices, or ways of life? Or do they undermine any prescriptive capacity we might have to place a priority on toleration in such circumstances, perhaps even precluding the possibility of engaging in toleration altogether?

Keywords

Relativism · Pluralism · Skepticism · Indifference · Value pluralism · Goods · Toleration

Introduction

> Three degrees of latitude reverse all jurisprudence; a meridian decides the truth. Fundamental laws change after a few years of possession; right has its epochs....... Truth on this side of the Pyrenees, error on the other side. (Pascal, *Pensées*, V, 294)

Relativism is a contested term but, broadly speaking, can be understood as describing a situation in which we lack the normative resources to make categorical distinctions and objective evaluations between competing moral values, practices, or ways of life, and so lack the capacity to prioritize these in some sort of authoritative order. Relativism has had its adherents and its critics over the centuries. But what is its relationship to toleration? It is to this question that this chapter is directed.

It is not possible, however, to consider relativism (and its relationship to toleration) without discussing two closely related concepts – skepticism and pluralism. We shall consider the possible connections between skepticism, relativism, and pluralism before considering the relationship of each to toleration and also to intolerance. For our purposes, the key questions are: Can one really place a priority upon toleration, as the preferred means of responding to diversity, conflict, and disagreement, categorically affirming it in preference to all alternatives, if one is a skeptic, a relativist, or a pluralist? Or are there features of skepticism, relativism, or pluralism which undermine our capacity to affirm toleration (in preference to its alternatives) and engage in it altogether? Further, does the relationship between relativism, skepticism, and pluralism, on the one side, and toleration on the other, alter if toleration is understood not as a "practice" but as a "disposition"?

20 Toleration and Its Possibilities: Relativism, Skepticism, and Pluralism

To answer these questions, this chapter will begin with a brief look at skepticism and relativism. It then discusses the conditions of toleration (those conceptual features that make toleration possible) before investigating the relationship between toleration and the "good," distinguishing between arguments for toleration premised on an "affirmation" of a specific "good" and arguments for toleration premised on a specific "orientation" toward "goods" in general. It then seeks to define skepticism and relativism before considering pluralism and its relationship to toleration. It then considers relativism and skepticism and their relationship to toleration. It also considers the relationship of all three to intolerance. The chapter also briefly looks at "indifference" as a foundation of toleration – a foundation quite distinct from relativism, skepticism, and pluralism insofar as "indifference" refers not to a philosophical outlook concerning the external world but to an emotional trait within individuals. Finally, the chapter considers whether the relationship of relativism, skepticism, and pluralism to toleration alters if toleration is understood as a "disposition" rather than as a "practice."

Relativism and Skepticism I

There are some who are comfortable with the possibility of relativism and skepticism and some who find these possibilities difficult to endure. The eighteenth-century skeptic, David Hume, advanced a relativist position when he declared: "Tis not contrary to reason to prefer the destruction of the whole world to the scratching of my finger" (Hume 1960: bk. II, pt. iii, sec. iii, 416). Immanuel Kant, on the other hand, developed his "critique of pure reason" precisely in order to refute the skepticism of Hume, and in so doing also sought to subvert the moral relativism which (as Hume makes clear in the preceding statement) arises from his skeptical belief that "reason" cannot authoritatively decide between competing moral choices (Kant 1949: V53; Kant 1964: B19–20, B127–28, A760–69/B788–97).

Yet despite Kant's attempt to find, in his "critique of pure reason," a bulwark against skepticism and relativism, both constitute a genuine presence in contemporary Western liberal democracies. Jeremy Waldron, however, has argued that in practice, relativism within contemporary liberal democracies is quite rare. It is not often, Waldron insists, that relativism is advanced as a basis for moral judgments:

> Most of the time when people state moral positions, they say, "Murder is wrong", not just that it is *regarded as wrong* around here; or they say, "The subordination of children to fathers is the right way for families to be organized", not just that this is the way their culture has *chosen* to organize the family structure. They may be aware that other cultures do things differently, but that is an awareness of opposition or disagreement, not merely cultural difference. Thus, when *we* say, "All humans are created equal", or "Slavery is wrong", we do not intend to qualify or limit that with a cultural reference such as, "This is just what we in the West happen to think". We intend the categorical and universal character of these utterances to be taken at face value. (Waldron 1999: 310)

The Conditions of Toleration

The conceptual possibility of toleration, as much as its practice, relies on a series of conditions. Depending on the conception of toleration we wish to advance, it is possible to argue that only if these conditions are in place is toleration, as a practice, possible.

In the first place, toleration requires something to be "tolerated." This might be a person possessing a particular identity, or a person expressing a set of beliefs, or engaging in particular practices, or living a particular lifestyle. Such a person, if committed to these identities, beliefs, or practices, will seek to engage in them free from intrusion or interference from others. Let us therefore say that the first condition of toleration (1) is that such a person seeks a "liberty" to act in a specific way free from the interference of others.

The second condition of toleration resides in the opposition of others to the exercise of this "liberty." It is a widespread assumption within the literature that to "tolerate" something is to refrain from interfering with that to which we are *averse* and which, other things being equal, we would prefer did not exist (Cohen 2004: 71; Jones 2007a: 384–85, 2012: 266–67; Scanlon 2003: 187; Vernon 1997: 53, 71; Waldron 1997: 351; Horton 1994: 8; Coffey 2000: 10). As D.D. Raphael puts it: "Toleration is the practice of deliberately allowing or permitting a thing of which one disapproves" (Raphael 1988: 139). By contrast, if we positively approve of something, then, arguably, we are not "tolerating" it at all but rather supporting or endorsing it. The second condition of toleration (2), therefore, is that some individual must have an aversion to the "liberty" being sought (or those seeking it) under Condition 1, and therefore possess a disposition to interfere with this liberty in some way.

A third condition of toleration (3) is that the person with the disposition to interfere confronts a set of reasons why they should not act on this disposition, their continuing aversion to the "liberty" whose exercise is sought under Condition 1 notwithstanding. These "reasons" encountered under Condition 3 therefore constitute reasons for toleration.

Actual toleration (Condition 4) takes place when this person decides to *act* on the "reasons" they have encountered under Condition 3, thereby *not* interfering with the "liberty" whose exercise is sought under Condition 1, their continuing aversion to that liberty (Condition 2) notwithstanding. Such toleration therefore depends on the person with the disposition to interfere affirming the reasons for toleration, arising under Condition 3, in preference to the counter-reasons, arising under Condition 2, why they *should* interfere with and impede the "liberty" in question.

The fifth condition of toleration (5) is that those possessing the aversion to the "liberty" sought under Condition 1 have not only the disposition but the *capacity* to interfere with, and perhaps prevent, its exercise. After all, if we are averse to a particular identity, belief, or practice, have a disposition to interfere with it, but lack the capacity to do so effectively, then our putting up with or enduring it is not a case of "toleration," but rather a case of helpless impotence (see Jones 2007a: 384–385. See also Jones 2007b: 10).

Debate exists in the literature concerning how efficacious must be this "capacity" to interfere with the "liberty" in question. Must it extend to a total capacity to preclude the exercise of the liberty or might it only be a capacity to impede it in some way? And must this be an *actual* capacity to interfere or might it be a capacity that exists solely in the mind of the person seeking to engage in toleration (see Raphael 1988: 139; Jones 2007a: 384–385, 395n; Galeotti 2002: 22, 89; Cohen 2004: 93–94; Horton 1996: 28; Balint 2014: 267–268; Mendus 1989: 9; Newey 2001: 317–318; Williams 1996: 19)? Irrespective of its definition or scope, this "capacity" constitutes our fifth condition of toleration. For a more detailed discussion of these five conditions of toleration, see ▶ Chap. 40, "Toleration and Religion."

Toleration and the "Good"

"Goods" exist either as ends in themselves or are considered "good" because they are a means to some even more important end. Within contemporary liberal political philosophy, a distinction is often made between the "right" and the "good" (see Rawls 1972: 31–32) – and given that both could broadly be defined as that which *ought to be*, a further definition of the "good" is necessary. John Rawls identifies the "right" as those normative and regulative constraints within which individuals, within a liberal polity, make their choices and direct their actions, while the "good" is that goal to which those choices and actions are directed and (within these constraints) seek to achieve (Rawls 1972: 31–32). In this respect, the "good" is that ideal, however complex or manifold, which individuals will seek to realize, often altering or adapting their choices, actions, or commitments to do so. It is this definition of the "good" which is adopted here.

Toleration can arise, as a prescriptive choice, either on the basis of our "affirmation" of a particular "good" or on the basis of a particular "orientation" towards such "goods" in general. In each case, the crucial locus at which such considerations apply is Condition 3 – the "reasons" we adopt for toleration. These reasons will be informed either by our "affirmation" of a particular "good" or our "orientation" towards "goods" in general, and the justification of toleration (to which these reasons give rise) will therefore be premised on either one or the other of these.

"Affirmation" of a "Good"

The first consideration concerns reasons for toleration arising from our affirmation of a particular good. If we possess reasons in favor of toleration, this may be because toleration is either a "good" in itself or is a means to some other "good." Generally, toleration is understood in the latter sense – as a means to some other "good." This "good" might be the "good" of civil peace. Toleration would therefore be endorsed, in such circumstances, because we affirm the "good" of "civil peace," and toleration is considered an important means to this end. One of the arguments that John Locke advanced, seeking to convince ruling authorities in seventeenth-century England to tolerate "Dissenters" (Protestants unwilling to outwardly conform to the Church of England) was that such toleration was an important means to ensure civil peace – avoiding the violent reaction which might otherwise arise should Dissenters be denied toleration for the religious liberties that they seek. As Locke advised these ruling authorities:

> Since force is a wrong way to bring dissenters off from their persuasions. . . . .it will certainly prevail much less with those to be your friends who steadfastly retain their persuasion and continue in an opinion different from you. He that differs in an opinion is only so far at a distance from you, but if you use him ill for that which he believes to be right, he is then at perfect enmity. The one is barely a separation, but the other is a quarrel; nor is that all the mischief which severity will do among us as the state of things is at present, for force and harsh usage will not only increase the animosity but number of enemies. (Locke 1993: 207. See also Tate 2016a: 84–89)

On the other hand, one reason why we might endorse toleration is because it is an important means to the "good" of "individual autonomy." In such cases, toleration would be considered worthwhile because, by tolerating others, and so refusing to interfere with the choices they make, we are upholding their "individual autonomy." This is the view of Bernard Williams:

> If toleration as a practice is to be defended in terms of its being a value, then it will have to appeal to substantive opinions about the good, in particular, the good of individual autonomy. (Williams 1996: 24. See also Raphael 1988: 139; Kymlicka 1996: 95)

In contrast, Anna Elisabetta Galeotti has insisted that toleration is a means of affirming the "good" of "equal respect" (Galeotti 2002: 6). This is so when toleration is extended to previously excluded groups within the polity via a "public recognition of their differences" (Galeotti 2002: 6). In this context, in order to affirm the "good" of "equal respect," we affirm toleration (in the form of "public recognition of differences") as a means to this end. As Galleoti states:

> Toleration can be seen as responding to and satisfying requirements of justice if it is understood as a recognition of excluded, marginalized, and oppressed identities. It can, however, work as a form of recognition only if it is considered symbolically as a public gesture intended to legitimize the existence of differences and place them on the same footing as the habits and practices of the majority. (Galeotti 2002: 11. See also Galeotti 2002: 103, 116–17)

In each of the examples above, toleration is affirmed as a worthwhile practice because it is a means of achieving important "goods." In each case, reasons for toleration (Condition 3) are articulated in terms of the capacity of toleration to achieve such "goods." Reasons for toleration have moral weight in such circumstances, and are therefore a persuasive basis for overriding our aversion (Condition 2) to that seeking toleration, because, prior to endorsing such reasons, we have already endorsed or affirmed the "good" which these "reasons" (via the practice of toleration) seek to uphold. The worth of toleration, in these examples, is therefore ultimately premised upon our prior "affirmation" of particular "goods."

Such "goods" also help define the "scope" and "limits" of toleration. The "scope" of toleration encompasses all that which falls *within* the auspices of toleration and so is entitled not to be interfered with. The "limits" of toleration demarcate this sphere of noninterference from all that falls *outside* the scope of toleration and so is (potentially) capable of being proscribed. Those beliefs, practices, or commitments seeking toleration under Condition 1 are more likely to fall within the *scope* of toleration, and not be interfered with, if they are not entirely inconsistent with the "good" to which such toleration is perceived as a means. There are peculiar variations on this. If toleration is justified because not interfering with others advances the "good" of "autonomy," we may choose to tolerate (i.e., not interfere with) a person's choices even though these choices undermine their own autonomous behavior (e.g., drug addiction). John Stuart Mill, for instance, declared that a person's own well-being was insufficient reason to interfere with their liberty (Mill 1971: 73).

Conversely, beliefs, practices, or commitments seeking toleration are more likely to fall outside the *limits* of toleration if they are perceived as transgressing the "good" to which toleration is perceived as a means. For instance, if toleration is justified in terms of the "good" of civil peace, it would be unlikely that the expression of beliefs or practices likely to endanger civil peace would be perceived as falling within the *scope* of toleration (and so be subject to non-interference). Rather, they would be likely to be perceived as falling outside the *limits* of toleration and so be proscribed.

"Orientation" Towards "Goods"

However, just as it is possible for toleration to be justified in terms of an "affirmation" of a particular "good," so it may be possible for toleration to be justified in terms of an "orientation" towards "goods" in general. In such contexts, toleration is justified not because it is a means of achieving a particular "good." Rather, toleration arises from an "orientation," informed by a specific evaluative disposition, toward "goods" in general.

Three relevant "orientations" toward "goods" which might, in some circumstances, underwrite toleration, are skepticism, relativism, and pluralism. For instance, it *might* be possible for individuals to affirm reasons for toleration (Condition 3) arising from a skeptical, relativist, or pluralist "orientation" toward "goods" in general. The equivocation ("might") arises because the one clear difference, we shall see, between toleration underwritten by an "affirmation" of a particular "good," and toleration arising from an "orientation" towards "goods" in general, is that the latter is a far less certain basis upon which to justify toleration.

Indeed, whether toleration is possible on the basis of either a relativist, skeptical, or pluralist "orientation" toward "goods" will be discussed later in this chapter. For the moment, the important point to remember is the one just made – that a justification of toleration in terms of an "affirmation" of a particular "good" is a much more indubitable and categorical basis upon which to premise toleration than an "orientation" towards "goods" in general. This is because, in the former case, toleration is affirmed because it itself is conceived as a means to the "good" in question. Unless some more effective "means" can be found, the worth of toleration is clearly demarcated in terms of its instrumental capacity to achieve or realize this "good," or produce circumstances which make this realization or achievement more likely. In the case of toleration justified in terms of an "orientation" to "goods" in general, by contrast, matters are much more indirect and uncertain, with some "orientations" to "goods" being unable to justify toleration at all. Consequently, the relationship between skepticism, relativism, and pluralism on the one hand and toleration on the other is much more equivocal and tenuous than a relationship between toleration and the "affirmation" of particular "goods" like "autonomy," "civil peace," or "equal respect."

Relativism and Skepticism II

Skepticism and relativism are relevant to toleration in that either may give rise to reasons (Condition 3) why we ought to engage in toleration. Later in the chapter we shall determine if each is able, in terms of these reasons, to provide sufficient justification for toleration, capable of overriding the aversion (Condition 2) which offers a set of contrary reasons why toleration should not take place. But first we must determine what, for the purposes of our argument, constitute "relativism" and "skepticism," and why they can be described, generically, as involving a particular "orientation" toward "goods" in general.

Skepticism

Skepticism arises from an epistemological judgment concerning the possibility of knowledge. Richard Popkin distinguishes, in this respect, between what he calls "academic scepticism" and "Pyrrhonian scepticism." Academic skepticism is the belief that no knowledge is possible; Pyrrhonian skepticism (named after the ancient Greek philosopher, Pyrrho of Elis – c. 360–275 BC) is the belief "that there [is] insufficient and inadequate evidence to determine if any knowledge [is] possible," with the result that "one ought to suspend judgment on all questions concerning knowledge" (Popkin 1979: xiii–xv). Either of these types of skepticism can be affirmed once an individual has made a conscious intellectual judgment that one or the other of these epistemological propositions is a valid account of the state of human knowledge, or parts of it.

Skepticism, as a fundamental epistemological position, may impact on our "orientation" towards "goods" in general. After all, to affirm a particular norm, ideal, belief, or practice as "good" is, in many cases, to claim a knowledge of it as "good," or to appeal to some other criteria which authorizes or substantiates the matter in question as "good." Without such knowledge, such criteria, or some other authoritative means to ascertain the worth or value of the matter in question, there would be a disinclination to affirm it as "good" at all. Consequently, skepticism, in throwing doubt on all such claims to certitude, potentially affects our "orientation" toward "goods" in general. In cases where we possess certitude concerning the worth or value of a particular ideal, belief, or practice, we have little hesitation in affirming it as a "good," and perhaps orienting our actions in accord with it. However, in the context of skepticism, which denies such certitude, we are less likely to orient our actions in this way because we lack the certitude that the matter in question really is a "good" at all.

Relativism

Relativism is a highly contested term, capable of multiple meanings. In its broadest sense it is most understandable when contrasted to its opposite. This opposite is an absolute belief in the possibility of indubitable, veridical, and objective judgment, and the knowledge such judgement yields. Immanuel Kant, with the full force of late eighteenth-century Enlightenment optimism, described his own age as one where "reason" (in either its "pure" or "practical" form) would provide the basis for such judgment, not least through an authoritative critique of its own claims, thereby determining both the scope and the limits of its authority and veracity:

> It is obviously the effect not of levity but of the matured judgement of the age, which refuses to be any longer put off with illusory knowledge. It is a call to reason to undertake anew the most difficult of all its tasks, namely, that of self-knowledge, and to institute a tribunal which will assure to reason its lawful claims, and dismiss all groundless pretensions, not by despotic degrees, but in accordance with its own eternal and unalterable laws. This tribunal is no other than the *critique of pure reason.* (Kant 1964: Axi–xii. See also Kant 1964: Axiia)

Kant's statement is definitive of eighteenth-century Enlightenment ambitions – not least, its ambitions for "reason" (however defined). "Reason" was to be the authoritative criterion of "truth," "knowledge," "morality," and all other prescriptive and normative outcomes, thereby precluding the possibility of an uncertain "relativism." As Alasdair MacIntyre tells us:

> It was a central aspiration of the Enlightenment, an aspiration the formulation of which was itself a great achievement, to provide for debate in the public realm standards and methods of rational justification by which alternative courses of action in every sphere of life could be adjudged just or unjust, rational or irrational, enlightened or unenlightened. So, it was hoped, reason would displace authority and tradition. Rational justification was to appeal to principles undeniable by any rational person and therefore independent of all those social and cultural particularities which the Enlightenment thinkers took to be the mere accidental clothing of reason in particular times and places. (MacIntyre 1988: 6. See also MacIntyre 1990: 172; Hiley 1988: 119)

A relativist would reject all such possibilities. They would insist that no indubitable epistemological or moral criterion exists on the basis of which such authoritative propositions can be advanced and such conclusive judgments reached, categorically excluding their alternatives. Everything, for a relativist, is ultimately contestable precisely because there are no ultimate or authoritative criteria, transcending particular histories, societies, or cultures, by which rival claims can be categorically prioritized or determined. Richard Bernstein provides such a definition of relativism, distinguishing it from its alternative (which he calls "objectivism") as follows:

> By "objectivism" I mean the basic conviction that there is or must be some permanent, ahistorical matrix or framework to which we can ultimately appeal in determining the nature of rationality, knowledge, truth, reality, goodness, or rightness...The objectivist maintains that unless we can ground philosophy, knowledge, or language in a rigorous manner we cannot avoid radical skepticism.
>
> The relativist not only denies the positive claims of the objectivist but goes further. In its strongest form, relativism is the basic conviction that when we turn to the examination of those concepts that philosophers have taken to be the most fundamental – whether it is the concept of rationality, truth, reality, right, the good, or norms – we are forced to recognize that in the final analysis all such concepts must be understood as relative to a specific conceptual scheme, theoretical framework, paradigm, form of life, society, or culture.... For the relativist, there is no substantive overarching framework or single metalanguage by which we can rationally adjudicate or univocally evaluate competing claims of alternative paradigms. (Bernstein 1983: 8)

Indeed, even the authoritative conception of reason advanced by Enlightenment thinkers such as Kant, in which "reason" is an entity capable of acting as a "tribunal" of evaluation for all competing claims, is rejected by "relativists," not least because they are likely to perceive "reason" itself as a multiple, disaggregated concept, based on culturally specific foundations, and so also open to contestation. As Bernstein writes:

> [W]hen we turn to something as fundamental as the issue of criteria or standards of rationality, the relativist claims that we can never escape from the predicament of speaking of "our" and "their" standards of rationality – standards that may be "radically incommensurable." (Bernstein 1983: 8)

Of course, this does not mean that relativists are cognitively or ethically "paralyzed," in a solipsistic fashion, unable to make choices or judgments because incapable of providing ultimate justification for these in terms of absolute, unconditional, or indubitable criteria. On the contrary, relativists will recognize that different choices or judgments often fall within specific "paradigms" of thought or value which, within themselves, provide authoritative standards for evaluation. Thomas Kuhn described the history of science in terms of the displacement of such "paradigms" by others (Kuhn 2012). Kuhn famously argued that competing scientific "paradigms" are defined by an "incommensurability" in which their respective proponents must "fail to make complete contact with each other's viewpoints" (Kuhn 2012: 147). But *within* paradigms, Kuhn declared, rational argument and adjudication is possible because all within the paradigm agree upon the authoritative standards by which such adjudication is to take place (Kuhn 1977: 297–98).

20 Toleration and Its Possibilities: Relativism, Skepticism, and Pluralism

Such "paradigms" need not refer only to a theoretical framework of scientific understanding, as in Kuhn's writings. They may also refer to "traditions," "cultures," and relatively self-enclosed "ways of life" – any entity sufficiently hermetic to be capable of providing its own authoritative standards of meaning, evaluation, and justification (see MacIntyre 1997: 221–222). Needless to say, any process of adjudication and justification that arises *within* such frameworks is likely to be, in an ultimate sense, self-referential, affirming some norms, values, and practices within the framework in terms of other norms, values, and practices also arising within the same framework, which are themselves affirmed, in turn, by others, etc. Richard Rorty fully acknowledged and endorsed such self-referentiality when he declared:

> [A] circular justification of our practices, a justification which makes one feature of our culture look good by citing still another, or comparing our culture invidiously with others by reference to our own standards, is the only sort of justification we are going to get. (Rorty 1989: 57. See also Rorty 1982: 173–74; Rorty 1995a: 207–08, b: 212, 213)

John Rawls identified this same process of self-referentiality, arising within specific cultures, as the ultimate source of justification for political norms, declaring:

> I should emphasize that what I have called the "real task" of justifying a conception of justice is not primarily an epistemological problem. The search for reasonable grounds for reaching agreement rooted in our conception of ourselves and in our relation to society replaces the search for moral truth interpreted as fixed by a prior and independent order of objects and relations, whether natural or divine, an order apart and distinct from how we conceive of ourselves. The task is to articulate a public conception of justice that all can live with who regard their person and their relation to society in a certain way. And though doing this may involve settling theoretical difficulties, the practical social task is primary. What justifies a conception of justice is not its being true to an order antecedent to and given to us, but its congruence with our deeper understanding of ourselves and our aspirations, and our realization that, given our history and the traditions embedded in our public life, it is the most reasonable doctrine for us. We can find no better basic charter for our social world. (Rawls 1980: 518–19)

It is only when individuals are capable of abstracting from such self-referential and self-confirming contexts, enabling them to compare paradigms, cultures, and traditions with each other, that they might arrive at a realization that only *within*, and not *between*, such frameworks do criteria for authoritative judgments exist. In this respect, their relativism, if it arises at all, arises as a "metaethical" perspective, which emerges only once they are capable of abstracting sufficiently from their own hermetic context to perceive the relationship of that context to others quite different from their own. Gordon Graham provides a definition of "relativism" which incorporates this metaethical perspective as follows:

> Relativism holds that for some evaluative questions there is no right answer. At the level of particular judgments between people operating within some shared framework, we can apply the notions of correct and incorrect. But when evaluative disputes arise, or seem to arise, between conceptual frameworks, they are rationally irresolvable. (Graham 1996: 53)

It would certainly seem to be the case that skepticism is one avenue by which "relativism" might be reached. After all, if we are not convinced concerning the capacity of individuals to acquire epistemic or moral certitude, we are unlikely to affirm the possibility of these same individuals reaching indubitable conclusions regarding rival propositional claims, whether concerning knowledge, morality, or any other object of evaluation. Our skepticism, in this respect, might, in these circumstances, lead us to a relativist outlook. And just like a skeptical outlook, a relativist outlook will affect our "orientation" towards "goods" in general.

Toleration, Skepticism, and Relativism

Toleration first emerged in Europe as one means by which state authorities or individuals within society were able to respond to the reality of religious difference ushered in by the Reformation of the sixteenth century (see ► Chap. 40, "Toleration and Religion"). When toleration was practiced by governments in the sixteenth, seventeenth, and eighteenth centuries, it was often practiced by individual monarchs, as part of the panoply of their personal rule. As Glen Newey tells us:

> When the ideal of toleration was formulated by thinkers such as Locke, Bayle, Walwyn, Milton and Spinoza during the early modern period, the predominant form of government in Europe was personal and prerogative rule – such as Louis XIV's "l'état, c'est moi". The sovereign stood as individual person to the collectivity of the citizenry or subjects. (Newey 2001: 324. See also Jones 2007a: 383–84)

When it came to matters of religion, such monarchs were unlikely to be skeptics or relativists. They were likely to believe they knew, with all the certitude of conviction, what constituted religious "truth" and what constituted "error." When they tolerated another religious faith, therefore, it was not usually because they were in doubt about the "truth" of their own religion, or the "error" of that which they tolerated (see Rawls 2005: xxiii–xxiv). Rather, such toleration would be enjoined for a range of other reasons, including purely pragmatic ones, concerning the need to maintain civil peace within their territory in a context of religious diversity (see ► Chap. 40, "Toleration and Religion").

In such contexts, religious toleration only occurred when the reasons in favor of toleration outweighed, in a ruler's mind, the adverse consequences of tolerating a religious faith to which they were averse. The same applied to anything else such rulers decided to tolerate. In each case, toleration occurred when the ruler encountered reasons (Condition 3) which convinced them to engage in toleration (Condition 4), their continuing aversion to that which was seeking toleration (Condition 2) notwithstanding. For the reasons explained above, skepticism and relativism were not, generally, a part of this equation.

In contemporary liberal democratic societies, by contrast, skepticism and relativism, as philosophical, ethical, and epistemological outlooks, are far more widespread. And for many, a commitment to relativism is often causally related, as a necessary precondition, to toleration. Allan Bloom argued that it is precisely this connection between relativism and toleration which exists within the minds of university students within the USA:

> There is one thing a professor can be absolutely certain of: almost every student entering the university believes, or says he believes, that truth is relative......They are unified only in their relativism and in their allegiance to equality. And the two are related in moral intention. The relativity of truth is not a theoretical insight but a moral postulate, the condition of a free society, or so they see it......That it is a moral issue for students is revealed by the character of their response when challenged – a combination of disbelief and indignation: "Are you an absolutist?", the only alternative they know, uttered in the same tone as "Are you a monarchist?" or "Do you really believe in witches?"......The danger they have been taught to fear from absolutism is not error but intolerance. Relativism is necessary to openness, and this is the virtue, the only virtue, which all primary education for more than fifty years has dedicated itself to inculcating. Openness – and the relativism that makes it the only plausible stance in the face of various claims to truth and various ways of life and kinds of human beings – is the great insight of our times. (Bloom 1988: 25–26)

The perspective that Bloom identifies in his students – in which relativism is associated with toleration and "absolutism" with intolerance – is widely held. Gordon Graham has identified (but not endorsed) such a point of view as follows:

> [B]ecause relativism holds that unconditional truth cannot be ascribed to any one moral or political view, relativism in turn provides support for toleration; if no one belief or set of beliefs is superior to any other in terms of truth, all must be accorded equal respect. Conversely, an objectivist metaethics implies the endorsement of just one set of proscriptions and prescriptions as true, which are thus regarded as absolutely forbidden or required. This in turn legitimizes suppressing other erroneous views. Thus a belief in toleration requires us to subscribe to relativism; conversely, the rejection of relativism licences suppressing moral variation on the general ground that "error has no rights." (Graham 1996: 44)

Thus, on the basis of these views, we see that the context in which toleration, today, is sometimes practiced – whereby the reasons for toleration (Condition 3) arise on the basis of a commitment to relativism – is very different from the way in which toleration was practiced by earlier European monarchs. If an individual engages in toleration *because* they are a skeptic or a relativist, with the result that their unwillingness to repudiate a belief, practice, or way of life is because they are not convinced it is wrong, then not only the motivations of such toleration but also its intrinsic qualities are likely to be different to one who engages in toleration (such as our European monarchs above) in full (and aversive) knowledge that what they are tolerating is "untrue," "immoral," "unjust," or in some other way in error. After all, in the latter case, toleration, despite the scope and permission it provides for alternative beliefs, practices, or ways of life, is a censorious process, in which the object of toleration (arising under Condition 1) is not conceded any sort of equal status with more mainstream and accepted practices, but rather is a reality which those engaging in toleration would prefer did not exist (see the account of Condition 2 above). In the case of toleration arising on the basis of skepticism or relativism, by contrast, the reasons for toleration (Condition 3) emerge, in part, because the authoritative normative criteria on the basis of which such unequal evaluation arises are absent altogether.

Nevertheless, despite these differences between toleration based on skepticism or relativism and toleration arising from other foundations, we have seen that the view that there is a relation (perhaps even a causal relation) between toleration and relativism is widespread (the association between skepticism and toleration, on the other hand, is, we shall see, less widely endorsed). But such recognition of this association is no warrant for its validity. As discussed earlier, one of the key questions for our purposes (investigated further below) is: Can one really engage in toleration as a practice if one is a relativist? Or does relativism produce conditions which undermine the possibility of toleration altogether?

Pluralism as an Empirical Reality

Pluralism is distinct from relativism and has both an empirical and a normative dimension. A pluralist society, at an empirical level, is a society characterized by a deep level of diversity. Such diversity can be of a social, cultural, religious, ethnic, racial, philosophical, or moral kind. Such "diversity" is "deep" in the sense that it cannot be reduced to a single value or single way of life or a common anterior value or way of life. Another way of describing this is by saying that in a pluralist society there is a "diversity" of conceptions of the "good." As Anna Elisabetta Galeotti tells us:

> [P]luralism is conceived of as the plurality of the conceptions of the good, i.e. what each individual thinks worthwhile and valuable in life. The problem is that in contemporary societies there are many conceptions of the good and, often, they are not compatible. Indeed, since they have to do with ultimate values, final meanings, and basic principles, their diversity is a potential source of conflict. Moreover, in many cases, they are incommensurable, since they embody alternative and irreducible interpretations of what is valuable and why. Finally, they cannot be adjudicated, insofar as there is no common, publicly accepted way of making a reasonable judgment about them, or of defining priorities. (Galeotti 2002: 29)

Certainly, John Rawls was of the view that contemporary liberal democratic societies were "plural" in this sense, incorporating different religious, philosophical, and moral conceptions of the "good." Rawls altered key elements of his philosophical position, first articulated at length in *A Theory of Justice*, precisely because of what he believed was this inescapable fact of plurality and diversity within contemporary liberal democracies. Referring to his doctrine of "justice as fairness," at the center of *A Theory of Justice*, Rawls conceded that, because of the plurality and diversity of contemporary liberal democratic societies, where citizens endorse very different conceptions of the "good," he could no longer assume (as he had in that earlier text) that "justice as fairness" could be affirmed by all citizens within such societies as a comprehensive moral and philosophical doctrine (Rawls 2005: xv–xvii). The most, he insists, that those unable to endorse "justice as fairness" in such comprehensive terms can do is affirm it as a "political" doctrine, applying only to "political" matters, quite distinct from the life matters encompassed by their comprehensive moral and philosophical doctrines (Rawls 2005: xviii–xxi, 374–75). In other words, Rawls ultimately arrived at the view that it was "unrealistic" to assume that citizens, within liberal democratic politics, were capable of reaching a comprehensive moral or philosophical consensus on such principles as "justice as fairness," because their moral and philosophical commitments were too plural and diverse to allow for any such substantive agreement (Rawls 2005: xvi, xvii). Rawls describes such "pluralism" within contemporary liberal democratic societies as follows:

> Now the serious problem is this. A modern democratic society is characterized not simply by a pluralism of comprehensive religious, philosophical, and moral doctrines but by a pluralism of incompatible yet reasonable comprehensive doctrines. No one of these doctrines is affirmed by citizens generally. Nor should one expect that in the foreseeable future one of them, or some other reasonable doctrine, will ever be affirmed by all, or nearly all, citizens. Political liberalism assumes that, for political purposes, a plurality of reasonable yet incompatible comprehensive doctrines is the normal result of the exercise of human reason within the framework of the free institutions of a constitutional democratic regime. . . . The fact of a plurality of reasonable but incompatible comprehensive doctrines – the fact of reasonable pluralism – shows that, as used in *Theory*, the idea of a well-ordered society of justice as fairness is unrealistic. (Rawls 2005: xvi–xvii)

Pluralism, Relativism, and Skepticism

There is no obvious link between pluralism and skepticism. The reason is that it is possible to conceive of a pluralist society, of the type which Rawls describes above, in which individuals endorse diverse (and at times incompatible) religious, philosophical, and moral comprehensive doctrines, but in which none of these doctrines endorse skepticism.

On the other hand, there is a possible link between pluralism and relativism. This is because although these diverse comprehensive doctrines, in and of themselves, might be just as devoid of relativism as they are of skepticism, nevertheless from the viewpoint of a person perceiving such a society from an aggregate or synoptic perspective, they might perceive that *between* these comprehensive doctrines (just as *between* Kuhn's scientific paradigms above) there is no authoritative criterion of evaluation or adjudication, capable of prioritizing one comprehensive doctrine in relation to another in terms of any transcendent standard of value.

The result, therefore, is that from this "metaethical" perspective, relativism might be the inevitable consequence of such pluralism. After all, in the absence of an overarching evaluative framework capable of encompassing and adjudicating between competing comprehensive doctrines, there is no authoritative basis for affirming (on any transcendent criteria) one comprehensive doctrine in preference to another.

Pluralism as a Normative Ideal

Although acknowledging the irreducible plurality of contemporary liberal democracies, John Rawls did not, for the purposes of his "political liberalism," affirm any metaethical position such as relativism, or any comprehensive epistemological perspective such as skepticism (see Rawls 2005: 150, 375). This is because, from the perspective of such "political liberalism," relativism or skepticism would themselves be a "comprehensive" doctrine, and Rawls is insistent that his "political liberalism" does not rely on any such doctrine: "We try, so far as we can, neither to assert nor to deny any particular comprehensive religious, philosophical, or moral view, or its associated theory of truth and the status of values" (Rawls 2005: 150. See also Rawls 2005: 375).

But while Rawls does not arrive at a metaethical position as a result of his recognition of the empirical reality of pluralism within liberal democracies, other theorists do. Foremost among these are those who refer to themselves as "value pluralists." "Value pluralists" conceive of contemporary liberal democracies, at an empirical level, as "pluralist," insofar as such polities incorporate a diversity of "values" (embodied in what Rawls would call "comprehensive doctrines") each affirming a particular set of "goods." However, "value pluralists" go further and insist (in normative terms) that, so long as these "values" are conducive to an overall ideal of "human flourishing," all have worth, with the result that their normative significance is affirmed. But none can be accorded a definitive priority over any of the others, because none exhaust the diverse modes by which human beings might "flourish":

> The core of value-pluralism considered as an ethical theory is the claim that the human good harbours rival perfections. Its consequence is that no single way of life exhausts the possibilities of human flourishing. A diversity of ways of life is good because there are many kinds of life – many, no doubt, yet to be invented – that human beings find worth living. (Gray 2000a: 331–32. See also Gray 2000b: 9)

Yet in addition to affirming a diversity of "values" (and the "goods" to which they refer) value pluralists insist that such diversity is irreducible because such values are "heterogeneous." The "heterogeneity" of "values" refers to the fact that these "values" (and the "goods" to which they refer) cannot be reduced to a single criterion of worth, with the result that no "comprehensive rank-ordering" is possible between them (Galston 1999: 770). As William Galston states:

> Objective goods cannot be fully rank-ordered. This means that there is no common measure for all goods, which are qualitatively heterogeneous. It means that there is no summum bonum that is the chief good for all individuals. It means that there are no comprehensive lexical orderings among types of goods. (Galston 2002: 5)

The result, Galston says, is that "[b]ecause there is no uniquely rational ordering or combination of such values [or the 'goods' to which they refer] no one can provide a generally valid reason, binding on all individuals, for a particular ranking or combination. There is therefore no rational basis for restrictive policies whose justification includes the assertion that there is a unique rational ordering of value" (Galston 1999: 775. My addition).

"Value Pluralism" and Relativism

We saw above that from a metaethical perspective, in which societies are perceived as irreducibly "plural," relativism might be a logical outcome. However if by "relativism" we mean a thoroughgoing inability to arrive at categorical and authoritative judgments concerning the relative worth of competing values, then value pluralists are not "relativists" of this thoroughgoing kind.

It is true, as we have seen, that value pluralists acknowledge the "heterogeneity" of values, meaning that they acknowledge that the values present in human societies "cannot be reduced to a common measure of value" with the result that no objective "rank-ordering" is possible between them (Galston 1999: 770, 775). Further, value pluralists recognize the "incompatibility" of values, meaning that they realize that values often give rise to mutually exclusive claims or demands which cannot be combined or reconciled (Moore 2009: 245), with the result that (in Isaiah Berlin's words in a passage below) "tragic" choice is often necessary between them.

Yet this does not commit value pluralists to a thoroughgoing relativism. The reason is that the "heterogeneous" values that value pluralists acknowledge as having worth possess this worth precisely because they are conducive to "human flourishing." For this reason, although value pluralists cannot categorically choose between such values, assigning each a priority relative to the others in some overall rank-ordering, they can identify these same values as having normative worth precisely because of their relationship to "human flourishing." "Human flourishing" is therefore a norm affirmed by value pluralists on a nonrelativist basis, and against which the worth of all other values can be determined. Relativists, by contrast, are not able to assign such normative significance in such a transcendent manner at all, because they lack the authoritative criteria to do so.

Further, such "human flourishing" provides a norm not only enabling value pluralists to assign normative worth but also enabling them to deny it. This is because a "value" which undermined such "flourishing" would not be considered a worthwhile "value" by value pluralists at all, and so would be thoroughly repudiated. In this way, value pluralists are able to make a categorical distinction between those values which have normative worth and those which do not, precisely because the one nonrelative value (or "good") they affirm is "human flourishing." William Galston acknowledges the capacity of value pluralists to make such distinctions as follows:

> Value pluralists believe there is a wide range of ways in which human beings can flourish, but they do not believe there is no distinction between developed and stunted lives, or no reason to prefer development to stunting. Children who grow up without attachments to parents and peers, in circumstances of pervasive physical insecurity, disconnected from all

potential sources of meaning and purpose in their lives, are harmed from the standpoint not of some but of all viable conceptions of flourishing. (Galston 1999: 776–77)

On this basis, Galston refuses to identify value pluralism with relativism:

Value pluralism is not relativism. The distinction between good and bad, and between good and evil, is objective and rationally defensible. (Galston 2002: 5)

While value pluralists can assign values a normative significance if they are conducive to "human flourishing," we have seen that they cannot, on some meta-ethical basis, categorically choose between them. In this respect, Galston's declaration in the passage above notwithstanding, we might say that value pluralists are committed to a *partial* relativism. While they can categorically distinguish (in normative terms) between those values which are conducive to "human flourishing" and those which are not, and can assign (in line with Galston above) the adjective of "good" to one and "evil" to the other, they cannot (on a metaethical basis) categorically distinguish (in some lexical order of priority) between "good" values themselves, precisely because all, in their different ways, are conducive to "human flourishing," and (being "heterogenous") none are reducible to the other.

In contrast, when it comes to their own personal lives (involving "ethical" as distinct from "metaethical" choice) value pluralists are capable of making such categorical distinctions between values conducive to "human flourishing." This is because, in reference to their *own* personal "flourishing," value pluralists possess an authoritative criterion for determining which of these "values" (and therefore which "goods") are preferable to others. Their own personal "flourishing," after all, is singular, not plural, and so there will only be certain goods, values, or practices which (according to their own estimation) are conducive to it, allowing them to categorically exclude all others. In this respect, once value pluralists move away from a metaethical perspective and apply value choice to their own personal life, they are unlikely to be "relativist" at all.

"Value Pluralism" and Toleration

Are value pluralists likely to affirm toleration? We saw above that value pluralists are capable of affirming (nonrelative) distinctions between values, and they do so on the basis of whether such values are or are not conducive to "human flourishing." As such, they have clear and authoritative criteria for refusing toleration to values which fall short of this normative threshold.

But when it comes to the "values" that are conducive to "human flourishing," toleration, at least as a practice, is more difficult. On the one hand, value pluralists recognize and affirm the diversity of ways of life to which such values, and the goods to which they refer, give rise. For this reason, they are willing to affirm the entitlement of individuals, on the basis of their own liberty, to make their own choices, free from the interference of others, concerning these "values," and the

20 Toleration and Its Possibilities: Relativism, Skepticism, and Pluralism

ways of life they endorse (Moore 2009: 244–45, 245–46). Isaiah Berlin makes this connection between value pluralism and the defense of individual freedom of choice as follows:

> [I]t seems to me that the belief that some single formula can in principle be found whereby all the diverse ends of men can be harmoniously realised is demonstrably false. If, as I believe, the ends of men are many, and not all of them are in principle compatible with each other, then the possibility of conflict – and of tragedy – can never wholly be eliminated from human life, either personal or social. The necessity of choosing between absolute claims is then an inescapable characteristic of the human condition. *This gives its value to freedom.....as an end in itself*, and not as a temporary need, arising out of our confused notions and irrational and disordered lives, a predicament which a panacea could one day put right. (Berlin 2008: 214. Emphasis added)

But while this willingness to affirm the free choices of others concerning values conducive to "human flourishing" provides a reason, in terms of Condition 3, why value pluralists should not interfere with these choices, or the ways of life to which they give rise, and instead allow individuals to make their own decisions on these matters, such noninterference does not (in terms of our five conditions above) amount to toleration. This is because another element of toleration – the aversion present in Condition 2 – is absent, and that is because the values conducive to "human flourishing," which assist in providing "reasons" for noninterference (Condition 3), do not elicit aversion on the part of value pluralists. This is because "human flourishing" is a norm that value pluralists endorse.

Value pluralists are, however, capable of *intolerance*, and this is because they have a clear criterion (centered on "human flourishing") for determining whether specific values, and the goods associated with them, lack worth and so (ceteris paribus) should be repudiated. Such a criterion provides them with reasons for their intolerance, and the aversion which underwrites it. Conversely, should value pluralists, under different circumstances, find reasons, under Condition 3, for not interfering with such otherwise impermissible values, they would be capable of toleration because, in this instance, the aversion required under Condition 2 would now exist.

Relativism and Toleration

Unlike value pluralists, thoroughgoing relativists lack an indubitable criterion to categorically affirm any particular identity, belief, or practice as a "good," or reject it as an "evil." After all, as we have seen above, something is either "good," in and of itself, or "good" because it is an instrumental means of achieving some other "good." In each case, something is only "good" (within our frame of reference) if we possess a criterion for authoritatively determining it to be so, to the exclusion of its opposite.

Thoroughgoing relativists, lacking such criteria, are unable to indubitably endorse any particular identity, belief, or practice as "good" in preference to available alternatives. For this reason, they will have difficulty affirming the worth of toleration if this worth depends on the "affirmation" of a particular "good."

But while relativists may not be able to affirm toleration based on the "affirmation" of a particular good, are they able to do so based on their "orientation" towards goods in general? The "orientation" of relativists to such "goods" is that they lack authoritative means to decide between them. We saw above that some have suggested that precisely such relativism provides a "reason" for toleration (Condition 3). Michael Wreen has advanced (but not endorsed) such a view as follows:

> Assume that relativism is true. Then if proponents of two different moral codes find themselves disagreeing about some moral matter – abortion, say – there's no ultimate proof that either can offer, no way for either to conclusively refute the other or conclusively establish her own position. That being the case, neither has the right to force her views on the other, or punish the other for violating the moral code she thinks correct. (Wreen 2001: 333)

According to this perspective, "relativism" provides a reason for toleration because, as a result of their "orientation" towards "goods" in general, relativists lack the normative basis to condemn another's beliefs or practices. Lacking a normative capacity to condemn these beliefs or practices, they have no normative entitlement to interfere with them, precluding them as an alternative, and so should not interfere. An "absence of a reason for interference" is thereby presented, in this context, as a "reason for toleration" (Condition 3). Although it is not a *positive* reason for toleration, such as the reasons that arise from perceiving toleration as a means to a particular "good," it is a reason for toleration that arises from an absence of a reason to engage in toleration's opposite – an absence that arises from the relativist's "orientation" towards "goods" in general.

But it is precisely this "orientation" towards "goods" in general that ultimately undermines relativism as a basis for toleration. Why is this the case? The answer is that in a relativist world, an "absence of a reason for interference" is insufficient to underwrite a categorical "reason for toleration." This is because just as relativism is not capable of advancing a normative case for interference (with the result, we have seen, that it elicits an "absence of reason" to interfere), neither can it preclude interference, because to preclude interference relativists would have to declare, on some prescriptive basis, that such interference was morally impermissible, and so ought to be categorically rejected as an option. Yet it is precisely this conclusion that thoroughgoing relativists (as a result of their "orientation" towards "goods" in general) lack the normative resources to affirm. They cannot categorically affirm one moral position, to the exclusion of its opposite, because they lack the normative resources to categorically affirm any moral position at all. The result is that they have no indubitable basis by which they can declare that interference (and therefore intolerance) should *not* take place even though they possess an "absence of reason" to interfere. Hans Oberdiek makes clear the incapacity of relativists to affirm toleration (to the exclusion of its opposite) identifying, as a specific class of "relativists," "subjectivists" who believe the origin of all value resides in individual subjective preference:

If any subjectivist claims that tolerance is something *everyone* of whatever persuasion should adopt, then he would be unjustifiably privileging tolerance by claiming (contrary to his avowed position) that it has some transsubjective basis. If *everything* we cherish rests, in the end, on mere subjective preference, then so too does a cherished commitment to toleration. Why should that be any different? And just as there may be an explanation but no justification for any of our other commitments, so there might be an explanation but no justification for our commitment to toleration. The support tolerance draws from subjectivism, therefore, turns out to be shaky indeed. (Oberdiek 2001: 15–16)

To sum up, therefore, we have seen that because relativism is incapable of categorically affirming any normative position to the exclusion of its opposite, relativists are unable to declare that interference (and therefore intolerance) should *not* take place even though (as a result of their relativism) they possess an "absence of reason" to interfere. The result is that because this "absence of reason" to interfere, when advanced by relativists, cannot, in and of itself, preclude interference, it is insufficient to underwrite a categorical "reason for toleration" (Condition 3).

But how do relativists fare concerning the other important precondition for toleration – the aversion, possessed by those engaging in toleration, toward the object of toleration itself (Condition 2)? Here, I think, they are on stronger ground. After all, relativism is a philosophical position. It arises from a conscious assumption that authoritative criteria for determining, on some transcendent basis, the relative worth of "goods" or "values," do not exist.

But this does not mean that relativists cannot feel, at a purely personal level, an aversion to particular beliefs, practices, identities, or ways of life, if such aversion arises on a purely emotive or affective basis, rather than from philosophical judgments that involve a reference to values. Relativism, being a philosophical judgment, only affects outcomes informed by such judgments. An emotive or affective aversion may have no relation to such judgments at all.

So we see, therefore, that relativists and value pluralists are incapable of toleration for contrary reasons. While relativists possess the aversion necessary under Condition 2, they lack the capacity to indubitably affirm categorical "reasons" for toleration under Condition 3. Conversely, while value pluralists possess the capacity to affirm "reasons" for toleration under Condition 3, they lack (in the case of values conducive to "human flourishing") the aversion toward the object of toleration necessary under Condition 2.

Others in the literature have also denied that relativism is capable of justifying toleration, but for somewhat different reasons to those which I identify above. Geoffrey Harrison's repudiation of this idea is dependent on a dichotomy he advances between relativism as a metaethical position and toleration as a practice which (he says) can only acquire import from the values internal to a "particular moral system":

Relativism is a metaethical theory, and its truth or falsity is a question for an outside observer. Advocating tolerance or being tolerant are activities which are internal to particular moral systems – the activities of participants. There is nothing that the relativist, qua relativist, can say either for or against tolerance from a moral point of view. The moment he does this he ceases to be an observer of morality and becomes a user of a moral system.... .If tolerance is to be defended, or, come to that, attacked, it may be from a Christian or Kantian or utilitarian point of view, but it must be from *some* point of view. There is no such thing as a moral judgment made from a morally neutral or "extramoral" position. (Harrison 1976: 131–32)

Michael Wreen has advanced a similar view, distinguishing relativism (as a metaethical position) from any first-order moral position endorsing toleration:

Considered simply as such, relativism entails neither tolerance nor intolerance, nor, indeed any first-order value. Another, more sweeping way to put the point is that relativism has no implications for the contents of a moral code, nor even the partial contents of a moral code. Relativism is a piece of meta-ethics, not normative ethics, and in and of itself, about as morally neutral as can be. (Wreen 2001: 332)

Relativists and Intolerance

However, while relativists may not be capable of toleration (at least toleration understood in terms of our five conditions above), is it the case that, like value pluralists, relativists are capable of intolerance? Certainly, like value pluralists, we have seen that they possess the capacity for the (affective or emotive) aversion necessary to underwrite such intolerance with performative intent. After all, as we have seen, such aversion, if it arises from an affective or emotive basis, is not dependent on the sort of evaluative judgments which would be affected by relativism. But unlike value pluralists, relativists lack the moral criteria to categorically specify certain values, beliefs, or practices as impermissible and therefore as deserving of intolerance. Just as the absence of such capacity for moral discrimination undermines the capacity of relativists to categorically affirm "reasons" for toleration (Condition 3), is it the case that it also undermines any "reasons" they might have for intolerance?

Arguably not. This is because when it comes to "intolerance," "reasons" for intolerance, independent of the aversion that first arouses such a disposition, may not be necessary at all. After all, one of the roles of "reasons" for toleration (Condition 3) is to override the aversion (Condition 2) which encourages us to act intolerantly (i.e., in a manner contrary to that advocated by the "reasons" arising under Condition 3). Such "reasons" (Condition 3) are therefore a necessary condition of any act of toleration. In the case of intolerance, by contrast, aversion alone is arguably sufficient to underwrite intolerant actions, with the result that, in such contexts, aversion becomes its own sufficient "reason" for intolerance. There is no need, therefore, for there to be the "intolerant" equivalent of Condition 3, providing additional "reasons" for intolerance over and above the aversion that is the initial impetus for it. The result, therefore, is that relativists (on the basis of their aversion alone) are capable of intolerance.

Skepticism and Toleration

In ▶ Chap. 40, "Toleration and Religion," I pointed to a venerable tradition of religious toleration, first arising in Europe in the sixteenth century, and purporting to base itself on skeptical assumptions concerning religious truth. Nevertheless, just as some within the literature have suggested that toleration is not possible on the basis of relativism, others have claimed it is not possible on the basis of skepticism. As Richard Vernon states:

> The conceptual issue is whether it makes sense to say that a sceptic exercises tolerance. Tolerance is clearly manifest in cases where people have hostile views about something, as well as the power to suppress the object of their hostility, but do not do so for some overriding reason. If their hostile views are undermined by scepticism, as they should be, then the category of toleration seems out of place since, if people are not hostile to something, they do not need to explain why they do not use their power to suppress it; whereas the sceptic who does have hostile views about something simply presents an interesting case of psychological conflict. (Vernon 1997: 53. See also Vernon 1997: 71; Gray 1995: 19; Tuck 1988: 26, 32–33, 35; Galston 1982: 625)

I argued above that relativists are not capable of affirming toleration in preference to its alternatives because relativism is not capable of yielding categorical reasons for toleration (Condition 3). Richard Vernon, in the passage above, is claiming that skeptics are not capable of engaging in toleration because skepticism undermines aversion as a condition of toleration (Condition 2). John Gray makes a similar point. He insists that the practice of toleration will involve categorical judgments in favor of some goods (thereby justifying toleration) and against others (thereby justifying intolerance). Such categorical judgments trade on a certitude and incontrovertibility concerning the worth or otherwise of such goods. It is this certitude and incontrovertibility which is inconsistent with skepticism, because skepticism (like relativism) is incapable of yielding such indubitable conclusions. For this reason, Gray implies, skepticism is incapable of underwriting toleration:

> Toleration is unavoidably and inherently judgemental. The objects of toleration are what we judge to be evils. When we tolerate a practice, a belief or a character trait, we let something be that we judge to be undesirable, false or at least inferior; our toleration expresses the conviction that, despite its badness, the object of toleration should be left alone. This is in truth the very idea of toleration, as it is practiced in things great and small. Toleration is not, then, an expression of scepticism, of doubt about our ability to tell the good from the bad; it is evidence of our confidence that we have that ability. A tolerant person, or a tolerant society, does not doubt that it knows something about the good and the true; its tolerance expresses that knowledge. Indeed, when a society is tolerant, its tolerance expresses the conception of the good life that it has in common. (Gray 1995: 1820)

We see, therefore, that there are strong grounds, within the basic conceptual features of toleration, which leads some to believe that toleration is inconsistent with skepticism. The result, according to these views, is that "[m]oral skepticism does not necessarily lead to toleration" (Levine 1999: 5).

Yet once again, as with relativism, skepticism arises from a philosophical judgment. It depends on individuals engaging in an explicit judgment that skepticism is the appropriate epistemological position to adopt in response to a set of propositions or some other data. Aversion (as we saw in the case of relativists) can arise at an emotive or affective level and so have no relation to philosophical judgment at all. Contrary to Vernon, therefore, if the skeptic's aversion arises at this non-philosophical level, it is possible that a skeptic might feel an aversion to whatever is the object of toleration, thereby fulfilling Condition 2, their skepticism notwithstanding.

But a key question is whether a skeptic is thereby in the same situation as a relativist – capable of feeling aversion (Condition 2) to the object of toleration but unable to categorically affirm the reasons for toleration (Condition 3) that would be sufficient to preclude the intolerance to which such aversion would otherwise give rise? At one level, it might be thought that the situation is the same insofar as skepticism, like relativism, is generally thought to render its proponents incapable of categorically affirming positive moral positions that exclude rival alternatives. After all, the affirmation of such positions depends on an ability to indubitably affirm some values or goods in preference to others, and to do so on the basis of authoritative criteria. And in the view of many, it is precisely such criteria that skeptics (like relativists) lack.

Skeptics Versus Relativists

On the other hand, is there a possible difference between skeptics and relativists in this regard? Relativists are unable to endorse toleration in any specific instance because they are unable to affirm (on a categorical basis) "reasons" for toleration (Condition 3) capable of precluding toleration's opposite. This is so when these "reasons" are dependent on the "affirmation" of particular "goods." But we have seen that such inabilities also arise when these "reasons" are dependent on the relativist's "orientation" towards "goods" in general. Is the skeptic in the same position?

For the present, let us assume that skepticism prevents skeptics from affirming reasons for toleration (Condition 3) based on an "affirmation" of particular "goods." This is because, like relativists, skeptics lack the normative resources to categorically endorse some "goods" in preference to others. A thoroughgoing skeptic, after all, will be as "skeptical" about propositions concerning the worth of such "goods" as they will be about any other proposition. However, while skeptics and relativists are in the same position regarding toleration based on the "affirmation" of particular "goods," are they in the same position when it comes to toleration based on an "orientation" towards "goods" in general?

Consider the following scenario. An inveterate racist has an aversion to people of a particular race which he has possessed since a child. This is because, since a child, he has always been taught by parents and significant others the variety of reasons why they believe the race in question is beneath contempt. These reasons have no doubt informed his aversion to the race (and may be the impetus for it) but the persecution (intolerance) of the race in which he has engaged since a child has always been consciously justified, in his own mind, by these reasons, and not by his aversion.

But as he has grown older, he has become a thoroughgoing skeptic, and this skepticism has extended to his belief in the reasons instilled in him since childhood concerning the inferiority of the race in question. No longer believing in these reasons, he no longer possesses motives (based on such reasons) to engage in intolerance toward this race, and so ceases to do so. Further, in deeply doubting what he had hitherto believed were reasons for intolerance, it is possible that, eventually, he may no longer feel an aversion for the race in question. In such a circumstance, where such an aversion is absent, although he no longer engages in intolerance (with the result that noninterference is the outcome of his skepticism), it is not possible (in terms of our five conditions above) to identify this noninterference as toleration, because aversion (Condition 2) is absent.

But given that the ex-racist's aversion may not be coextensive with the "reasons" instilled in him for intolerance, but instead may arise, in part, from affective or emotive sentiments independent of those reasons, such aversion may not be eradicated by the skepticism he has subsequently applied to those "reasons" and which has vitiated their normative import. The result is that while he may no longer possess "reasons" for intolerance, and has therefore ceased to engage in the persecution associated with it, he may still possess, at an affective or emotive level, an aversion to the race in question. In such a situation, by no longer engaging in persecution (but still possessing an aversion to the race in question), the ex-racist, in not interfering with members of that race, is engaging in toleration.

The reason for such toleration (Condition 3) arises not from any affirmation of a particular "good." Rather, it arises from the skeptic's "orientation" to "goods" in general. This orientation gives rise (as in the case of relativists) to an "absence of a reason for interference" (skepticism depriving the ex-racist of the reasons he once possessed to interfere). But we saw, in the case of relativism, that this "absence of a reason for interference" was not sufficient to amount to a categorical reason for toleration, because, when advanced by relativists, such a reason lacked the capacity to preclude toleration's opposite (such an outcome arising from relativists' incapacity to categorically affirm a moral position to the exclusion of competing positions).

This is not the case with skepticism in the example above. By the ex-racist acknowledging that intolerance, in order to possess normative justification, requires reasons for its practice, and by skepticism denying the cogency of these reasons, skepticism does (in the example above) preclude toleration's opposite. After all, if the ex-racist now engaged in intolerance, without the reasons he once possessed to justify this, such expression of his aversion would (in his own terms) lack any reasonable warrant, because it was precisely such reasons which were once the sole rationale for his intolerant behavior. Consequently, in the case of the ex-racist, the "absence of a reason for interference," which skepticism provides, definitely precludes (in normative terms) the possibility of toleration's opposite, thereby constituting a categorical reason for toleration (Condition 3). The result is that although skepticism (like relativism) is incapable of providing justification for toleration premised on an "affirmation" of a particular "good," it is (unlike relativism) capable of providing a justification for toleration based on an "orientation" towards "goods" in general.

If skeptics are capable of toleration, are they capable of intolerance? If skepticism acts as a solvent on our aversion, intolerance is also precluded, since the pretext for the intolerance is the aversion. On the other hand, if (a) the aversion arises from affective or emotive foundations unrelated to the sort of intellectual judgements affected by skepticism, and (b) if, as in our example of the relativist above, the aversion is its own sufficient reason for intolerance, then (c) a skeptic might, in such an instance, be capable of intolerance since the basis for their intolerance would be impervious to their skepticism.

I have argued elsewhere that skepticism is the one secular reason capable of convincing the religiously devout to engage in toleration in cases where they confront that (such as blasphemy) which, upon the basis of their faith, they find abhorrent (see Tate 2016a: 240–42, b: 668–674; ; see also ▶ Chap. 40, "Toleration and Religion"). The discussion above has sought to advance a more general proposition that skepticism is capable of providing categorical reasons for toleration (Condition 3), sufficient to preclude toleration's opposite, in cases where the "reasons" for toleration are based, not on the "affirmation" of a particular "good," but on a skeptical "orientation" towards "goods" in general.

"Indifference" and Toleration

In addition to skepticism, relativism, and pluralism, some have identified "indifference" as a basis for toleration. We saw above that "indifference" is a condition quite distinct from relativism, skepticism, and pluralism insofar as it refers not to a philosophical outlook concerning the external world but to an emotional trait within individuals. Bernard Williams is among the philosophers who perceives "indifference" as a possible basis for toleration. He states: "Indifference is no doubt one route to toleration as a practice; it can scarcely be denied that toleration of religious variation has increased with a decline of enthusiasm for religion and religious issues" (Williams 1991: 204).

Certainly increasing secularization within societies can have, as one of its manifestations, an increasing religious "indifference" among ever-larger sections of the population, with the result that vociferous religious divisions inherited from a more religiously minded age are attenuated. But the key question is whether we can follow Williams and characterize this process as giving rise to an increasing "toleration"?

Whereas "reasons" for toleration, underpinned, perhaps, by a commitment to "autonomy" or "equal respect," if efficacious, override the motives for intolerance arising from aversion, they may not vitiate the aversion itself. The latter often remains, but in cases of toleration it is not acted upon due to the persuasive impact of the reasons for toleration arising under Condition 3. By contrast, we saw that relativism and skepticism, underwriting "reasons" for toleration, may vitiate the aversion, acting as a solvent upon it, if the aversion arises from the sort of considerations undermined by skepticism or relativism, but not if it arises from emotive or affective sources unaffected by these.

"Indifference," by contrast, acts as a solvent upon the aversion, irrespective of the aversion's source. This is because "indifference" and "aversion" are mutually exclusive. The more "indifference" we possess for something, the less "aversion" we feel for it. Indeed, even Williams concedes this: "[W]ith indifference and skepticism the point will be reached at which nobody is interested enough in the disagreements for there to be anything to put up with, and toleration will not be necessary" (Williams 1996: 25). In making this declaration, Williams adequately accounts for "indifference" as a solvent upon aversion, but misses the caveat we create for skepticism above, wherein there are circumstances in which skepticism does not "dissolve" (i.e., vitiate) aversion but rather provides a "reason" (Condition 3) why its imperatives ought not to be acted upon.

Consequently, if "indifference" is fully efficacious as a "reason" for toleration, not only will it "override" aversion, it will vitiate it altogether. Should this occur, although noninterference is the result, and the "liberty" sought under Condition 1 is thereby secured, toleration (understood in terms of our five conditions above) has not taken place because Condition 2 is absent altogether.

For this reason, just as it was suggested above in our discussion of Condition 2 that if we are positively in favour of something, then, arguably, we are not "tolerating" it, so if we are wholly "indifferent" to something, toleration is equally impossible. The reason, in each case, is because "indifference" and "endorsement" both vitiate aversion. If Bernard William's "indifference" is a source of religious toleration, as he claims above, this is only the case if "indifference" is partial, and aversion therefore still in place, in which case "indifference" (constituting a "reason" for toleration under Condition 3) might provide sufficient motivation not to act on the aversion represented by Condition 2.

Toleration as a "Disposition"

So far we have referred to toleration in terms of our five conditions above. When toleration is understood in such terms it is conceived as a "practice." However, it is possible to conceive of toleration in much wider terms, as a "disposition" that a person possesses and which they exhibit in relation to the world around them. When a person is described, for instance, as possessing a "tolerant" attitude of mind, it is to this "disposition" that reference is being made.

Certainly this is how Allan Bloom, in the passage quoted earlier, conceives of the "toleration" of his students. They possess a "tolerant" attitude of mind to all that is around them, in relation to which they endeavor not to interfere in an "intolerant" manner. When "toleration" is understood in these terms, as a "disposition," it is synonymous with attitudes such as "acceptance," "non-judgementalness," "open-mindedness," etc.

But what is also significant is that when toleration is understood as a "disposition," aversion to objects of toleration (Condition 2) is potentially *absent*, and so no longer a necessary condition of toleration itself. After all, the presence of such aversion would conceivably be at odds with the "acceptance," "non-judgmentalness," and "open-mindedness" characteristic of toleration as a "disposition."

Of course, it might be possible to conceive of aversion as still *present*, within toleration as a "disposition," if "acceptance," "open-mindedness," and "non-judgmentalness" are exercised as "reasons" for toleration, arising under Condition 3, intended to override the reasons for intolerant behavior arising under Condition 2. But in such circumstances, the agent of toleration is arguably placed in a position of cognitive dissonance, because like "indifference" above, "acceptance," "non-judgmentalness," and "open-mindedness" are qualities directly at odds with aversion, in the sense that the more "acceptance" we feel for something the less aversion we will possess. For this reason, the qualities of toleration as a "disposition" (open-mindedness, etc.) are more likely to be exercised in the absence of aversion.

In this respect, we can identify a qualitative difference between toleration as a "practice" and toleration as a "disposition." This difference arises from the fact that aversion is present as a condition of toleration in one but is potentially absent in the other.

Indeed, it is precisely this difference between toleration as a "practice" and toleration as a "disposition" that is traded upon in a paradox to which reference is sometimes made in the toleration literature. This is the paradox that one way to find more opportunities to engage in toleration as a practice is to have a more intolerant disposition to the world in general. As John Horton has put it: "[H]ow tolerant a person or group is, will be in part a function of the range of actions or practices to which the person or group has a negative attitude. So, apparently, the wider the range of negative attitudes, the wider the scope for practicing toleration" (Horton 1994: 16). This statement reflects a paradox precisely because our everyday understanding of a "tolerant" person (exhibiting toleration as a "disposition") does not include the "negative attitude" (aversion) present in toleration as a practice. Rather, it presumes the person in question possesses an attitude of mind in which such aversion is absent.

Horton then seeks to resolve this paradox by providing a wider conception of "toleration" which seeks to encompass, within a single definition, both of our conceptions of toleration – toleration as a "practice" (or what Horton calls a "behavior") and toleration as a "disposition" (or what Horton calls an "attitude"):

> [W]e also talk of tolerant attitudes as well as tolerant behaviour. In characterising an attitude as tolerant we are typically interested in more than the fact that people have a disposition not to interfere with some actions which they find objectionable. We are also interested in what sort of actions they find objectionable. We do not think of a tolerant person as someone with a host of intense and unreasonable antipathies to a wide range of activities commonly thought to be innocuous, successfully struggling to restrain himself from acting on them but, at least in part, as someone who is not inappropriately judgemental about how others

behave. Toleration, therefore, seems to require more than not acting, or even having the disposition to act, restrictively towards those actions which are found objectionable. It also presupposes not having an excessive or inappropriate range of objections to how others act. The restraint involved in toleration is not exclusively of action but also of judgment. (Horton 1994: 17)

I think Professor Horton's attempt to resolve the paradox by incorporating, within a single definition of "toleration," both toleration as a "practice" and toleration as a "disposition," ultimately fails. The reason is not simply that one conception of toleration involves a necessary condition (aversion) that the other does not. The reason is that the presence of this condition, within one conception of toleration, is inconsistent with the exercise of toleration in the other. This is evident in Horton's account in the passage above. Horton makes clear that although toleration as a "behavior" requires aversion to be present, genuine "tolerance" of mind requires an "attitude" in which it is absent. Given that the "behavior" and the "attitude" (according to Horton's account above) are both necessary features of his single conception of "toleration," it is difficult to see how an agent can exhibit both to any significant degree when one involves a condition (or an absence of a condition) that is inconsistent with the other.

The result is a contradiction at the center of Horton's expanded definition of "toleration." An alternative view to Horton, which avoids this contradiction, is to declare that far from being encompassed in a single definition of toleration, toleration as a "practice" and toleration as a "disposition" are in fact two qualitatively distinct conceptions of "toleration," and this because one involves a condition (aversion) which, in ordinary circumstances, is absent in the other.

Toleration as a "Disposition": Relativism, Skepticism, and Pluralism

Is it possible, therefore, to agree with Professor Bloom that the relativism of his students makes toleration as a "disposition" possible, even though, as we have seen, relativism is incapable of underwriting toleration as a "practice"? Are his students able to sustain their nonaversive and open-minded attitude to all that surrounds them on the basis, alone, of the relativism that Bloom ascribes to them?

The answer is "no." This is despite Bloom's insistence to the contrary, describing the relativism of his students as the normative basis of their toleration which makes their "openness" and "non-judgmentalness" toward others possible. As Bloom puts it above: "Relativism is necessary to openness......Openness – and the relativism that makes it the only plausible stance in the face of various claims to truth and various ways of life and kinds of human beings – is the great insight of our times"

But Bloom is mistaken that it is relativism that underwrites, justifies, and makes possible his students' toleration and the "openness" which is its primary manifestation. This is because we have seen that relativism is incapable of categorically affirming any moral position to the exclusion of another. Relativism, in and of itself, is therefore as incapable of indubitably affirming "openness" as it is of affirming its opposite, because incapable of affirming either to the exclusion of the other. What *is* capable of affirming "openness" (and the toleration with which it is associated) is the *other* moral commitment that Bloom ascribes to his students – "equality." As Bloom states in the earlier passage above, his students are "unified only in their relativism and in their allegiance to equality," adding that "relativism" and "equality" are, in this context, "related in moral intention."

If, in confronting another, we consider them an "equal," then this is a normative commitment capable of underwriting specific moral positions to the exclusion of their opposite, and so justifying the behavior that arises in accord with such moral positions. Such a commitment to "equality" is certainly capable of underwriting toleration, understood as the "openness" (and noninterference) which, according to Bloom, is its primary manifestation among his students. After all, to act obtrusively, censoriously, or with interdiction in relation to others is not to treat them "equally." To allow these others the same liberties as one allows oneself, not least by not interfering with them, is (ceteris paribus) to treat them "equally." It is the latter which is the manifestation of "toleration" ("openness") that Bloom highlights among his students. Yet it is a toleration underwritten not by the "relativism" that Bloom identifies but by the "equality" which, he says, is "related" to this relativism in "moral intention." It is "equality," not relativism, that gives rise, in these circumstances, not simply to an "absence of reason to interfere," but a positive reason not to interfere. Such a reason is sufficiently robust, in normative terms, to exclude its opposite, and so constitutes a categorical reason for toleration.

So Bloom is mistaken that it is relativism which underwrites his students' toleration. But he is equally mistaken that this relativism is "related" to "equality" in "moral intention." Relativism is as incapable of categorically affirming "equality" as a moral value, to the exclusion of its opposite, as it is of affirming any other moral position. Far from the two being related to each other in "moral intention," we might say that Bloom's students cease to be relativists the moment they affirm "equality" as a categorical commitment. Such "equality" underwrites their toleration precisely because it is a value which these students affirm on nonrelative grounds, with the result that it is capable of normatively excluding toleration's opposite. The source of such a commitment to "equality," therefore, must reside somewhere other than their "relativism." To return to our wider inquiry, therefore, we must conclude, on the basis of this analysis of Bloom's students, that relativism is as incapable of justifying toleration as a "disposition" as it is of justifying toleration as a "practice."

Does skepticism fare better than relativism as a normative foundation for toleration as a "disposition"? We saw above that skepticism was capable, in specific circumstances, of justifying toleration as a "practice." This is because, by giving rise to an "absence of a reason for interference," it undermined the "reasons" an agent possessed to act on their aversion and so removed justification for the intolerant behavior that would otherwise arise on the basis of those reasons. Without a justifiable reason to act on an aversion, noninterference, and so toleration, we saw, was the possible result.

But it is less apparent that skepticism can underwrite a general "disposition" to engage in tolerant behavior. After all, in such a context, we have seen, aversion is likely to be absent. While skepticism may give rise to an "absence of a reason for interference" when it comes to a specific aversion, is it possible that when it comes to a much wider ambit, concerning a tolerant disposition in general, skepticism finds itself in the same position as relativism – unable to categorically exclude toleration's opposite? After all, for skepticism to give rise to an "absence of a reason for interference," there perhaps needs to be a reason to interfere, whose normative import skepticism undermines (as in our racism example above). While such reasons to interfere arise in the context of specific aversions, directed to specific objects of toleration, they are unlikely to exist in the general context of toleration as a "disposition," in which aversion is absent. On the other hand, with skepticism incapable of giving rise to reasons to interfere, a skeptic lacks any reasonable warrant for interference in general, and as we saw with our racism example above, such an "absence of a reason for interference" is capable, in some circumstances, of constituting a reason for toleration. On this basis, it is possible that skepticism might be capable of underwriting toleration as a "disposition." Of course, relativists also lack any reasonable warrant for interference, but unlike the sceptic in our racism example above, they also lack any reasonable warrant not to interfere, and so for this reason are not capable of precluding toleration's opposite.

Are "value pluralists" capable of justifying toleration as a "disposition"? We saw above that the one reason value pluralists could not underwrite toleration as a "practice" was because they did not possess an aversion (Condition 2) to all that is conducive to "human flourishing." Given that toleration as a "disposition" does not, at least in the account provided above, require aversion as a necessary condition, value pluralists might be able to endorse toleration as a "disposition." But in this case, "toleration" (given the absence of aversion) could not be understood as anything other than the wholehearted endorsement and approval, by value pluralists, of anything conducive to "human flourishing."

In the context of such wholehearted endorsement, we are left with the question perennial within the toleration literature, and first raised in our discussion of Condition 2 above: If we wholeheartedly support, endorse, or approve of something, are we in fact "tolerating" it at all?

Conclusion

The discussion above has sought to investigate the relationship between relativism, skepticism, and pluralism. It has also sought to investigate the relationship of all three to toleration and also to intolerance. It has concluded that relativism, skepticism, and pluralism produce different outcomes in regard to both the possibility and the justification of toleration and intolerance. We have seen that they also produce different outcomes depending on whether toleration is understood as a "practice" or a "disposition." We have seen that whereas a justification of toleration in terms of "autonomy," "respect," or some other specific norm (where toleration is perceived as a means to such ends) constitutes a justification of toleration on the basis of an "affirmation" of a specific "good," a justification of toleration in terms of relativism, skepticism, or pluralism is a justification based upon an individual's "orientation" to "goods" in general. We saw that the former is a much more robust basis for justifying toleration than the latter.

Summary and Future Directions

Relativism, skepticism, and pluralism are perceived by many as indelible features of our moral universe. Consequently the question of their relationship to key political issues such as toleration is a perennial one. Given that relativism and pluralism refer to circumstances of diversity, and given that it is these same circumstances of diversity that often give rise to demands for toleration, it is inevitable that the question of the relationship between relativism, skepticism, pluralism, and toleration will continue to arise both in the present and in the future.

References

Balint P (2014) Acts of tolerance: a political and descriptive account. Eur J Polit Theo 13(3):264–281

Berlin I (2008) Two concepts of liberty. In: Hardy H (ed) Liberty. Oxford University Press, Oxford, pp 166–217

Bernstein RJ (1983) Beyond objectivism and relativism. Science, hermeneutics, and praxis. University of Pennsylvania Press, Philadelphia

Bloom A (1988) The closing of the American mind. How higher education has failed democracy and impoverished the souls of. Today's Students. Penguin, London

Coffey J (2000) Persecution and toleration in Protestant England, 1558–1689. Pearson Education Ltd, Edinburgh Gate

Cohen AJ (2004) What toleration is. Ethics 115(1):68–95

Galeotti AE (2002) Toleration as recognition. Cambridge University Press, Cambridge

Galston WA (1982) Defending liberalism. Am Polit Sci Rev 76(3):621–629

Galston WA (1999) Value pluralism and liberal political theory. Am Polit Sci Rev 93(4):769–778

Galston WA (2002) Liberal pluralism. The implications of value pluralism for political theory and practice. Cambridge University Press, Cambridge

Graham G (1996) Tolerance, pluralism and relativism. In: Heyd D (ed) Toleration. An elusive virtue. Princeton University Press, Princeton, pp 44–59

Gray J (1995) Enlightenment's wake. Politics and culture at the close of the modern age. Routledge, London

Gray J (2000a) Pluralism and toleration in contemporary political philosophy. Political Studies 48 (2):323–333

Gray J (2000b) Two faces of liberalism. Polity Press, Cambridge

Harrison G (1976) Relativism and tolerance. Ethics 86(2):122–135

Hiley DR (1988) Philosophy in question. Essays on a Pyrrhonian theme. University of Chicago Press, Chicago

Horton J (1994) Three (apparent) paradoxes of toleration. Synthesis Philosophica 9(1):7–20

Horton J (1996) Toleration as a virtue. In: Heyd D (ed) Toleration. An elusive virtue. Princeton University Press, Princeton, pp 28–43

Hume D (1960) In: Selby-Bigge LA (ed) A treatise of human nature. Oxford, Clarendon Press

Jones P (2007a) Making sense of political toleration. Br J Polit Sci 37(3):383–402

Jones P (2007b) Can speech be intolerant? In: Newey G (ed) Freedom of expression. Counting the cost. Cambridge Scholars Publishing, Cambridge, pp 9–29

Jones P (2012) Legalising toleration: a reply to Balint. Res Publica 18(3):265–270

Kant I (1949) Critique of practical reason. In: Kant I (ed) Critique of practical reason and other writings in moral philosophy. Chicago University Press, Chicago, pp 118–260

Kant I (1964) Critique of pure reason (trans: Smith NK). Macmillan, London

Kuhn TS (1977) Second thoughts on paradigms. In: Kuhn TS (ed) The essential tension. Selected studies in scientific tradition and change. University of Chicago Press, Chicago, pp 293–319

Kuhn TS (2012) The structure of scientific revolutions, 4th edn. University of Chicago Press, Chicago

Kymlicka W (1996) Two models of pluralism and tolerance. In: Heyd D (ed) Toleration. An elusive virtue. Princeton University Press, Princeton, pp 81–105

Levine A (1999) Introduction: the prehistory of toleration and varieties of skepticism. In: Levine A (ed) Early modern skepticism and the origins of toleration. Lexington Books, Lanham, pp 1–20

Locke J (1993) An essay concerning toleration. In: Wootton D (ed) Political writings. Penguin, London, pp 186–210

MacIntyre A (1988) Whose justice? Which rationality? University of Notre Dame Press, Notre Dame

MacIntyre A (1990) Three rival versions of moral enquiry: encyclopaedia, genealogy, and tradition. University of Notre Dame Press, Notre Dame

MacIntyre A (1997) After Virtue. A study in moral theory, Duckworth, London

Mendus S (1989) Toleration and the limits of liberalism. Macmillan, London

Mill JS (1971) Utilitarianism, liberty, representative government. Everyman, London

Moore MJ (2009) Pluralism, relativism and liberalism. Polit Res Q 62(2):244–256

Newey G (2001) Is democratic toleration a rubber duck? Res Publica 7(3):315–336

Oberdiek H (2001) Tolerance. Between forbearance and acceptance. Rowman & Littlefield Publishers, Inc, London

Popkin RH (1979) The history of scepticism from Erasmus to Descartes, rev. edn. Koninklijke Van Gorcum & Comp, Assen

Raphael DD (1988) The intolerable. In: Mendus S (ed) Justifying toleration. Conceptual and historical perspectives. Cambridge University Press, Cambridge, pp 137–154

Rawls J (1972) A theory of justice. Oxford University Press, Oxford

Rawls J (1980) Kantian constructivism in moral theory. J Philos 77(9):515–572

Rawls J (2005) Political liberalism, rev. edn. Columbia University Press, Columbia

Rorty R (1982) Consequences of pragmatism. University of Minnesota Press, Minneapolis

Rorty R (1989) Contingency, irony, and solidarity. Cambridge University Press, Cambridge

Rorty R (1995a) On ethnocentrism: a reply to Clifford Geertz. In: Rorty R (ed) Objectivity, relativism, and truth, Philosophical papers, vol I. Cambridge University Press, Cambridge, pp 203–210

Rorty R (1995b) Cosmopolitanism without emancipation: a response to Jean-François lyotard. In: Rorty R (ed) Objectivity, relativism, and truth, Philosophical papers, vol I. Cambridge University Press, Cambridge, pp 211–222

Scanlon TM (2003) The difficulty of tolerance. Essays in political philosophy. Cambridge University Press, Cambridge

Tate JW (2016a) Liberty, toleration and equality. John Locke, Jonas Proast and the letters concerning toleration. Routledge, New York

Tate JW (2016b) Toleration, skepticism and blasphemy: John Locke, Jonas Proast and Charlie Hebdo. Am J Polit Sci 60(3):664–675

Tuck R (1988) Scepticism and toleration in the seventeenth century. In: Mendus S (ed) Justifying toleration. Conceptual and historical perspectives. Cambridge University Press, Cambridge, pp 21–36

Vernon R (1997) The career of toleration. John Locke, Jonas Proast, and after. McGill-Queen's University Press, Montreal

Waldron J (1997) Locke: toleration and the rationality of persecution. In: Dunn J, Harris I (eds) Locke, vol II. Edward Elgar Publishing, Cheltenham, pp 349–374

Waldron J (1999) How to argue for a universal claim. Columbia Hum Rights Law Rev 30(2):305–314

Williams B (1991) Subjectivism and toleration. Griffiths AP A.J. Ayer: memorial essays. Cambridge University Press, Cambridge, 197–208

Williams B (1996) Toleration: an impossible virtue? In: Heyd D (ed) Toleration. An elusive virtue. Princeton University Press, Princeton, pp 18–27

Wreen M (2001) How tolerant must a relativist be? Public Aff Q 15(4):329–339

Toleration, Reasonableness, and Power

21

Thomas M. Besch and Jung-Sook Lee

Contents

Introduction	398
Toleration: Concept and Conceptions	399
Respect, Respect Toleration, and Justification	401
Power and Non-domination	404
True Toleration and Non-domination?	406
Reasonableness?	409
Discursive Equality?	412
Summary and Future Directions	415
References	416

Abstract

This chapter explores Rainer Forst's justification-centric view of non-domination toleration. This view places an idea of equal respect and a corresponding requirement of reciprocal and general justification at the core of non-domination toleration. After reconstructing this view, this chapter addresses two issues. First, even if this idea of equal respect requires the limits of non-domination toleration to be drawn in a manner that is equally justifiable to all affected people, equal justifiability should not be understood in terms of Forst's requirement of reciprocal and general acceptability. Second, for the equal justifiability of relevant constraints to ensure non-domination outcomes, discursive equality must be understood in substantive, purchase-sensitive terms. This means that a justification-centric view of non-domination toleration stands or falls with the participation value of

---

T. M. Besch (✉)
School of Philosophy, Wuhan University, Wuhan, Hubei, China

Department of Philosophy, The University of Sydney, Sydney, NSW, Australia
e-mail: thomas.besch@whu.edu.cn; thomas.besch@sydney.edu.au

J.-S. Lee (✉)
School of Social Sciences, UNSW Sydney, Sydney, NSW, Australia
e-mail: js.lee@unsw.edu.au

© The Author(s), under exclusive licence to Springer Nature Switzerland AG 2022
M. Sardoč (ed.), *The Palgrave Handbook of Toleration*,
https://doi.org/10.1007/978-3-030-42121-2_22

what it regards as the standards of justification. This places reasonably contested matters of value at the heart of such views.

Keywords

Respect · Toleration · Justification · Non-domination · Discursive equality · Reasonableness · Discursive influence

---

Introduction

Can a practice of toleration impose constraints without instantiating domination? This chapter explores Rainer Forst's seminal justification-centric view of non-domination toleration (2003a, b; Forst 2017a). In a nutshell, this view finds a form of equal respect and a corresponding requirement of reciprocal and general justification at the core of non-domination toleration. For Forst, practices of toleration can instantiate non-domination toleration only if they respect all affected people as moral-political equals. To this end, he claims, these practices must only impose constraints that are justifiable to all affected people by reasons that they can equally accept – which aims to capture a "Kantian republican" sense of non-domination (Forst 2013). On this basis, Forst insists that practices of toleration should draw the limits of toleration in terms of the requirement of reciprocal and general justification.

While this view, or its underlying commitment to a demanding form of equal respect, has merits, it gives rise to two concerns. First, even if non-domination toleration is possible only where people are suitably respected as equals and this calls for the equal justifiability of relevant constraints, there are reasons not to construe the kind of justification that is called for here in terms of a Forst-type reciprocal and general justification. Given the purposes of non-domination toleration, then, it is an open question what constitutes equal justifiability.

Second, that salient constraints are justifiable in practices of justification that accord people a formally equal justificatory say does not secure non-domination outcomes unless this say allows each person to exercise a suitable level of discursive influence in justification, or on its outcomes – that is, unless this say has suitable "discursive purchase" (Besch 2019a, p. 471f). This means that the kind of discursive equality at the core of a justification-centric conception of non-domination toleration must be understood in substantive, "purchase-sensitive" terms (Besch 2019a, p. 475f). This places important, yet reasonably contestable matters of value at the heart of such a conception. And it asks us to focus on the "participation value" (Besch 2019a, p. 468) of standards of justification, and to engage the question of how the good of discursive influence can permissibly or justly be allocated across diverse constituencies.

Below, these two issues are addressed against the background of a reconstruction of Forst's view. Section "Toleration: Concept and Conceptions" considers salient aspects of the concept and some conceptions of toleration. As the focus of this chapter is on respect toleration, section "Respect, Respect Toleration, and

Justification" elaborates on respect, respect toleration, and the idea of justification that Forst intertwines with these things. Section "Power and Non-domination" attends to the notions of power and non-domination. To complete the reconstructive part of the discussion, section "True Toleration and Non-domination?" puts these things together and specifies the contours of Forst's view of non-domination toleration. Section "Reasonableness?" then engages the idea of the reasonable that does important work in Forst's view of reciprocal and general justification. Once the question arises what "reasonable" means in this context, shortcomings of the view at hand emerge. Section "Discursive Equality?" addresses the idea of discursive equality that underpins Forst's thinking about justification and non-domination toleration. It emerges that discursive equality is compatible with problematic forms of domination unless discursive equality is understood in suitably substantive, purchase-sensitive terms. This points toward matters of value that bear on how standards of acceptability-based justification are defined, or their participation value is calibrated–matters that are more fundamental than justifications by these standards. Section "Summary and Future Directions" concludes.

Toleration: Concept and Conceptions

To provide some needed background, this section addresses the concept and conceptions of toleration; it will do so following Forst's account (Forst 2003a, b). The section begins with a note on a salient supposition of toleration.

While all toleration involves noninterference with an object of toleration, or what is being tolerated, social toleration – that is, interpersonal or intergroup relationships of toleration – supposes in tolerators some power to interfere with toleratees and assumes in toleratees a corresponding vulnerability. Betty's noninterference with Paul's drinking instantiates toleration only if she can interfere with it and hence only if Paul is vulnerable to that interference. Toleration thus supposes patterns of power. These need not be asymmetrical: for example, where toleration is mutual, it may not be. And the vehicles through which toleration is enacted need not take the form of individual acts or omissions. Vehicles of toleration can vary widely – for example, they can involve collective actions or omissions, policies and practices, norms and institutions, legislation, incentive schemes, "justification narratives" (Forst 2017a, pp. 55–74), and so forth.

Given such patterns of power, all toleration involves an "objection" component and an "acceptance" component (Forst 2017a, p. 78; 2003a, b; King 1998; McKinnon 2006). The tolerator must take it not only that there is something about the object of toleration that is objectionable or rejectable, but also that there is something about that object that is acceptable, merits approval, or is respectable. That toleration requires objection *and* acceptance has led some theorists to question whether toleration is coherent, viable, or desirable (Fletcher 1996; Mendus 1988; Newey 2013; Scanlon 2003; Williams 1996). In this chapter, it is assumed that toleration can be coherent and desirable.

Next, in toleration the acceptance component "trumps" the objection component: there must be "positive reasons which trump the negative ones in the relevant context," so that the object of toleration is "considered to be wrong, but not intolerably wrong" (Forst 2003b, p. 72). For example, Betty might disapprove of the health effects of Paul's drinking, but since she also sees it as an expression of his autonomy that she has overriding reasons to respect, she does not interfere with it. The tolerator's acceptance reasons, however, may or may not be reasons that the toleratee can accept as such acceptance reasons.

Not least, all toleration is normatively bounded – a matter that will be relevant later. As Forst highlights, a practice of toleration involves two boundaries, or normative lines. One line separates things that are accepted from things that are rejected but tolerated: this line indicates where acceptance ends and toleration begins (Forst 2003b, p. 72). Another line separates these things from things that are rejected as intolerable: this line marks the outer boundary of toleration, and it is often referred to as the limit of toleration. Forst also refers to this latter line as the "rejection" component in toleration (Forst 2017a, p. 78).

It is not always apparent where practices of toleration actually draw these lines, or on what grounds they do so. And, normatively, it is often contested where these lines should be drawn and on what grounds this may be done. Particularly relevant here is the line that marks the outer boundary, or the limit of toleration. That toleration has limits is sometimes taken to call into question whether any practice of toleration can *truly* be tolerant – rather than merely imposing on people some conception of what is intolerable that is dogmatic, arbitrary, parochial, or oppressive. The idea that there cannot be true toleration is sometimes referred to as a "paradox" of toleration – a problem that raises deep challenges for a normative view of toleration (Besch 2010; Forst 2003a, b; Newey 2013; Rossi 2013). This issue will be revisited later.

Next, at least four conceptions of toleration can be distinguished: permission, coexistence, respect, and esteem toleration. As only respect toleration matters here, the other three are only briefly mentioned. In permission toleration, tolerators grant toleration, or relevant permissions, from a position of (assumed or actual) superiority in order to advance their own ends. For example, "an authority permits one or several minorities to live in accordance with their beliefs ... provided that they do not challenge the supremacy of this authority" (Forst 2017a, p. 78). Coexistence toleration is symmetrical and instrumental: the parties instrumentally tolerate one another as a *modus vivendi* (Forst 2003b, p. 74). For example, two hostile religious groups agree to no longer interfere with one another in order to avert their own destruction. Esteem toleration is symmetrical, too, but it expresses a form of "mutual recognition," albeit one that reflects a "fuller, more demanding" form of recognition than the one expressed in respect-toleration (see below) (Forst 2003b, p. 75). Esteem toleration is based on "ethical esteem" of tolerated beliefs as "ethically attractive and held for good reasons," although this esteem is "reserved," insofar as tolerators regard these beliefs as less attractive than their own (ibid). For example, Muslim Betty and Christian Paul positively value each other's religions as forms of monotheism, although each believes their own faith to be closer to the truth.

21 Toleration, Reasonableness, and Power
401

What matters here is what Forst calls the respect conception of toleration. Respect toleration is symmetrical and moral, rather than instrumental: it expresses a form of moral respect (Darwall 1977). In respect toleration, the parties may "hold incompatible ethical beliefs about the good and right way of life," but they "respect each other as moral-political equals in the sense that their common framework of social life should ... be guided by norms that all parties can equally accept" (Forst 2003b, p. 74). Elsewhere, Forst adds:

> Although [the parties] differ sharply in their respective notions of the good and of salvation, they accord each other a status as equals which states that generally valid norms must rest on reasons that all those affected can accept *equally* and do not favour one side ... The "authority" to "bestow" liberties... resides ... in a process of general legitimation that provides for a special level of justification in questions of principle. (Forst 2017a, p. 79)

This ties respect toleration to equal acceptability justification. When Betty respect-tolerates Paul, she respects him as a moral-political equal, or as an equal authority of justice and justification – and hence as someone who has, or should be accorded, a discursive status such that moral or political things (such as norms, institutions, and social structure) that affect Paul must be justifiable to Paul on the basis of reasons that are equally acceptable by him. Hence, to respect-tolerate people in this sense commits to the view that where they are relevantly affected, they are owed justifications by reasons that are equally acceptable by them.

Not least, the above depicts respect toleration as interagentive in the narrow sense of a relationship between individual agents, but respect toleration can also be an intergroup phenomenon, or a group-level response of one social group to another such group (Galeotti 2002). In this chapter, it is assumed that toleration is interagentive in a wide sense: it can instantiate as a relationship between individual or collective agents.

Respect, Respect Toleration, and Justification

This brings us to the idea of equal respect that Forst-type respect toleration implicates. The idea of robust discursive equality that this kind of toleration entails will be discussed later, given the idea of equal respect that it builds on. It hence is useful to now elaborate on this idea and to register, as well, that respect toleration can be premised on different ideas of respect.

To start with, Forst's rendering of respect toleration is not doctrinally innocuous. It conceptualizes respect toleration in a manner that ties it to a particular view of respect and a particular kind of justification. And of course it is contested what kind of reason giving, if any, proper respect for other people calls for (Carter and Ferretti 2013; Rossi 2013; Besch 2010, 2018, 2019b). Even assuming that proper respect for other people is a kind of recognition respect that responds to morally important features of them – to mention just a few prominent candidates, these features might be their capacity for agency, autonomy, personhood, or their being free and equal, reasonable people, and so on (Darwall 1977; Raz 1986; Macedo 1991; Postema 1995; Kymlicka 1996; Rawls 2005; Larmore 2015) – it is open how we should respond to these features. This point can be elaborated by contrasting two ideas of equal respect that would yield different views of respect toleration.

First, consider the familiar view that equal respect requires treating others as equal *recipients* of justice. On such a view, conduct or social structure that affects people can respect them properly only insofar as it is just in a *substantive* sense – that is, it must accord with the content of justice, or the rights, liberties, or opportunities that just social structure allocates to people. Equal respect in this sense is a *conception-dependent* constraint the content of which is given by, or is defined in terms of, a (putatively) authoritative, reasonable, or justifiable conception of justice. Consequently, respect toleration in this sense commits to noninterference with other people – or their conceptions of what is good, right or true, their choices, practices, or forms of life, and so forth – only insofar as the content of justice calls for it, as defined accordingly.

One upshot: prior to knowing what justice calls for, substantively speaking, equal respect in the conception-dependent sense leaves open whether actions, practices, or institutions that relevantly affect people must be justifiable to them on the basis of reasons that they can equally accept – rather than, for example, reasons that they could or would accept at some high level of idealization (e.g., when fully rational or perfectly responsible epistemically), or reasons that actually apply to them whether or not they realize that this is so (Wall 2016; Steinhoff 2015; Besch 2010, 2019a, b).

A different view of equal respect typically is in play in "recognitive" conceptions of acceptability-based public justification (Besch 2019b, p. 613; see also section "Discursive Equality?", below). On such views, equal respect is not simply something the content of which is defined by a putatively authoritative conception of justice. Rather, it is (primarily) a constraint on the justifications that people are owed in relevant moral or political matters, including justifications of the standards and values of justice that (putatively) just social structure applies to them. The idea here is that a justification of moral or political things must accord each relevant person a meaningful level of discursive influence in justification, or on its outcomes, so as to respect each person not simply as a recipient, but as an *equal co-author* or *equal authority* of justification (Forst 2017a, p. 134; 2017b, p. 545). Where equal respect is construed in such *justification-constraining* terms, it is often conjoined with three other views (for relevant things, such as conduct, practices, or social structure, φ):

(i) φ, to equally respect relevant people, needs to accord with principles or values that are justifiable to them by reasons that are equally acceptable by them (the *equal acceptability requirement*),

(ii) While people must have a meaningful say in justification, they must have some measure of influence on what can or cannot count as justifiable to, or equally acceptable by, them (the *discursive influence requirement*).

Not least, (i) and (ii) often come intertwined with a constructivism requirement according to which relevant moral or political things *depend* for some relevant moral or political merit on their equal acceptability:

(iii) The principles or values referred to in (i) are *valid* (or *right*, or *reasonable*) only if they are justifiable to all relevant people by reasons that are equally acceptable by them (the *constructivism requirement*).

These views mark different elements of the idea that others should be respected as equal authorities of justification in the justification-constraining sense. Equal respect, when it is construed along such lines, takes the form of *discursive respect* and requires that people be accorded a form of *robust discursive equality* (Besch 2014, 2019a; this is discussed further below).

What does this entail at the site of toleration? When premised on justification-constraining respect, respect toleration calls for noninterference if and when interference – or principles, values, or policies, and so on, that would call for interference – cannot be justified to all affected people by reasons that, in a suitably meaningful sense, are equally acceptable by them. Plainly, this can point us in different directions than a practice of respect-toleration that builds on respect in the conception-dependent sense. What conception-dependent respect-toleration calls for cannot be identified independently from the contents of a conception of justice. But what a putatively authoritative conception of justice prescribes might not also be justifiable by reasons that, in some suitably meaningful sense, each of the relevantly affected can equally accept.

Forst construes equal respect primarily in a justification-constraining sense. As he puts it in a passage quoted earlier, in exercising respect toleration, people "respect each other as *moral-political equals* in the sense that their common framework of social life should … be guided by norms that all parties *can equally accept*" (emphasis added). This refers to Forst's requirement of reciprocal and general acceptability (or RGA, for short), understood as a requirement of justification. According to RGA, moral or political normative claims, to be justified, or valid, must be *equally* acceptable, or non-rejectable, by *all* affected people; at stages Forst takes this to require that justifications be based on reasons that no-one can reasonably reject (Forst 2017a, p. 28f; 2012, p. 21; 2010; 2013; Besch 2010; see also section "Reasonableness?", below). However, to respect people as moral-political equals, or as equal authorities of justification, is to respect them as people to whom justifications are owed in matters that affect them that meet RGA – and this means to respect them as equal authorities of justification (Forst 2017a, pp. 134, 6ff).

This ties equal respect to variant of the equal acceptability requirement and the constructivism requirement (see above). It also ties it to a variant of the discursive influence requirement. Forst assumes that where reason giving meets RGA, it accords affected people a qualified veto-right that (putatively) protects or helps to protect them from domination (Forst 2001, p. 168f; 2010, p. 719). Evidently, the assumption here is that people can use these veto rights to bring to bear their voice on what can or cannot count as justifiable to them. It is on the basis of this assumption that Forst attributes to reciprocal and general justifications an emancipatory or protective function and finds them at the normative core of a "basic structure of justification" that enables true non-domination (Forst 2017a, pp. 6f, 131–137; 2013, p. 155). Hence, justifications that meet RGA (putatively) accord people a measure of discursive influence in justification.

What matters for this chapter is only respect toleration in the second, justification-constraining sense. While the focus is on Forst's view here, the issues to be explored later are not specific for his approach. Forst, of course, is not the only theorist who construes respect toleration in justification-constraining terms. Seminal on the point is Rawls-type political liberalism – which strongly influences Forst. As Rawls observes, "political liberalism applies the principle of toleration to philosophy itself" (Rawls 2005, p. 10). The label "toleration" here refers to a respect-based commitment to avoid reasonable disagreement in public justification – or a principle of justificatory neutrality (Larmore 2015, pp. 68–74). For Rawls and other political liberals, political power can properly respect reasonable citizens as free and equal, and hence be legitimate, only if it is publicly justifiable to them on grounds they can equally accept (Besch 2012). Yet values, conceptions, or doctrines fail to be so acceptable when reasonable citizens reasonably disagree about them. Thus, no conception of justice can provide a basis for a publicly justifiable, legitimate exercise of political power unless it avoids reasonable disagreement – a conclusion that motivates the project of a political liberalism. In short, political liberalism adopts a justification-constraining idea of equal respect – that is, a demanding form of discursive respect (Besch 2018) – and shapes in this light its view of public justification.

Power and Non-domination

Next, the relationship between toleration and power is discussed, starting with remarks on power.

As Allen (2015) observes, power can be present as *power-over* or domination, *power-to* or agentive resource, or *power-with* or a form of collaborative agentive empowerment. What matters here is only power-over. In clear-cut cases, power in this form is or entails a relationship of influence between individual or collective agents such that one agent α (in the role of power agent) imposes constraints on another agent β (in the role of power subject). This relationship may or may not be symmetrical (e.g., α and β might each occupy the role of power agent and power subject vis-à-vis each other), it may or may not be voluntary, and it may or may not be morally or otherwise objectionable. In less than clear-cut cases, an interagentive schema does not or not clearly apply. For example, in the case of "systemic" domination, a "system of social relations" rather than any particular individual or collective agent, subjects all agents to its "functional imperatives" (Azmanova 2018, p. 69). Other cases involve interagentive power, but power agents merely administer power rather than also sourcing it. For example, where government officials use the powers attached to their offices to impose constraints on people, they may act as power agents, but they do not source the power they administer – that source resides in the institutions that appoints them to their offices and that attaches to these offices the relevant powers.

The focus of this chapter is on a particular kind of power-over, namely, domination. When α dominates β (in the sense relevant here), α exercises power over β. If domination entails power-over, what distinguishes it from other kinds of power-over? This chapter considers a *republican* answer to this question. Roughly, republican views tend to conceptualize the phenomenon of domination by considering in what way (if any) agents can bring to bear their perspective or will on the constraints that apply to them. Specifically, they take domination to occur where agents cannot relevantly influence what constraints apply to them.

For instance, on Pettit's (2012) control-centric account, a government dominates citizens when they cannot make use of relevant political or social tools, such as political participation rights or opportunities for political speech, to exercise a relevant level of control over the political or legal constraints that the government applies to them. More relevant now, however, is Forst's justification-centric, "Kantian republican" view (Forst 2013). On this view, political power instantiates domination when it imposes constraints on people that are not justifiable to them "reciprocally and generally," or on grounds that all affected people can equally accept (e.g., ibid., pp. 157, 159f). How so?

Forst adopts a justification-centric version of an "arbitrary power" conception of domination (Lovett 2010, Chapter 4). For Forst, domination occurs when people are subjected to arbitrary constraints, while he construes constraints as arbitrary if and when they lack "adequate justification" (Forst 2013, p. 155) or "legitimate reason" (ibid., 157). And in moral or political contexts, non-arbitrariness calls for justifications on the basis of reasons that are equally acceptable by all affected people. The upshot: if β is subjected to constraints, φ, this does not instantiate domination so long as φ is justifiable by reasons that β can equally accept. Consequently: if we do not know or have reasons to doubt whether φ is so justifiable, then we do not know or have reasons to doubt whether β's subjection to φ instantiates non-domination power-over.

In essence, this conjoins two familiar views: it grafts a view of non-domination as justifiable subjection onto an idea of equal (discursive) respect as calling for justifications on grounds that relevant people can equally accept. On this view, the good of equal (discursive) respect is the key good that stands to be secured where power over others is exercised; accordingly, justifiable subjection is conceptualized in terms that reflect a view of what it takes to properly secure that good. And so the idea becomes that non-domination power-over must impose suitably justifiable constraints, where this is interpreted as calling for equal acceptability justifications.

Before moving on, two things need to be highlighted. First, the view of non-domination in play here has a political ring, but it applies not only to political power in the narrow sense of state power. Forst's focus is on (non-)arbitrary constrains in a wide sense. He understands "arbitrariness"

> in a social sense, whether it assumes the form of arbitrary rule by individuals or by part of the community (for example, a class) over others, or of the acceptance of social contingencies that lead to asymmetrical positions or relations of domination and are defended and accepted as an unalterable fate, even though they are nothing of the sort. Arbitrary rule is the rule of some people over others without legitimate reason, that is, *domination*, and where struggles are conducted against injustice they are first and foremost directed against forms of domination of this kind. (Forst 2013, p. 157)

Arbitrary constraints need not be political to constitute domination. Thus, in the domain of the political and elsewhere, non-domination power-over requires constraints that people are subjected to be justifiable to them on equally acceptable grounds – only in this case can the imposition on them of these constraints suitably respect them as moral-political equals.

Second, also a justification-centric view of (non-)domination must place importance on something in the way of control over the constraints that apply to agents. The *justifiability* of relevant constraints can plausibly distinguish domination power-over from non-domination power-over only insofar as justification is understood in terms that allocate power subjects a relevant measure of *influence* on what constraints apply, or may apply, to them. Thus, much here depends on the level of discursive influence that agents can exercise in justification. And this puts center stage what we called earlier the discursive influence requirement. Forst is not unaware of this. If the constraints that α imposes on β are *not* equally acceptable by β, Forst, it seems, would insist that α should see this as a reason *not* to impose these constraints on β. After all, he takes it that people should be respected as moral-political equals, and he often puts this point also by saying that this involves according them a (qualified) *veto* right in matters that affect them (Forst 2001, p. 168f; 2010, p. 719).

The point: a justification-centric view must give importance to control or influence over constraints, although it might foreground reason giving – or "institutionalized justification procedures" (Forst 2013, p. 159) – as a method through which control or influence is exercised.

True Toleration and Non-domination?

This section addresses the theme of non-domination toleration. It has often been argued that toleration can involve domination (Galeotti 2002; Forst 2003a, b; Honohan 2013). Practices of toleration distinguish between things that are counted as tolerable and things that are seen as intolerable, (strictly) impermissible, or as proper objects of reproach, punishment, prosecution, or other negative social sanctions. And when views of the limits of toleration are legally, politically, or otherwise imposed on agents, they take the form of constraints on them, or their agency. Thus: at least when practices of toleration impose their views of these limits in the form of such constraints, they involve power-over. If this is so, what does it take for such practices to instantiate non-domination toleration?

To start with, when do questions of toleration arise? According to Forst,

the context in which the question of toleration between citizens arises is a context of justice: what is at issue here is the just – that is, mutually justifiable – legal and political structure for a pluralistic community of citizens with different ethical beliefs. Claims for toleration are raised as claims for justice, and intolerance is a form of injustice, favouring one ethical community over others without legitimate grounds. (Forst 2003b, p. 76)

This understands "the question of toleration" in terms of the question of when exercises of political power – specifically, legal or political constraints – are just or justifiable. For Forst, then, toleration and political non-domination are different sides of the same coin. Either way, the key normative issue is whether salient constraints properly respect people as moral-political equals. And either way, constraints can do so only if they are justifiable by reasons that are equally acceptable by relevant people.

To elaborate, consider first real or true toleration – as opposed to practices of toleration that distinguish between the tolerable and the intolerable in terms that are intolerant. This relates to one of the "paradoxes" of toleration, that is, the "paradox of drawing the limits" (Forst 2003a, p. 38ff; 2003b, p. 70ff). Says Forst:

> All toleration necessarily implies intolerance toward those who are seen as intolerable ... The concept of tolerance makes no sense without certain limits, though as soon as these are substantively defined, tolerance seems to turn into nothing but intolerance. There is thus no "true" tolerance. To resolve this paradox a conception of toleration must show how far its limits can be drawn in a mutually justifiable and non-arbitrary way. (Forst 2003b, p. 72)

However, the paradox can be overcome if the limits of toleration are drawn in terms that suitably respect all affected people as moral-political equals, and that cannot be rejected reasonably. To this end, this line must be drawn on the basis of RGA itself, the requirement of reciprocal and general acceptability (Forst 2003b, pp. 76–78). (This notion of "drawing" or "defining" the limits of toleration refers not merely to the intellectual activity of defining those limits, but also to the social, legal or political imposition or enforcement of views of these limits.)

Two main lines of thought are in play here. First, of course, Forst puts to work the idea that people should be respected as moral-political equals – or as equal authorities of justice or justification, or, as he also says, as agents who are equally "worthy of being given adequate, justifying reasons in matters that affect them," or who have an equal "right to justification" (Forst 2003a, pp. 76f, 81). As such, agents are owed reciprocal and general justifications in matters that affect them. Thus, social structure that imposes on them a view of the limits of toleration must be justifiable to them on grounds that they can equally accept, while respect toleration – where "respect" is understood as discursive respect, in a justification-constraining sense – is a "superior" kind of toleration (Forst 2003a, p. 76).

Second, since the limits of toleration must be drawn in terms that do not depend for their justification on grounds that can reasonably be rejected, they should be drawn on the basis of RGA itself. That is, to draw these limits in a way that suitably respects people, they must be drawn in terms that are justifiable on grounds that are equally acceptable by all affected people. For Forst, this calls for a justification on grounds that no affected person can reject reasonably. And here, he looks to RGA: for Forst, RGA cannot be rejected reasonably. Thus, he offers RGA as a standard by which to draw the limits of toleration. Accordingly,

> [c]itizens are tolerant if they accept the boundary set by the criteria of reciprocity and generality as both delineating the justifiability of mutually binding norms and the limits

of toleration. Tolerant citizens are 'reasonable' in accepting that (. . .) an *ethical objection* does not amount to a legitimate *moral rejection*; and they also see that they have a moral duty to tolerate all those ethical beliefs and practices that they disagree with but that do not violate the threshold of reciprocity and generality (trying to force their views on others). Such a violation of the basic right to justification is a form of intolerance that cannot be tolerated. (Forst 2003b, p. 78; Forst's emphasis)

Persons are tolerant to the extent that . . . they tolerate all other views within the bounds of reciprocity and generality. (Ibid., p.78)

Being tolerant . . . means seeking reasonable justification, accepting reasonable disagreement within the limits of reciprocity and generality, and being aware of the different contexts of justification that persons are part of. (Ibid., p. 81)

This suggests the following view (for a candidate object of toleration, φ):

1. Practices of toleration must respect all affected agents as moral-political equals, or as equal authorities of justification.
2. To this end, the (legal, political) limits of toleration must be drawn in terms that are reciprocally and generally justifiable.
3. Thus, the (legal, political) limits of toleration must be drawn in terms that do not depend for their justification on grounds that can reasonably be rejected.
4. Practices of toleration should (legally, politically) limit toleration on the basis of RGA itself.
5. Hence: if (legally, politically) interfering with φ would *not* be reciprocally and generally justifiable, φ is tolerable; but if (legally, politically) interfering with φ *is* so justifiable, then φ is intolerable.

This appears to be the core of Forst's normative conception of non-domination toleration. Claims (2) to (5) draw out what practices of toleration must be like to properly instantiate (1), while the notion of "reciprocal and general justification" in (2) refers to justifications on the basis of reasons that are equally acceptable by all affected people.

Forst believes that his view overcomes the "paradox of drawing the limits." When the line between the tolerable and the intolerable is drawn in terms of RGA, it is drawn in a manner that extends equal respect to all affected people:

By drawing the 'limits of toleration' with the help of the criteria of reciprocity and generality, we draw them . . . in the widest possible way given the existence of a large diversity of world-views, without sacrificing one for the sake of the unjustifiable claims of another. Thus there is not arbitrary substantive content that defines the tolerable; this content is open to dispute and argument, and protection is given to those voices in danger of being marginalized. Those who violate the basic norm of mutual respect implied by that cannot claim to be the victims of intolerance. (Ibid., p. 82)

Hence, if the limits of toleration are drawn in suitably justifiable terms, practices of toleration do not dominate: the constraints that they impose will respect each affected person as moral-political equals.

Reasonableness?

This conception of non-domination toleration has limits. The role that it accords to an idea of equal (discursive) respect has much moral appeal. But there are reasons to doubt the coherence of this conception. To explain why, this section begins with comments on the idea of the reasonable at work in Forst's conception of non-domination toleration. After that, section "Discursive Equality?" will address the idea of equal respect on which this conception builds, or the kind of discursive equality it entails.

Recall: Forst claims that practices of toleration must respect people as moral-political equals, but can do so only if the standards by which these practices draw the limits of toleration – that is, the standards that serve as their criterion of toleration – cannot reasonably be rejected. On this basis, Forst offers RGA as a criterion of toleration. But is RGA reasonably non-rejectable? Consider the content Forst builds into his idea of reasonableness:

> The *epistemological* element of being reasonable consists in an insight into the finitude of both theoretical and practical reason in finding 'final' answers to the question of the good that all can agree on … [and] in an insight into the possibilities of reason, that is, the capacity of reaching mutually justifiable normative answers. [This commits to] the task of finding and defending justifiable reasons, because this is what reasonable and finite persons … owe to each other. (…) [T]he *normative* element of being reasonable implies this form of respect for others as reasonable and worthy of being given adequate reasons; that is respect for their basic right to justification. Both elements in combination (…) are the basis for the acceptance and the recognition of the threshold of reciprocity and generality. They provide the essential reasons for being tolerant. Being tolerant thus means seeking reasonable agreement within the limits of reciprocity and generality, and being aware of the different contexts of justification that persons are part of. (Forst 2003b, p. 80f)

This effectively defines into reasonableness (i) a commitment to respect people as moral-political equals in Forst's justification-constraining sense, and (ii) a commitment to the view that people are owed reciprocal and general justifications in moral or political matters that affect them, that is, justifications that meet RGA. Although reasonableness so construed is philosophically interesting and these commitments are, to some extent, morally attractive, various concerns arise.

First, these commitments *can* be rejected reasonably – unless we first define reasonableness in philosophically partisan terms. As Moore (1996) observes, as far as the meaning of the word "reasonable" in ordinary discourse is concerned, "reasonable" people are committed to reason-giving, or justification, and they take it that other people are worthy of reason-giving and moral consideration. But a commitment to reason-giving, or justification, is not a commitment to Forst-type reciprocal and general justification. And a commitment to the view that people merit moral consideration is not a commitment to accord them equal respect, or to respect them as moral-political equals in a justification-constraining sense. The point: people can be "reasonable" in an ordinary discourse sense of the word even if they deny, doubt, or do not act in accordance with, the view that people should be respected as a moral-political equal in a justification-constraining sense, or the view that other people are owed reciprocal and general justifications, or the view that the goodness of good, justifying reasons depends on their equal acceptability by all affected people, and so forth.

Second, Forst has reasons not to define the commitments referred to in (i) and (ii), above, into his idea of reasonableness. On the one hand, this must render the claim that RGA is reasonably non-rejectable trivial, if not viciously circular. It is unsurprising that reasonable people *in Forst's sense* – say, *reasonable-F* people – cannot coherently reject RGA. After all, reasonableness-F is construed as involving a commitment to reciprocal and general justification. Hence, the claim that RGA, or adopting RGA as a criterion of toleration, is reasonably-F non-rejectable (or equally acceptable, or non-rejectable, by reasonable-F people) cannot carry justificatory weight: the circle is too narrow.

On the other hand, other things being equal Forst cannot index a criterion of toleration to the perspective of reasonable-F people without undermining his own, inclusive intentions. On his view, a practice of non-domination toleration must respect *all* affected people as moral-political equals, while this calls for justifications on the basis of reasons that *all* affected people can equally accept. What matters for non-domination toleration hence cannot merely be a criterion of toleration that is equally acceptable only by reasonable-F people: this would be objectionably exclusionary also by Forst's own lights.

A third issue relates to two potentially *competing* requirements at work in Forst view. Recall: on this view, a practice of non-domination toleration must respect people as moral-political equals. To this end, he claims, it must draw the limits of toleration in terms that are justifiable to all affected people by reasons they can equally accept. But he insists that these limits must be drawn in reasonably non-rejectable terms (i.e., reasonably-F non-rejectable terms). Thus, he claims:

(i) A criterion of toleration must be justifiable by reasons that are equally acceptable by all affected people.
(ii) A criterion of toleration must be reasonably non-rejectable.

However, what is the relationship between (i) and (ii)? (i) and (ii) can point in different directions: that φ cannot be rejected "reasonably" (on some definition of the term or other) does not mean that φ is justifiable by reasons all affected people can equally accept – and vice versa. And if (i) and (ii) can point in different directions, what condition must a practice of toleration meet to suitably respect people as moral-political equals?

Things are complicated further by the obscurity of what (putative) reasons must be like to count toward justification. According to RGA, reasons can justify salient claims only if they are reciprocally and generally acceptable, or non-rejectable. This has so far been interpreted in terms of the requirement that suitably justifying reasons must be equally acceptable (reciprocity) by all affected people (generality). But this simplifies. Forst sometimes suggests that a (candidate) reason to φ is a reciprocally and generally acceptable (or non-rejectable) reason to φ only if no relevant person can "reasonably" reject φ's (alleged) status as such a reason – that is, only if φ's (alleged) role as such a reason is reasonably non-rejectable (Forst 2012, p. 21). Roughly, this understand (i), above, in terms of (ii): if we want to know whether a candidate criterion of toleration is justifiable by reasons that are equally acceptable by all affected people, then we need to consider whether it is reasonably non-rejectable.

Premising reciprocity and generality on some reasonableness constraint addresses an important need. All conceptions or practices of acceptability-based justification must somehow qualify the kind of acceptability or non-rejectability that they regard as contributing to justification: for equal acceptability to justify, it must also be respectable, or *authoritative*–for example, it must be rational, coherent, epistemically responsible, or, as it were, reasonable. Acceptability-based justification hence is normatively indexed to the authoritativeness constraints that it (openly or tacitly) adopts. However, such constraints often are in their own right contested. This is so especially where these constraints are nontrivial – that is, where they impose requirements that not all relevant people always meet anyway. Thus, premising reciprocity and generality on an idea of reasonableness inevitably raises deeper questions of justification: much here hinges on the content of the idea of reasonableness that comes in here and whatever reasons there are to premise reciprocity and generality on it.

It emerged earlier that Forst's notion of the reasonable is potentially problematic, given its content. Forst's explicit comments on the meaning of the notion of reasonable non-rejectability appear to compound matters. He stresses that while he takes the phrase "reasonably non-rejectable" from Scanlon, he "interpret[s]" it in terms of his criteria of reciprocity and generality in order to "more precisely *define the meaning of "reasonable"* than Scanlon did" (Forst 2012, p. 272; emphasis added). This is in play when Forst more recently writes:

> Adapting Thomas Scanlon's formulation ("not reasonable to reject"), I believe that moral justification requires that norms must rest on reasons that are not reciprocally and generally rejectable. (Forst 2017a, p. 28f)

But then Forst seems to hold that a reason, φ, is a "reciprocally and generally" acceptable (or non-rejectable) reason only if φ, or its role as a reason, is "reasonably" non-rejectable, while φ, or its role as a reason, can qualify as "reasonably" non-rejectable only if it is "reciprocally and generally acceptable" (or non-rejectable). As this seems to be circular, it raises the question how anything could *non-arbitrarily*, without mere *stipulation*, be claimed to be reciprocally and generally justifiable (see also Besch 2020). This threatens to collapse the view of justification onto which Forst grafts his view of non-domination toleration.

The point: even if practices of toleration instantiate non-domination toleration only if they extend equal (discursive) respect to all affected people, and even if such practices must only impose constraints that are equally justifiable to each affected person, there are reasons not to understand the kind of justification called for here in terms of a Forst-type conception of reciprocal and general justifiability. It remains open what constitutes the kind of equal justifiability that is needed for the purposes of non-domination toleration.

Discursive Equality?

This section focuses on the idea of discursive equality that underpins Forst's conception of non-domination toleration. As discussed earlier, this conception places a demanding form of equal respect at the heart of non-domination toleration. For Forst, practices of toleration must respect people as moral-political equals, or as equal authorities of justification, but can do so only if the constraints that they impose on people are justifiable to them by reasons that they can equally accept. Thus, on this conception, each affected person has or should have an *equal justificatory say* in relation to such constraints – a say, moreover, that allows people to exercise some relevant level of discursive influence on what constraints apply or may apply to them. In other words, equal respect here requires that relevant people be accorded a robust form of discursive equality (Besch 2019a).

The idea of discursive equality marks a familiar theme. Variants of the idea are typically in play in recognitive conceptions of moral or political justification (Besch 2019b, p. 613). On such views, justification practice must suitably cohere with or express proper respect for or recognition of actual people. Specifically, such views take it that justification can properly respect people as equals only where it accords them a meaningful equal justificatory say. Thus, such views tend to construe the standards of justification in terms that idealize less, rather than more, so as to ensure that people can exercise their say in justification in a manner that relevantly tracks their actual voice and perspective (Besch 2019b, pp. 608–614). Accordingly, such views foreground the participation value (Besch 2019a, p. 468) of justification as a key dimension in which to calibrate the normativity of the standards of justification. Salient examples include the views of public justification advanced by political liberals like Rawls (2005), Macedo (1991), Larmore (2015), or Forst's conception of reciprocal and general justification.

Despite its prominence and moral appeal, the idea of discursive equality is not without problems. One feature of this elusive idea is particularly relevant here: discursive equality is compatible with forms of domination unless it is construed in suitably substantive terms. But it is not obvious what these terms should be, while any substantive view of discursive equality is likely to attract reasonable disagreement. This further complicates the idea of a justification-centric, republican form of non-domination toleration.

Consider first the difference between *formal* and *substantive* discursive equality (Besch 2019a, p. 473f). Recall that all acceptability-based justification must qualify the kind of acceptability that it regards as justifying: for equal acceptability to justify, it must also be authoritative. Now, the authoritativeness constraints that justification practice adopts can accord people more or less discursive influence in justification, given their actual voice or perspective, or their actual deliberative resources (as opposed to the voice or perspective or deliberative resources that they would bring to bear in justification if they perfectly satisfied the relevant authoritativeness constraints) (Besch 2019a, p. 4271f; Besch 2019b, pp. 606–611). For example, if rejections must be ideally rational or fully reasonable (on some definition of what this takes or other) in order to negatively contribute to φ's justification status, actual people can have very little discursive influence in justification. What Paul is actually committed to reject or cannot actually accept coherently can be very different from what he could or would reject if he was ideally rational or fully reasonable. And if this difference is large enough, then Paul's actual voice and perspective can be deprived of any real discursive influence in justification or on its outcomes.

One upshot is this: a justificatory say – more generally, discursive standing – can be (or fail to be) equal in more than one respect. It can be (or fail to be) equal in a *formal* sense as a matter of the consistent application of relevant standards and constraints to people, and in a *substantive* sense as a matter of the discursive influence that an application of these things to people allows them to exercise in justification, or on its outcomes. Roughly, a justification practice, JP, accords α and β formally equal discursive standing when JP accords α and β a justificatory say and applies to each the same standards and constraints, such as the same authoritativeness constraints. But JP accords α and β substantively equal discursive standing only if their discursive standing allows them to exercise the same level of discursive influence in justification, or on its outcomes – that is, only if their discursive standing has the same discursive purchase (Besch 2019a, p. 417f; 2019b, p. 606f; 2014, p. 216ff).

The following example helps to clarify the distinction at work here, and it substantiates that formal discursive equality is compatible with domination. Let JP1 be a justification practice that adopts a negative variant of an equal acceptability requirement (Besch 2019a, p. 474f):

> JP1 φ is valid if and only if no affected person can authoritatively reject (i.e., in JP1, all affected people have a justificatory say vis-à-vis φ, and JP1 applies the same standards, including its authoritativeness constraint, ψ, throughout).

> JP1's constituency includes Dominant Group and Marginal Group. Over time, Dominant Group has used its social influence and "occlusion" power (Jenkins and Lukes 2017), to define ψ in terms of values that it accepts and Marginal Group rejects: JP1 recognizes discursive input as authoritative, or as positively or negatively contributing to justification, only insofar as this input is compatible with the values of Dominant Group.

JP1 satisfies formal discursive equality: in JP1, it is true of each agent that φ can count as justified or valid only if φ cannot authoritatively be rejected by that agent. But JP1 does not also instantiate substantive discursive equality; and the way in which it fails to do this is problematic. Members of Marginal Group do not have equal influence in justification, or on its outcomes; they do not have (substantively) "equal opportunity for political influence" (Cohen 2006, p. 242), or (substantively) equal opportunity "to participate in the process of public deliberation" (Peter 2009, p. 67), or do not enjoy equal substantive inclusion (Dieleman 2015, p. 803). JP1 filters, brackets, or hypotheticalizes their voice or perspective in a way in which it does not filter, bracket, or hypotheticalize the voice or perspective of members of Dominant Group. And so JP1's authoritativeness constraint can make it impossible for members of Marginal Group to effectively contest or reject the values of Dominant Group. Thus, JP1 entrenches the dominance of Dominant Group, and it turns justification practice itself into a vehicle of domination, or forms of it, such as "hermeneutic" domination (Catala 2015).

Consequently, in order to attain non-domination outcomes, it is not enough to ensure that relevant constraints are justifiable in justification practices that accord people a formally equal justificatory say. It must also be the case that their justificatory say is not problematically or impermissibly unequal, or too low, in discursive influence. This suggests that the kind of discursive equality that is called for here is purchase-sensitive (Besch 2019a, p. 475f): if we assume that discursive equality requires a formally equal justificatory say, we have reasons to assume, as well, that discursive equality depends on the level of discursive influence that the having of such a say allows each agent to exercise in justification, or on its outcomes, given their actual voice and perspective. But what level of discursive influence is the right level?

This is not the place to delve into this vexing question, or to engage competing views on the matter (e.g., see Forst 2013, p. 165; Besch 2019b, pp. 618–621; Besch 2019a, pp. 476–485). Merely two things can be highlighted. First, there are reasons to construe the kind of discursive equality that underpins Forst's conception of non-domination as purchase-sensitive. To attain non-domination outcomes, an equal justificatory say must allow people to exercise a suitable level of discursive influence in justification. *How much* or *how little* influence this calls for is an open question – and one that appears to involve deeper matters of value. This is so if it is true that a high level of discursive influence, or "high-purchase discursive standing," is an "inclusive enabler good," or "a good that we value, or have reasons to value, and that helps to protect and support the pursuit of a wide (but not unlimited) range of conceptions of what is good, right, or true" (Besch 2019a, p. 427f). The matter at hand, then, appears to raise questions about the permissibility, justness, or the desirability of ways to allocate a potentially highly important discursive good.

Second, the matter at hand concerns the conditions under which a standard like RGA can confer authority. Consider:

(i) In terms of what idea of the reasonable should we define the authoritativeness constraints of reciprocal and general justification (e.g., for the purposes of a justification of the constraints that practices of toleration impose on people)?

That no relevant person can "reasonably" reject φ cannot justify φ if an objectionable idea of the reasonable is in play. And an idea of the reasonable is objectionable if it leaves people with too little discursive influence or entails impermissible interpersonal differences in discursive influence. If so, then questions like the following mark a theme that is constitutive for the authority, or normativity, of reciprocal and general justification:

(ii) How much discursive influence in justification, or on its outcomes, should the justificatory say of relevant people allow them to exercise (in their own right, and vis-à-vis others)?

If we do not know how (ii) must be answered, then we do not know how we may interpret, or calibrate, the normative content of standards like RGA. But if this is not known, then we do not know whether the fact that salient constraints are justifiable by such a standard can really justify them, constitute their authority, or secure non-domination outcomes.

It is an open question how the participation value of standards like RGA must be calibrated in order to ensure non-domination outcomes. And this question invites much reasonable disagreement. More than one pro tanto reasonable view is available about the conditions that justification standards must meet to permissibly allocate the good of discursive influence across diverse constituencies (e.g., consider the views sampled in Besch 2019a, pp. 476–485).

Thus, the theme of discursive equality marks a gateway to deeper questions of value. It puts the participation value of justification at the center of a justification-centric conception of non-domination toleration, and it asks us to (re)consider the idea of non-domination toleration in this light. Even if a practice of toleration only imposes constraints that are justifiable by reasons that all relevant people can equally accept authoritatively, or cannot authoritatively reject, non-domination outcomes are not guaranteed. For the question remains whether the authoritativeness constrains that are in play suitably allocate discursive influence. And if this matter invites reasonable disagreement, there will be reasonable disagreement at the heart of a duly accountable conception of non-domination toleration.

Summary and Future Directions

This chapter focused on the idea of non-domination toleration, or its normative form, through the lens of a discussion of Forst's republican conception of non-domination toleration. Non-domination toleration in Forst's sense requires that practices of toleration draw the limits of toleration in a manner that is suitably justifiable to relevant people – that is, the legal, political, or other constraints that spring from its view of these limits must be justifiable to all affected people on the basis of reasons that are equally acceptable by them. After reconstructing this conception, this chapter interrogated the idea of reasonableness that comes with the idea of reciprocal and general justification on which Forst premises non-domination toleration. And it addressed the idea of equal respect, or one key implication of it, that reciprocal and general justification builds on and that is at the heart of the republican understanding of non-domination that underpins Forst's view of non-domination toleration.

The chapter pointed toward two issues. First, even if non-domination toleration is possible only where people are suitably respected as equals and salient constraints are equally justifiable to them, the kind of justification called for here arguably should not be understood in terms of Forst-type reciprocal and general justifiability: for it is not clear what it means for (putatively) justifying reasons to be "reciprocally and generally" acceptable, or to be "reasonably" non-rejectable.

Second, given the purposes of non-domination toleration, equal (discursive) respect calls for a form of discursive equality that is not just formal, but purchase sensitive. If practices of toleration must only impose constraints that are justifiable by reasons that people can equally accept authoritatively, then non-domination outcomes are not ensured if the authoritativeness constrains that are in play do not allocate discursive influence permissibly, or justly.

But what allocation of this potentially highly important discursive good does non-domination toleration call for? On this, the jury is still out.

References

Allen A (2015) Feminist perspectives on power. In: Zalta EN (ed) Stanford encyclopedia of philosophy. The Metaphysics Research Lab, Center for the Study of Language and Information (CSLI), Stanford University, Stanford

Azmanova A (2018) Relational, structural and systemic forms of power: the 'right to justification' confronting three types of domination. J Polit Power 11(1):68–78

Besch TM (2010) Diversity and the limits of liberal toleration. In: Ivison D (ed) The Ashgate research companion to multiculturalism. Routledge, London, pp 75–94

Besch TM (2012) Political liberalism, the internal conception, and the problem of public dogma. Philoso Public Issues 2(1):153–177

Besch TM (2014) On discursive respect. Soc Theory Pract 40(2):207–231

Besch TM (2018) Public justification, inclusion, and discursive equality. Dialogue: Can Philos Rev/Revue Canadienne de Philosophie 57(3):591–614

Besch TM (2019a) On robust discursive equality. Dialogue: Can Philos Rev/Revue Canadienne de Philosophie 58(3):465–490

Besch TM (2019b) On justification, idealization, and discursive purchase. Philosophia 47 (3):601–623

Besch TM (2020) Forst on reciprocity of reasons: a critique. South J Philos (in press)

Carter I, Ferretti M (2013) Introduction, special issue on toleration and respect. J Appl Philos 30 (3):191–194

Catala A (2015) Democracy, trust, and epistemic justice. Monist 98(4):424–440

Cohen J (2006) Is there a human right to democracy? In: Sypnowich C (ed) The egalitarian conscience: essays in honour of GA Cohen. Oxford University Press, Oxford, pp 226–248

Darwall SL (1977) Two kinds of respect. Ethics 88(1):36–49

Dieleman S (2015) Epistemic justice and democratic legitimacy. Hypatia 30(4):794–810

Fletcher G (1996) The instability of tolerance. In: Heyd D (ed) Toleration: an elusive virtue. Princeton University Press, Princeton, pp 158–172

Forst R (2001) Towards a critical theory of transnational justice. Metaphilosophy 32(1–2):160–179

Forst R (2003a) Toleranz im Konflikt. Suhrkamp, Frankfurt am Main

Forst R (2003b) Toleration, justice and reason. In: McKinnon C, Castiglione D (eds) The culture of toleration in diverse societies. Manchester University Press, Manchester

Forst R (2010) The justification of human rights and the basic right to justification: a reflexive approach. Ethics 120(4):711–740

Forst R (2012) The right to justification: elements of a constructivist theory of justice. Columbia University Press, New York

Forst R (2013) A Kantian republican conception of justice as non-domination. In: Niederberger A, Schink P (eds) Republican democracy: liberty, law and politics. Edinburgh University Press, Edinburgh, pp 154–168

Forst R (2017a) Normativity and power: analyzing social orders of justification. Oxford University Press, Oxford

Forst R (2017b) Noumenal alienation: Rousseau, Kant and Marx on the dialectics of self-determination. Kantian Rev 22(4):523–551

Galeotti AE (2002) Toleration as recognition. Cambridge University Press, Cambridge

Honohan I (2013) Toleration and non-domination. In: Dobbernack J, Modood T (eds) Tolerance, intolerance and respect. Palgrave politics of identity and citizenship series. Palgrave Macmillan, London, pp 77–100

Jenkins D, Lukes S (2017) The power of occlusion. Journal of Political Power 10(1):6–24

King PT (1998) Toleration. Frank Cass Publishers, London

Kymlicka W (1996) Multicultural citizenship: a liberal theory of minority rights. Oxford University Press, Oxford

Larmore C (2015) Political liberalism: its motivation and goals. In: Sobel D, Vallentyne P, Wall S (eds) Oxford studies in political philosophy, vol 1. Oxford University Press, New York, pp 63–88

Lovett F (2010) A general theory of domination and justice. Oxford University Press, Oxford

Macedo S (1991) Liberal virtues: citizenship, virtue, and community in liberal constitutionalism. Oxford University Press, Oxford

McKinnon C (2006) Toleration: a critical introduction. Routledge, New York

Mendus S (1988) Justifying toleration: conceptual and historical perspectives. Cambridge University Press, Cambridge

Moore M (1996) On reasonableness. J Appl Philos 13(2):167–178

Newey G (2013) Toleration in political conflict. Cambridge University Press, Cambridge

Peter F (2009) Democratic legitimacy. Routledge, New York

Pettit P (2012) On the people's terms: a republican theory and model of democracy. Cambridge University Press, Cambridge

Postema GJ (1995) Public practical reason: an archeology. Soc Philos Policy 12(1):43–86

Rawls J (2005) Political liberalism, Expanded edition. Columbia University Press, New York

Raz J (1986) The morality of freedom. Clarendon Press, Oxford

Rossi E (2013) Can tolerance be grounded in equal respect? Eur J Polit Theo 12(3):240–252

Scanlon TM (2003) The difficulty of tolerance: essays in political philosophy. Cambridge University Press, Cambridge

Steinhoff U (2015) Against equal respect and concern, equal rights, and egalitarian impartiality. In: Steinhoff U (ed) Do all persons have equal moral worth? On 'basic equality' and equal respect and concern. Oxford University Press, Oxford, pp 142–172

Wall S (2016) The pure theory of public justification. Soc Philos Policy 32(2):204–226

Williams B (1996) Toleration: an Impossible Virtue? In: Heyd D (ed) Toleration: an elusive virtue. Princeton University Press, Princeton, pp 18–27

Toleration and Reasonableness

22

Roberta Sala

Contents

Introduction 420
Human Fallibility, Religion, and Politics in Locke's Thought 421
    Epistemic Division and Public Reason in John Rawls 426
    A More Than Tolerant Public Debate 434
Summary and Future Directions 435
References 436

Abstract

This chapter focuses on the two notions of toleration and reasonableness and on the ways in which they may relate to each other. The core idea is that reasonableness acts as prerequisite for toleration or even a source of it. Being reasonable makes one well-disposed to being tolerant. The reciprocal implications of reasonableness and toleration will be perused through a comparison between John Locke's and John Rawls's respective ideas. At the end of the debate about Rawlsian reasonableness and its relevant flaws, the challenge for future research is to go on revisiting such notion in order to make it more and more inclusive and tolerant.

Keywords

Religion · Faith · State/church · Consensus · Public judgment · Probability · Disagreement · Liberalism · Peaceful society · Method of avoidance · Epistemic division · Abortion · Public reason

---

R. Sala (✉)
Faculty of Philosophy, Vita-Salute San Raffaele University, Milan, Italy
e-mail: sala.roberta@unisr.it

© The Author(s), under exclusive licence to Springer Nature Switzerland AG 2022
M. Sardoč (ed.), *The Palgrave Handbook of Toleration*,
https://doi.org/10.1007/978-3-030-42121-2_31

419

Introduction

This chapter focuses on two notions, namely, toleration and reasonableness, and on the ways in which they relate to each other. The core idea is that reasonableness acts as prerequisite for toleration or even a source of it. Being reasonable makes one well-disposed to being tolerant. The reciprocal implications of reasonableness and toleration will be perused through a parallel reading of the well-known works by John Locke and John Rawls concerning toleration. In fact, what follows intends to trace a path of a possible comparison between the interpretations that the authors give to the two notions of toleration and reasonableness, without any pretension of exhaustiveness.

In the first section, some considerations about reasonableness and toleration in Locke will be introduced, aiming to show how the awareness of the limits of human understanding leads to self-restriction in individuals' liberty as a necessary premise of public life and deliberation. Then, toleration will be recalled as both a strategy to assure peaceful coexistence among people and groups holding different beliefs and as the individual availability to tolerate people in spite of their beliefs, given the intrinsic limits of human understanding. As it will be shown, Locke offers a variety of reasons for toleration, political to theological, epistemic to moral, with the aim of defending toleration as "virtuous" for both individuals and society. In the end, Lockean toleration can be construed as the precondition for recognizing our epistemic limits, hence for the assumption of reasonableness as that disposition to see oneself and others as moral partners and epistemic peers; an ideal of interpersonal relationship, based on mutual respect; and an ideal of peaceful cohabitation in which religious pluralism can be accommodated.

In the second section, similar considerations will be offered with regard to Rawls' thought. Specifically, the argument will start by recalling the author's invitation to apply the principle of toleration to philosophy. Such invitation entails the adoption of the so-called method of avoidance, meaning that, in public debate, no philosophical position should be invoked to ground any deliberation given the pluralism of the "comprehensive doctrines," be they philosophical, metaphysical, or religious. Thus, toleration applied to any "comprehensive" position is a precondition for the public discourse to host different moral, religious, or philosophical views. The idea is that each one should see her belief or even truth from outside, i.e., as if that would be others' belief or truth. Such ability to see oneself from outside, even taking her own truth as others would take it, possibly as a mere opinion, is called reasonableness. Such "double point of view," so to speak, is made possible by reasonableness: it implies a sort of epistemic modesty, which reminds of the awareness of the limits of reason as mentioned above. Reasonableness is needed when pursuing a fair and peaceful cohabitation. Then, some criticism against Rawlsian theory will be summarized, in order to point out the flaws of reasonableness since it ends out as a strategy of exclusion, not to say of intolerance toward the so-called "unreasonable" people. As they are not ready to be reasonable – in the sense in which they are expected to be – they are being excluded from citizenry, and their exclusion seems to testify the failure of reasonableness, unable to act as effective precondition for a fair

22 Toleration and Reasonableness

liberal society. In the third section, a revision of the notion of reasonableness will be proposed. Then, some conclusions will be drawn.

Human Fallibility, Religion, and Politics in Locke's Thought

Locke develops his theory of toleration according to several lines. One of these entails an epistemic view in which toleration results from the acknowledgment of human limits in understanding and deliberating. In such a view, toleration is somehow connected with reasonableness, as it will be shown as follows.

Starting by reasonableness, in a nutshell, Locke holds reasonable those people who are ready to tolerate others since they are ready to recognize the limits of their own capability of understanding and in general of private judgments. They are reasonable inasmuch as they acknowledge in themselves and others the same cognitive limits and similar biases in making judgments.

Reasonableness is here represented as a sort of epistemic attitude somehow requested by both ineluctable uncertainty and probability as features of human knowledge. The awareness of their inescapable cognitive limits, in fact, must not prevent people from living and arranging their coexistence accordingly. Quoting Locke, "the understanding faculties being given to man, not barely for speculation, but also for the conduct of his life, man would be at a great loss if he had nothing to direct him but what has the certainty of true knowledge [...] In the greatest part of our concernments, [God] has afforded us only the twilight, as I may so say, of probability; suitable, I presume, to that state of mediocrity and probationership he has been pleased to place us in here; wherein, to check our overconfidence and presumption, we might, by every day's experience, be made sensible of our short-sightedness and liableness to error" (Locke 1999a [1690], IV, XIV.1–1).

In other words, probability is enough in such matters, in which absolute certainty cannot be attained (Locke 1999a [1690], IV.1.3). Albeit they are matters of disagreement, they make up political life, the management of which requires the capability of judgment. Such capability is needed in fact to lead everyday life and to make all decisions. More precisely, Locke defends the idea of a reasonable judgment as required by a public justification: the latter should aim at achieving public good like peace or legal order against any divisive political decision. Hence, reasonableness is needed for people to adopt a "vocabulary of judgement" as the precondition for public deliberation over matters of public importance (Casson 2011, pp. 9–10).

The relevance attributed to reasonableness shows Locke's concern for public debate and deliberation, being they threatened by the religious fanaticism he could experience personally when he was young. In fact, Locke could observe how individuals, specifically religious believers, asserting their moral and political claims, did not attempt to articulate them in terms comprehensible to others (Locke 1976–1980, I, 30). By contrast, they maintained to be guided by a divine inner light, intelligible only by people similarly illuminated (Hoff 2015) and, accordingly, to be invested by God to impose their truth on others in their presumed interest, be it religious, moral, or political. Against such pretentions, Locke trusts in public reasonableness to be intended as citizens' compliance with authority in charge of judging and deciding what should be applied to all publicly and equally, given the multiplicity of individual judgments and their different degree of probability. In contrast to private judgments, often contrasting one another, public judgment – a sort of *ante litteram* public reason – serves as a conciliating decision-making strategy in the face of disagreement.

It is worth pointing out that public judgment is not to be seen as alternative to private ones: authority – in charge of formulating public judgment – is legitimated insofar as it is consented by those who are subjected to it. Individuals are aware that their private judgment is at risk of factiousness. It is precisely because people are likely to be or become unreasonable – i.e., factious – that the question of political judgment arises. They may become unreasonable, and they are conscious of running this risk. Thus, they subscribe to a consensual authority, legitimized by the instance of a coordination or even homogenization of private judgments, in order to prevent conflicts and political disorder (Locke 2016 [1690], II.13). In Lockean words, agents join together in an effort to "avoid, and remedy the inconveniences of the state of nature, which necessarily follow from every man's being judge in his own case" (Locke 2016 [1690], II.90). Political authority responds to the challenge of private judgments; it is the solution to the conflicts that emerge on the basis of such judgments, being they different and contrasting (Locke 2016 [1690], I.6). To sum up, the inevitable flow of private judgments necessitates political authority in the first place. Being aware of such inconveniences entails a sort of reasonableness, enabling people to join a political contractual community by consenting on it.

In such a perspective, reasonableness can be regarded also as that moral disposition enabling people to see themselves and others as partners in a political enterprise. To detail, the contract among people to establish a political community is not based on a series of individual promises, rather it springs out of a general attitude of willing cooperation and trust (Locke 1997). A social contract is realizable because people are both rational and reasonable: they are rational, and then they may be aware that the political authority as a coordination power is needed to find a solution to disagreement, especially when this is likely to transform itself into conflict or even war. Beyond that, people may be reasonable insofar as they recognize their human fellows as moral agents on an equal footing. It means that they are aware that, on public issues, human beings can only reach degrees of consensus, given that probability is the epistemic status of their acquirements (Besussi 1987). As said above, they will be able to come to different judgments, not to truth. To put it more clearly, reasonableness is not to eradicate disagreement, but, again, it is "to ensure a common vocabulary within which disagreement can take place. A common language of judgement serves as a homogenizing agent that allows heterogeneity to arise without disaster" (Casson 2011, p. 19). Said that, reasonableness is not to eradicate truth as well.

Indeed, Locke is not skeptical about truth in general and about religious truth specifically. As said above, Locke starts by recognizing human fallibility: it is a matter of fact that human beings are not exempt from the possibility of being in error. The ones who are well-disposed to recognize limits in themselves and in others, hence who are ready to defend individuals' moral agency, moral equality, and publicity, will take on a "legislative point of view" (Tuckness 2002, p. 6). It means that everyone is entitled to wonder whether the state should use the force to impose what is believed true or valid. Given the deep disagreement on truths like the religious ones, what is at stake are the principles to be adopted to guide political decisions and possibly to exercise political force. The "legislative point of view" is to be adopted when principles justifying force are contested: in such a situation, people should wonder whether they would want others to act on the same principles that they propose to act on, recognizing that others may disagree about them, and apply controversial terms differently. Said that, the legislator or anyone who acts as legislator is not requested to be skeptical about religious truths: all that is requested is to assume a neutral and pluralistic approach to deal with any religious controversies.

The same happens, for instance, with public good, upon which there is large disagreement. No political interference should be allowed about what can be defended by persons as their good, especially when such good is somehow religious: toward it, toleration is the right solution. By contrast, when the goods at stake are inviolable rights such as life, freedom, and property, political authority must intervene to protect them against any possible threat or menace. Those rights are not a matter of toleration: they are not disputable and must be enforced (Locke 2016 [1690], VIII). When considering conflictual conceptions of the good, persons should take on the abovementioned "legislative point of view" that is now playing as an attitude of reasonableness that enables people to keep the distance from their own (contested) truth. It means that people will wonder whether their own moral positions are consistent with the background assumptions of judgmental equality, equal respect, equal freedom, and publicity. It means also that they will not take the necessity of a political decision as given: let us remember the case for an "Appeal to Heaven," the last remedy left to people when a tyrant is governing upon them. In the absence of a "judge on earth," people invoke the judge in heaven – God or the law of nature – that is, they decide to rebel against the political power (Locke 2016 [1670], III, 20–21). Lastly, it means also that people will wonder whether they would want others to interpret and act upon another conception of good that they put forward, realizing that others will interpret it as a public good differently than in the past.

To conclude on this point, Locke shows to conceive of reasonableness as a precondition for deliberating over political issues in the absence of a "real" agreement or, even, in the face of deep disagreement. Since people are not equipped to eradicate partiality and uncertainty from political life, given their intrinsic limitations, an impartial judge is needed to decide for all in accordance or even disagreeing with individuals' private judgments. Being these the circumstances, people are rational enough to legitimate an authority to make collective decisions. The task of authority is to ensure the convergence of different private judgments on public issues. People are also reasonable enough to share the public judgment as formulated by the authority and to comply with its decisions.

Now, in light of what has been said above, it should be clear why reasonableness implies toleration and why toleration results from everybody's recognition of the limits of deliberation on public issues, especially when they are controversial. Normatively, toleration is to be adopted by individuals when they realize that, given the limits all humans share, nobody knows the right solution to disagreement; pragmatically, toleration is to be adopted to face disagreement because it is not convenient to impose any truth or even coerce people to believe in a truth they do not hold as such.

In details, in Locke's theorizing, toleration rests on multiple reasons: political, moral, theological, and epistemic (Locke 2016 [1689]). Those reasons are deeply intertwined: mutual toleration is requested among individuals and groups, given that nobody has been granted of any divine power or truth. Symmetry among people, since they are equal as creatures, preserves anyone from being subjected to any political authority with regard to religious faith. In Locke's words, no one can impose religion on others as nobody knows more about dogmas than any other. God gives nobody the authority to coerce others with regard to religion or with the way in which to worship him.

Said that about the symmetry among human beings, it is crucial that faith consists in an inward persuasion of mind. Quoting Locke, the "Care of Souls is not committed to the Civil Magistrate any more than to other Men [...] God has ever given any such Authority to one Man over another, as to compell any one to his Religion" (Locke 2016 [1689], p. 128). Similarly, no church – given that churches are free associations for Locke – can rely on political power either to enforce religion on non-believers or to punish dissenters. In short, a principle of separation between politics and religions is here at stake: it entails that political and religious authorities have different functions, aims, and means. On the one hand, the "Power of Civil Government relates only to Mens Civil Interests; is confined to the care of the things of this World; and hath nothing to do with the World to come"; on the other hand, churches are free and voluntary societies, the end of which is the public worship of God and the salvation of souls. "Nothing ought, nor can be transacted in this Society, relating to the Possession of Civil and Worldly Goods. No Force is here to be made use of, upon any occasion whatsoever" (Locke 2016 [1689], p. 130; p. 133).

In addition to the previous consideration about the incoercibility of inner conviction, Locke propounds also another argument for respect, albeit with different words. The idea is that any conscientiously held beliefs are to be respected and belief holders should be respected too, even in the case that their beliefs were false. Freedom of conscience must take priority over any conception of truth. Such words should not be interpreted as "profession of skepticism," if any. Skepticism is not the appropriate justification of toleration, let alone of reasonableness. In fact, skepticism fails to provide a persuasive argument for toleration, as it undermines the other moral principles it might be combined with as part of a larger argument for toleration. Skepticism, in fact, denies any moral principle and claims that this counts as a reason for toleration. In such view, toleration ends being likely to resemble a laissez-faire strategy, in which anything goes with the risk of disorder and disrespect. The problem with the skeptic argument for toleration is far from the Lockean one.

The theological background of the whole Lockean doctrine justifies the limits of toleration, namely, a virtue, insofar as it rests on epistemic and moral premises.

The conclusion so far is that individuals and groups should exercise mutual toleration. That is, no religious reasons can justify infringements of civic goods, i.e., life, freedom, and property, and no political means can be adopted to convert people or even persecute them because of heresy or apostasy or any other sin. Individuals and groups are free to adhere to their religion provided that they will not use religion as an instrument for violating others' freedom. No religious belief is allowed to threaten the life, liberty, and property of people, which are civic goods, the protection of which is the task of political authority.

Similar conclusion about the illegitimacy of physically coercing people on the basis of religious reasons is supported by a theological argument which recalls Latitudinarian assumptions. Namely, Locke follows the Latitudinarian theologians who envisaged a wide ambit of "things indifferent," i.e., matters that were not prescribed by Scripture, hence open to human choice and local convention. About such "things indifferent," toleration is invoked as the right way to deal with them, by leaving them to human initiative. The background idea is the one already mentioned: God requires that he be worshipped, but he is not prescriptive about the manner of worship. The only necessary truth is the belief that Christ is the Messiah and Saviour (Locke 1999b [1695]). What it is necessary to believe to save oneself is accessible to any human creature, and no special competence is required. On the track of this theological premise – the Latitudinarism of Locke – some points introduced above can be better clarified.

So briefly explained the matter of "things indifferent," a question that might arise is whether an authority is allowed to decide what is indifferent and what is not (Goldie 2016, p. xvii). The point is that the notion of "things indifferent" can easily lead to an argument for intolerance: if something is a "thing indifferent," then nobody has good reason to object to it on conscientious grounds. "Things indifferent" could be imposed by authority, not because God requires it, but rather for the sake of order. This risk is realistic: in fact, Locke warns that "Faith is not Faith without believing" (Locke 2016 [1689], p. 128). It means that religious belief is a matter of inward conviction; hence conscience cannot be forced. To punish somebody for not worshiping God "correctly" cannot bring about genuine belief. Thus, it is nonsense that anybody should enforce the truth, let alone a religious one, especially in a world of divided religions.

To put it differently, no intolerance should be consequent to latitudinarianism, but precisely the opposite, a horizontal toleration among confessions: "for every Church is Orthodox to it self; to others, Erroneous or Heretical. Whatsoever any Church believes, it believes to be true; and the contrary thereunto it pronounces to be Error. So that the Controversie between these Churches about the Truth of their Doctrines, and the Purity of their Worship, is on both sides equal; nor is there any Judge, either at *Constantinople*, or elsewhere upon Earth, by whose Sentence it can be determined" (Locke 2016 [1689], p. 135). Again, there cannot be any room for a "material" power to impose any "thing indifferent" as necessary: not only because conscience cannot be forced – thus no religious faith can be imposed – but because insofar as they are indifferent, such things cannot be a "material" affair. What a political authority may have the right to do is only to prevent one from imposing their convictions on others by force and threat. The consent which people can realistically give to an authority provides reasons for restricting the scope of the public good so that it does not, for example, encompass religious ends, which are not properly object of public decision. In the end, the theory of "things indifferent" acts as a theological basis for toleration, insofar as believers are entitled to choose to adhere to any Christian confession and worship God correspondently. No imposition on religious matter is consequently justified.

In sum, Locke's thinking on toleration has shown how various are the reasons for tolerating believers of different churches, that is, different truth-bearers. Roughly, it may be said that the very basis for toleration is a sort of reasonableness, construed as the awareness of the limits of human understanding and judgment. It means that reasonable people, notwithstanding their different inner beliefs, are able to tolerate each other: as believers, they see themselves and others as equal creatures, to whom God left freedom in choosing the external aspects of worship, the so-called things indifferent. As citizens, they agree on stopping political struggles on matter of faith: such struggles are not legitimated neither by God, who wants sincere faith and not an imposition of it, nor by the laws of nature, which prescribe all people mutual and equal respect for basic goods such as liberty, freedom, and property. Any possible restrictions of these goods must be justified on the basis of political reasons, not religious ones. In few words, Lockean toleration expresses the separation of politics and religion, in the variety of aspects in which this distinction may be declined.

Epistemic Division and Public Reason in John Rawls

The notion of toleration is to be applied, first of all, to philosophy. By using these words, Rawls defends a fundamental premise of his political liberalism, that is, the idea that a fair society – a desirable one – should rest on a political conception of justice, not on a comprehensive one (Rawls 1985). To understand correctly the meaning of the sentence above, Rawls' crucial argument has to be recalled: for a society to be just, stability for the right reasons must be assured. Thus, a just society cannot but rest on a "political, not metaphysical," conception of justice. Indeed, metaphysics, morals, religions, and comprehensive doctrines, in general, have always been battlefields as they deal with deeply divisive matters. When such doctrines are at stake, it is likely for conflicts to arise. In order for a society to be fair, within which people can coexist safely and freely, such conflicts must be avoided or at least resolved and peace stably installed.

Clearly, in Rawls's conception of justice – as depicted in *Political Liberalism* (Rawls 2005) – stability is crucial. A just society is first of all a stable one, but it must be *rightly* stable, that is, for the "right reasons," that is, moral ones. In order for a society to be stable for the right reasons, the pluralism of comprehensive doctrines must be taken seriously. A society in which pluralism is forbidden or ignored is not properly just, rather it would be one in which people should conform to the same doctrines, be they metaphysical, moral, or religious. Put it differently, people with different truths should pretend to share the same, publicly claiming it is the one on which they agree. Said that, the crucial point is how pluralism and stability can rightly cohere. It is apparent how the former can realistically turn to menace the latter. Pluralism involves a certain degree of conflict or at least of disagreement. The point is how to conciliate disagreeing doctrines, especially when such disagreement is deep, even irreconcilable. The answer is in spite of doctrinal disagreement, political agreement is feasible insofar as pluralism is reasonable. Reasonableness is to Rawls the keyword of his just and stable society.

The argument will develop as follows: firstly, the Rawlsian project of political liberalism should be clarified, in order to understand better why a theory of justice should transform itself into a political conception; secondly, an explanation of the dangerous relationship between truth and politics should be offered, in order to introduce reasonableness as the essential element of political liberalism, being it a political virtue, an epistemic device, or even a requirement for justice; it will be shown how reasonableness and public reason are mutually bounded. Thirdly, some criticism to reasonableness as expression of intolerance will be discussed.

Let us start by the first clarification. The original aim of Rawls's thought is to argue for a just society, as presented in his seminal work *A Theory of Justice* (Rawls 1999). Stability is central in this work; it presupposes, in individuals, a kind of motivational priority centered on a sense of justice, which instills in the citizens of the well-ordered society the motivation to support the right institutions over time (Rawls 1999, Chap. VIII). Some years later the publication of *A Theory of Justice*, happened in 1971, Rawls began to consider the way stability was assured as unsatisfactory. Taking note of the profound differences, which necessarily exist at the level of the moral psychology of the people who inhabit the pluralistic society, means for Rawls to opt for defending justice as fairness as a political conception, to be sustained by different points of view. Such a "political turn" (Weithman 2010) is necessary in order to pursue the feasibility of justice as an ideal with a chance of being realized, albeit partially. In the face of pluralism, stability remains a problem to be addressed and resolved. The problem of political liberalism is rephrased like this: "how is it possible for there may exist over time a stable and just society of free and equal citizens profoundly divided by reasonable though incompatible religious, philosophical and moral doctrines? Put another way: how is it possible that deeply opposed though reasonable comprehensive doctrines may live together and all affirm the political conception of a constitutional regime?" (Rawls 2005, p. xviii). Foreseeably, the answer is "yes": people deeply divided by different comprehensive doctrines may coexist peacefully and stably provided that they are reasonable. It means that what they are required to do is to converge on a set of political principles such as freedom, equal respect, and mutual tolerance in order to reach a stable peaceful coexistence. Being reasonable is equivalent, here, to being aware of each person's limits in understanding, knowing, and practical reasoning.

In detail, according to Rawls, reasonableness implies two conditions: the acknowledgment of the so-called burdens of judgment (namely, the limits of human understanding) and the recognition of pluralism (namely, the fact of the pluralism of philosophies, moralities, and religions which inhabit a plural society). Backed by the abovementioned awareness of one's own cognitive limits and of the plural results of practical reasoning within free institutions, people can be reasonable insofar as they are enabled to adopt the "method of avoidance": it entails renouncing the truth or, better, renouncing to appeal to the truth to settle disputes that may arise in the domain of politics. Such an avoidance responds to the objective of the stability of a well-ordered society, which is pursued through the morally motivated support (whatever the moral reasons and whatever the doctrines from which they are drawn) of the right institutions. Abstention from truth is so thus functional to stability, being it an essential element for a just society. The method of avoidance, or, as it has been called alternatively, the epistemic abstinence, corresponds to the application of toleration to philosophy, mentioned above. Rawls says: "we must apply the principle of toleration to philosophy itself. The hope is that, by this method of avoidance, as we might call it, existing differences between contending political views can at least be moderated, even if not entirely removed, so that social cooperation on the basis of mutual respect can be maintained" (Rawls 1985, p. 231). (This quotation goes on: "Or if this is expecting too much, this method may enable us to conceive how, given a desire for free and uncoerced agreement, a public understanding could arise consistent with the historical conditions and constraints of our social world." Rawls is emphasizing the relevance of social and political context for realizing a peaceful coexistence with others, in a real not abstract world.)

Secondly, the matter is the intrinsically conflictual relationship between politics and truth. Rawls fears the political consequences of truth when it is brought into politics, as the historical example of Europe after the Reform testifies (Rawls 2005, pp. xxiii-xxvi). A politics of toleration was defended – as Locke did in his works – as the best solution to contain the conflicts among religions. In Rawls's terms, the same should happen with the comprehensive doctrines when they are incompatible: they cannot be hosted in politics at the same time. What their holders must do is to agree on a few political principles, adopted as a "module" (Rawls 2005, p. 145), that differently can fit into various reasonable comprehensive doctrines. How such a module can fit, it is one's own task. In fact, Rawls says it is left to citizens individually as part of their liberty to settle how they think such political principles and values are related to other values in their comprehensive doctrine (Rawls 2005, p. 140). By saying this, Rawls assumes political values as free-standing but potentially coherent with one's own comprehensive values, according to a sort of "justificatory neutrality" (Maffettone 2010, p. 290): that is to say, that everyone finds for themselves the reasons for supporting the institutions in their own comprehensive doctrine. It is clear that, consistently with the method of avoidance, Rawls's intention is not to go into the justifications that individuals have for supporting the right institutions out of respect for their freedom of conscience and thought. The political principles are now the content of a political conception of justice that may or may not be in continuity with the individual comprehensive doctrines that make it their own, each from its own perspective. What is required of citizens is not to agree on the same comprehensive doctrines – i.e., on the same truth – but only to converge on the political conception of justice from each one's own position, achieving that overlapping consensus which, given the motivating reasons that each person is able to find by herself, within her own doctrine, guarantees stability to the institutions. Such ability is the same met above: reasonableness.

Reasonableness takes the place of truth in politics, as the method of avoidance prescribes. To avoid the troubles caused by conflicts of truths, reasonable people accept to abstain from defending publicly their truth. The qualification of "reasonable," initially attributed to the pluralism of the reasonable comprehensible doctrines, is now attributed to citizens who are able to find in their reasonable doctrine the reasons which support political values and principles of justice. Reasonableness is independent of the content of the reasons everyone can find and of their truth. It is reasonableness that enables citizens to reach an overlapping consensus on political principles; it is because they are reasonable that they find the link between their comprehensive values and the political principles. Moreover, when it is necessary, i.e., in cases of conflict between one's own comprehensive values and the political principles of justice, reasonableness pushes reasonable people to suspend judgment on one's own truth as well as on those of others: what counts is the possibility that they identify an overlapping area inhabited by political values, which can be shared by all. The judgment of truth on one's own and on others' reasons is suspended, and what counts is their convergence: the abstention from truth is the first move to pursue the political objective of consensus as a response to the problem of stability. It is, indeed, the fundamental requirement to respond to the question of stability in the face of the challenge of pluralism.

Another relevant issue concerns the relationship, if any, between reasonableness and skepticism. According to Rawls, the defense of reasonableness should not be interpreted as skepticism: the willingness to avoid invoking truth in the public debate does not mean for Rawls to renounce supporting that truth; it just means being prepared to take seriously the fact that there are many reasonable comprehensive doctrines and relative truths within liberal society and that no reasonable person can be asked to renounce the contents of his or her own truth in order to give priority to the principles of justice. The effort that should be made is to adopt the perspective of public reason, namely, what is required of reasonable people is to be ready to explain to each other, with regard to questions of justice, how their political choices can be mutually acceptable in the light of shared political values. They can do so without denying their deeper values and without becoming skeptic about the truth they hold.

To sum up, in Rawlsian political liberalism, toleration – that is, the application of it to the truth, one's own and others – and reasonableness are reciprocally linked. Toleration must be "applied to philosophy," being "philosophy" an umbrella notion which comprises metaphysics, morals, religion, and their respective truths. The application of toleration to truth is necessary in order to avoid inevitable conflicts that would burst when metaphysics, morals, religion, and in general comprehensive doctrines should be brought in the political debate. The application of toleration to such doctrines means also that truth is suspended in political debates: not truth but reasonableness should occupy the political space, in order to assure peaceful and stable coexistence among people who reach an overlapping consensus on the same principles of justice. Abstinence from truth in politics does not imply skepticism: it requires only the adoption of a public reasoning ordered to realize a just society.

Thirdly, the Rawlsian account of reasonableness has been largely disputed. Critics raised the following points.

(a) Reasonableness itself is an elusive notion. Although Rawls declares that reasonableness and truth do not exclude each other, since being reasonable does not mean renouncing truth but only avoiding the claim to truth in public debate, many critics contested precisely such an epistemic division. It is precisely the recognition of the "burdens of judgement" that has been objected, with its outcome of epistemic division between what people are allowed to bring into public discourse and what they are not. In a nutshell, reasonableness seems here an arbitrary principle of division between publicly presentable reasons and reasons that must remain private. The paradigmatic case of abortion can help illustrate this point. According to Rawls, in questions such as that of abortion, unanimity of views is not to be expected. He believes that, according to the perspective of public reason, enabled by reasonableness, any reasonable balance of conflicting values (namely, the respect for human life, an ordered reproduction of political society, the equality of women) will give a woman a qualified right to decide whether or not to end her pregnancy during the first trimester (Rawls 2005, p. 243, f. 32). Given the deep disagreement about the status of human embryo and the uncertainty about how it should be treated, especially when compared with other requirements such as women's freedom, all reasonable citizens should accept the outcome of a vote as binding on all under the majority rule. It is possible, of course, that some people may reject certain legitimate decisions. It may happen, for example, that the decision to recognize the right to abortion is contested by Catholics. In such contestation, Rawls adds Catholicism proves to be a comprehensive doctrine uncapable of assuming public reason since it does not support a reasonable balance or ordering of political values on the issue.

Comprehensibly, these words arose a lot of criticisms, since Catholics cannot accept being labelled as unreasonable. In their view, any request for epistemic division between their truth (the one about the embryo) and the requirements of public reason (the invitation to do without claiming the truth in debating political issue such as abortion) is in fact unreasonable and cannot but be rejected. According to Catholics – to go on with the example – reasonableness in Rawls's view should thus be criticized as it causes discriminatory outcomes. The epistemic division imposed by public reason intolerably forces them to remain silent about what is fundamental to them, as in the case of abortion. Following Joseph Raz, if a person gives up asserting her truth in cases like this, it would be tantamount to letting other people's truths take over. If one believes that abortion should be forbidden because it is a murder, she has a strong reason to believe that it should be forbidden, whether others share it or not (Raz 1990).

Similar considerations have been made by religious authors who argue against the method of avoidance as the precondition for participating into the public debate: believers cannot accept to bracket the truth when debating with fellow citizens on public issues. Believers can be good citizens by professing their faith, indeed by bringing the reasons of faith into the public debate and thus contributing to shaping more authentically the just society (Weinstock 1994; Wenar 1995; Weithman 2002; Perry 2003). The basic conviction is that the Rawlsian idea of public reason is too exclusive or too binding if not even discriminatory toward the bearers of religious visions, imposing on believers sacrifices in terms of defending their own truth more than it imposes on others. Greenawalt, putting himself from the point of view of believers, grasps the dilemma they are faced with when they are asked to assess how much space their comprehensive doctrines leave to loyalty to the institutions (Greenawalt 1995). Back to the case of abortion, if abortion represents an offence for the Catholic believer because it is comparable to a very serious harm inflicted on a human being, it is difficult to confine the believer's reason to faith alone, since the argument of harm is valid for all. A case like this one shows the arbitrariness of the epistemic constraint that imposes restrictions on the reasons in defense of the embryo; it also shows the arbitrariness of the a priori distinction between what can be valid publicly and what is considered the expression of private beliefs. But that the value of the embryo's life is a private belief is something that Catholics are not prepared to accept.

Another criticism is raised by Brian Barry. According to Barry (1995), the appeal to the reasonableness of individuals is contradictory, asking them to put aside their comprehensive doctrines and, at the same time, asking them, by virtue of their reasonableness, to find within their doctrines the reasons to reasonably support the conception of justice. Similarly, Glen Newey says that Rawls's reasonable pluralism is in fact a reasonable skepticism (Newey 2011). The idea of reasonable pluralism – Newey clarifies – should allow to hold two contrasting beliefs, e.g., the belief that p (say, a belief in God) is reasonable and the belief that not-p (say, atheism) is reasonable. This entails that whatever makes a belief reasonable cannot necessarily make its negation unreasonable. But to state that it is reasonable to believe p, and that it is reasonable to believe not-p, seems to be no less than to say that reason cannot decide whether to believe one or the other. If reason cannot decide between the conflicting doctrines, then there are insufficient grounds for believing in any one's doctrine rather than any of the others. Now, as it will be exposed below, such undecidability does not necessarily lead to skepticism: it can be the expression of an epistemic disagreement, which asks for some political management.

(b) In defending reasonableness, Rawls seems to fall into a vicious circle. To understand this objection, it is useful to recall the reasons why Rawls introduced the concept of reasonableness: for the political life to be just and peaceful, one in which political decisions are legitimate, i.e., justified on the basis of reasons that everyone is willing to share, it is necessary for all citizens to adopt an attitude of reasonableness. Reasonable citizens are able to set aside their comprehensive reasons and to share the same public reasons. Rawls's intention to see reasonableness as the premise for liberal legitimacy is thus clear. But one cannot but see a risk of circularity: it consists in the fact that a political conception is considered legitimate because it is reasonable, and it is reasonable because it is based on shared reasons; such reasons are shared because they are reasonable, and they are reasonable because they are supported by reasonable people (Habermas 1995; Estlund 1998; Boettcher 2004).

To put a remedy to such objections – *pace* Rawls – it is necessary to ground reasonableness in a moral theory and to adopt the point of view of a philosophical truth that allows to argue for the priority of reasonableness over people's own truths (Talisse 2003). Reasonableness must be theoretically based, in order to get out of the impasse of argumentative circularity. In spite of Rawls's bias against any theoretical premise, in arguing for reasonableness, he should realize that he is presupposing, without declaring it, a strong normative basis that remains hidden in order not to contradict the intention of abstention from truth. To put it differently, the more a theory takes into account the fact of pluralism, declaring its independence from one specific position, the more such theory loses theoretical depth, and consequently it is not able to assure stability. At the end, there is no positive result: obliged to remain on the surface not to assume any specific position, a theory is deemed to be unable to cope with pluralism. A solution to this justificatory dilemma, as it has been called, consists in rephrasing reasonableness in order to be more inclusive, as it will be dealt with below.

(c) Another question remains open in the Rawlsian account of reasonableness, that is, the issue of the so-called unreasonable people. Too dismissively, Rawls mentions them as the ones who are not reasonable, being unavailable to subscribe to the requirements of reasonableness, first of all the acceptance of epistemic division as they see it as a betrayal of truth. Again, unreasonable are the believers who are reluctant to give up the truth while debating public issues such as abortion. Such people are ready to violate these terms whenever they have the convenience and circumstances allow it (Rawls 2005, pp. 48–50):

> if it were possible, they would suppress freedom of conscience and thought. The unreasonable person – Rawls holds – is inclined to consider her own doctrine as the only one true and to impose it on others.

Rawls adds a few words about the unreasonable people; he believes that unreasonableness is a fact of public life, as mere pluralism is a fact as well. This means that just institutions have the task of holding them off – like wars and diseases – so that they do not threaten political justice (Rawls 2005, p. 64, f. 19). It can be said, in short, that Rawls's treatment of the unreasonable persons is a form of tolerance combined with efforts of accommodating them within society; such efforts aim at preserving a peaceful coexistence, with the hope that the unreasonable people, living in a just society and enjoying the benefits of stability, can gradually appropriate political values.

Of course, the treatment of the unreasonable to be contained like war and disease arouses widespread dissent, especially among the ones who reject the label of unreasonable and the consequent exclusion from the public debate. The strategy adopted by Rawls proves to be discriminatory against those who do not share political values as they are not universal values at all. On the contrary, they are values of a part of citizenry, the one supporting the moral values of liberalism; what Rawls intends to do is imposing such values to all. The Rawlsian task of pragmatically extending the legitimacy of the institutions also to non-liberal people turns out, in fact, to be exclusive: Rawls' reasonableness does not apply to everyone; first it does not apply to those who do not accept to suspend their truth in public debate (Friedman 2000).

There is a point that is rightly raised here: when Rawls speaks of unreasonable people, he does not make clear who they are. He says that they are the ones who do not accept the requirements of reasonableness. But practically it is not clear if he is referring to a unique category of people or more categories. The problem, therefore, is to address the question of the type of treatment to be given to the unreasonable people, not as a whole, but to groups of "differently unreasonable" ones, whose differences must be taken seriously. In fact, one thing is the position of those who consider reasonableness as too restrictive if not discriminatory because it obliges believers to bracket their truths while taking part into public debate; another is the position of those who would impose their truth on others. Both cases are against the idea of reasonableness: but if those who hold the first position dispute reasonableness as exclusive and even discriminatory, at the price of silencing their beliefs, those who refer to the second position are undoubtedly unreasonable.

In conclusion, the evident flaw of the Rawlsian debate about unreasonableness concerns truth or, better, the political exclusion of truth. To make some points in defense of Rawls, it is important to emphasize firstly that reasonableness has been figured out by Rawls as that virtue of citizens willing to participate into the democratic game. One becomes reasonable because one grasps the spirit of democracy, which for Rawls is essentially constituted by a continuous exchange of reasons between citizens who are aware of the limits of reason and who respect others. Secondly, in the background of the political intent, the accusation that the adoption of reasonableness discriminates against religious positions, Catholic first, is at least controversial; reasonableness in fact does not create any asymmetry between religious and non-religious people. Rather, Rawls's notion of reasonableness aims at standing against any form of sectarian interpretation of liberal-democratic political life, be such interpretation religious or not. What Rawls asks of believers as well as non-believers is to refrain from invoking the whole truth when fundamental political issues are at stake, committing themselves to justify their choices and actions to others.

Another issue is whether this bracketing makes sense or not: actually, this is the fundamental matter of liberalism, be it comprehensive or political, like the Rawlsian one. Now, having reaffirmed the task of a methodological distancing from truth for political, not philosophical or religious, purposes (the so-called method of avoidance), it remains unavoidable that this task is much more problematic for those who identify themselves with a religious affiliation. If it is true that there is no aprioristic preclusion of the public debate for believers, the conditions of access, especially the epistemic division required to enter it, are certainly the cause of not always unreasonable discontent. This criticism of liberalism, however, goes beyond the scope of this chapter.

A More Than Tolerant Public Debate

The purpose of this section is to revise the idea of reasonableness, in order to rescue it to respond to some criticisms. Let us start by recalling one of the most relevant objections to reasonableness – the one concerning its supposed exclusivism, as it would show to be unhospitable toward variously intended differences. According to such objection, reasonableness puts constraint on pluralism – so pluralism is much less pluralistic than it is in reality. If so, reasonableness is not able to solve the problem of stability: on the one hand, because some individuals may have reasons to oppose the political conception of justice in the name of what they consider to be true, as the Catholics mean to do in the case of abortion, and, on the other hand, because public reason, that is, the point of view from which people are asked to bracket their truth in public debate on the assumption of their reasonableness, seems unable to explain how principles of justice may be compatible with comprehensive doctrines. In other words, it is not clear how to link public reasons and comprehensive beliefs and how it would be possible given that one should avoid speaking of whatever truth, included, then, the logic truth.

Now, further arguments can be adopted to defend reasonableness again. First, *pace* Rawls, one can recognize the limits of her own understanding without being prevented to engage in a public debate bringing her own truth. Differently from Rawls, truth is not necessarily a threat for politics. People can continue defending their truth even in public and hold liberal political values (e.g., religious toleration). What it is not allowed is, as repeatedly seen, to enforce such truth on others.

In order to rescue reasonableness from its harsher criticisms, a thinner conception of reasonableness can be propounded, intended as the readiness to abide by fair terms of social cooperation, without the additional requirements that Rawls ascribes to it, especially the willingness to recognize the epistemic division (Bonotti 2011). Corresponding to such a thinner idea of reasonableness, there is a thinner, less severe notion of unreasonableness: there may be unreasonable people who show to be ready to cooperate with others without sharing fundamental liberal values such as equal respect. Even if they are in Rawlsian terms unreasonable, because, for example, they refuse to bracket their truth in public fora, they cannot be seen as unreasonable in the sense of intolerant or fanatics: they neither interfere with other people's decisions nor impose their beliefs on others. Such unreasonable people are willing to enter permanently into cooperation even though they do not accept the epistemic division or pluralism (Sala 2013). In conclusion, a thinner reinterpretation of the Rawlsian idea of reasonableness may preserve the more inclusive features of political liberalism while rejecting its more exclusionary attributes.

Another reflection can be added at this point: beyond a thinner notion of reasonableness, there is room to reconceive it also as the admission that people in a same citizenry are likely to disagree without a chance to come to an agreement. The idea is that the interests of some people are reasons to offer to others, without commitment to act only on grounds the former would recognize as reasons. Each one should be able to acknowledge that important among others' interests is the ability to guide their own lives, including participation in collective life, according to considerations they recognize as reasons. There may remain a deep disagreement among people, whose positions may be totally irreconcilable. Recognizing such disagreement is entirely compatible with rejecting the idea that others should be regarded as mere obstacles to one's own ends (Ebbels-Duggan 2010).

To overtake the paradox of reasonableness, so called because it requires citizens to avoid any appeal to the beliefs they hold more strongly when they are engaged in a public deliberation over political matters, it is salient to assume the epistemic idea that disagreement cannot be solved but that it can somehow be managed in the public domain (Liveriero 2015). Again, the paradox may be resolved by distinguishing between public reasons that are employed within the political domain and comprehensive reasons by which citizens might support the very same political justice. Such distinction allows to speak properly of reasonable pluralism, in which two individuals may be both justified in holding beliefs supported by their own comprehensive reasons and yet incompatible with each other. This amounts to saying that two individuals do not agree on the very same comprehensive reason in favor of a principle of justice, but they do converge on defending the same principles as valid.

The recognition of the fact that people may agree on some contents while disagreeing on the reasons supporting them is crucial for overcoming what has been called a paradox; in fact, there is no paradox but the recognition of human fallibility and of the consequent epistemic disagreement. Disagreement is a human fact characterizing any aspect of our life, specifically the public one.

Such a reformulation of disagreement sheds new light on the very notion of reasonableness. In this frame, to be reasonable means to be ready to recognize that nobody, when facing specific issues, has any epistemic authority to impose her beliefs that are justified by her own comprehensive reasons as ultimate truths to other citizens. In this view, reasonableness turns to be the virtue that allows individuals to understand reciprocity as well as accepting the epistemological limits we share as fallible agents.

Thus, if people accept the fallibility of human knowledge, when challenged by the disagreement, they are required – for epistemic reasons – to adopt an attitude of epistemic humility and of toleration toward the others, so recognized as peers (Leland and Wietmarschen 2012). They are ready to share the epistemic authority, and, in such way, they show to be reasonable agents. This implies that they are keen also to engage in public deliberation over political matters that are undecided and on which there is large disagreement. In the end, toleration might be defined as a fundamental normative consequence of the fact that reasonable agents may disagree even strongly but that they are ready to recognize mutually their being political partners.

Summary and Future Directions

This chapter aimed at focusing on the relationship between reasonableness and toleration. To do that, it took clue from the Lockean doctrine of toleration intended not only as the political strategy to combine religious differences and disarm conflicts but also as a cognitive readiness to recognize the limits of human reason. Moreover, true faith is an inward conviction; hence no force can do anything in converting dissenters. Reasonableness plays here a multiple role: it is the sign of a sincere believer; it is the quality of a citizen, who still believes in God; and it is the background of a society in which political institutions and the ecclesiastic ones are recognized in their different aims, functions, and means. In few words, reasonableness is a quality of a tolerant society in which all differences can be accommodated, provided that none of them should threat public order nor deny the existence of God.

Beyond Locke, the position of Rawls on reasonableness and toleration has been perused. It showed some similarities to the Lockean one: reasonableness as the recognition of the limits of human reason, then as the principle for an epistemic division between truth and what can be publicly justified as true, and, ultimately, as that source of epistemic humility enabling people to tolerate each other's doctrine in order to endorse a general mutual acceptance and respect. In spite of the efforts made by Rawls to argue for reasonableness, many criticisms have been advanced to point out the flaws of this notion and even the failure in its fundamental aim, that it putting moral, religious, and philosophical pluralism, on the one hand, and political stability, on the other, together. In a nutshell, the Rawlsian reasonableness turns to be less tolerant than expected. More words should be devoted to revise such notion, to make it more inclusive and effective in pursuing a society that is as just as possible.

References

Barry B (1995) John Rawls and the search for stability. Ethics 105:874–915
Besussi A (1987) John Locke. La ragionevolezza della politica. In: Veca S (ed) Filosofia, politica e società. Bibliopolis, Napoli, pp 9–45
Boettcher JW (2004) What is reasonableness? Philos Soc Crit 30(5–6):597–621
Bonotti M (2011) Religious political parties and the limits of political liberalism. Res Publica 17:107–123
Casson D (2011) Liberating judgement. Fanatics, skeptics, and John Locke's politics of probability. Princeton University Press, Princeton/Oxford
Ebbels-Duggan K (2010) The beginning of community: politics in the face of disagreement. Philos Q 60(238):50–71
Estlund D (1998) The insularity of the reasonable: why political liberalism must admit the truth. Ethics 108(2):252–275
Friedman M (2000) John Rawls and the political coercion of unreasonable people. In: Davion V, Wolf C (eds) The idea of a political liberalism. Essays on Rawls. Rowman & Littlefield, Lanham, pp 16–33
Goldie M (2016) Introduction. In: Second treatise on government [1670] & a letter concerning toleration [1689]. Oxford University Press, Oxford, pp ix–xxiii
Greenawalt K (1995) Private consciences and public reasons. Oxford University Press, New York/Oxford
Habermas J (1995) Reconciliation through the public use of reason. Remarks on John Rawls's *Political liberalism*. J Philos 92(3):109–131
Hoff S (2015) Locke and the nature of political authority. Rev Polit 77(1):1–22
Leland RJ, van Wietmarschen H (2012) Reasonableness, intellectual modesty, and reciprocity in political justification. Ethics 122(4):721–747
Liveriero F (2015) The epistemic dimension of reasonableness. Philos Soc Crit 41(6):517–535

Locke J (1976–1980) Letter to Father [1660]. In: De Beer E (ed) Correspondence of John Locke, vol 1. Clarendon, Oxford, pp 136–137

Locke J (1997) Essays on the law of nature [1663–1664]. In: Goldie M (ed) Political essays. Cambridge University Press, Cambridge, pp 79–133

Locke J (1999a) In: Manis J (ed) An essay concerning human understanding [1690]. Electronic classics series. Pennsylvania State University, Hazleton

Locke J (1999b) The reasonableness of Christianity as delivered in the scriptures [1695] edited with an introduction, notes, critical apparatus and transcriptions of related manuscripts by J C Higgins-Biddle. Clarendon Press, Oxford

Locke J (2016) Second treatise on government [1670] & a letter concerning toleration [1689]. Edited by M Goldie. Oxford University Press, Oxford

Maffettone S (2010) Rawls. An introduction. Polity, Oxford

Newey G (2011) Toleration as sedition. Crit Rev Int Soc Pol Phil 14(3):363–384

Perry M (2003) Under god? Religious faith and liberal democracy. Cambridge University Press, Cambridge

Rawls J (1985) Justice as fairness. Political, not metaphysical. Philos Public Aff 14(3):223–251

Rawls J (1999) A theory of justice [1971]. Belknap Press at Harvard University Press, Cambridge

Rawls J (2005) Political liberalism [1993]. Columbia University Press, New York/Chichester

Raz J (1990) Facing diversity: the case of epistemic abstinence. Philos Public Aff 19(1):3–46

Sala R (2013) The place of 'unreasonable' people beyond Rawls. Eur J Polit Theory 12:253–270

Talisse R (2003) Rawls on pluralism and stability. Crit Rev 15(1–2):173–194

Tuckness A (2002) Locke and legislative point of view. Toleration, contested principles, and the law. Princeton University Press, Princeton/Oxford

Weinstock D (1994) The justification of political liberalism. Pac Philos Q 75:165–185

Weithman P (2002) Religion and the obligations of citizenship. Cambridge University Press, Cambridge

Weithman P (2010) Why *Political liberalism*? On John Rawls's political turn. Oxford University Press, Oxford

Wenar L (1995) *Political liberalism*: an internal critique. Ethics 106:32–62

International Toleration

23

Pietro Maffettone

Contents

Introduction	440
Categorical Differences and Nonliberal Political Communities	441
Peace, Political Autonomy, and Self-determination	444
Pluralism, Sovereignty, and Political Realism	446
International Toleration and Liberal Foreign Policy	448
Summary	452
Future Directions	452
Conclusion	453
References	453

Abstract

This chapter discusses the idea of international toleration. It does so by exploring a wider question to which "international toleration" only constitutes one of the possible answers. The basic question addressed is the following one: how should the foreign policy of liberal democratic states be structured with respect to nonliberal and nondemocratic ones (nonliberal, for short)? The answer will depend on the nature of those nonliberal political communities. International toleration will be appropriate, for prudential reasons, in a limited number of cases. Difficult political circumstances may lead liberal political communities not to interfere with morally abhorrent nonliberal societies. However, a more respectful kind of international toleration is also possible provided that nonliberal political communities display two important features, namely, respect for their citizens' basic interests in political autonomy and peace. Internally self-determining and externally peaceful nonliberal

---

The author would like to thank Giulia Bistagnino, Federica Liveriero and Sebastiano Maffettone for detailed comments.

P. Maffettone (✉)
Political Science Department, University of Napoli, Federico II, Naples, Italy
e-mail: pietro.maffettone@unina.it

© The Author(s), under exclusive licence to Springer Nature Switzerland AG 2022
M. Sardoč (ed.), *The Palgrave Handbook of Toleration*,
https://doi.org/10.1007/978-3-030-42121-2_12

political societies are entitled to respectful toleration. They are, following Rawls, equal members in good standing of international society and liberals are to respect their freedom and independence.

Keywords

Liberal democracy · Foreign policy · International toleration · Rawls · Decent peoples · Self-determination · Sovereignty · Pluralism · Political autonomy · Peace

---

Introduction

This chapter discusses the idea of international toleration. It does so by exploring a wider question to which "international toleration" will only constitute one of the possible answers. The basic question addressed is the following one: how should the foreign policy of liberal democratic states be structured with respect to nonliberal and nondemocratic ones (nonliberal, for short)? Let us unpack the meaning of this basic question. The idea of "foreign policy" here refers to something that is much broader and perhaps more foundational than its conventional usage. When the latter is invoked, foreign policy usually stands for a specific branch of government activity comprising issues such as international treaties, membership in international organizations, decisions concerning international economic relations, etc. Here, instead, the expression is taken to refer to the basic features of a general political attitude. Such general political attitude will be guided by reasons of some kind (either prudential or moral in nature) and will likely result in more specific forms of policy decisions, and/or official declarations in the relevant fora, and/or long-term strategic visions about a country's place in international society (here see especially Rafanelli 2019). Examples of different kinds of foreign policies can range from outright opposition, to different forms of toleration, unproblematic acceptance, or positive endorsement.

To illustrate, Iran is defined by the USA as a "rogue state" and thus, leaving aside specific policy decisions, it is not considered, by the USA, as a member in good standing of international society (see Hoyt 2000; O'Reilly 2007). The USA and the UK actively cooperate on a range of sensitive issues and have an especially close relationship on security matters. They cooperate closely in a number of important fora, such as the UN, and often cite their mutual undertakings as best described by the idea of a "special relationship" (see Dumbrell 2009). The USA and France have had their disagreements over time (most recently, over the 2003 invasion of Iraq), but US foreign policy takes it for granted that France is a free and independent country on the world stage and thus entitled to respect by the USA. The situation with countries such as China is somewhat more complex. Its human rights record, and especially its consistency in repressing anything close to political dissent, its constant refusal to observe foreign (especially USA) intellectual property rights, the manipulation of its currency to foster export led growth, and its far from peaceful stance in the South China sea, all contribute to foster a rather more suspicious attitude on the part of the USA (Jisi and Ran 2019). Toleration guided by prudential reasons might best describe the current situation. Finally, consider US relations with Jordan. While the two countries have been cooperating closely on many issues including security matters in the Middle East, disagreements about Jordan's human right and democratization efforts and about US military interventions in the regions abound. Here, it is not implausible to portray the US attitude as one of respectful toleration. Jordan is recognized as a member in good standing of international society entitled to its freedom and independence. Yet, the way in which the country is governed is often at odds with the US (official) concern for freedom of expression, democratic rule, and women's rights among other issues.

A liberal democracy, in the minimal sense adopted here, is a state controlled by a democratically elected government which guarantees the individual rights that are associated with the constitutional tradition. In real life, whether a specific country actually fits the description of a liberal democratic state just offered will be, most likely, a matter of degrees (but see Doyle 2006). The issue, however, is not to individuate genuine liberal democracies in the real world but rather to understand what moral (or prudential) reasons apply to their choice of foreign policy towards nonliberal states. Finally, the expression "nonliberal states" simply refers to all other forms of nonliberal political organization. This definition of nonliberal states is purely negative, and, fully compatible with the existence of qualitatively different kinds (morally speaking) of nonliberal political regimes (more on this below). In this picture, then, we can say that a liberal democratic foreign policy vis-à-vis nonliberal states may be one of outright opposition, it may accept the existence of such states as unproblematic or even desirable, or, alternatively, it might be guided by the idea that such states should be the object of toleration.

What, then, is the appropriate foreign policy of liberal states vis-à-vis nonliberal ones? Much will depend on the nature of the nonliberal state under consideration, yet even taking the latter into account, the likely answer will exclude unproblematic acceptance or positive endorsement. This kind of conclusion may initially appear to be trivial. It is not. First, it depends on the ability to qualitatively distinguish different kinds of nonliberal societies. Second, it excludes any kind of morally relativistic answer to the question asked (i.e., an answer that would not see any ground for making moral distinctions between nonliberal states). Third, it clearly suggests, at least intuitively, that toleration is important since it offers the only plausible alternative to outright opposition. Before moving on to the substance of the discussion, a word about the language employed. The expressions "political community" or "political society" refer to a modern state together with its government. In addition, the expression "international toleration" refers to toleration in international society, understood as a society of states, not nations.

Categorical Differences and Nonliberal Political Communities

Recall that a liberal democracy has been defined as a state controlled by a democratically elected government and which guarantees for its citizens a list of individual rights that is familiar from the constitutional tradition (I shall not provide a list of those rights, but the rights covered by Rawls' first principle of justice in *A Theory of Justice* (1971, 1999) can act as a plausible referent.). The definition is compatible with different kinds of methods to make sure that a government is democratically accountable. All such methods will however require to feature the familiar idea that each person has one vote, and that the highest executive and legislative offices in the country are the object of regular competitive electoral procedures. Similarly, this description of a liberal democracy is compatible, within limits, with different understandings of which individual rights ought to be protected, and will allow many interpretations of the concrete meaning for such rights, and assignment of relative priority among them. Thus, according to this stipulative definition, countries such as India, Sweden, the USA, the UK are all plausibly understood as liberal democracies even though some feature a federal system of governance and some do not, some are republics and one is not, some directly elect the head of the executive and some do not, and the background political cultures of each is markedly different from the others and thus likely to lead to significant variations in the list of rights that they are going to accord to their citizens. All of this seems rather obvious.

A more complex question is what to say about states that do not fit the description of a liberal democratic state and that have been, in the introduction, generically labeled nonliberal states. Though the widespread enthusiasm for the "end of history" narrative that followed the collapse of the Soviet Union in the 1990s is long gone, political philosophers (as opposed to political scientists, see Hudson 2005; Krotz 2002) have generally been reluctant to say much in the way of making sophisticated distinctions. More specifically they have been reluctant to specify criteria that would allow one to clearly and *categorically* distinguish different kinds of nonliberal states *from a moral point of view*. Political philosophers, and most reasonable persons for that matter, know that nonliberal states are not all the same even when one assesses them through the moral lenses provided by a broadly liberal account. Yet they tend to gloss over a crucial distinction: whether such differences are categorical or just a matter of degrees. Why is that so? Many would be inclined to say that this outcome results from what might be called a persistent unease with respect to international political pluralism (see Ferrara 2015).

To put things in a slightly different way, one is tempted to conclude that while the internal political features of the members of international society vary extensively, *a great deal of liberal international political theory seems to work under the assumption that the only permissible way of organizing political society is according to a fully liberal democratic model*. Other models or ways of organizing political institutions, in this picture, would simply exhibit different degrees of "moral deficiency" depending on their institutional distance from the reference model (i.e., liberal democratic). Many, however, have found the latter to be a counterintuitive stance (here see Maffettone 2020; Jenkins 2010; Reidy forthcoming).

Clearly, an intuition just is what the word suggests, an intuition, not an argument. But one can provide a sketch of the basic elements that seem to speak in favor of its pro tanto plausibility, if not its appeal. The first element underpinning its plausibility derives from the black and white picture of international politics that would seem to be implicitly relied upon by the opposite conclusion. While "liberal democracies versus the rest" makes for a clear and uncompromising characterization of the international political landscape, it does not strike many observers as one that should easily be taken for granted. One reason not to do so is that it may be portrayed as exceedingly moralistic. Here, "moralistic" does not refer to a complex doctrine or kind of ethical fault, but to rather to an oversimplification of what seems to be, prima facie, a very complex moral problem. Put differently, one might legitimately suspect that a view like "liberal democracies vs. the rest" would run the risk of being moralistic, at least insofar as a central aspect of any view being moralistic is its implicit attempt to oversimplify something most people are bound to consider, on due reflection, very complicated morally and politically speaking. And there is no doubt that such moral and political complexity is a feature of the internal institutional organization of a political society. For such internal organization is bound to be the result of a host of interconnected factors, including the interaction between a culture, its values, and innumerable past historical circumstances.

Second, consider the range of political societies that populate the international political landscape. More specifically, think of, for example, the different kinds of nonliberal regimes that often appear in the news: North Korea, Singapore, China, Brunei, Jordan, Iran, Saudi Arabia, Vietnam, Cuba, and Morocco. As anyone minimally in touch with international politics would be able to recognize, the defining political features of the aforementioned polities are very diverse. This is not just in light of their formal constitutional make-up, though of course, the latter is important. To a significant extent, these differences seem relevant when we consider how these countries perform when one judges, even from a liberal perspective, how a given basic structure is organized. We often ask whether a given basic structure is just, whether government power is legitimately used within it, but also whether the way in which a society is run is compatible with developing central elements or aspects of the human experience, that is, the ability to flourish even according to a very thin account of what human flourishing might require.

And there is no denying that being placed in these different societies would allow us to gain radically different perspectives and thus give radically different answers about the extent to which such benchmarks pertaining to political morality are met, if at all. To see this in the plainest way possible, one might entertain the following thought experiment: would anyone be indifferent towards these different countries if they were forced to live in one of them for a significant length of time? The predictable answer would be "surely not." The question then is: why would that be so? Many would be inclined to believe that the nature of the answer would be of a qualitative kind, rather than simply of a quantitative kind, so to speak. Put differently, the answer would be guided by the intuition that these societies are categorically different and not simply, to a lesser or greater extent, imperfect versions of the only acceptable model of political organization, namely, the liberal democratic model. To put things in yet another way, the idea that the only morally distinctive feature of all the aforementioned political regimes is that they are, to a greater or lesser extent, all nonliberal may strike at least some as counterintuitive.

These observations, it should be stressed, are fully compatible with accepting the overall superiority of the liberal democratic model over other forms of internal political organization. Their point or purpose, rather, is to invite caution. For while one might justifiably entertain the idea that a given regime is superior to its alternatives, this does not, on its own, translate into an argument for the conclusion that all other kinds of regimes are equal and equally impermissible.

Peace, Political Autonomy, and Self-determination

Nonliberal societies are categorically different. This is, in itself, an interesting result, but were this to be the only outcome of the present discussion the reader might legitimately, given the purpose of this chapter, feel underwhelmed. The next question she is likely to ask is: what criteria could be used to distinguish these different categories of nonliberal political communities?

Two such criteria stand out as eminently plausible and widely accepted. They are based on two distinct political interests that citizens qua citizens have. The interests are political autonomy and peace. That citizens have, as individual citizens, an interest in peace is not particularly controversial. That they do can be easily gleaned from what the absence of peace would entail. Citizens also have an interest in political autonomy, and such interest is served by democratic government. A liberal democracy is a state controlled by a democratically elected government. At the very least, this suggests that the state, the apparatus that ultimately wields coercive force within its jurisdiction, is controlled by a body of persons that have been *authorized* to use coercive force on behalf of citizens, that is, the ones over which such force will ultimately be used. Seen in this light, coercive political arrangements are not simply "monopolized violence" but exhibit some link with the will of those over whom the coercion is exercised; democratic rule allows us to paint a picture of a political community in which citizens are considered agents, and their interactions as a scheme of willing cooperation rather than a system of command by force (see Stilz 2019).

What *is the best way* to express respect for citizens' interests in political autonomy and peace? The standard liberal answer is that respect for political autonomy is best expressed by democratic forms of government and peace by adherence to the standards of just war theory. These are, to be sure, not uncontroversial answers — answers that rely on specific assumptions. The first is that democratic government is not only a means to guarantee political equality but also, if not mainly, a system of government that protects political autonomy. The second is that just war theory's aim is to limit war and thus promote peace, and that, in the long run, it will achieve this better than available alternatives compatible with minimal justice requirements.

There are different institutional models of democracy (see Held 1996), and thus, different ways in which authorization to govern might be granted by citizens in a democratic country. Yet it is widely acknowledged that all such ways require specific *preconditions* to be in place. This is one of the key roles of the second criterion that has been used, in this chapter, to define a liberal democracy; namely, that to be a liberal democracy, a political society needs to guarantee the rights that are familiar from the constitutional tradition. To be clear, such rights serve more than this purpose alone and their justification does not rest exclusively on the particular function under consideration here. Yet, many would argue that one of their most important functions is indeed to guarantee the correct kind of background conditions for government to be not simply for the people but also of the people and by the people, to paraphrase Lincoln.

That the ideal of a liberal democratic polity is the best way to express respect for citizens' interests in political autonomy and peace is not necessarily to say, however, that it is the only possible way to do so. There *could be* other kinds of polities that, while not liberal democratic, are externally peaceful and have internal institutions such that the use of coercive power by the state over its citizens expresses a sufficient measure of respect for the value of political autonomy. Honing in on political autonomy, then, the key question is the following one: is there a way of exercising state power over citizens that is not the one displayed by liberal democratic institutions and that yet expresses a sufficient measure of respect for the value of political autonomy?

The short answer to the latter question is "yes." The slightly longer answer has often been thought to require a detour via the idea of self-determination (see Cohen 2006; Beitz 2009). The link between self-determination and political autonomy is relatively clear. In a self-determining political community, all basic political arrangements are not simply the result of the use of brute force by the state, but have a strong connection to the will of those on the receiving end of state power. Thus, the institutional set-up of a self-determining political community shows a sufficient measure of respect for citizens' interests in political autonomy.

A further key question, then, is: can a political society be internally self-determining in the absence of democratic institutions? Two basic intuitions seem to pull in opposite directions. Those who deny that there can be self-determination without democracy would simply point out that in the absence of democratic procedures, there is no clear way of knowing what the collective will of citizens is and no clear mechanism to guarantee that governments obey it were we to know what such will actually is (for a discussion see Buchanan 2003). Those who are in favor of the idea that even in the absence of a democratic system of governance there can be genuine self-determination often point out that to require a country to be liberal democratic would deny its citizens choice over one of the most significant aspects of their common political life: the choice of how to structure their political system at the most basic or fundamental level (see Altman and Wellman 2009). How can these competing arguments be balanced?

Those who are in favor of the conclusion that the citizens of *some* nonliberal states can be internally self-determining would certainly concede that the liberal democratic model of governance is *the most reliable one* to the extent that we are interested in knowing what citizens collectively want and make sure that government decisions stably track what citizens collectively want. And this is so for a number of reasons. First, because the rights that are familiar from the constitutional tradition and that are at the core of the liberal democratic model allow for *genuinely free* public deliberation by protecting freedom of conscience and expression and by permitting political dissent. Second, because a liberal democratic model of governance offers very clear incentives for governments to use the powers that citizens delegate to them, including the power to use coercive force through the state, in ways that track the collective will of the citizens themselves.

However, they would point out that, even accepting the aforementioned picture, it seems perfectly possible that there might be other, perhaps less reliable but still reasonably acceptable, ways of obtaining similar results, for example, Rawls' account of a decent consultation hierarchy in his *The Law of Peoples* (1999: 61). What is important is that, in a given political society, citizens are able to deliberate about, and subsequently establish, what they collectively want and that their government's decision-making generally tracks the outcome of their public deliberations.

What institutional features should a country have for it to be self-determining even if not democratic? There have been various proposals in the literature (see Blake 2013; Stilz 2019; Rawls 1999; Forster 2014). Whatever the details of the best account, all of them will include, at a minimum, the following provisions: (a) meeting the requirements of basic justice (perhaps in the form of respect for human rights); (b) respect for the main elements of the rule of law; (c) the existence of set of procedures for the formation and communication of the collective political will of citizens and thus protection for the individual rights (such as freedom of conscience and of expression) that are necessary preconditions for public deliberation; and (d) the ability to express dissent.

Pluralism, Sovereignty, and Political Realism

Given the two criteria that would serve the purpose of making categorical distinctions among nonliberal societies, and thus guide a liberal state's choice of foreign policy, one plausible conclusion seems to follow. The conclusion is that toleration (or, more specifically, "respectful toleration," see below) is reserved for externally peaceful countries that also express a sufficient measure of respect for the value of political autonomy through their internal institutional arrangements. In order to see the attractiveness of that conclusion, let us start by discussing a number of hypothetical objections. Some, for example, might be tempted to say that diversity in international society should be valued rather than tolerated or opposed. Others would be inclined to say that one of the core principles of international society, namely, respect for sovereignty, prevents us from adopting anything other than an accepting stance vis-à-vis nonliberal political societies. Others still would want to recall the importance of the realist tradition in international political life and argue that the question of a liberal state's foreign policy toward nonliberal societies is fundamentally mistaken ab initio.

Let us proceed by reversing the order in which these objections have been stated. Realists would be inclined to stress that a state's foreign policy is likely to be guided considerations of a nonmoral nature, that is, states, liberal or not, generally conduct their foreign policy by pursuing their rational interests (see Donnelly 2000). If one takes the latter to be a purely descriptive claim, then, it cannot be a valid objection to the account sketched in this chapter. The simple reason for that conclusion is that the basic question that is being addressed here is a normative one. More accurately, it is (largely) a *morally* normative question. If the Realist complaint is, instead, to be interpreted as a claim about prudential imperatives, then it is indeed more plausible. And yet far more controversial. Few deny that, in politics as in the everyday lives of individuals, prudential normative reasons have some role to play. What is far less obvious is what weight, or degree of priority, they should be given and why.

What about respect for sovereignty (here see Jones 2018: 223–242)? Much will depend on how one develops the objection. There seem to be two main ways to do so. On one interpretation, one ought to respect sovereignty because of what sovereignty might plausibly protect, from a moral point of view, namely, political pluralism in international politics. Yet if that is the objection, then, it is fundamentally misguided. By invoking sovereignty in this fashion, one would allow the concept to mask rather than illuminate the issue at hand. Unless one wants to adhere to some kind of relativistic view of political diversity, then, one is unlikely to find all forms of political pluralism worth protecting. After all, just as few believe that there is much to say in favor of torturing babies, most also think that there is not much to say, morally speaking, in favor of allowing, for example, Sudan to stay sovereign over its people and territory. If sovereignty is an instrument that is used to protect some forms of political pluralism, then, one ought to provide an account of which forms of political pluralism are worth protecting. And that is precisely the role that an account of international toleration is meant to perform. The account might be wrong about specifics, but invoking sovereignty will not really show why that might be the case.

On a different interpretation of the respect for sovereignty argument, the latter is not to be considered as playing a prevalently moral function. According to a well-known constructivist account, one can think of sovereignty as a "constitutive rule of the game" in international society (see Kratochwil 1995). Glossing over several complexities, it can be argued that if sovereignty is not taken seriously, then the "game of international politics" would cease to exist (at least as it is currently "played"). Yet, to believe that a given institution is a cornerstone for the functioning of a given political system is not to say much about the specific shape that the institution ought to take or might plausibly take for it to play the function we assign to it. Less abstractly, even if one accepts the constructivist objection in defense of sovereignty, the latter does not really tell in favor of a specific account of sovereignty. It certainly can be observed that one such account, "sovereignty as dominium," for example, suggests itself as the most obvious answer, but that does not exclude, ipso facto, other understandings. This is what relatively recent attempts at couching sovereignty as a "responsibility to protect (R2P)" have been, inter alia, aimed at: to provide a version of the institution of sovereignty that would still allow international political life to function as we know it and yet to which we might also be morally reconciled to.

Finally, let us consider the idea that one ought to accept and value diversity in international society. The latter can be presented as an argument concerning liberal self-understanding. Put differently, the claim might be that liberalism is standardly conceived of as a political philosophy that looks favorably upon diversity. Different stories can lead to that conclusion, but a concern for freedom or autonomy are generally seen as its main sources. If a liberal state is, internally, inclined to accept different ways of life, why shouldn't it do the same internationally? The basic answer, as convincingly argued by K.C. Tan (2000), is that there is a clear disanalogy between the two aforementioned set of circumstances. The first refers to diversity within a shared liberal political structure, the second to a form of diversity between distinct, some liberal some nonliberal, political structures. Those structures being, in nonliberal countries, often far less internally welcoming toward diversity than those in liberal states usually are. Diversity within the framework of liberal institutions affirms liberalism; diversity between different kinds of political institutions, some liberal some nonliberal, does not necessarily do the same. So, at the very least, liberals who are critical rather than enthusiastically happy with international political pluralism are not using double standards, nor are they being incoherent. Clearly enough, even internationally, many forms of cultural differences will certainly be judged very favorably by most liberal individuals and states, or at the very least, they will accept that their existence is not necessarily to be regretted. But the shape of the basic structure of a political society is not equivalent to shape of its aesthetic, literary, social, or culinary traditions. To be liberal just is to believe that individuals are entitled to specific prerogatives (i.e., that they have certain rights) and political systems that deny individuals those rights will never be the object of indifference much less approval from a liberal perspective.

Have we gone too far? Having concluded that diversity about political institutions is not something that liberals are bound to look favorably upon or be indifferent to, haven't we come full circle and determined that the only foreign policy of a liberal state toward a nonliberal society ought to be opposition? The answer is "no," and, predictably, the idea of toleration is central to the possibility of finding additional options.

International Toleration and Liberal Foreign Policy

At least one element is shared among most analyses of the concept of toleration (see Cohen 2004; Galeotti 2002, for authoritative discussions of the concept). First, that to tolerate something, one needs both to disapprove of it and find some reason to override that disapproval. In addition, moving from concept to conception, the main task of an account of toleration is often taken to be that of offering a justification for the fact that when one tolerates something opposition to what is tolerated is in fact overridden. More precisely, when toleration does occur, our opposition to what is tolerated remains intact, yet we find reasons that override, rather than cancel, our opposition and thus refrain from acting upon it. In other words, when we tolerate something, we clearly oppose it and continue to find that thing wanting in some fundamental or key way. But we are also brought to the conclusion that it would be inappropriate to interfere with it, and thus we must find something of value *in allowing* the tolerated action, agent, or belief continuing their existence undisturbed, so to speak. How can these insights be applied to liberal foreign policy? One potential implication would be that it is possible to conceive of a limited range of cases in which liberal states might not approve of the political make-up of a given society but might nonetheless decide to tolerate it.

A first account of the circumstances of international toleration would portray the latter as merely "putting up" with the object of toleration. It would understand the main justification for it as either prudential or at the very least consequentialist in nature. For example, some would argue that, especially within the remit of international political life, it is implausible to believe that only *morally* normative reasons apply. The normative reasons that apply to international political life ought to, at the very least, include prudential considerations. This is especially the case when matters of war and peace are at stake. To illustrate, a liberal state might be within its rights in opposing a nonliberal state given that, hypothetically, it does not allow its citizens any input in the political process and denies them even the most basic individual rights. Yet, the liberal state in question might come to the conclusion that its outright opposition would be ineffective, and in fact even damaging to the welfare of both its citizens and the citizens of the nonliberal state. Outright opposition might, for example, make the likelihood of war higher than it would otherwise be. Thus, even though the liberal state might be justified in openly opposing the nonliberal one, it might decide to adopt a more tolerating stance for fear of the potential consequences (both for the well-being of its own citizens and of that of the citizens of the "tolerated country"). The case of North and South Korea comes to mind. Here, a tolerant foreign policy might take the form of a mere absence of interference. Whether this kind of reasoning is going to be purely prudential or whether it is a form of consequentialism guided by a desire to avoid extreme implications for human welfare will, in real life political, be difficult to ascertain (much will depend, it might be argued, on the priority that is given to internal welfare). What is worth noting, given our purposes, is that the kind of toleration that is envisaged in these cases is based on a clear form of regret; regret that existing political circumstances do not allow a liberal state to be more explicit about the moral faults of a given nonliberal society.

Can there be reasons for tolerating a class of nonliberal societies other than on prudential or consequentialist grounds? Are there circumstances in which toleration might involve respect instead of merely signaling the need to put up with something that it would be too costly (morally or politically) to alter? Answering these questions is a complex task. For what has to be shown is that a nonliberal society is both deficient in some important ways and yet worthy of a kind of toleration that comes with respect and recognition for its standing in international society. There are different avenues to argue for that particular conclusion.

To being with, recall that in the previous part of the chapter, a brief sketch was offered of the institutional features of a political society (one might call it, adapting Rawls' expression, a decent political society) that is nonliberal and yet internally self-determining and externally peaceful. The fact that a decent nonliberal political society, ex hypothesis, is externally peaceful takes care of one of the two core moral commitments of liberal states. A decent nonliberal society shows some form of fundamental respect for human life by abiding by the principles of just war theory. It does not consider the use of military force as an acceptable means to its political ends. On this score, a decent nonliberal political society would simply be "equivalent" to a just liberal polity. A decent nonliberal political society is also internally self-determining. It is not a democratically governed country but its system of institutions displays a commitment to basic justice through its respect for human rights and has clear mechanisms for the formation of the collective will of its citizens and for government accountability. In other words, a decent nonliberal society is structured in such a way that its institutions show a sufficient measure of respect for citizens' interest in political autonomy and peace.

In this picture, liberal states can reason in the following way: while a decent nonliberal political community is not fully just, its adherence to political principles and practices that lead to external peacefulness and to a sufficient respect for the political autonomy of citizens provide reason enough to liberal states for refraining from any kind of interference (see Reidy 2010). This is, it should be noted, a different kind of predicament compared to noninterference based on prudential or consequentialist reasons: the justification for noninterference is here deontological and sees decent nonliberal societies as *entitled* to a specific kind of treatment, not simply as receiving such treatment for contingent reasons. However, even if one accepts that much, it is still unclear whether a decent nonliberal society is entitled to a form of toleration that includes respect by liberal states and their recognition of its equal standing in international society, and if so, why.

There are at least three different avenues to establish the latter conclusion. To move forward, let us concentrate on citizens' interest in political autonomy. As we have seen, even a decent nonliberal society is in some sense deficient given that it is not fully liberal democratic. But the nature of this deficiency, the way in which we portray it, may vary and is clearly important for the general structure of an account of the grounds for international toleration.

One option is to portray a decent nonliberal society as engaged in a similar project compared to a liberal one, but to be less successful at it, so to speak. A tolerant but respectful stance toward a decent nonliberal society is possible because liberal states recognize that decent nonliberal political communities are travelling in the same moral political direction, though they are doing so by walking a different, and less attractive, path. The respectful toleration that decent nonliberal societies are owed, in this picture, is akin to the respect that might be owed to those who, thoughtfully and credibly, make a mistake in good faith about something that is deemed to be important (here see Stilz 2019). If the mistake is indeed made in good faith, and if it does not push the agent too far off from what is believed to be the correct answer, then one might be justified in respecting their conscientious efforts.

A second kind of approach would instead rely on the idea of reasonable disagreement. It would start by observing that international society is characterized by strong forms of pluralism about political organization. In part, this is due to reasons that one is unlikely to find attractive. Colonialism and imperial conquests, class struggles, wars, economic exploitation, etc., all come to mind. And it seems rather patent that the outcomes of such historical interactions would not incline many observers to judge the resulting pluralism as welcome. But that is not the only option. One can also ask whether something akin to the *reasonable* pluralism of world views that is generated by liberal institutions within liberal political communities can obtain internationally. For example, one might conjecture, for it can only be a conjecture, that some of this pluralism has more benign origins. To illustrate, one might highlight the way in which religious and cultural traditions that have their roots in the very distant past have slowly interacted with political movements and have, over time, shaped the structure of local political institutions. One might, in addition, come to believe that something like the burdens of judgment apply to these processes of historical evolution and that at least some versions of political organization, some nonliberal societies, owe their internal make-up to choices that one might deem all things considered wrong, but not unreasonable (see Avila 2007). In this picture, liberal states respectfully tolerate at least some nonliberal political communities because they come to realize that their political institutions are reasonable attempts at protecting the basic interests of their citizens. Such attempts are mistaken from the perspective of a liberal society and from that specific perspective liberals are allowed to hold on to some regret for how things are. However, within the bounds of international society, they, perhaps begrudgingly, recognize the equal standing of a particular class of nonliberal political communities.

A third option would alter the nature of the reasoning used to determine the appropriate foreign policy for a liberal state. So far, the argument that has been developed relied on a specific methodology to assess answers to the basic question set out at the beginning of the chapter. It started by outlining what might plausibly be taken to be some of the key commitments of a liberal political community. It then implicitly assumed that its foreign policy would be guided, for the most part, by the adoption of the liberal democratic model of governance as a form of (qualitative) selection tool. There is, however, a (partly) more indirect strategy. The strategy, following Rawls's approach in his *The Law of Peoples* (1999), would start by asking what kind of principles of justice for international relations would be adopted by liberal democratic peoples. Once these principles are in place, it would then ask whether there are nonliberal political communities that can abide, for the right reasons, by the same principles of justice liberals have given to themselves. In this picture, what principles liberal peoples decide to select will be crucial to determine the extent to which nonliberal peoples can abide by them. Yet, such principles might be, for reasons that are independent form a desire to be tolerant (see Maffettone 2015, 2020), weak enough for some non-liberal political communities to adhere to them. Assuming the plausibility of this picture, one would then have to concede that those nonliberal peoples would be, from a public political perspective, beyond reproach. They would be entitled to equal standing in international society because they would simply follow, for the right reasons, the very same principles of international justice that liberal peoples have selected as their preferred account of the normative bases of international politics. Liberal peoples would still tolerate those nonliberal societies since they would be entitled to believe that those societies are clearly wrong when it comes to the shape of their internal political institutions. However, from the perspective of international political morality, those political communities would not be at fault: liberals would lack a public basis for condemning them.

So far, we have explored three justificatory strategies in favor of what we might call respectful international toleration. Is there a way to select one over the others? In part, this will depend on the kinds of trade-offs one is inclined to make. All three strategies have a shared goal and face a similar kind of tension: they want to offer reasons for respectful toleration while still holding on to liberal commitments. The first strategy seems to score well on the affirmation of the superiority of the liberal paradigm, but then seems relatively weaker in justifying respect for nonliberal societies. The second is instead much more credible as a justification for respectful toleration. However, it suggests a problematic relativization of the standing of liberal political morality: liberal democracy cannot be portrayed as the best form of political organization from a universal perspective since other kinds of political organizations can also be seen as reasonable. The third and final one tries to offer some form of reconciliation. It combines a clear justification for respectful toleration since some nonliberal political communities turn out to be beyond reproach internationally (they abide by a liberal account of international justice). Yet, it does so without drifting toward relativism. In this picture, one would hold the following view: liberal democracy is the best form of domestic political organization, but is not required for membership in good standing of international society.

Summary

The chapter addressed one basic question: how should the foreign policy of liberal democratic states be structured with respect to nonliberal and nondemocratic ones (nonliberal for short)? It was argued that the answer depends on the nature of the nonliberal political communities under consideration. International toleration will be appropriate, for prudential reasons, in a limited number of cases. Difficult political circumstances may lead liberal political communities to not interfere with morally abhorrent nonliberal societies. However, a more respectful kind of international toleration is also possible provided that nonliberal political communities display two important features, namely, a sufficient measure of respect for their citizens' interests in political autonomy and peace. Internally self-determining and externally peaceful nonliberal political societies are entitled to respectful toleration.

Future Directions

The main goal of international political morality is to combine peace and justice, and international toleration is an attempt at fostering such goal. If that is indeed the case, then, all liberals have reason to think harder about international toleration, and whatever the preferred account of it, to promote it as an important way of engaging nonliberal societies.

Conclusion

The chapter addressed one basic question: how should the foreign policy of liberal democratic states be structured with respect to nonliberal and nondemocratic ones (nonliberal for short)? It was argued that the answer depends on the nature of the nonliberal political communities under consideration. International toleration will be appropriate, for prudential reasons, in a limited number of cases. Difficult political circumstances may lead liberal political communities to not interfere with morally abhorrent nonliberal societies. However, a more respectful kind of international toleration is also possible provided that nonliberal political communities display two important features, namely, a sufficient measure of respect for their citizens' interests in political autonomy and peace. Internally self-determining and externally peaceful nonliberal political societies are entitled to respectful toleration. They are, following Rawls, equal members in good standing of international society and liberals are to respect their freedom and independence.

References

Altman A, Wellman CH (2009) A liberal theory of international justice. Oxford University Press, New York
Avila M (2007) Defending a law of peoples: political liberalism and decent peoples. J Ethics 11:87–124
Beitz C (2009) The moral standing of states revisited. Ethics Int Aff 23(4):325–347
Blake M (2013) Justice and foreign policy. Oxford University Press, New York
Buchanan AB (2003) Justice, legitimacy, and self-determination: moral foundations for international law. Oxford University Press, Oxford
Cohen AJ (2004) What toleration is. Ethics 115(1):68–95
Cohen J (2006) Chapter 3: Is there a human right to democracy? In: Sypnowich C (ed) The Egalitarian conscience: essays in Honour of G.A. Cohen. Cambridge University Press, Cambridge
Donnelly J (2000) Realism and international relations. Cambridge University Press, Cambridge
Doyle MW (2006) One world, many peoples: international justice in John Rawls's the law of peoples. Perspect Polit 4(1):109–120
Dumbrell J (2009) The US–UK special relationship: taking the 21st-century temperature. Br J Polit Int Rel 11(1):64–78
Ferrara A (2015) The democratic horizon. Cambridge University Press, Cambridge
Forster A (2014) Peace, justice and international order: decent peace in John Rawls' the law of peoples. Palgrave Macmillan, London
Galeotti AE (2002) Toleration as recognition. Cambridge University Press, Cambridge
Held D (1996) Models of democracy, 2nd edn. Polity Press, Cambridge
Hoyt PD (2000) The 'rogue state' image in American foreign policy. Glob Soc 14(2):297–310
Hudson VM (2005) Foreign policy analysis: actor-specific theory and the ground of international relations. Foreign Policy Anal 1(1):1–30
Jenkins M (2010) Political liberalism and toleration in foreign policy. J Soc Philos 41(1):112–136

Jisi W, Ran H (2019) From cooperative partnership to strategic competition: a review of China–U.S. relations 2009–2019. China Int Strategy Rev 1:1–10

Jones P (2018) Essays on toleration. Rowman & Littlefield International, London

Kratochwil F (1995) Chapter 2: Sovereignty as dominium: is there a right of humanitarian intervention? In: Mastanduno M, Lyons G (eds) Beyond Westphalia? National Sovereignty and international intervention. Johns Hopkins University Press, Baltimore

Krotz U (2002) National role conceptions and foreign policies: France and Germany compared. Program for the Study of Germany and Europe, Minda de Gunzburg Center for European Studies, Harvard University, Working paper 02.1. http://aei.pitt.edu/63712/

Maffettone P (2015) Toleration, decency and self-determination. Philos Soc Crit 41(6):537–556

Maffettone P (2020) International toleration: a theory. Routledge, London

O'Reilly KP (2007) Perceiving rogue states: the use of the 'rogue state' concept by U.S. foreign policy elites. Foreign Policy Anal 3:295–315

Rafanelli L (2019) Promoting Justice Across Borders. Polit Stud https://doi.org/10.1177/0032321719875402

Rawls J (1971) A theory of justice. Harvard University Press, Cambridge

Rawls J (1999) The law of peoples. Harvard University Press, Cambridge

Reidy D (forthcoming) Rawls, law-making and liberal democratic toleration: from Theory to Political Liberalism to The Law of Peoples. Jurisprudence

Reidy D (2010) Human Rights and Liberal Toleration. Can J Law and Jurisprudence 23(2):287–317.

Stilz A (2019) Territorial sovereignty: a philosophical exploration. Princeton University Press, Princeton

Tan KC (2000) Toleration, Diversity, and Global Justice (Penn State Press, 2000)

Toleration and Tolerance in a Global Context

24

Vicki A. Spencer

Contents

Introduction 456
Confucianism 457
Islam 461
"Hinduism" 465
Buddhism 469
Summary and Future Directions 472
References 473

Abstract

Although toleration is often seen as a modern and quintessential liberal value that is distinctly Western in origin, scholars are increasingly challenging that perception. As long as religious and moral differences have existed amongst people, the question of how one ought to treat them has existed. Non-Western intellectual traditions offer a range of approaches that have often been far more inclusive than conformity to the standard Western conception of toleration as principled non-interference enables. This chapter explores four non-Western intellectual traditions – Confucianism, Islam, "Hinduism," and Buddhism – and sketches some of their approaches to diversity in theory and practice. Each tradition shows the importance of toleration when irreconcilable views exist, but they differ over the extent of self-restraint they recommend, their justifications for toleration, and the forms it assumes in practice. Each also offers to varying degrees a more appreciative and magnanimous approach to difference, called in this chapter tolerance. Rather than the "hands-off" state neutrality that liberal advocates of toleration often support, or the communal and hierarchical toleration of the Ottoman Empire, other traditions consider the state has a legitimate role to play

---

V. A. Spencer (✉)
Politics, School of Social Sciences, University of Otago, Dunedin, New Zealand
e-mail: vicki.spencer@otago.ac.nz

© The Author(s), under exclusive licence to Springer Nature Switzerland AG 2022   455
M. Sardoč (ed.), *The Palgrave Handbook of Toleration*,
https://doi.org/10.1007/978-3-030-42121-2_45

in the patronage of diverse sects as a means not just to tolerate, but to honor, them. This chapter shows there is more than one pathway to a tolerant society, but what unites these traditions with contemporary liberal proponents of toleration is their common desire to combat intolerance.

> **Keywords**
>
> Toleration · Tolerance · Pluralism · Confucianism · Islam · Ottoman Empire · Hinduism · Buddhism · Emperor Ashoka

Introduction

In contemporary Western philosophy, toleration is defined as the principled non-interference in others' opinions, beliefs, and practices that one morally disapproves of or, at least, dislikes. Due to this objection component it is distinguished from mere indifference; the person who tolerates needs to care about her point of difference with those views or practices she tolerates. The principled nature of the objection also means it differs from mere forbearance or "putting up" with difference. One's self-restraint is motivated by a principled belief in noninterference that overrides the objection to the belief or practice that one holds. Not all forms of engagement and interference are therefore excluded. Toleration prohibits coercive mechanisms of conformity through state interference, but it does not rule out persuasion and rational engagement or critique between individuals in the private sphere. It is also always limited; although the limits vary among philosophers, neither intolerance nor direct harm to others is tolerated. Defined in this way, toleration is often seen to be a quintessential liberal value (Spencer 2018a; Cohen 2004; Nicholson 1985).

Yet the idea that toleration is a uniquely liberal value and one that is often thought to have originated during the seventeenth-century European Reformation has been increasingly challenged in recent years. Cary Nederman (2000, 2016) along with other scholars of medieval European thought have firmly established an extensive body of literature existed during the Middle Ages in favor of toleration (Shogimen 2018), while Rainer Forst (2011) traces the term *tolerantia* to the ancient Roman philosopher Cicero in around 46 BCE. And just as seventeenth- and eighteenth-century European philosophers from John Locke (1983) to Voltaire (1994) were fully aware of the greater toleration accorded under the Ottoman Empire to non-Muslims than was enjoyed by many Christian denominations in most European jurisdictions at the time, Western political theorists are again beginning to pay greater attention to non-Western models and ideas of toleration (Spencer 2018c, Stepan and Taylor 2014, Kymlicka 1996).

By examining the concept of toleration within a global context, this chapter focuses on four traditions of thought: Confucianism, Islam, "Hinduism," and Buddhism. It is impossible here to offer a comprehensive examination of any one of these traditions, never mind all four. Each has a long and complex history and is characterized by a multitude of interpretations and practices. The objective is the far narrower one of sketching some of the resources in these different traditions on which a more global approach toward toleration could be based. As Forst (2011, p. 2) writes, "toleration is a general human concern and is not confined to any particular epoch or culture. For as long as there has been religion, the problem of people of different beliefs and the problems of heretics and nonbelievers has existed." It is the way these different traditions have approached the cultural and religious heterogeneity in their midst that opens the pathway to expand our understanding of different conceptions of toleration even when the term itself might not be employed in a particular tradition.

As Michael Walzer (1997) argues, there are many pathways to a tolerant society; the standard Western conception of toleration is only one path. If we are to widen our field of vision, the appropriateness of exclusively applying the contemporary Western definition is therefore questioned. For the sake of clarity, I will continue to use the term "toleration" in the standard way with the proviso that I will include pragmatic and instrumental justifications for its adoption that are sometimes excluded due to the requirement to have a principled belief in noninterference in the normative definition above. By contrast, I will use the term "tolerance" to denote a more positive approach to difference at both the individual and institutional level. Tolerance, in this usage, entails a belief that something positive, like the relinquishing of bigotry, acceptance, understanding, or a broadening of one's perspective, is potentially gained through one's encounter with difference. It does not always mean that disagreements or differences are eliminated, but the strong objection component characteristic of toleration is lacking as tolerance requires seeing other's beliefs and practices as part of an ethically valuable life.

It might be objected from the outset that textual evidence and practices in these traditions could just as easily be employed to support intolerance. Yet the same would be the case in any comprehensive review of the history of Western philosophy and politics. As Wendy Brown (2006) also argues, even liberal toleration has often gone hand-in-hand with Western intolerance in the international sphere. The crude dichotomy between the tolerant West and intolerant Others is open to serious challenge. An examination of non-Western approaches reveals a rich array of resources in a wide variety of intellectual traditions across the globe to combat intolerance.

Confucianism

Confucian philosophy is over 2500 years old. *The Analects*, a record of Confucius' (551–479 BCE) ideas and teachings, is seen as the fundamental text in the tradition. His ideas were developed further by Mencius (c. 379–288 BCE) and Xunxi (c. 340–245 BCE) whose teachings together constitute the classical tradition of Confucianism, the main focus of this section. Central to Confucian thought is a perfectionist political philosophy in which politics and morality coincide; the Zhou dynasty during which Confucius lived was suffering from extensive political disorder and corruption and the solution he offered was to combine Zhou's system of rites with a new ethics that fostered a particular conception of the moral person (Liu 2006; Chan 2003).

The idea that Confucianism is perfectionist in nature so a Confucian state ought to endorse and promote a particular conception of the good life might immediately disqualify it for some liberals from being an appropriate candidate for the basis of a tolerant state. Many liberals believe a neutral state that is characterized by the state acting like an umpire between competing conceptions of the good life represents the embodiment of toleration in political terms. But such a conclusion would be far too quick. The extent to which a state can be morally neutral is a highly contested issue, but even advocates of neutrality admit that intolerance is unacceptable. At the very least, a neutral state therefore fosters the virtue of toleration, although admittedly rarely in a proactive way.

An important distinction needs to be drawn between a strong and weak perfectionist state. Strong perfectionism employs coercive force to impose the state's conception of the good life on its citizens. Laws against homosexual acts and those that limit marriage to a union between a heterosexual couple are examples of strong perfectionism with the state interfering in the private morality and activities of its citizens. Weak perfectionism, by contrast, tends to encourage or discourage certain forms of behavior rather than use coercive mechanisms. Examples include government advertisements discouraging smoking or excessive drinking and the provision of funds to the arts and museums to ensure a state has a diverse array of cultural activities without complete reliance on market forces. Toleration of diverse moralities and practices is entirely compatible with weak perfectionism since toleration does not exclude disagreement or rational persuasion. But weak perfectionism also opens the possibility to promote tolerance with some liberal theorists maintaining quintessential liberal values like freedom and diversity require proactive protection from the state (Raz 1986; Taylor 1985). The relevant issues, therefore, are the kind of values Confucianism fosters and its teachings on the use of force.

The highest virtue that Confucians aspire to is the embodiment of *ren*, which is variously translated as benevolence, compassion, love, or humanity. But no single English word fully captures its complexity; as the expression of humanity, *ren* encompasses a number of different virtues from self-examination and self-improvement to caring for and respecting others. It also entails the abilities to sympathize and empathize with others. Confucius believed this moral quality is innate in every human being; however, it requires people to engage in self-cultivation and constant learning to nurture it. For politics, it means that the state and its leaders should have an active role in ensuring the welfare and well-being of their people (Zhang 2010; Chan 2003).

State leaders should not, however, employ the coercion characteristic of strong perfectionism. JeeLoo Liu (2006, p. 50) maintains that the Confucian Golden Rule – "Do not impose on others what you yourself do not desire" – promotes a policy of noninterference by not assuming one has knowledge of what is good for others. Leading by example and moral education in accord with a weak perfectionism are the recommended pathways toward encouraging others to lead a virtuous life, not through the use of coercive legal mechanisms. As Confucius said, "Guide them by edicts, keep them in line with punishments, and the common people will stay out of trouble but will have no sense of shame. Guide them by virtue, keep them in line with the rites and they will, besides having a sense of shame, reform themselves" (Lau 1995, 3.3).

There are clearly right and wrong ways to behave in Confucian morality. Such judgment can lead to a sense of superiority in determining the amount of virtue others possess, and Joseph Chan (2008) indicates that there was no concept of equality between different cultures and ethical systems in the classical Chinese political tradition. Confucius judged, for example, that "Barbarians with their rulers are inferior to Chinese states without them" (Lau 1995, 3.5). Far from the kind of relativist doctrine that claims all cultures are equally valid, Confucius insisted that everyone would benefit from the cultivation of *ren* and by practicing the rites. Yet this insistence is consistent with the Western conception of toleration that neither rules out disagreements nor a sense of superiority in those who tolerate others they consider wrong or whose views and practices they morally disapprove of.

Importantly, too, in Confucian philosophy this moral hierarchy does not mean barbarians are considered less human; they possess the innate capacity of *ren* and the ability to practice the rites. "Men are close to one another by nature," Confucius taught, "They drift apart through behaviour that is constantly repeated" (Lau 1995, 17.2). If members of barbarian states developed Confucian virtues and practiced the rites, Chan (2008) maintains that they would then be regarded as equals. Moreover, in relations with barbarian states, Confucius insisted on the continued practice of virtuous behaviour in the same way Confucians were expected to behave virtuously toward their fellow Chinese: "While at home hold yourself in a respectful attitude; when serving in an official capacity be reverent; when dealing with others give of your best. These are qualities that cannot be put aside, even if you go and live among the barbarians" (Lau 1995, 13.19).

The use of persuasion, over violence, is a central Confucian edict of governance. When the disciple "Chi K'and Tzu asked Confucius 'What would you think if, in order to move closer to those who possess the Way, I were to kill those who do not follow the Way?' Confucius answered, 'In administering your government, what need is there for you to kill? Just desire the good yourself and the common people will be good. By nature the gentleman is like wind and the small man is like grass. Let the wind sweep over the grass and it is sure to bend'" (Lau 1995, 12.19). The self-restraint in the use of coercion that characterizes toleration is therefore recommended when something is improper (Yu 2018). In a discussion between two disciples in Book 19 of the *Analects* "Tzu-hsia says, 'You should make friends with those who are adequate and spurn those who are inadequate.' In reply, "Tzu-chang said, 'That is different from what I have heard. I have heard that the gentleman honours his betters and is tolerant of the multitude and that he is full of praise for the good while taking pity on the backward'" (Lau 1995, 19.3).

Toleration has its limits as it does in liberal philosophy. Kam-por Yu (2018) nevertheless indicates that even in the case of evil, criticism ought to be directed at the deed and not at the person. "To attack evil," Confucius said, "as evil and not evil of a particular man, is that not the way to reform the depraved?" (Lau 1995, 12.21).

Despite the aim of harmony in Confucian philosophy, criticism over important issues when conducted in this manner is acceptable. Confucius was himself critical of the actions of the political leaders of his time for their failure to adhere to Zhou's system of rites and therefore act as exemplars in attaining *ren*. Later, Mencius rejected in strong terms the two rival schools of thought in his time, the philosophy of Yang Zhu and that of Mozi, emphasizing the importance of combating their ideas in speech: "I wish to follow in the footsteps of the three stages in rectifying the hearts of men, laying heresies to rest, opposing extreme actions, and banishing excessive views. I am not fond of disputation. I have no alternative. Whoever can, *with words*, combat Yang and Mo is a true disciple of the sages" (Lau 2003 3B:9; Chan 2003). At the same time, however, Mencius admonished those who castigated former followers of Yang and Mozi, and instead counseled that "When they come to us, accept them" (Lau 2003, 7B:26; Ivanhoe 2000). Focusing on the deed, rather than the person, Yu (2018) argues, opens the pathway toward forgiveness when people transform.

It is a Confucian objective to help others live virtuously. According to Confucius, "a benevolent man helps others to take their stand in that he himself wishes to take his stand, and gets others there in that he himself wishes to get there" (Lau 1995, 4.30). It is through practicing the rites that one takes one's stand, but blind obedience to the rites was not Confucius' intention. He understood that new circumstances required revision of social conventions and a plurality of ethical judgments by individuals was necessary in different situations (Chan 2003; Liu 2006). Despite the importance placed on respecting one's parents, in *The Classic of Filial Piety* of the Han dynasty Confucius clarifies that neither respect nor obedience means following all of one's father's commands. Rather, he states, "'In the face of whatever is not right, the son cannot but remonstrate with his father'" (cited in Madsen 2008, p 8). The same advice is repeated with respect to wives and their husbands in *The Classic of Filial Piety for Women* (Madsen 2008).

Salient differences nonetheless exist between the Confucian and modern liberal conceptions of toleration. While the latter is often seen to be based on a right to negative liberty that equates freedom with a lack of constraints on one's words and deeds unless one directly harms another physically, Confucian toleration is founded on sympathy, which entails a duty to care about the consequences of one's deeds and words (Chan 2008; Yu 2018). Thus, Confucius recommends not only self-restraint in the use of coercive measures but also in criticism of small errors. Failure to do so, he says, will only "bring ruin to great plans" (Lau 1995, 25.27). One ought never despise others or demean, humiliate, or slander them. Civility, respect, and understanding toward and for others need to temper one's self-righteousness in condemning others with whom one disagrees or whose deeds one disapproves of (Lau 1995, 17.24). The intolerance displayed in treating others contemptuously and without sympathy, should not be tolerated (Yu 2018).

Such self-restraint, as Yu (2018) argues, goes beyond the standard Western conception of toleration which allows criticism and disapproval in speech without any clearly stated limitations. Since it is only coercive mechanisms of constraint that are prohibited, critics like Anne Phillips (1999) indicate that toleration and contempt can easily coexist. Yet some liberal thinkers have also been attuned to the need to engage in self-restraint beyond the non-coercion entailed in toleration. The emphasis Confucius placed on civility and self-examination when we meet others with whom we disagree is similar, for example, to John Locke's (1975, 4.14.4, 4.16.2) advice to be "careful to inform our selves, [rather] than constrain others" and to cultivate "*Friendship, in the diversity of Opinions*" while avoiding treating others "as obstinate and perverse." And Locke (1983) stipulated that a magistrate should not extend toleration to churches whose leaders failed to encourage their congregation to adopt a tolerant disposition toward other churches (Spencer 2018b). Thus, despite their many differences, both Confucius and Locke understood the need to promote a deeper conception of tolerance as a more positive and proactive virtue in order to create a tolerant society.

In Confucianism, this positive approach to diversity is further supported by the virtue of *kuan* that Yu (2018, p 219) indicates is often translated as "tolerance," although "it literally means being broad-minded, bighearted, open, and accommodating. It is highly positive and not something chosen reluctantly as a result of compromise" because a higher-order value restrains one's desire to interfere in a belief or practice that one disapproves of. Being open-minded and accommodating to diverse perspectives are regarded as essential requirements of an enlightened ruler. "Multiplicity," Yu (2018, p 220) adds, "is regarded as good. As a result, it is a virtue to preserve the existing variety and a greater virtue to promote further transformation." Importantly, though, the aim of this transformation is not elimination of the difference, but "a transformation of the underlying unity to accommodate the new element" through a "magnanimous learning process" (Angle 2012, p 79). Tolerance along with the self-restraint characteristic of toleration coexist as essential values in Confucian philosophy.

Islam

Both values are equally evident in Islamic philosophy and practice. The youngest of the traditions to be examined here, Islam dates from the seventh century, although it has a long history of tolerating diversity, one that European thinkers during the seventeenth and eighteenth centuries admired as a feature of the Ottoman Empire. The Ottomans were highly successful for centuries in ruling over a vast landmass that at the height of their empire linked the three continents of Europe, Asia, and Africa, and incorporated a diverse array of cultures and religions. Karen Barkey (2018) indicates that a policy of pragmatic toleration toward non-Muslim religious groups was firmly established by the fifteenth century, but even as the Ottomans conquered the Balkans in the early fourteenth century a policy of accommodation, known as *istimalet* (securing goodwill), was followed to gain the indigenous population's cooperation while incorporating churches and monasteries into the Ottoman administrative system. The Ottomans were not neutral about their own religion as Barkey (2018) shows; the empire was undeniably Muslim, but the sultans chose to institute a policy of positive inclusion. Ottoman toleration was thus permissive, but it was not equal.

The extent of this permissiveness and the level of noninterference non-Muslim communities enjoyed are evident in surviving imperial documents. One example scholars point to is the Treaty of Galata negotiated with an envoy from Galata after the conquest of Constantinople in 1413. In its text, Sultan Mehmed II (1451–1481) committed to protect "'their religious customs and fundamentals, in whatever way the ceremonies and fundamentals of their religion have so far been customarily enacted'" ensuring that "'their churches shall remain in their hands,'" and "'they shall worship according to their customs.'" Also, in accord with the noninterference required in the concept of toleration, the treaty guaranteed that no one would be "'converted to Islam without his consent'" (cited in Barkey 2018, p 91).

The privileges non-Muslims enjoyed under Ottoman toleration were nonetheless limited. The contractual arrangements contained in The Treaty of Galata stipulated, for example, that in exchange for the sultan not turning their churches into mosques the Christians had to agree not to "'ring gongs or church bells'" or erect new churches (cited in Barkey 2018, p 91). The negotiated agreement was unquestionably based on an asymmetrical power relationship in which the weaker minority needed to make certain concessions to the dominant power not to face persecution (Halbertal 1996). Restrictions on non-Muslims varied in different periods and parts of the empire, but there were typically codes of conduct regulating dress, housing, and transportation. Jews and Christians were forbidden to build taller houses than Muslims, wear Muslim dress, or ride horses which would display their wealth. At times, sultans issued edicts on these matters such as the 1631 edict of Sultan Murad IV in which he declared that

> infidels are not to mount a horse, wear a sable fur, fur caps, European silk velvet, and satin. Infidel women are not to go about in the Muslim style and manner of dress and wear "Paris" overcoats. Thus they are to be treated with contempt, made submissive, and humbled in their clothes, and style of dress. For some time, however, these rules have been neglected. (cited in Barkey 2008, p 120–21)

The sultan's intention was not only to demarcate Muslim and non-Muslims, but also to confirm the inferiority of non-Muslims and even "humiliate" them. The concept of toleration does not preclude contempt, but it does restrict one's ability to interfere in the beliefs and behaviors of those being tolerated. Ottoman practice not only fell short of the state neutrality many contemporary liberals support, but also on the level of noninterference the concept of toleration prescribes in theory. In practice, however, discriminatory measures have been no less a feature of toleration regimes in the West. In France under the Edict of Nantes (1598), Protestants could only build new churches in certain locations and under license, and the Toleration Act (1689) in England granted freedom of religion to nonconformist Protestants in exchange for their loyalty to the king but not to Catholics. It is also evident from the sultan's lament that these rules were not always enforced. In reality, Barkey (2018) indicates that the Ottomans were often either unable to implement such regulations or lacked the will to enforce them; new synagogues were, for example, built, and negotiations to adjust and reassess such rules were commonplace.

The protection Ottoman toleration provided non-Muslims is further evident in the willingness of the empire to accept refugees fleeing persecution in Christendom. Jews had experienced what some have referred to as a "Golden Age" in Muslim Spain. When they were forced to leave during the Spanish *reconquista* in the fifteenth century they found a safe haven in the Muslim-majority Ottoman empire as did those who migrated from Portugal, Italy, and Central Europe (Barkey 2008; Afsaruddin 2018; Shah-Kazemi 2010). A letter written by the Rabbi Isaac Tzarfati in 1454 is testament to the advantages Ottoman toleration bestowed on Jews compared to their treatment in Christian Europe. In response to his friends seeking help, the Rabbi urged them to leave "'the tyrannical laws, the compulsory baptisms and the banishments that occur in Germany'" for Turkey. "'Is it not better for you to live under Muslims than the Christians?'" he asked, claiming that "'Here every man may dwell at peace under his own vine and fig tree. Here you are allowed to wear the most precious garments. In Christendom, on the contrary, you dare not even venture to clothe your children in red or in blue, according to our taste, without exposing them to the insult of beaten black and blue, or kicked green and red...leave this accused land forever'" (cited in Barkey 2018, p 92). Non-Muslims were *tolerated* by the Ottomans in an unequal relationship, but such treatment was a considerable advantage for them over the persecution they experienced in Christendom.

The freedom and privileges granted to non-Muslims were at the same time more extensive than the toleration of individual non-Muslims in the practice of their faith due to the semi-autonomous status of their communities, what scholars refer to as the *millet* system. Three *millets* were established in the fifteenth century in addition to the Muslim one: the Greek Orthodox community was recognized in 1454, the Armenian Orthodox in 1461, and the Jews unofficially in the same period (Barkey 2008). The Ottomans incorporated the existing ecclesiastical structures into the empire's fiscal and administrative system which enabled taxes to flow to the center while empowering local religious leaders to conduct their own affairs according to their own laws and customs. The community leaders acted as the intermediaries between the state and the communities and were responsible for the collection of state taxes. Penial issues remained under the jurisdiction of the Islamic courts, but civil and family issues including births, deaths, and marriages were settled by local religious courts (Barkey 2008). Unlike the separation of church and state characteristic of liberal toleration, Ottoman toleration reinforced religious power over civic matters.

Historical precedents existed in early Muslim history for the Ottoman's communal approach to diversity. Both religious and tribal diversity existed in Medina when the Prophet Muhammed emigrated there from Mecca. In what is known as the Pact or Constitution of Medina of 623, the Prophet recognized and legitimated all the various Muslim tribes in Mecca and Medina as well as the Jews of different tribes and the polytheists, who Reza Shah-Kazemi (2010) indicates formed the majority of the population. Each enjoyed religious and legal autonomy while they simultaneously comprised a single community based on a commitment to ensure peaceful coexistence and to assist each other if attacked by outsiders. This pact then provided the basis for the agreement that the second caliph 'Umar ibn al-Khattab (584–644) reached with the Christian population in Jerusalem in 638 in which he guaranteed protection of their lives, goods, and churches as long as they did "'not initiate anything [to endanger] the general-security'" (cited in Sachedina 2007, p 65).

In return for the protection of their properties and religious institutions, non-Muslims were expected to pay a poll tax to the Muslim authorities. It had been commonplace for Arabic tribes to impose a tax on aliens and this historical institution was adopted by early Islamic jurists and continued by the Ottomans. In the early period, the tax was levied on adult men for the protection provided by the authorities in lieu of having to join the army. If they joined the army, they were not required to pay and, in one famous example, the second caliph refunded the tax to an Arab Christian tribe he was unable to protect from Byzantine aggression. It was a progressive form of taxation with the poor and dependents exempt from payment and the amount increasing in proportion to one's wealth. It is also noteworthy that poor non-Muslims were provided stipends from the state treasury (Sachedina 2007; Afsaruddin 2018; El Fadl 2002). There is nonetheless evidence that at certain times the poll tax became onerous, and Barkey (2008) indicates that to avoid it whole communities sometimes converted to Islam under the Ottomans. Asma Afsaruddin (2018) further notes that after the ninth century it was increasingly seen as a sign of inferiority.

Scholars indicate a pragmatic element to the flexibility and accommodation that characterized the Islamic approach to diversity. In the early years, Muslims were numerically in a minority position that meant non-Muslims had a certain degree of bargaining power (Sachedina 2007). The sheer size of the Ottoman empire and its economic interests in ensuring taxes flowed to the center meant incorporating local institutions and the cooperation of local leaders was highly strategic. Peaceful coexistence benefitted both the tolerated non-Muslims and the state (Barkey 2018, 2008). Yet there are reported instances of sultans showing a genuine interest in the diversity within their empire. Mehmed II is said, for example, to have visited a Christian church during mass and inquired about Christian laws and rites. Barkey (2018) also relates the story of Sultan Süleyman the Magnificent (1520–1566) when asked about exterminating the Jews. In response, he pointed to a vase of diverse flowers to indicate that while each flower is unique and beautiful in itself by complementing each other they created a greater beauty through their interaction. And since each of the nations he ruled over contributed to the wealth and reputation of his empire, he considered it wise to maintain that situation.

Textual evidence in the Qur'an shows that tolerant principles and practices are foundational in Islam. Freedom of religion is firmly protected in verse 2:256 which decrees "There is no compulsion in religion" (also see Khalidi 2008, 18:29). In other verses (Pickthall 1992, 30:22, 5:48), human diversity is legitimated as a divine creation and the right to judge over religious disputes and the question of salvation is placed exclusively in the hands of the Lord (Pickthall 1992, 30:59, 22:67). While delegitimizing coercive measures toward non-believers, the Prophet counsels Muslims to "endure patiently" and not "grieve" for nonbelievers or be "in distress." Muslims disagree with non-Muslims on the right path, but consistent with the concept of toleration the Prophet only considered persuasion through "fair exhortation" and the use of reason as appropriate means to convince them to change their path (Pickthall 1992, 16:126–127; Afsaruddin 2018; Shah-Kazemi 2010, 173–176, El Fadl 2002, 15–18, 99–100).

Afsaruddin (2018) argues, however, that the concept of tolerance better suits the Qur'anic ethos due to its endorsement of pluralism. The Arabic word *al-tasamuh*, usually translated as tolerance, does not mean merely to tolerate people but to be magnanimous toward one another. Qur'an 5.48, moreover, declares human diversity is God's will:

> For every community We decreed a law and way of life. Had God willed, He could surely have made you a single community, but in order to test you in what He revealed to you. So vie with one another in good works! (Khalidi 2008)

Qur'an 49:13 further explains the purpose of this diversity is to encourage people to "to come to know one another" (Khalidi 2008), thus going well beyond toleration. The Muslim Emperor Akbar, who ruled India in the late sixteenth century, is perhaps the best known early exemplar of this principle. Not only did he guarantee freedom of religion for his largely non-Muslim subjects, he promoted dialogue among Sikhs, Hindus, Jains, Jesuits, Zoroastrians, and Carvaka atheists in weekly meetings and ensured his court was replete with non-Muslim advisers, intellectuals, and artists. He is thus credited with developing the foundations for a form of state neutrality; albeit one that embraces religious diversity in public spaces rather than the French *laïcité* model that attempts to eliminate it in favor of secularism (Bilimoria 2018; Sen 2005).

"Hinduism"

Many scholars (Mocka 2018; Shukla-Bhatt 2018; Bilimoria 2018; Davis 2008; Parekh 2007) argue that tolerance, rather than toleration, also better captures the Hindu approach to religious diversity. Such is the nature of its pluralism that the term "Hinduism" itself needs some clarification as it is a relatively recent and European construction that misleadingly implies there is a single religion with a common body of beliefs and practices. Yet no single text or Hindu canon exists and there is no formal organizational structure that dictates an authoritative doctrine or set of practices. Hindus can even be atheists and, in the Indian Constitution, Jains, Buddhists, and Sikhs are categorized as Hindu. The term "Hindu" is, in fact, geographically rooted and originally referred to all those living east of the River Indus. It is often used even today to refer to anyone living in India, although at a certain historical point it also came to refer to people participating in a common "civilization," or way of life, of which religion is only one part (Parekh 2007; Doniger 2014).

The porousness and openness of the Hindu religion makes it additionally challenging to define. Throughout its history, new gods, goddesses, rituals, practices, and texts have appeared. Purushottama Bilimoria (2018, p 161) notes that it had no difficulty, for instance, in incorporating with certain adaptations "both the Buddha and Jesus (with Mary) within its ever-expanding pantheon of 333,003+¼ gods!"

Scholars agree, however, that there are certain shared ideas and practices among Hindus, despite the caveat that not all Hindus accept each of them. While acknowledging the challenges this multifariousness poses, the Indian Supreme Court settled on the following definition: "Acceptance of Vedas with reverence [which distinguishes it from Jainism and Buddhism]; recognition of the fact that the means or ways to salvation are diverse and realization of the truth that the number of gods to be worshiped is large, that indeed is the distinguishing feature of Hindu religion" (cited in Dasarathi et al. 2017). Pluralism is therefore at its definitional core in legal terms.

This pluralism can be traced to the oldest known Hindu text, the *Rig Veda* ("Knowledge of Verses"), which dates from around 1500 BCE and is the first of three Vedas. There is a multiplicity of gods: Indra is the god of rain and the king of gods, Varuna is the god of oceans and moral law, Yama is the god of death, Agni is the god of fire, etc. A situation would determine which god an individual would pray to. During a drought, for example, a worshipper would pray to Indra and then Agni during a sacrifice (Shukla-Bhatt 2018; Doniger 2014). Yet, at the same time, a deeper unity underlies this diversity. In verse 1.164.46, the poet explains that the different gods are all manifestations of a single truth: "They say it is Indra, Mitra, Varuna, Agni, and also it is the winged, well-feathered (bird) of heaven [=the Sun]. Though it is One, inspired poets speak of it in many ways. They say it is Agni, Yama, Mātariśvan" (Jamison and Brereton 2014). "The One" therefore assumes multiple forms, although these divinities are understood simultaneously to exist as different entities each with their own individual characteristics and deeds attributed to them. Neelima Shukla-Bhatt (2018, p 143) indicates that the verse is therefore interpreted not as an erasure of difference in favor of sameness, "but as the recognition of a deeper unity, which is distinct from uniformity."

This unity, or oneness, underlying Hindu pluralism was more explicitly developed in the philosophical collection of texts, the *Upanishads*, also known as the Vedenta, and written over a thousand-year period from 200 BCE. A regularly cited passage employed to demonstrate this foundational monism relates a teacher's response to a student repeatedly inquiring how many gods really exist. The teacher initially replies, "Three and three hundred, and three and three thousand," next, "Thirty-three," then, "Six," then, "Three," then, "Two," then, "One and a half," and finally, "One" (Olivelle 1995, 3.9.1). This oneness is not, however, confined in the *Upanishads* to the gods; a number of passages and images propagate the monist view that a single universal being (often called *Brahman*) permeates all living creatures. The image of smoke emanating from a fire in which wet wood was used occurs, for instance, three times as a metaphor for all things emanating from the "great being" (Bilimoria 2018, p 161). In two other famous passages, a father explains to his son the all-pervading reality first with a group of varied vessels that have clay in common and then with salt dissolved in water. The salt cannot be seen but it nonetheless exists in every drop of the water (Shukla-Bhatt 2018).

The idea that we cannot see reality in its entirety is particularly salient in the grounding of the concept of Hindu tolerance. Since *Brahman,* or God, is infinite, he can never be grasped completely by the finite human mind. Human beings are situated in a certain time and place and they therefore see reality from their particular standpoint. The Hindu parable of the six blind men that also appears in Jain and Buddhist texts captures this many-sided nature of reality. The six men who had heard of an elephant coming to their village wanted to touch it. As each touched a different part of the elephant, they described its characteristics differently. Each was correct as a wise man passing by informed them, but each invariably had only a partial perspective of the ultimate reality of the elephant. Bhikhu Parekh (2007) maintains that the same is the case with God who reveals himself in different forms at various points in history depending on the needs of particular societies. All religions possess truth but the truths each reveal differ; none provides "the final and definitive knowledge of God" (Parekh 2007, p 339). It follows, Parekh argues, that all religions deserve not merely to be tolerated, but to be equally respected.

The respect Hindus have extended toward members of different religions in history is extensively documented. A large Christian community, for instance, existed in Kerala by the fourth century, Zoroastrians and Muslims arrived in India from the seventh century, and Jews as early as the fall of Jerusalem in 70 CE with each enjoying freedom of religion. Yet the freedom of conscience central to Hindu thought does not translate into neutrality of governance in a liberal sense with the state acting as an umpire between competing and bounded religions. Jews, for instance, were granted a self-governing district in the Hindu kingdom of Cochin (Parekh 2007; Sen 2005), while Hindu kings in Nepal's Kathmandu Valley actively encouraged and patronized Buddhist sites and traditions as well as Hindu ones from the late fourteenth century to the eighteenth century. Situated in close proximity to each other, Anne Mocka (2018) indicates the kings of the region were highly competitive also in their religious patronage, which they saw as integral to their role as kings. Unlike liberal neutrality and toleration, there was genuine appreciation for and celebration of both the Hindu and Buddhist religions by state authorities with the king "an active, often enthusiastic, participant in religious matters, cultivating the presence of consecrated divine beings in his realm and increasing the scope and grandeur of public religious activity" (Mocka 2018, p 125).

But while there are many notable cases that exemplify Hindus' recognition of the legitimacy of other religions, Parekh (2007) draws a salient distinction between equal respect and the idea of equal worth that sees each religion possessing equal moral and spiritual excellence. Eternal damnation does not await non-Hindus and different religious methods are deemed valuable to those who practice them, but a hierarchy of value exists in central Hindu texts between different pathways to the highest state, usually called *moksa* or *nirvana*. Krishna's teaching to Arjuna on the battlefield in the *Bhavagad Gita* – a seven hundred verse scripture and part of the epic *Mahabharata* dated around the second century BCE – illustrates this point. In an oft-quoted passage to exemplify Hindu tolerance and echoing the idea of the "one in the many," Krishna declares that whatever god people follow, they are following him. Richard H. Davis (2008) nonetheless shows that this inclusivism is combined with a hierarchy of practices. In reviewing yoga practices, for instance, Krishna indicates the most accomplished "yogin" recognizes and contemplates his divine nature and thus "attains to the peace that lies in me, beyond *nirvana*" (Van Buitenen

1981, 6.14–15). And in a later passage, sacrifices to Krishna unreservedly provide the most direct path to him and are therefore the most spiritually effective and rewarding:

> Even they who in good faith devote themselves to other deities really offer up their sacrifices to me alone, Kaunteya, be it without proper rite. For I am the recipient of all sacrifices and their master, though they do not really recognize me and therefore slip. To the Gods go they who are avowed to the Gods, to the ancestors (*pitr*) go they who are avowed to the ancestors, to the ghouls (*bhuta*) go those who are avowed to the ghouls, to me go they who sacrifice to me. (Van Buitenen 1981, 9.23–25)

This kind of hierarchal ranking, also evident in the *Upanishads*, can lead in Vedantic philosophy to a badge of inferiority for those who worship anything other than the "Absolute" so that toleration, rather than the appreciation associated with tolerance, might be a more apt description of the Vedantic position (Minor 1982). It is, at the very least, a matter of dispute among scholars. Shukla-Bhatt (2018) argues, by contrast, such ranking need not lead to the moral disapproval and endurance associated with toleration when differences in the material world are perceived as a mosaic that is synthesized in an underlying universal and divine reality. She also shows how the pluralist interpretation encapsulated in the concept of "the one in the many" has been handed down through the ages in devotional lyrics of poet-saints written in vernacular languages and widely spread to the general populace throughout India by traveling performers, unlike the largely inaccessible classics written in the ancient language of Sanskrit.

Hindu tolerance is nevertheless limited by its very tolerance. Hindus have particular difficulty with accepting those who wish to proselytize and engage in missionary activities with Christian missionaries still viewed suspiciously today. Parekh (2007) argues that this stance is similar to the liberal argument against tolerating the intolerant. But while co-existence has been common to both, the Hindu position differs from the liberal one that accepts persuasion as valid and guarantees freedom of expression. By contrast, Hindus perceive an intolerance in the attempt of missionaries to work actively to destroy alternative religions by attacking and ridiculing them and attempting to convert their adherents rather than stopping at the point of claiming perfection. Indeed, the behavior of bigoted Christian missionaries provides ample evidence for this position and led the pluralist German philosopher and Lutheran Minister, Johann Gottfried Herder (1744–1803), to have similar qualms about the role of Christian missionaries in the late eighteenth century (Spencer 2012). This critical stance, moreover, does not mean that Christians are necessarily unacceptable in all circumstances. While the Swami Vivekananda (1863–1902), founder of the Ramakrishna mission, was, for instance, highly critical of such missionaries in his lecture series in Detroit in 1894, he reportedly welcomed Christians who were true servants and missionaries of Christ's teachings toward the downtrodden (Ray and Ray 2018). Not all forms of speech are, however, tolerable.

The pluralist view that there are many worthwhile paths to God and the exclusivist view that there is only one and its adherents are duty-bound to save all others are competing and irreconcilable beliefs. In the interests of peaceful coexistence and

24 Toleration and Tolerance in a Global Context

non-coercion the pluralist is therefore bound to revert to toleration of the exclusivist view she disapproves of over the positive acceptance of difference associated with tolerance. This conundrum permeates the thought of Sarvepalli Radhakrishnan (1888–1975), a central figure in propagating the idea of Hindu tolerance in the West as a statesman, philosopher, and the president of UNESCO. Radhakrishnan emphasized the idea of "the one in the many" as a basis for universal acceptance. Yet Robert N. Minor (1982) indicates his "tolerance" only accepted and appreciated other religions to the extent that they fitted his conception of religion. He taught, for example, that religions had to relinquish their partisan behavior and consider the entire world, not just their own communities. This position accords with the liberal position toward the intolerant, but it does mean that on this issue Radhakrishnan displayed toleration rather than tolerance.

Buddhism

The same quandary permeates the Buddha's teachings in the Tipitaka, a central text in Theravada Buddhism, the dominant form of Buddhism practiced in South and South-east Asia and the focus of this section. Scholarly texts on Buddhism commonly portray the Buddha's style of teaching as an open and respectful one. Peter Harvey (2013, p 30), for example, maintains that "He did not mind if others disagreed with him, but censured misinterpretations of what he taught. He showed even-mindedness when gaining disciples" and in the case of one general recommended he should continue to support Jain monks in addition to his desire to support Buddhist ones (Harvey 2013; Gard 1962). He emphasized, too, that one should not follow a particular path because of tradition or what some authoritative or persuasive figure considered best, but by following one's own inner judgment (Harvey 2013), a perspective with which liberal philosophers would readily agree. Yet, like Confucius, the Buddha goes further than the negative freedom often associated with liberal toleration by encouraging civility from his monks even in the face of those who would disparage the Buddha and their principles: "you should not," he said, "be angry, resentful or upset on that account," but "you must explain what is incorrect" (Walshe 1995, 1.5). Rational persuasion, rather than coercion or disparagement of others, was the method of disputation the Buddha recommended to his monks.

At the time of the Buddha's life (c. fifth to fourth century BCE) there were many competing sects and philosophical perspectives with numerous religious teachers wandering eastern India so disputations were commonplace in public parks and halls set up by laypeople (Gard 1962). Far from the indifference evident in a live-and-let attitude or the positive acceptance and celebration of other views associated with tolerance that Western scholars and journalists often attribute to Buddhism, Ben Schonthal (2018) indicates that numerous stories in the Tipitaka show the Buddha on a mission to prove the incorrectness of opposing views and convert his opponents to his teachings. Indeed, the Tipitaka is replete with "wrong views" the Buddha denounces. Just in his teaching on The Supreme Net, which begins with the above advice to his monks, he identifies 62 wrong views. Those who hold them are said to do so due to craving, confusion, stupidity, corruption by pleasure or envy, or evasiveness and, in the latter case, he disparagingly refers to the ascetics and Brahmins as "Eel-Wrigglers" (Walshe 1995, 2.28). In conclusion, the Buddha draws an analogy between the minds of the ascetics and Brahmins and fish trapped and caught in a fisherman's net (Walshe 1995, 3.72).

When dealing with views the Buddha deemed wrong there is therefore a degree of disapproval, and certainly dislike, evident. His self-restraint is, however, principled rather than pragmatic due to his views on kindness and non-violence toward all living creatures. His teachings therefore exhibit the standard Western conception of toleration. Schonthal (2018, p 184) nonetheless provides a more critical perspective arguing that "what seems to be recommended is a stance of guarded vigilance against the adoption of any wrong views that might impede one in understanding and following the Buddha's way to nirvana" and thus "exiting what would otherwise be an endless cycle of births and rebirths." Wrong views are therefore "potentially hazardous." Thus, the kind of epistemological humility evident, for instance, in Locke's case for toleration is absent. Locke was a devoted, albeit unorthodox and minimalist Protestant and he wrote *The Reasonableness of Christianity* (1695) to persuade people to that path. But he considered spiritual issues to be a matter of faith and not knowledge. Truth over spiritual matters is ultimately discoverable but only on Judgement Day, and salvation is a matter for God to decide, not human beings (Spencer 2018b).

By contrast, as the awakened one, the Buddha is portrayed in the Tipitaka as the one who possesses access to the truth regarding the right path toward nirvana. There is thus an asymmetrical power relationship between the Buddha and others, while Locke (1975, 4.16.4) saw us all as living in a state of "mutual Ignorance" with human fallibility a fundamental hallmark of the human condition. Locke strongly criticized the intolerant and he thought one ought to subject one's religious beliefs to reason. He also, like the Buddha, thought some views "absurd" (Locke 1983, p 46), but Locke's epistemology meant he did not engage in the kind of strong condemnation of "wrong views" regarding one's chosen spiritual path that is found in the Tipitaka (Spencer 2018b). The sense of superiority in the Buddha's position therefore means it conforms to a hierarchical conception of toleration. Due to his principled self-restraint it is nevertheless compatible with the broad, standard Western definition. Schonthal (2018, p 184) further indicates that although the Buddha adopts an epistemological discrimination in his determination of wrong and right views, it was not accompanied with "a posture of social discrimination, positive or negative." Although he strongly disagreed with others, like Locke, he considered it a matter for individuals to decide which path they would take, not for him or a magistrate to influence them coercively.

The Tipitaka is, however, only one source of early Buddhist views and a more proactive embracing of difference exists in the inscriptions left behind by India's first Buddhist emperor, Ashoka Maurya. Ashoka reigned over most of the Indian subcontinent from 268 until 232 BCE and issued a series of edicts that were inscribed into rocks, cave walls, and stone pillars. He was not a Buddhist at the time of his succession and he appears to have converted about ten years into his reign. The edits issued following his conversion address a range of topics from administrative justice and morality to dedications of shelter for the monks in caves and Ashoka's activities as a lay Buddhist. The Indian historian Romila Thapar (1961) indicates that the edits fall into two categories: personal inscriptions to Buddhist monks and nuns, and public pronouncements that he intended his subjects to abide by. The Fourteen Major Rock Edicts placed along the border of the empire and the Pillar Edicts placed in important cities and on roadsides belong in the second category. They also appear to have been read out at public meetings and dispersed throughout the empire in various forms to disseminate the emperor's instructions (Thapar 1961).

Two of the Major Rock Edicts address the topic of religious diversity with the seventh explicitly guaranteeing freedom of religion in the emperor's declaration that he "wishes members of all faiths to live everywhere in his kingdom" (Nikam and McKeon 1959, p 51). Rajeev Bhargava (2014) indicates that some scholars maintain that due to similarities between the existing religious sects at the time, with Jainism and Buddhism both offshoots of Hinduism, Ashoka's tolerance would not have been controversial. Yet Buddhists disagreed at many levels with Vedic values that meant they rejected, among other things, the killing of animals in ritual sacrifices and the caste system. Notably, however, Ashoka did not thereby state he would merely endure the diversity in his kingdom; he appears to have welcomed and appreciated it and encouraged the intermingling of members of different sects throughout his empire. That he considered it necessary to issue this edict, moreover, suggests it was a necessary reassurance to his non-Buddhist subjects.

Rock Edit Twelve further extends Ashoka's policy of tolerance by promoting equal respect for all faiths:

> The faith of others all deserve to be honoured for one reason or another. By honouring them, one exalts one's own faith and at the same performs a service to the faith of others. By acting otherwise, one injures one's own faith and also does disservice to that of others. For if a man extols his own faith and disparages another because of devotion to this own and because he wants to glorify it, he seriously injures his own faith. (Nikam and McKeon 1959, p 51–52)

The kind of disparagement that we saw Hindus objected to from Christian missionaries, but liberals often accept in the interests of a right to freedom of expression, was therefore not tolerated by Ashoka. This intolerance was considered essential to ensure that different faiths were not merely tolerated but honored with this more demanding requirement necessitating more self-restraint. Thus, as was also evident in Confucian philosophy, not all speech was deemed acceptable. Ashoka stipulated that one needs to guard "one's speech to avoid extrolling one's own faith and disparaging the faith of others improperly or, when the occasion is appropriate, immoderately" (Nikam and McKeon 1959, p 51). There is an important recognition here that harm is inflicted upon others through disrespectful and immoderate speech and it should therefore not be tolerated. But, as Bhargava (2014) indicates, the civility Ashoka's edict displays goes far beyond toleration by requesting his subjects equally to desist from immoderate praise of their own faith.

Ashoka's recognition that all faiths have valuable attributes lay the groundwork for his proactive tolerance. He was sufficiently wise to include a pragmatic element in his appeal to the self-interest of worshippers to protect the integrity of their own faith by not acting dishonorably. But the central key he identified to fulfill his desire to create a tolerant society was the need for his subjects to understand and know each other's faiths:

> King Priyadarśī ["the benevolent one"] desires men of all faiths to know each other's doctrines and to acquire sound doctrines. Those who are attached to their particular faiths should be told that King Priyadarśī does not value gifts or honors as much as growth in the qualities essential to religion in men of all faiths. ... The objective of these measures is the promotion of each man's particular faith and the glorification of Dharma. (Nikam and McKeon 1959, p 52, 26)

The meaning of the final sentence and, in particular, the term "Dharma" is subject to some debate among scholars. In Indian philosophy, the term *dharma* has had various ethical, metaphysical, and religious meanings (Gard 1962). The question that begs, however, is whether Ashoka was imposing the Buddhist understanding of it in which case, rather than tolerance, a strong case could be made that he only *tolerated* other religions to the extent that they conformed to Buddhist principles, which the state privileged and protected above all others (Schonthal 2018).

There is no doubt that in other edicts Buddhist principles were privileged in the same manner that Christian principles are currently privileged in many Western states with the recognition, for example, of Christian festivities as public holidays but not those of other religions. In Pillar Edict Five, for instance, Ashoka ordered that certain animals could not be killed at all and some others could not be castrated, branded, or killed on Buddhist holy days, and in Rock Edit Nine he was highly critical of ceremonies with no discernible utility unlike the ceremony of the Dharma. But, at the same time, he did not impose the Buddhist principle of complete abstinence of killing all living creatures. Nor did he abolish capital punishment, although he gave some reprieve on it being carried out. Thapar (1961) further indicates that Ashoka cannot be accused of partiality toward Buddhist leaders over Hindu Brahmans, treating them with the same respect in the edicts. The ceremony of Dharma, for instance, includes "liberality" to both and they are mentioned as equals to be respected when "Dharma" is explained in Rock Edict Four (Nikam and McKeon 1959, 46, 31). The edicts were designed to promote moral values and Ashoka assigned officers everywhere with the task of spreading and promoting "Dharma." His state was thus a perfectionist one, although persuasion rather than regulation was his stated preferred method to inculcate his moral values (Thapar 1961). And while it would have been impossible for those values not to have reflected Buddhist principles at all, he intentionally adapted them to be sufficiently broad to promote respect and civility toward other faiths in his dominions.

Summary and Future Directions

This sketch of Confucian, Islamic, Hindu, and Buddhist approaches to diversity has shown that they have far more in common with the standard Western definition of toleration than is often assumed. Going beyond toleration, all of the traditions, moreover, exhibit varying degrees of the more proactive appreciation of and engagement with diversity characteristic of tolerance. It does not follow that they are necessarily incongruent with Western perspectives. An examination of various approaches toward diversity in Western philosophy would likewise show that some past thinkers and many contemporary theorists have advocated a greater embracement and recognition of difference than the standard conception of toleration enables. Nonetheless, toleration has admittedly been the main preoccupation of Western liberal philosophy, while tolerance has played a more prominent role in, for instance, the Hindu tradition. Unlike the Western tradition of toleration, the self-restraint required in Confucian philosophy and Ashoka's edicts also extends further to disbar disparagement and denigration of others and their views. There is a far greater recognition in these non-Western traditions of the harm that can be inflicted on people through speech than has existed in the liberal tradition. The justifications in favor of toleration and tolerance also differ between traditions and yet in their common attempt to overcome intolerance these theories possess a family resemblance that unites them.

The failure of a philosophical and/or political tradition to adopt the contemporary liberal idea of toleration does not thereby mean it promotes intolerance. The privatization of religion might be the most suitable model for the West, but it is illegitimate to insist on its uniform application when alternative models potentially create greater respect for diverse others and may be better suited to different contexts. In the period of the Ottoman Empire, its sultans were also far more inclusive of difference than Western leaders. A more informed cross-cultural approach to conceptions of toleration and tolerance is important, however, not only to overcome misperceptions often perpetuated in the West and to lay the groundwork for more respectful international relations. Non-Western theories and models provide many insights from which we can learn to do better than merely tolerate diverse others. The fact that traditions which have focused on tolerance have not been immune to strains of intolerance is also instructive for Western theorists attempting to develop more positive approaches to accommodate difference. A positive appreciation of difference is, moreover, not always possible; when irreconcilable conflicts exist, toleration is equally essential to our peaceful coexistence if we wish to respect those differences and have the ability to deny tolerance to the intolerant.

References

Afsaruddin A (2018) Tolerance and pluralism in Islamic thought and praxis. In: Spencer VA (ed) Toleration in comparative perspective. Lexington Books, Lanham, pp 99–117

Angle S (2012) Contemporary Confucian political philosophy: toward progressive Confucianism. Polity Press, Cambridge

Barkey K (2008) Empire of difference: the Ottomans in comparative perspective. Cambridge University Press, Cambridge

Barkey K (2018) The Ottomans and toleration. In: Spencer VA (ed) Toleration in comparative perspective. Lexington Books, Lanham, MD, pp 81–98

Bhargava R (2014) Beyond toleration: civility and principled coexistence in Ashokan edicts. In: Stepan A, Taylor C (eds) Boundaries of toleration. Columbia University Press, New York, pp 173–202

Bilimoria P (2018) The limits of intolerance: a comparative reflection on India's experiment with tolerance. In: Spencer VA (ed) Toleration in comparative perspective. Lexington Books, Lanham, pp 159–177

Brown W (2006) Regulating aversion: tolerance in the age of identity and empire. Princeton University Press, Princeton

Chan J (2003) Confucian attitudes toward ethical pluralism. In: Madsen R, Strong TB (eds) The many and the one: religious and secular perspectives on ethical pluralism in the modern world. Princeton University Press, Princeton, pp 129–153

Chan J (2008) Territorial boundaries and Confucianism. In: Bell D (ed) Confucian political ethics. Princeton University Press, Princeton, pp 61–84

Cohen AJ (2004) What toleration is. Ethics 115(1):68–95

Dasarathi A, Neelakantan M, Khanna V (2017) What does it mean to be a Hindu? How the Supreme Court of India has defined Hindus. Citizens for Justice and Peace https://cjp.org.in/what-does-it-mean-to-be-a-hindu/. Accessed 10 Nov 2020

Davis RH (2008) Tolerance and hierarchy: accommodating multiple religious paths in Hinduism. In: Neusner J, Chilton B (eds) Religious tolerance in world religions. Templeton Foundation Press, West Conshohocken, pp 360–376

Doniger W (2014) On Hinduism. Oxford University Press, Oxford

El Fadl KA (2002) The place of tolerance in Islam. Beacon Press, Boston

Forst R (2011) Toleration in conflict: past and present. Cambridge University Press, Cambridge

Gard RA (1962) Buddhism. George Braziller, New York

Halbertal M (1996) Autonomy, toleration, and group rights: a response to Will Kymlicka. In: Heyd D (ed) Toleration: an elusive virtue. Princeton University Press, Princeton, pp 106–113

Harvey P (2013) An introduction to Buddhism: teachings, history, and practice, 2nd edn. Cambridge University Press, Cambridge

Ivanhoe PJ (2000) Confucian moral self cultivation, 2nd edn. Hackett, Indianapolis

Jamison SW, Brereton JP trans (2014) The Rigveda: the earliest religious poetry of India, vol. 1. Oxford University Press, Oxford

Khalidi T trans (2008) The Qur'an. Viking, London

Kymlicka W (1996) Two models of pluralism and tolerance. In: Heyd D (ed) Toleration: an elusive virtue. Princeton University Press, Princeton, pp 81–105

Lau, CD trans (1995) The analects. The Chinese University Press, Hong Kong

Lau, CD trans (2003) Mencius, rev. edn. The Chinese University Press, Hong Kong

Liu JL (2006) An introduction to Chinese philosophy: from ancient philosophy to Chinese Buddhism. Blackwell, Oxford

Locke J (1975) An essay concerning human understanding, Nidditch P H ed. Clarendon Press, Oxford

Locke J (1983) A letter concerning toleration, Popple W trans, Tully J ed. Hackett, Indianapolis

Madsen R (2008) Confucian conceptions of civil society. In: Bell D (ed) Confucian political ethics. Princeton University Press, Princeton, pp 3–19

Minor RN (1982) Sarvepalli Radhakrishnan on the nature of "Hindu" tolerance. The Journal of the American Academy of Religion 50(2):275–290

Mocka A (2018) Tolerance in Nepal Mandala: communal relations and religious patronage in Malla-era Kathmandu. In: Spencer VA (ed) Toleration in comparative perspective. Lexington Books, Lanham, pp 121–139

Nederman G (2000) Worlds of difference: European discourses of toleration, c. 1100–c. 1550. Pennsylvania State University, University Park

Nederman G (2016) Medieval toleration through a modern lens: a "judgmental" view. Oxford Studies in Medieval Philosophy 4:1–26

Nicholson P (1985) Toleration as a moral ideal. In: Horton J, Mendus S (eds) Aspects of toleration: philosophical studies. Methuen, London, pp 158–173

Nikam NA, McKeon R trans (1959) The edicts of Asoka. Chicago University Press, Chicago

Olivelle P trans (1995) Upaniṣads. Oxford University Press, Oxford

Parekh B (2007) Hindu theory of tolerance. In: Bilimoria P, Prabhu J, Sharma R (eds) Indian ethics: classical traditions and contemporary challenges, vol 1. Ashgate, Aldershot, pp 337–349

Phillips A (1999) The politicisation of difference: does this make for a more intolerant society? In: Horton J, Mendus S (eds) Toleration, identity, and difference. Macmillan, Basingstoke, pp 126–145

Pickthall M (1992) The meaning of the glorious Koran. David Campbell Publishers, London

Ray S, Ray AB (2018) Truth Swami Vivekananda taught the US at Detroit – lasting significance of his teachings. Prabuddha Bharata 123(8):587–596

Raz J (1986) The morality of freedom. Clarendon Press, Oxford

Sachedina A (2007) The Islamic roots of democratic pluralism. Oxford University Press, Oxford

Schonthal B (2018) The tolerations of Theravada Buddhism. In: Spencer VA (ed) Toleration in comparative perspective. Lexington Books, Lanham, pp 179–196

Sen A (2005) An argumentative Indian: writings on Indian history, culture, and identity. Farrar, Straus, and Giroux, New York

Shah-Kazemi R (2010) Tolerance. In: Sajoo AB (ed) A companion to Muslim ethics. I.B. Taurius, London, pp 167–186

Shogimen T (2018) William of Ockham and medieval discourses on toleration. In: Spencer VA (ed) Toleration in comparative perspective. Lexington Books, Lanham, pp 3–21

Shukla-Bhatt N (2018) The one in the many in the songs of poet-saints of medieval India: a cultural stance on tolerance. In: Spencer VA (ed) Toleration in comparative perspective. Lexington Books, Lanham, pp 141–158

Spencer VA (2012) Herder's political thought: a study of language, culture, and community. University of Toronto Press, Toronto

Spencer VA (2018a) Introduction. In: Spencer VA (ed) Toleration in comparative perspective. Lexington Books, Lanham, pp ix–xxii

Spencer VA (2018b) Human fallibility and Locke's doctrine of toleration. In: Spencer VA (ed) Toleration in comparative perspective. Lexington Books, Lanham, pp 41–59

Spencer VA (ed) (2018c) Toleration in comparative perspective. Lexington Books, Lanham

Stepan A, Taylor C (eds) (2014) Boundaries of toleration. Columbia University Press, New York

Taylor C (1985) Atomism. In: Taylor C (ed) Philosophy and human sciences: philosophical papers, vol 2. Cambridge University Press, Cambridge, pp 187–210

Thapar R (1961) Aśoka and the decline of the Mauryas. Oxford University Press, Oxford

Van Buitenen JAB (1981) The Bhagavadgita in Mahabharata. University of Chicago Press, Chicago

Voltaire (1994) A treatise on toleration and other essays, McCabe J trans. Prometheus Books, New York

Walshe M trans (1995) The long discourses of the Buddha. Boston: Wisdom Publications

Walzer M (1997) On toleration. Yale University Press, New Haven

Yu K (2018) Two conceptions of tolerating in Confucian thought. In: Spencer VA (ed) Toleration in comparative perspective. Lexington, Lanham, pp 217–233

Zhang Q (2010) Humanity or benevolence? The interpretation of the Confucian *ren* and its modern implications. In: Yu K, Tao J, Ivanhoe PJ (eds) Taking Confucian ethics seriously: contemporary theories and applications. State University of New York, New York, pp 53–72

Two Models of Toleration

25

Will Kymlicka

Contents

Introduction 478
Rawls on the Lessons of the Reformation 479
The Group Autonomy Model and the Ottoman Millet System 480
Individual Rights and Autonomy 484
Comprehensive Versus Political Liberalism 487
The Issue of Nonliberal Minorities 492
Summary and Future Directions 495
References 496

Abstract

According to John Rawls, the "obvious lesson" to draw from the Wars of Religion between Catholics and Protestants is the need for religious tolerance. He further assumes that religious tolerance should take the form of individual freedom of conscience. There is, however, a second model of religious tolerance that Rawls does not consider: group autonomy. In the group autonomy model, exemplified by the millet system of the Ottoman Empire, each religious group tolerates other religions while enforcing religious orthodoxy within their own group, at the expense of individual rights to dissent or defect. This chapter explores the different normative structures of these two models of tolerance. The former model is often seen as a distinctly "liberal" conception of religious toleration, in part because it better protects individual autonomy. However, recent defenses of liberalism – including Rawls' own "political liberalism" – have attempted to downplay the importance of individual autonomy within liberal theory. And this raises the question whether political liberalism can defend the individual conscience model of religious toleration over the group autonomy model or whether

W. Kymlicka (✉)
Department of Philosophy, Queen's University, Kingston, ON, Canada
e-mail: kymlicka@queensu.ca

© The Author(s), under exclusive licence to Springer Nature Switzerland AG 2022
M. Sardoč (ed.), *The Palgrave Handbook of Toleration*,
https://doi.org/10.1007/978-3-030-42121-2_9

liberals must instead appeal to the "comprehensive" value of individual autonomy.

Keywords

Individual autonomy · Group autonomy · Group rights · Political liberalism · Civil rights · Millets · Religion · Apostasy · Proselytization · John Rawls

---

Introduction

According to John Rawls, the "obvious lesson" to draw from the Wars of Religion between Catholics and Protestants is the need for religious tolerance. He further assumes that religious tolerance should take the form of individual freedom of conscience. There is, however, a second model of religious tolerance that Rawls does not consider: group autonomy. In the group autonomy model, exemplified by the millet system of the Ottoman Empire, each religious group tolerates other religions while enforcing religious orthodoxy within their own group, at the expense of individual rights to dissent or defect.

Liberals have traditionally defended the former model, in part because it better protects individual autonomy. However, some recent defenses of liberalism – including Rawls' own "political liberalism" – have attempted to downplay the importance of individual autonomy within liberal theory, on the grounds that autonomy is a controversial, even sectarian, value. Rawls assumes that liberals can maintain their support for the individual freedom of conscience model of religious toleration without appealing to the "comprehensive" value of individual autonomy. But he reaches this conclusion in part by ignoring the possibility of securing toleration through group autonomy. Once we recognize that there are indeed these two viable models for securing inter-religious toleration, any defense of the individual freedom of conscience model may require taking a stand on the moral and political significance of individual autonomy.

I begin by reviewing Rawls' account of the "obvious lessons" of the Reformation and how it ignores the possibility of a group autonomy approach to toleration (section "Rawls on the Lessons of the Reformation"). I then spell out some of the details of the group autonomy model and how it secures toleration between groups at the expense of individual freedom within groups (section "The Group Autonomy Model and the Ottoman Millet System"). I then turn to Rawls' later work, particularly his claim that liberals should defend their views on "political" and not "comprehensive" grounds (section "Individual Rights and Autonomy"). Against Rawls, I argue that liberals must give a more comprehensive defense of liberal values if they are to adequately defend individual liberty within groups (section "Comprehensive Versus Political Liberalism"). I conclude with some suggestions about how liberal democratic regimes should deal with minorities who reject liberal ideals (section "The Issue of Nonliberal Minorities").

Rawls on the Lessons of the Reformation

In his later work, John Rawls argued that "we must draw the obvious lessons of our political history since the Reformation and the Wars of Religion" – namely, that we must recognize and accommodate "the plurality of conflicting, and indeed incommensurable, conceptions of the good affirmed by the members of existing democratic societies" (Rawls 1987: 13; 1985: 225, 249). In the sixteenth century, both Catholics and Protestants sought to use the state to support their conception of true faith and to oppose the other. After innumerable wars and civil strife, both faiths learned that only the oppressive (and futile) use of force could ensure adherence to a single comprehensive religious doctrine. Both faiths now accept that "a practicable political conception for a constitutional regime cannot rest on a shared devotion to the Catholic or Protestant faith" (Rawls 1987: 5).

According to Rawls, this development of religious tolerance was one of the historical roots of liberalism. Liberals have simply extended the principle of tolerance to other controversial questions about the "meaning, value and purpose of human life" (Rawls 1987: 4). Unless oppressive state force is employed to prevent it, the members of a democratic society will invariably endorse different views about the highest ends in life, just as they endorse different religious views. Some will view civic participation or communal cooperation as our highest end, while others will view individual accomplishment as the greatest good. Any conception of justice which hopes to serve as the basis of political legitimacy, therefore, "must be one that widely different and even irreconcilable comprehensive doctrines can endorse" (Rawls 1989: 235). Hence, liberal "neutrality" on questions of the good accepts and extends the lessons of the Reformation.

Rawls' interpretation of the lessons of the Reformation has been very influential, but I think questions can be raised about it. The need for religious tolerance is indeed obvious. But there is more than one form of religious toleration. In the context of Western democracies, tolerance took a very distinctive form – namely, the idea of individual freedom of conscience. It is now a basic individual right to worship freely, to propagate one's religion, to change one's religion, or indeed to renounce religion altogether. To restrict an individual's exercise of these liberties is seen as a violation of a fundamental human right. Rawls views this as the most natural form of religious toleration. Indeed, as we will see, he often writes as if it is the only form of toleration. He simply equates "the principle of toleration" with the idea of individual freedom of conscience.

There is, however, a second model of toleration, based on group autonomy rather than individual liberty. In both models, religious communities are protected from oppression, but in very different ways. The Rawlsian model protects each religious community by separating church from state. It removes religion from the public agenda, leaving adherents of the competing doctrines free to pursue their beliefs in private churches. In the group autonomy model, on the other hand, church and state are closely linked. Each religious community is granted official status and a substantial measure of self-government. In the "millet system" of the Ottoman Empire, for example, Muslims, Christians, and Jews were all recognized as self-governing units (or "millets") within the Empire.

There are a number of important differences between these two models. For the purposes of this chapter, the most significant is that the group autonomy model need not recognize any principle of *individual* freedom of conscience. Since each religious community is self-governing, there is no external obstacle to basing this self-government on religious principles, including the enforcement of religious orthodoxy. Hence, there may be little or no scope for individual dissent within each religious community and little or no freedom to change one's faith. In the millet system, for example, the Muslims did not try to suppress the Jews, and vice versa, but they did suppress heretics within their own community. Heresy (questioning the orthodox interpretation of Muslim doctrine) and apostasy (abandoning one's religious faith) were punishable crimes within the Muslim community. Restrictions on individual freedom of conscience also existed in the Jewish and Christian communities. The millet system was, in effect, a federation of theocracies.

My aim is not to defend this second model. On the contrary, like Rawls, I believe that the liberal system of individual liberty is a more appropriate response to pluralism for contemporary societies. My aim, rather, is to see what sorts of reasons liberals can give to defend their commitment to individual liberty. The "obvious lesson" of the Wars of Religion is that diverse religions need to tolerate each other. It is less obvious why we must tolerate dissent within a religious (or ethnic) community.

Rawls has not, I think, adequately addressed this question. In fact, I believe that Rawls' later work on "political liberalism" has obscured the basis for this liberal commitment to individual liberty. In order to see the challenge here, we need to explore in a bit more depth the group autonomy model.

The Group Autonomy Model and the Ottoman Millet System

A paradigmatic example of the group autonomy model is the Ottoman millet system. The Ottoman Turks were Muslims who conquered much of the Middle East, North Africa, Greece, and Eastern Europe during the fourteenth and fifteenth centuries, thereby acquiring many Jewish and Christian subjects. For various theological and strategic reasons, the Ottomans allowed these minorities not only the freedom to practice their religion but also a more general freedom to govern themselves in purely internal matters, with their own legal codes and courts. For about five centuries, between 1456 and the collapse of the Empire in World War 1, three non-Muslim minorities had official recognition as self-governing communities (or "millets") – the Greek Orthodox, the Armenian Orthodox, and the Jews – each of which was further subdivided into various local administrative units, usually based on ethnicity and language. Each millet was headed by the relevant church leader (the Chief Rabbi and the two Orthodox Patriarchs).

The legal traditions and practices of each community, particularly in matters of family status, were respected and enforced through the Empire. However, while they were free to run their internal affairs, their relations with the ruling Muslims were tightly regulated. For example, non-Muslims could not proselytize, they could only build new churches under license, and they were required to wear distinctive dress so that they could be recognized. There were limits on inter-marriage, and they had to pay special taxes, in lieu of military service. But within these limits, "they were to enjoy complete self-government, obeying their own laws and customs." Their collective freedom of worship was guaranteed, together with their possession of churches and monasteries, and they could run their own schools (Runciman 1970: 27–35, Braude and Lewis 1982: 1–34).

While the millet system was generally humane and tolerant of group differences, it was not a liberal society, for it did not tolerate individual dissent within its constituent communities. It was, rather, a deeply conservative, theocratic, and patriarchal society, antithetical to the ideals of personal liberty endorsed by liberals from Locke to Kant and Mill.

The various millets differed in the extent of their enforcement of religious orthodoxy. There were many periods during the 500-year history of the millets in which liberal reformers within each community pushed for constitutional restrictions on the power of the millet's leaders. And indeed, in the second half of the nineteenth century, some of the millets adopted liberal constitutions. This makes clear that the idea of according special rights of self-government to minority communities is not itself illiberal, *if this communal self-government respects the civil rights of its members*. It is useful, therefore, to distinguish two kinds of group rights that can be attributed to minority communities: rights of the group *against the larger society*, which we can call "external protections," and rights of the group *against its own members*, which we can call "internal restrictions." The former are consistent with liberal views of freedom and equality, if they protect a vulnerable minority from the impact of the majority of economic or political decisions. Such external protections may include land claims, language rights, guaranteed representation in political institutions, veto power over certain kinds of policies, and so on. Internal restrictions, by contrast, involve giving the group the right to limit the basic civil and political rights of its members – for example, by legally prohibiting heresy or apostasy. Such internal restrictions are a threat to liberal values (Kymlicka 1995: chap. 3).

If we apply this distinction to the Ottoman Empire, we can see that the millet system involved both external protections and internal restrictions. It not only protected minority religions from being subject to domination or oppression by the majority, but it also involved significant restrictions on the freedom of individuals within each group to question or reject church doctrine. The Ottomans accepted the principle of tolerance, where that is "understood to indicate the willingness of a dominant religion to coexist with others" (Braude and Lewis 1982: 3), but did not accept the quite separate principle of individual freedom of conscience.

This system of toleration is very different from that which evolved in the West, although it is interesting to note that the two systems had similar historical origins.

The Ottoman restrictions on the building and location of non-Muslim churches were similar to the system of "licensed co-existence" established under the Edict of Nantes (1598). Under that Edict, which ended the Wars of Religion, Protestants in France could only build new churches in certain locations and only with a state license. In the West, however, state-licensed coexistence between Protestants and Catholics gradually evolved into a system of individual freedom of conscience. This never occurred in the Ottoman Empire.

As noted above, there were some liberal reformers who questioned the legitimacy of theocratic rule. Some Jews and Christians in the Ottoman Empire had extensive contact with the West. They brought back Enlightenment ideas of freedom and reason and, like liberals in the West, challenged the rule of "obscurantist" religious leaders who maintained power by keeping the people fearful and ignorant (Davison 1982: 332; Braude and Lewis 1982: 18–19, 3031; Karpat 1982: 159–163). These reformers wanted to secularize, liberalize, and democratize the millet system and use it as the basis for national self-government by the various national groups in the Empire. The Ottoman rulers actually sided with these liberal reformers in 1856 and demanded that the non-Muslim millets adopt new and more democratic constitutions (Davison 1982: 329; Braude and Lewis 1982: 22–23). However, unlike in the West, liberal reformers were a small minority, and the Patriarchs were able to maintain their hold on the reins of power, albeit with ever-decreasing relevance.

The influence of Western ideas was just one of many external influences which ultimately combined to undermine the millet system (along with economic competition, military force, and diplomatic meddling). But its internal dynamics were remarkably stable. As Braude and Lewis note, "for nearly half a millennium, the Ottomans ruled an empire as diverse as any in history. Remarkably, this polyethnic and multireligious society worked. Muslims, Christians, and Jews worshipped and studied side by side, enriching their distinct cultures" (Braude and Lewis 1982: 1).

The millet system, therefore, offers a viable alternative form of religious tolerance to Rawlsian liberalism. It does not deny the obvious lesson of the Wars of Religion that religions need to coexist. Indeed, the existence of the millets probably saved the Ottoman Empire from undergoing these wars. In fact, this is arguably the more natural form of religious tolerance. The historical record suggests that "in practice, religions have usually felt most violently intolerant not of other religions but of dissenters within their own ranks" (Elton 1984a: xiii). This was true of paganism in antiquity (Garnsey 1984: 24) and of leading figures in the English Reformation, such as Thomas More (Elton 1984b: 174–175, 182–183).

The Ottoman millet system is the most developed form of the group autonomy model of religious tolerance. But variations on that model can be found in many other times and places, including many contemporary liberal democracies. Consider the following three cases:

1. Both Canada and the United States exempt a number of long-standing religious sects (e.g., Mennonites, Doukhobours, Amish, and Hutterites) from laws regarding the mandatory education of children. Members of these sects can withdraw their children from schools before the legal age of 16 and are not required to teach

the usual school curriculum. Parents worry that if their children received this broader education, they would be tempted to leave the sect and join the wider society (Janzen 1990: chaps. 5–7).

2. Britain has recently received a considerable number of Muslim immigrants from its former protectorates and colonies. Some traditional practices in their country of origin violate current British law, including various forms of gender discrimination in relation to decisions about child custody or property division upon divorce. Some Muslim leaders have called for a millet-like system in Britain, which would allow Muslims to apply their own personal status laws regarding family status (Poulter 1987; Parekh 1990; Modood 1993).

3. American Indian tribes have a legally recognized right to self-government. As part of this self-government, tribal governments are not subject to the American Bill of Rights. Some tribes have established a theocratic government that discriminates against those members who do not share the tribal religion. For example, the Pueblo deny housing benefits to those members of the community who have converted to Protestantism (Weston 1981; Robinson 2003).

In all these cases, as with the Ottoman millets, there are debates within the group about the extent to which the exercise of group autonomy should be subject to liberal rights constraints. Some liberal reformers want to prevent internal restrictions on the civil rights of individual members. However, in each of these cases, some leaders within the group have sought the legal power to restrict the liberty of their own members, so as to preserve traditional religious practices. They are seeking to establish or maintain a system of group autonomy which protects communal practices, not only from external oppression but also from internal dissent, and this often requires exemption from the constitutional or legislative requirements of the larger society.

Various justifications are offered for such demands for group autonomy. In the case of Indigenous peoples, for example, there are appeals to principles of self-determination; in the case of the Amish, Doukhobours, and Hutterites, there were historic promises at the time of immigration. But these demands are also, sometimes, justified in terms of the value of "tolerance." And indeed, they do embody a particular conception of toleration. But it is not the sort of tolerance Rawls has in mind. These groups do not want the state to protect each individual's right to freely express, question, and revise her religious beliefs. On the contrary, this is precisely what they object to. What they want is the power to restrict the religious freedom of their own members, and they want the exercise of this power to be exempted from any requirement to respect individual rights.

Hence, the idea of group autonomy is a live issue in many democracies. Yet, Rawls never considers this model of tolerance. He talks about "the principle of tolerance" (e.g., Rawls 1987: 18), as if there was just one, which he equates with the idea of freedom of conscience. Indeed, he often writes as if respect for individual rights is the only way to accommodate pluralism. Consider his claim that the liberal commitment to individual rights was accepted "as providing the only alternative to endless and destructive civil strife" (Rawls 1987: 18). Or his claim that parties in his "original position" would see the fact of pluralism as sufficient grounds for adopting a principle of individual rights:

> We need only suppose in the first stage that the parties assume the fact of pluralism to obtain, that is, that a plurality of comprehensive doctrines exists in society. The parties must then protect against the possibility that the person each party represents may be a member of a religious, ethnic, or other minority. *This suffices for the argument for the equal basic liberties to get going.* (Rawls 1989: 251, my emphasis)

Indeed, Rawls sometimes writes as if a religiously diverse society had never existed before the birth of liberalism:

> The success of liberal institutions may come as a discovery of a new social possibility: the possibility of a reasonably harmonious and stable pluralist society. Before the successful and peaceful practice of toleration in societies with liberal political institutions there was no way of knowing of that possibility. It can easily seem more natural to believe, as the centuries' long practice of intolerance appeared to confirm, that social unity and concord requires agreement on a general and comprehensive religious, philosophical or moral doctrine. (Rawls 1987: 23)

But the "successful and peaceful practice of toleration" existed in the Ottoman Empire long before England's Toleration Act. Even if we endorse Rawls' liberal conception of tolerance, the millet system is a useful reminder that individual rights are not the only way to accommodate religious pluralism.

Individual Rights and Autonomy

If Rawls had considered the group autonomy model, what would he have said about it? At one level, the answer is clear: insofar as the millet system involves restricting basic individual civil liberties, it violates his first principle of justice which states that "each person has an equal right to the most extensive system of equal basic liberties compatible with a similar scheme of liberty for all." But how can he defend individual liberty as a superior model of toleration than group autonomy?

Most liberals would object to the millet system on the grounds that it makes it difficult or impossible for people to question or revise their religious commitments. It does not impose religious views on people, in the sense that there is no forced conversion. But nor does it allow people to judge for themselves what parts of their inherited religious faith are worthy of their continued allegiance and why.

One way to express this objection is to say that the millet system restricts individual autonomy. It limits individual's ability and freedom to judge the value of inherited practices and to thereby form and revise their own conception of the good. Many liberals explicitly appeal to this idea of autonomy as the basis for their defense of individual rights. Consider the following passage from J.S. Mill's *On Liberty*:

It would be absurd to pretend that people ought to live as if nothing had been known in the world before they came into it; as if experience had as yet done nothing towards showing that one mode of existence, or of conduct, is preferable to another. Nobody denies that people should be so taught and trained in youth as to know and benefit by the ascertained results of human experience. *But it is the privilege and proper condition of a human being, arrived at the maturity of his faculties, to use and interpret experience in his own way. It is for him to find out what part of recorded experience is properly applicable to his own circumstances and character.* (Mill 1982: 122, emphasis added)

For Mill and other liberals, a basic argument for civil rights is that they help ensure that individuals can make informed judgments about the inherited practices of the community. For example, mandatory education ensures that children acquire the capacity to envisage alternative ways of life and rationally assess them. Freedom of speech and association (including the freedom to proselytize or dissent from church orthodoxy) ensures that people can raise questions and seek answers about the worth of the different ways of life available to them. Since the millet system restricts these civil rights, it harms a basic interest of people, by leaving them unable to rationally assess the worthiness of their current ends and to revise their ends accordingly.

I will call this the "Millian" or "autonomy" argument for civil rights – that is, the view that we have a basic interest in being able to rationally assess and revise our current ends. These labels may be misleading, since Mill never used the term autonomy, and this is only one of his arguments for civil rights. Moreover, there are other conceptions of autonomy present in the liberal tradition. However, I believe that this particular conception of autonomy – Buchanan (1975) calls it the "rational revisability" conception of autonomy – is central to Mill's defense of individual rights, and to many other liberal theorists.

It is important to distinguish this conception of autonomy from others that have been defended within (or attributed to) the liberal tradition. Some people think that the exercise of autonomy is intrinsically valuable, because it reflects our rational nature (this view is ascribed to Kant). Others believe that nonconformist individuality is intrinsically valuable (this view is often ascribed to Mill). What I am calling the Millian conception of autonomy, however, is simply the claim that the capacity for rational revisability enables us to assess and learn what is good in life, and why. It presupposes that we have an essential interest in revising those of our current beliefs about value which are mistaken (On these different views of autonomy, see Kymlicka 1989: chap. 4.).

In his early work, Rawls seemed to endorse the Millian argument. He says that members of a liberal society have the capacity "to form, to revise, and rationally to pursue" a conception of the good. It is important to note that Rawls explicitly mentions the capacity to *revise* one's conception of the good, alongside the capacity to pursue one's *existing* conception. Indeed, he suggests that the latter "is in essential respects subordinate" to the former. Exercising our capacity to form and revise a conception of the good is a "highest-order interest," in the sense of being "supremely regulative and effective." People's interest in advancing their existing conception of the good, on the other hand, is simply a "higher-order interest." While it is, of course, important to be able to pursue one's existing conception of the good, the capacity to evaluate and revise that conception is needed to ensure that it is worthy of one's continued allegiance (Rawls 1980: 525–528).

Hence, people have a highest-order interest in standing back from their current ends and assessing their worthiness:

> As free persons, citizens recognize one another as having the moral power to have a conception of the good. This means that they do not view themselves as inevitably tied to the pursuit of the particular conception of the good and its final ends which they espouse at any given time. Instead, as citizens, they are regarded as, in general, capable of revising and changing this conception on reasonable and rational grounds. Thus it is held to be permissible for citizens to stand apart from conceptions of the good and to survey and assess their various final ends. (Rawls 1980: 544)

This capacity to survey and assess our ends is, in fact, one of the two fundamental "moral powers" (along with the capacity for a sense of justice) that define Rawls' "conception of the person." And, like Mill, Rawls defends civil liberties in terms of their contribution to the realizing and exercising of this moral power (Rawls 1980: 526).

Some communitarians deny that we can "stand apart" from (some of) our final ends. According to Michael Sandel, some of our final ends are "constitutive" ends, in the sense that they define our sense of personal identity (Sandel 1982: 150–165; cf. MacIntyre 1981: chap. 15; Bell 1993: 24–54). It makes no sense, on his view, to say that my final ends might not be worthy of my allegiance, for these ends define who I am. Whereas Rawls claims that individuals "do not regard themselves as inevitably bound to, or identical with, the pursuit of any particular complex of fundamental interests that they may have at any given moment" (Rawls 1974: 641), Sandel responds that we are, in fact, "identical with" at least some of our final ends. Since these ends are constitutive of people's identity, there is no reason why the state should not reinforce people's allegiance to those ends.

This communitarian conception of the self as defined by constitutive ends is one possible basis for the group autonomy approach to tolerance. Sandel himself rarely discusses the question of group autonomy, and he often qualifies his idea of constitutive ends in such a way that suggests that people can, after all, stand back and assess even their most deeply held ends. Hence, he and other contemporary communitarians might well object to the sorts of individual restrictions imposed by some group autonomy systems (e.g., D'Entreves 1990).

However, a millet-like system can be seen as a sort of hypercommunitarianism. It assumes that people's religious affiliation is so profoundly constitutive of who they are that their overriding interest is in protecting and advancing that identity and that they have no interest in being able to stand back and assess that identity. Hence, the millet system limits people's ability to revise their fundamental ends and prevents others from trying to promote such revision.

This is perhaps most obvious in the prohibition on proselytization and apostasy. If we assume that religious ends are constitutive of people's identity, then proselytization is at best futile and at worst an inherently harmful attempt to tempt people away from their true identity. This is indeed one reason why systems of group autonomy often seek to limit or prohibit proselytization, or its secular equivalents (e.g., the attempts of the Amish to prevent their children from learning about the outside world in schools).

The liberal model, on the other hand, gives people access to information about other ways of life (through proselytization) and indeed requires people to learn about these options (through mandatory education) and allows people to radically revise their ends (apostasy is not a crime). These aspects of a liberal society only make sense, I think, on the assumption that we have an interest, not only in pursuing our existing conception of the good but also in being able to assess and potentially revise that conception. The liberal model assumes that revising one's ends is both possible and sometimes desirable. It assumes that people's current ends are not always worthy of their continued allegiance and that exposure to other ways of life helps people make informed judgments about what is truly worthwhile.

Comprehensive Versus Political Liberalism

So in his earlier work, Rawls clearly endorses the Millian view that we have a basic interest in assessing and potentially revising our existing ends. In his later work, however, Rawls wants to avoid appealing to this conception of autonomy, which he now sees as "sectarian," in the sense that it is an ideal which is "not generally, or perhaps even widely, shared in a democratic society" (Rawls 1987: 24, 1993). He wants to find an alternative basis for defending civil rights, one which can be accepted even by those who reject the conception of the person implicit in the Millian argument.

His proposal is not to reject the autonomy argument entirely, but rather to restrict its scope. In particular, he wants to continue appealing to it in *political* contexts, while avoiding it in other contexts. The idea that we can form and revise our conception of the good is, he now says, strictly a "political conception" of the person, adopted solely for the purposes of determining our public rights and responsibilities. It is not, he insists, intended as a general account of the relationship between the self and its ends applicable to all areas of life or as an accurate portrayal of our deepest self-understandings. On the contrary, in private life, it is quite possible and likely that our personal identity is bound to particular ends in such a way as to preclude rational revision. As he puts it,

it is essential to stress that citizens in their personal affairs, or in the internal life of associations to which they belong, may regard their final ends and attachments in a way very different from the way the political conception involves. Citizens may have, and normally do have at any given time, affections, devotions, and loyalties that they believe they would not, and indeed could and should not, stand apart from and objectively evaluate from the standpoint of their purely rational good. They may regard it as simply unthinkable to view themselves apart from certain religious, philosophical and moral convictions, or from certain enduring attachments and loyalties. These convictions and attachments are part of what we may call their 'nonpublic identity.' (Rawls 1985: 241)

So Rawls no longer assumes that people's religious commitments are revisable or autonomously affirmed. He accepts that these ends may be so constitutive of our identity that we cannot stand back from them and subject them to assessment and revision. However, in political contexts, we ignore the possible existence of such constitutive ends. As *citizens*, we continue to see ourselves as having a "highest-order interest" in our capacity for autonomy, even though as *private individuals* we may not see ourselves as having or valuing that capacity. Rawls' conception of the person, based on the two moral powers of justice and autonomy, continues to provide the language of public justification in which people discuss their rights and responsibilities as citizens, although it may not describe their "non-public identity" (Rawls 1980: 545).

Hence, Rawls distinguishes his "political liberalism" from the "comprehensive liberalism" of Mill. As we have seen, Mill thinks that people should exercise autonomy in both public and private contexts. Mill's argument that people should be able to assess the worth of inherited social practices applies to all areas of life, not just political life. Indeed, he was mostly concerned about the way people blindly followed popular culture and social customs in their everyday personal affairs. Hence, Mill's liberalism is based on an ideal of rational reflection that applies to human action generally and that is intended "to inform our thought and conduct as a whole" (Rawls 1987: 6).

Rawls worries that many people do not accept Mill's idea of autonomy as a principle governing human thought and action generally. However, he thinks that such people can nonetheless accept the idea of autonomy if it is restricted to political contexts, leaving them free to view their nonpublic identities in quite different ways. People can accept his political conception "without being committed in other parts of their life to comprehensive moral ideals often associated with liberalism, for example, the ideals of autonomy and individuality" (Rawls 1985: 245).

Is this a coherent position? The challenge is to explain why anyone would accept the ideal of autonomy in political contexts unless they also accepted it more generally. If the members of a religious community see their religious ends as constitutive, so that they have no ability to stand back and assess these ends, why would they accept a political conception of the person which assumes that they do have that ability (and indeed a highest-order interest in exercising that ability)?

One answer Rawls might give is that everyone can accept his political conception because those who do not generally value the capacity for autonomy can simply refrain from exercising it in private life. While a liberal society allows rational assessment and revision of one's ends, it does not compel it. Hence, he might argue, even if this view of autonomy conflicts with a religious minority's self-understanding, that there is no cost to accepting it for political purposes.

But there is a cost to nonliberal minorities from accepting Rawls' political conception of the person – namely, it precludes any system of group autonomy that limits the right of individuals to revise their conceptions of the good. For example, it precludes a religious minority from prohibiting apostasy and proselytization or from preventing their children learning about other ways of life. The minority may view these civil liberties as harmful. But if, for the purposes of political debate, they accept the assumption that people have a highest-order interest in exercising their capacity to form and revise a conception of the good, then they have no way to express their belief in the harm of allowing proselytization and apostasy.

Consider the Canadian case of *Hofer v Hofer*, which dealt with the powers of the Hutterite Church over its members. The Hutterites live in large agricultural communities, called colonies, within which there is no private property. Two lifelong members of a Hutterite colony were expelled for apostasy. They demanded their share of the colony's assets, which they had helped create with their years of labor. When the colony refused, the two ex-members sued in court. They objected to the fact that they had "no right at any time in their lives to leave the colony without abandoning everything, even the clothes on their backs" (Janzen 1990: 67). The Hutterites defended this practice on the grounds that freedom of religion protects a congregation's ability to live in accordance with its religious doctrine, even if this limits individual freedom.

The Canadian Supreme Court accepted this Hutterite claim. But it is far from clear that the Hutterite claim can be defended, or even expressed, within the language of Rawls' "political liberalism." As Justice Pigeon noted in dissent, the usual liberal notion of freedom of religion "includes the right of each individual to change his religion at will." Hence, churches "cannot make rules having the effect of depriving their members of this fundamental freedom." The proper scope of religious authority is therefore "limited to what is consistent with freedom of religion as properly understood, that is freedom for the individual not only to adopt a religion but also to abandon it at will." Justice Pigeon thought that it was "as nearly impossible as can be" for people in a Hutterite colony to reject its religious teachings, because of the high cost of changing their religion, and so they were effectively deprived of freedom of religion (*Hofer v Hofer* et al. (1970) 13 DLR (3d) 1).

Justice Pigeon's view, it seems to me, is most consistent with Rawls' "political liberalism." Pigeon is assuming, as Rawls says we should for the purposes of political argument and legal rights, that people have a basic interest in their capacity to form and revise their conception of the good. Hence, he concludes, the power of religious communities over their own members must be such that individuals can freely and effectively exercise that capacity. The power of religious authorities clearly cannot be such as to make it effectively impossible to exercise that capacity. Were the Hutterites to accept Rawls' conception of the person, then they too would have to accept the view that freedom of religion must be interpreted in terms of an individual's capacity to form and revise her religious beliefs.

It is important to emphasize that this argument for civil rights does not imply that the goal is to *maximize* the development and exercise of the capacity to form and revise a conception of the good. As Rawls rightly notes, it would be "absurd" to try to maximize "the number of deliberate affirmations of a conception of the good." Rather, "these liberties and their priority are to guarantee equally for all citizens the social conditions essential for the adequate development and the full and informed exercise of these powers" (1982: 47–49). In Justice Pigeon's view, the Hutterites do not provide the social conditions essential for the "adequate development" and "informed exercise" of autonomy.

Hence, Rawls' strategy of endorsing autonomy only in political contexts, rather than as a general value, is unlikely to succeed. Accepting the value of autonomy for political purposes inevitably enables its exercise more generally, an implication that will only be favored by those who endorse autonomy as a general value. Rawls fails to explain why people who reject his conception of the person in private life should endorse it as a political good. Rawls may be right that "within different contexts we can assume diverse points of view toward our person without contradiction so long as these points of view cohere together when circumstances require" (Rawls 1980: 545). But he has not shown that these points of view do cohere. On the contrary, they clearly conflict on issues of intragroup dissent such as proselytization, apostasy, and mandatory education.

Although I do not have the space here to demonstrate this, I think the same critique applies to other recent attempts to defend liberalism without appeal to the value of autonomy, whether it is Galston's defense of "Reformation" liberalism (in contrast with "Enlightenment" liberalism) (Galston 1995), or Larmore and McCabe's defense of "modus vivendi" liberalism (in contrast with "Kantian" liberalism) (Larmore 1987; McCabe 2010), or Sleat and Levy's defense of a more "realist" liberalism or "liberalism of fear" (in contrast with "High Liberalism") (Sleat 2013; Levy 2000). In each case, the authors suggest that liberalism can be defended in terms of the value of tolerance and civil peace, without appeal to the value of personal autonomy. However, they do not explain why groups which reject the value of personal autonomy would endorse a model of tolerance that prioritizes individual freedom of conscience when the group autonomy model can equally secure inter-group tolerance and civil peace at lower cost to their beliefs.

Why did not Rawls see this conflict? Perhaps because he assumed that his political conception is the only one that can protect religious minorities from the intolerance of the majority. Recall his claim that the fact of pluralism is sufficient ground for endorsing individual rights:

> We need only suppose in the first stage that the parties assume the fact of pluralism to obtain, that is, that a plurality of comprehensive doctrines exists in society. The parties must then protect against the possibility that the person each party represents may be a member of a religious, ethnic, or other minority. This suffices for the argument for the equal basic liberties to get going. (Rawls 1989: 251)

Rawls here implies that the only viable way to prevent persecution between groups is to allow freedom of conscience for individuals. But this is a mistake – one can ensure tolerance *between* groups without protecting tolerance of individual dissent *within* each group. A system of group autonomy ensures the former without ensuring the latter. If we want to defend civil rights for individuals, therefore, we must go beyond the need for group tolerance and give some account of the value of endowing individuals with the freedom to form and revise their final ends.

Rawls is mistaken, therefore, to suppose that he can avoid appealing to the general value of individual autonomy without undermining his argument for the priority of civil rights. The mere fact of *social plurality*, disconnected from any assumption of *individual autonomy*, cannot by itself defend the full range of liberal freedoms. Rawls' belief that social plurality can defend individual liberty, even in the absence of individual revisability, is made most explicit in "Basic Liberties and Their Priority." In that article, Rawls distinguishes two arguments for freedom of conscience. On the first argument, conceptions of the good are "regarded as *given and firmly rooted*; and since there is a plurality of such conceptions, each, as it were, non-negotiable, the parties recognize that behind the veil of ignorance the principles of justice which guarantee equal liberty of conscience are the only principles which they can adopt." On this view, freedom of conscience protects religious minorities. Without freedom of conscience, people may find, once they drop the veil of ignorance, that they "belong to a minority faith and may suffer accordingly." On the second argument, conceptions of the good are "seen as *subject to revision* in accordance with deliberative reason, which is part of the capacity for a conception of the good." On this view, freedom of conscience protects individuals who wish to change their faith, because there "is no guarantee that all aspects of our present way of life are the most rational for us and not in need of at least minor if not major revision" (Rawls 1982: 25–29, my emphasis). Rawls claims that these two arguments "support the same conclusion" (1982: 29) – that is, recognizing the *plurality* of conceptions of the good within society has the same implications for individual liberty as affirming the *revisability* of each individual's conception of the good. But they do not support the same conclusion on issues such as proselytization, which is an essential liberty on the second argument, but a futile and disruptive nuisance on the first argument. If people's private identity really is tied to certain ends, such that they have no interest or ability to question and revise them, then group autonomy may be a superior response to pluralism. If individuals are incapable of revising their inherited religious commitments or if it is not important to enable individuals to exercise that capacity, then the millet system may best protect and advance those constitutive ends.

This is hardly a novel conclusion. On the contrary, this is what defenders of group autonomy have often argued. They believe that once we drop the assumption that autonomy is a general value, then religious and ethnic groups should be allowed to protect their members' constitutive ends by restricting certain individual rights (Sandel 1990; Kukathas 1992; McDonald 1991; Newman 2011).

If liberals wish to defend individual freedom of conscience, they must reject the idea that people's ends are beyond rational revision. At one point, Rawls seems to do just this. He notes that some people think of themselves as being incapable of questioning or revising their ends, but he suggests that this may be inaccurate: "our conceptions of the good may and often do change over time, usually slowly but sometimes rather suddenly," even for those people who think of themselves as having constitutive ends. For example, "On the road to Damascus Saul of Tarsus becomes Paul the Apostle" (Rawls 1985: 242).

This is an important point. No matter how confident we are about our ends at a particular moment, new circumstances or experiences may arise, often in unpredictable ways, that cause us to reevaluate them. This is the beginning of an argument for why people should be free to stand back and assess their ends. But Rawls makes no attempt to elaborate on it. He does not explain why it is important for people to be able to make these kinds of changes or how this capacity should be legally and socially encouraged (e.g., through education or freedom to proselytize).

The Issue of Nonliberal Minorities

Why is Rawls so reluctant to affirm the Millian argument and explicitly endorse autonomy as a general human interest? What is wrong with Mill's "comprehensive" liberalism? The problem, Rawls says, is that not everyone accepts this ideal of autonomy and so appealing to it in political life would be "sectarian":

> As comprehensive moral ideals, autonomy and individuality are unsuited for a political conception of justice. As found in Kant and J.S. Mill, these comprehensive ideals, despite their very great importance in liberal thought, are extended too far when presented as the only appropriate foundation for a constitutional regime. So understood, liberalism becomes but another sectarian doctrine. (Rawls 1985: 246)

Mill's defense of civil rights rests "in large part on ideals and values that are not generally, or perhaps even widely, shared in a democratic society," and hence "cannot secure sufficient agreement" (Rawls 1987: 6, 24).

This is a legitimate point, but Rawls overstates it and draws the wrong conclusion from it. The idea that we have an interest in being able to assess and revise our inherited conceptions of the good is very widely shared in Western democratic societies. (Rawls' fear that the Millian conception of autonomy is not widely shared arguably depends on conflating this conception of autonomy with the other, more controversial, conceptions discussed earlier.) There are some insulated minorities who reject this ideal, and these groups pose a challenge for liberal democracies, since they often demand group autonomy that conflicts with individual civil rights. We cannot simply ignore this demand or ignore the fact that they reject the idea of autonomy.

But Rawls' strategy is no solution to the questions raised by the existence of nonliberal minorities. His solution is to continue to enforce individual rights, but to do so on the basis of a "political" rather than a "comprehensive" liberalism. This obviously does not satisfy the demands of nonliberal minorities. They want a form of group autonomy that takes precedence over individual rights. Rawls' political liberalism is as hostile to that demand as Mill's comprehensive liberalism. The fact that Rawls' theory is less comprehensive does not make his theory more sympathetic to the demands of nonliberal minorities.

Rawls does briefly discuss the demands of some traditional religious groups (e.g., the Amish) for exemption from mandatory education and argues that his political liberalism is more sympathetic to this demand than Mill's comprehensive liberalism. Whereas comprehensive liberalism "may lead to requirements designed to foster the values of autonomy and individuality as ideas to govern much if not all of life," political liberalism "has a different aim and requires far less," since it is only concerned with promoting a liberal ideal of citizenship ("the state's concern with [children's] education lies in their role as future citizens"). As a result, Rawls says, political liberalism "honors, as far as it can, the claims of those who wish to withdraw from the modern world in accordance with the injunctions of their religion, provided only that they acknowledge the principles of the political conception of justice and appreciate its political ideals of person and society" (Rawls 1988: 267–268).

However, this requirement that the Amish must "appreciate" the political liberal's "ideals of the person and society" is precisely what is at issue. Many religious communities object to these ideals and to any form of education built upon them. Mennonites and Hutterites in Canada have objected to some of the materials they are required to teach their children because these materials promote an ideal of citizenship that is in conflict with their religious ideals of person and society. While the government talked about preparing children for the rights and duties of citizenship, Mennonites saw "a different purpose of education ... to prepare their children for life in their communities" (Janzen 1990: 97). Similarly, the Hutterites are "concerned not primarily with the potential for rationality but with, as they see it, the need for obedience. They argue that education should reorient the individual's self-regard and nurture a desire to abide by the will of the community" (Janzen 1990: 143). These groups do not see political liberalism as honoring their claims, and as a result, they have sought exemption from precisely the sort of education that Rawls' "political liberalism" insists upon. On issues of mandatory education, as on issues of prohibiting apostasy and proselytization, there is simply an unbridgeable gap between liberal commitments to individual rights and the sort of group autonomy that some nonliberal religious groups seek. Framing these liberal commitments as "political" rather than "comprehensive" does not remove the gap.

How then should a liberal state treat nonliberal minorities? To begin with, we need to distinguish two very different questions that Rawls conflates: First, what kind of provision for religious and ethnic minorities is consistent with liberal principles? Second, should liberals impose their views on communities that do not accept liberal principles? The first is a question of *identifying* a defensible liberal theory of tolerance; the second is a question of *imposing* that liberal theory.

With respect to the first question, I believe that the most defensible liberal theory is based on the value of autonomy and that any form of group autonomy that restricts the civil rights of group members is therefore inconsistent with liberal principles of freedom and equality. The Ottoman millet system was therefore seriously deficient from a liberal point of view.

But that does not mean that liberal states can impose those principles on groups that do not share them. There are a number of further steps that are required before we can determine how, if at all, liberal states should act. Once we know what an appropriate liberal conception of minority rights is, we can then determine how much it coincides with, or differs from, the wishes of a particular minority. Once we have determined the extent of any disagreements, then we are faced with the question of state action. This in turn will depend on many factors, not least the question whether the state has legitimate authority in the first place. In the case of Indigenous peoples, for example, the state may never have acquired the legitimate right to govern them (or their territory) in the first place or may only have acquired that power under the terms of a treaty that reserved certain self-governing powers to Indigenous peoples. Even where the state's authority to govern a particular community or territory is undisputed – as perhaps with many immigrant groups – there are still many factors to consider, including the severity of rights violations within the minority community, the extent to which specific subgroups within the minority are particularly vulnerable (the so-called minority within minority issue), the degree of consensus in the community on the legitimacy of restricting individual rights, the ability of dissenting group members to leave the community if they so desire, the existence of historical agreements with the minority community (e.g., historical promises made to religious groups), the likely efficacy of the proposed intervention, and so forth (Kymlicka 1995: chap. 8).

The question of imposing liberalism comes therefore a number of steps after the question of identifying a liberal theory. Much important work has been done in recent years exploring these additional steps (e.g., Shachar 2001; Spinner-Halev 2000), often the heading of "multicultural feminism," given that women tend to be disproportionately subject to internal restrictions within group autonomy models (e.g., Okin 1999; Deveaux 2006; Song 2007; Rubio-Marin and Kymlicka 2018). There has been a particularly lively debate on the right of exit. For some commentators, the right of exit is sufficient to justify internal restrictions (e.g., Kukathas 1992). As the case of *Hofer v Hofer* shows, however, the exercise of a right of exit can often be very difficult. Most commentators, therefore, have argued that a right of exit must be robust, not merely formal, and that even with robust rights of exit, there still need to be other safeguards to protect the interests of vulnerable "minorities within minorities" (Okin 2002; Eisenberg and Spinner-Halev 2005; Mazie 2005; Borchers and Vitikainen 2012).

While there remains much disagreement about how to specify these safeguards, there is widespread agreement that we cannot simply jump from identifying a liberal theory to imposing it on nonliberal groups. Indeed, in many cases, there will be little room for coercive intervention. Relations between majority and minority groups should be determined by peaceful negotiation, not force (as with international relations). This means searching for some basis of agreement. If two groups do not share basic principles and cannot be persuaded to adopt the other's principles, then they will have to come to some kind of accommodation. In cases where the minority rejects liberal values, then the resulting agreement may well involve recognizing group autonomy. And, as noted above, contemporary liberal societies do, in fact, recognize some millet-like structures – for example, education exemptions for the Amish. But this is a compromise, not the instantiation, of liberal principles, since it violates a fundamental liberal principle of freedom of conscience. Hence, liberal reformers inside the group would seek to promote their liberal ideas through reason or example, and liberals outside would lend their support to any efforts the community makes to liberalize.

Rawls seems to conflate these two questions of identifying and imposing a liberal theory of justice. His "political" conception of liberalism is not, I think, an adequate answer to either question. It does not adequately *identify* a defensible liberal theory, since he leaves it entirely unclear why citizens (but not private individuals) have a highest-order interest in their capacity to form and revise a conception of the good. It does not adequately answer the question of *imposing* liberalism, since it would enforce liberal rights in minority communities that may have a strong social consensus in favor of group autonomy and a strong historical claim to them as well.

Rawls is right to worry about the existence of ethnic and religious minorities that reject the value of autonomy. But his response is off target. In the face of such minorities, Rawls has become less willing to defend comprehensive liberalism but is still willing to impose liberal political institutions. A more appropriate response, I believe, is to continue defending comprehensive liberalism based on autonomy as a general value, but become more cautious about imposing the full set of liberal political institutions on nonliberal minorities.

Summary and Future Directions

I have described two models of religious tolerance: a liberal model based on individual liberty and a hypercommunitarian model based on group autonomy. Both recognize the need for different religious communities to coexist and hence are consistent with the fact of religious pluralism in modern societies. However, they disagree fundamentally on the role of individual freedom within religious communities. The group autonomy model allows each group to limit the religious liberties of its own members so as to protect the constitutive ends and practices of the community from internal dissent. The liberal model insists that each individual has a right to freedom of conscience, including the right to question and revise her religious beliefs, and so allows for proselytization, heresy, and apostasy.

Rawls has consistently endorsed the liberal model, and his theory of justice precludes any system of group autonomy that limits freedom of conscience. But his justification for this preference has become increasingly obscure. In his earlier work, he seemed to defend the liberal model on the ground that people have a basic interest in their capacity to form and revise their conceptions of the good, so as to ensure that these conceptions are worthy of their continued allegiance. This autonomy argument is a familiar liberal argument for civil rights. Indeed, liberals are often defined as those who support toleration because it is necessary for the promotion of autonomy. As Mendus notes, "the autonomy argument is sometimes referred to as the characteristically liberal argument for toleration" (Mendus 1989: 56).

In his later writings, however, Rawls wants to avoid this autonomy argument, which he views as "sectarian," and insensitive to the views of certain religious and ethnic minorities. His solution is to abandon any form of liberalism that relies on a "comprehensive" ideal such as autonomy and rely instead on a "political" conception of the person as free and equal. But this strategy, I have argued, does not work. It simply leaves it unclear why a liberal state should assign priority to civil rights, without, in fact, being any more sympathetic to the demands of nonliberal minorities. A more appropriate response, I believe, is to continue to defend comprehensive liberalism, but to recognize that there are limits to our ability to implement and impose liberal principles on groups that have not endorsed those principles.

References

Bell D (1993) Communitarianism and its critics. Oxford University Press

Borchers D, Vitikainen A (eds) (2012) On exit: interdisciplinary perspectives on the right of exit in liberal multicultural societies. Walter de Gruyter

Braude B, Lewis B (1982) Introduction. In: Braude L (ed) Christians and Jews in the Ottoman empire. Holmes and Meyer

Buchanan A (1975) Revisability and rational choice. Can J Philos 5:395–408

D'Entreves MP (1990) Communitarianism and the question of tolerance. J Soc Philos 21(1):77–91

Davison R (1982) The millets as agents of change in the nineteenth-century Ottoman empire. In: Braude B, Lewis B (eds) Christians and Jews in the Ottoman empire. Holmes and Meyer

Deveaux M (2006) Gender and justice in multicultural liberal states. Oxford University Press

Eisenberg A, Spinner-Halev J (eds) (2005) Minorities within minorities: equality, rights and diversity. Cambridge University Press

Elton GR (1984a) Introduction to special issue on persecution and toleration. Stud Church Hist 21: xiii–xv

Elton GR (1984b) Persecution and toleration in the English reformation. Stud Church Hist 21:163–187

Galston W (1995) Two concepts of liberalism. Ethics 105:516–534

Garnsey P (1984) Religious tolerance in classical antiquity. Stud Church Hist 21:1–27

Janzen W (1990) Limits of liberty: the experiences of Mennonite, Hutterite, and Doukhobor communities in Canada. University of Toronto Press

Karpat K (1982) Millets and nationality: the roots of the incongruity of nation and state in the post-Ottoman era. In: Braude B, Lewis B (eds) Christians and Jews in the Ottoman empire. Holmes and Meyer

Kukathas C (1992) Are there any cultural rights? Political Theory 20(1):105–139

Kymlicka W (1989) Liberalism, community, and culture. Oxford University Press

Kymlicka W (1995) Multicultural citizenship. Oxford University Press

Larmore C (1987) Patterns of moral complexity. Cambridge University Press

Levy J (2000) The multiculturalism of fear. Oxford University Press

MacIntyre A (1981) After virtue: a study in moral theory. Duckworth

Mazie S (2005) Consenting adults? Amish rumspringa and the quandary of exit in liberalism. Perspect Polit 3(4):745–759

McCabe D (2010) Modus vivendi liberalism: theory and practice. Cambridge University Press

McDonald M (1991) Should communities have rights? Reflections on liberal individualism. Can J Law Jurisprud 4(2):217–237

Mendus S (1989) Toleration and the limits of liberalism. Humanities Press

Mill JS (1982) On liberty. Penguin

Modood T (1993) Kymlicka on British Muslims. Anal Krit 15(1):87–91

Newman D (2011) Community and collective rights: a theoretical framework for rights held by groups. Bloomsbury Publishing

Okin SM (1999) Is multiculturalism bad for women? Press, Princeton University

Okin SM (2002) 'Mistresses of their own destiny': group rights, gender, and realistic rights of exit. Ethics 112(2):205–230

Parekh B (1990) The Rushdie affair: research agenda for political philosophy. Pol Stud 38:695–709

Poulter S (1987) Ethnic minority customs, English law, and human rights. Int Comp Law Q 36(3):589–615

Rawls J (1974) Reply to Alexander and Musgrave. Q J Econ 88(4):633–655

Rawls J (1980) Kantian constructivism in moral theory. J Philos 77(9):515–572

Rawls J (1982) The basic liberties and their priority. Tanner Lect Human Values 3:1–87

Rawls J (1985) Justice as fairness: political not metaphysical. Philos Public Aff 14(3):223–251

Rawls J (1987) The idea of an overlapping consensus. Oxf J Leg Stud 7(1):1–25

Rawls J (1988) The priority of right and ideas of the good. Philos Public Aff 17(4):251–276

Rawls J (1989) The domain of the political and overlapping consensus. N Y Univ Law Rev 64(2):233–255

Rawls J (1993) Political liberalism. Columbia University Press

Robinson A (2003) Cultural rights and internal minorities: of Pueblos and Protestants. Can J Polit Sci 36(1):107–127

Rubio-Marín R, Kymlicka W (eds) (2018) Gender parity and multicultural feminism: towards a new synthesis. Oxford University Press

Runciman S (1970) The Orthodox churches and the secular state. Auckland University Press

Sandel M (1982) Liberalism and the limits of justice. Cambridge University Press

Sandel M (1990) Freedom of conscience of freedom of choice. In: Hunter J, Guinness O (eds) Articles of faith, articles of peace. Brookings Institute

Shachar A (2001) Multicultural jurisdictions: cultural differences and women's rights. Cambridge University Press

Sleat M (2013) Liberal realism: a realist theory of liberal politics. Manchester University Press

Song S (2007) Justice, gender, and the politics of multiculturalism. Cambridge University Press

Spinner-Halev J (2000) Surviving diversity: religion and democratic citizenship. JHU Press

Weston W (1981) Freedom of religion and the American Indian. In: Nichols R (ed) The American Indian: past and present, 2nd edn. Wiley

Modus Vivendi Toleration

26

Manon Westphal

Contents

Introduction 500
Modus Vivendi 501
A Modus Vivendi Perspective on Toleration 504
    The Traditional Conception of Toleration 506
    Accommodative Toleration 507
Liberal Democracies as Arrangements of Modus Vivendi Toleration 510
    Modus Vivendi Liberalism and the Limits of Toleration 510
    A Modus Vivendi Perspective on the Crisis of Liberal Democracies 512
Summary and Future Directions of Research 515
References 517

Abstract

This chapter outlines a modus vivendi perspective on toleration. A modus vivendi is an arrangement that balances conflicting interests and enables peaceful coexistence under conditions of disagreement and conflict. First, the chapter defines the notion of modus vivendi toleration. John Horton has convincingly argued that a modus vivendi perspective rehabilitates the traditional understanding of toleration according to which being tolerant means to refrain from interference with the practices of others. However, the creation of modus vivendi arrangements also requires what will be called accommodative toleration: those who are party to a conflict need to accept that views which they reject influence collective decisions. Second, the chapter addresses the context of liberal democracies and the challenges posed by right-wing populism to outline potential contributions of a modus vivendi perspective to the debate on the current crisis of liberal democracies. David McCabe has shown what it means to read the liberal state as a modus vivendi and specified the limits of toleration in the liberal state from a modus

---

M. Westphal (✉)
Institute of Political Science, University of Münster, Münster, Germany
e-mail: manon.westphal@uni-muenster.de

© The Author(s), under exclusive licence to Springer Nature Switzerland AG 2022   499
M. Sardoč (ed.), *The Palgrave Handbook of Toleration*,
https://doi.org/10.1007/978-3-030-42121-2_14

vivendi point of view. The chapter argues that a modus vivendi interpretation of the current crisis of liberal democracies highlights the wide range of political possibilities within these limits. What is needed in the current situation are renegotiations of existing institutions and practices that might result in fundamental reforms provided that they respect the requirements of modus vivendi toleration.

Keywords

Acceptance · Accommodative toleration · Crisis · Disagreement · Conflict · Democracy · John Horton · Liberalism · Liberal democracy · David McCabe · Modus vivendi · Populism

---

Introduction

Modus vivendi theorists argue that, contrary to an often negative resonance to the term, the concept of modus vivendi deserves more attention in political theory debates about diversity and conflict. A political theory of modus vivendi recognizes that disagreement, power, and self-interests are central to politics and that the acceptance of political arrangements is often merely "'grudging', 'wary' and 'reluctant'" (Horton 2006: 164). It takes seriously the "non-ideal, mundane and quotidian character of politics" (Horton 2010a: 437) without losing sight of the cooperative element of politics. From a modus vivendi perspective, the task of a political processing of conflicts is to generate "broadly consensual" arrangements (Horton 2010a: 438). One reason for discussing the topic of toleration through a modus vivendi lens is that this perspective might contribute something new to the debate on toleration. Because modus vivendi as a positive political concept is still a "nascent idea" (Horton 2010a: 432), a modus vivendi perspective might bring some distinctive and possibly novel considerations to the debate. A second reason why it might be worthwhile to specify the relationship between modus vivendi and toleration is that the concept of modus vivendi has some obvious affinities with the notion of toleration: if a modus vivendi is in place where parties who are divided by their disagreement accept certain rules and decisions as arrangements that they can live with, the functioning of modus vivendi politics seems to depend on the willingness of the involved actors to tolerate other views and ways of life (Horton 2011, 2019a).

The chapter outlines the notion of modus vivendi toleration and describes some practical implications of this notion by applying it to the current crisis of liberal democracies. The first part focuses on the concepts of modus vivendi and toleration. Here, the chapter draws especially on the work of John Horton, who has developed the most advanced theory of modus vivendi to date and who also presents important considerations on the nature of the relationship between modus vivendi and toleration. In particular, Horton argues that a modus vivendi perspective rehabilitates the traditional understanding of toleration, which is sometimes also called "mere" toleration. However, the chapter argues that neither the vertical relationships between the state and the citizens nor the horizontal relationships among citizens can be relationships of mere toleration alone. In addition to "mere" toleration, modus vivendi toleration includes what will be called *accommodative toleration*. Accommodative toleration implies that the coercive rules of the state contain concessions to the different views that exist in a diverse political community and that citizens are willing to accept that political demands which defend views and practices that they reject influence the shape of modus vivendi arrangements. Accommodative toleration thus contributes to a fuller description of modus vivendi toleration without, however, making it collapse into a respect conception of toleration.

In the second part, the chapter relates its discussion of modus vivendi toleration to the current crisis of liberal democracies, which finds its expression, even if not exclusively, in the recent political success of right-wing populists. Because modus vivendi theorists emphasize the independence of modus vivendi from liberalism – modus vivendi arrangements do not have to be liberal – they have seldom shown interest in the nature of liberal forms of political order. David McCabe (2010) is an exception in this regard. His theory of modus vivendi liberalism shows what it may mean to theorize the liberal state through a modus vivendi lens. However, while McCabe offers a modus vivendi interpretation of the liberal state and, as part of that project, specifies what the *limits of toleration* in a liberal state are, the current crisis of liberal democracies urges modus vivendi theorists to draw attention to the wide range of political possibilities *within* these limits. A modus vivendi perspective suggests reading the current crisis as a situation where the broad acceptance of previous modus vivendi arrangements has eroded and political processes are needed that enable renegotiations of those arrangements. Importantly, this does not mean that a modus vivendi perspective is uncritical of the demands of populists. Reading the increased political support of right-wing populists as reflecting an eroded acceptance of the status quo does not mean that populists offer adequate responses to the question what potential renegotiations of the status quo might look like. In addition, a modus vivendi perspective limits the range of potential outcomes of renegotiations. Any renegotiated arrangement must respect the substantive limits to toleration in the liberal state that McCabe described and meet the requirements of accommodative toleration as described in this chapter.

The chapter thus shows what a political theory of modus vivendi has to contribute to the debate on toleration in political theory and also demonstrates that there is some considerable potential for applying modus vivendi theorizing to debates on current political challenges that have not played a central role in the work of modus vivendi theorists so far. It concludes with some considerations on possible directions of future research on the topic.

Modus Vivendi

Central to the concept of modus vivendi is the notion of peaceful coexistence (Gray 2000: 105; Horton 2010a: 438; Rossi 2010: 27; Willems 2016: 297). Modus vivendi arrangements are "institutions that enable us to live together in peace under circumstances of disagreement and conflict" (Wendt 2016: 351). There exist two fundamentally different views of modus vivendi in the literature (Westphal 2019: 2–3). One sees modus vivendi as a deficient form of political order. This view has been famously presented by John Rawls in *Political Liberalism* (2005). For Rawls, a modus vivendi is an inherently unstable arrangement that results from a clash of interests among parties who are "ready to pursue their goals at the expense of the other" (Rawls 2005: 147). Because a modus vivendi results from the coincidental "convergence of self- or group interests" (Rawls 2005: 147), it depends entirely "on happenstance and a balance of relative forces" (Rawls 2005: 148). Rawls gives the example of the conflict between Catholics and Protestants in the sixteenth century to illustrate this feature of a modus vivendi. Because at that time "[b]oth faiths held that it was the duty of the ruler to uphold the true religion [...] the acceptance of the principle of toleration would indeed be a mere modus vivendi, because if either faith becomes dominant, the principle of toleration would no longer be followed" (Rawls 2005: 148). Similar descriptions of modus vivendi can be found elsewhere. According to Daniel Weinstock, for instance, a modus vivendi "results from the playing out of purely strategic and tactical dynamics" (Weinstock 2017: 639). Those who are party to a modus vivendi "are motivated by the wish to sue whatever advantage they can in order to maximize the extent to which their preferences are satisfied" (Weinstock 2017: 639).

A different view of modus vivendi has been presented by theorists whose work can be located within the broader strand of political theory that is often referred to as political realism. Realists are united by the understanding that political theory should avoid moralist forms of reasoning and instead develop arguments from a consideration of the dynamics of real politics such as those related to disagreement, conflict, and power (e.g., Galston 2010; Rossi and Sleat 2014). John Horton points out that "[o]ne of the principal motivations behind the modus vivendi approach is better to capture at least some of those aspects of the political that the realist critique argues liberal moralism neglects" (Horton 2010a: 437). By contrast with Rawls and other authors who consider modus vivendi a deficient form of political order, this second group of authors highlights the political achievements of modus vivendi. It is this group that this chapter refers to when it speaks of modus vivendi theorists.

John Gray's work and especially *Two Faces of Liberalism* (2000) established the understanding that defenders of a positive view of modus vivendi share: modus vivendi arrangements create something genuinely positive by enabling "individuals and communities with conflicting values and interests" to interact peacefully in circumstances of disagreement and conflict (Gray 2000: 105). Gray is somewhat ambiguous about the extent to which modus vivendi arrangements express liberal values. He characterizes modus vivendi as one neglected "face" of liberalism, but also emphasizes that modus vivendi arrangements need not be liberal. Modus vivendi arrangements are shaped by relevant contexts and by what those who live in relevant contexts consider important to enable peaceful coexistence. "The terms of such *modi vivendi* will be constrained by a universal minimum morality which specifies a range of generically human goods and bads; but within the vast range of legitimate *modi vivendi* there are many that do not embody the full range of liberal freedoms" (Gray 1998: 20).

Some critics of Gray's theory question that his account of a universal minimal morality actually achieves the independence of liberalism that Gray, at least in central passages of *Two Faces of Liberalism*, argues is characteristic of modus vivendi (see, e.g., McCabe 2019; Talisse 2000). On the one hand, the avoidance of at least several of the human evils that Gray refers to in his specification of the universal minimal morality does not already render relevant regimes liberal. For instance, he mentions the evils of "genocide," the "suppression of minorities, or of the majority," humiliation, the destruction of the "common environment," or "religious persecution" (Gray 2000: 107). On the other hand, Gray also gives examples of universal goods that seem to be more closely related to liberal states, such as "a rule of law and the capacity to maintain peace, effective representative institutions, and a government that is removable by its citizens without recourse to violence" (Gray 2000: 107). Drawing a line between the minimal morality of modus vivendi and a distinctly liberal morality is an important challenge for modus vivendi theorists who follow Gray's line of argument and refer to notions of universal human goods and bads to specify the meaning of modus vivendi.

John Horton, who has presented the most fully developed theory of modus vivendi to date (Horton 2006, 2010a, 2019a, b), offers a different definition of modus vivendi. Rather than describing the content of universal goods and evils, Horton identifies "two constitutive components" of modus vivendi (Horton 2010a: 438). The first is "an ongoing concern with the conditions of peace and security, by which is meant primarily the avoidance of serious civil disruption and the maintenance of a level of social order that is at least sufficient to enable the parties subject to it to live minimally worthwhile lives" (Horton 2010a: 438). This does not mean that peace and security are "necessarily overriding all other goods" in a modus vivendi, but that they are "peculiarly fundamental goods of politics" that "have at least instrumental value to almost everyone" (Horton 2010a: 438). The second constitutive component of modus vivendi is that it "has to be broadly 'acceptable' or 'agreeable' to those who are party to it, even if only reluctantly and for diverse reasons" (Horton 2010a: 439).

Horton specifies the acceptance criterion of modus vivendi as follows. First, acceptance must not be a product of "clear, wilful, systematic and comprehensive deception by those with political power" (Horton 2010a: 439). Second, different sorts of reasons can motivate parties to accept a modus vivendi arrangement. "[A] modus vivendi can be arrived at by drawing on whatever resources – moral, intellectual, cultural, pragmatic, etc., as well as self-interest – are available in helping the parties to reach it" (Horton 2010a: 439; see also Rossi 2010: 27). Third, Horton argues that acceptance has a subjective and an objective component (Horton 2019b): not only people's expressed views count as indicators of acceptance but also their behavior. If people, for instance, participate in the regular institutions and procedures of a political order and benefit from the cooperation that this order enables, such participation should be seen as an evidence of their acceptance of the existing arrangements (Horton 2019b: 140). Even if this specification leaves open important questions, that is, how one distinguishes between a chosen and a coerced compliance with modus vivendi arrangements, it shows how a political theory of modus vivendi can define acceptance in a way that enables it to keep a distance from idealizing or moralist argument. The understanding that political arrangements fail to meet the acceptance criterion only if there exist, in addition to articulated criticisms, forms of behavior that express an unwillingness to live under those arrangements, clearly marks a difference to theories that define the expression of consent, or public justifiability as criteria of acceptance. Where people refuse to give their consent to, or deny the justifiability of existing arrangements, but do not openly confront these arrangements, the acceptance criterion of modus vivendi is met.

On the basis of his positive definition of modus vivendi, Horton defends the notion of modus vivendi against the negative assessments of its critics. For instance, he questions Rawls's claim that a modus vivendi is necessarily unstable. On the contrary, "a modus vivendi may be quite robust and persist for a considerable length of time" (Horton 2006: 162). Especially in view of the benefits of social and political peace, parties might be "wary, on ethical and prudential grounds, about seeking to exploit short-term shifts of power in their favour" (Horton 2006: 162). Because of its adaptiveness to context, modus vivendi "may encourage a political culture of negotiation, compromise and flexibility" and thereby contribute to the stability of political cooperation (Horton 2006: 162). Horton also challenges the view that modus vivendi might be a "proposal to grant legitimacy to more or less whatever is the outcome of the free play of brute political power" (Horton 2006: 164). He points to the acceptance criterion to show why such a view is misled: because a modus vivendi must find the acceptance of those who are subject to it, "it is not the ruthlessly, coercive imposition of a particular set of arrangements by one party on another" (Horton 2006: 164). The acceptance criterion of modus vivendi limits the extent to which power can be used to create modus vivendi arrangements that disadvantage the views and concerns of some groups.

The positive view of modus vivendi will be the basis of the discussion of the relationship between modus vivendi and toleration in this chapter. This does not mean that the negative assessments of modus vivendi do not require closer attention – they certainly present challenges that a political theory of modus vivendi, which aims to exploit the potentials of modus vivendi, must consider. However, since the objective of this chapter is to describe possible contributions of modus vivendi to the debate on toleration, it focuses on those specifications of modus vivendi that identify some considerable potentials of the concept.

A Modus Vivendi Perspective on Toleration

It seems worthwhile to consider in more detail the relationship between modus vivendi and toleration not only because a perspective that sheds light on often neglected qualities of modus vivendi might contribute something distinctive to the debate on toleration. A specification of modus vivendi toleration can also contribute to the development of a political theory of modus vivendi. While it is often stressed that modus vivendi arrangements require the acceptance of those who are subject to them, it is seldom specified what sorts of political virtues or attitudes parties must have to be able to contribute to a modus vivendi. In the literature on modus vivendi, the perspectives of those who are parties to a modus vivendi are not at the center of attention (for interesting exceptions see Fossen 2019; Schweitzer 2019). If Horton (2019b) is right that there exists a natural affinity between modus vivendi and toleration, an intensification of the debate on the relationship between modus vivendi and toleration might address this lacuna of modus vivendi theorizing.

The central reason why there is a substantial overlap between the concepts of modus vivendi and toleration is that "both have the desirability of finding ways of living peaceably together at their heart" (Horton 2019a: 13). The previous section showed how such desirability is at the heart of modus vivendi: a modus vivendi is "an acceptable and workable, peaceful settlement, which allows citizens to go about their ordinary business and at least does not prevent them from living worthwhile lives" (Horton 2019a: 13). Toleration, on the other hand, can be defined as the "willingness to put up with (i.e. to permit) the actions of others, by a person, group or institution that disapproves of them" that creates "a willed refusal to interfere coercively with what is regarded as the objectionable behaviour of others" (Horton 2019a: 2; see also Horton 1996: 28). To the extent that "it offers people a way to live together without requiring them to treat ways of life that they regard as seriously objectionable and even immoral as of equal value [. . .]," toleration "can function as an important conceptual and practical resource in helping to institute a modus vivendi" (Horton 2019a: 13).

Modus vivendi and toleration can thus be seen as complementary: while a modus vivendi comprises the collection of practices and institutions that constitute the arrangements of a situation of peaceful coexistence, toleration is a combination of attitude ("willingness to put up") and behavior ("refusal to interfere") on the part of those who contribute to a modus vivendi. Even if tolerance is not bound to modus vivendi, because it can also be exercised "in circumstances where there is nothing like a modus vivendi in place" (Horton 2019a: 13), it is difficult to imagine a modus vivendi in the absence of a willingness of parties to put up with views that they reject.

Contra such a view, Glen Newey has argued that modus vivendi and toleration are in tension with each other because toleration presumes that parties have the power to intervene with the practices of others. Such power, however, is usually absent in a situation of modus vivendi. "Modus vivendi seems typically to arise when two or more parties strike a compromise because none has enough power to force through its preferred regime" (Newey 2017: 426). On the one hand, Newey is right to stress that non-interference is not an expression of toleration where parties' only reason to refrain from interference is a lack of power to interfere. Toleration requires forbearance in the sense that the objection that a party holds "is intentionally not acted upon in a way that negatively interferes with the behaviour to which there is objection" (Horton 2019c: 193). On the other hand, Newey's argument presumes a narrow understanding of modus vivendi which rather resembles Rawls's conception than that of those who have a positive view of modus vivendi (see section "Modus

Vivendi"). The latter argue that a whole range of reasons can motivate parties to create a modus vivendi, including "moral, intellectual, cultural, pragmatic" reasons (Horton 2010a: 439). Against the background of this conception, "instances of modus vivendi which do not comprise toleration" (Kühler 2019: 236) in the sense that they result merely from a stalemate of power, appear as rather specific instances of modus vivendi. Oftentimes, power is distributed asymmetrically among parties and interfering with the practices of others is a real option at least for some. Since modus vivendi arrangements as understood in this chapter must be "broadly 'acceptable' or 'agreeable'" (Horton 2010a: 439) to those who are subject to them, the powerful must choose not to make use of that option, or at least only interfere to a degree that does not render the respective arrangements unacceptable for others. Otherwise, they would lose their standing as modus vivendi arrangements. It thus seems that although a modus vivendi can be more or less tolerant, for example, provide more or less extensive opportunities for groups to live according to their worldviews or cultural practices, there "will likely be severe limits" to the possibility of an intolerant modus vivendi (Horton 2019a: 13).

The Traditional Conception of Toleration

In view of the nuanced debates about manifold possibilities to define toleration (see, e.g., Balint 2017; Forst 2013; Galeotti 2004; Newey 2013; Walzer 1997), it should be specified what sort of toleration can be seen as matching especially well with the notion of modus vivendi. There exist two views on this in the literature. The first view is that there is a natural affinity between modus vivendi and the *traditional understanding of toleration* (Horton 2011, 2019a). According to the traditional understanding, toleration means a "willingness to put up with (i.e. to permit)" views or actions that one finds objectionable (Horton 2019a: 2). From a modus vivendi perspective, advantages of this understanding of toleration are that it recognizes "the antagonistic nature of many conflicts between divergent values and ways of life," that it "allows some play for the inequalities of power that are typically airbrushed out of ideal political theory" and that it "acknowledges that the complex interweaving of interests, ideals and power, of self-interest, prudence and morality, is an ineliminable feature of any plausible understanding of political life" (Horton 2011: 296). The second view, which has been outlined by Michael Kühler (2019), is that modus vivendi can also be thought of as implying a respect-based form of toleration. Kühler refers to Rainer Forst's definition of a respect conception of toleration and describes as one possible instantiation of modus vivendi a "*moral conception* of modus vivendi" which "closely resembles the moral conception of toleration, in that it could very well likewise comprise the necessary condition of fundamental moral respect and recognition of others in society" (Kühler 2019: 247).

Theorists who have criticized the traditional conception of toleration often condemn its "negative, condescending, judgemental character" (Horton 2019a: 3). Elisabetta Galeotti, for instance, argues that the traditional conception of toleration presents "too narrow a model" to the extent that it "does not meet the quests for identity, respect, dignity, recognition, and justice, implicitly posed by minority groups as groups" (Galeotti 1993: 596). Similarly, James Bohman argues that a democratic understanding of toleration "demands more of citizens than the silent toleration of reasons and attitudes that they abhor" (Bohman 2003: 758). "If we regard the persons whom we tolerate as citizens, then we must as such also regard them as entitled to put forth reasons that are valuable from their perspective" (Bohman 2003: 758). However, the idea that toleration should be exercised for reasons of justice and mutual respect stands in some considerable tension with the notion of modus vivendi.

As has been shown above, modus vivendi theorists assume that power, interests, and emotions severely limit the role that morality plays in politics. If modus vivendi theorists took the view that toleration should be exercised out of reasons of respect, this would create a tension with that fundamental premise. Sune Lægaard (2013), in a critical discussion of Forst's theory, argues that the respect conception of toleration as described by Forst is not only "extremely optimistic, in that it presupposes that people under conditions of competitive pluralism will be able to agree on where the distinction between moral norms and ethical values should be drawn" (Lægaard 2013: 534). In practice, it is also "very likely to be counterproductive, in that the respect conception focuses on exactly the kinds of disagreements that might exacerbate conflict rather than contain it" (Lægaard 2013: 534). An important reason why modus vivendi "is not from the outset committed to ideals of impartiality or equal recognition or respect, but only to the idea of an acceptable and workable, peaceful settlement" (Horton 2019b: 13) is that modus vivendi theorists share Lægaard's emphasis of the disputed nature of justice (e.g., Gray 1998: 29, 2000: 80; Horton 2010a: 436, b: 71). Because they highlight that political action is not always guided by moral considerations and that there is considerable disagreement about what views deserve respect, modus vivendi theorists could not incorporate a respect conception of toleration without thereby introducing the sort of moral argument into their theorizing that they aim to abandon.

Thus, Horton makes an important step toward a definition of modus vivendi toleration when he exposes the tension between respect conceptions of toleration and modus vivendi and argues that there exists instead a special affinity between modus vivendi and the traditional understanding of toleration. However, modus vivendi toleration requires further specification – it cannot rely on the traditional understanding of toleration only. The subsequent section shows why, in addition to the traditional understanding of toleration, modus vivendi toleration might have to include what can be dubbed *accommodative toleration*.

Accommodative Toleration

Modus vivendi requires more than toleration as defined by the traditional conception because the sole willingness to refrain from interference with the practices of others is often insufficient to create arrangements that are accepted by those subject to them. At least two considerations demonstrate why the members of groups that are merely tolerated in a polity in the sense that they are left in peace and free to exercise practices that are important to them are unlikely to accept the relevant arrangements. First, people often think that they deserve more than being merely tolerated. Horton has described this in his earlier work on toleration as follows:

> Generally, to be the object of tolerance is a welcome improvement on being the object of intolerance, but typically people do not wish themselves or their actions to be the object of either. Only when people themselves accept that what they are doing is in some respect objectionable is toleration likely to satisfy them. Otherwise, they do not want to be subject to the negative valuation that tolerance necessarily seems to carry with it. Hence the frequently observed pattern that what begins, when people are faced with intolerance, as a demand for toleration becomes transformed into a demand for more than *mere* toleration, once intolerance is no longer a threat. The demand for more than mere tolerance is the demand that what one is or does no longer be the object of the negative valuation that is an essential ingredient of toleration. (Horton 1996: 35–36)

If people do not want to be objects of negative evaluation and have an interest in finding more than that, they have a motivation to reject arrangements that merely tolerate them. That means that in order to find the acceptance of those who live under it, a modus vivendi arrangement might have to offer something more positive.

The second reason why a political theory of modus vivendi cannot rely on the traditional understanding of toleration only is that some conflicts are difficult to be solved by means of mere toleration. In a number of cases, political conflicts do not arise because groups demand the freedom to exercise certain practices in the absence of interference by others, but because groups have different views of how collective rules and institutions should look like. To give examples from different policy fields, consider political conflicts that arise because parties hold opposing views of how organ donation and transplantation practices should be regulated, or about how inheritance law should be organized. It is difficult to see how relevant demands could be made objects of toleration in the traditional sense, because what is at stake in such conflicts are not practices that could be performed if the state refrains from interference. Thus, even if toleration in the traditional sense is a workable response to some conflicts – for instance where exemptions from general laws allow groups of society to realize their cultural practices – it cannot be a workable response to all conflicts.

A political theory of modus vivendi that recognizes the shortcomings of the traditional understanding of toleration but keeps a distance from respect conceptions of toleration requires a form of toleration that goes beyond a mere willingness to put up with views or practices that one finds objectionable without, however, demanding a commitment to mutual respect. A form of toleration that might play that role is what can be called *accommodative toleration*. What accommodative toleration requires depends to some extent on the relevant actor. It is common understanding that the state and citizens can act as tolerators (Zuolo 2013: 289). A specification of how accommodative toleration requires more than the traditional conception of toleration and less than a respect conception of toleration must consider both the role of the state and the role of citizens.

As far as the role of the state is concerned, accommodative toleration requires political responsiveness to the diversity of political views among the citizenry. If people are unlikely to accept political arrangements unless these arrangements offer something positive to them, the state should not only permit groups to live according to their views and practices but, instead, define and act according to collectively binding rules that recognize the views and demands of different groups to some extent. To do so, modus vivendi arrangements could, for instance, take the form of compromises that include concessions to different views. To be sure, in order to avoid moralist argument, modus vivendi theorists must refrain from defining the requirements of political responsiveness in specific ways. The exact range of views that should be recognized and the degree to which the recognition of different views should be fairly balanced should be left to be determined by what those who are involved in relevant contexts consider acceptable solutions to political conflicts. However, what political responsiveness excludes are situations where matters of common concern are decided one-sidedly despite the existence of different views of how that matter should be dealt with among the citizenry. In situations of this sort, the state fails to exercise accommodative toleration.

As far as citizens are concerned, accommodative toleration requires a willingness to put up with views and practices that one finds objectionable not merely in the sense of refraining from interference with such views and practices, but in the sense of accepting, or enduring, that those who hold such views and act according to such practices participate in and are sometimes granted concessions in negotiations of collectively binding rules. In the absence of such a willingness on the part of the citizens, it seems difficult to imagine how the actions of the state could be expressive of accommodative toleration in the described sense. From a modus vivendi perspective, the rules that guide the actions of the state in the present represent modus vivendi arrangements that are the outcomes of previous political processes where disputed issues were negotiated. Political processes cannot generate modus vivendi arrangements that guide the actions of the state in ways that reflect political responsiveness as described above if those who contribute to those processes – either actively, by participating in relevant negotiations, or passively, by expressing their acceptance or rejection of negotiated arrangements – are unwilling to put up with some political influence on the part of actors who make political demands in defense of views and practices that they reject. In that sense, accommodative toleration requires a willingness to accept that those who hold views that one finds objectionable participate in and are sometimes granted concessions in political negotiations of collectively binding rules.

The necessity to theorize modus vivendi toleration in terms of accommodative toleration does not mean that toleration in the form of a mere willingness to refrain from interference with the practices of others is not important for modus vivendi. First, some views and practices might be unsuited objects of accommodative toleration, for instance because their political influence would undermine the conditions of peaceful coexistence. Toleration as determined by the traditional conception might be the most that can be granted such views. Second, the degree to which modus vivendi requires accommodative toleration depends on what those who are subject to the arrangements in a given context accept as terms of peaceful coexistence. In some cases, the attitudes and forms of behavior that the traditional conception of toleration describes may suffice to create arrangements that meet the broad acceptance on which modus vivendi arrangements depend. However, because actors are often unwilling to accept arrangements that merely tolerate them and because some conflicts are difficult to be solved through arrangements of mere toleration, modus vivendi, at least in a significant number of cases, requires that political responses to conflict are given in the spirit of accommodative toleration.

Liberal Democracies as Arrangements of Modus Vivendi Toleration

This section aims at putting the above considerations of what it may mean to theorize toleration from a modus vivendi perspective to the context of liberal democracies. For an obvious reason, liberal democracy has not received much attention in the modus vivendi literature to date – as has been shown, modus vivendi theorists emphasize that modus vivendi is not bound to liberal ideas. However, even if this conceptual independence of modus vivendi is central to the capacity of a political theory of modus vivendi to represent more than just an addendum to liberal political theory, it is worthwhile to examine what views open up if liberal democracy is considered through a modus vivendi lens. A modus vivendi reading might enable distinct and potentially novel perspectives on liberal democracy. In the current situation, where liberal democracies are severely challenged by developments such as the recent political success of right-wing populists, it seems more important than ever to reflect on the nature and tasks of liberal democracy and to probe what different political theory perspectives might have to contribute to such reflections.

Modus Vivendi Liberalism and the Limits of Toleration

David McCabe (2010) is at present the only modus vivendi theorist who has developed a modus vivendi interpretation of the liberal state. McCabe considers a political theory of modus vivendi liberalism capable of overcoming an important deficit of mainstream liberal theory, which is that it often pays insufficient attention to the view of a critic of liberal principles. He sees this as a deficit because people who "either endorse some illiberal vision of political association or are unsure of the appeal of the liberal account" make up the "really important audience" for defenders of the liberal state (McCabe 2010: 7). In light of their understanding that coercive rules must be justifiable to those who are subject to them, liberals must take seriously the concerns of the illiberal critic. Otherwise it is not clear how "liberal states can reasonably claim authority over him" (McCabe 2010: 7). McCabe argues that liberal theories focusing on notions of well-being, the principle of autonomy, or political reasonableness have not successfully dealt with this task (McCabe 2010: part II). He contends that a political theory of modus vivendi liberalism (MVL) is much better equipped to include the critic into the liberal project.

McCabe defines MVL as comprising two considerations. The first is "the recognition that many citizens endorse normative frameworks that recommend as ideal illiberal models of political association" (McCabe 2010: 133). The second consideration is "that many citizens see the existence of the state either as an unchangeable fact of modern life or as something that contributes vitally important goods" (McCabe 2010: 133). Under such conditions, the liberal state can represent a "compromise among citizens who recognize the value of ordered political life" and recognize that pluralism renders it impossible for them to realize "the political vision recommended by their distinct normative frameworks" (McCabe 2010: 133).

> MVL thus rests on a wager: that citizens will tolerate others' having broad liberties and accept that state power will not be used to advance their particular normative framework, in exchange for the assurance that their own liberties will be protected and that neither they nor their children will be subject to paternalist measures reflecting norms they reject. (McCabe 2010: 133)

Regarding the motivation for people to take such a tolerating stance, McCabe's explanations are to some extent ambivalent. On the one hand, when he discusses the relationship between MVL and the justificatory requirement of liberalism, McCabe argues that also the illiberal critic "recognizes the equal moral status of all persons, including those who endorse mistaken values" (McCabe 2010: 159). The above quote, on the other hand, allows a different reading of the assumed willingness to tolerate other views and practices: people might understand toleration not as a virtue that they have a duty to fulfill but, instead, as part of a bargain which they have to deliver if they want to enjoy the benefits of ordered political life that the liberal state provides. The latter specification, at least, harmonizes with the notion of accommodative toleration as described above.

McCabe also addresses the limits of toleration in the liberal state. It is not the case that modus vivendi theorists should "consider solely the requirements of civil order and forgo appeal to moral ideals" (McCabe 2010: 136). "What distinguishes MVL as I understand it is not its rejection of moral ideals, but instead its commitment to minimal moral universalism grounded in a presumption that the interests of all persons matter equally" (McCabe 2010: 138). According to McCabe, a minimal moral universalism is a "thin morality" that comprises "a core set of human rights which the MVL state is committed to protect and which draw the limits of the tolerable" (McCabe 2010: 138). Like Gray, McCabe refers to the notion of human evils to describe the content of such a minimal moral universalism. Basic human rights "rule out such evils as slavery and severe or permanent bodily harm, while guaranteeing access to such things as education, basic physical and psychological needs, and security" (McCabe 2010: 138). By contrast with Gray (see section "Modus Vivendi"), McCabe obviously does not face the task of defending his account of a "thin morality" as independent of liberal morality. Since MVL aims at a modus vivendi reconstruction of the liberal state, the "thin morality" must rather be specified in a way that renders it a plausible definition of a moral threshold that no liberal state must fail to meet and is likely to find the acceptance of people with different worldviews.

The notion of basic human rights, which McCabe illustrates with the above examples, seems to be a suitable basis to deal with that task. A state that does not protect persons from dangers such as "slavery" or "severe or permanent bodily harm" and that does not ensure access to "education, basic physical and psychological needs" (McCabe 2010: 138) could hardly count as a liberal state. In addition, the provisions of basic human rights have some considerable potential to be acceptable to people with different worldviews, even if they might have different reasons to accept them. While liberal citizens consider the implied principles as expressions of what is morally right, illiberal citizens might not view provisions like equal access to education morally desired objectives but nevertheless accept the authority of such provisions, for instance because they receive important things in return, such as peace and security and other benefits of collective institutions (McCabe 2010: 159). Thus, basic human rights seem to provide a good basis for determining the limits of toleration in a liberal state. To be sure, a question that would have to be addressed in more detail in order to flesh out where the limits of toleration are to be drawn, is what exactly the relevant list of basic human rights should include. However, rather than dealing with this important question of specification, this chapter draws attention to a blind spot of MVL.

While McCabe shows how the liberal state can be read as a modus vivendi arrangement and how it is possible to define the limits of toleration in the liberal state, he does not pay much attention to the continuously negotiated character of modus vivendi arrangements and the considerable range of possibilities for specifying modus vivendi arrangements *within* the limits of modus vivendi toleration. Especially if modus vivendi theory is to be applied to provide some reflections on the current crisis of liberal democracies, it is these features of modus vivendi that should be put at the center of the debate.

A Modus Vivendi Perspective on the Crisis of Liberal Democracies

The crisis of liberal democracies is of course not an entirely new phenomenon. About one and a half decades ago, Colin Crouch (2004) famously identified tendencies of "post-democracy" in liberal democracies such as a too strong influence of experts in politics and a lack of broad political debates on fundamental political matters. However, the recent rise of right-wing populism has contributed to a deepening of the crisis of liberal democracies and a widespread perception of the situation *as* a crisis. Some observers view recent developments as expressing the emergence of an illiberal democracy (e.g., Mounk 2018). Following Chantal Mouffe, who identifies the specificity of liberal democracy to consist in a need to balance the "logic of liberalism" and its focus on individual rights with the "logic of democracy" and its focus on democratic self-government (Mouffe 2000: 93), these crisis diagnoses can be seen as indicating developments that challenge existing liberal democracies from opposite directions. While post-democracy analyses point to tendencies that weaken democratic self-government, analyses that interpret right-wing populism as advancing the vision of an illiberal democracy highlight that what is under attack in the current situation is especially institutions expressing the liberal logic of liberal democracy.

This section shows what a modus vivendi perspective might contribute to a debate on how the current crisis should be interpreted and what measures might be in place to respond to it. Recall that Horton (2019b) argues that the acceptance of modus vivendi arrangements finds expression not only in explicit approval but also in people's behavior. On the one hand, this renders a political theory of modus vivendi considerably tolerant of criticism of the status quo: because it assumes that people also express their acceptance of existing arrangements by participating in the regular institutions and practices of those arrangements, that part of the citizenry that is seen to contribute to the legitimacy of modus vivendi arrangements is often significantly bigger than it would be if only articulated views of those arrangements counted as expressions of acceptance. On the other hand, the behavioral conception of acceptance endows a political theory of modus vivendi with a capacity for critique where people express, through their behavior, that they do not accept the existing arrangements. In the current situation in liberal democracies, the increased number of votes for populist parties can be read as such an expression. Even if citizens who vote for populist parties still participate in regular election procedures, they do so by giving support to parties that articulate fundamental criticisms of the status quo and often present themselves as the alleged "only real alternative to the system" (Mouffe 2005: 67). From that perspective, the increased political support of populist and especially right-wing populist parties in liberal democracies shows that a consider-able number of citizens express, through their behavior, that they reject the existing arrangements and thereby put into doubt the legitimacy of the status quo.

If a modus vivendi perspective reads the current situation as a situation where at least a significant part of the citizenry withdraws its acceptance of existing arrange-ments and thereby contributes to a crisis of legitimacy, the question is how liberal democracies should respond to this crisis. Recall at this point Horton's response to Rawls's concern about the instability of a modus vivendi. One of the reasons why a modus vivendi, contra Rawls's assessment, might in fact prove to be considerably stable is that it "may encourage a political culture of negotiation, compromise and flexibility" (Horton 2006: 162). Because it takes to be legitimate what parties identify as workable terms of peaceful coexistence, modus vivendi theory has no inbuilt affinity to the status quo. Where the acceptance of existing arrangements ceases, these arrangements no longer serve their political purpose and need to be renegotiated if compliance through coercion is to be avoided (Horton 2010a: 441). It is exactly this openness toward frequent renegotiations and political renewal that can contribute to the overall stability of a political order: by allowing redefinitions of social institutions and practices, a political order might adapt to changed circum-stances to again find that sort of broad acceptance that modus vivendi requires. A modus vivendi reading thus suggests that liberal democracies should respond to the current political situation by providing possibilities to renegotiate existing arrangements. Liberal democracies should not just defend their institutions and practices as they currently exist but enable political processes where the shape of these institutions and practices can be renegotiated.

A modus vivendi perspective leaves broad scope for substantially different views to contribute to such renegotiations and it is largely nonrestrictive as regards potential outcomes of such renegotiations. Since a modus vivendi does not necessarily involve the accommodation of *all* views and concerns or an *equal* accommodation of views and concerns, outcomes may realize the concerns of some more than those of others, and they may not contain concessions to some views at all. In particular, the proposed modus vivendi perspective does not imply an uncritical stance toward the views and political demands of right-wing populists. For at least three reasons, it would be inappropriate to interpret the modus vivendi case for responding to the current "populist moment" (Galston 2017) with renegotiations of existing institutions and practices of liberal democracy as legitimizing the political projects of right-wing populists: a modus vivendi perspective defines certain substantive limits of toleration in the liberal state, it highlights the diversity of reasons that motivate people to vote for right-wing populist parties, and it insists on the need to realize renegotiations in ways that reflect the requirements of accommodative toleration. Consider each of these points in turn.

Regarding the first, a brief reminder of McCabe's argument suffices. MVL shows that a modus vivendi interpretation of the liberal state implies a moral minimum that sets limits to what can legitimately be decided in politics (see section "Modus Vivendi Liberalism and the Limits of Toleration"). As a consequence, where the views and demands of right-wing populists threaten the content of this moral minimum, they must be excluded also by newly negotiated modus vivendi arrangements in a liberal democracy. Such views cannot be more than objects of mere toleration by a liberal state.

In addition, it is important to distinguish between the policy agendas of right-wing populist parties and the views and concerns of citizens who vote for these parties. The modus vivendi reading of the current situation as a crisis that demands renegotiations of the institutions and practices of liberal democracies focuses on the voting behavior of a considerable part of the citizenry, not on the existence of right-wing populist parties as such, and the motivations of citizens to vote for populist parties are not necessarily reflected by the policies of these parties. Because modus vivendi theorists emphasize that the reasons which motivate political action are often multiple (see section "Modus Vivendi"), they should be skeptical that all citizens who vote for right-wing populist parties do so only or primarily because they identify with the policy agendas of those parties. To be sure, some voters give their votes for purely ideological reasons. Others, however, may identify only with some elements of these agendas and disagree with others. Yet others may only vote for right-wing populist parties because they see no other way of expressing their dissatisfaction with the status quo in a meaningful way. The assumption that people vote for populist parties for different reasons finds some support in the populism literature. For instance, studies dealing with the causes of populism often point out that the recent political success of populist parties cannot be explained without considering the current cultural and economic circumstances in liberal democracies (see, e.g., Galston 2017; Inglehart and Norris 2016; Manow 2018). Such findings indicate that any full explanation of citizens' dissatisfaction with the status quo must include a complex set of factors among which socioeconomic inequalities and cultural divisions play an important role. That means that political actors who make proposals for renegotiating existing institutions and practices in ways that address these issues directly could speak more effectively to the views and concerns that motivate many citizens to express their dissatisfaction through their voting behavior than the right-wing populists parties which have benefited from that voting behavior.

Third, the above argument about the need to interpret modus vivendi toleration as comprising accommodative toleration shows that a modus vivendi case for reading the current crisis of liberal democracies as a situation where existing institutions and practices should be made subject to renegotiations also implies certain standards of how such renegotiations should look like. Section "Accommodative Toleration" defined accommodative toleration as a willingness to put up with views and practices that one finds objectionable in the sense of accepting, or enduring, that those who hold such views and act according to such practices participate in and are sometimes granted concessions in political negotiations. Where political actors do not display such a willingness, they do not make legitimate contributions to the sort of political renegotiations that appears desirable from a modus vivendi perspective in the current situation. Consider, for instance, potential renegotiations of the rules and practices that determine forms of dealing with cultural diversity in a liberal democracy. If a political actor denies the legitimate existence of cultural diversity and attempts to exclude others from such negotiation processes, or demands the implementation of rules that would prevent certain cultural groups from articulating their views and demanding recognition of their views in future negotiation processes, that actor would violate the standards of modus vivendi toleration.

Accommodative toleration thus not only enables a fuller description of modus vivendi toleration than the traditional understanding of toleration taken in isolation. It also endows a political theory of modus vivendi with important means to specify and defend the proposal that the response to the current crisis of liberal democracies should consist in a renegotiation of existing institutions and practices against the potential objection that it might thereby take on an uncritical stance toward the views and demands of right-wing populists.

Summary and Future Directions of Research

This chapter developed some considerations on what it may mean to theorize toleration from a modus vivendi perspective. First, it separated negative from positive views of modus vivendi and argued that it is worthwhile to probe what positive views of modus vivendi might contribute to the debate on toleration (section "Modus Vivendi"). According to a positive understanding of the term, modus vivendi arrangements are political arrangements that serve conditions of peace and order and are broadly accepted among those who live under these arrangements even if the reasons for acceptance can vary and may also include purely pragmatic reasons as well as self-interest. Second, the chapter described the notion of modus vivendi toleration (section "A Modus Vivendi Perspective on Toleration"). Drawing especially on the work of John Horton, it showed that a political theory of modus vivendi does not share many theorists' principled concerns about the traditional understanding of toleration. In some cases, a willingness of political actors to refrain from interference with the views and practices of others may not only be the most that can be achieved but may also suffice to create arrangements of peaceful coexistence. However, the chapter also argued for an addendum to modus vivendi toleration. Because people are often unwilling to accept arrangements that do not recognize their views to some positive extent and because some political conflicts are difficult to be solved through means of mere toleration, *accommodative toleration* is a central component of modus vivendi toleration. Accommodative toleration requires the state to act on the basis of arrangements that contain concessions to different views, and it requires citizens to accept that others who hold views that they find objectionable participate in and are sometimes granted concessions in political negotiations. Third, the chapter applied the modus vivendi perspective to liberal democracies (section "Liberal Democracies as Arrangements of Modus Vivendi Toleration"). Drawing on McCabe's MVL, it showed how the liberal state can be read as an instance of modus vivendi and how a modus vivendi perspective specifies the limits of toleration in a liberal state. However, a modus vivendi analysis of the current crisis of liberal democracies draws attention to possibilities of renegotiating institutions and practices within these limits. Because the significant number of votes that populist parties receive can be interpreted as a substantial part of the citizenry withdrawing their acceptance of institutions and practices in their current forms, what is needed are political renegotiations of these forms. While a modus vivendi perspective leaves considerable room for such renegotiations to create new institutions and practices, it demands adherence to the moral minimum, which defines the limits of toleration in a liberal state, and it requires participants to accept the influence of other views and concerns on political decisions as defined by the notion of accommodative toleration.

There seem to be especially three important tasks of future research on modus vivendi and toleration. First, the relationship between the components of modus vivendi toleration: the chapter has shown that modus vivendi toleration cannot consist of the traditional conception of toleration alone and should also include accommodative toleration, but an important question is how exactly these forms of toleration complement each other and how much of which is needed to enable modus vivendi politics. Second, the conditions of modus vivendi toleration: a fuller picture of modus vivendi toleration requires an examination of the practical conditions that are necessary for, or conducive to the realization of modus vivendi toleration, for instance in terms of socioeconomic conditions or the institutional design of political processes. Third, the actors of modus vivendi toleration: while this chapter distinguished between the role of the state and the role of citizens in its definition of accommodative toleration, it is vital to also consider the role of collective actors like political parties and political movements to be able to further specify the meaning of modus vivendi toleration in the context of possible renegotiations of the institutions and practices in liberal democracies. As has been argued in the section "A Modus Vivendi Perspective on the Crisis of Liberal Democracies," a consideration of the multiple reasons that may motivate citizens to vote for right-wing populist parties renders a modus vivendi perspective aware that other political actors might be able to effectively address the concerns that motivate the voting behavior of at least many of those who contribute to the current electoral success of right-wing populists. However, it should be asked who could articulate such responses in ways that contribute to a stabilizing renewal of liberal democracy – is it political parties, either the existing ones or new ones, or is it political movements, or both? These are some of the topics and questions that a future development of a modus vivendi perspective on toleration should address. (An earlier draft of this chapter was presented at the panel "Challenges to Liberal Democracy: Reacting to Populism and Extremism" at the 2019 ECPR General Conference in Wroclaw. I am especially grateful to Uğur Aytaç, Giulia Bistagnino, Chiara Destri, and John Horton for their helpful written comments on the draft and to Thomas Altmeppen, Manuel Biertz, Sabrina Görisch, Oliver Hidalgo, Michael Kubiak, Claudia Ritzi, and Ulrich Willems for a helpful discussion at the Political Theory Colloquium in Trier in September 2019.)

References

Balint P (2017) Respecting toleration: traditional liberalism and contemporary diversity. Oxford University Press, Oxford
Bohman J (2003) Deliberative toleration. Political Theory 31(6):757–779
Crouch C (2004) Post-democracy. Polity, Cambridge
Forst R (2013) Toleration in conflict. Past and present. Cambridge University Press, Cambridge
Fossen T (2019) Modus vivendi beyond the social contract: peace, justice, and survival in realist political theory. In: Horton J, Westphal M, Willems U (eds) The political theory of modus vivendi. Springer, Heidelberg, pp 111–127
Galeotti AE (1993) Citizenship and equality: the place for toleration. Political Theory 21(4):585–605
Galeotti AE (2004) Toleration as recognition. Cambridge University Press, Cambridge
Galston WA (2010) Realism in political theory. Eur J Polit Theo 9(4):385–411
Galston WA (2017) The populist moment. J Democr 28(2):21–33
Gray J (1998) Where pluralists and liberals part company. Int J Philos Stud 6(1):17–36
Gray J (2000) Two faces of liberalism. Polity Press, Cambridge
Horton J (1996) Toleration as a virtue. In: Heyd D (ed) Toleration: an elusive virtue. Princeton University Press, Princeton, pp 28–43
Horton J (2006) John Gray and the political theory of modus vivendi. Crit Rev Int Soc Pol Phil 9(2):155–169
Horton J (2010a) Realism, liberal moralism and a political theory of modus vivendi. Eur J Polit Theo 9(4):431–448
Horton J (2010b) Reasonable disagreement. In: Dimova-Cookson M, Stirk PMR (eds) Multiculturalism and moral conflict. Routledge, Abingdon/New York, pp 58–74
Horton J (2011) Why the traditional conception of toleration still matters. Crit Rev Int Soc Pol Phil 14(3):289–305

Horton J (2019a) Toleration and modus vivendi. In: Critical review of international social and political philosophy (online first), 1–19. https://doi.org/10.1080/13698230.2019.1616879

Horton J (2019b) Modus vivendi and legitimacy. In: Horton J, Westphal M, Willems U (eds) The political theory of modus vivendi. Springer, Heidelberg, pp 131–148

Horton J (2019c) Conceptualising toleration. Crit Theory Int Soc Polit Philos 23(2):191–196

Inglehart RF, Norris P (2016) Trump, brexit, and the rise of populism: economic have-nots and cultural backlash. Faculty Research working paper series (Harvard Kennedy School), pp 1–52

Kühler M (2019) Modus vivendi and toleration. In: Horton J, Westphal M, Willems U (eds) The political theory of modus vivendi. Springer, Heidelberg, pp 235–253

Lægaard S (2013) Toleration out of respect? Crit Rev Int Soc Pol Phil 16(4):520–536

Manow P (2018) Die Politische Ökonomie des Populismus. Suhrkamp, Frankfurt am Main

McCabe D (2010) Modus vivendi liberalism. Theory and practice. Cambridge University Press, New York

McCabe D (2019) Modus vivendi as a global political morality. In: Horton J, Westphal M, Willems U (eds) The political theory of modus vivendi. Springer, Heidelberg, pp 149–167

Mouffe C (2000) The democratic paradox. Verso, London/New York

Mouffe C (2005) The 'end of politics' and the challenge of right-wing populism. In: Panizza F (ed) Populism and the mirror of democracy. Verso, London/New York, pp 50–71

Mounk Y (2018) The people vs. democracy. Why our freedom is in danger and how to save it. Harvard University Press, Cambridge, MA

Newey G (2013) Toleration in political conflict. Cambridge University Press, Cambridge

Newey G (2017) Modus vivendi, toleration and power. Philosophia 45(2):425–442

Rawls J (2005) Political liberalism. Expanded Edition. Columbia University Press, New York

Rossi E (2010) Modus vivendi, consensus, and (realist) liberal legitimacy. Public Reason 2(2):21–39

Rossi E, Sleat M (2014) Realism in normative political theory. Philos Compass 9(10):689–701

Schweitzer K (2019) Motives and modus vivendi. In: Horton J, Westphal M, Willems U (eds) The political theory of modus vivendi. Springer, Heidelberg, pp 223–233

Talisse RB (2000) Two-faced liberalism: John Gray's pluralist politics and the reinstatement of enlightenment liberalism. Crit Rev 14(4):441–458

Walzer M (1997) On toleration. Yale University Press, New Haven/London

Weinstock D (2017) Compromise, pluralism, and deliberation. Crit Rev Int Soc Pol Phil 20(5):636–655

Wendt F (2016) The moral standing of modus vivendi arrangements. Public Aff Q 30(4):351–370

Westphal, Manon (2019) Theorising Modus Vivendi. In: Horton, John/Westphal, Manon/Willems, Ulrich (eds.): The Political Theory of Modus Vivendi. Heidelberg: Springer, 1–27

Willems U (2016) Wertkonflikte als Herausforderung der Demokratie. Springer VS, Wiesbaden

Zuolo F (2013) Toleration and informal groups: how does the formal dimension affect groups' capacity to tolerate? Eur J Polit Theo 12(3):288–305

Multiculturalism and Toleration

27

Sune Lægaard

Contents

Introduction 520
Multiculturalism and Toleration as Different Ways of Responding to Diversity 521
Multiculturalism and Toleration as Positive and Negative Attitudes to Difference 523
Multiculturalism and Toleration as Modes of Accommodation 525
Toleration and Multiculturalism as Descriptive Concepts and Normative Ideals 527
Justifications for Toleration and for Multiculturalism 529
The Multiculturalism Challenge to Liberal Toleration 530
Responding to the Multiculturalism Challenge 532
Multiculturalism and Toleration at Different Levels 534
Summary and Future Directions 537
References 538

Abstract

Multiculturalism has two main meanings. One is the descriptive fact of cultural, ethnic, and religious diversity within a society, the other is a set of normative claims that the state should recognize, respect, and accommodate such diversity. Toleration is classically understood as the relation between two agents where one objects to something about the other, has the power to interfere with the other, but refrains from doing so. Multiculturalism and toleration thus both concern cases involving differences. Nevertheless, multiculturalism and toleration involve quite different attitudes to differences. Where toleration is concerned with differences toward which someone has a negative attitude, multiculturalism in the normative sense prescribes a positive attitude to differences. Furthermore, multiculturalism as a set of policies is often formulated and motivated in contrast to policies of toleration. According to many proponents of multiculturalism, toleration is not enough and might even be part of a problematic and unjust way of handling

---

S. Lægaard (✉)
Department of Communication and Arts, Roskilde University, Roskilde, Denmark
e-mail: laegaard@ruc.dk

© The Author(s), under exclusive licence to Springer Nature Switzerland AG 2022   519
M. Sardoč (ed.), *The Palgrave Handbook of Toleration*,
https://doi.org/10.1007/978-3-030-42121-2_23

differences. Multiculturalism therefore often demands that states move "beyond" toleration, i.e., from a negative to a positive attitude and from non-interference to active support and accommodation. The chapter analyzes the relation between multiculturalism and toleration. It distinguishes between claims of toleration and multiculturalism at the state level and the citizen level, respectively, which makes clear that toleration and multiculturalism might in fact be compatible in several respects.

Keywords

Acceptance · Accommodation · Difference · Diversity · Equality · Minority · Multiculturalism · Objection · Power · Tolerance · Toleration · Recognition · Respect

Introduction

Toleration and multiculturalism are both ways of relating to differences. However, toleration and multiculturalism are often thought to be at odds with each other due to the attitude they each involve to differences. Here is a recent statement of this widespread view about the relation between the two:

> *Multiculturalism is not just anti-discrimination, the sameness of treatment and the toleration of 'difference', but also a respect for difference. This respect is not simply about equal rights despite differences but also about equality as the accommodation of difference in the public space, which is shared, rather than dominated, by the majority... This genuine equality requires dropping the pretence of 'difference blindness' and allows marginalized minorities to also be visible and explicitly accommodated in the public sphere. This equality will sometimes require enforcing uniformity of treatment and eliminating discrimination against (for example) religious affiliation, and it may also require the recognition of distinctive disadvantages (such as measures to increase the number of women in a legislature) or special needs (such as the provision of halal meat in state schools).* (Modood 2019: 200–201)

Furthermore:

> *despite the unpopularity of the term 'multiculturalism', as doubts about certain policies and anxieties about certain minorities continue, mainstream public discourses are also conceiving of this diversity not merely in terms of toleration (putting up with something negative), but in terms of the positive inclusion for minorities who do not have to assimilate or conform to the norms and attitudes of the majority... this multiculturalist sensibility – the idea that 'difference' is not an unfortunate fact to be put up with but a difference worthy of equality and respect.* (Modood 2019: 201–202)

Multiculturalism and toleration are contrasted both at the conceptual level, i.e., as a matter of what toleration and multiculturalism means, and at the level of political prescriptions, where the supposed conflict between toleration and multiculturalism is often a version of the debate between liberalism and multiculturalism. This chapter analyzes the relation between multiculturalism and toleration and examines different versions of the alleged contrast or incompatibility between them as different ways of relating to diversity.

For present purposes, the relevant concept of toleration is the classical one characterized by five conditions (or components), namely, 1. difference, 2. objection, 3. power, 4. acceptance, and 5. non-interference. Briefly stated, this means that a relation between two parties is one of toleration if there is a difference in some respect between them, where one party (the tolerator, or subject of toleration) objects to how the other party is different (the object of toleration), has the power to act on this objection by interfering with the other party, but simultaneously has other reasons of acceptance that override the reasons for interference, and therefore refrains from interfering. All of these conditions or components will be discussed further below. There are of course other ways of understanding toleration, but this classical concept is the relevant one here precisely because it is the one assumed in contrasts between multiculturalism and toleration, as the quotes from Modood indicate.

Similarly, for present purposes, multiculturalism is also characterized by a number of conditions or components, namely, 1. difference, 2. acceptance, and 3. accommodation. Just as briefly stated, this means that multiculturalism in the sense of interest here, which is multiculturalism as a normative view or policy prescription, requires some party standing in a relation characterized by difference to adopt a positive attitude of acceptance regarding this difference and to act toward the different party in a way that accommodates the difference. These conditions or components will also be discussed further below.

The chapter proceeds as follow. The first section describes and compares multiculturalism and toleration as different ways of relating to diversity. The second section discusses in which senses multiculturalism and toleration involve positive and negative attitudes to differences, respectively. The third section considers how and in which senses we can understand both multiculturalism and toleration as modes of accommodation. The fourth section presents how toleration as well as multiculturalism can be both descriptive concepts and normative ideals, which leads to the fifth section on different justifications for them as normative ideals. The sixth section focuses on recent articulations of the so-called multiculturalism challenge to liberal toleration, and the seventh section discusses some responses to this challenge. The final section distinguishes between toleration and multiculturalism at different levels and discusses the issue of compatibility on this basis. The compatibility question is of interest as a way of understanding multiculturalism and toleration, because some arguments for as well as against multiculturalism assume incompatibility, and in order to understand which theoretical categories we should use to describe and discuss actual cases involving differences.

Multiculturalism and Toleration as Different Ways of Responding to Diversity

Both multiculturalism and toleration are responses to diversity. Historically, toleration in Europe was formulated and discussed in relation to the religious differences that developed after the reformation and gave rise to the wars of religion in the sixteenth and seventeenth centuries (Kaplan 2007). In this context, many people considered religious differences as extremely problematic. They not only believed that the true religious faith determined salvation for the individual but also linked this to the authority of the state and the loyalty of subjects toward their ruler. Religious diversity was therefore a problem. This provided reasons for limiting this diversity – be it in the form of forced conversion, restriction, or outright exclusion or even extermination of those with different beliefs. Religious toleration developed in this context as the idea and practice of not interfering with religious differences, of allowing people to hold differing religious beliefs and to practice their faith, at least within limits.

Whereas the standard idea of toleration in western political philosophy developed out of this case of religious toleration, the general idea of toleration has subsequently been extended to other kinds of differences, e.g., differences of opinion, political differences, gender and racial differences, sexual preferences, family patterns, etc. Toleration can accordingly be a response to many kinds of differences. What makes some difference a possible object of toleration is that someone holds a negative view of the difference in question, whether it be different religious practices, sexual preferences, or family patterns that diverge from the social norm in a given context.

Multiculturalism is a more recent idea, formulated in especially Canada and Australia in the 1970s as part of a rejection of the up until then dominant idea that these countries should have a white and English-speaking population. Multiculturalism thus started out as an opening to linguistic diversity, e.g., the recognition of French as on a par with English in Canada, but subsequently extended to ethnic differences (first of all of indigenous peoples, but also of blacks) and related cultural differences. Multiculturalism was subsequently, especially in Europe, increasingly linked to differences due to immigration, first conceived of in terms of nationality, which included ethnic, cultural and linguistic differences. However, after the Rushdie Affair and the French *Affaire du Foulard*, these differences were gradually reconceptualized as expressions of religious diversity (Horton 1993; Galeotti 2002).

Even though the word "multiculturalism" suggests that multiculturalism is about *cultural* diversity, the differences relevant to multiculturalism are thus not linked to a specific conception of culture. The underlying consideration informing multiculturalism is (cf. the opening quotes) that it concerns differences relevant for the fair inclusion and integration of minority groups as full and equal citizens (Kymlicka 1995; Modood 2007). The reasoning informing multiculturalism thus starts out from ideals of equality and inclusion and picks out the relevant types of differences in a given social context on this basis, rather than stipulating what counts as relevant differences beforehand, e.g., on the basis of some abstract account of culture.

Toleration and multiculturalism are accordingly both responses to a potentially very broad range of differences. A difference is a potential object of toleration if someone objects to it, whereas a difference is a potential object of multiculturalism if it is relevant for the fair and equal inclusion of minority groups. As long as a difference is somehow socially salient, it is a potential object of both toleration and multiculturalism (cf. social salience as a precondition for discrimination in Lippert-Rasmussen 2014).

When one says that both toleration and multiculturalism are responses to diversity, this on the one hand presupposes a non-evaluative understanding of diversity. At this stage, "diversity" is not a value; it is a fact to which both toleration and multiculturalism responds. On the other hand, the differences in question are not independent from evaluative questions either, since the relevant differences are determined by the presence of negative attitudes in the case of toleration and by being linked to positive ideals of fairness and inclusion in the case of multiculturalism. It is not culture, ethnicity, or religion *as such* that is of concern to multiculturalism; it is rather cultural, ethnic, or religious differences that function or are treated in a certain way (e.g., by exposing the members of social groups to exclusion, domination, or discrimination).

Whereas there is a link of the non-evaluative fact of difference to evaluative perspectives in both toleration and multiculturalism, the link is different in the two cases. The presence of negative attitudes to some difference is itself a given fact in the case of toleration; toleration takes its point of departure the fact that someone objects to something. Multiculturalism understood as a positive policy prescription, on the other hand, requires a decision about which forms of diversity are relevant to fairness and inclusion and thus warrant the appropriate positive attitudes. Any plausible version of multiculturalism has to base this decision on principled considerations, which usually have to do with the minority position in which some socially salient groups find themselves in a given society. Multiculturalism thus takes its point of departure in an assessment of the situation of minority groups as being unfair in some way (although see Patten 2020 for a discussion of the applicability of multiculturalism to majorities). However, toleration also gives rise to similar questions at a later stage. Whereas toleration itself is a descriptive fact – simply that someone decides not to interfere with something to which he or she objects – there is a further normative question about when we *should* be tolerant and toward *which* differences. This move from descriptive to normative turns the focus toward the acceptance component, which relies on normative values or principles that will themselves pick out what makes a given kind of difference apt for toleration.

Multiculturalism and Toleration as Positive and Negative Attitudes to Difference

The main difference between multiculturalism and toleration is that they involve opposed attitudes to differences, in a certain sense. At a general level, one might say that toleration is a negative response to differences and multiculturalism is a positive response. However, this statement has to be qualified and explained. First, there are several senses in which one can say that toleration is a negative response and multiculturalism a positive response.

The first sense in which toleration is a negative response to differences is the one captured by the objection component. People are normally only said to tolerate something when this is something they do not like, disapprove of, or otherwise find some fault with or would rather be without. In the classic case of religious toleration, the objection stemmed from disagreement about the true faith and from the related belief that people who did not adhere to the true faith could not be loyal subjects or trustworthy co-citizens. In the case of sexual difference, objection might be due to the belief that, say, homosexuality is unnatural or against God's will. Objection can also consist in a base and unreflective sense of disgust or derive from traditional practices of exclusion and stigmatization, e.g., of gays (this presupposes a wide view of what can qualify as an objection, which fits with a view of toleration as a descriptive concept rather than as a moralized ideal, cf. the discussion below).

The second sense in which toleration is a negative response to differences is the one captured by the non-interference component. This means that toleration consists in not interfering or otherwise exercising the power someone has to act on his or her objection to something. Religious toleration thus consisted in allowing people to hold and to some extent practice religious beliefs diverging from the official faith and not subjecting them to persecution based on their beliefs. Toleration of homosexuality can similarly consist in not criminalizing homosexuality or not attacking gays. So at the level of action, toleration is characterized by the absence of exercises of power. However, the negative attitude to the difference in question remains.

Multiculturalism, on the other hand, is a positive response to differences. As in the case of toleration, this covers two different senses, one concerning *attitudes* to difference and the other actual *acts* or *policies*. The first sense in which multiculturalism is a positive response to difference is the one formulated by Modood in the opening quotes in terms of "respect for difference." This can mean different things and involve different values or principles, however. One possible reason for the idea that differences are not an unfortunate fact to be put up with but are worthy of equality and respect is instrumental. In a classically Millean perspective, for instance, diversity might be a good thing simply because it contributes to a manifold of perspectives and experiments in living that might enter the marketplace of ideas and bring humanity closer to true beliefs and fulfilling ways of life. In Will Kymlicka's liberal theory of multiculturalism (1989, 1995), what he calls "societal cultures" function as "contexts of choice" that are prerequisites for meaningful choices and thus for equal opportunities. Diversity might also be an effect of something else that is positively valued. According John Rawls's political liberalism (1996), for instance, pluralism is a natural consequence of free institutions. Diversity might also be valued intrinsically, e.g., for aesthetic reasons.

The most prominent and common varieties of multiculturalism, including the one expressed in the opening quotes, however, involves some form of recognition that different ways of life are legitimate presences in society and thus should be treated equally by the state. Therefore, even though multiculturalism is sometimes formulated as the view that diversity in general and/or specific cultures are valuable *as such*, multiculturalism as a political view is more often and more plausibly a recognition of the legitimacy of different ways of life (both Taylor 1994, Galeotti 2002, and Modood 2007 exemplify the tension between formulations of recognition as affirmation and legitimacy). One way to capture these two ways of understanding the attitude to difference involved in multiculturalism is by appeal to Stephen Darwall's distinction between "appraisal respect" and "recognition respect"

(2006). Appraisal respect is an attitude of positive appraisal of a person – or, in the case of multiculturalism, of socially salient groups – or their merits. Positive appraisal of a culture thus amounts to saying that this is a good culture, e.g., because of its magnificent history, beautiful language, interesting traditions, or evaluation in light of some other qualitative standard. Appraisal respect of cultures thus implies that some cultures might be better than other cultures. Even though multiculturalists sometimes use language resembling appraisal respect, this kind of positive evaluation is not suited to multiculturalism understood as an egalitarian political view. Multiculturalism is better understood in terms of recognition respect, which is the disposition to give appropriate weight or consideration in one's practical deliberations to some fact about the object – here, of a group identity – and to regulate one's conduct by constraints derived from that fact. In multiculturalism, recognition respect of group identities is based on some underlying principle that all ways of life are equally legitimate within certain limits, e.g., insofar as they do not violate human rights or something similar.

The second sense in which multiculturalism is a positive response to difference concerns the kinds of acts or policies that follow from this positive attitude. Multiculturalism at the policy level consists in official acts of recognition of minority cultures, of support for minority cultures, or of reform of rules and institutions in order to accommodate minorities. Canadian multiculturalism thus classically involved recognizing official languages besides English and introducing different jurisdictions in Quebec and for indigenous peoples. Classic cases of multiculturalism in Britain rather concern exemptions of some groups from certain generally applicable rules, e.g., rules about the wearing of safety helmets or uniforms. Multiculturalism might also involve the extension of public support to minority faith schools or granting of official status to minority religions in addition to an established church. The point of such policies is partly to express positive recognition, partly to counteract specific burdens or inequalities that minorities face, both in order to include minorities on an equal footing.

Both toleration and multiculturalism thus include the two levels of attitudes and acts (cf. Lægaard 2010). Nevertheless, the relation between the two levels is different in the case of toleration and of multiculturalism. Where toleration consist in *not doing* what would follow from the negative attitude, i.e., refraining from acting on one's objection, multiculturalism consist in *doing* what follows from the positive attitude, i.e., to give tangible expression to the recognition of minority groups as legitimate participants in society.

Multiculturalism and Toleration as Modes of Accommodation

Even though accommodation was initially used only to characterize multiculturalism, one can understand both multiculturalism and toleration as ways of accommodating differences (Kymlicka 2012; Balint 2017: 8–9) but in different senses, for different reasons and by different means. In extension of the previous discussion, one might say that toleration is negative accommodation (accommodation despite objection and by means of non-interference within limits), whereas multiculturalism is positive accommodation (accommodation as recognition and by means of active support or reshaping of the social context). Any claim that some act or policy accommodates someone (be it a person or a group) implicitly assumes some standard of comparison or baseline relative to which the act or policy is accommodative.

In the case of toleration, the baseline is the counterfactual behavior that people would engage in if they acted on their objections. In the classic case of religious toleration, this meant persecuting religious dissenters. Therefore, any policy that falls short of persecution could – in a seventeenth century context – be said to be a form of toleration and accommodation, even if it is still far from anything resembling religious freedom or equal treatment of religions. In a more contemporary context, the de-classification of homosexuality as a psychological disorder might count as a form of toleration and accommodation (assuming that there still are prevalent beliefs about the divergent nature of homosexuality). This understanding of the sense in which toleration is a form of accommodation, which relates this to a baseline set by the objection component and the power component (i.e., people's ability to act on their objection) explains a common variety of criticisms of toleration. This criticism sees toleration as itself problematic because it describes a situation where someone still objects to and have power over others, where the absence of interference happens at the discretion of the objectors and does not guarantee equal treatment of those subjected to the combination of objection and power (see, e.g., Bessone 2013).

In the case of multiculturalism, there are two different ways of understanding the baseline (Lægaard 2017: 159). On a commonsensical understanding, the baseline is how the society in question previously treated a minority group. A society might have rules in place that burden members of a particular religious minority, e.g., because members of this group have beliefs about obligatory dress that conflict with the public rule (e.g., Sikh turbans, Islamic headscarves, Jewish skullcaps). If the state exempts members of the group from this general rule or revises the rule so that it no longer burdens them, then this would count as accommodation. This actual or temporal understanding measures accommodation relative to what was actually the case previously. There is also a more theoretical understanding of multicultural accommodation according to which the baseline is not previous actual regulations but by what would be permitted by an ideal liberal standard. This kind of baseline is assumed in discussions that see multiculturalism as a contrast to liberalism (e.g., Barry 2001). On this latter theoretical understanding, a measure only counts as multicultural accommodation if it offers "special" treatment of a group that, because it diverges from an ideal liberal standard of equal treatment, in some sense constitutes unequal treatment (similar to criticisms of affirmative action as reverse discrimination). On this theoretical understanding, reforming public rules so that they no longer burden minorities while still achieving their public aim (e.g., by making dress codes compatible with religious headwear) is not a form of multicultural accommodation, whereas it would be on the actual/temporal understanding. The theoretical understanding is thus more suited to debates that pit multiculturalism against liberalism as ideal theoretical models, whereas the actual/temporal understanding is more suited to real-world discussions focused on the ability of specific minorities to live as they want to or discussions about a particular society's ability to handle diversity.

In both the case of toleration and in the case of the actual/temporal understanding of multiculturalism, the baseline for describing toleration and multiculturalism as forms of accommodation are non-ideal states of affairs. This shows how both toleration and the actual/temporal understanding of multiculturalism are what might be called practice-oriented notions designed to capture situations in the real world rather than ideal theoretical models of what an ideal society should be like. This explains some of the criticisms directed at both the notion of toleration and against multiculturalism; both are in many cases actions or policies that would not be part of a perfectly just society. If one assesses toleration and multiculturalism against ideal standards, they will accordingly often fall short. If one, to the contrary, assess them against counterfactual or actual/temporal baselines, they qualify as forms of (however imperfect) accommodation.

This suggests that toleration and multiculturalism are suited for so-called political realism perspectives, understood as approaches that take real-world circumstances of politics, such as the prevalence of power, interest conflicts, and disagreement, as given and reject so-called moralism, which political realists understand as the imposition of normative standards from outside of politics (Williams 2005). The affinity with political realism arguably has a conceptual basis in the case of toleration (Kühler 2019). In the case of multiculturalism, this possible affinity with realism might be indirectly evident through the appeal of many multiculturalist theorists to a contextualist approach that takes contingent facts about the context of actual cases to play an important role in the argument for multiculturalism (cf. Lægaard 2015). This real-world focus also points in the direction of another central discussion, namely, whether toleration and multiculturalism are descriptive concepts or normative ideals.

Toleration and Multiculturalism as Descriptive Concepts and Normative Ideals

Debates about multiculturalism standardly distinguish between a descriptive and a normative sense of multiculturalism. The descriptive sense simply reports the demographic fact that a given society is diverse in some sense, e.g., due to the presence of indigenous peoples, national minorities, or groups of immigrant origin with a culture, language, or religion different from the majority within the society in question. The descriptive sense is non-evaluative in that it does not say anything about whether this diversity is good or bad. The normative sense, in contrast, is the claim that the state should pursue certain policies in order to accommodate this diversity in a just way. Normative multiculturalism is thus both evaluative, in that it criticizes certain policies as inadequately accommodative, and prescriptive, in that it directs the state to adopt certain policies. Multiculturalism policies typically include measures to ensure that minority groups are not unfairly burdened by general rules, which might take the form of exemptions from generally applicable rules or the reformation of these rules or other kinds of policies that recognize or support minorities. It is possible to refer to such multiculturalism policies in a non-prescriptive way as well. This means that the descriptive sense can both refer to the demographic fact of diversity or the fact that certain multiculturalism policies are in place (for an example of the latter, see the multiculturalism policy index, cf. Banting and Kymlicka 2013).

Toleration has both descriptive and normative aspects as well. It is nevertheless often more complicated to distinguish these, and there is some controversy as to whether and how this can be done (Balint 2017, Chap. 4). On the one hand, the general concept of toleration seems to be a purely descriptive concept. It picks out and describes a relation holding between two agents characterized by the presence of difference, objection, power, acceptance, and resultant non-interference. To say that two people stand in a relation of toleration is not in itself to say whether this is a good or a bad thing; this fact might be regrettable, either because the presence of objection or power are problematic or because the difference in question is so objectionable that this should not be overridden but should rather lead to intolerance.

On the other hand, there are clear normative elements of the concept of toleration. The objection component can involve moral disapproval. This is, for instance, the case if members of one group sincerely believe that the practices of another group, e.g., practices of infant circumcision or ritual slaughter, are reprehensible and wrong. The crucial element of toleration, however, is the acceptance component, which denotes the reasons why the tolerator refrains from acting on the objection. Even though the acceptance component can be instantiated by purely strategic or pragmatic considerations, e.g., a purely self-interested concern for the consequences of interfering, most discussions of toleration focus on acceptance for moral reasons. Standard cases of toleration thus involve an objection that is overridden by moral considerations, e.g., based on a principle of respect for others or ideas of autonomy or freedom, which provide reasons for not interfering even if one thinks that what others do is wrong.

According to views that focus on particular conceptions of toleration where the acceptance component is already specified in moral terms, e.g., Rainer Forst's "respect conception of toleration" (Forst 2013), or discussions that proceed on the assumption that toleration is a moral virtue (Heyd 1996), toleration is an irreducibly normative notion, which cannot be applied without making moral judgments. Even if one does not accept such moralized specifications of the notion of toleration, it is still true that the application of the concept will almost always happen in a normative context; the reason for focusing on relations of toleration is that we usually want to discuss what we should tolerate and why. It is therefore crucial to distinguish between the aim of the discussion and the concept of toleration used in the discussion. For some purposes, even if the aim is to have a normative discussion, a descriptive concept will be appropriate – if for no other reason, because a moralized concept will often pre-judge the normative question by assuming that we already have answers to the normative questions (Lægaard 2013a).

Even if one adopts a descriptive concept of toleration, there is then the further question when someone should be tolerant. If the concept itself is descriptive, then it is not able to answer this question on its own. The concept is then, in Rainer Forst's words, "normatively dependent" (2013: 32), which means that we only get an answer to the normative question by inserting a normative principle. It then furthermore becomes clear that there are several possible principles that could function as reasons for acceptance. These are different justifications for toleration.

The same goes for multiculturalism. Given a descriptive understanding of multiculturalism policies, it is still an open question whether and why a state should adopt these policies. The answer to this question depends partly on the facts of the matter (what is the situation of minority groups in the society in question), partly on which normative principle one invokes to assess this situation.

Justifications for Toleration and for Multiculturalism

One thing is what multiculturalism and toleration mean conceptually and how we can compare them at this level; another thing is what the justification might be for requirements of multicultural accommodation or of toleration. Both types of responses to diversity can be justified in different ways, some of them on more or less similar normative grounds (e.g., some kinds of liberal concern with individual freedom and equality), others more divergent or outright conflicting (e.g., multiculturalism based on corporate groups rights as opposed to toleration based on individual autonomy, although see Levey 2012 for an argument for the compatibility of liberal autonomy and multiculturalism). In the case of toleration, the justification for requirements of toleration relates to the acceptance component, i.e., the reason why some agent should not act on a reason for objecting to some difference.

For present purposes, the most interesting question is what the relation is between justifications for toleration and justifications for multiculturalism. There are two possibilities that are interesting to consider. One is that justifications for toleration and for multiculturalism might appeal to conflicting principles or considerations, the other is that toleration and multiculturalism might be based on the same normative premises. Both possibilities are present in discussions that identify toleration with a liberal approach to diversity and view multiculturalism as an approach that departs from liberalism. Multiculturalism might depart from liberalism in different ways, and this departure might be viewed as either a good or a bad thing.

Standard narratives about the relation between liberalism and multiculturalism take liberalism to be an individualist and difference-blind approach focused on treating citizens equally and according to neutral rules that do not take a stance regarding citizens' conceptions of the good, ways of life, or identities. Some responses to this view of liberalism sees it as both impossible and as inadequate in the sense that it fails to identify and address group specific injustices. This then provides a point of departure for arguments about the need to go "beyond" liberalism and instead or additionally adopt multiculturalism policies (Lægaard 2013b: 53–54). On this way of viewing the relation between multiculturalism and liberalism, it is a good thing that multiculturalism goes beyond liberalism. A prominent example of this is Will Kymlicka's liberal theory of multiculturalism (1989, 1995), which argues that state neutrality is impossible and liberal individualism inadequate in order to secure equality between individuals for members of minority groups. Kymlicka thus argues for minority rights as justified on liberal grounds. Insofar as his view is correct, multiculturalism and liberalism are justified based on the same principles.

There is also a competing narrative, which shares the same understanding of liberalism and the claim that multiculturalism goes beyond liberalism. However, this narrative sees this as a bad thing. According to this narrative, the fact that multiculturalism goes beyond liberalism constitutes a threat to equal treatment, individual freedom, and state neutrality. Brian Barry's classic criticism of multiculturalism (2001) is a prominent example of this narrative. To the extent that this criticism of multiculturalism is correct, this means that multiculturalism is an illiberal view. This can be the case because the consequences of multiculturalism policies involve infringements of liberal rights or principles or because multiculturalism is itself based on illiberal principles, e.g., collectivist ideas about the primacy of the group over the individual. To the extent that the latter is the case, multiculturalism and liberalism are justified on the basis of conflicting normative premises.

This controversy is of interest for present purposes insofar as toleration is a feature of the liberal approach to diversity. This might be the case because the liberal framework allows citizens to object to each other on grounds of the differences between them. Liberalism leaves objections in place, due to the liberal requirement of neutrality, but requires citizens not to act on their objections, which many people see as providing a reason for acceptance required for toleration. However, there is a debate about whether and in which sense this is really toleration. Toleration also requires power to interfere and citizens in a liberal state regulated by constitutional rights protecting individual freedom might not have this power in the relevant sense, at least not if the right are effectively enforced (Heyd 2008). The resulting non-interference would then not qualify as toleration since citizens do not fulfil the power component required for toleration. Against this objection, others argue that it makes sense to understand the liberal state as securing an ideal of toleration (Jones 2018).

Insofar as we can meaningfully see toleration as a feature of liberal approaches to diversity, the relation between toleration and multiculturalism turns on which of the sketched narratives is correct. This will naturally not be something that can be settled on the basis of the general concepts of toleration and multiculturalism – precisely because they allow that requirements of toleration and multiculturalism can be justified in different ways. For some justifications, toleration and multiculturalism will be at odds, either at a fundamental level of justifying principles or at the derivative level of prescribed actions. For other justifications, there need not be any conflict. In order to consider this issue, it is therefore necessary to look at particular instances of the debate between toleration and multiculturalism, one of which will be the focus of the next section.

The Multiculturalism Challenge to Liberal Toleration

A recent treatment of the relation between toleration and multiculturalism can be found in Peter Balint's book *Respecting Toleration* (2017). Balint's discussion of this issue both provides a good presentation of the debate and offers a particular view of how we can understand both toleration and multiculturalism in this debate.

According to Balint, what he calls *The Multicultural Challenge* claims that:

the traditional liberal approach to diversity has failed to accommodate minorities adequately, and that fair accommodation requires some sort of positive respect or recognition of minority practices, ways of life, or identities. Those supporting this position have been wary of liberal toleration and neutrality because of its perceived bias towards the majority and its failure to see that treating ways of life fairly may require treating minorities differently. (Balint 2017, p. 3)

Balint acknowledges that the multicultural critique *is* on to something:

people should be able to live divergent lives, and too often liberal states have both explicitly and implicitly favoured dominant groups. Insisting that those who wish to lead divergent lives are still free to do lots of other things, or are simply holding themselves back with their beliefs, or are subject to the same rules as everybody else, or need to properly integrate, is both to privilege the status quo unnecessarily and unfairly, and to fail to be adequately tolerant. (Balint 2017, p. 9)

Balint formulates the *Multicultural Challenge* by using the notions of "respect for difference" and "recognition" as contrasts to toleration. This is common in debates about multiculturalism, among proponents as well as critics of multiculturalism, cf. the quotes from Modood in the introduction.

As is evident from these remarks, there are several different ways of understanding the notions of respect for difference and recognition, which generate different ways of understanding the supposed conflict between multiculturalism and toleration. Assuming the standard concept of toleration characterized by objection and non-interference, one way of understanding the notions of respect for difference and recognition is simply as ways of relating to diversity that either reject the objection component or require more in terms of action than non-interference, or both (cf. the section on multiculturalism and toleration as positive and negative responses to diversity). The objection component of toleration denotes a negative attitude to specific differences. Respect for difference and recognition are sometimes (e.g., in the second quote from Modood) used as labels for positive attitudes to diversity. The standard understanding of toleration furthermore takes it to consist in non-interference at the level of acts. Respect for difference and recognition are often used (e.g., in the first quote from Modood) as labels for policies that go beyond toleration in the sense that they offer positive support or otherwise accommodate diversity. So respect for difference and recognition can refer to positive ways of relating to diversity both at the level of attitudes and at the level of acts or policies. An obvious possibility is that they link these two levels so that the positive attitude to diversity is part of the justification for the supportive policies and/or that these policies are supposed to express the positive attitude to diversity.

There is also a different, more theoretical way of understanding the notion of respect for difference, namely, as a more fundamental normative principle that can justify multiculturalism policies. Proponents of multiculturalism sometimes apparently use the notion of respect for difference and related terms to denote values or normative considerations distinct from those they take to lie at the basis of traditional liberalism. However, it is often unclear what this use of "respect for difference" more precisely means and whether it really captures a distinctive principle (Lægaard 2013c).

Despite these different uses, it is clear that many theorists, both proponents of multiculturalism and defenders of toleration, operate with this kind of contrast, which as suggested can be understood as relating both to the level of attitudes to diversity and to the level of policies. This suggests a conflict between toleration and multiculturalism, where proponents of the latter view the former as either something to be rejected (at the level of attitudes) and/or something that is an inadequate response to diversity (at the level of policies).

One response to this conflict is to try to reinterpret toleration in a way that includes respect for difference (e.g., Addis 1997). Rainer Forst has tried to capture this kind of view under the label of what he calls the "esteem conception" of toleration (2013: 31–32). However, as Forst notes, this is a difficult exercise, which either threatens to remove the distinctiveness of toleration or will have to limit or qualify the positive attitude to differences.

Responding to the Multiculturalism Challenge

Balint's general response to the multiculturalism challenge has two parts. One is to reinterpret the standard concept of toleration to include a broader repertoire of approaches to diversity. Since the multicultural challenge is posed at the level of how states relate to diversity (rather than at the level of individual attitudes and actions), the response to it in terms of toleration has to articulate toleration as a general *political* practice.

Balint proposes a permissive conception of political toleration according to which the standard sense of toleration characterized by objection (what Balint calls "forbearance toleration") is only one among a range of possible forms of toleration. Toleration in Balint's permissive sense also includes indifference – what is usually discussed under the heading of neutrality – and respect for difference (2017: 28–32). Given that respect for difference is the kind of positive attitude to diversity and the related positive policies of accommodation that characterizes multiculturalism, Balint's conceptual widening of toleration makes multiculturalism a sub-species of toleration.

The other part of Balint's response to the multiculturalism challenge is to engage with the justification underlying the challenge. The challenge is normally justified with reference to claims that liberal states practicing what Kymlicka (1995) called "benign neglect" and others call "difference blindness" do not really succeed in treating minorities and majorities equally. The criticism is that liberal neutrality is not neutral in practice but favors the majority. If liberalism merely consists in being difference blind, then it will not be able to detect and rectify the relations of domination and privilege already established in the social and political *status quo* of a given society. Balint agrees with this claim but points out that this is a criticism properly directed at the practice of actual liberal states rather than at liberalism as a theory. He then further argues that there are ways of practicing toleration that not only avoid the problems in liberal practice identified by proponents of the multiculturalism challenge but also are preferable to the kinds of policies suggested by proponents of respect for difference.

The first part of Balint's response to the multiculturalism challenge seems to run into the same problem that Forst identified for the esteem conception of toleration, namely, that the distinctiveness of toleration disappears if we relax the requirement of objection. Balint is not the first theorist to suggest such a widening of the notion of toleration. Walzer (1997), for instance, used the term to denote the entire spectrum of attitudes to diversity spanning from resignation, over indifference and openness to enthusiastic endorsement. Nevertheless, this widening and relaxation of the concept makes the description of something as a case of toleration much less informative. It may even make the term toleration redundant, since the removal of the requirement of objection means that we can describe these cases without using the concept of toleration but instead simply use freedom or non-interference (Ceva 2020; Galeotti 2019).

The second part of Balint's response to the multicultural challenge is independent from the first in the sense that whereas the first concerns the objection component, i.e., the attitude part of the concept of toleration, the second part concerns the kind of policies that a liberal state should pursue in relation to diversity. Balint approaches this question based on a liberal concern with ensuring the freedom of citizens to be able to live their life as they want to. Given this underlying justification for toleration, Balint's claim is that liberal states should as far as possible adopt a "hands off" approach, which means that the state should withdraw and not privilege any ways of life (Balint 2017: 64). The underlying idea is that any state interference, especially of the positive kind required by respect for difference where the state tries to actively support certain ways of life, will limit individual freedom more than a state that stands back and does not interfere at all.

While this part of Balint's argument looks like a very traditional form of liberalism, he adds a novel aspect in his discussion of difference-sensitivity (2017: 61–63, although this has some resemblance to the "dynamic" view of toleration in Wolff 2003). In the received narrative about the conflict between liberalism and multiculturalism mentioned above, liberalism is often associated with ideas of difference-blindness and multiculturalism is then in contrast supposed to be difference-sensitive. Balint, however, argues that a liberal state can and should be difference-sensitive. This means that a liberal state should not just keep rules in place if they at the time of implementation did not favor any ways of life over others. This is because societies develop and new ways of life appear, e.g., due to immigration. If the state is to remain neutral, it must continuously monitor whether established rules manage to treat different groups equally in terms of allowing them to live their life as they want to. The state should be sensitive to whether the emergence of new ways of life means that established rules are no longer neutral – and in that case, it should change the rules. Therefore, a liberal state should be difference-sensitive, but this does not mean that it should actively support minorities, as respect for difference is usually understood; rather, it means that the state should withdraw support in every case where it turns out that this does not treat all present groups equally in terms of their freedom.

While Balint's view of difference-sensitivity provides a much more plausible understanding of what liberalism requires than the traditional (and often not very considered) slogan of difference-blindness, his claim that this is better realized by the state being "hands off" is debatable. Not only is it unclear exactly what it means for a state to be "hands off," it also seems that there are many cases where state interference and regulation is needed to ensure equal freedom for citizens, e.g., in enforcing non-discrimination (Lægaard 2020, as more or less acknowledged by Balint 2020).

Whatever one thinks of his substantive view, this discussion of Balint's response to the multiculturalism challenge suggests that the standard narrative, according to which toleration and multiculturalism are opposed and irreconcilable, is overstated and at least stands in need of qualification. There are other ways of doing this than by broadening the concept of toleration. The final section considers a different way of relating the two.

Multiculturalism and Toleration at Different Levels

Toleration is usually formulated as a pattern of action at the individual level. When motivating the components of toleration, we normally appeal to examples involving persons standing in a relation to other persons. While being designed to apply to interpersonal relations, we also use the term at the level of the state, which raises the question about the meaning and legitimacy of toleration by the state (Jones 2018). This means that toleration can in principle be applied both at the level of individuals and at the political level (even through there are then debates about whether and in what sense toleration at either level really are genuine forms of toleration).

Similarly, multiculturalism can both be a (state) policy and an individual requirement. Many of the already noted examples of multiculturalism policies are policies at the state level, e.g., official acts of recognition, schemes of support, or changes in legislation. Many multiculturalism policies are often implemented at intermediate levels, e.g., at the level of city councils. Nevertheless, for present purposes, this also qualifies as a part of the political level (albeit one in some respects closer to the individual citizens). However, while this is a less common usage, multiculturalism can also denote requirements at the individual level. Some discussions of multiculturalism raise the possibility that a multicultural society requires not only certain state policies but also a specific attitude towards diversity from individual citizens – what Modood called a "multiculturalist sensibility." This is for example evident in views according to which citizens in a multicultural society should show respect for the religious convictions of others, e.g., by refraining from using their freedom of speech to ridicule the religion of other citizens. Such a view can be held simultaneously with the liberal view that the state should not criminalize such utterances. This combined view then articulates multiculturalism as what one may call a multicultural social ethos, i.e., as a set of values supposed to inform the actions of individual citizens in civil society (Lægaard 2011, 2014).

Given that we can articulate toleration as well as multiculturalism at both the political and the individual level, the compatibility question divides into several sub-questions. One question is whether toleration and multiculturalism might be compatible by each being the appropriate response to diversity at its own level, i.e., that toleration might for instance, be the appropriate response at the level of individual behavior while multiculturalism might be the appropriate response at the political level of policies. Another question is whether there are senses in which toleration and multiculturalism can be compatible at the same level.

The first possibility is that toleration and multiculturalism might be appropriate responses to diversity at different levels. The most obvious possibility is the one already noted, namely, that multiculturalism is primarily a state policy, whereas toleration is mainly an individual requirement. This fits with the fact that multiculturalism is most commonly formulated as a matter of policies and toleration as a feature of interpersonal relations. This possibility shows that there need not be any contradiction between toleration and multiculturalism, because the subject of the negative and the positive attitudes to diversity might be different, namely, individuals and the state, respectively, and the different requirements at the level of actions might address different actors, again, private citizens, and public authorities. It also shows that some criticisms of multiculturalism to the effect that it is a totalitarian ideology, which violates citizens' liberty to have negative views of, e.g., other religions or ways of life, can be relaxed insofar as multiculturalism concerns what the state should do rather than what individuals should do. State multiculturalism can thus retain certain aspects of a liberal approach to the relation between state and citizens, according to which the state should not meddle with what citizens believe or how they live their life.

The converse scenario is also a possibility, i.e., the case where the state upholds classic liberal neutrality or benign neglect toward differences in society, and in that sense is a tolerant state, but where citizens are motivated and behave according to a multicultural social ethos. This is also a case of full compatibility, since the attitudes and actions required by toleration and multiculturalism, respectively, concern different agents. The main question in this scenario rather is whether we should count a neutral liberal state as really being tolerant, since it arguably does not fulfill the objection component. As already noted, Balint's permissive view of toleration countenances this possibility. Multiculturalism is then not a state policy but rather a moral requirement on citizens.

Finally, these two split-level scenarios can even be combined, as long as the different requirements of toleration and multiculturalism do not concern the exact same thing. A state might, for instance, be tolerant in the sense of being neutral in many respects, but might adopt multiculturalism policies in very specific respects. A state might, for instance, recognize both the majority church and minority religious associations but otherwise adopt a stance of benign neglect both regarding issues of culture and ethnicity. As long as the positive attitude expressed by recognition of religious groups does not generalize beyond recognition of them *as* religious groups, there is in principle not a problem with the state being neutral about other forms of diversity, even if the same people are members of the religious groups and other socially salient groups.

While there are therefore several ways in which toleration and multiculturalism might be compatible, the most interesting question is whether they are compatible at the same level and in the same respects. This initially looks more doubtful. Precisely because multiculturalism and toleration are positive and negative responses to diversity in the senses discussed earlier, it seems that they rule each other out if applied to the same subjects and with respect to the same differences. A person or state cannot both object to and endorse some specific different way of life or practice. This is the reason why toleration and multiculturalism are commonly assumed to be incompatible.

However, there might be ways in which this incompatibility does not hold, even for the same the subject and object of toleration and multiculturalism. One way in which compatibility might be possible has to do with the type of reasons or evaluations involved. If the types of reasons involved in objection and acceptance are not of the same kind, then they might not strictly speaking contradict each other, even if they concern the same object. This possibility is similar to the strategy for dissolving apparent paradoxes of toleration by categorizing reasons for objection and reasons for acceptance as different kinds of reasons. Forst's respect conception of toleration (2013) is a prominent example of this, according to which objections are expressions of people's conception of the good and reasons for acceptance derive from a principle of justice (in Forst's case, a right to public justification). According to Forst, this shows how reasons for acceptance can override reasons for objection without negating or annulling the latter. This shows how toleration is possible, since reasons for objection persist even though people motivated by their sense of justice will not act on them.

Might multiculturalism and toleration be compatible in a way analogous to the way in which reasons for objection and reasons for acceptance according to Forst can persist side by side? Multiculturalism and toleration seem incompatible because they require a positive and a negative attitude to differences, respectively. Nevertheless, as noted in the above discussion of how we should understand multicultural recognition, we can both interpret multicultural recognition as appraisal respect and as recognition respect in Darwall's sense. The obvious tension with toleration arises if we understand multicultural recognition as requiring positive appraisal of differences, as sometimes suggested by proponents of multiculturalism (e.g., Taylor 1994). Multiculturalism then requires a positive evaluation of differences as good in some sense. This does seem incompatible with toleration, which requires a negative evaluation of differences. However, if the attitude to differences involved in multicultural recognition is not one of positive appraisal respect but rather a form of recognition respect, then the same relation seems to hold between the attitudes involved in toleration and multiculturalism as between objection and acceptance as understood in Forst's respect conception of toleration. As argued above, it is more plausible to understand multiculturalism as an egalitarian political view in terms of recognition respect, i.e., as recognition of the legitimate presence of different ways of life, rather than as a requirement of positive appraisal respect of the differences in question. If this is the case, there is a reason to doubt the common view that toleration and multiculturalism are incompatible.

Therefore, multiculturalism and toleration might be compatible at the level of the attitudes involved. What about the acts required? Toleration requires refraining from interfering, whereas multiculturalism requires some active steps to positively support or accommodate differences. Initially, it might seem that there is an incompatibility here since it is not possible both to do nothing and to do something with respect to the same thing at the same time. However, on closer inspection, this is not really what toleration and multiculturalism require – this way of formulating the actions required is too general and not sufficiently specific (cf. Lægaard 2010). Toleration does not require doing nothing; it specifically requires that someone does not act on the reasons provided by his or her objection to some difference. This is compatible with doing very many different things, as long as the agent in question refrains from negatively interfering in the ways that the objection would otherwise suggest doing. Similarly, multiculturalism does not require just doing something; it requires accommodating minority groups in the way required to express recognition of them as legitimate presences or to overcome or counteract unfair barriers to their equal inclusion. There is therefore no general reason to think that the acts required by toleration and multiculturalism are incompatible. However, it is also not possible to say beforehand that they are compatible; this depends on what the objections are and especially on what the circumstances for minority groups are in the society in question and which multicultural policies are required to ensure accommodation in this context. What toleration or recognition required in practice is a partly contextual question (cf. Bardon and Ceva 2019).

Summary and Future Directions

Multiculturalism and toleration are different ways of relating to diversity involving positive and negative attitudes to differences, respectively. Both can be understood as modes of accommodation relative to different baselines and both can be descriptive concepts as well as normative ideals. Multiculturalism and toleration finally are alike in that they can both, as normative ideals, be justified in different ways. The justification for them has implications for the issue about whether there is a conflict or tension between multiculturalism and toleration, which has been exemplified both by the so-called multiculturalism challenge to liberal toleration and liberal criticisms of multiculturalism. This issue of compatibility depends, however, on the exact justifications for toleration and multiculturalism as well as on at which level they are taken to apply as normative ideals.

In light of the complexity of both toleration and multiculturalism and the resulting many different ways in which they can relate to each other, future directions in the discussion of these relations have to take the complexities into account rather than merely focus on the more general contrast in terms of positive or negative attitudes to differences. This requires discussing toleration and multiculturalism in specific respects and at specific levels rather than in the abstract. Such studies are likely to qualify and move beyond the established narratives about incompatibility and will often have to take a more contextually sensitive approach in order to consider the specific barriers to inclusion addressed by multiculturalism and the specific objections to differences underlying toleration.

References

Addis A (1997) On human diversity and the limits of toleration. In: Shapiro I, Kymlicka W (eds) Ethnicity and group rights. New York University Press, New York, pp 112–153

Balint P (2017) Respecting toleration: traditional liberalism & contemporary diversity. Oxford University Press, Oxford

Balint P (2020) Toleration, neutrality, and freedom: a reply. Crit Rev Int Soc Pol Phil 23(2):203–211

Banting K, Kymlicka W (2013) Is there really a retreat from multiculturalism policies? New evidence from the multiculturalism policy index. Comp Eur Polit 11:577–598

Bardon A, Ceva E (2019) The ethics of toleration and religious accommodations. In: Lever A, Poama A (eds) The Routledge handbook of ethics and public policy. Routledge, London, pp 434–446

Barry B (2001) Culture and equality. Polity, Cambridge

Bessone M (2013) Beyond liberal multicultural toleration: a critical approach to groups' essentialism. Eur J Polit Theo 12(3):271–287

Ceva E (2020) The good of toleration: changing social relations or maximising individual freedom? Crit Rev Int Soc Pol Phil 23(2):197–202

Darwall S (2006) The second-person standpoint. Harvard University Press, Cambridge, MA

Forst R (2013) Toleration in conflict. Cambridge University Press, Cambridge

Galeotti AE (2002) Toleration as recognition. Cambridge University Press, Cambridge

Galeotti AE (2019) Rescuing toleration. Crit Rev Int Soc Pol Phil. https://doi.org/10.1080/13698230.2019.1616882

Heyd D (ed) (1996) Toleration: an elusive virtue. Princeton University Press, Princeton

Heyd D (2008) Is toleration a political virtue? In: Williams MS, Waldron J (eds) NOMOS XLVIII: toleration and its limits. New York University Press, New York, pp 171–194

Horton J (ed) (1993) Liberalism, multiculturalism and toleration. Macmillan, Basingstoke

Jones P (2018) Essays on toleration. Rowman & Littlefield, London

Kaplan BJ (2007) Divided by faith. Harvard University Press, Cambridge, MA

Kühler M (2019) Toleration and modus vivendi. In: Horton J, Westphal M, Willems U (eds) The political theory of modus vivendi. Springer, Cham

Kymlicka W (1989) Liberalism, community and culture. Oxford University Press, Oxford

Kymlicka W (1995) Multicultural citizenship. Oxford University Press, Oxford

Kymlicka W (2012) Multiculturalism: success, failure, and the future. Migration Policy Institute, Washington, DC

Lægaard S (2010) Recognition and toleration: conflicting approaches to diversity in education? Educ Philos Theory 42(1):22–37

Lægaard S (2011) A multicultural social ethos: tolerance, respect, or civility? In: Calder G, Ceva E (eds) Diversity in Europe: dilemmas of differential treatment in theory and practice. Routledge, Abingdon, pp 81–96

Lægaard S (2013a) Toleration out of respect? Crit Rev Int Soc Pol Phil 16(4):520–536

Lægaard S (2013b) State toleration, religious recognition and equality. In: Dobbernack J, Modood T (eds) Tolerance, intolerance and respect: hard to accept? Palgrave Macmillan, Basingstoke, pp 52–76

Lægaard S (2013c) What does 'respect for difference' mean? In: de Latour SG, Balint P (eds) Liberal multiculturalism and the fair terms of integration. Palgrave, Basingstoke, pp 34–53

Lægaard S (2014) The paradox of civility: the case of the Danish cartoons controversy. In: Göle N (ed) Islam and public controversy in Europe. Ashgate, Farnham, pp 123–136

Lægaard S (2015) Multiculturalism and contextualism: how is context relevant for political theory? Eur J Polit Theo 14(3):259–276

Lægaard S (2017) Multiculturalism and secularism: theoretical understandings and possible conflicts. Ethnicities 17(2):154–171

Lægaard S (2020) Accommodating toleration: on Balint's classical liberal response to the multiculturalism challenge. Crit Rev Int Soc Pol Phil 23(2):212–218

Levey GB (2012) Liberal autonomy as a pluralistic value. Monist 95(1):103–126

Lippert-Rasmussen K (2014) Born free and equal? Oxford University Press, Oxford

Modood T (2007) Multiculturalism: a civic idea. Polity, Cambridge

Modood T (2019) Essays on secularism and multiculturalism. Rowman & Littlefield, London

Patten A (2020) Populist multiculturalism: are there majority cultural rights? Philos Soc Crit, First published February 6, 2020. https://doi.org/10.1177/0191453720903486

Rawls J (1996) Political liberalism, Expanded edition. Columbia University Press, New York

Taylor C (1994) Multiculturalism: examining the politics of recognition. Princeton University Press, Princeton

Walzer M (1997) On toleration. Yale University Press, New Haven

Williams B (2005) In the beginning was the deed. Princeton University Press, Princeton

Wolff J (2003) Social ethos and the dynamics of toleration. In: McKinnon C, Castiglione D (eds) The culture of toleration in diverse societies: reasonable tolerance. Manchester University Press, Manchester, pp 147–160

Recognition and Toleration

28

Cillian McBride

Contents

Introduction 542
How "Recognition" Became Associated with the Politics of "Difference" 544
Is Toleration an Outmoded Response to Contemporary Pluralism? 545
What Is "Recognition" and Is It Centrally Concerned with "Cultural" Differences? 547
Recognition, Abstraction, and Domination 550
Domination and the Public Expression of Difference 553
Recognition Versus Toleration Revisited 555
Summary and Future Directions 557
Future Directions for Research 559
References 560

Abstract

Is "recognition" a more "difference friendly" alternative to toleration, replacing objection and forbearance with positive acceptance and inclusion? Is toleration ill-suited to responding to contemporary differences between groups and identities and can appeals to equal respect and rights themselves be complicit in intolerance? It is suggested here that the apparent attractiveness of recognition of positive acceptance of particular identities relies on a flawed reading of the history of toleration and of the politics of difference and a very limited account of the concept of recognition. Contrasts between religious and cultural groups and between belief and identity are less clear-cut than is typically supposed, and recognition struggles by marginalized groups are more concerned with the achievement of equality than the culturalist reading supposes. An expanded understanding of the idea of recognition reveals that not all disesteem is illegitimate and that positive esteem recognition can itself be complicit in maintaining social hierarchies. It also reveals that questions about lack of respect and esteem

---

C. McBride (✉)
Queen's University Belfast, Belfast, UK
e-mail: c.mcbride@qub.ac.uk

© The Author(s), under exclusive licence to Springer Nature Switzerland AG 2022
M. Sardoč (ed.), *The Palgrave Handbook of Toleration*,
https://doi.org/10.1007/978-3-030-42121-2_16

cannot be separated from questions about the power of others to grant or withhold recognition. A comprehensive understanding of recognition struggles underscores the need for continued reflection on the value and limits of toleration.

Keywords

Recognition · Toleration · Respect · Esteem · Domination · Equality · Dignity · Stigma · Identity · Culture · Abstraction

Introduction

For many, the idea of "recognition" has come to represent the possibility of an alternative to toleration, or at least to toleration as "traditionally" conceived (Galeotti 1997: 226). Sometimes we find recognition presented as a form of toleration itself, although this is a little puzzling as recognition is presented as a form of positive acceptance in contrast to the grim forbearance associated with the traditional notion of toleration (Galeotti 2002; Walzer 1997). In any case, toleration and "recognition" are presented as distinct modes of responding to cultural diversity in modern societies (Walzer 1997: 2) The core of the concept of toleration is the combination of an "objection" component, i.e., a negative attitude towards some person or group of persons, with an "acceptance" component that would justify a policy of non-interference (King 1976: 44–51). There is also a third component in theories of toleration: an account of the limits of toleration which sets out when intervention is permitted or required (Forst 2013: 18–23). Where the objection component is absent, there is no question of toleration. Aversion is built into the idea of toleration at the ground level. This lies at the heart of the contrast between toleration and "recognition" at least as it is commonly understood in the context of multicultural political theory. Recognition is thought to involve a positive attitude of acceptance or inclusion (Jones 2006a: 28). This makes it attractive to critics of toleration who believe that we can and should overcome the negative attitudes central to toleration and move "beyond" the traditional conception (Galeotti 1997) towards the positive recognition, perhaps even celebration, of "differences" (Walzer 1997). Sometimes this is presented as a reconceptualization of toleration "as" recognition, i.e., without the objection component (Galeotti 1997; Jones 2006b: 126n) but for the sake of clarity it seems preferable to stick to the standard usage of toleration as always involving objection, and to understand the issue as a conflict between "recognition" and toleration.

Objections to toleration are not new: Paine praises France's revolutionary government for establishing a "universal right of conscience" and rejecting both "toleration and intoleration" (Paine 2000: 94). A state which upholds the equal rights of its citizens does not "tolerate" any of its citizens as it does not differentiate between them in the sense that the state makes disapproving ethical judgements about some set of citizens and yet forbears to interfere with them. The state upholds equal rights and limits its judgements to whether or not it is required to intervene and coerce.

Paine rejects the policy of toleration which affords rulers the freedom to establish their chosen faith but with the option of extending toleration to select groups of others. The essence of this model of toleration, the "permission" conception (Forst 2007), is that toleration is entirely at the discretion of the prince, who would typically forbear to interfere for prudential, rather than principled reasons.

In the language of contemporary republicanism the permission conception of toleration represents a form of *domination*, for the absence of interference does not secure the freedom of the tolerated. Instead, they are constantly exposed to the possibility of uncontrolled interference in their lives (Pettit 1996, 2012). While the absence of active persecution is, no doubt, a good thing, from this perspective one is still dominated under the permission conception because one must live every day with the thought that this permission could be withdrawn on the whim of the ruler. Consequently, one must learn to keep one's head down and avoid rocking the boat if one does not wish to excite the ire of the ruler. This is clearly inconsistent with enjoying an equal standing in society.

Defenders of toleration, accepting these arguments against the permission conception, have typically abandoned the idea of toleration as state policy as inconsistent with equality. Instead, they have turned to toleration, or "tolerance," which is typically associated with open-mindedness and a reluctance to rush to judgement, as a virtue which should be practiced by citizens with respect to one another (Horton 1998). There has been a shift, if you like, from a "vertical" model of toleration, in which the state tolerates citizens, to a "horizontal" model of toleration, in which citizens tolerate one another. The acceptance component here relies not on a view about whether one can get away with persecution, but on moral grounds, typically respect for autonomy.

This move reconfigures toleration to render a version of it consistent with equal respect. The challenge to toleration, however, is not restricted to the permission conception, but also applies, it seems, to the respect conception. The respect conception retains the objection component, while providing a robust egalitarian basis for the acceptance component in place of the arbitrary will of the powerful. It is thought that the idea of equal respect is itself a source of hostility to certain forms of social "difference" and that the move to the recognition of social, typically understood as "cultural" difference avoids reliance on the homogenizing thrust of traditional notions of equal respect. This then is the structure of the argument for replacing toleration with recognition: a) the overcoming of the objection component and b) the rejection of appeals to equal respect or dignity as the basis of the acceptance component. This is typically presented in terms of a shift from valuing others "despite" their differences to valuing them "as" different, and as a move towards "full inclusion" or minority or marginalized people (Galeotti 2002).

Is the idea of moving "beyond" toleration is plausible and does "recognition" genuinely offer an alternative? This suggestion poses a number of questions. Is the common assumption that we are now in a new era which demands new tools for coping with the diversity of modern societies plausible? How well is the concept of recognition understood in mainstream Anglo-American political theory and has it become too closely associated with a certain sort of multicultural politics? For such a popular concept it has received surprisingly little critical attention in these circles. Have partisans of the "recognition of difference" got a sufficiently complex understanding of how recognition functions and in particular is there enough attention paid to the way positive acceptance can also be morally problematic? Is the standard multicultural view of recognition too narrowly focused on the problem of remedying recognition deficits? A broader view of recognition as an iterated process, a struggle as Hegel pictured it, poses additional questions about *who* has the power to recognize, questions that do not seem to be taken into account in these debates. Finally, if we take a more comprehensive view of the politics of recognition, might that view actually make the issue of objection more, rather than less prominent?

How "Recognition" Became Associated with the Politics of "Difference"

While the idea that our relationship to ourselves is mediated by our relations with others has its origins in Hegel (1977: 111), recognition was introduced into Anglo-American political theory by Charles Taylor in the context of debates about multiculturalism (1994). On this view, our relations to others are not external to us such that they could be drastically altered without producing any corresponding change in our selves. Rather, these relations are constitutive of who we are and changes in our social relations can also alter our sense of ourselves. This social model of selfhood essentially blurs the line between self and other. While some accounts of the social constitution of the self have a strongly deterministic quality to them, with the self appearing as the product of anonymous disciplinary techniques, relying on the complicity of subjects with these techniques (Foucault 1995), Taylor understands the process of self-constitution to be an intersubjective, "dialogical" process (1994: 33). The ethical lesson he seeks to draw from this account of the nature of the self is that this illuminates the special vulnerability we have to attacks on the social relations, identities, and practices which make us who we are. On an atomistic model of the self these things are clearly external but on the dialogical model they are internal. This means that the claim that "sticks and stones may break my bones but names can never hurt me" is fundamentally mistaken – the negative attitudes of others towards the identities and practices which constitute my sense of self have the power to reach inside me and cause me real harm. This is not understood as mere offence to the extent that our dialogical constitution renders us vulnerable to internalizing these negative views. Through internalization we can come to interpret ourselves through the lens of others' aversions, effectively becoming "imprisoned" by denigrating stereotypes (1994: 25).

Taylor goes on to connect this account of our constitutive vulnerability to the misrecognition of others to a larger historical narrative about the bifurcation of the politics of recognition in the modern era. The Enlightenment gave rise to a politics focused on equal dignity aimed at transforming social and political relations so that they better reflected the underlying moral equality of all persons. Taylor argues, however, that this politics (in fact he distances himself from this claim by ascribing it to critics) that this project has a strongly homogenizing dynamic on account of its emphasis on our common humanity as the basis of our equal moral status. This results in a politics which assumes that the achievement of equality requires us to park our identities at the door as it were. Taylor argues that this is a special problem for a certain sort of "procedural liberalism" but it appears to be more generally tied to a particular vision of modernity as the disembedding of modern subjects from their concrete attachments and identities. As such, it also played a central role in Marxism's account of human emancipation, making it a key strand of left politics for much of the late nineteenth and twentieth centuries. The recent rise of identity politics, however, represents an alternative politics of recognition which resists the privileging of our common humanity, a politics of difference that insists on the acknowledgment of the *value* of our particular identities. This politics of difference entails a revaluation of differences which are no longer to be regarded as incidental, contingent features of our moral personhood – we are to be valued *because* of our differences not in spite of them (1994: 38–9).

Is Toleration an Outmoded Response to Contemporary Pluralism?

Taylor's narrative about the emergence of the "politics of difference" as a new force, countering an older Enlightenment politics of dignity, is shaped by the sense that the tectonic plates of left politics were shifting by the 1980s with the apparent decline of class politics and the rise of "new social movements" centered on struggles over race, gender, ethnicity, sexuality, and the environment. There are two points to note about this backdrop. Firstly, there is a genuine difference between a politics of class which, on the Marxist view, aimed at the abolition of class differences altogether through the abolition of the property relations that constituted them, and a politics that aims at reordering relations between groups without abolishing all differences between them (although some contemporary gender politics aims at abolishing gender binaries). The second thing to note, however, is that the claim that this is a radically new politics, at odds with Enlightenment concerns with equal dignity, itself seems unduly influenced by the assumption that class politics, however conceived, is the default politics of modernity rather than merely the dominant politics of liberal democracies in the post-war era. Taking a longer view of the modern struggles against religious discrimination, slavery, imperialism, and patriarchy throughout the nineteenth and twentieth centuries suggests rather that perhaps the roots of this "politics of difference" lie in the very Enlightenment that it is, on Taylor's account reacting against. While Taylor would, no doubt, insist that there are key differences in how the claims of marginalized groups are now articulated, it is not immediately obvious that he is right about this and other recognition theorists have challenged his reading of the politics of identity, as we shall see. There is no doubt, however, that the apparent displacement of class politics did contribute to the impression that new conceptual tools were becoming necessary.

With respect to toleration, this contributed to the thought that liberal toleration had become an obstacle to reflection on the question of social difference because it is fundamentally concerned with moral disagreements between *individuals*, rather than with deep-seated cultural differences involving *groups* (Galeotti 2002: 5). Now it may well be the case that academic philosophy discussions do indeed home in on moral disagreements and discuss them in abstract ways as if they simply involved conflicts between individuals, but this is perhaps a criticism best directed at a certain contemporary style in philosophy (Wolff 2010) rather than at the historical tradition of liberal thought about the issue of toleration. This tradition is very much concerned with deep-seated conflicts between groups seeking to persecute nonmembers and/or shield themselves from such group-based persecution.

A related suggestion is that while toleration was traditionally concerned with differences about beliefs, modern conflicts concern conflicts involving "ascribed" social identities, i.e., *unchosen* identities. Here the problem is that the idea of social ascription looks like an unhelpful simplification, especially from the point of view of a recognitive account of the self (Jones 2006b: 142). Rather than being passive recipients of social identities impressed upon us by others, the recognition perspective understands social identities as the (revivable) outcome of a dialogue, sometimes a struggle, always a set of interactions between multiple agents, in which the power to ascribe identities may be very unequally distributed and may be challenged or internalized to varying degrees. The internalization process itself reveals that social identities are not mere labels applied by others, but rather involve a complex network of beliefs and commitments on the part of those involved. Even if social identities are not *chosen* as such, neither are they wholly outside our control, rather they always involve efforts and commitment to live up to their normative demands. This is a clear implication of the Taylor's point that there are no sharp lines to be drawn between the self and surrounding norms and practices and is an important implication of the recognitive understanding of the self.

If religious differences, between Christians at least, appear as if they have been largely defused in Western countries, then this has been the product of hard-won political struggles in which the theory and practice of toleration has played a central role. These conflicts are not plausibly thought of as academic differences about matters of individual belief. As Forst notes, toleration was historically always concerned with regulating attempts to interfere with the public, communal, and practice of religions by groups of people: "although it is the freedom of conscience of the individual that is defended, this is supposed to open up the social space for the *communal* exercise of religious worship and for a plurality of ecclesiastical organizations" (2013: 172). It is a misreading of the history of toleration, not to mention of religious beliefs and practices, to suppose that these are concerned with individuals and not groups and with one's private relationship to God rather than with the public expression of religious differences whether in the form of the wearing of religious dress and symbols or acts of public worship, including processions, etc. (practices not confined to Catholicism, as the example of Northern Ireland shows).

When we turn to controversies such as those involving the wearing of the hijab, etc. by Muslims in France and beyond, it is not obvious that these pose radically new problems for which the tools of toleration are inappropriate. They concern expressions of religious faith in public, a question that has always been an issue in debates about toleration. Indeed, those countries which have opted to ban such modes of dress in public spaces appear to be practicing an all too familiar form of religious intolerance and in so doing violating the liberal idea that religious faith should be a matter of private choice or commitment and not the business of the state unless the rights of others are being violated. Such bans are politicizing, not privatizing, religious expression and it is not obvious that toleration is complicit in this rather than notions of civic unity or *laïcité* (Laborde 2002), or that it offers the wrong sort of guidance on what to think of such cases. The history of toleration is the history of managing and combating antipathies to "alien" religious groups and contemporary Islamophobia appears to be simply the latest episode in a long history of sectarian intolerance.

In addition to the misleading contrast between individual and groups is the persistent tendency to treat "difference" in *cultural* terms when the cases discussed are typically those which concern religious groups (Parekh 2000: 198–199; Brown 2009: 14). Not only does this obscure the degree to which these debates are focused on traditional issues of *religious* toleration and the expression of *religious* differences in public in modes of dress and other practices, it also displaces concerns with gender, race, and sexuality. These twin assumptions, that we have moved from a concern with individuals to a concern with groups and that these groups should be thought of as cultural rather than religious, serve to obscure underlying historical continuities and contribute to the arguably mistaken view that the tools of toleration must be outmoded and unsuitable for coping with contemporary problems (Galeotti 2002).

What Is "Recognition" and Is It Centrally Concerned with "Cultural" Differences?

In debates about cultural difference and toleration "recognition" is usually thought to be a unified good which simply involves "symbolic" acceptance by the majority. Taylor, unlike many others, distinguishes between *two* modes of recognition, one focused on equal dignity and the other on the recognition of difference, but his historical reconstruction of the politics of recognition appears to suggest that the politics of equal dignity has now run its course and is serving only as a fetter, obstructing the recognition of difference. Axel Honneth, who has developed a systematic theory of social recognition from the same Hegelian point of departure, distinguishes, however, between three main modes of recognition, love, respect, and esteem (Honneth 1995). Love in the form of care is the recognition children are supposed to receive in early infancy and it fosters a basic bodily self-confidence. Respect is something everyone is entitled to simply in virtue of their common humanity, or, more specifically, their "personhood." Respect is a sort of special high status to which all are equally entitled and which is itself undifferentiated (Waldron 2012: 33). While we speak of "earning" respect or "losing" respect as if respect requires us to act in certain ways, this is not "respect" in the deeper moral sense of something we owe to each other and which we may in turn demand of others in virtue of our equal moral status. When we use "respect" in the sense that we must "earn" it by our efforts we are talking rather about social esteem, which is indeed sensitive in many cases to our actions. Esteem is focused on our particular posing features while respect attaches to our common moral status. Taylor's politics of difference can be interpreted as focused on one particular form of social esteem – that concerned with the value of cultural identities and practices.

Honneth argues that social recognition shapes our relations to ourselves. Honneth, at least initially, appears to think of this in fairly deterministic terms while others take this to be a more interactive process (McBride 2013). For Honneth, social recognition as love, respect, and esteem is necessary if we are to form positive relations to ourselves, bodily self-confidence, self-esteem, and self-respect. These positive self-relations are necessary if we are to realize our capacity for agency. There is then a recognition threshold we must cross in order to realize our capacity for freedom as self-determination and as self-realization. While some have criticized him for psychologizing the recognition (Fraser 2003), i.e., as little more than a narcissistic demand for affirmation of one's identity, it seems clear that his account is actually firmly rooted in the Hegelian/Marxist tradition of thought concerned with identifying the social and political conditions of human freedom.

While Honneth identifies three central forms of recognition, others simply distinguish between two different modes of respect: recognition respect, which comes into play when others figure in our deliberations as equal moral persons, and esteem respect, which attaches to their particular achievements (Darwall 1977). For clarity, it may be more helpful to follow Honneth in treating these as two different modes of recognition, esteem and respect. We should also note that Darwall restricts esteem – his appraisal respect – to traits and performances for which we can be held responsible, it may be more helpful to distinguish between esteem we can be held responsible for and social esteem as social status or prestige which attaches to certain groups who share a particular lifestyle and/or stocks of social capital (Jones 2006a: 32–33; Weber 1978: 932; Bourdieu 1984). How are we to think of the relations between respect and esteem? Taylor's narrative might encourage to suppose that we need to let the egalitarian politics focused on the realization of equal dignity or respect fade into the background as the new politics of cultural esteem comes to the fore. Honneth and others clearly think of them as coexisting and answering distinct needs. Clearly, however, there can be tensions between them. We can see these playing out in two common ways.

Firstly, while critics of toleration appear to want to eliminate or minimize the place for objection in social life in the name of recognition as acceptance, it is clear that recognition does not always signify acceptance and inclusion. There can be negative esteem recognition, i.e., disesteem, and we should not assume that this is always unjustified (Jones 2006b: 128). I might, for example, disesteem a colleague who has let me down in some way. While I might keep these thoughts to myself, equally I might give them practical expression, avoiding his company and warning others about his lack of trustworthiness. Disesteem might reasonably lead to the withholding of associational goods and deserved reputational damage in this case. While I do not esteem this person, I may combine this attitude with respect recognition, respecting him as a moral equal even if he is also a poor colleague. My respect for him sets limits to how far one might go in expressing disesteem – it should restrain me from sending him hate mail or whipping up a twitter mob against him, for example. Here respect and negative esteem recognition, a form of recognition which attends closely to my colleague's traits and actions, may be legitimately combined.

It is tempting to assume that we should always seek to avoid negative recognition, but disesteem and the *expression* of that disesteem may be consistent with equal respect. This was a familiar thought to eighteenth-century moralists from Shaftesbury through to Hume and Smith. Smith and Hume both regarded our sensitivity to social esteem as a guide to leading a moral life – the good man cared for the good opinion of his peers and took care not to act in ways that might provoke their disesteem (Hume 1978: 491; Smith 2009: 138–139). Only the vicious and arrogant were indifferent to the esteem judgements of others. While the value of respect recognition lies in the way it secures one's equal standing among others, the point of esteem recognition is to distinguish one from others, whether in positive or negative ways. Much of the politics of recognition is concerned with combating forms of disesteem which are inconsistent with equal respect, but it is also the case the disesteem has an important role to play in the social relations between equals. Where it is attached to actions for which we are responsible it can serve as a valuable form of informal social regulation, encouraging us to live up to normative expectations and discouraging us from violating them (Brennan and Pettit 2006). In discussions of recognition and toleration it is tempting to overlook the negative force of much recognition and also to assume that objections to others are always objectionable.

If deserved disesteem within the bounds of underlying respect is reasonable and socially necessary for the maintenance of justified norms of behavior, social disesteem attached to status groups works against respect recognition. Social and political struggles to secure respect must always struggle against the penalization of certain identities and their expression through social stigmatization, stereotyping, and status distinction more generally (stigmatization is simply the most extreme form of status inequality). Social norms often serve the interests of powerful groups by stigmatizing certain identities and practices such that it is understood to be deeply shameful to be the bearer of that identity (Goffman 1968) and stereotyping certain groups in ways that weight social expectations against them. Opportunities may be closed to certain groups of people or only available on pain of drastic self-refashioning and repositioning. Stigma, stereotyping, and status differentials, more generally, rely not on treating others as "invisible" but on making them *visible in particular ways* regardless of their wishes. This does not entail the absence of recognition, but rather the refusal to recognize the personhood of others, i.e., their equal moral status, through insisting on seeing them *only* in terms of their particular group identity or some aspect of that identity in more extreme forms of objectification, e.g., relating to women purely as sex objects, for example. This is not a matter of the simple *absence* of recognition, but of the displacement of respect recognition by more particular forms of recognition. Respect recognition, on this view, does not require us to be "difference blind" in the sense that we pretend that social difference does not exist, rather it operates as a reminder that others are not simply their particular role or identity, but always also persons and entitled to be considered as such (Kant 1996: 83). Stigma, stereotyping, and status deprivation all entail a determination to repress this thought and relate to others without regard to their equal status. This reading of recognition struggles as struggles for equal respect and against (negative) forms of particular recognition is at odds, however, with Taylor's account which treats them rather as struggles to affirm the value of particular cultural identities and practices and sees respect recognition as essentially a form of intolerance.

Honneth (2003: 122) rejects Taylor's treatment of respect recognition, regarding it as little more than a caricature of egalitarian thought which misrepresents respect recognition as a form of homogenizing legal recognition. He also objects to his interpretation of the so-called "politics of difference" suggesting that it is a misreading to interpret these struggles as exclusively, or even primarily, concerned with seeking social esteem for cultures and social identities – rather these struggles have historically centered on the achievement of *equal respect* both in formal, legal, terms but also in informal, social terms. It is a mistake, then, to suppose that there is a contrast to be drawn nineteenth- and late twentieth-century political struggles on the grounds that the former were concerned with achieving recognition of equal status, while the latter are concerned with the affirmation of particular identities. Rather these can more readily be understood as struggles for equal respect and the rights it mandates which entail the overcoming of various forms of stigma and low status, i. e., of demeaning forms of recognition. Recognition turns out to be more complex than it is commonly understood to be in debates about culture and toleration, encompassing respect and esteem, and also both negative and positive attitudes, which can be combined in more or less problematic ways. If some forms of disesteem need not undermine equal respect, is it possible that some forms of positive esteem can themselves run counter to equal respect?

Recognition, Abstraction, and Domination

While Honneth essentially thinks that the politics of recognition is focused on overcoming stigma, securing esteem for one's social contributions, and respect for one's status as an equal, Taylor sees it as a rebellion against a politics of equal human dignity. Marginalized groups, he claims, want to be recognized *as* different, not *despite* their differences. It is not immediately clear what this means, however (Bird 2004), and Taylor ultimately draws surprisingly tentative conclusions about what this might entail. Taylor's analysis of the problem turns on the idea that respect recognition entails a morally problematic form of abstraction which must be remedied by turning to particular, i.e., esteem focused recognition. There are two problems with this argument. Firstly, the politics of difference itself turns out to involve abstraction. Secondly, esteem recognition of marginalized identities may be as much of a trap as a solution. Thirdly, a closer examination of how recognition struggles are constituted reveal that the standard account of the politics of recognition is too narrowly framed and consequently obscures a set of pressing questions about who has the authority to claim or extend recognition.

The critique of abstraction insists that "difference blindness" renders social difference invisible in some sense and that this is oppressive because it requires us to abstract from our particular social identities (Galeotti 2002; Taylor 1994; Young 1990). If equal dignity seeks the source of our moral status in our common capacity for personhood, then all of our other, differentiating, particular features must be viewed, so the argument goes as merely contingent features of ourselves. As such any attachments to them must be of correspondingly little value. Respect recognition involves an abstraction from the totality of our features and does them not only symbolic violence, but also underwrites policies and attitudes that prize homogeneity and uniformity. This is a version of the romantic critique of the "spirit of abstraction" (Schiller 2016: 19) which is aimed at the way modern civilization abstracts the individual subject from the organic community in which she/he is situated, and similarly abstracts this subject's capacity for rationality from the totality of their being (Herder 2002: 324). On this view then, taking the abstract notion of the "person" as the basis of egalitarian morality and politics does violence to our embodied, situated nature and is oppressive to the extent that it requires us to slough off these things, central to our particular identities as mere contingencies, the role of "recognition" then is to affirm the importance of these aspects ourselves, retrieving them from the apparent normative oblivion to which the politics of respect for human dignity has consigned them. In this way, the critique of abstraction presents the politics of equal dignity as a form of intolerance.

If we turn, however, to Frantz Fanon's (2008) account of the recognition politics of colonialism a different picture emerges. Taylor's account of the politics of recognition relies primarily on a Herderian concern for cultural pluralism and is driven by a concern with the revaluation of minority cultures. Fanon, however, draws directly on Hegel's account of the dialectic between master and slave and the struggle for recognition that they engage in (Hegel 1977: 111–119). This struggle entails a clash of expectations between the parties involved and the attempt to transform the expectations of the other, thereby transforming the way each recognizes the other. Where the politics of difference assumes a simple "recognition deficit" – the absence of appropriate recognition which it is in the gift of the majority to provide, the Hegelian metaphor of a struggle for recognition assumes a much more complex process in which one must struggle to liberate oneself from one mode of recognition in order to demand another, thereby transforming social expectations and self-relations of the parties involved.

Fanon presents the first phase of the colonial struggle for recognition as one in which the colonized seek to emulate the white other, seeking recognition through assimilation by conforming to the norms of the colonizer (2008: 170–172). When this fails, however, a common reaction is to opt instead to emphasize the distance between the colonizer and the colonized by rejecting the project of assimilation and embracing one's "difference." Fanon regards this move as a trap rather than a step towards emancipation as one is still driven by the desire to secure the recognition of the master, albeit this time in the form of recognition of one's "difference."

In addition, one is abstracting from one's totality of being, by presenting oneself purely in terms of one's differentiating particularity. In so doing, the colonized are simply colluding with the expectations of the colonizer: the white master does not need much encouragement to see the black slave as irredeemably "other" as this is how he's been viewed all along. As Sartre observes in the foreword to the *Wretched of the Earth*, it is the recognition of the colonizer which has "brought the native into existence" (Fanon 1965: 28), i.e., through conceiving of the other as a "native" and expecting him to live up to stereotypical expectations. Fanon believes that the turn to assertion of difference does not emancipate because it does not emancipate the colonized from the desire to be recognized, i.e., esteemed by the colonizer. While the demand for equal respect is a demand made of the master the fact that it is a *demand* for something one is *entitled* to, rather than a *request* for the *gift* of esteem to be granted which makes it consistent with the sort of relative independence which members of a community of equals enjoy.

Fanon's insightful interpretation of the master/slave dialectic brings three important points into focus. Firstly, it reveals the one-sidedness of the critique of abstraction by pointing to the way that abstraction from the totality of one's identity can work in two ways: by abstracting from one's particularity – the abstraction that Taylor is concerned with and which he takes to be characteristic of "procedural liberalism," but also by abstracting from personhood by seeing others, or indeed oneself, purely in terms of a particular identity or role (Jones 2006a: 31). This latter form of abstraction is clearly a form of disrespect, as suggested by Kant: we must never treat others simply as a means but always also as an end in themselves (Kant 1996: 83). While Kant is thinking here of the wrong of recognizing people purely as their roles, the problem is clear: recognition focused purely on particular features to the exclusion of their personhood is an abstraction which is also a serious wrong. This is not to say that homogenizing insistence of uniformity it not wrong, but it does suggest that the wrong does not lie simply in the fact of abstraction itself.

The second point raised by Fanon's account is that positive esteem recognition for others' particular cultures and identities is not necessarily a liberating move. Both this recognition and the desire for it can instead serve to trap people in subordinate social relations. Esteem and affection for the exotic other is not the same as respect and can easily be compatible with a condescending, infantilizing attitude to the object of one's recognition, something all too familiar in the context of colonialism and in race relations (Saïd 2003). Legal scholar Patricia Williams (1997: 20–24) warns against the way that such relations can take a voyeuristic and even appropriative form rather than being characterized by genuine respect. The combination of these attitudes with the desire of some marginalized people to be esteemed in this way can serve to stabilize unequal social relations rather than forming the basis for inclusion on the basis of equality.

The third issue that Fanon's Hegelian account of recognition as a struggle raises are the limits of framing the recognition of members of marginalized groups as the simple overcoming of a "recognition deficit" through the granting of recognition by the more advantaged. Fanon rightly objects to the idea of recognition as a gift in the control of the powerful rather than as an entitlement to be demanded as a right by the powerless. The deficit model adopts a truncated, one-sided image of the recognition relations rather than taking into account the need to struggle against preexisting forms of particular recognition, positive or negative, and in so doing fails to place in question the authority of the powerful to grant or withhold recognition and the claim to be recognized as having this authority. We are not, then, dealing with the simple distribution of some good to overcome a deficit, but rather with a complex struggle to restructure social relations, a struggle against unequal authority relations. Recall that this was the same problem posed by the permission conception of toleration: that one party had the power to grant or withhold toleration. Now we see that recognition, at least in the form of the recognition of difference, has precisely the same structure and is therefore liable to the same criticism. For this reason, we should be skeptical of the suggestion that "recognition" should be preferred to toleration.

Domination and the Public Expression of Difference

How might we explain the wrong of "abstraction" if Taylor's romantic account is insufficient? Recall that permission conception of toleration is objectionable because it purports to afford a measure of freedom to marginalized groups, but in fact constitutes a form of domination even if it does not entail active persecution.The tolerated must keep their heads down and not draw attention to themselves in public because they must fear that whatever permission they are currently afforded can be withdrawn at any time. A common complaint, then, about toleration is that it discourages the expression of difference in public. In the case of the permission conception this is literally true. Is it also true of the respect conception of toleration? Certainly, we can read Taylor's account of the politics of equal dignity as a form of symbolic hostility to the expression of difference. Sometimes this is connected to the complaint that toleration "privatizes" differences, but here we must be careful, for privatization here is quite different to privatization in the sense that one is to be discouraged from expressing one's differences in public spaces. Privatization as conceived in liberal political theory (as opposed, say, to more general criticisms of the individualism of modern societies, which may or may not be traced back to liberal ideals) entails drawing a normative line around certain beliefs, actions, and practices to secure them against state intervention. Normative privatization, then, can have the effect of securing the freedom of members of marginalized groups to express their differences in public spaces. Indeed, from this point of view, those countries which ban the public wearing of the veil by Muslim women are pursuing an illiberal policy which denies equal rights of self-expression to those women.

While we have reason to reject certain claims made by the proponents of the "recognition of difference" regarding both the nature of recognition and it's relation to toleration, this does not mean that we should reject the suggestion that people may have interests in expressing and seeking recognition for various aspects of their identities. Rather, the problem lies with the way proponents of the "recognition of difference" frame this issue, and in particular their reliance on the revived romantic critique of abstraction.

On Taylor's view abstraction itself, or rather one form of abstraction, is the problem. But perhaps the problem is not abstraction per se, but exposure to domination connected to one's identity, i.e., one's vulnerability to uncontrolled interference in one's life. The "recognition of difference" relieves on a one-sided notion of abstraction and a similarly limited understanding of social recognition and this hampers its analysis of identity-related domination. The central issue is not, on reflection, the failure to recognize particular identities, but rather the failure to recognize the rights of individual group members to manage which aspects of themselves they may wish to bring to bear in social contexts. We do not normally insist on bringing our "full" selves to bear in ordinary social interactions with friends and colleagues. Instead, we typically limit access to ourselves and expect others to similarly limit their own presentation of self in such contexts. In managing our own presentation of self we abstract, i.e., select from all of the true things we might choose to reveal or simply to foreground about ourselves. The wearing of masks, i.e., the freedom to conceal or reveal as we please, is, as sociologist Richard Sennett has observed, an essential feature of sociability (Sennett 1977: 15). It is not abstraction which is the problem but the way that unequal social and political power affects our freedom to manage our presentation of self (Goffman 1990).

On the intersubjective model of selfhood, we do not enjoy sovereign, i.e. absolute, control over our self-presentation (Markell 2003) but we may enjoy considerable discretion over how we choose to present ourselves. However we choose to present ourselves we can never exclude the possibility that we are opening ourselves up to dialogues that may come to alter our understanding of ourselves. It would be unreasonable to demand absolute freedom to control my self-understanding and still less to seek to control others' interpretations of me and evaluations of my merits. It is not unreasonable, however, to seek equal freedom to control my self-presentation, and to deny others' the power to dominate my choices in this respect. My judgements about what to foreground and what to leave in the background in a given context should not be constrained by the thought that I cannot afford to draw attention to myself and thereby risk persecution.

The domination critique focuses on the ways that we may unfairly disadvantaged with respect to our identities. When people are unfairly disadvantaged, i.e., denied access to important social goods, rights, liberties, and opportunities, etc., on account of their identity, their self-management is typically compromised in two ways: firstly, they discouraged them from openly presenting themselves in ways that expose them to this disadvantage. Where possible, they must conceal their identity from others in order to shield themselves from domination and disadvantage. Secondly, they may find that they must adapt to repressive social expectations by conforming to stereotypical expectations and adopting a variety of deferential modes of self-presentation, or by seeking to conform to the norms of dominant groups. In this case, there is an additional risk to one's self-respect associated with complicity in norms that ensure one's own subordination (Hill 1991).

One might object that not all identities lend themselves to these adaptive strategies – race and sex, for example, involve visible physical characteristics that render concealment difficult while many religious or sexual minorities can more easily conceal their identities. What we can say is that the incentive to adopt deferential modes of interaction may be more common for those for whom strategies of concealment or "passing" are not readily available. In any case, it is not the availability of an adaptation strategy that matters from a moral point of view: it is unjust that some should have to consider adopting such strategies because they are subject to domination. Where marginalized groups adopt muted forms of self-expression in public spaces or in workplaces, the problem is not one of abstraction from their particular identities in the name of equality, but rather a basic denial of equal respect prompting them to modify their self-presentation for fear of the consequences of not doing so. It is the lack of respect recognition for the equal personhood of others that explains the wrongness of the pressure to assimilate and repress particularizing identities not a failure to directly value these identities themselves (Jones 2006a: 30–32).

Recognition Versus Toleration Revisited

While the idea that "recognition" as acceptance, i.e., positive esteem should replace toleration is widespread, it turns out that the philosophical proponents of the "recognition of difference" ultimately shy away from such strong conclusions. This is because they are ultimately unwilling to endorse the claim that there is a right to esteem recognition for cultural practices and identities. Respect can plausibly be demanded as a right, a right which can be backed by the power of the state if necessary. Even if someone lacks the corresponding *attitude* of respect, they can be compelled to *treat* others with respect. This is not an unreasonable imposition on our liberty as no has the right to treat others as less than equals. One might object that the outward performance of esteem can also be performed by flatterers regardless of their true views, and can be demanded or commanded by high-status persons of their social inferiors. The difference is that while it is legitimate to demand equal respect, it not obviously legitimate to demand the esteem which one takes to be one's due. This is because there may be a much greater range of reasonable disagreement in matters of social esteem because we value the freedom of persons to make and express evaluative judgements, and because it is all too common to meet people whose esteem expectations are obviously unreasonable, such as those of white supremacists, sexists, etc. (such expectations are essential to the norms constituting social hierarchy after all).

Galeotti argues for recognition as the positive acceptance of marginalized groups, rejecting (contra Honneth) the idea that systems of equal rights already constitute a form of recognition. Galeotti also, however, believes that this public recognition of difference must also be rendered compatible with the notion of state neutrality. This complicates matters as a commitment to neutrality (which, Galeotti notes, is a relatively recent addition to liberalism) is typically understood to bar the state from making specifically ethical judgements about its citizens and their particular ethical projects and ways of life. The state, on this view, guards the equal rights of its citizens, but ought not engage in additional *ethical* judgements about the value of their projects, identities, or cultural practices (the history of actual states, of course, suggests a different picture). This is the thrust of Paine's rejection of "toleration" and "intoleration." How, then, may the state extend "recognition" to marginalized identities beyond recognition of the equal right to have and express one's commitments and identities?

Galeotti acknowledges that a neutral liberal state must not engage in the direct evaluation of marginalized identities: endorsing some but rejecting others, over and above any considerations about rights violations is clearly not neutral, or impartial, and risks setting the state on a path away from pluralism and towards the encouragement land enforcement of particular ethical views. That does not look like a recipe for securing the pluralism which "recognition of difference" is supposed to promote. Her solution, in effect, is to take a step back from the evaluation of any particular social difference and to focus more on the phenomenon of difference in general: "positive recognition, even though only symbolic, requires a positive consideration of the difference in question, and this goes beyond a merely neutral stance. By positive consideration I do not mean a positive evaluation of the difference, but, rather, a special attention intended as a sign of its public acceptance" (2002: 74). She goes on to say that: "The non-neutral but positive attitude needed is, in any case, justified by the neutral principle of the rectification of injustice. Moreover the public positive attitude which characterizes symbolic recognition can be neutrally extended to all differences, and is, hence, impartial" (2002: 74). This position appears to be a fudge: attention in the form of consideration is different from positive evaluation precisely because the outcome of consideration need not always be positive, but if this attention itself is supposed to signal positive acceptance, then we are back to the first-order evaluation of identities and practices. This is supported by her suggestion that recognition in this sense amounts to "the declaration that different identities and practices are just as legitimate and valuable as those that constitute the social norms" (2002: 73–74). This is an unambiguously positive form of esteem recognition. Elsewhere, she adopts a different formulation, suggesting that public recognition aims only at recognizing that the identity in question is valuable for members of the group in question (2002: 104).

The problem with the first of these is that it goes too far: for any given identity or culture, we cannot say in advance whether it is genuinely is as legitimate as any other or that it is worthy of esteem. Galeotti insists that positive recognition should not extend to identities that depend on or are complicit in rights violations, of course, but this cannot be decided in advance of any investigation of an identity. Furthermore, cultures and identities that stop short of legal rights violations but which, nonetheless, embody subordinating norms cannot obviously be seen as deserving of esteem. The second of these formulations – that we recognize that identities and practices have value for those who subscribe to them – seems to not go far enough as recognition of this fact does not itself imply any positive evaluation. Even identities that are bound up with persistent rights violations may be valued by those who inhabit them, and yet the practices connected to these identities may be subject to legal intervention as well as social disesteem, so this form of recognition seems to fall well short of the positive acceptance desired.

Taylor, by contrast, is not concerned with liberal neutrality – his account of the divergent politics of recognition is intended as a critique of the homogenizing tendencies of "procedural liberalism" after all. He is, however, aware that there may be significant disagreement about the value of particular cultural identities (Jones 2006: 124) and that this counts against the idea that there might be a general right to esteem recognition for particular cultural identities even if the suggestion that recognition should be viewed as a basic human need looks like a possible grounding for such a right. It is certainly plausible that some recognition claims do ground rights, but these seem to be confined to claims for the recognition of equal status and do not extend to social esteem per se. If we do have a need for some basic esteem recognition, we might think that, like other important goods such as love and friendship, we cannot claim this directly as a right. At most, we could be said to have a right to equal opportunities to achieve social esteem. This would certainly count against the stigmatizing and stereotyping, positive and negative, of social identities, which all restrict these opportunities. It would not commit us to esteeming others who do not deserve our esteem such as those who enjoy unearned high social status or those whose self-worth depends on the subordination of others.

Taylor appears to think of the recognition of difference in much this way: mindful of the fact that not all cultural identities are going to be worthy of esteem, he suggests in the end that rather than a right to recognition, we should rather aim to be approach other cultures with an open mind as to their value. There should, he suggests, be a "presumption" that other cultures may have value, with the caveat that this should be no more than "a starting hypothesis" and not a right (1994: 66–68). This leaves open the possibility that we may have reason to reject some claims to esteem recognition, even if we owe everyone fair consideration of their claims. In the end, the case for the recognition of difference falls far short of claiming that everyone has an automatic right to recognition in the sense of positive acceptance or esteem for their identity. Once we allow not only for reasonable disagreement about the value of cultures and identities, but also for the possibility that may be cases in which it would be entirely wrong to extend such recognition, it seems that the "recognition of difference" does not turn out to pose a serious challenge to toleration at all.

Summary and Future Directions

The case for moving beyond toleration, or reinterpreting it as "recognition," relied in part on historical narratives which presented contemporary controversies about culture and identity as representing a sharp break with earlier controversies about religious differences and the politics of equal dignity. The motivation behind the turn to recognition as positive acceptance was the thought that such a move would allow us to eliminate the objection component which is essential to toleration. The key assumption here seemed to be that recognition as positive acceptance is morally unproblematic while objections to culture and identity taken to be normally rooted in intolerance. A supposed contrast between belief and identity seemed to explain this latter assumption, the thought being that people may reasonably disagree with beliefs but an objection to a social identity looks like it can only be explained as the product of prejudice. While there is general agreement that the permission conception of toleration represents a form of domination and inconsistent with equal respect, the "recognition" critique of toleration goes further than this, suggesting that not only is recognition in the form of equal rights inadequate (Galeotti 2002: 96) it may itself represent a form of intolerance.

We have seen, however, that there are reasons to query the way critics of toleration have framed the problem to which "recognition" is thought to be the solution. It is clear that the history of religious toleration is a history of struggles about the toleration of groups, not individuals, and about collective practices and public forms of expression. The tool of toleration is not obviously ill-suited to coping with contemporary controversies, which often turn out to concern religious groups, whether these are Muslims seeking to wear religious dress in public contexts, or fundamentalist Christians opposing equal rights for gay people. The assumption that we can draw a bright line between identity and belief is also dubious, especially if one adopts a recognitive view of the self which entails a blurring of the lines between self and other and between self-understandings and the normative expectations that constitute social identities.

At the level of conceptual propriety the attempt to contrast toleration with "recognition" overlooks the way that conceptions of toleration are already constituted by recognitive attitudes. In the case of the permission conception this is limited to recognition as stigmatization of the tolerated group, of course, while in the case of the respect conception, there is a combination of disesteem and equal respect. Too often, then, the idea of "recognition" is treated simply as a synonym for positive social esteem, rather than being analyzed into its different modes. This over-simplified account of recognition has two further implications. Firstly, it fails to come to terms with the way that positive esteem recognition can be compatible with disrespect and wider inequalities. Secondly, it encourages us to frame the problem of misrecognition as one of simply supplying others with the recognition they currently lack, rather than taking a more comprehensive view of the relations involved. Once we do this, however, it becomes clear that relations of respect and esteem are inextricably linked to struggles for power and authority. Just as we might object to the idea that some should enjoy the unconstrained power to tolerate or not, we might also object to the idea that some should enjoy the unconstrained power to withhold or grant recognition. The question of *who* has the *power* to recognize and whether this can be justified is obscured in the standard Anglo-American accounts of the politics of recognition.

While the permission conception of toleration has no philosophical defenders nowadays, this does not mean that it does not have an afterlife in the social attitudes of citizens who persist in the belief that they are specially entitled to determine who is worthy of toleration and who is not. This belief obviously remains an obstacle to recognizing others as having equal standing in our political communities. The suggestion that many popular objections to marginalized identities and practices have their basis in prejudice rather than in reasonable ethical disagreement also seems very plausible. Similarly the suggestion that we should not automatically think of social pluralism as a problem to be managed if not indeed overcome. Finally, the claim that at least some interpretations of equality may amount to a form of intolerance is also plausible. The stronger versions of these claims, however, that the pursuit of equality is necessarily aimed at stifling the expression of social differences, or that we could, or should, in principle, eliminate the objection component that makes intolerance and toleration possible, are deeply implausible.

A comprehensive politics of recognition, concerned with challenging low status, stigma, and stereotyping, positive and negative, and the power relations that maintain these, will be primarily driven by a concern for achieving equal respect. It may prompt the revision and abandonment of many objections on the grounds that they are inconsistent with respect and are rooted in prejudice, but it cannot eliminate the phenomenon of objection as many objections will turn out to be reasoned, even if there may be reasonable disagreement about the force of these objections. Social difference cannot easily be separated from the deeper ethical differences that exist in modern societies and the prospect of a deep and wide consensus on the value of all social identities and practices seems to be neither possible nor desirable. If we may revise views about what constitutes a reasonable objection without eliminating objection per se, then it seems there is going to be an ongoing role for the virtue of toleration: objections that nonetheless must be restrained by a more fundamental respect for others' authority over their own lives will remain a feature of our societies. More than that, however, a genuine politics of recognition that is conceived as a complex, ongoing, transformative struggle for equality will discover new sources of objection over and above those involving negative esteem and stigmatization. Some of these might be matters about which there may be reasonable disagreement, but others may entail serious departures from equal respect to the point of allowing or encouraging rights violations. In this way, a comprehensive politics of recognition will not only have the potential to alter our views about what is objectionable, but also where we should place the limits of toleration. We have no reason, then, to suppose that recognition, properly understood, constitutes an alternative to toleration. Once we expand our appreciation of the ways our lives are shaped by struggles for social recognition, it must be evident that questions about toleration and its limits must continue to play an important role.

Future Directions for Research

The motivation for turning to recognition was the assumption that there was a sharp discontinuity between the circumstances in which the modern practice of toleration was formed and our contemporary context, i.e., the rediscovery of culture and community in the 1980s and 1990s. That this assumption has been so readily accepted among political theorists raises a question about the way normative political theory is practiced. Future research in toleration might benefit from a more thoroughly contextual approach, for example. This might focus more attention on the way political theorists frame the problems they are concerned with. In the case of the cultural turn in political theory, such an approach might help to bring the romantic influence on our understandings of the nature and value of culture into focus. It might also prompt us to consider whether there are in fact deeper continuities between liberal toleration and "cultural recognition" which are obscured by the narrative of discontinuity. For example, whether "cultural recognition" effectively privatizes cultural practices in the same way liberal toleration is said to have privatized religion. Finally, the concept of recognition remains largely unanalyzed in Anglo-American political theory, thanks to its identification with "cultural recognition." Future research should perhaps pay closer attention to the importance of the recognition of equal standing and possible conflicts with esteem recognition. It would also be worth focusing more attention on the role of recognition in driving social and political conflict. Placing the idea of a struggle for recognition at the center of future work on toleration and recognition might also be helpful for thinking through the politics of toleration in an era marked by populist culture wars. In this context, we may find that we need to find ways to preserve toleration rather than seek to move beyond it, and to ask whether cultural norms are working *against* equal recognition, rather than seeking recognition *for* cultures.

References

Bird C (2004) Status, identity, and respect. Political Theory 32:207–232
Bourdieu P (1984) Distinction. Routledge, London
Brown W (2009) Regulating aversion: tolerance in the age of identity and empire. Princeton University Press, Princeton
Darwall S (1977) Two kinds of respect. Ethics 88:36–49
Fanon F (1965) The wretched of the earth. Penguin, Harmondsworth
Fanon F (2008) Black skin white masks. Pluto Press, London
Forst R (2007) 'To tolerate means to insult' toleration, recognition, and emancipation. In: Owen D, van den Brink B (eds) Recognition and power. Cambridge University Press, Cambridge, pp 215–237
Forst R (2013) Toleration in conflict. Cambridge University Press, Cambridge
Foucault M (1995) Discipline and punish. Vintage, New York
Galeotti AE (2002) Toleration as recognition. Oxford University Press, Oxford
Goffman E (1968) Stigma. Penguin, Harmondsworth
Goffman E (1990) The presentation of self in everyday life. Penguin, Harmondsworth
Hegel GWF (1977) Phenomenology of spirit. Clarendon Press, Oxford
Herder JG (2002) This too a philosophy of history of humanity. In: Philosophical writings. Cambridge University Press, Cambridge
Hill T (1991) Servility and self-respect. In: Autonomy and self-respect. Cambridge University Press, Cambridge, pp 4–18
Honneth A (1995) The struggle for recognition. Polity, Cambridge
Honneth A (2003) Redistribution as recognition: a response to Nancy Fraser. In: Fraser N, Honneth A (eds) Redistribution or recognition? Verso, London, pp 110–197
Horton J (1998) Toleration as a virtue. In: Heyd D (ed) Toleration: an elusive virtue. Princeton University Press, Princeton, pp 28–43
Hume D (1978) A treatise of human nature. Clarendon Press, Oxford
Jones P (2006a) Equality, recognition and difference. Crit Rev Int Soc Pol Phil 9:23–46
Jones P (2006b) Toleration, recognition and identity. J Polit Philos 14:123–143
Kant I (1996) Groundwork of the metaphysic of morals. In: Practical philosophy. Cambridge University Press, Cambridge

28 Recognition and Toleration

King P (1976) Toleration. St Martin's Press, London

Laborde C (2002) On republican toleration. Constellations 9:167–183

Markell P (2003) Bound by recognition. Princeton University Press, Princeton

McBride C (2013) Recognition. Polity Press, Cambridge

Paine T (2000) Rights of man in political writings. Cambridge University Press, Cambridge

Parekh B (2000) Rethinking multiculturalism. Macmillan, Basingstoke

Pettit P (1996) Freedom as antipower. Ethics 106:576–604

Pettit P (2012) On the people's terms. Cambridge University Press, Cambridge

Pettit P, Brennan G (2006) The economy of esteem. Oxford University Press, Oxford

Saïd E (2003) Orientalism. Penguin, London

Schiller F (2016) On the aesthetic education of man (1795). Penguin, London

Sennett R (1977) The fall of public man. Cambridge University Press, Cambridge

Smith A (2009) The theory of moral sentiments (1759). Penguin, London

Taylor C (1994) The politics of recognition. In: Gutmann A (ed) Multiculturalism. Princeton University Press, Princeton, pp 25–74

Waldron J (2012) Dignity, rank, and rights. Oxford University Press, Oxford

Walzer M (1997) On toleration. Yale University Press, New Haven

Weber M (1978) Economy and society, vol 2. University of California Press, Berkeley

Williams P (1997) Seeing a colour-blind future. Virago, London

Wolff J (2010) Fairness, respect and the egalitarian ethos revisited. J Ethics 14:335–350

29
Toleration and Dignity

Colin Bird

Contents

Introduction 564
Dignity 564
Toleration for the Sake of Dignity 567
Indignity, Disrespect, and the Intolerable 576
Summary and Future Directions 580
References 582

Abstract

A commitment to the protection of human dignity and the value of toleration seem, at first glance, to go hand in hand. Both, after all, seem to require a sensitivity to the diversity of alternative ways of life. Despite this commonality, this chapter however suggests that their relationship is more complicated than one might initially suppose. It considers two ways in which they may be connected. First, it asks whether a principle of respect for the dignity of the individual person can motivate an expectation of tolerance. This dependence is less straightforward than it appears at first and makes sense only under rather special assumptions. Second, the chapter considers whether taking human dignity seriously requires societies to be intolerant in certain cases, i.e., those in which agents face treatment that threatens the value of human dignity. It concludes, therefore, by exploring some ways in which a commitment to dignitarian values may create pressure to narrow the range of acceptable toleration further than many liberal writers are normally prepared to accept.

C. Bird (✉)
Department of Politics, Program in Political Philosophy, Policy, and Law, University of Virginia, Charlottesville, VA, USA
e-mail: colinbird@virginia.edu; cpb6f@virginia.edu

© The Author(s), under exclusive licence to Springer Nature Switzerland AG 2022
M. Sardoĉ (ed.), *The Palgrave Handbook of Toleration*,
https://doi.org/10.1007/978-3-030-42121-2_29

Keywords

Toleration · Human dignity · Pluralism · Human rights · Natural law · Liberalism · Kant · Freedom of conscience · Free speech · Harassment · John Rawls · Ronald Dworkin · Jeremy Waldron

Introduction

Claims about human dignity, or about the "dignity of the individual," might bear on the issue of toleration in at least two ways: first, as *grounds* for an expectation of tolerance toward others and, second, as the basis for elaborating various *archetypes* of the intolerable. In the former, more familiar capacity, appeals to the dignity of persons, groups, or states purport to justify a tolerant attitude toward, or perhaps a duty to tolerate, them. When used in this first way, dignitarian arguments imply that respect for the dignity of individuals prohibits certain forms of intolerance.

Although it has received less attention from theorists of toleration, the second possibility is no less important. At least since World War II, the language of human dignity has routinely been mobilized to characterize outrages, atrocities, and other forms of mistreatment that are "beyond the pale" of civilized interaction. That is why genocide, torture, slavery, rape, persecution, and other forms of personal degradation come up so frequently in discussions of human dignity. Behind this second line of thought lies a powerful intuition: that these are abuses so unconscionable that neither any civilized society nor any consequentialist calculation of costs and benefits could ever condone them.

Although consistent and likely related in various ways, these two ways of understanding the relation between toleration and dignity are nonetheless distinct. Indeed, in some sense, they move in opposing directions. In the first, claims about dignity purport to explain why toleration is justified in a range of cases. In the second, by contrast, intuitions about what we can never tolerate help to specify the content of a commitment to protecting human dignity. Where the first canvasses reasons for toleration and against intolerance, the second suggests that respect for the dignity of the person may actually require certain kinds of intolerance. In what follows, each of these possibilities is discussed independently (Sections "Toleration for the Sake of Dignity" and "Indignity, Disrespect, and the Intolerable"). A concluding section (Section "Conclusion") considers the relationship between them. Before doing any of this, however, I begin with some orienting remarks about the concept of dignity itself.

Dignity

For several overlapping reasons, the idea of human dignity is currently enjoying something of a vogue in social and political thought. First, thanks above all to the seminal work of John Rawls (Rawls 1999), much recent moral, political, and legal theory invests strongly in assumptions drawn from Kantian ethics – especially Kant's emphasis on "respect" as the key ingredient in moral motivation and his allied contrast between the "price" of things and the "dignity" of the human person. These dignitarian ideas played a key role in Rawls's influential attack on utilitarianism. According to him, utilitarianism cannot properly respect the "inviolable" dignity of individuals because it is willing to sacrifice the welfare of a few in order to promote that of a greater number.

Another reason for renewed interest in dignitarian ideas reflects the increasingly cosmopolitan outlook of contemporary political philosophy. Governments and their citizens are now more globally interdependent than ever before, and few now think that the scope of political judgment can be confined within the boundaries of the nation-state. However, if political arguments must address a diverse, global audience, they need to appeal to values that have some universal, cross-cultural appeal. Many accordingly have turned to the idea of "human dignity" to serve as a suitably accessible category that can cover the minimal requirements for humane and decent institutions. The gravest abuses that humans can inflict on each other – violent assault, genocide, racial or ethnic oppression, slavery, human trafficking, and other forms of brutal economic exploitation, torture and intimidation, and religious persecution – all seem to undermine a dignified human existence. Insofar as that thought can be endorsed by any reasonable person, regardless of their religious or cultural background, one has some reason to hope that the idea of human dignity is a universal cosmopolitan value from which political argument can proceed.

That hope is reflected in the frequent recourse to dignitarian ideas within contemporary human rights discourse. More generally, the idea that basic rights, whether human, natural, or moral, are grounded on the dignity of the person is a familiar one. Robert Nozick offers an exemplary statement of the logic underlying such claims, arguing that if "[We]. . .are inviolate individuals, who may not be used in certain ways by others as means or tools or instruments or resources. . .," then we must be treated "as persons having individual rights with the dignity this constitutes" (Nozick 2013, pp. 333–334). Nozick prosecutes this argument on behalf of a strongly libertarian position, but proponents of a wide variety of views have found the root idea attractive. One reason for its broad appeal is that the requirement of respect for the dignity of individuals seems to unite a concern for their freedom and equality within a single, robust formula. As Ronald Dworkin put it, in elaborating his famous "liberal" principle of "equal concern and respect":

> What does it mean for the government to treat its citizens as equals? That is, I think, the same question as the question of what it means to treat all its citizens as free, or as independent, or with equal dignity. (Dworkin 1985, p. 191)

According to Dworkin, freedom and equality need not be conceived as separate and competing values, to which political theories might attach different weights. Properly understood, rather, they refer to different aspects of the same underlying value – the dignity of autonomous individuals, and the "equal respect" it commands.

Despite the gathering interest in concepts of dignity, no clear consensus as to how they should be construed currently exists. Indeed, the renewed intellectual attention they have lately attracted has if anything underlined their unsettled character. Still, recent philosophical discussion has at least clarified where legitimate dispute about the construal of dignitarian ideas surfaces. Three main areas of uncertainty about the meaning and import of the concept of dignity are relevant to the discussion below.

First, and most basically, there is dispute about whether dignitarian categories are of any philosophical use at all. Much dignity-skepticism is inspired by the very unsettledness of the concepts itself, and the concomitant concern that appeals to dignity is of rhetorical or merely ornamental significance only. As the utilitarian Peter Singer has remarked:

> Philosophers frequently introduce ideas of dignity, respect, and worth at the point at which other reasons appear to be lacking, but this is hardly good enough. Fine phrases are the last resource of those who have run out of arguments. (Regan and Singer 1976, p. 89)

Several other forms of dignity-skepticism deserve mention. Some have been concerned that dignitarian idioms are tainted by their historical associations with honor-culture, hierarchy, exclusion, sexism, and violence. Respect and dignity are, after all, central values for *Mafiosi* and gang culture more generally. Others have worried that the traditional idea that persons have inherent dignity is essentially a religious one, harking back to Christian notions of the *imago dei*, and therefore unsuited for use in secular political discussion (Waldron 2002). This suspicion is to some extent reinforced by commentators with religious sympathies who look to ideas about the dignity of the human person to reintroduce traditional spiritual values they see has threatened by an excessively secularized culture (Wolterstorff 2010).

A second area of uncertainty involves a central ambiguity about whether we should think of dignity primarily as a *status-concept* or as a form of personal *worth*. Although often elided, this contrast turns out to be very important. Sometimes, when we speak of someone's dignity, we are placing them in a formal hierarchy, as when we describe diplomats as "dignitaries." Yet while an ambassador has "dignity" in this status-related sense, and a taxi driver lacks it, it doesn't follow that their "worth" as human beings differs. Indeed, in many contexts, we would say that they are worthy of the same respect despite their differing formal rank. Torturing a taxi driver is presumably no less a denial of his worth and dignity than torturing an ambassador would be of hers. The same ambiguity between status and worth crops up elsewhere. Consider the term "gentleman." In some contexts, dignifying someone as a "gentleman" is simply to place him within a recognized hierarchy – a member of the "gentry," above the peasantry but below nobility. In others, describing someone as a "gentleman" is a term of endearment, equivalent to (something like) "a decent guy" or a "fine fellow." The former usage locates someone in a formal space of status relations, and the latter makes a judgment of personal worth. What goes for the concept "gentleman" also goes for that of "dignity." When considering the role of dignity concepts in political argument, it often matters whether we are using them in a status-related or worth-related sense (Lucy 2017; Bird 2018). As we shall see, arguments about toleration are a case in point.

A third source of variance in our construal of dignity derives from the fact that sometimes we think of it as a property or possession of the individual person and sometimes as a more diffuse social quality. On a traditional religious understanding – one that figures prominently in "pro-life" arguments about abortion, for example – human dignity is *inherent* in the person. To the extent that we adopt this construal, we will think of violations of human dignity as assaults on something that is identified with the victim. Thus, one might say that in raping or torturing others, rapists and torturers take their victim's dignity away: but clearly one can only take something away if it was with them in the first place. When construed in this mode, dignitarian claims tend to have a strongly individualist tenor, oriented fundamentally toward the protection of persons and their entitlements.

However, we often also think of dignity as a social quality. It is doubtful, for example, that one can endorse a status-based conception of dignity and treat a person's dignitary status as if it is straightforwardly inherent in them. To call someone a "dignitary" is to say as much about their relations to their political society as about their personal attributes. In a broader sense, dignity is also often an ambient quality, as when we speak about the dignified atmosphere of a religious rite, or the way that degrading social conditions refract indignity and humiliation. And the language of "human dignity" naturally implies that dignity is as much an attribute of the species as it is one of individuals. Even Kant, who can come across as an obsessively individualist thinker, sometimes foreshadows the increasingly fashionable idea that dignity lies at the core of a "common humanity" in which all people and cultures share. So, in considering how toleration and dignity are related, then, we need not be confined to thinking about the impact of tolerance or intolerance on specific people. The question of how they contribute to, or detract from, human dignity as a broader cultural achievement may be no less relevant.

Toleration for the Sake of Dignity

On standard accounts, toleration presupposes disapproval of what is tolerated: one can tolerate only what one finds objectionable; conversely, one cannot tolerate something to which one is indifferent or that attracts one's approval. The need to justify toleration of P arises, then, precisely when agents have at least a prima facie reason to disapprove, discourage, and perhaps suppress P. Looking to an expectation of respect for dignity to motivate toleration in such cases is at once natural and problematic.

It is natural because, as Kantians especially emphasize, that expectation seems to carry exactly the preemptive, categorical force, needed to override the reasons to not tolerate something objectionable. This is at least in part due to the connotations of deference and obedience carried by our ordinary notions of respect. When we admonish children to "respect their parents," for example, it is almost always when a child resists or rejects her parents' expectations. The point of the statement is to urge the child concerned to "suck it up," to set aside their personal aversion to whatever it is their parents are asking of them, and to comply regardless.

Citing a principle of respect for dignity as the basis for a stance of tolerance is nonetheless problematic because the relation between toleration and respect is a famously uneasy one. We have already noted that tolerating something presumes that one has reasons to disvalue it. Yet commentators have made much of the fact that, in contrast, to respect P is to somehow positively affirm P's value. In the light of this contrast, one might think that respect and tolerance correspond to two quite distinct attitudes to the pluralism and disagreement that characterize modern society.

For example, those who today urge "respect for diversity" suggest that the dizzying array of conflicting approaches to religious devotion, artistic endeavor, political activity, cultural reproduction, educational aspiration, psychological self-exploration, etc. represented among the citizenry of liberal societies is something to be celebrated. This way of thinking tends to sidestep the inconvenient conflicts that arise when agents despise each others' commitments. It instead focuses on the desirability of a rich plurality of alternative ways of life. But, for precisely that reason, one might doubt that it supports toleration, for here the claim is not that agents should suspend their disapproval of others who live in ways they find offensive but rather that they should positively welcome the presence of those others. So, while tolerant societies will normally be quite diverse, not all diverse societies need be tolerant.

As a case in point, consider the modern university, which today promotes research and teaching of different kinds in highly diverse areas; even within particular disciplines, contrasting approaches and topics are often represented. Although there are certainly genuine tensions between some academic disciplines, for the most part, scholars positively value the wide range of studies pursued in the modern university. Indeed, many would regard that diversity as among its chief glories, perhaps citing its connection to Enlightenment ideals of dignity – the autonomous pursuit of rational inquiry, critical thinking, wisdom, knowledge, clarity of thought, the open exchange of ideas, human ingenuity, etc. In a striking discussion, St. Augustine connected glory with clarity, and one might well see the kaleidoscopic variety of the modern academy as an important aspect of what Avishai Margalit has called humanity's "reflected glory" (Margalit 1998). Insofar as we identify this "reflected glory" with a form of dignity, we are implicitly operating with a conception of dignity as social and ambient rather than narrowly individualist.

In such a perspective, however, the protean character of modern academic research, which (at its best) both manifests the prodigious ingenuity of the human mind and its often heroic efforts to clarify its understanding of the world, is not sustained by toleration, but rather by a kind of mutual respect in which scholars and students affirm the dignity and worth of their highly varied intellectual vocations. A university in which professors of history, physics, economics, or philosophy merely tolerated each other, and who therefore refrain from acting on their aversion to their colleagues' research, would surely lack something crucial. Yet insofar as the ethos sustaining the modern university requires participants to celebrate heterogeneity for the sake of (something like) the dignity of human inquiry, it won't be one centered on the value of tolerance, but rather on a positive ideal of mutual respect.

If one assumes, on these grounds, that dignitarian mutual respect and toleration represent two quite different ways of responding to diversity, two possible implications for politics seem available. One emphasizes a contrast between universities and other institutions in civil society and the normal context of political life: it proceeds from the observation that the forms of diversity and disagreement that divide citizens of modern liberal states are far deeper and less easily reconciled than those that develop under the umbrella of narrower associations like universities. After all, the diversity of academic disciplines within the university is still bounded by a rough, but still circumscribed, consensus on the legitimate goals of education. Since no analogous consensus about the ends of government exists, one might think public cooperation typically occurs among citizens who hold opposed, even incompatible, beliefs about the purposes of political association. Toleration, rather than a strong, dignity-grounded conception of mutual respect, might then be a more appropriate way of accommodating pluralism at the level of politics. For proponents of this line, whatever role ideals of respect and human dignity have in private or local settings like a university, they have little application to the larger-scale, more encompassing context of political association. In the public sphere, such ideals must yield to a more modest expectation of tolerance.

Alternatively, one might assimilate the two cases but then conclude that the seeming appropriateness of a model of toleration in political contexts is to the detriment of our current way of understanding the state. To aim for a tolerant modus vivendi is, on this view, to set our expectations of public life too low: we should aim ultimately to realize a political settlement that more closely resembles the university model. Rainer Forst quotes Goethe articulating something like this suggestion: "Tolerance should be a temporary attitude only: it must lead to recognition. To tolerate means to insult" (Forst 2007). Transcending mere tolerance and achieving a richer, mutually affirmative regime need not require a highly homogenous political society in which everyone shares the same values, proclivities, and cultural orientation. To the contrary, as with universities, diversity would not only persist in such a society but also be positively valued as a vital incident of human dignity and hence an occasion for sincere mutual respect. Efforts to eliminate difference or enforce cultural homogeneity would be seen as a threat to human dignity and the wide range of ways in which it can manifest itself in the lives of peoples and cultures (Galston 2002; Raz 2009).

Both of these possibilities are worth thinking about, but we are limited to them only if we assume that the models of tolerance and mutual respect are at odds. Many will however resist that assumption and find it rather artificial: can't toleration and dignitarian ideals of respect be mutually supportive in various ways? The idea that practices of toleration might be justified for the sake of dignity and mutual respect still looks like a reasonable proposal. Consider three possible ways in which they might be linked.

(1) *Toleration as a condition for respect.* First, toleration might be necessary but not sufficient for mutual respect: a society in which people are willing to tolerate

each other even when they strongly disapprove of their beliefs and activities would then be a required foundation for a dignitarian culture of civility and respect to eventually develop. Without a foundation of toleration, dignity and mutual respect cannot be achieved.

Some support this line of thought by appealing to the historical trajectory of Western theism. On a now standard narrative, modern ideas about toleration first emerged within the Christian tradition in the aftermath of the European Reformation and the ensuing wars of religion. As Christians struggled to come to terms with the subsequent fracturing of their tradition into myriad dissenting sects, they eventually mastered the urge to be intolerant of blasphemy, heresy, apostasy, etc. and learned to live peacefully together despite often profound doctrinal disagreements. Arguably, however, Christianity, and theistic religions more generally, is now moving beyond mere tolerance and increasingly embraces a mutually respectful ecumenism in which religious differences are affirmed as positively valuable rather than as occasions for the more grudging forbearance of toleration which, as Goethe suggested, implicitly insults those tolerated. This narrative, if it has any plausibility, lends credence to the claim that practices of toleration are necessary way-stations on the road to affirmative recognition and hence that they are requirements of a more demanding dignitarian ideal of respect for diversity. But for the prior emergence of dispositions of tolerance within theism, the richer forms of respect for religious difference that today's theists often embrace would never have stood a chance, or so one might maintain.

This tempting line of argument however confuses two distinct ideas: (a) that practices of toleration are the typical precursors, or preconditions for the emergence, of an ethos of mutual respect within divided communities and (b) that, unless one tolerates P, one cannot respect P. But these ideas are not at all the same.

(a) is an empirical generalization postulating that one circumstance (the emergence of mutual respect among members of a diverse community) tends to succeed another (the entrenchment of tolerant attitudes within such communities): here, tolerance is to mutual respect as puberty is to adulthood. But to depict that generalization as establishing some sort of necessary condition for dispositions of mutual respect, one would have to believe that the growth of such dispositions within diverse communities is *always* preceded by a "transitional" phase of mere toleration. No doubt this progression is often observed, as the case of theism perhaps illustrates, but it is implausible to think that it must be followed in all cases. It's not as if the mutual respect of the contemporary university required a prior régime in which warring academic disciplines merely tolerated each other. Why not think that, under the right conditions, an ethos of mutual respect can arise spontaneously, without needing any antecedent preparation in the form of a culture of bare tolerance?

In contrast, (b) does suggest that mutual respect has certain necessary conditions and that tolerance is among them. Unlike (a), however, it is not an empirical claim proposing that mutual respect is consequent upon prior practices of toleration. Rather, (b) asserts that, while it may not be sufficient for an agent to respect P, an attitude of tolerance toward P is an essential ingredient in her respecting P. However, while it has the right form given the aim of specifying a necessary condition for respect, this claim is substantively implausible, for reasons Goethe clearly appreciated: if tolerance of P presupposes disapproval of P, it is hard to see that respect for P could possibly be among its necessary conditions. If anything, it seems more plausible to say that disrespect for P is a necessary condition for tolerance of P. We are back to the original problem of reconciling the attitudes of respect and tolerance.

This difficulty is easy to overlook because tolerance and respect manifest themselves *behaviorally* in ways that are often hard to distinguish. Divided communities practicing toleration and those cultivating mutual respect will, for example, be similarly unlikely to interfere in, suppress, criminalize, or officially discourage activities in which only some of its members have strong interests. The contrast between tolerance and respect consists less in differences in outward treatment than in the internal attitudes that motivate it. Although harder for observers to verify, that attitudinal contrast is clear enough introspectively: imagine yourself tolerating my rudeness, insults, offensive beliefs, sycophancy, hypocrisy, malodorous pet, etc.; now imagine the emotions likely to accompany your respect for a trusted expert, an artistic or literary tradition, an order issued by a legitimate authority, a venerable institution or political leader, etc. When one does this, one cannot fail to notice their quite different psychological character.

Notice that this difference is not a matter of the pleasantness or unpleasantness of the feelings associated with each: the tolerant person may enjoy the sense of pride and even of contemptuous superiority that sometimes accompanies a willingness to bear something one dislikes or repudiates; and respect is often experienced as a form of intimidation or an onerous sense of obligation or duty. The point is not that adopting a tolerance or respectful stance is agreeable or disagreeable, but rather that each stance presupposes contrasting evaluative attitudes toward their objects. In respecting P, one thinks of it as somehow valuable, as important, as reckonable, or as mattering in a way that requires that it be preserved, honored, affirmed, taken seriously, or treated well. In tolerating Q, one thinks of it as in some way unworthy, contemptible, or objectionable, even as one refrains from interfering with it.

We are still seeking some way of reconciling these attitudes.

(2) *Tolerance and equal civic status.* A second reconciliation strategy involves the idea that the sort of dignity that matters in political contexts consists in an abstract civic status that citizens enjoy and that is constituted by a familiar set of basic liberal democratic rights – to freedom of speech, association, and worship, to vote and participate in democratic self-determination, and to legal protections for person, property, and individual autonomy. Jeremy Waldron and others have rightly emphasized the long-standing association between dignity and concepts of rank, status, and authority (Waldron 2002, 2015). Even today, we refer to state officials as "dignitaries," and the US Supreme Court has explicitly defended the legal doctrine of sovereign immunity as an incident of the state's dignity. As its 2002 decision in *Federal Maritime Commission v. South Carolina State Ports Authority* puts it, "The preeminent purpose of state sovereign immunity is to accord States the dignity that is consistent with their status as sovereign entities." Many writers in the liberal tradition conceptualize individual persons as independent mini-sovereigns in an

analogous sense, answerable to no one but themselves in matters that concern only them. Indeed, Richard Tuck has argued that our notion of the "sovereign individual" itself grew out of the idea of state sovereignty constructed by classical theorists of the social contract (especially Grotius and Hobbes) in the seventeenth century (Tuck 2009). Not surprisingly, contemporary writers like Arthur Ripstein have identified respect for the dignity of the individual with a willingness to recognize agents' personal sovereignty to pursue their own purposes, as long as they don't infringe on the similar independence of anyone else (Ripstein 2006, 2009). For Ripstein, liberal rights to security of person and property are all predicated on this primordial title to personal sovereignty.

This second approach offers an apparently propitious reconciliation of toleration and mutual respect by implicitly distinguishing between their targets. You practice a religion that I find superstitious, sentimental, and self-righteous. You find my atheism Godless, amoral, and crass. Each of us, then, has reasons to disapprove of our respective attitudes to religion. When we tolerate our respective religious attitudes, we clearly aren't affirming or respecting them. But we could certainly adopt such a stance of tolerance toward each other's views out of mutual respect for our status as persons wielding sovereign independence over our own lives. Here, what is tolerated are agents' beliefs, attitudes, and practices; what is respected is the dignity of the agents themselves, understood as a status that agents enjoy as putatively free and equal citizens, and in virtue of which they have the discretion to lead their lives as they see fit.

This approach has wide appeal, and many "liberal" thinkers today endorse it. Yet it is not without difficulties. Most of these stem from its strongly juridical conception of dignity and mutual respect. Its implicit understanding of dignity is tied to a particular liberal democratic conception of citizenship in which the "rule of law" guarantees citizens the rights of civic equality. This approach seems limited by its heavy reliance on the de facto existence of legal and moral conventions that confer the privileges of liberal citizenship on agents. Where those conventions are indeed in force and widely accepted, this strategy for reconciling toleration and mutual respect will be available, but what about societies whose de facto criteria for citizenship contradict familiar liberal ideals of freedom and abstract equality? In such societies, many citizens will lack the formal status of civic equality that liberal democratic institutions would confer on them. Women may lack equal rights with men, freedom of religion may not be guaranteed, rights of political participation may be restricted only to certain groups, and non-discrimination protections may not exist.

These inequalities are uncontroversially objectionable, but in societies where they are enshrined and reinforced in customs, culture, and the law, citizens can't appeal to already recognized legal or positive conventions conferring equal status on all to justify their removal. Rectifying them would require the law and other conventional norms to newly recognize all citizens as equals, but since that is what needs justifying in this case, some independent reason to confer that status must be provided. How can a claim about agents' respective status as equals be at the same time the premise and the conclusion of such an argument?

The obvious response is to say that the right to be treated as an equal is not just an artifact of existing conventions but is rather a pre-conventional entitlement owed to all human beings *as such*. To take this line is to follow the classical tradition of natural law, which assumes that human beings, independent of any system of positive law, enjoy certain basic "natural" rights to be treated justly and fairly. As hinted earlier, however, one reason why commentators have been attracted to ideas about human dignity is that they point toward a view that has the same structure of a natural law theory without making the assumption – on which critics of "natural rights" theories from Hume and Bentham have seized – that "rights" can exist and be recognized apart from positive legal conventions. According to such critics, thinking of a "right" as something "natural" is simply a category mistake: the only rights anyone can be said to enjoy are those created by positive law. One could think, however, that even if human beings *as such* cannot have "natural rights" in any strict sense, their inherent dignity still gives everyone decisive reasons not to mistreat them. The most compelling way to articulate this thought is to assert, recalling a distinction drawn earlier, that dignity is less a formal status and more a kind of intrinsic worth possessed by individuals. In this view, dignity names a form of value possessed by human beings that makes them worthy of respect, acceptance, care, consideration, and perhaps love. Since they are patently inconsistent with such dispositions, cruelty, violence, persecution, and similar abuses are quite naturally conceived as failing to take their dignity and worth seriously. But we don't need the concept of a "right" to think this. Cruelty, one could argue, is simply inhumane in a plain, pre-conventional sense. And one could press this view while agreeing fully with critics of natural law theory that redescribing such abuses as violations of a "natural right" adds only confusion.

This looks like a strong reply, but one could reasonably complain that its value-based construal of dignity is actually a departure from, not a version of, the second strategy for reconciling tolerance and respect that we're currently assessing. In fact it points toward a third reconciliation strategy that I will shortly consider. Taken by itself, however, the purely juridical, status-based conception of dignity envisaged by the second approach seems too weak to capture the powerful intuition behind the reply.

Consider, for example, its use of the metaphor of personal "sovereignty." To enjoy "sovereignty" is to wield a kind of authority over a jurisdiction; its legitimate exercise is presumably limited by the need to respect the rights of other sovereign agents and by any background law or formal body of rules that confer such sovereignty. But can our "worth" as human beings, which is what the idiom of dignity purports to be capturing, really be just a matter of our standing and authority in this formal sense? If this is all there is to "dignity," we seem to be back in the orbit of a natural rights theory, and it is no longer clear that the dignitarian element in the claim is adding anything but ornamental shrubbery to what remains an essentially rights-based view. These considerations put pressure on at least one strand of Kantian thinking about dignity and respect – that which grounds the personal autonomy (or "sovereignty" over one's own choices) of agents on the recognition of, and unconditional submission to, a "moral law." As many critics of Kant have pointed out, the more a theory emphasizes these juridical metaphors, the less clearly it will require respect for *people* and their dignity (Parfit 2011; Honig 1993). Instead, it will require only respectful obedience to legalistic abstractions like the "moral law," the personal sovereignty, or the idea of a natural right. This arguably alienates dignity from the flesh-and-blood human concerns with which the concept is usually associated.

To press the same worry from a different angle, consider the powerful intuition that the most egregious forms of demeaning treatment (rape, slavery, torture, etc.) exemplify outrages against human dignity. Is our dignitarian aversion to these abuses really nothing more than a concern about disobeying the personal sovereignty of their targets? If so, then dignity-based objections to (say) slavery or torture amount to the complaint that slave owners or torturers disobey their victims. Yet to suggest that the main problem about torture or slavery is that they are species of insubordination surely understates the problem and is in any case rather strange. A less antiseptic characterization would be that slavery, rape, torture, etc. strip people of their very humanity, or deny their value as human beings, and that this is what brings a concern for the dignity of persons into view. But such formulations presuppose a conception of dignity and respect centered on notions of human *worth*, not on the thinner gruel of juridical status.

(3) *Toleration, autonomy, and conscience.* With that in mind, consider now a third, and more promising, strategy for grounding toleration on a principle of respect. Like the second, it distinguishes the objects of respect and tolerance, following something like the pattern of the Christian injunction to "hate the sin, love the sinner," though a more precise rendition of the operative thought might be "respect the offender by tolerating their offenses." Unlike the second approach, however, it ditches a narrowly juridical conception of dignity in favor of one centered on the value and worth of certain basic capacities agents share. Rainer Forst (2007), Martha Nussbaum (2008), and Nicholas Wolterstorff (2015) have all recently pursued variants of this idea as grounds for expectations of tolerance.

Forst's account, which builds on the writings of the seventeenth-century French proponent of toleration Pierre Bayle, grounds toleration in the "demand to respect each other's moral autonomy as a reason-giving and reason-receiving being." Forst's investment in an idea of individual autonomy may recall the Kantian idea of personal sovereignty and indeed is influenced by Kant's understanding of human agents as morally accountable beings. But it focuses less on autonomy as an abstract civic status, or a form of sovereign law-giving, and more on its importance as the guarantor of existentially authentic self-exploration. The sort of autonomy in question doesn't just consist in wielding authority over a personal jurisdiction, but rather is constituted by the independent search for a "religious and cultural" identity that agents can affirm "as their own...and as one worth having." The desire to be recognized as an autonomous being in this sense is not, as Forst says, just a desire to be esteemed for who one is and what one does. The fulfillment of that desire would obviate toleration by others, for one cannot tolerate something one positively esteems. The need for toleration arises precisely because freeing autonomous agents to develop themselves on their own terms will predictably lead some to pursue forms of life others will find difficult to accept. Still, behind these inevitable differences in outlook lies a common interest in being "able to live a worthy life" as one personally understands it. Forst identifies that common interest with a desire to "be treated justly in one's dignity as a moral being" and characterizes it as the "main motive. . .for fair toleration" (Forst 2007).

Nussbaum's version of this approach is indebted to the thought of Roger Williams, a seventeenth-century Anglo-American Puritan cleric who helped found the settlement of Providence, Rhode Island. Although himself deeply devout, Williams was an early advocate (and, in Providence, a practitioner) of the doctrine of church-state separation and of religious liberty quite generally. As Nussbaum glosses him, Williams's case for toleration appeals fundamentally to the "preciousness and dignity of the individual human conscience." Williams regarded the faculty of conscience as a universal human attribute, "found in all mankind, more or lesse, in Jewes, Turkes, Papists, Protestants, Pagans, etc." But it can flourish only under conditions in which it is given free rein to develop itself as its individual bearers wish. In a striking image, Williams compares intolerance and persecution to "spirituall and soule rape." On his characterization, the persecutor:

> speakes so tenderly for his owne, hath yet so little respect, mercie or pitie to the like consciencious perswasions of other Men[.] Are all the Thousands of millions of millions of Consciences, at home and abroad, fuell onely for a prison, for a whip, for a stake, for a Gallowes? Are no Consciences to breath the Aire, but such as suit and sample his?

Nussbaum suggests that Williams's arguments for liberty of conscience (which he called "the most precious and invaluable Jewel") anticipate even very recent theories of toleration. As she reads it, for example, Williams's image of a tolerant society, in which citizens whose conscientious beliefs are often incongruent nonetheless converge around a common affirmation of a purely secular civil order, foreshadows John Rawls's notion of an "overlapping consensus."

In a similar vein, Nicholas Wolterstorff has defended toleration on the grounds that religious, and no doubt other conscientious, commitments mobilize "remarkable, amazing" human capacities. Wolterstorff singles out two capacities that have special relevance for the question of toleration: the capacity to "interpret reality and one's place therein" and the capacity to form what he calls a "valorized identity," by which he means the ability to order one's commitments and priorities according as they correspond to one's deepest sense of self. These capacities invite wonder, respect, and even awe, and for Wolterstorff, they serve both to flesh out our sense of human dignity and as grounds for toleration. As he sums it up:

> So far as we know, no other creatures that dwell on earth possess these capacities to anywhere near the same degree, if, indeed, they possess them at all. Not only are human persons remarkable on account of possessing these capacities, they also have great worth on account of possessing them. On account of possessing these hermeneutic and valorizing capacities, along with others, human persons are precious. They have multifaceted dignity. They are to be prized. Something of great worth is lost when these capacities are destroyed or lost. . .being treated in ways that befit that worth will quite obviously include having the civil right to free exercise of their religions.

Rather like Roger Williams, then, Wolterstorff fears that persecution and intolerance debase their victims by failing to give their awe-inspiring capacities (conscience, self-interpretation, the ability to identify oneself with certain values or ideals) the space to flourish. In these views, toleration is required because, without it, too many facets of human dignity would remain stunted and unexpressed.

This third reconciliation strategy may face some legitimate resistance. One might note important differences of emphasis between the accounts of Nussbaum, Wolterstorff, and Forst and worry that, on closer inspection, these conceal hidden problems. Wolterstorff regards his capacity argument, for example, as justifying a "natural right" to toleration, but as earlier suggested, many have wanted to distance a dignity-based approach from theories of natural rights. Another concern is that all of these arguments ground dignity on capacities (ability to appreciate and give reasons, the exercise of conscience, the power to interpret oneself and place in the world) that may not be equally distributed among the human population. Such capacities are often (what Margalit has termed) "graded traits" in that some possess them to a high degree, others far less so. This may threaten the assumption that dignity is a quality in which all agents can claim an equal share.

Although worth considering, these objections don't decisively refute the general approach taken by Forst, Wolterstorff, Nussbaum, and others. It is certainly the strongest of the three reconciliation strategies we have considered. To the extent the value of human dignity figures in the justification of toleration, it seems a safe bet that it will do so by relying on some version of this third approach.

Indignity, Disrespect, and the Intolerable

Some indignities are tolerable (e.g., the humiliation of unrequited love or of abject defeat in competitive sport), and some intolerable indignities cannot be avoided (e. g., the agonies and infirmities of aging or disease). This might lead one to doubt that describing something as an "affront" to, or "assault" on, human dignity need imply that it should never be tolerated or that it falls beyond the limits of reasonable toleration. But this inference overlooks the important point that assaults on *human* dignity, as we ordinarily understand them, form a subset of all possible indignities. Undergoing a digital rectal exam, whether performed for medical or security-related reasons, is certainly to suffer an indignity, but few would describe it as a violation of *human* dignity. We reserve that idiom for those outrages that we take to be so grave as to be beyond any possible justification or excuse – rape, wanton cruelty, torture, genocide, etc. – and hence intolerable.

The border dividing "mere" indignities from those patterns of conduct, forms of treatment, social practices, institutional routines, etc. that should be condemned as intolerable threats to human dignity is bound to be a fuzzy one: no sufficiently sharp criterion of "gravity" exists to map it with any precision, and reasonable people will often disagree at the margins about whether an abuse is serious enough to count. Still, two conditions seem necessary for something to plausibly constitute an affront to human dignity:

(1) It must somehow categorically threaten the value of dignity, so that no ulterior consideration could possibly justify it and hence that its prevention, elimination, or punishment carries overriding importance.

(2) Its unconscionable quality must be appreciable by any reasonable, psychologically well-adjusted agent, regardless of their background or outlook.

If duly elaborated, the first condition would explain the sense in which dignity is urgently at stake in the relevant transactions and the second why the indignities involved are objects of universal, human concern, transcending the particularities and idiosyncrasies of culture and personality. The powerful meme "shock the conscience of mankind," first introduced in 1946 in a UN General Assembly Resolution on Genocide, has stuck because it captures the universalist tenor of the second condition particularly well. Put together, these two conditions postulate a common point of view from which certain social circumstances and modes of treatment offend deep intuitions about what it is to live as a human being, rather than an animal, or an exploitable resource, commodity, or mere object.

Since most of the literature on toleration has been concerned to explain its value and importance, it has understandably focused on cases in which tolerance goes against the grain but still seems appropriate all things considered. In focusing on affronts to human dignity, however, we are considering cases in which no overriding reason for tolerating P exists and hence where societies ought to actively suppress P. Such cases won't justify toleration in other, more ambiguous ones, but it can clarify where the scope of reasonable tolerance in any decent, civilized society runs out. After all, no tolerant society can tolerate everything, and no one thinks that refusing to tolerate murder, rape, racial discrimination, battery, theft, or fraud, all of which might reasonably be thought to assail victims' dignity, is inconsistent with a public commitment to toleration.

Commentators sometimes insinuate that there is something hypocritical about toleration insofar as it refuses to tolerate those disposed toward intolerance. Stanley Fish thus criticizes Michael Walzer's decision, announced at the outset of his book *On Toleration*, to dismiss without argument the claims of "monolithic religious or totalitarian political regimes." Fish counters: "it seems odd to begin a book on tolerance by ruling out forms of thought and organization without even giving them a hearing" (Fish 1997, p. 2256). But Fish's imputation of hypocrisy is wholly unwarranted. Admitting that some things should not be tolerated is no embarrassment to a theory of toleration. Indeed, it is hard to understand how toleration could be valuable at all unless there are some circumstances in which we are prepared to withdraw it. The interesting question is why certain forms of intolerance are required and what that tells us about how tolerant we can be. Intolerance of the intolerant is not paradoxical but an implicit component of any coherent conception of toleration.

Since at least some required forms of intolerance are likely justified on the grounds that they are necessary to defend human dignity, the question arises: what forms of intolerance may a broadly tolerant society embrace for the sake of human dignity? As I have said, rape, torture, persecution, and genocide are easy cases: few would deny that a tolerant society can and should refuse to tolerate these abuses for the sake of human dignity. Other examples are more ambiguous. Consider one recent case.

In December 2019, the French court sentenced Didier Lombard, the former CEO of the telecommunications company now known as Orange, to several months in jail for his role in a spate of employee suicides and attempted suicides that occurred when he was in charge. Lombard was convicted on a charge of "moral harassment" whose definition in the French labor code is as follows: "repeated acts having as their object or effect a deterioration of an employee's working conditions likely to (i) infringe his rights or dignity, (ii) alter his physical or mental health, or (iii) compromise his promotion." Lombard had taken over the company – *France Télécom* – at a time when it had recently been privatized. Lombard believed that, in order to be competitive, he would have to reduce the company's workforce by 20%. Few employees wished to be laid off, however, and the strong protections against being fired at will enjoyed by French civil servants remained in force. Unable to dismiss them forthwith, Lombard embarked on a campaign to pressure employees to quit, by assigning them meaningless jobs, demoting them, or ostracizing them. His explicit aim, as he is reported to have said, was to induce employees to leave "by the door or the window." Working conditions became so toxic that one employee stabbed himself in the abdomen during a meeting, albeit not fatally. Another worker, who did succeed in taking their own life, left a suicide note complaining of "management by terror" at the company. All told, 19 employees committed suicide and at least another 12 attempted suicide during Lombard's tenure.

In punishing Lombard, several of his colleagues, and the company itself, for "moral harassment," the French court implicitly asserted that the power of managers over their employees in the workplace can be abused in ways that no civilized society should tolerate. Since the moral harassment statute explicitly refers to infringements on workers' dignity, the court's decision was presumably informed by dignitarian expectations. Is this sort of intolerant intervention in the conduct of private life consistent with the ideal of a tolerant society?

That it is *required* seems doubtful. At least some liberal societies would be very reluctant to make Lombard's behavior an occasion for criminal conviction. In the United States, for example, Lombard would not have been constrained by the expectation of lifetime employment that European civil servants often enjoy, and he could have fired the employees he wanted to lose more or less at will. Suppose that, under something like the current US legal regime, several employees committed suicide after having been sacked by a company and left suicide notes citing their firing as the reason. It is hard to see how an employer could be held legally liable for this given that their firings were perfectly legal. US law of course does forbid various forms of workplace harassment – especially sexual harassment – but American jurisprudence has generally subsumed these abuses under the heading of discrimination rather than following the European view that these prohibitions protect workers' dignity (Friedman and Whitman 2003). And one could reasonably complain that the dignitarian principle underlying the French "moral harassment" statute opens the door to unacceptable legal interference in private life. After all, many suicides can plausibly be attributed to shabby or cruel treatment shown by spouses or intimate partners. Those who are subject to such cruelty might well describe themselves as suffering the indignity of humiliation, but, devastating as it may be personally, few would want the law to criminalize such behavior. This looks, in fact, like a paradigm case of toleration. No one disagrees that the vindictiveness, harshness, and callousness that partners, family members, and others display in private life are bad. So, if we conclude that society and the law should refrain from suppressing these forms of mistreatment, we are choosing to tolerate them.

On the other hand, it seems equally hard to say that these considerations are sufficient to show that ideals of toleration *prohibit* states from enacting statutes like the French "moral harassment" law. There needn't be a slippery slope from "moral harassment" in the workplace to more hectoring interference in the private lives of friends, families, and marital partners. For any number of reasons, relations between employers and employees in the workplace seem fitting objects of legal regulation in a way that the negotiation of intimate friendships don't. Still, the French case nonetheless underlines an important point: that a strong public commitment to upholding human dignity will tend to restrict the range of conduct that a society can regard as tolerable. Once the law or social norms, more generally, deem particular conduct an affront to human dignity, they effectively declare it intolerable – something that decent societies should never be prepared to accept, even for the sake of other benefits.

The same tendency can be observed in Jeremy Waldron's recent defense of hate speech regulations (Waldron 2014). Waldron's argument is, again, a dignitarian one: according to him, hate speech corrodes the dignitarian values on which civilized societies depend.

> Its aim is to compromise the dignity of those at whom it is targeted, both in their own eyes and in the eyes of other members of society. And it sets out to make the establishing and upholding of their dignity...much more difficult. It aims to besmirch the basics of their reputation, by associating ascriptive characteristics like ethnicity, or race, or religion, with conduct that should disqualify someone from being treated as a member of society in good standing.

To the extent that societies tolerate hate speech, on Waldron's view, they undermine the "general assurance of decent treatment and respect" on which agents' dignity depends. Hate speech regulations, for Waldron, are therefore required for liberal democracies to discharge their "affirmative responsibility for protecting the atmosphere of mutual respect."

In taking this line, Waldron is self-consciously opposing the standard position in American first amendment jurisprudence, according to which the appropriate remedy for hate speech is not government restriction, but "more speech." As Mill argued, when governments refuse to regulate speech on the basis of its content, citizens need not fear that what they say or write is subject to censorship or legal penalty; this frees people to speak their minds and to vigorously oppose and criticize the claims expressed by others. So, although the US first amendment protects hate speech, it also (on this view) guarantees the most propitious conditions for the effective criticism of such speech: a diverse and vital civil discourse capable of ruthlessly exposing nonsense, fraudulent claims and falsehoods propagated by others. Whether Waldron is right to reject this standard liberal defense of a highly permissive free speech régime is not an issue we can decide here. But Waldron's argument vividly illustrates the same point that emerged from our discussion of the French "moral harassment" case: for good or ill, the tendency of dignitarian thinking is to narrow the domain of reasonable tolerance more than many "liberal" thinkers would find appropriate.

Summary and Future Directions

This chapter has considered the relationship between toleration and dignity from two angles. From one direction, it has asked how far they are complementary, and even mutually supportive, values. The clear tensions between the attitudes of forbearance involved in toleration and the disposition of respect implicated in a concern for human dignity make their reconciliation far from straightforward. Significant as the tensions between them are, this chapter has surveyed several legitimate, albeit more and less successful, strategies for grounding expectations of toleration on a principle of dignitarian respect. From another direction, this chapter has also explored the possibility that a commitment to protecting human dignity establishes strong limits on the scope of acceptable toleration. Since our inherited idea of an "assault on human dignity" already includes the assumption that the relevant behavior is intolerable, that idea likely plays a role in our intuitive sense of the scope and limits of toleration. The plausibility of this last claim also clarifies an important point about the character of toleration as a political value, one that is worth highlighting in conclusion.

Some political values, like justice, welfare, or human flourishing, refer to positive ideals with definite content, implying desiderata that we ought to expect our institutions to satisfy. By elaborating the content of these desiderata, the political theorist can in principle guide those committed to the relevant ideals to clearer judgments about which practices, conduct, institutions, etc. they should regard as legitimate or illegitimate or worthy of being preserved and supported rather than eliminated or reformed. But other political values – "peace" might be an obvious candidate – refer not so much to ideals with a clear positive content as to desirable modes of political co-habitation defined by the *absence* of certain evils (to stick with "peace" as an example: enmity, conflict, violence, discord, insecurity, etc.). A value of this latter kind doesn't itself ground clear desiderata by which political societies should judge their ideal performance; rather it is itself a desideratum whose importance derives from the need to stave off various other abuses. In such a case, understanding why (say) peace matters requires that we appreciate why enmity, insecurity, violence, etc. are independently problematic.

Toleration is a political value of this second kind. If it is a desideratum of just and decent forms of public life, it is not because it defines a positive ideal that enables us to rank better and worse political arrangements, but because we have independent reasons to reject certain modes of intolerance as unacceptable. In this sense, toleration is a "trouser-concept" in J. L. Austin's sense (Austin and Warnock 2010). A trouser-concept designates something that can only be specified negatively, as the absence of some opposing quality. In these cases, a concept's antonyms "wear the trousers," to use Austin's unfortunately sexist terms. Austin took the word "real" to be an exemplary case. In his view, the effort to specify "reality" or the "real" *as such*, as if these terms refer to something positive, uniform quality, is a fool's errand; we should instead recognize that our concept of the real is as complex and multifaceted as the various ways in which we recognize things as "unreal": as "phony," "artificial," "illusory," etc. The same naturally applies to our concept of toleration, which probably doesn't name a single, simple thing that we can define independently of judgments about how agents can display intolerance and why it is objectionable, or sometimes desirable, for them to do so. To the contrary, our understanding of certain attitudes or modes of conduct as "tolerant" may depend more fundamentally on a prior apprehension of certain archetypes of "intolerance."

If so, then when we refer to individuals tolerating each other or to societies that are tolerant, we are pointing to the absence of specific types of intolerance – interference, discouragement, suppression, criminalization, denunciation, dishonor, marginalization, discrimination, curtailment of right and privileges, etc. No society can abjure these entirely: at least some things *should* be interfered with, discouraged, suppressed, criminalized, denounced, frowned upon, marginalized, discriminated against, and treated as grounds for withdrawing or modifying social entitlements. Ultimately, claims about the character and value of toleration must depend on implicit judgments about when intolerance of these different sorts is appropriate or inappropriate. Rather than trying to positively specify "toleration" as a simple quality, we will make more progress by thinking through when specific modes of intolerance are required and when they are prohibited. This line of inquiry promises the most fertile source of insight for future research into the relationship between toleration and the requirements of human dignity.

Sometimes pleas for tolerance are criticized for promoting a culture that is reluctant to be "judgmental" and that numbs agents' critical reactions to each other. Such objections are however doubly misguided. On the one hand, they underestimate the extent to which tolerance requires disapproval of, or even contempt for, what is tolerated. A tolerant society won't be populated by blithely indifferent naïfs who simply shrug when they confront others very different from them. To the contrary, toleration will be at its most robust precisely when the agents who practice it are quite open about their discomfort with the things they are nonetheless prepared to tolerate. Rather than refusing to acknowledge their distaste toward conduct they find offensive, such agents instead recognize overriding reasons to set it aside and exercise self-restraint. In so doing, they display a humility, modesty, and even magnanimity that arguably foster dignified social relations and an atmosphere of mutual respect. On the other hand, the image of tolerance as a stance of insipid neutrality cannot be reconciled with any general defense of toleration committed to upholding the conditions for human dignity. If we are justified in tolerating some things in the name of human dignity, it follows that there are other things we should never tolerate.

References

Austin JL, Warnock GJ (2010) Sense and sensibilia. Reprint. Oxford Univeresity Press, London

Bird C (2018) The theory and politics of recognition. In: The Oxford handbook of distributive justice. Edited by Serena Olsaretti. Oxford University Press, Oxford

Dworkin R (1985) A matter of principle. Reprint edition. Harvard University Press, Cambridge, MA

Fish S (1997) Mission impossible: Settling the just bounds between church and state. Colum L Rev 97(8):2255–2333

Forst R (2007) "To tolerate is to insult" toleration, recognition, and emancipation. In: Brink D, Owen D (eds) Recognition and power: Axel Honneth and the tradition of critical social theory. Cambridge University Press, Cambridge

Friedman GS, Whitman JQ (2003) The European transformation of harassment law: discrimination versus dignity. Columbia J Eur Law 9:241

Galston WA (2002) Liberal pluralism: the implications of value pluralism for political theory and practice. Cambridge University Press, Cambridge, UK

Honig B (1993) Political theory and the displacement of politics. Contestations. Cornell University Press, Ithaca

Lucy W (2017) Law's judgement. Hart Publishing, London

Margalit A (1998) The decent society, vol 1. Harvard University Press paperback ed. Harvard University Press, Cambridge, MA

Nozick R (2013) Anarchy, state, and Utopia. Reprint edition. Basic Books, New York

Nussbaum M (2008) Living together: The roots of respect. University of Illinois Law Review 5:1623–41

Parfit D (2011) On what matters. The Berkeley Tanner lectures. Oxford University Press, Oxford/New York

Rawls J (1999) A theory of justice, 2nd edn. Belknap Press: An Imprint of Harvard University Press, Cambridge, MA

Raz J (2009) The morality of freedom. Reprinted. Clarendon Press, Oxford

Regan T, Singer P (eds) (1976) Animal rights and human obligations. Prentice-Hall, Englewood Cliffs

Ripstein A (2006) Beyond the harm principle. Philos Public Aff 34(3):215–245

Ripstein A (2009) Force and freedom: Kant's legal and political philosophy. Harvard University Press, Cambridge, MA

Tuck R (2009) The rights of war and peace: political thought and the international order from grotius to Kant. Reprint. Oxford University Press, Oxford

Waldron J (2002) God, Locke, and equality: Christian foundations in Locke's political thought. Cambridge University Press, Cambridge/New York

Waldron J (2014) The harm in hate speech. First Harvard University Press paperback edition. Harvard University Press, Cambridge, MA/London, UK

Waldron J (2015) Dignity, rank, and rights. Edited by Meir Dan-Cohen. Reprint edition. Oxford University Press, New York

Wolterstorff N (2010) Justice: rights and wrongs. Princeton University Press, Princeton

Wolterstorff N (2015) Toleration, justice, and dignity. Lecture on the occasion of the inauguration as professor of Dirk-Martin Grube, Free University of Amsterdam, September 24, 2015. Int J Philos Theol 76(5):377–386

Toleration and Respect

30

John William Tate

Contents

Introduction	584
Conditions of Toleration	585
State and Individual Toleration	587
Multiculturalism	587
The Liberal Tradition and "Respect"	588
"Features" Versus "Persons"	591
Galeotti and Respect	594
Niqab and Burqa	594
The Niqab, Burqa, and "Equal Respect"	595
Blasphemy	597
Rival "Respects"	598
Blasphemy and Free Speech	599
"Mutual Exclusivity"	600
"Respect" as a Contested Term	601
Whose Intolerance?	603
"Universalization"	604
"Nonuniversalization"	606
"The Question"	607
"Clear and Present Danger"	609
Conclusion	611
Summary and Future Directions	611
References	611

Abstract

"Respect" is a highly resonant norm carrying significant moral weight. It is therefore a norm which will inevitably be contested, in terms of its meaning and application to specific circumstances, given that many will want to associate

---

J. W. Tate (✉)
Discipline of Politics and International Relations, Newcastle Business School, College of Human and Social Futures, University of Newcastle, Newcastle, NSW, Australia
e-mail: John.Tate@newcastle.edu.au

© The Author(s), under exclusive licence to Springer Nature Switzerland AG 2022
M. Sardoĉ (ed.), *The Palgrave Handbook of Toleration*,
https://doi.org/10.1007/978-3-030-42121-2_40

their own entitlements with it. This chapter focuses on the relationship between "respect" and toleration. It considers the manner in which "respect" has been used as a norm to justify toleration and to what extent its meaning and application is contested in this context. It also looks at the history of "respect," within the liberal tradition, and the entitlements and obligations with which, within this tradition, it has been associated. The chapter then seeks to apply the concepts of toleration and "respect" to specific circumstances, centered on the burqa, niqab, and the free speech issue of blasphemy. This application shows once more how "respect" is a highly contested and contentious norm, both in terms of its meaning and the attempts of competing parties to associate their agenda with it. The chapter ends by focusing more intensively on issues of "respect" as they apply to free speech and toleration. This focus centers, once again, on blasphemy and considers the extent to which blasphemous speech ought to be tolerated, and the "free speech" imperatives underwriting such toleration "respected," if it gives rise to violent consequences.

Keywords

Toleration · Multiculturalism · Respect · John Locke · Immanuel Kant · John Stuart Mill · Niqab · Burqa · Blasphemy

---

Introduction

"Respect" is a contentious norm. Like many highly value-laden norms, its meaning, in specific circumstances, as well as the outcomes associated with it, is not always self-evident and so is subject to contestation. This does not mean that the norm lacks legitimacy in and of itself. It is precisely because so many accord legitimacy to "respect" that the norm is so highly contested, with each party seeking to associate it with their own aspirations and commitments. But the legitimacy of anybody's claim to "respect," as well as its meaning, implications, or applications in any specific circumstance, is often open to question and dispute.

This chapter will discuss the relationship between toleration and "respect." It will do so by tracing the origins of "respect," as a distinctive norm within the liberal tradition, before applying the norm to two high-profile toleration disputes which have arisen in liberal democratic polities in recent years. These are, firstly, the issue of burqas and niqabs and, secondly, the issue of blasphemy. These disputes have given rise to demands for toleration and its contrary. Further, such disputes have made clear that "respect" is a highly contested norm, capable of being advanced by competing parties, often in ways fundamentally at odds with each other.

In using terms such as "blasphemy," the author is aware that, like "respect," these are contested in their meaning, with "blasphemy" (like "heresy") being very much a matter that is in the eye of the beholder. Nevertheless, for our purposes, "blasphemy" is what religious adherents perceive it to be, since it is their response that determines whether "blasphemy" is at issue, thereby transforming the situation into one in which toleration (for either party involved in the dispute) is at stake. The chapter will pursue issues of "respect" and toleration in the context of blasphemy further by asking to what extent blasphemous speech ought to be tolerated, and the "free speech" values underwriting such toleration "respected," when such speech gives rise to violent consequences, as it has done in recent decades.

The chapter will begin by outlining the conceptual and practical conditions of toleration. It then distinguishes between toleration undertaken by individuals and toleration undertaken by state authorities. It raises the issue of "respect" by linking it to the contemporary policy of multiculturalism, before discussing it in the context of the liberal tradition. The chapter then links toleration to "respect" in terms of a distinction, sometimes made within toleration studies, between "features" and "persons." The chapter then applies the concepts of toleration and "respect" to niqabs, burqas, and blasphemy, identifying the rival (and often incompatible) claims to "respect" arising among competing parties in these disputes, before analyzing whether such rival claims can be resolved by a criterion of "universalization." Finally, the chapter asks to what extent it is possible to tolerate blasphemous speech and accord "respect" to the "free speech" values underwriting such toleration, when such speech gives rise to violent consequences.

Conditions of Toleration

The conceptual and practical possibility of toleration arises on the basis of a number of key conditions. Within the toleration literature, there is much debate concerning these conditions (see ▶ Chap. 40, "Toleration and Religion"). While some toleration theorists identify numerous conditions (see Cohen 2004: 78–94), it is possible to prioritize the main ones. In schematic terms, toleration depends upon (a) the existence of a party seeking toleration; (b) something (i.e., an "object") for which toleration is sought; (c) the existence of a second party disposed to deny this toleration based on the aversion they feel for this "object" or those seeking toleration for it; and (d) a willingness on the part of this second party to ultimately allow such toleration, based on specific "reasons" for toleration, the aversion they feel for the "object" of toleration notwithstanding. We can refer to the "object" of toleration (the identity, belief, or practice for which toleration is sought) as a "liberty," insofar as it is characterized by a demand on the part of an individual or group to be entitled to pursue or advance this "object" free from interference. We can formalize these schematic features into five specific conditions of toleration as follows:

1. A person or group seeking an entitlement to exercise a particular "liberty," concerning their identity, beliefs, practices, or some other aspect of their lives, thereby demanding that others refrain from interfering with this liberty.
2. An aversion to this liberty (or those seeking to exercise it) on the part of those who do not wish this liberty to be exercised, and therefore a disposition, on their part, to interfere with this liberty.

3. A recognition, on the part of those disposed to interfere, that the individuals seeking to exercise this liberty nevertheless have some entitlement to do so. This entitlement arises either on the basis of specific values or norms prioritizing this entitlement, or it arises on the basis of pragmatic considerations, on the part of those disposed to interfere, concerning why such liberties ought to be permitted. These normative and pragmatic considerations constitute "reasons" for toleration and ought to be weighed, by those with the disposition to interfere, against the reasons counseling interference, and therefore a refusal of toleration, arising under Condition 2.

4. A willingness on the part of those with the disposition to interfere to (i) evaluate the competing and conflicting imperatives arising, respectively, under Conditions 2 and 3, and conclude that the reasons for toleration, under Condition 3, ought to outweigh the reasons for interference, under Condition 2, their continuing aversion to the "object" of toleration (Condition 2) notwithstanding; and (ii) arrive at a concerted decision to act on this conclusion and refrain from interfering with the liberties sought under Condition 1.

5. There is a fifth condition of toleration widely debated within the literature. It refers to the extent to which the "disposition to interfere," identified under Condition 2, ought to be translatable into an actual "capacity to interfere." Toleration scholars differ on the extent to which this "capacity" needs to be fully efficacious. Some insist on such efficacy, declaring that those with the disposition to interfere must be capable of fully expunging the liberties sought under Condition 1, thereby completely reversing toleration if they wish. Others suggest this "capacity" needs only to be partial, enabling those averse to these liberties to materially hinder their exercise, should they wish, but not necessarily extending to a capacity to fully expunge them. Others insist it is sufficient if those with the disposition to interfere merely have a *belief* that they possess such capacity, even if they do not in actual fact. On these questions see Raphael 1988: 139; Jones 2007a: 384–85; Galeotti 2002: 22, 89; Cohen 2004: 93–94; Horton 1996: 28; Balint 2014: 267–268; Mendus 1989: 9; Williams 1996: 19. Some version of this "capacity" is a necessary condition of toleration because if a party, possessing a disposition to interfere with and impede the "liberty" advanced under Condition 1, recognizes that they are impotent to do so, then far from their noninterference being explicable in terms of "reasons" for toleration arising under Condition 3, the reason for their "noninterference" is their powerlessness to do otherwise. For an expanded account of these five conditions of toleration, see ▶ Chap. 40, "Toleration and Religion"

What is clear from the above is that toleration is a practice that involves engagement between two parties, one seeking toleration and the other with the initial disposition to oppose it. It is also a practice that involves conflicting imperatives, with those granting toleration only doing so once they have affirmed "reasons" for toleration that override (but do not expunge) their continuing aversion to, and desire to interfere with, that for which toleration is sought. As Glen Newey tells us: "[T]he tolerator has to feel the competing pull of reasons for intervention and reasons for restraint" (Newey 2001: 317).

State and Individual Toleration

Much of the political history of toleration over the last 500 years within the European world has involved political authorities exercising toleration via a practice of granting liberties to minority groups within their jurisdiction. This involved a willingness on the part of these authorities not to exercise the instruments of force at their disposal, or the legal instruments of prohibition, to intrude upon the liberties sought by these minority groups or individuals within these societies, and also a willingness to protect these minorities or individuals from hostile majorities, when these liberties (and the dissident or nonconformist activities that arose from them) elicited a widespread aversion within the wider society or among the political authorities themselves. On why such state toleration is possible even if state authorities do not share this aversion to these liberties (or those seeking to advance them) see ▶ Chap. 40, "Toleration and Religion"

However as well as occurring at this state level, toleration can also occur *between* individuals or groups within society. We exercise toleration on a daily basis when we do not seek to physically or verbally interfere with persons or practices to which we are averse, when such physical or verbal interference has the potential to preclude, prevent, or otherwise impede these persons or those practices. Sometimes our aversion is premised on a moral objection to these persons or practices – for instance, when we perceive parents in the street behaving in what we believe are unfair or arbitrarily coercive ways towards their children. Sometimes our aversion is purely aesthetic, affective, or emotive – as when, for instance, we are confronted by loud and obtrusive conversations in a train or bus emitted by other passengers. Toleration theorists have differed as to whether the aversion, on which toleration is premised, must be a moral aversion or whether it can instead be an affective or emotive aversion such as that identified above (Horton 1996: 29–30; Cohen 2004: 88–90; Balint 2014: 264, 266–67; Raz 1986: 401–02; Raphael 1988: 139; see also other ▶ Chap. 40, "Toleration and Religion").

Multiculturalism

John Stuart Mill, in his famous essay, *On Liberty*, argued that as society becomes more integrated and organized, it is the intolerance of the "majority" of society, acting as a collective, censorious body, rather than government, which constitutes the greatest threat to individual liberty (Mill 1971: 67–68). Mill argued that the most onerous imperative of such integrated societies is a demand for conformity, impinging on individuals, to society's basic norms and mores and therefore a willingness to persecute dissident minorities who refuse to conform. As Mill put it:

> The will of the people. . .practically means the will of the most numerous or the most active *part* of the people; the majority, or those who succeed in making themselves accepted as the majority; the people, consequently *may* desire to oppress a part of their number; and precautions are as much needed against this as against any other abuse of power. . . . . .Protection, therefore, against the tyranny of the magistrate is not enough: there

needs protection also against the tyranny of the prevailing opinion and feeling; against the tendency of society to impose, by other means than civil penalties, its own ideas and practices as rules of conduct on those who dissent from them. (Mill 1971: 67–68)

Over the last 50 years, some liberal democracies have deliberately adopted a more plural conception of society than the conformist society feared by Mill, centered on "multiculturalism." Here society is understood not in terms of a homogenous entity, capable of collectively enforcing its norms, but rather in terms of a plurality of racial, ethnic, cultural, and religious groups who occupy the social space. Such groups, in the context of multiculturalism, have "rights" to express their particular identities, both in private and, to some extent, in the public sphere.

Certainly there has been criticism, emanating from within liberal democracies, of this ideal of multiculturalism in recent years. German Chancellor Angela Merkel, responding to a perceived absence of migrant integration in Germany, declared, in 2010, that multiculturalism in Germany had "failed utterly," and in 2015 that "[m]ulticulturalism leads to parallel societies and therefore remains a 'life lie'" (Noack 2015). In 2011, British Prime Minister, David Cameron, explained Islamic extremism in the United Kingdom, in part, in terms of a failure of "state multiculturalism":

[W]e have allowed the weakening of our collective identity. Under the doctrine of state multiculturalism, we have encouraged different cultures to live separate lives, apart from each other and apart from the mainstream. We've failed to provide a vision of society to which they feel they want to belong. We've even tolerated these segregated communities behaving in ways that run completely counter to our values. (Cameron 2011)

Yet others defend the ideal of multiculturalism and its importance as a source of individual liberty and dignity for individuals possessing diverse racial, ethnic, cultural, and religious backgrounds. The Canadian philosopher, Charles Taylor, has justified "multiculturalism" in terms of what he calls a "politics of recognition," which is in turn premised (he argues) on the values of "equal respect" and individual "dignity." As Taylor writes:

[T]he demands of multiculturalism build on the already established principles of the politics of equal respect. If withholding the presumption [of cultural worth] is tantamount to a denial of equality, and if important consequences flow for people's identity from the absence of recognition, then a case can be made for insisting on the universalization of the presumption as a logical extension of the politics of dignity. Just as all must have equal civil rights, and equal voting rights, regardless of race or culture, so all should enjoy the presumption that their traditional culture has value. (Taylor 1994: 68. My addition)

The Liberal Tradition and "Respect"

This connection between "equal respect" and the ideal of individual "dignity," which Taylor advances in the passage above, is not new. It has had a presence within the liberal tradition since its inception. The liberal tradition has "plural" foundations in the sense that these foundations are made up of a number of fundamental values, none more foundational than the other, and none reducible to the other or to a more elementary anterior value (Tate 2008: 993–1002, 2016a: 35–36). "Equal respect" for individuals, it can be argued, is one of these fundamental values, foundational to the liberal tradition, as are values of right to life, privacy, private property, and fundamental liberties such as freedom of speech (Tate 2008: 993, 2016a: 36).

John Locke is widely recognized as a seminal figure within the liberal tradition (McClelland 1996: 242; Macintyre 1997: 250; Plamenatz 1963: 214). As well as being committed to an ideal of religious toleration, premised on the entitlement of individuals to freely express their religious faith so long as this is not at odds with state security or civil order (Locke 1993a, b; see ▶ Chap. 51, "John Locke and Religious Toleration"), Locke was also committed to an ideal of "equal respect" for individuals.

Locke's ideal of "equal respect" arises from his fundamental belief in individual equality. He argues that this equality arises from the fact that all individuals are the "workmanship" of God, "all the Servants" of this "one Sovereign Master," and have an equal status for this reason (Locke 1965: II § 6). Within a prepolitical state of nature, Locke tells us, such "equality" means that "all the Power and Jurisdiction" between individuals "is reciprocal, no one having more than another: there being nothing more evident, than that Creatures of the same species and rank promiscuously born to all the same advantages of Nature, and the use of the same faculties, should also be equal one amongst another without Subordination or Subjection" (Locke 1965: II § 4). Such "equality," with its injunctions against "subordination" or "subjection," therefore imposes limits on how individuals may appropriately treat each other, since their equal status as "God's creatures" means they are not "made for one another's uses, as [Locke tells us] the inferior ranks of Creatures are for ours" (Locke 1965: II § 6. My addition).

It is these normative assumptions concerning individual equality, and the limits they impose on how individuals might legitimately treat each other, which underwrite, within Locke's political philosophy, an ideal of "equal respect" between individuals. Locke believed such ideals concerning equality, and the limits they imposed on mutual behavior, were embodied in natural law (which he believed expressed the will of God), and it is from this same natural law that he believed individuals derived the "natural rights" on the basis of which they advanced their normative entitlements to be treated with "equal respect," not least their entitlement to exercise specific individual liberties without interference. On Locke's conception of natural law as reflecting the will of God, see Locke 1965, II, § 6, 8, 135, 142, 195; on Locke's belief that natural law embodies entitlements to individual liberty and equality and gives rise to "natural rights" to these entitlements, see Locke 1965, II, § 4, 6–13, 22, 54, 57, 87, 128, 135, 142, 171, 172, 190, 195.

Immanuel Kant, another foundational figure within the liberal tradition, made such claims concerning "equal respect" explicit. For Kant, the "only object of respect" is the moral law, legislated by our rational will (Kant 1949a: 401n. See also Kant 1949b: V73–78, 81, 117). But on the basis of this "respect" for the moral law, Kant argues, it is possible to have "respect" for persons: "The direct determination of the will by the law and the consciousness of this determination is respect.... The only object of respect is the law, and indeed only the law which we impose on ourselves and yet recognize as necessary in itself.... All respect for a person is only respect for the law (of righteousness, etc.) of which the person provides an example" (Kant 1949a: 401n). Kant insisted that if we are to act "morally" (as opposed to pragmatically) within the world, we must act in accordance with the moral law, which means we can never treat other individuals as "means" to our own ends but only as "ends in themselves" (Kant 1949a: IV 428, 429, 430, 433, 437–38). As the following passage indicates, Kant believed that to treat others as "ends in themselves," rather than as "means," and therefore to treat them "morally," was to treat them with "respect," and such "respect" was equal (and so ought to be reciprocal) between individuals because each individual was entitled to such "respect" given their equal status as "persons" (i.e., "ends in themselves"). In this way, Kant, like Locke, perceived "respect" as regulating relationships between human beings, placing limits on how they might legitimately treat one another:

> Now, I say, man and, in general, every rational being exists as an end in himself and not merely as a means to be arbitrarily used by this or that will. In all his actions, whether they are directed to himself or to other rational beings, he must always be regarded at the same time as an end.... [R]ational beings are designated 'persons', because their nature indicates that they are ends in themselves, i.e., things which may not be used merely as means. Such a being is thus an object of *respect* and, so far, restricts all [arbitrary] choice. (Kant 1949a: IV 428, 429. Emphasis added)

Contemporary liberals have also sought to advance "equal respect" as a norm, seeking to regulate the actions of individuals toward each other in these terms. Charles Larmore, for instance, insists that the sort of "political liberalism" espoused by twentieth-century liberals such as John Rawls can only be sustained in terms of a prior moral foundation of "respect for persons," whose validity, he tells us, "must be understood as antecedent to the democratic will" (Larmore 2008: 140). Like Locke and Kant, Larmore insists that such "respect" places limits on how individuals are entitled to treat each other:

> Respect for beliefs is simply a belief about their justifiability within the other's perspective; so it is not itself an obligation we could bear toward others. Respect for persons, however, is not just a belief that others have a capacity for developing beliefs justifiable within their own perspective.... [I]t is an obligation to treat others in a certain way because of that fact.... (Larmore 1987: 64)

In each case, we see that "respect" is upheld at a number of points within the liberal tradition. Further, such respect is understood as applying equally, and therefore reciprocally, between individuals and, when applied to specific circumstances, places normative limits on how individuals are entitled to treat each other. When behavior is perceived as inconsistent with this ideal of "equal respect," then, if "respect" is to be upheld, there is a prima facie obligation that the behavior ought to be curtailed.

Of course, matters become more complex when the behavior in question is legitimated by *other* foundational liberal values (such as freedom of speech) since, in such circumstances, the liberal entitlements of "speech" and "respect" find themselves (and the practices they justify) at odds. In fact, matters are even more protracted than this. In the discussion above, it was suggested that "equal respect" is one among a number of fundamental values foundational to the liberal tradition. But in practice, it is possible for liberal proponents of each of these fundamental values to advance them in terms of demands for "respect." So for instance, we shall see, in the context of blasphemy, that although religious devotees demand that blasphemers "respect" their religious beliefs, or their God, and so cease their blasphemy, blasphemers can insist, in response, that religious devotees "respect" the fundamental liberal value of "freedom of speech," underwriting entitlements to engage in such blasphemy. In such contexts, involving rival and incompatible demands for "respect," it is difficult (perhaps impossible) for "respect" to be accorded "equally" to the respective parties, since what is demanded by each of the parties, in terms of "respect," is incompossible (mutually exclusive) with the result that "respect" cannot be accorded to one party, in such circumstances, without denying it to the other. It is this intraliberal conflict, involving rival (and incompossible) claims to "respect," arising on the basis of competing liberal values, that renders such disputes so difficult for liberals to resolve.

"Features" Versus "Persons"

"Respect" can play a significant role in making the practice of toleration possible. We saw that the conditions of toleration include an aversion (Condition 2) on the part of some to that which seeks toleration (Condition 1). In such circumstances, dominant groups (including, at times, political authorities themselves) may have difficulty conceding permission to beliefs or practices that they abhor. In more extreme cases, the very identities of some minority groups elicit such aversion, with the result that dominant groups (with the disposition to interfere) sometimes seek to discriminate against these minority groups and impose upon them a legal and social regime of inequality. How is it possible, in such circumstances, to secure "toleration" of such minority groups, resulting in a situation where the aversion of dominant groups (Condition 2) is not acted upon and, instead, dominant groups affirm "reasons" for toleration (Condition 3) that convince them not to act on their disposition to interfere, with the result that toleration (Condition 4) takes place, the continuing aversion of these dominant groups to the object of toleration (or the persons seeking it) notwithstanding?

The concept of "respect" can play an important role, in such circumstances, in making such toleration possible. The basis upon which it can do so is by providing "reasons" for toleration (Condition 3) capable of overriding the aversion (Condition 2) which councils that toleration not take place. Of course, there are many possible "reasons" for toleration, but "respect" for the person or groups seeking toleration is one of them. This "respect" is possible when those with the disposition to interfere make a distinction, under the auspices of Condition 3, between (i) the beliefs, practices, and various other features (including features of persons) for which toleration is sought and which are therefore the "object" of toleration under Condition 1 and (ii) the persons themselves, associated with such "objects," who are seeking such toleration. While those with the disposition to interfere may find that their aversion to the object of toleration identified in (i) might preclude toleration, nevertheless if they acquire a "respect" for the person (ii) advancing this object and seeking toleration for it, this could be one means whereby "reasons" for toleration (Condition 3) might be possible, a continuing aversion to the object of toleration (Condition 2) notwithstanding.

Such "respect" for persons might arise on any number of grounds. One might be the grounds identified by Kant above, wherein he conceived of "persons," irrespective of their contingent features, as "ends-in-themselves." By according individuals such status as "ends-in-themselves," one is obligated (on Kantian grounds) to treat them in a manner which is consistent with "respect" for this status, irrespective of how averse one might be to their contingent features or practices (where these contingent features or practices presumably include all that falls outside their status as "ends-in-themselves"). To use the terms applied by Stephen Darwall, we can say that in treating individuals as "ends-in-themselves," irrespective of our attitude to their contingent features or practices, we are according them "recognition respect" as distinct from "appraisal respect." "Appraisal respect" arises on the basis of our positive appraisal of a person's "character-related features"; in contrast, "recognition respect" arises from "the moral requirements that are placed on one by the existence of other persons," irrespective of their contingent features, with the result that one is "willing to constrain one's behaviour in ways required by that fact" (Darwall 1977: 41, 44, 45).

In line with the requirements of "recognition respect," treatment of individuals as "ends-in-themselves" means that they are not to be treated as a "means" to another's ends – which is precisely what occurs when their contingent beliefs or practices (or, indeed, they themselves) are interfered with, due to the aversion of others, in ways detrimental to their personal liberty. In other words, "respect" for the status of such individuals as "ends-in-themselves" requires refraining from such interference, thereby providing a "reason" for toleration (Condition 3). Charles Larmore makes this point in his passage above, distinguishing between one contingent feature of "persons" (their "beliefs") and arguing that, irrespective of our aversion to such "beliefs," we can nevertheless tolerate such "beliefs" on the basis of our "respect" for the "persons" who possess them. Larmore elucidates this further by distinguishing between "sympathy" and "respect." "Sympathy," he declares, can only arise when we are capable of conceiving of ourselves as sharing the beliefs or practices of others, whereas "respect" arises on the basis of obligations to these others irrespective of their beliefs or practices (Larmore 1987: 63). As Larmore puts it: "Respect for persons is an attitude that we can adopt, just about however much we may disagree with them about the nature of the good life" (Larmore 1987: 65).

In this way, the distinction between (i) the contingent features of persons (including their specific identities, beliefs and practices) and (ii) the persons exhibiting these – wherein we have an aversion to one but a "respect" for the other – assists us in affirming a reason for toleration (Condition 3) that may convince us not to interfere with these persons and the liberties they seek to exercise under Condition 1. Such a distinction between (i) "features" and (ii) "persons" makes this possible because in basing our reasons for toleration (Condition 3) on a "respect" for persons qua persons, rather than upon their contingent features or practices which are the objects of toleration, we are not being asked to permit these features or practices because of any value intrinsic to themselves but rather solely on the basis of the "respect" we accord to the persons whose features or practices they are. In this way, our aversion to these features and practices (Condition 2) can remain, but toleration (Condition 4) still be possible because the reasons for toleration arising under Condition 3 ("respect" for persons qua persons) are separate from the features and practices seeking toleration under Condition 1. As Peter Jones puts it, "we accept that what matters to them should matter to us because it matters to them" (Jones 2006: 133).

However, contrary to Larmore's contention above that "respect" for a person "is an attitude that we can adopt, just about however much we may disagree" with that person concerning "the nature of the good life," there are conceivable limits to this process. As Peter Jones states: "Some beliefs may be so absurd, so depraved, so evil, so outrageous, that they do not deserve our respect; indeed, they may deserve our disrespect" (Jones 2011a: 89. See also Larmore 1987: 64). In such cases, our aversion (Condition 2) to the expression of such beliefs or practices may be so extreme that it begins to undermine the "respect for persons" upon which we have relied as a reason for toleration of such beliefs and practices (Condition 3). The result is an inherent tension in the use of "respect for persons" as a reason for toleration. Our desire, in such cases, to rely on this "respect" as a reason for toleration, allowing us to tolerate the features or practices (i) of others irrespective of the intrinsic merit of the latter, butts up against an erosion of that "respect" (and therefore its weight as a reason for toleration) when those "features" or "practices" are so repugnant to ourselves that they elicit our extreme aversion. The result is that it is not always possible to maintain a hermetic distance between our "respect" for persons (ii) and the features, beliefs, and practices (i) for which they seek toleration, affirming a "respect" for one irrespective of the merits of the other. In the circumstances in which such distance collapses, toleration has reached its limits.

Of course, "respect" can operate in other ways as a means for individuals to arrive at "reasons" for toleration (Condition 3). In addition to "respect for persons," it is possible to have "respect" for specific norms or values. These norms might include the norm of "autonomy," where tolerating the beliefs or practices of another, irrespective of our aversion to the latter, is justified because our noninterference enhances the "autonomy" of the person subject to such toleration (see Galeotti 2002: 39–40; Williams 1996: 23). As with "respect" for persons, this "respect" for "autonomy" provides a "reason" for toleration separate from the beliefs or practices (i) which are the object of toleration. In this way (subject to the possible limits identified in the paragraph above), the intrinsic merit of the "objects" for which toleration is sought is, once again, irrelevant to the reasons why toleration takes place, thereby allowing those engaging in toleration to concede permission to such objects despite their continuing aversion to them.

Galeotti and Respect

"Respect," as a basis for toleration, has been most systematically advanced by the Italian toleration theorist, Anna Elisabetta Galeotti. Like the Canadian philosopher, Charles Taylor, in his conception of multiculturalism above, Galeotti links "respect" to "public recognition," arguing that those whose identities have been excluded from full recognition or acceptance within the public spheres of liberal democracies seek toleration as a means to this end, where such public recognition is itself a means of ensuring their equal "respect." As Galeotti puts it:

> If what is really at stake in contemporary issues of toleration is equal respect and social standing for minority groups, rather than equal liberties for individuals, then the issue of public toleration must be addressed not simply in terms of the compatibility between liberal institutions and various cultures or practices, but in terms of contests over the inclusion of distinct identities and their bearers in the polity via the public recognition of their differences. (Galeotti 2002: 6. See also Galeotti 2002: 103, 116–17)

In the following passage, we see that Galeotti promises such "public recognition" on the basis of the same distinction outlined above between (ii) "persons," on the one hand, and (i) their contingent features (such as "beliefs" and "practices") on the other, affirming toleration via "respect" for the one, irrespective of our aversion to the other. Referring to the toleration controversy which has arisen within some liberal democracies concerning Muslim women's entitlements to wear the burqa and niqab, Galeotti argues that we should "tolerate" the wearing of such garments, irrespective of our aversion to them, because of our "respect" for the Muslim women who deport themselves in this attire:

> I contend that toleration of social differences in public should...aim at the recognition of those differences as legitimate options of a pluralist liberal democracy, hence redrawing the map of social standards and including their bearers as equals......If wearing a veil does not harm anyone, it should have the same public consideration as having a tattoo, getting one's body pierced, or wearing a wig, and such an option, whether familiar or odd, should be considered legitimate out of *respect for the people who endorse it* and for their reasons, *whether we share them or not......*Toleration as recognition is then neither *permission* nor *acceptance...*but is instead *legitimation*: a public declaration that a given practice, if it does not infringe on any right, is a legitimate option of the pluralist society. (Galeotti 2015: 102. Emphasis added. See also Galeotti 2010: 447–48)

Niqab and Burqa

The burqa and the niqab have produced significant controversy within specific liberal democratic polities within recent years. Both have been the subject of legislative ban in Europe and elsewhere. Concerning Europe, there have been total bans on wearing these garments in public places in France, the Netherlands, Denmark, Austria, Belgium, and Bulgaria (Müller 2019).

France was the first European polity to ban the burqa and niqab but couched this in legislation banning all full-face coverings in "public places." Section 1 of Law no. 2010-1192 of October 11, 2010, states: "No one may, in public places, wear clothing that is designed to conceal the face" (Law no. 2010-1192, Section 1). In Section 2 of the legislation, "public places" are defined broadly, comprising "the public highway and any places open to the public or assigned to a public service" (Law no. 2010-1192, Section 2). The law does not apply if the face covering "is justified for health or occupational reasons, or if it is worn in the context of sports, festivities or artistic or traditional events" (Law no. 2010-1192, Section 2). The French *Conseil Constitutionnel* also ruled that the law does not apply in those circumstances where it infringes upon "religious freedom in places of worship open to the public" (Conseil Constitutionnel 2010).

The French parliamentary vote supporting this legislation was overwhelming. On July 13, 2010, the *Assemblée Nationale* passed the legislation by an almost unanimous margin of 335 votes in favor, 1 vote against, and 3 abstentions (Spielmann 2014: 9). On September 14, 2010, the same law was affirmed in the *Sénat* by a similar margin of 246 votes in favor and 1 abstention (Spielmann 2014: 9).

The Niqab, Burqa, and "Equal Respect"

According to Galeotti in the passage above, the issue of the niqab and burqa is a relatively clear case wherein, due to the absence of any obvious infringement of the "rights" of others or "harm" to third parties, those seeking to wear such garments ought to be accorded toleration to do so consistent with their "equal respect," with the result that, by state and society permitting such attire, the public identity of those wearing such garments is accorded full "recognition." As Galeotti states:

> I contend that only by treating citizens as equals is [equal respect] properly granted by means of an individualizing act of recognition. Hence I hold that when democracy is confronted with this type of claim [in this case, the hijab in French public schools], it should recognize the legitimate visibility of the difference under discussion, unless there is evidence of real harm to a third party. (Galeotti 2010: 448. My addition)

However, "equal respect" is a reciprocal term. After all, "respect" is only "equal" if it is "equal" between contending parties. Consequently, inherent within this term is an implicit assumption of reciprocity, wherein "respect" ought to apply equally to all relevant parties in a dispute. The result is that it is possible, in such circumstances, for conflict to arise between parties due to rival, and conflicting, claims to "respect." Indeed, it is even possible that such rival claims to "respect" might be incompossible (mutually exclusive), where the respective claims are so diametrically at odds that it is not possible to accord "respect" to one party without denying it to the other. We shall see below that blasphemy, and the contending claims to which it gives rise, at times possesses this quality.

For Galeotti, there are presumably no circumstances of such "mutual exclusivity" in the context of the niqab or burqa. This is because according "respect" to Muslim women by allowing them to wear such garments in the public sphere does not (according to Galeotti in her first passage above) produce a countervailing circumstance – such as the violation of another's "right" or a "harm" to a third party – in which "respect" would (as a result) not be reciprocally applied.

The French Parliament, however, perceived things differently. As we shall see below, it declared that Muslim women wearing the burqa and niqab in public does produce "harm" to third parties. The result was that, from the perspective of the French Parliament, the demand that the burqa and niqab be tolerated in the public sphere gave rise to rival claims of "respect" – claims that could potentially produce the circumstances of "mutual exclusivity" referred to above wherein it is not possible to accord "respect" to one party without denying it to the other.

This perspective is apparent in the explanatory memorandum which constituted the preface to the French parliamentary bill banning the burqa and niqab. The memorandum begins by asserting Parliament's commitment to the key values of the French Republic – "liberty, equality, fraternity" – which, it says, "form the foundation-stone of our social covenant," "guarantee the cohesion of the Nation," and "underpin the principle of respect for the dignity of individuals and for equality between men and women" (Explanatory Memorandum 2010: 8).

The first "harm" which the memorandum identifies as arising from the burqa and niqab is that "the wearing of the full veil is the sectarian manifestation of a rejection of the values of the Republic" – and this because it negates "the fact of belonging to society for the persons concerned" and "brings with it a symbolic and dehumanising violence, at odds with the social fabric" (Explanatory Memorandum 2010: 8). Among the republican values allegedly "rejected" by the "wearing of the full veil," the memorandum identified "fraternity":

> The defence of public order is not confined to the preservation of tranquillity, public health or safety. It also makes it possible to proscribe conduct which directly runs counter to rules that are essential to the Republican social covenant, on which our society is founded. The systematic concealment of the face in public places, contrary to the ideal of *fraternity*. . . . falls short of the minimum requirement of civility that is necessary for social interaction. (Explanatory Memorandum 2010: 8. Emphasis added)

However, the memorandum goes further and identifies other "harms" to third parties arising from the burqa and niqab. Whereas we might say that for Galeotti, it is the "dignity" of Muslim women which is primarily at stake in the controversy, given that a public proscription of the burqa or niqab denies them "recognition," and therefore "equal respect," in the public sphere, the French Parliament both reverses and extends this assumption. It insists that the "dignity" of Muslim women, far from being affirmed, is denied by their wearing the burqa or niqab, even if they make a voluntary choice to do so, and, further, insists that the "dignity" of others in society is also at stake given the physical separation produced by such garments:

> [T]his form of public confinement, even in cases where it is voluntary or accepted, clearly contravenes the principle of respect for the dignity of the person. In addition, it is not only

about the dignity of the individual who is confined in this manner, but also the dignity of others who share the same public space and who are thus treated as individuals from whom one must be protected by the refusal of any exchange, even if only visual. (Explanatory Memorandum 2010: 8)

The French Parliament gives some idea of why they believe the "dignity" of Muslim women is denied by their wearing the burqa or niqab – insisting that irrespective of any voluntary choice to do so, the garment is intrinsically demeaning for women, denying their equality with men in French society:

Lastly, in the case of the full veil, worn only by women, this breach of the dignity of the person goes hand in hand with the public manifestation of a conspicuous denial of equality between men and women, through which that breach is constituted. (Explanatory Memorandum 2010: 8)

What we see, therefore, in contrasting Galeotti's perspective to that of the French Parliament, is that considerations of "respect" (or also, in this case, "dignity") are inherently contested. Whereas Galeotti sees only "respect" for Muslim women as being at stake in any question concerning the toleration of the niqab and burqa, with no other obvious "harms" to third parties, the French Parliament reverses this, seeing the "dignity" and "equality" of Muslim women (and their associated "respect") being denied by the niqab and the burqa and insisting that the "dignity" and "respect" of third parties who confront the niqab and burqa in public places are also at stake. Further, these competing claims to "respect" are mutually exclusive (and therefore incompossible) in the sense that it is not possible to accord "respect" to Muslim women (in Galeotti's sense) without (in the view of the French Parliament) denying it to both Muslim women and others in French society, because to accord "respect" to Muslim women (on Galeotti's terms) requires affirming their entitlement to wear the burqa and niqab in public, but it is precisely this which, the French Parliament insists, produces the opposite outcome.

Consequently, what is constituted and required by "respect," and who is perceived to have a legitimate claim, in any particular circumstance, not to have their "respect" violated, will be one of the contestable issues at stake in many disputes over toleration. When individuals disagree over who has an entitlement to "respect," what "respect" requires or demands, and therefore what actions are in accord with "respect," rival claims become likely. "Respect" will be most contested, and the conflicts to which it gives rise most intractable, when such rival claims are characterized by circumstances of "mutual exclusivity" (incompossibility) such as those identified above.

Blasphemy

Rival claims to "respect," characterized by circumstances of "mutual exclusivity," are likely to arise in the context of blasphemy. Blasphemy has become an increasingly prominent matter within liberal democracies in recent years. In 1997 and 2011, in Sydney and Avignon, there were public protests in reaction to an exhibition of

Andres Serrano's 1987 photograph, *Piss Christ*. In each case, Christians staged protests outside the venues exhibiting the photograph, and in each case, the Perspex protective shield, protecting the photograph, was attacked and mutilated (Chrisafis 2011; Hunt 2013).

More violent responses to perceived instances of blasphemy arose in the reaction of some Muslims to the publication of Salman Rushdie's novel, *The Satanic Verses*, in 1988, and the publication, on September 30, 2005, of 12 cartoons of the Prophet Muhammad by the Danish newspaper, *Jyllands-Posten*. According to Flemming Rose, the editor who commissioned these cartoons, *Jyllands-Posten,* received "104 registered death threats" within 5 months of publication, and he estimates that by 2014, the cartoons were directly related to 200 deaths around the world (Rose 2006, 2014).

Muhammad cartoons were also directly related to 12 deaths at the *Charlie Hebdo* editorial offices in Paris on January 7, 2015, among the deceased being the magazine's editor, 4 cartoonists, and 3 other editorial staff (Withnall and Lichfield 2015). *Charlie Hebdo* had previously placed cartoons of the Prophet Muhammad on their front cover, and witnesses heard the gunmen yell, as the shootings occurred, "God is Great," and "We have avenged the Prophet Muhammad" (BBC 2015).

Similar violence has arisen more recently in relation to Muhammad cartoons. On May 3, 2015, police shot and killed two men who sought to embark on a gun attack targeting the "First Annual Muhammad Art Exhibit and Contest," organized by the *American Freedom Defense Initiative*, at the Curtis Culwell Centre, in Garland, Texas. One security officer was shot in the ankle by the attackers, but no attendees at the contest were injured (Conlon and Sgueglia 2015). On Friday October 16, 2020, a French secondary school teacher, Samuel Paty, was beheaded on his way home from school, in the town of Conflans-Sainte-Honorine, just outside of Paris, in retaliation for his showing Muhammad Cartoon material in class as part of a classroom discussion on free speech and blasphemy, and concerning which a parent had posted a complaint on social media (McAuley 2020; Williamson 2020).

Rival "Respects"

Rival claims to "respect" can arise in such extreme circumstances. On the one hand, those engaging in alleged acts of blasphemy can draw, for their justification, not only on the foundational liberal value of freedom of speech but also on Enlightenment values which insist on free inquiry in all matters, including religion. Immanuel Kant conceived of his own age as an "age of Enlightenment" (Kant 1991: 58) and insisted that such "Enlightenment" requires the "freedom to make *public use* of one's reason in all matters" (Kant 1991: 55). He therefore associated "Enlightenment" with freedom of inquiry and the "criticism" to which such inquiry often gives rise. As he put it in 1781:

> Our age is, in especial degree, the age of criticism, and to criticism everything must submit. Religion through its sanctity, and law-giving through its majesty, may seek to exempt

30 Toleration and Respect

themselves from it. But they then awaken just suspicion, and cannot claim the sincere respect which reason accords only to that which has been able to sustain the test of free and open examination. (Kant 1968: Axiia)

The liberal value of freedom of speech or the Enlightenment value of freedom of inquiry, therefore, provides the basis upon which those engaged in alleged acts of blasphemy can insist that their entitlement to do so be "respected," and not interfered with by others. In this way, such "respect" constitutes a reason (Condition 3) for tolerating such forms of expression. On the other hand, those religionists outraged by such blasphemy can insist that either their own religious feelings or their God has been denied "respect" in such circumstances and that appropriate remedial action be taken.

The result is the likelihood of rival and mutually exclusive claims to "respect" arising between contending parties in blasphemy disputes. Such rival claims are "mutually exclusive" because any concession of "respect" to blasphemers in such circumstances, tolerating their speech and refusing to preclude or punish its expression, is not possible without (in the mind of religionists opposed to the blasphemy) denying "respect" for the latter's religious beliefs or their God.

Blasphemy and Free Speech

Enlightenment commitments in defense of freedom of speech were clearly espoused at the time of the *Jyllands-Posten* publications of the Muhammad cartoons. The Danish Prime Minister at the time, Anders Fogh Rasmussen, courted controversy by refusing to meet the diplomatic representatives of Muslim countries who sought to protest against the cartoons (Rostbøll 2009: 625–26, 2011a: 12, 2010: 406). A year later, Rasmussen, in an interview in *Jyllands-Posten*, was unapologetic, explicitly appealing to Enlightenment values in defense of his position. As he put it:

> The Enlightenment has been the driving force behind European development and decisive for why we have come as far as we have. Therefore, we have something here (i.e. freedom of expression), with regard to which we cannot give one millimetre. (Rasmussen 2006)

Others, in defense of Muhammad cartoons, have also appealed to values of freedom of speech, whether grounded in liberal or Enlightenment commitments. A victim of the *Charlie Hebdo* shootings, Stéphane Charbonnier, the editor of the magazine, was insistent, prior to his death, that religion, and in particular the religion of Islam, fell well within the ambit of such free speech entitlements:

> If we can poke fun at everything in France, if we can talk about anything in France apart from Islam or the consequences of Islamism, that is annoying. (BBC 2011)

This sentiment was expressed somewhat more graphically by the editor in chief of *Charlie Hebdo*, Gerard Biard, in an interview in *Le Monde* in 2012. As he put it:

If we say to religion, 'You are untouchable', we're fucked. (Nelson 2015)

Yet while such positions demand "respect" for free speech, many Muslims opposed to the cartoons also articulated their opposition in terms of the "respect" which, they insisted, the cartoons denied to their God or their Prophet or their own religious convictions. To this end, Danish political scientist, Christian F. Rostbøll, declared that one of the primary discursive divisions in the public debate that arose within Denmark as a result of the *Jyllands-Posten* cartoons was a division between Enlightenment and liberal values of freedom of speech, on the one hand, and the "respect" which, many believed, had been denied to the religious feelings of Muslims on the other:

> Of the dividing lines in the Danish public debate about the cartoons, the one drawn between standing firm on Enlightenment values versus giving in to the demand for respect for religious feelings is of particular interest from the perspective of political theory. This way of framing the debate was widespread among those who defended the publication of the cartoons. . . . . . .The critics of the cartoons in Denmark saw them as an expression of disrespect for the religious feelings of Muslims, indeed as one among many contributions to a pervasive anti-Muslim and anti-immigrant public discourse. A Muslim organization, characteristically, pitted their right to freedom of religion against the right to print the 'deeply disrespectful' cartoons. (Rostbøll 2009: 625–26. See also Rostbøll 2011b: 387)

"Mutual Exclusivity"

Galeotti argues that even if it was not possible to accord "respect" to Muslim opponents of the cartoons by agreeing to their demands for punitive action against *Jyllands-Posten* or the cartoonists (action which, she says, would have "crucially jarred with liberal constitutional principles") nevertheless she insists that "respect" could have been accorded to Muslims within the wider context in which the debate over the cartoons took place, not least by Prime Minister Rasmussen agreeing to meet with Muslim diplomatic representatives:

> Institutions behave and speak through their officials and representatives. In the case of the Danish cartoons, for example, a claim contrasting. . . .freedom of expression was advanced by Muslim groups so as to prevent the publication of allegedly blasphemous representations of Muhammad. The government could not forbid the cartoons' publication, because political censorship of the free press crucially jarred with liberal constitutional principles. Neverthe-less, the refusal of the Danish government to receive the imams and discuss the problem with them was also a clear sign of institutional disrespect which fuelled the controversy. If democratic institutions have to stick to certain principles, like freedom of expression, there are nevertheless various modes and attitudes of carrying out such an uncompromising stand. (Galeotti 2010: 448)

In this way, Galeotti insists that the Muhammad cartoons affair, as it arose in Denmark, was not inevitably characterized by a "mutual exclusivity" involving rival and incompossible claims to "respect." On the contrary, she insists, it was possible to show "respect" to Muslims opposed to the cartoons, within the wider public context in which debate over the cartoons took place, while still upholding "respect" for free speech values by refusing to engage in the punitive action some Muslims demanded against *Jyllands-Posten* or the cartoonists.

For the religiously devout, however, what is often at stake in circumstances of blasphemy is not simply their own religious feelings but their belief that their God or their Prophet has been desecrated, defiled, or impugned (Mendus 1990: 9; Jones 1990: 419, 2011a: 88). The sort of "institutional respect" offered by Galeotti above will therefore be of little use if, in the minds of at least some of the religiously devout, it is their God who must be avenged, not their own religious feelings. In such cases, it is possible that only a punitive response – of either the legal or illegal variety – will be deemed appropriate by at least some of those seeking such vengeance.

Of course, only a very small minority of religious adherents are likely to be intent on engaging in violent acts of retribution against alleged blasphemers or those believed responsible for propagating the blasphemy (though as the *Charlie Hebdo*, Samuel Paty, and other attacks indicate, a small minority is all it takes to result in a profound loss of life). Many among the religiously devout will instead seek legal avenues of redress. Some may remain averse to the blasphemy but not respond at all. However, irrespective of this, what is most likely is that in circumstances of blasphemy in which a religious devotee believes their God or Prophet has been desecrated, defiled, or impugned, such a devotee will find themselves in a situation of "mutual exclusivity," regarding matters of "respect," in relation to those who have engaged in such blasphemy. This is because any claim to "respect," advanced by the blasphemers, seeking to uphold their entitlement to engage in the blasphemy, will not be perceived by the devotee as compatible with the claims to "respect" arising from their religious convictions.

"Respect" as a Contested Term

So once again we see that, just as in the case of niqabs and burqas, "respect," in the context of blasphemy, is a contested term. Each party is capable of advancing rival claims to "respect," and, when these are perceived by each party to be directly at odds, it is not possible to satisfy one claim without denying the other. Indeed, as with the burqa and niqab, blasphemy can also produce situations where the very meaning and content of "respect" – and therefore what it requires in any specific circumstance – can itself be open to dispute.

Consider, for instance, the publication of the Muhammad cartoons by *Jyllands-Posten* in 2005. The editor of *Jyllands-Posten*, Flemming Rose, claims he commissioned the cartoons with a specific intent – to push back what he saw as an increasing self-censorship on the part of writers and artists in Denmark when it came to matters of Islam (Rose 2006, 2014: 32, 2015). He therefore claimed the cartoons were published for legitimate reasons of public interest, and so were not a scurrilous, "disrespectful," or gratuitous attack on Muslims or their religion (Rose 2006, 2015).

Others have contested this, suggesting that the motives of *Jyllands-Posten* in commissioning and publishing the cartoons resided in an absence of "respect" for Muslims. As Christian Rostbøll states:

> If the cartoons had been published in an atmosphere that was otherwise characterized by mutual respect and attempts to try to understand and listen to Danish Muslims, there would have been no reason for moral reproach of *Jyllands-Posten*. But that was clearly not the case. The atmosphere of Danish public debate has for some years, not least since the election in 2001 (and subsequent reelection) of a government that relies on the support of the far-right Danish People's Party, been very hostile toward Muslims, and *Jyllands-Posten* has been a main contributor to this hostility. In this context, it is difficult to see the cartoons only as a legitimate critique of religiously justified terrorism and not also and primarily as part of an antagonistic discourse toward Muslims. (Rostbøll 2009: 627)

One of Flemming Rose's Danish journalist colleagues sent him an email, soon after the publication of the cartoons, where she imputed similar motives to him and *Jyllands-Posten*, thereby once again insisting that the publication of the cartoons arose from an absence of "respect" for Muslims:

> Dear Flemming Rose,
> I'll make this brief: I'm very proud of having been brought up in a country that prides itself on its broad-mindedness, tolerance, openness, and enlightenment. Therefore, I'm mortified and ashamed to have to share this country and this line of work with *Jyllands-Posten*, whose Muhammad cartoons to the best of my convictions are borne by the exact opposite: embarrassing ignorance, intolerance, lack of respect and distasteful arrogance. As a journalist I will always seek to protect and fight for the right of individuals to speak freely. But to drape oneself in the mantle of free speech in order to publish a series of contemptuous depictions of other people's religion is in my opinion downright shameful. We shudder now at Nazi depictions of the Jews prior to and during World War II. In the future we will also shudder at *Jyllands-Posten's* depiction of an entire world religion. (Rose 2014: 65)

Rose deeply regrets the loss of life that has arisen in the context of the cartoons, but he is unapologetic about their publication (Rose 2006, 2015). He insists that the cartoons raised genuine issues of freedom of speech in Danish liberal democracy in regard to matters of religion (Rose 2006, 2015).

But for our purposes, what is significant is how Rose is able to problematize and in fact reverse the accusations concerning "respect" leveled against him and *Jyllands-Posten*. One way in which Rose does so is by insisting it is not *he* that denied "respect" to Muslims and their religion by publishing the cartoons. Rather, he insists that it is those Muslims opposed to the cartoons, and insisting on a punitive response to their authors or publishers, who are displaying "disrespect," since they are refusing to abide by the basic principles of the liberal democratic polity in which the cartoons were published, which insists on a fundamental entitlement to freedom of speech in matters of religion:

> What do you do when people adhering to a faith or ideology insist that others with different convictions submit themselves to taboos outside sacred places? Over the years, my answer to that challenge has been consistent. If a believer demands that I, as a nonbeliever, observe his

taboos in the public domain, he is not asking for my respect, but for my submission, and that is incompatible with a liberal democracy. (Rose 2015)

Rose then problematizes the issue of "respect" even further by insisting that far from demonstrating "disrespect" to Danish Muslims, the publication of the cartoons has accorded them "equal respect" by treating them like any other member of Danish society, not immune from criticism or satire but subject to the same exigencies of free debate and open inquiry as all other Danish citizens:

> The cartoonists treated Islam the same way they treat Christianity, Buddhism, Hinduism and other religions. And by treating Muslims in Denmark as equals they made a point: We are integrating you into the Danish tradition of satire because you are part of our society, not strangers. The cartoons are including, rather than excluding, Muslims. (Rose 2006. See also Rose 2014: 48, 2015)

So "respect" is a contested and contentious norm, not only in the sense that rival claims to "respect" are open to dispute but also because its meaning, content, or implications in any specific circumstance is also open to contestation. For instance, we saw that how the French Parliament understood "respect," in relation to the niqab and burqa, was very different to those who believed that "respect" for Muslim women had been violated by the proscription of these garments in the French public sphere. Similarly, Flemming Rose understands "respect," in the context of the Muhammad cartoons, very differently from his critics. What they perceive as his denial of "respect" to Muslims he perceives as an act of "respect," treating Danish Muslims as "part of" Danish society, not as "strangers."

Consequently, in such circumstances, not only are we confronted with incompossible claims to "respect," thereby giving rise to what I have called circumstances of "mutual exclusivity." We are also confronted with a situation in which what can be said to constitute "respect" is itself open to question. The result is that the meaning and import of "respect," in any particular circumstance, is often not self-evident and is therefore one of the matters which will be open to contestation in any dispute concerning toleration.

Whose Intolerance?

Let us assume that speech that intentionally produces offense or some other form of harm to others can be characterized as an act of intolerance (see Newey 2011: 225; Jones 2011b: 446). Toleration would therefore consist of individuals, with a propensity to engage in such speech, choosing not to do so, their continuing aversion to the addressee of such speech notwithstanding. On the other hand, these same individuals could (on the basis of the liberal and Enlightenment norms identified above) insist that their entitlement to engage in such speech be "respected," with the result that "intolerance" consists in denying them this "respect."

In such cases, therefore, it may be that, in matters of speech, we confront not only rival and incompossible claims to "respect" but rival and incompossible claims to "toleration," with the result that we are once again mired in the circumstances of "mutual exclusivity" identified above. For instance, Peter Jones concedes that deliberately placing a "pig's head" in a synagogue or mosque, knowing this would offend the attendants of such places of worship, is an "intolerant" action (Jones 2011b: 446. See also Jones 2007b: 20). But as Jones identifies "intolerance" as the curtailment of agency (Jones 2007a: 397–98, 2011b: 446), he would also have to concede that any attempt to prevent individuals from placing the "pig's head" in the mosque or synagogue is also an "intolerant" action. We are therefore confronted with the "symmetry" of rival and incompossible claims to "toleration," identified by Glen Newey, in which to accord toleration to one party inevitably results in "intolerance" toward the other (Newey 2001: 315, 320–21, 2011, 2013: 51). It is precisely such situations that I have identified in terms of circumstances of "mutual exclusivity" above.

But this does not mean that such rival claims to "toleration" or "respect" are morally equivalent, with the result that no evaluative choice is possible between them. The relative validity of these rival claims will be determined by whatever criterion we adopt to enable us to make a choice between them. This does not mean that the choice, arising from such a criterion, is the legitimate or correct one. Such legitimacy depends, after all, on the perceived legitimacy of the criterion itself (about which opinions may differ) and the validity of its application to the specific circumstances (which may also be subject to dispute). But criteria do exist by which a choice between such rival and incompossible claims is possible.

"Universalization"

One means of deciding between rival and incompossible claims is to apply a criterion of "universalization." This is a criterion, its roots residing in the Kantian categorical imperative, which seeks to evaluate the worth of a norm by determining if it is capable of being affirmed by all relevant parties in all similar contexts. John Rawls' "original position" seeks to replicate such processes of "universalization" via the "veil of ignorance," and Rawls identifies the antecedents of this procedure in Kant (Rawls 1980: 11–12, 140–41). In this respect, "universalization" is an important criterion that some use to test the validity of norms and principles. As Gerald Dworkin states:

> It is by now widely accepted that those who act and claim moral justification for their conduct must be prepared to accept as legitimate certain universalizations of their action. There must be consistency in conduct, a refusal to make special pleas in one's own behalf or to consider oneself an exception to general principles. One way of testing this consistency is to ask of someone proposing to engage in a certain course of action, "What if everyone did that?" (Dworkin 1974: 491)

If we assume that the religiously devout perceive in blasphemy an offense primarily against their God or perhaps against their own religious commitments (with the result that they demand the blasphemy not take place or be punished if it does) and the alleged blasphemers perceive in their blasphemy an affirmation of liberal or Enlightenment norms concerning freedom of speech and inquiry (with the result that they believe the blasphemy should take place with impunity), then the rival claims to "respect," to which these demands give rise, are mutually exclusive and so incompossible, since it is not possible to meet the requirements of "respect" for one party without denying it to the other.

However, it is possible to decide between these competing positions by utilizing our criterion above and determining which of the claims to "respect," advanced by either party, is capable of "universalization." The norm for which the blasphemers seek "respect" (freedom of speech) *is* capable of "universalization." This is because such a norm is capable of being generalized to all parties in the dispute. The blasphemers engage in the freedom of speech that gives rise to blasphemy, and their critics engage in the freedom of speech that morally objects, castigates, or in some way denies legitimacy to that choice. To affirm the principle of free speech, advanced by the blasphemers, does not preclude according the same entitlement to the opposing party (even if it is not an entitlement the opposing party is seeking). Both parties engage in such freedom of speech by articulating positions in opposition to each other. The result is that a "universalization" of the norm of "free speech," in the context of blasphemy disputes, is possible.

However, it is not possible to "universalize" the norm for which the critics of blasphemy seek "respect." The outcome they seek is that the blasphemy be either precluded, so that it does not take place, or punished if it does, when it grossly impugns the God, or the religious convictions, of the devout. If we were to articulate this as a norm, we might say that speech should not take place (or be punished when it does) if it impugns an individual's deepest conscientious convictions.

But the problem with such a norm is, as John Locke told us in the late seventeenth century, there is "nothing so indifferent which the consciences of some or other do not check at" (Locke 1993a: 191). In other words, there is no obvious limit to the conscientious convictions upon which some might seek to impose a censorial limit on speech, insisting such censorship is a necessary condition of "respect" for such convictions in circumstances where they risk being deeply offended. Even if the narrower norm of limiting speech only when it offends *religious* convictions was affirmed, the same problem would arise insofar as there is no obvious limit to those convictions that might be identified as "religious" and so have a prima facie entitlement to impose such limitations. The result of such open-endedness, Locke says, is that it is not possible to accord "a toleration of men in all that which they pretend, out of conscience, they cannot submit to," as this will "wholly take away all the civil laws, and all the magistrate's power" (Locke 1993a: 191). In the circumstances described above, it will also "wholly take away" any definite boundaries concerning the liberties, in relation to speech, upon which (it might be thought) others should not intrude.

But even if it was possible to arrive at a determinate conception of what conscientious convictions ought to give rise to prima facie limits on speech, the entitlement to impose such limits does not arise from a norm that can be "universalized" because (unlike freedom of speech) it is not a norm that can be reciprocally applied to all parties in a dispute. We saw that the norm of freedom of speech could be applied to the religiously devout, outraged by blasphemy, even if this was not a norm that they were seeking. But the alternative norm (limits on speech for the sake of conscientious convictions) cannot be applied to the rival party engaging in blasphemy because *their* conscientious convictions demand no such limits on speech at all. It is not, therefore, a norm capable of being generalized to all parties in a dispute and so not a norm that can be affirmed by the "universalization" criterion.

The fact that only the norm advanced by the blasphemers (freedom of speech) is capable of "universalization" in the context of blasphemy disputes does not necessarily make it the correct norm to endorse in all such contexts and therefore the one to which "respect" ought to be accorded. After all, there may be many reasons why, given multiple considerations, a society (or its political authorities) may not wish to tolerate blasphemy, and the adoption of a "universalization" criterion will not, in and of itself, legitimate blasphemy in the face of such objections. Anna Elisabetta Galeotti, for instance, suggests that limits on some types of speech (such as blasphemy) may be justifiable when such speech stigmatizes or diminishes those minorities whom we wish, for the sake of justice, to grant "public recognition" comparable to more dominant groups (Galeotti 2002: 111–12). In the context of such commitments, the "universalization" criterion may (in the view of key decision-makers) have neither weight nor relevance.

However, although it may not be the appropriate criterion to endorse in all contexts, what the above discussion of the "universalization" criterion makes clear is that, when confronted with rival, mutually exclusive, and incompossible claims to "respect," we are not entirely helpless. It is possible to prioritize between such rival claims, determining whose claims to "respect" ought to be "tolerated" in such contexts and whose ought to be denied. But all such outcomes are dependent on the criterion we choose to facilitate this process, and because such criteria are not self-validating, their legitimacy in any specific context will itself be dependent on multiple considerations subject to the judgment of the individuals or authorities concerned.

"Nonuniversalization"

Sometimes such mutually exclusive claims to "respect" are adjudicated, and toleration achieved, by applying the very opposite criterion to "universalization." We saw above that in the context of successful "universalization," each rival party is accorded the same rights and entitlements. This is then conceived to be the "toleration" that each party enjoys. But at times, "toleration" may be achieved by *denying* each rival party the entitlements they seek. While such denial might not itself be conceived as an act of "toleration," nevertheless in some circumstances it is

30 Toleration and Respect

understood to achieve "tolerant" outcomes (i.e., a more "tolerant" society where civil peace between rival parties is the norm).

An example of this arose in colonial Australia. White colonists within the Australian colonies in the nineteenth century were primarily of English, Scots, and Irish descent. Needless to say, many brought the rival animosities not only of their respective nationalities but also of the Anglican, Presbyterian, and Catholic religions with them. One way in which some of the colonial authorities in Australia sought to repress this animosity and ensure that the religious sectarian conflict, evident in the old countries, was not reproduced in the Australian colonies, was to *deny* the entitlements of rival parties to religious and nationalist expression:

> The worst sectarian violence in our history occurred in Melbourne in 1846 when Catholic and Protestant mobs fired on each other on the anniversary of the Battle of the Boyne. But note the response. The colony's mini-parliament immediately passed a law banning processions held to commemorate festivals, anniversaries, or political events related to any religious or political differences between her Majesty's subjects. Banners and music calculated to provoke animosity were forbidden. The poisonous cycle of demonstration and counter demonstration by which Northern Ireland keeps alive its troubled past was nipped in the bud. (Hirst 2005: 14)

Thus, we see that different criteria to ensure "toleration" (and different conceptions of what constitutes "toleration" itself) can be applied in response to rival parties seeking to advance mutually exclusive claims. Sometimes this might involve according to each party the same entitlement (the "universalization" criterion above) and at other times might involve an equal and reciprocal denial of their respective demands (as in the example immediately above). Which criterion is applied will itself be a matter of contestation and (ultimately) political negotiation and judgment between rival groups and other interested parties or authorities.

"The Question"

In 1994, Eugene Genovese wrote an "open letter to the Left," which was published in *Dissent* magazine. It was entitled "The Question," and it asked why the Left had not yet openly acknowledged the appalling and needless loss of life inflicted on populations governed by Communist regimes, not least Stalin's Soviet Union (Genovese 1994).

Genovese's "question" requires those with strong moral or political commitments to be morally accountable for the consequences of those commitments. I think the same can be asked of those (such as myself) who believe that free speech entitlements should extend (as the Enlightenment insisted) to all matters of religion, including blasphemy, any aversion we might have to blasphemy itself notwithstanding. The question that thereby arises is whether "respect" for the free speech norms underwriting blasphemy, and therefore the demand that blasphemy be tolerated, can be justified given the appalling loss of life that the violent reaction to blasphemy sometimes produces. The Muhammad cartoons are perhaps the most obvious instance of this.

Answers to such questions are, at some level, affected by subjective perceptions concerning the literary weight or worth of the blasphemy concerned. As Peter Jones states:

> [R]espect for beliefs is likely to count for most when assaults on people's beliefs are merely gratuitous, that is when they have no serious purpose or no purpose that justifies their not giving countervailing weight to what matters to others. The difficulty is, of course, that whether an act is merely gratuitous is often disputed between its perpetrators and objectors. (Jones 2011a: 89)

This sort of differential is evident in Jeremy Waldron's respective responses to Salman Rushdie's *The Satanic Verses*, published in 1988, and the Muhammad cartoons published by *Jyllands-Posten* in 2005. Waldron was unequivocal in his defense of Rushdie's novel, despite the loss of life that had resulted from it. It is not suggested here that Rushdie intended to engage in blasphemy or sought deliberately to cause offense to Muslims with his novel. But from the perspective of many Muslims, including the Ayatollah Khomeini who, in 1989, passed a public death sentence on Rushdie, such was the outcome.

Waldron insisted that no quarter should be given to the "intolerance" displayed by those Muslims outraged by Rushdie's novel and seeking to harm either Rushdie or those associated with the novel:

> [T]he relativist approach is of no use in the Rushdie affair. That 'their' ways are not our ways is now the problem, not the solution. The question is whether we shall have free expression *in the world* or not – whether some of the inhabitants of the world are to be threatened with death by others for what they write.. . . . It may be a lost cause, but we must do everything we can to make the case for freedom of expression, freedom from this sort of terror, to those with whom we share the world. Without that, legal or international protection for literary freedom is as fragile and as fearful as the police line that is guarding Salman Rushdie at this moment. (Waldron 1993: 135–36)

Yet when it came to the cartoons published by *Jyllands-Posten* in September 2005, Waldron was of a very different point of view. Although he did not declare that the cartoons ought to have been subject to either censorship or penalty, he did insist that their publication was "unnecessary and offensive" – the clear corollary being that, on the basis of any mature, level-headed judgment, they should not have been published at all:

> To the debate about the Islam-terrorist connection, I suspect that.. . . even the Danish cartoons (portraying the Prophet Mohammed as a bomb-throwing terrorist) make some sort of twisted contribution; and I believe they should be tolerated as such. I do not mean that these contributions are admirable. In my view there is something foul in the self-righteousness with which Western liberals have clamored for the publication and republication of the Danish cartoons in country after country and forum after forum. Often the best they could say for this was that they were upholding their right to publish the cartoons. But a right does not give the rightbearer a reason to exercise the right one way or another, nor should it insulate him against moral criticism. My view is that the exercise of this right was unnecessary and offensive; but as I have now said several

times, offensiveness by itself is not a good reason for legal regulation. (Waldron 2010: 1652–53)

It is true that not all the Danish Muhammad cartoonists sought to draw cartoons that vilified Islam or the Prophet Muhammad. One was critical of *Jyllands-Posten's* motives in soliciting and publishing the cartoons, referring to the newspaper's editors as "reactionary provocateurs" (Henkel 2006: 4). Nevertheless others did vilify in ways that caused offense.

On this basis, Waldron articulates what he perceives to be a clear qualitative distinction between *The Satanic Verses* and the Danish Muhammad cartoons. He perceives the violence elicited by the former as a serious threat to free speech which we must stoically resist, while perceiving the latter as a scurrilous assault upon Muslim sensibilities that ought not to have occurred and ought to be subject to "moral criticism." No doubt Waldron's distinction between the two is premised, to a significant degree, not only on his estimation of their respective literary weight or merit but also on what he perceives as the respective intent informing both publications. And yet, in his defense of Rushdie, Waldron made no such distinctions, and offered no such qualifications, insisting that *all* manner of speech and publication ought to be defended in matters of religion:

> Persons and peoples must leave one another free to address the deep questions of religion and philosophy the best way they can, with all the resources they have at their disposal. In the modern world, that may mean that the whole kaleidoscope of literary technique – fantasy, irony, poetry, word-play, and the speculative juggling of ideas – is unleashed on what many regard as the holy, the good, the immaculate, and the indubitable. (Waldron 1993: 140)

So how should we confront "the question" when it comes to blasphemy? Should we make the same distinction as Waldron, seeing some publications as laudatory and others, such as the Muhammad cartoons, as "unnecessary" and therefore regrettable? Or should we side with the editors of *Charlie Hebdo* or Flemming Rose who (in line with Waldron's statement immediately above) were unapologetic (in their accounts provided above) concerning their entitlement to engage with religion on *any* terms? How we respond to these options will determine the extent to which we are willing to "tolerate" blasphemy, despite the violence to which it can give rise, and therefore the extent to which we are willing to "respect" norms of freedom of speech and freedom of inquiry which provide "reasons" for this toleration, however averse we might be to the blasphemy itself.

"Clear and Present Danger"

However, if we view the Muhammad cartoons from the opposite end of the evaluative spectrum (not in terms of the intent of the cartoonists but rather in terms of the violent consequences to which the cartoons have given rise), do we arrive at different conclusions concerning "respect" and "toleration"? Even so robust a defense of freedom of speech as the US First Amendment has elicited judicial judgments which have sought to limit free speech entitlements in proportion to the negative consequences to which such speech is capable of giving rise. Justice Oliver Wendell Holmes, delivering the opinion of the court in an espionage case just over 100 years ago, provided the authoritative precedent in this regard. He insisted that entitlements to freedom of speech under the First Amendment diminish depending on the immediacy of the "evils" such speech is likely to produce:

> [T]he character of every act depends upon the circumstances in which it is done. . . . The most stringent protection of free speech would not protect a man in falsely shouting fire in a theatre and causing a panic. . . . The question in every case is whether the words used are used in such circumstances and are of such a nature as to create a *clear and present danger* that they will bring about the substantive evils that Congress has a right to prevent. It is a question of proximity and degree. (Holmes 1919: 52. Emphasis added)

Justice Holmes' statement arose in the circumstances of a trial focusing on speech critical of government during wartime. The circumstances of blasphemy are, of course, quite different. The "evils" to which blasphemous speech is likely to give rise is violence on the part of those outraged by the blasphemy, not threats to national security. But the same "question" arises. Is defense of such speech justified when it produces such deleterious consequences?

One answer is as follows. If we are willing to reduce the extent to which we are willing to "tolerate" speech (and therefore "respect" free speech principles) depending on the amount of violence such speech is likely to elicit, then we are allowing the scope of such "toleration" (and the freedom it makes possible) to be determined by the most "intolerant" members of the community (those willing to respond to such speech with violence). If we allow the "intolerant" to determine the scope of our "tolerance" in this way, then we are creating for ourselves a highly illiberal political culture, with no limit on the possible incursions upon our free speech liberties.

Yet does this mean that, at times, enduring the violent response of the intolerant is the necessary cost of free speech? It is if this is speech we wish to tolerate ahead of other priorities, perhaps because we perceive the entitlement to engage in such speech as fundamental to our liberties or the liberties of others, and if we wish to avoid a situation where the scope of those liberties is determined by the most intolerant within the community. Whether any particular instance of public speech fulfills such conditions will (as with *The Satanic Verses* and the Muhammad Cartoons above) be a matter of individual judgment. But if we perceive such expression as fundamental to our liberties, or to the Enlightenment norms we endorse, then enduring the violent response of the intolerant (if it cannot be forestalled) is the necessary cost of free speech.

Of course, one other option is to try to convince the small minority, willing to engage in such violence, to tolerate the speech they find abhorrent, and so forego such violence altogether. Needless to say, such toleration, in the context of blasphemy, is difficult for the religiously devout, when they believe their God or their Prophet has been desecrated, defiled, or impugned. Such is the extremity of the aversion such blasphemy elicits among the devout that it is likely to undermine whatever reasons they might ordinarily consider, under Condition 3, to tolerate such blasphemy. The author has argued elsewhere that the only nonreligious basis upon which the religiously devout might find reasons (under the auspices of Condition 3) to tolerate blasphemy is a skepticism concerning the truth claims of revealed religion – but a skepticism that nevertheless leaves the full plenitude of their religious faith intact (see Tate 2016b: 668–674, 2016c: 240–42). Only such skepticism, it is argued, provides reasons, outside of the religion of the devout, why they might choose to tolerate blasphemy, thereby reconciling their religious faith with liberal or Enlightenment principles centered on freedom of speech.

Conclusion

We see that "respect" can play an important role in enabling individuals to find "reasons" for toleration (Condition 3), and allowing them to engage in toleration (Condition 4), their continuing aversion to that which they are tolerating (Condition 2) notwithstanding. However, "respect" is, in many circumstances, a contested and contentious norm, whose implications, when applied to specific circumstances, are not always clear and which may give rise to mutually exclusive claims between competing parties, resulting in rival and competing claims to "toleration." But it is precisely the moral weight that we accord to "respect," and the normative legitimacy associated with the concept itself, that makes it such an ardent object of contestation between competing parties, since all are eager to claim its imprimatur for themselves.

Summary and Future Directions

We have seen that "respect" has a long history within the liberal tradition. We have also seen that it has links, as a norm, to the idea of "toleration" and can provide reasons why toleration ought to prevail as a means of dealing with that to which we are averse. But "respect" is always "respect" for a specific value, practice, identity, or some other entity. Consequently, it can inform rival claims for "toleration," underwriting the demands of each side in a dispute. It is for this reason, among others, that it is inherently contested, both in terms of its content and in its application to specific circumstances, because rival claims to "respect," and so rival claims to toleration, often give rise to circumstances of mutual exclusivity, with all the intractable conflict this involves. For this reason, it is likely that there will continue to be a close relationship between "respect" and "toleration," as well as a continuing contestation surrounding the norm of "respect," for many years to come.

References

Balint P (2014) Acts of tolerance: a political and descriptive account. Eur J Polit Theo 13(3):264–281
BBC (2011) French satirical paper Charlie Hebdo attacked in Paris. BBC News. http://www.bbc.com/news/world-europe-15550350

BBC (2015) Charlie Hebdo attack: three days of terror. BBC News. http://www.bbc.com/news/world-europe-30708237

Cameron D (2011) PM's speech at Munich security conference. GOV.UK. https://www.gov.uk/government/speeches/pms-speech-at-munich-security-conference

Chrisafis A (2011) Attack on 'blasphemous' art work fires debate on role of religion in France. The Guardian. https://www.theguardian.com/world/2011/apr/18/andres-serrano-piss-christ-destroyed-christian-protesters

Cohen AJ (2004) What toleration is. Ethics 115(1):68–95

Conlon K, Sgueglia K (2015) Two shot dead after they open fire at Muhammad cartoon event in Texas. CNN. http://edition.cnn.com/2015/05/03/us/mohammed-drawing-contest-shooting/index.html

Conseil Constitutionnel (2010) Decision of the Constitutional Council of 7 October 2010. In: S.A.S. v. France, (2014) ECHR 695, application no. 43835/11: 30

Darwall SL (1977) Two kinds of respect. Ethics 88(1):36–49

Dworkin G (1974) Non-neutral principles. J Philos 71(14):491–506

Explanatory Memorandum (2010) Law no. 2010-1192 of 11 October 2010. In: S.A.S. v. France (2014) ECHR 695, application no. 43835/11: 25

Galeotti AE (2002) Toleration as recognition. Cambridge University Press, Cambridge

Galeotti AE (2010) Multicultural claims and equal respect. Philos Soc Crit 36(3–4):441–450

Galeotti AE (2015) The range of toleration: from toleration as recognition back to disrespectful tolerance. Philos Soc Crit 41(2):93–110

Genovese ED (1994) The question. Dissent (Summer):371–376

Henkel H (2006) 'The journalists of *Jyllands-Posten* are a bunch of reactionary provocateurs': the Danish cartoons controversy and the self-image of Europe. Radic Philos 137(May/June):2–7

Hirst J (2005) Sense & nonsense in Australian history. Black Inc, Melbourne

Holmes OW (1919) Schenck v. United States, 249 U.S. 47

Horton J (1996) Toleration as a virtue. In: Heyd D (ed) Toleration. An elusive virtue. Princeton University Press, Princeton, pp 28–43

Hunt E (2013) Andres Serrano 'Piss Christ' triggers religious fury and court battle in 1990s trials. Herald Sun. https://www.heraldsun.com.au/news/law-order/andres-serrano-piss-christ-triggers-religious-fury-and-court-battle-in-1990s-trials/news-story/5e997822f57fce0ea4dcdf066ef7b79e?sv=8f3949d369ec826f3eb00d5b75d3d27d

Jones P (1990) Respecting beliefs and rebuking Rushdie. Br J Polit Sci 20(4):415–437

Jones P (2006) Toleration, recognition and identity. J Polit Philos 14(2):123–143

Jones P (2007a) Making sense of political toleration. Br J Polit Sci 37(3):383–402

Jones P (2007b) Can speech be intolerant? In: Newey G (ed) Freedom of expression: counting the costs. Cambridge Scholars Publishing, Newcastle, pp 9–29

Jones P (2011a) Religious belief and freedom of expression: is offensiveness really the issue? Res Publica 17(1):75–90

Jones P (2011b) Political toleration: a reply to Newey. Br J Polit Sci 41(2):445–447

Kant I (1949a) Foundations of the metaphysics of morals. In: I Kant, Critique of practical reason and other writings in moral philosophy (trans: Beck LW). University of Chicago Press, Chicago, pp 50–117

Kant I (1949b) Critique of practical reason. In: I Kant, Critique of practical reason and other writings in moral philosophy (trans: Beck LW). University of Chicago Press, Chicago, pp 118–260

Kant I (1968) Critique of pure reason (trans: Smith NK). Macmillan, London

Kant I (1991) An answer to the question: 'what is enlightenment?'. In: Reiss H (ed) I Kant, Political writings. Cambridge University Press, Cambridge, pp 54–60

Larmore C (1987) Patterns of moral complexity. Cambridge University Press, Cambridge

Larmore C (2008) The autonomy of morality. Cambridge University Press, Cambridge

Law no. 2010-1192 of 11 October 2010. In: S.A.S. v. France (2014) ECHR 695, application no. 43835/11: 2

Locke J (1965) In: Laslett P (ed) Two treatises of government. New American Library, New York

30 Toleration and Respect

Locke J (1993a) An essay concerning toleration. In: Wootton D (ed) J Locke, Political writings. Penguin, London, pp 186–210

Locke J (1993b) A letter concerning toleration. In: Wootton D (ed) J Locke, Political writings. Penguin, London, pp 390–436

MacIntyre A (1997) After virtue. A study in moral theory. Duckworth, London

McAuley J (2020) Gruesome details emerge in beheading of French teacher who showed students Muhammad Cartoons. Washington Post. https://www.washingtonpost.com/world/gruesome-details-emerge-in-beheading-of-french-teacher-who-showed-students-mohammed-cartoons/2020/10/17/9bcaeedc-107b-11eb-b404-8d1e675ec701_story.html

McClelland JS (1996) A history of Western political thought. Routledge, London

Mendus S (1989) Toleration and the limits of liberalism. Macmillan, London

Mendus S (1990) The tigers of wrath and the horses of instruction. In: Commission for Racial Equality (ed) Free speech. Report of a seminar. Commission for Racial Equality, London, pp 3–17

Mill JS (1971) On liberty, in JS Mill, utilitarianism, liberty, representative government. Everyman's Library, London, pp 61–170

Müller M (2019) Where are 'burqa bans' in Europe? DW. https://www.dw.com/en/where-are-burqa-bans-in-europe/a-49843292

Nelson L (2015) Charlie Hebdo: its history, humour and controversies explained. Vox, 7 Jan 2015. https://www.vox.com/2015/1/7/7511001/charlie-hebdo-attack-paris

Newey G (2001) Is democratic toleration a rubber duck? Res Publica 7(3):315–336

Newey G (2011) Political toleration: a reply to Jones. Br J Polit Sci 41(1):223–227

Newey G (2013) Toleration in political conflict. Cambridge University Press, Cambridge

Noack R (2015) Multiculturalism is a sham, says Angela Merkel. The Washington Post. https://www.washingtonpost.com/news/worldviews/wp/2015/12/14/angela-merkel-multiculturalism-is-a-sham/

Plamenatz J (1963) Man and society, vol I. Longman, London

Raphael DD (1988) The intolerable. In: Mendus S (ed) Justifying toleration. Conceptual and historical perspectives. Cambridge University Press, Cambridge, pp 137–154

Rasmussen AF (2006) "Interview". In: J. Hansen, Jyllands-Posten havde ret til at bringe de tegninger – punktum [Jyllands-Posten had a right to publish those cartoons – period], an interview with Anders Fogh Rasmussen, Jyllands-Posten, October 1, quoted in CF Rostbøll, The use and abuse of 'universal values' in the Danish cartoon controversy. Eur Polit Sci Rev 2 (3):401–422

Rawls J (1980) A theory of justice. Oxford University Press, Oxford

Raz J (1986) The morality of freedom. Clarendon Press, Oxford

Rose F (2006) Why I published those cartoons. Washington Post. http://www.washingtonpost.com/wp-dyn/content/article/2006/02/17/AR2006021702499.html

Rose F (2014) The tyranny of silence. How one cartoon ignited a global debate on the future of free speech. Cato Institute, Washington

Rose F (2015) Why I published cartoons of Muhammad and don't regret it. Huffpost. https://www.huffpost.com/entry/why-i-published-cartoons-of-muhammad_b_6709650

Rostbøll CF (2009) Autonomy, respect, and arrogance in the Danish cartoon controversy. Political Theory 37(5):623–648

Rostbøll CF (2010) The use and abuse of 'universal values' in the Danish cartoon controversy. Eur Polit Sci Rev 2(3):401–422

Rostbøll CF (2011a) Freedom of expression, deliberation, autonomy and respect. Eur J Polit Theo 10(1):5–21

Rostbøll CF (2011b) From the standpoint of practical reason: a reply to Tønder. Political Theory 39 (3):386–393

Spielmann D (2014) S.A.S. v. France, ECHR 695, application no. 43835/11

Tate J (2008) Free speech or equal respect? Liberalism's competing values. Philos Soc Crit 34(9): 987–1020

Tate J (2016a) Free speech, toleration and equal respect: the Bolt affair in context. Aust J Polit Sci 51(1):34–50

Tate J (2016b) Toleration, skepticism and blasphemy: John Locke, Jonas Proast and Charlie Hebdo. Am J Polit Sci 60(3):664–675

Tate J (2016c) Liberty, toleration and equality. John Locke, Jonas Proast and the letters concerning toleration. Routledge, New York

Taylor C (1994) The politics of recognition. In: Gutmann A (ed) Multiculturalism. Examining the politics of recognition. Princeton University Press, Princeton, pp 25–74

Waldron J (1993) Rushdie and religion. In: Waldron J (ed) Liberal rights. Collected papers 1981–1991. Cambridge University Press, Cambridge, pp 134–142

Waldron J (2010) Dignity and defamation: the visibility of hate. Harv Law Rev 123(7):1597–1657

Williams B (1996) Toleration: an impossible virtue? In: Heyd D (ed) Toleration. An elusive virtue. Princeton University Press, Princeton, pp 18–27

Williamson L (2020) France teacher attack: suspect 'asked students to point Samuel Paty out'. BBC News. https://www.bbc.com/news/world-europe-54581827

Withnall A, Lichfield J (2015) Charlie Hebdo shooting: at least twelve killed as shots fired at satirical magazine's Paris office. Independent. https://www.independent.co.uk/news/world/europe/charlie-hebdo-shooting-10-killed-as-shots-fired-at-satirical-magazine-headquarters-according-to-9962337.html